THE FACTS ON FILE
WORLD POLITICAL ALMANAC

FROM 1945 TO THE PRESENT

FOURTH EDITION

BY CHRIS COOK

REVISED BY
WHITNEY WALKER

■® Facts On File, Inc.

The Facts On File World Political Almanac, Fourth Edition

Copyright © 2001, 1995, 1992, 1989 by Chris Cook

All rights reserved. No part of this book may be reproduced or utilized in any form or by any means, electronic or mechanical, including photocopying, recording, or by any information storage or retrieval systems, without permission in writing from the publisher. For information contact:

Checkmark Books
An imprint of Facts On File, Inc.
11 Penn Plaza
New York NY 10001

Library of Congress Cataloging-in-Publication Data
Cook, Chris, 1945–
   The Facts on File world political almanac : from 1945 to the present / by Chris Cook; revised by Whitney Walker.—4th ed. / Revised by Whitney Walker.
      p. cm.
   Includes bibliographical references and index.
   ISBN 0-8160-4295-0 (hardcover) — ISBN 0-8160-4296-90 (softcover)
   1. World politics—1945– I. Facts on File, Inc. II. Title.
   D843.C5798 2001
   909.82—dc21   00-044222

Checkmark Books are available at special discounts when purchased in bulk quantities for businesses, associations, institutions or sales promotions. Please call our Special Sales Department in New York at (212) 967-8800 or (800) 322-8755.

You can find Facts On File on the World Wide Web at
http://www.factsonfile.com

Text design by Ron Monteleone and Joan M. Toro
Cover design by Cathy Rincon

Printed in the United States of America

MP BVC 10 9 8 7 6 5 4 3 2 1

This book is printed on acid-free paper.

CONTENTS

PREFACE AND ACKNOWLEDGMENTS

Bringing the *World Political Almanac* into the 21st century has been a rewarding challenge. This fourth edition updates key facts and figures from recent political developments within a single reference volume. The contents cover a range of topics, from heads of state and constitutional structure to diplomacy and warfare, as well as elections and political parties. Much of it is presented in readily accessible tabular or statistical form supplemented by biographical details on international figures and a glossary of political terms. Although no reference this size can be comprehensive, the goal of this almanac has been to provide information on the specific countries and events that will best serve most readers.

Since the first edition of this book, the world has seen the fall of communism in Eastern Europe and the end of apartheid in South Africa. As the 1990s drew to a close, both Boris Yeltsin and Nelson Mandela turned over their governments to a new generation of democratic leaders, but at the same time, military coups in Africa and Asia have plunged some countries back into dictatorship. The parties in Northern Ireland have made significant strides toward peace, but talks in the Middle East have suffered setbacks. And as most of the world works for a historic ban on atomic weapons, South Asia teeters on the verge of nuclear brinkmanship. Once again, the *World Political Almanac* records all these changes and more.

Thanks to Chris Cook for laying such excellent groundwork to make my job easier, and to Owen Lancer of Facts On File for supporting this new edition. And finally, thanks, as always, to Eric Reyes for his keen eye and sound advice.

Whitney Walker

CHAPTER 1

INTERNATIONAL POLITICAL ORGANIZATIONS AND MOVEMENTS

COMPARATIVE TABLE: DATES OF FORMATION OF INTERNATIONAL ORGANIZATIONS		
	Treaty	**Date of Formation**
Arab League	—	22 Mar 1945
Association of South-East Asian Nations (ASEAN)	—	7 Aug 1967
Caribbean Community (CARICOM)	4 July 1973	1 Aug 1973
Colombo Plan	28 Nov 1950	1 July 1951
Commonwealth	31 Dec 1931	—
Commonwealth of Independent States (CIS)	8 Dec 1991	8 Dec 1991
Council of Europe	5 May 1949	July 1949
Council for Mutual Economic Assistance (CMEA or COMECON)*	—	25 Jan 1949
Danube Commission**	18 Aug 1948	1949
European Communities (EC) (i) (ECSC)	18 Apr 1951	—
(ii) (EEC)	25 Mar 1957	—
(iii) (Euratom)	25 Mar 1957	—
European Free Trade Association (EFTA)	20 Nov 1959	3 May 1960
European Trade Union Confederation (ETUC)	—	Feb 1973
International Confederation of Free Trade Unions (ICFTU)	—	Dec 1949
North Atlantic Treaty Organization (NATO)	4 Apr 1949	24 Aug 1949
Organization of African Unity (OAU)	—	25 May 1963
Organization of American States (OAS)	—	30 Apr 1948
Organization for Economic Cooperation and Development (OECD)	14 Dec 1960	30 Sep 1961

COMPARATIVE TABLE:
DATES OF FORMATION OF INTERNATIONAL ORGANIZATIONS
(CON'T)

	Treaty	Date of Formation
Organization for European Economic Co-operation (OEEC)	—	16 Apr 1948
Organization of the Islamic Conference (OIC)	—	May 1971
Organization of Petroleum Exporting Countries (OPEC)	—	14 Sep 1960
The Secretariat of the Pacific Community (formerly the South Pacific Commission [SPC])	Feb 1947	July 1948
United Nations	26 June 1945	24 Oct 1945
Warsaw Pact***	—	14 May 1955
West European Union (WEU)	23 Oct 1954	6 May 1955
World Bank	27 Dec 1945	June 1946
World Confederation of Labour (WCL)	—	1968
World Federation of Trade Unions (WFTU)	—	3 Oct 1945
World Trade Organization (WTO)	—	1 Jan 1995

* Officially dissolved 28 June 1991.

** Effectively ceased to exist by 1990.

*** Effectively moribund as a military organization since 1990. Officially dissolved 1 July 1991.

ARAB LEAGUE
(LEAGUE OF ARAB STATES)

Date of Formation   22 March 1945

Headquarters

Until 1979   Cairo (Egypt)
1979–1990   Tunis (Tunisia)
Since 1990   Cairo (Egypt)

Aims

a)   To foster cultural, economic and communications links among member states.

b)   To mediate in disputes between Arab states.

c)   To represent Arab states in international negotiations.

d)   To coordinate the economic and diplomatic offensive against Israel.

History

In the early part of the 20th century the Arab world was largely divided into British and French spheres of influence. By 1943, however, seven states had substantially achieved independence. After a meeting in autumn 1944 they drew up the Alexandria Protocol, which committed them to the formation of a league rather than a unitary state or federation. The covenant was signed in Cairo in 1945. The League is regarded as a regional organization within the United Nations and has observer status at the United Nations General Assembly. The Iraqi invasion of Kuwait in 1990 placed major strains on the organization. The league has recently focused on the stalled Israeli-Palestinian peace process.

Structure

Council meets in any one of the Arab capitals, presided over by member states in turn. It meets twice a year with the main function of mediating disputes. Each member has one vote.

Political Committee consists of foreign ministers of member states.

Secretariat consists of administrative and financial offices and was moved to Tunis from Cairo in 1979 when Egypt was suspended from the League because of a bilateral treaty with Israel. The Secretariat returned to Cairo in 1990.

Secretary-General Since May 1991 Esmet Abdel Meguid (Egypt)

Past Secretaries-General

Mar 1945–Sept 1952	Abdul Azzem (Egypt)
Sept 1952–June 1972	Abdul Hassouna (Egypt)
June 1972–Mar 1979	Mahmoud Riad (Egypt)
June 1979–Aug 1990	Chedli Klibi (Tunisia)

Members

Algeria (joined 1962)
Bahrain (joined 1971)
Comoros (joined 1993)
Djibouti (joined 1977)
Egypt (suspended 1979, readmitted May 1989)
Iraq
Jordan
Kuwait (joined 1961)
Lebanon
Libya (joined 1953)
Mauritania (joined 1973)

Morocco (joined 1958)
Oman (joined 1971)
Palestine*
Qatar (joined 1971)
Saudi Arabia
Somalia (joined 1974)
Sudan (joined 1956)
Syria
Tunisia (joined 1958)
United Arab Emirates (joined 1971)
Yemen

---

* Not recognized as a sovereign state outside the Arab world.

ASSOCIATION OF SOUTH-EAST ASIAN NATIONS (ASEAN)

Date of Formation   8 August 1967

Headquarters   Jakarta (Indonesia)

Aims

a) To promote political, economic, social and cultural cooperation among the noncommunist states of Southeast Asia.

b) To increase trade between ASEAN countries and with the rest of the world.

History

The foreign ministers of Indonesia, Malaysia, the Philippines, Singapore and Thailand met in Bangkok to discuss a regional organization, and as a result signed the Bangkok Declaration. The first summit meeting was held in February 1976.

Structure

Heads of Government Meeting takes place whenever necessary.

Annual Ministerial Meeting of foreign ministers takes place in member countries on an alphabetical rotation.

Standing Committee consisting of the foreign minister of the host country and the ambassadors of the others carries on business between meetings.

Secretariat was established in Jakarta in 1967. The post of secretary-general revolves in alphabetical order every two years, while other officers remain for three years.

There are also five economic committees and three noneconomic committees.

Secretary-General   Since Jan 1998 Rodolfo Severino (Philippines)

Past Secretaries-General

Feb 1976–Feb 1978	Hartono Dharsono (Indonesia)
Feb–July 1978	Umarjadi Njotowijona (Indonesia)
July 1978–July 1980	Datuk Ali bin Abdullah (Malaysia)
July 1980–July 1982	Narciso Reyes (Philippines)
July 1982–July 1984	Chan Kai Yau (Singapore)
July 1984–July 1989	Phan Wannamethee (Thailand)
July 1989–July 1991	Rusli Noor (Indonesia)
July 1991–Dec 1997	Ajit Singh (Malaysia)

Members*

Brunei (joined 1984)	Malaysia	Singapore
Cambodia (joined 1999)	Myanmar (Burma) (joined 1997)	Thailand
Indonesia	Philippines	Vietnam (joined 1995)
Laos (joined 1997)		

Observer:
Papua New Guinea

Consultative partners:
China, Russia

CARIBBEAN COMMUNITY (CARICOM)

Date of Formation   Treaty, 4 July 1973; in force, 1 August 1973

Headquarters   Georgetown (Guyana)

Aims
a) Economic cooperation throughout the Caribbean Common Market.
b) Coordination of foreign policy of member countries.
c) Cooperation in areas such as education, health and tax administration.

History
The Treaty of Chaguaramas, which established the Caribbean Community and replaced the Caribbean Free Trade Association (founded in 1965), was signed by the prime ministers of Barbados, Guyana, Jamaica, and Trinidad and Tobago on 4 July 1973. It also set up a common external tariff for members of the Caribbean Common Market.

Structure
Heads of Government Conference is the main decision-making body. Its meeting in November 1982 was the first for seven years, but since then it has met annually. Decisions are made unanimously.

Common Market Council consists of a minister of government of each member.

Secretariat is led by a secretary-general elected by the conference for five yearly renewable terms.

There are also numerous institutions in which each state is represented by the appropriate minister, e.g., health, foreign affairs and labor.

---

* In July 1992 Vietnam and Laos took the first steps to full membership.

Secretary-General

Edwin Carrington
Deputy Secretary-General

(Trinidad and Tobago)
Louis Wiltshire (Trinidad and Tobago)

Past Secretaries-General

1974–Aug 1977
Aug 1977–Aug 1978
Nov 1978–Sept 1983
After Sept 1983–?

Alister McIntyre (Grenada)
Joseph Tyndall (Guyana) (acting)
Kurleigh King (Barbados)
Roderick Rainford (Jamaica)

Members

Anguilla (associate member)
Antigua and Barbuda (joined
   1974)
Bahamas (joined 1983)*
Barbados (joined Community,
   but not Common Market, in
   1983)
Belize (joined 1974)
Dominica (joined 1974)
Grenada (joined 1974)
Guyana

Haiti**
Jamaica
Montserrat (joined 1974)
St. Kitts-Nevis (joined 1974)
St. Lucia (joined 1974)
St. Vincent and the
   Grenadines (joined 1974)
Trinidad and Tobago
Turks and Caicos Islands (associ-
   ate member)
Suriname (joined 1995)

Observers

Aruba, Dominican Republic, Netherlands Antilles, Puerto Rico, Venezuela, Bermuda, Cayman Islands, Colombia, Mexico

COLOMBO PLAN

Date of Formation   Treaty, 28 November 1950; in force 1 July 1951

Headquarters   Colombo (Sri Lanka)

Aims

a) To promote the development of member countries in Asia.
b) To review economic and social progress and help accelerate this
    through cooperative effort.
c) To encourage development aid both to and within the area.

History

The original Plan was set up by seven Commonwealth countries and
was intended to last six years. Its life was extended by five yearly inter-
vals until 1980, when it was given an indefinite span.

---

* The Bahamas is a member of the Community but not the Common Market.
** Haiti has yet to satisfy all terms required for membership.

Although the Plan endeavors to deal with development in a coordinated multilateral way, negotiations for assistance take place in a direct bilateral fashion between donor and recipient countries.

Structure

Consultative Committee of ministers meets once every two years, preceded by a meeting of senior officials.

Colombo Plan Council meets three or four times a year in Colombo to review progress.

Colombo Plan Bureau is the permanent servicing, research and information disseminating organ. Since 1973 it has been operating a drug advisory program.

Colombo Plan Staff College exists to help members with technical education.

Director   U. Sarat Chandran (India)

Past Directors

Aug 1951–Sep 1953	G. M. Wilson (U.K.)
Sep 1953–Feb 1956	P. W. E. Curtin (Australia)
April 1956–Aug 1957	N. Keyitz (Canada)
Aug 1957–July 1959	R. H. Wade (New Zealand)
July 1959–Dec 1961	J. K. Thompson (U.K.)
Jan 1962–Mar 1964	S. Matsui (Japan)
Jan 1965–Mar 1966	J. L. Allen (Australia)
Mar 1966–June 1969	D. Alan Strachan (U.S.)
June 1969–Aug 1973	A. B. Connelly (Canada)
Aug 1973–Dec 1975	I. K. McGregor (New Zealand)
Jan 1976–Jan 1979	L. E. T. Storar (U.K.)
Jan 1979–Jan 1982	Noboru Yabata (Japan)
Jan 1982–Feb 1985	Erik Ingevics (Australia)
Feb 1985–Jan 1986	Donald R. Toussaint (U.S.)
Jan 1986–1991	Gilbert H. Sheinbaum (U.S.)

Members

Afghanistan (joined 1963)	Republic of Korea (joined 1962)
Australia	Laos (joined 1951)
Bangladesh (joined 1972)	Malaysia (joined 1957)
Bhutan (joined 1962)	Maldives (joined 1963)
Cambodia (joined 1951)	Myanmar (Burma) (joined 1952)
Fiji (joined 1972)	Nepal (joined 1952)
India	New Zealand
Indonesia (joined 1953)	Pakistan
Iran (joined 1966)	Papua New Guinea (joined 1973)
Japan (joined 1954)	Philippines (joined 1954)

Singapore (joined 1959)   Thailand (joined 1954)
Sri Lanka   United States (joined 1951)

THE COMMONWEALTH

Date of Formation 31 December 1931 ([U.K.] Statute of Westminster); redefined 1949

Headquarters London (United Kingdom)

Aims

Cooperation, consultation and mutual assistance among countries that accept "the Queen as the symbol of the free association of independent member nations and as such the Head of the Commonwealth."

History

Following resolutions at Imperial Conferences of 1926 and 1930, the Statute of Westminster affirmed that dominions are "autonomous communities within the British Empire, equal in status. . . . united by a common allegiance to the Crown and freely associated as members of the British Commonwealth of Nations." This definition was modified in 1949 when member countries accepted India's intention of becoming a republic while at the same time remaining a full member of the Commonwealth. There are now 16 Queen's realms, 30 republics and five indigenous monarchies within the Commonwealth.

Structure

Commonwealth Secretariat was established in 1965 to serve all members. It has observer status at the United Nations, disseminates information, organizes meetings, coordinates activities and provides expert technical assistance.

Commonwealth Heads of Government Meetings are held biennially. Until 1946, prime ministers' meetings were attended by Great Britain, Australia, Canada, New Zealand and South Africa. As countries became independent they began to attend, and in 1971 the meetings were renamed as delegations and were often led by executive presidents.

Commonwealth Finance Ministers Meetings are held annually.

Secretary-General Since June 1990 Emeka Anyaoku (Nigeria)

Past Secretaries-General*
July 1965–July 1975 Arnold Smith (Canada)
Aug 1975–June 1990 Sir Shridath Ramphal (Guyana)

---

* Prior to 1965 Commonwealth affairs were the purview of the British Foreign Office.

Members

Antigua and Barbuda (joined 1981)
Australia
Bahamas (joined 1973)
Bangladesh (joined 1972)
Barbados (joined 1966)
Belize (joined 1981)
Botswana (joined 1966)
Brunei (joined 1984)
Cameroon (joined 1995)
Canada
Cyprus (joined 1961)
Dominica (joined 1978)
Fiji (left 1987; rejoined 1997)
The Gambia (joined 1965)
Ghana (joined 1957)
Grenada (joined 1974)
Guyana (joined 1966)
India (joined 1947)
Jamaica (joined 1962)
Kenya (joined 1963)
Kiribati (joined 1979)
Lesotho (joined 1966)
Malawi (joined 1964)
Malaysia (joined 1957)
Maldives (joined 1982)
Malta (joined (1964)
Mauritius (joined 1968)
Namibia (joined 1990)
Nauru (joined 1968)
New Zealand
Nigeria (joined 1960)**
Pakistan (left 1972; rejoined 1989)
Papua New Guinea (joined 1975)
St. Kitts-Nevis (joined 1983)
St. Lucia (joined 1979)
St. Vincent and the Grenadines (joined 1979)
Seychelles (joined 1976)
Sierra Leone (joined 1965)
Singapore (joined 1965)
Solomon Islands (joined 1978)
South Africa (left 1961; rejoined 1994)
Sri Lanka (joined 1948)
Swaziland (joined 1968)
Tanzania (joined 1961)
Tonga (joined 1970)
Trinidad and Tobago (joined 1962)
Tuvalu (joined 1978)
Uganda (joined 1962)
United Kingdom
Vanuatu (joined 1980)
Western Samoa (joined 1970)
Zambia (joined 1964)
Zimbabwe (joined 1980)

Former Members

Ireland   left 1949

COMMONWEALTH OF INDEPENDENT STATES (CIS)

Date of Formation   Treaty of Alma-Ata, 21 December 1991, following the earlier Declaration of Minsk (8 December 1991 by Belarus, the Russian Federation and Ukraine).

Headquarters   Minsk (Belarus)

Aims

Its founding declaration committed its members to recognize the independence and sovereignty of other members, to respect human rights,

** Suspended in 1995.

including those of national minorities, and to observe existing boundaries. It was agreed to endorse the principle of unitary control of strategic nuclear arms and the concept of a "single economic space."

History

The CIS is a voluntary association of 11 (formerly 12) states formed when the Soviet Union disintegrated. Its history to date suggests it is little more than a forum to keep alive some vague form of cooperation after the demise of the old USSR. Early "agreements" were made at Minsk (14 February 1992, on strategic forces), Kiev (20 March 1992, on state frontiers) and Tashkent (15 May 1992, on collective security). By 1993 the Asian states were drifting away from the CIS.

Structure

The supreme organ of the CIS is a Council of Heads of State. Associated with the work of this Council is a Council of Heads of Government. Its common affairs are regulated by multilateral agreement rather than by central institutions.

Members

Armenia	Moldova (rejoined)
Azerbaijan (joined 1993)	Russia
Belarus	Tajikistan
Georgia (joined 1993)	Turkmenistan
Kazakhstan	Ukraine
Kyrgyzstan	Uzbekistan

COUNCIL OF EUROPE

Date of Formation   Treaty, 5 May 1949; in force, July 1949

Headquarters   Strasbourg (France)

Aims

To achieve greater unity among members and to safeguard and realize the ideals and principles that are their common heritage.

History

A conference of representatives of 26 European countries at The Hague in 1948 called for the creation of a united Europe, including a European Assembly. Following discussions by the Ministerial Council of the Brussels Treaty powers and a conference of ambassadors, the Statute of Council was signed in London in May 1949. Since then a complex system of structures and committees has been developed, which was streamlined to some extent in 1966. One hundred and fifteen conventions have been concluded.

Structure

Committee of Ministers meets in May and December, usually attended by foreign ministers.

Parliamentary Assembly meets in ordinary session three times a year for about one week. It consists of 170 parliamentarians elected or appointed by their national parliaments.

There are numerous standing committees of experts and commissions, the foremost of which is the European Commission. This investigates violations of the European Convention of Human Rights (1950) and, where necessary, refers cases to the European Court of Human Rights, set up in 1959.

Secretary-General Since September 1999 Walter Schwimmer (Austria)

Past Secretaries-General

Aug 1949–July 1953	Jacques Camille-Paris (France)
July 1953–May 1957	Léon Marchal (France)
May 1957–Jan 1964	Ludovico Benvenuti (Italy)
Jan 1964–May 1969	Peter Smithers (U.K.)
May 1969–May 1974	Lujo Toncic-Sorinj (Austria)
May 1974–May 1979	Georg Kahn-Ackermann (Federal Republic of Germany)
May 1979–May 1984	Franz Karasek (Austria)
May 1984–May 1989	Marcelino Oreja Aguirre (Spain)
May 1989–May 1994	Catherine Lalumière (France)
June 1994–Sep 1999	Daniel Tarschys (Sweden)

Members

Albania (joined 1995)
Andorra (joined 1994)
Austria (joined 1956)
Belgium
Bulgaria (joined 1992)
Croatia (joined 1996)
Cyprus (joined 1961)
Czech Republic (joined 1993)
Denmark
Estonia (joined 1993)
Finland (joined 1993)
France
Germany (joined 1951)
Greece (joined 1949, withdrew 1969, rejoined 1974)

Hungary (joined 1991)
Iceland (joined 1950)
Ireland
Italy
Latvia (joined 1995)
Liechtenstein (joined 1978)
Lithuania (joined 1993)
Luxembourg
Malta (joined 1965)
Moldova (joined 1995)
Netherlands
Norway
Poland (joined 1991)
Portugal (joined 1976)
Romania (joined 1993)

Russia (joined 1996)   Sweden
San Marino (joined 1992)   Switzerland (joined 1963)
Slovakia (joined 1993)   Turkey (joined 1949)
Slovenia (joined 1993)   Ukraine (joined 1995)
Spain (joined 1977)   United Kingdom

COUNCIL FOR MUTUAL ECONOMIC ASSISTANCE (CMEA or COMECON)*

Date of Formation   25 January 1949

Headquarters   Moscow (USSR)

Aims

a)   To assist the economic development of member states through sharing of resources and coordination of effort.

b)   To encourage the development of socialist economic integration.

History

The organization was originally formed in response to the Marshall Plan. Its early years were dominated by the Stalinist drive to self-sufficiency but during the 1950s there was an attempt to increase discussion on long-term coordination of effort. In 1962 Khrushchev attempted to convert CMEA into a supranational authority, but this failed, largely as a result of Romanian opposition. With the adoption of policies leading to market economies in Eastern Europe after the 1989 revolutions, Comecon had effectively ceased to function by the end of 1990. It was formally dissolved on 28 June 1991. The final act of Comecon was to vote to establish a new body, the Organization for International Economic Cooperation.

Structure

Session was the supreme authority. It was held in members' capitals under the chairmanship of the host country. Delegations were led by prime ministers; all countries had to be present and decisions had to be unanimous. The meeting in June 1984 was the first since 1969, and a further meeting took place in Warsaw in June 1985.

Executive Committee met every three months at deputy premier level.

There were numerous committees and seven standing conferences.

Secretaries

Jan 1949–Oct 1983   Nikolai Faddeyev (USSR)
Oct 1983–June 1991   Vyacheslav Sychev (USSR)

---

* Formally dissolved 28 June 1991.

Members

Albania (joined 1949, left 1961)
Bulgaria
Cuba (joined 1972)
Czechoslovakia
German Democratic
    Republic* (joined 1950)
Hungary
Mongolia (joined 1962)

Poland
Romania
USSR
Vietnam (joined 1978)
Yugoslavia (agreed to participate
    in the work of some CMEA
    bodies, 1964, but not an offi-
    cial member)

Observers

Afghanistan
Angola
Ethiopia

Lao People's
    Democratic Republic
Mexico

Mozambique
Nicaragua
Yemen

DANUBE COMMISSION**

Date of Formation Treaty, 18 August 1948; in force 1949–1990

Headquarters Since 1954 Budapest (Hungary)

Aims

a) To check that the provisions of the Belgrade Convention were car-
    ried out.
b) To establish a uniform buoying system on all the Danube's navigable
    waterways.
c) To establish basic regulations for the navigation of the river.

History

A meeting of countries on the Danube signed the Belgrade Convention
in August 1948. This reaffirmed that navigation from Ulm, Germany, to
the Black Sea should be free and open to nationals, merchant shipping
and merchandise of all states.

Structure

Commission consisted of one representative of each country on the Danube. It had legal status and its own seal and flag. Its elected officers had
diplomatic immunity.

President 1987–90 Veneline Kotzev (Bulgaria)

Past Presidents

1950–52 Teodor Rudenco
             Grigore Preoteasa (Romania)

---

* Until 1990.
** Effectively ceased to exist by 1990.

1953	Grigore Preoteasa (Romania)
1954–57	Endre Sik (Hungary)
1957–60	Karel Stekl (Czechoslovakia)
1960–63	Slavoljub Petrovic
	Mustafa Vilovic (Yugoslavia)
1963–66	Gueorgui Denisov
	F. E. Titov (USSR)
1966–69	Vassil Bogdanov (Bulgaria)
1969–72	Kurt Enderl (Austria)
1972–75	Ioan Cotot (Romania)
1975–78	Vaclav Moravec (Czechoslovakia)
1978–81	Istvan Roska (Hungary)
1981–84	Radovan Urosev (Yugoslavia)
1984–87	Vladimir Bazovsky (USSR)

Members

Austria	Hungary	USSR
Bulgaria	Romania	Yugoslavia
Czechoslovakia		

Guests   Since 1957 Federal Republic of Germany

EUROPEAN UNION (EU) (formerly European Community)

Date of Formation

18 Apr 1951	Treaty of Paris setting up European Coal and Steel Community (ECSC)
25 Mar 1957	Treaty of Rome setting up European Economic Community (EEC) and European Atomic Energy Community (Euratom)
8 Apr 1965	Treaty to merge executives; in force 1 July 1967
Feb 1992	Signing of Treaty on European Union (the Maastricht Treaty) agreed to in December 1991 by the heads of government
1 Nov 1993	Maastricht Treaty entered into force

Headquarters

Brussels (Belgium)	Council and Commission
Strasbourg (France)	European Parliament
Luxembourg (Luxembourg)	European Court of Justice
Frankfurt am Main (Germany)	European Central Bank

Aims

a) Ever closer union of the peoples of Europe.
b) Improvement of living and working conditions through concerted action to guarantee steady expansion, balanced trade and fair competition.
c) A reduction in the economic differences between regions.
d) Progressive abolition of restrictions on international trade.
e) Aid for overseas development.
f) Preservation and strengthening of peace and liberty.

History

The European Union is a collective term for three organizations with a common membership and, since 1967, a common executive. The ECSC originally had six members; Belgium, France, Federal Republic of Germany, Italy, Luxembourg and the Netherlands. The same six members signed the Treaty of Rome in 1957. Since then the membership has been enlarged with the entry of Denmark, Ireland and the United Kingdom on 1 Jan 1973, Greece on 1 Jan 1981, Spain and Portugal on 1 Jan 1986, and Austria, Sweden and Finland on 1 Jan 1995. Under the successive Lomé Conventions (the fourth was signed in 1989) the Community has trade agreements with 69 countries in Africa, the Caribbean and the Pacific. On 1 Jan 1999 the euro became the official currency of 11 Member States of the European Union.

Structure

European Parliament exercises democratic control over the running of the European Community. The first direct elections were held in June 1979, the second in June 1984, the third in June 1989 and the fourth in June 1994. Full public sessions are held for a week each month in Strasbourg. Its administration is in Luxembourg and its 18 specialist committees meet in Brussels for two weeks each month.

Council of Ministers consists of ministers of each member state and makes decisions on laws to be applied throughout the Community. Chairmanship is taken for six months in alphabetical order. The relevant ministers attend, e.g., agriculture ministers for farm policy, finance ministers for budgetary matters. Heads of government meet for "summits" two or three times a year.

Commission or executive civil service consists of 17 commissioners of all 15 nationalities with supporting staff. Commissioners are appointed for four years and are independent of both governments and the Council.

Court of Justice upholds the law in the implementation and interpretation of community treaties. It consists of 13 judges and six advocates-general appointed for a six-year term.

Court of Auditors has 12 members appointed to check the Community's finances. European Central Bank and the 11 national banks of the particpating member states constitute the Eurosystem, which formulates and defines the single monetary policy.

President of the European Parliament   Since July 1999   Nicole Fontaine (France)

President of the Commission   Since 1995   Jacques Santer (Luxembourg)

Past Presidents of the European Parliament

Mar 1958–Mar 1960	Robert Schuman (France)
Mar 1960–Mar 1962	Hans Furler (Federal Republic of Germany)
Mar 1962–Mar 1964	Gaetano Martino (Italy)
Mar 1964–Sep 1965	Jean Duvieusart (Belgium)
Sep 1965–Mar 1966	Victor Leemans (Belgium)
Mar 1966–Mar 1969	Alain Poher (France)
Mar 1969–Mar 1971	Mario Scelba (Italy)
Mar 1971–Mar 1973	Walter Behrendt (Federal Republic of Germany)
Mar 1973–Mar 1975	Cornelis Berkhouwer (Netherlands)
Mar 1975–Mar 1977	Georges Spénale (France)
Mar 1977–July 1979	Emilio Colombo (Italy)
July 1979–Jan 1982	Simone Veil (France)
Jan 1982–July 1984	Pieter Dankert (Netherlands)
July 1984–Jan 1987	Pierre Pflimlin (France)
Jan 1987–Dec 1989	Lord Plumb (U.K.)
Jan 1990–Dec 1991	Enrique Barón Crespo (Spain)
Jan 1992–July 1994	Egon Klepsch (Germany)
July 1994–Jan 1997	Klaus Hansch
Jan 1997–July 1999	Jose Maria Gil-Robles (Spain)

Past Presidents of the Commission

Jan 1958–June 1966	Water Hallstein (Federal Republic of Germany)
June 1966–May 1970	Jean Rey (Belgium)
May 1970–Mar 1972	Franco Malfatti (Italy)
Mar 1972–Jan 1973	Sicco Mansholt (Netherlands)
Jan 1973–Jan 1977	François-Xavier Ortoli (France)
Jan 1977–Jan 1981	Roy Jenkins (U.K.)
Jan 1981–Jan 1985	Gaston Thorn (Luxembourg)
Jan 1985–Jan 1994	Jacques Delors (France)

Members*

Austria (joined Jan 1995)	Italy
Belgium	Luxembourg
Denmark (joined Jan 1973)	Netherlands
Finland (joined Jan 1995)	Portugal (joined Jan 1986)
France	Spain (joined Jan 1986)
Germany	Sweden (joined Jan 1995)
Greece (joined Jan 1981)	United Kingdom (joined Jan
Ireland (joined Jan 1973)	1973)

EUROPEAN FREE TRADE ASSOCIATION (EFTA)

Date of Formation   Treaty, 20 November 1959; in force, 3 May 1960

Headquarters   Geneva (Switzerland)

Aims
a)   To achieve free trade in industrial goods among members.
b)   To assist in the creation of a general Western European market.
c)   To contribute to the expansion of world trade in general.

History

The Stockholm Convention that brought EFTA into being had the above three aims. The first was achieved three years before the planned date on 31 December 1966. Finland removed its remaining tariffs a year later and Iceland on 31 December 1979. The second objective was achieved in 1972 when the United Kingdom and Denmark joined the EEC and five other countries (Austria, Iceland, Portugal, Sweden and Switzerland) signed free trade agreements with the EEC. Finland negotiated a separate agreement in 1973 and Norway on 14 May 1973 after failure to join the EEC. This free trade in industrial goods applied to Spain from 1 May 1980 and to Greece from 1 January 1981. The third aim has also been achieved with an increase in total exports from $6.852 billion in 1959 to $225.6 billion in 1990. Agricultural products are generally excluded but there are some bilateral agreements.

EFTA played a major role in the 1990s in helping develop the European Economic Area and in assisting the countries of the former Soviet bloc.

---

* Norway signed the Treaty of Accession on 22 January 1972 but a referendum rejected the treaty by a narrow majority. Norway reapplied, but again voters rejected membership in 1995. In April 1994 Hungary became the first former communist country seeking to join. Cyprus, Turkey, the Czech Republic and Poland are among other countries that seek to join.

Structure

Council in which each country holds the chair for six months. It meets twice a year with ministers present. The heads of national delegations meet every other week.

There are nine standing committees.

Secretary-General   Aug 1994   Kjartan Johannsson (Iceland)

Past Secretaries-General

Sep 1960–Oct 1965	Frank Figgures (U.K.)
Oct 1965–May 1972	John Coulson (U.K.)
May 1972–Dec 1975	Bengt Rabaeus (Sweden)
Jan 1976–Sep 1981	Charles Muller (Switzerland)
Oct 1981–Nov 1981	Magnus Vahlquist (Sweden) (Acting)
Dec 1981–Apr 1988	Per Kleppe (Norway)
Apr 1988–Aug 1994	Georg Reisch (Austria)

Members

Austria
Denmark (left 1972 to join EEC)
Finland (associate from 1961, full member 1986)
Iceland (joined 1970)
Liechtenstein
Norway
Portugal (left 1985 to join EEC)
Sweden
Switzerland
United Kingdom (left 1972 to join EEC)

EUROPEAN TRADE UNION CONFEDERATION (ETUC)

Date of Formation   February 1973

Headquarters   Brussels (Belgium)

Aims

To deal with matters of interest to European working people, both inside and outside the EEC.

History

The ETUC was originally founded by 15 affiliates of the International Confederation of Free Trade Unions within Europe, but later accepted members from European affiliates of the World Confederation of Labor, the Irish Congress of Trade Unions and the Italian Communist Trade Union Center.

Structure

ETUC Congress meets every three years.

Executive Committee meets six times a year.

General Secretary   Mathias Hinterscheid (Luxembourg)

Members

Originally, trade unions from Austria, Belgium, Denmark, Finland, France, Federal Republic of Germany, Iceland, Italy, Luxembourg, Netherlands, Norway, Sweden, Switzerland, the United Kingdom and the proscribed Spanish union. Now (2000) comprises 58 national trade union confederations.

INTERNATIONAL CONFEDERATION OF FREE TRADE UNIONS (ICFTU)

Date of Formation   December 1949

Headquarters   Brussels (Belgium)

Aims

a) To promote the interests of working people and to secure recognition of workers' organizations as free bargaining agents.
b) To reduce the gap between rich and poor.
c) To defend fundamental and trade union rights.

History

The ICFTU was set up at a congress in London in 1949 as a breakaway from the World Federation of Trade Unions, which, because of pressure from East European unions, had become an organization giving unquestioning support to the policies of the USSR.

Structure

Congress meets every four years. The 17th meeting was in South Africa, in April 2000. Delegations vary according to membership of national federations.

Executive Board meets at least twice a year. Thirty-seven members are nominated by the Congress on an area basis for a four-year period.

There are various committees concerned with specific problems, e.g., atomic energy, and there are regional organizations in North and South America, Asia and Africa.

General Secretary   Bill Jordan   (United Kingdom)

Members (2000)

Approximately 125 million workers from 215 organizations in 145 countries.

INTERNATIONAL MONETARY FUND (IMF)

Date of Formation   27 December 1945

Headquarters   Washington, D.C.

Aims
To promote international monetary cooperation and facilitate balanced trade.

History
The IMF came into existence during the Bretton Woods conference, 1–22 July 1944, when 29 countries signed its Charter. The IMF began operations in Washington, D.C., in May 1946 with 39 members and commenced financial operations on 1 March 1947. Following the Great Depression, the IMF was established to encourage the unrestricted conversion of one currency into another, establish an unequivocal value for each currency, and eliminate the competitive devaluations that had halted investment and trade during the 1930s. The IMF's membership now includes all major countries. The formerly centrally planned economies of Eastern Europe and the former Soviet Union have become members and are at various stages of completing their transition to market economies. Cuba, Czechoslovakia (now the Czech Republic and Slovak Republic), Indonesia, and Poland have left the IMF, but all except Cuba eventually rejoined. The IMF is now well known to the general public for lending billions of dollars to the countries at the center of the Asian financial crisis and to Russia. In the 1980s, the IMF was associated with large loans connected with the debt crisis, and then, in the 1990s, with very large credits to Mexico, Russia and various Asian countries.

Structure
Board of Governors, one from each member, and an equal number of Alternate Governors, meets annually to deal with IMF matters. An Interim Committee gives the board advice on the functioning of the international monetary system. The IMF/World Bank Development Committee advises the Interim Committee on the special needs of poorer countries. An Executive Board meets at least three times a week to supervise implementation of policies set by member governments through the Board of Governors.

Managing Director   Horst Köhler (Germany)

Members
Approximately 182 member countries.

LEAGUE OF ARAB STATES
see ARAB LEAGUE

NORTH ATLANTIC TREATY ORGANIZATION (NATO)

Date of Formation   Treaty, 4 April 1949; in force, 24 August 1949

Headquarters

Paris (France)	Until 1967
Brussels (Belgium)	Since 1967

Aims

a) To settle disputes by peaceful means.
b) To contribute to the development of friendly and peaceful international relations.
c) To develop individual and collective capacity to resist attack.
d) To regard an attack on one as an attack on all.
e) To take all possible action to repel an attack under Article 51 of the UN Charter.

History

The Brussels Treaty of 17 March 1948 was signed on the initiative of the U.K. foreign secretary and pledged five Western European nations to come to each other's aid in the event of armed aggression. A Canadian initiative put forward the idea of a single mutual defense system involving North America too, and this led to the creation of the Atlantic Alliance. Following the collapse of communism in Eastern Europe, the fall of the Soviet Union and the dissolution of the Warsaw Pact, a fundamental review of NATO's objectives is now being undertaken. In 1994, NATO launched Partnership for Peace (PFP) to expand and intensify political and military cooperation throughout Europe; PFP now has 26 member countries. In 1996, Russian forces joined NATO's peace-keeping missions in Bosnia, and in May 1997, NATO and Russia signed a Founding Act on Mutual Relations, Cooperation and Security, in which both sides agreed to stop viewing each other as adversaries.

Structure

North Atlantic Council is the highest authority. It consists of permanent representatives of members and meets at ministerial level (either foreign or defense ministers) at least twice a year. At ambassador level it meets once a week. Decisions are by common consent, not majority vote. The secretary-general is the chairman and the presidency rotates among foreign ministers for one-year terms.

Military Committee consists of chiefs of staff and meets at least twice a year, but remains in permanent session at the level of military representatives.

There are three commands: the Atlantic Ocean Command, the European Command and the Channel Command. The North American sphere is covered by the Canada–U.S. Regional Planning Group.

Secretary-General   Oct 1999   Lord Robertson (United Kingdom)

Secretaries-General

Apr 1952–May 1957	Lord Ismay (U.K.)
May 1957–Mar 1961	Paul-Henri Spaak (Belgium)
Mar 1961–Apr 1961	Alberico Casardi (Acting; Italy)
Apr 1961–July 1964	Dirk Stikker (Holland)
Aug 1964–Oct 1971	Manlio Brosio (Italy)
Oct 1971–June 1984	Joseph Lŭns (Holland)
June 1984–July 1988	Lord Carrington (U.K.)
July 1988–Oct 1994	Manfred Worner (Germany)
Oct 1994–Dec 1995	Willy Claes (Belgium)
Dec 1995–Oct 1999	Javier Solana (Spain)

Supreme Allied Commanders, Europe

Dec 1950–Apr 1952	Dwight D. Eisenhower (U.S.)
Apr 1952–July 1953	Matthew Ridgway (U.S.)
July 1953–Nov 1956	Alfred M. Gruenther (U.S.)
Nov 1956–Jan 1963	Lauris Norstad (U.S.)
Jan 1963–July 1969	Lyman L. Lemnitzer (U.S.)
July 1969–Dec 1974	Andrew J. Goodpaster (U.S.)
Dec 1974–June 1979	Alexander Haig (U.S.)
June 1979–June 1987	Bernard Rogers (U.S.)
June 1987–June 1992	John R. Galvin (U.S.)
June 1992–Oct 1993	John Shalikashvili (U.S.)
Oct 1993–July 1997	George A. Joulwan (U.S.)
July 1997–May 2000	Wesley Clark (U.S.)
May 2000–	Joseph W. Ralston (U.S.)

Members

Belgium
Canada
Czech Republic (joined 1999)
Denmark
France (withdrew from Military Committee in 1966 while remaining member of Council)
Germany (joined 1955)*
Greece (joined 1952, withdrew from military structure after Turkish invasion of Cyprus in 1974, rejoined 1980)
Hungary (joined 1999)
Iceland
Italy
Luxembourg
Netherlands
Norway
Poland (joined 1999)
Portugal
Spain (joined 1982)
Turkey (joined 1952)
United Kingdom
United States

---

* When, of course, Germany was a divided nation.

ORGANIZATION OF AFRICAN UNITY (OAU)

Date of Formation   25 May 1963

Headquarters   Addis Ababa (Ethiopia)

Aims
a)   The furtherance of African unity and solidarity.
b)   The coordination of political, economic, cultural, health, scientific and defense policies of members.
c)   The elimination of colonialism in Africa.

History
After various attempts to set up an inter-African organization had failed, a meeting of heads of state or government in Addis Ababa in 1963 signed a charter setting up the OAU.

Structure
Assembly of heads of state meets annually.

Council of Ministers meets twice a year, generally foreign ministers.

Committee of Mediation, Conciliation and Arbitration was formed in 1964 and consists of 21 members elected for a five-year term.

Secretary-General   Since July 1989   Salim Ahmed Salim (Tanzania)

Past Secretaries-General
July 1964–July 1972	Diallo Telli (Guinea)
July 1972–July 1974	Nzo Ekangaki (Cameroon)
July 1974–July 1978	William Eteki Mbomua (Cameroon)
July 1978–July 1983	Edem Kodjo (Togo)
July 1983–July 1985	Peter Onu (Nigeria) (Acting)
July 1985–July 1989	Ide Oumarou (Niger)

Members
Algeria*
Angola
Benin*
Botswana
Burkina Faso*
Burundi*
Cameroon*
Cape Verde

Central African
   Republic*
Chad*
Comoros
Congo, People's
   Republic of the
Democratic Repub-
   lic of the Congo

Djibouti
Egypt*
Equatorial Guinea
Eritrea
Ethiopia*
Gabon*
Gambia
Ghana*

* Original members

Guinea*	Morocco* **	Sierra Leone*
Guinea-Bissau	Mozambique	Somalia*
Ivory Coast*	Namibia	South Africa
Kenya	Niger*	Sudan*
Lesotho	Nigeria*	Swaziland
Liberia*	Rwanda*	Tanzania*
Libya*	Saharan Repub-	Togo*
Madagascar*	lic**	Tunisia*
Malawi	São Tomé and	Uganda*
Mali*	Principe	Zambia
Mauritania*	Senegal*	Zimbabwe
Mauritius	Seychelles	

ORGANIZATION OF AMERICAN STATES (OAS)

Date of Formation   Treaty, 30 April 1948; in force, 13 Dec 1951

Headquarters   Washington, D.C. (U.S.)

Aims
a)   To achieve an order of peace and justice.
b)   To promote American solidarity.
c)   To strengthen cooperation among members.
d)   To defend sovereignty, integrity and independence of members.

History
In 1890 the International Union of American Republics was set up, which, in 1910, became the Pan American Union. Its original aim was cooperation and mutual understanding among the nations of the Western Hemisphere. Successive conferences broadened the scope of the work until the Ninth International Conference of American States in Bogota adopted the Charter of the Organization of American States. On 27 February 1970 the Protocol of Buenos Aires, modifying the 1948 charter, came into effect.

Structure
General Assembly held annually in member countries in turn.

Meeting of Consultation of Ministers of Foreign Affairs meets to consider urgent problems at the request of any member.

Permanent Council consists of one member from each country with the rank of ambassador. The office of chairman is held in alphabetical order for a three-month term.

---

* Original members
** The Saharan Republic was admitted in 1984 after Nigeria became the 30th member to recognize it. Morocco resigned in protest.

There are also four other councils: the Economic and Social Council, the Council for Education, Science and Culture, the Juridical Council and the Commission on Human Rights.

Secretary-General   Since March 1994   Cesar Gavira (Colombia)

Past Secretaries-General

May 1948–Aug 1954	Alberto Lleras Camargo (Colombia)
Aug 1954–Oct 1956	Carlos Davila (Chile)
Oct 1956–Feb 1968	José Mora Otero (Uruguay)
Feb 1968–May 1975	Galo Plaza Lasso (Ecuador)
May 1975–Mar 1984	Alejandro Orfila (Argentina)
Mar 1984–June 1984	Valerie McComie (Barbados) (Acting)
June 1984–Mar 1994	João Clemente Baena Soares (Brazil)

Members

Antigua and Barbuda (joined 1981)
Argentina (joined 1956)
Bahamas (joined 1982)
Barbados (joined 1967)
Belize
Bolivia
Brazil
Canada
Chile (joined 1953)
Colombia
Costa Rica
Cuba* (joined 1952)
Dominica (joined 1979)
Dominican Republic
Ecuador
El Salvador
Grenada (joined 1975)
Guatemala (joined 1955)
Guyana
Haiti
Honduras
Jamaica (joined 1969)
Mexico
Nicaragua
Panama
Paraguay
Peru (joined 1954)
St. Kitts-Nevis (joined 1984)
St. Lucia (joined 1979)
St. Vincent and the Grenadines (joined 1981)
Suriname (joined 1977)
Trinidad and Tobago (joined 1967)
United States
Uruguay (joined 1955)
Venezuela

ORGANIZATION FOR ECONOMIC COOPERATION AND DEVELOPMENT (OECD)

Date of Formation   Treaty, 14 December 1960; in force, 30 September 1961

---

* Excluded 1962 from activities but not from membership.

Headquarters   Paris (France)

Aims

a) To promote social and economic welfare throughout the OECD area by assisting members to formulate policies.
b) To contribute to the economic expansion of developing countries.

History

The OECD replaced the OEEC *(q.v.)* in 1961 when it ceased to be a purely European body and added development aid to its activities.

Structure

Council meets at heads of delegation level weekly and at ministerial level once a year.

Executive Committee consists of 14 members elected annually by Council.

There are three major committees—Economic Policy Committee, Development Aid Committee and Trade Committee—as well as over 200 specialized committees and working groups.

There are also five autonomous or semiautonomous bodies:

Development Centre, which began in 1963

Centre for Educational Research and Innovation, set up in 1968

International Energy Agency

Nuclear Energy Agency

Centre for Cooperation with European Economies in Transition

Secretary-General   Since June 1996   Donald Johnston (Canada)

Past Secretaries-General

Sep 1961–Sep 1969   Thorkil Kristensen (Denmark)
Sep 1969–Sep 1984   Emile van Lennep (Netherlands)
Sep 1984–June 1996   Jean-Claude Paye (France)

Members

Australia (joined 1971)	Germany	Netherlands
Austria	Greece	New Zealand (joined 1973
Belgium	Hungary (joined 1996)	Norway
Canada	Iceland	Portugal
Czech Republic (joined 1995)	Ireland	Spain
Denmark	Italy	Sweden
Finland (joined 1969)	Japan (joined 1964)	Switzerland
France	Luxembourg	Turkey
	Mexico (joined 1994)	United Kingdom
		United States

ORGANIZATION FOR EUROPEAN ECONOMIC COOPERATION (OEEC)

Date of Formation 16 April 1948 Replaced by OECD 1960

Headquarters Paris (France)

Aims

a) To work closely together for the economic reconstruction and well-being of Europe.

b) To achieve a sound European economy through the cooperation of members.

History

The Economic Cooperation Act, signed in Paris in April 1948, aimed to restore the European economy by the end of 1951. After the end of Marshall Aid in 1952, OEEC continued to operate until it was replaced in 1960 by OECD *(q.v.)*.

Structure

Council consisting of all members.

Executive Committee of seven elected by Council.

There were numerous technical committees.

Secretaries-General

Apr 1948–Apr 1955	Robert Marjolin (France)
Apr 1955–Sep 1960	Rene Sergent (France)
Sep 1960 until it became OECD	Thorkil Kristensen (Denmark)

Members

Austria	Greece	Spain (joined 1958)
Belgium	Iceland	Sweden
Canada	Ireland	Switzerland
(associate member)	Italy	Turkey
Denmark	Luxembourg	United Kingdom
France	Netherlands	United States (associ-
Germany	Norway	ate member)
(western)	Portugal	

ORGANIZATION OF THE ISLAMIC CONFERENCE (OIC)

Date of Formation May 1971

Headquarters Jeddah (Saudi Arabia)

Aims

a) To cooperate in economic, social, cultural, scientific and other spheres.

b) To eliminate racism and colonialism in all their forms.
c) To safeguard the holy places and support the struggle of Palestine and of all Muslim people.

History

The leaders of 24 Muslim states met at Rabat, Morocco, in September 1969 following the burning of the Al Aqsa Mosque in Jerusalem. Two further meetings of foreign ministers took place in Jeddah, Saudi Arabia, and Karachi, Pakistan, in 1970; the organization was established in May 1971 and its official charter adopted in 1972. There are currently (1994) 51 member states or states with observer status.

Structure

Summit Conferences are held every three years. The eighth conference took place in Iran in December 1997.

Conferences of Foreign Ministers take place annually.

There are also six specialized or standing committees.

Secretary-General   Azeddine Laraki (Morocco)

Members

Afghanistan (suspended Jan 1980)
Albania
Algeria
Azerbaijan
Bahrain
Bangladesh
Benin
Brunei
Burkina Faso
Cameroon
Chad
Comoros
Djibouti
Egypt (suspended May 1979, restored March 1984)
Eritrea

Gabon
The Gambia
Guinea
Guinea-Bissau
Indonesia
Iran
Iraq
Jordan
Kuwait
Kyrgyzstan
Lebanon
Libya
Malaysia
Maldives
Mali
Mauritania
Morocco
Niger

Oman
Pakistan
Palestine Liberation Organization
Qatar
Saudi Arabia
Senegal
Sierra Leone
Somalia
Sudan
Syria
Tunisia
Turkey
Uganda
United Arab Emirates
Yemen

Observers

Nigeria
The Turkish Federated State of Cyprus
Mozambique

Zanzibar (part of Tanzania) was given Conference membership in December 1992.

ORGANIZATION OF PETROLEUM EXPORTING COUNTRIES (OPEC)

Date of Formation 14 September 1960

Headquarters Vienna (Austria)

Aims

a) To unify the petroleum policies of members.
b) To safeguard the interests of members.
c) To devise methods of stabilizing prices in international oil markets.
d) To secure regular income for producers, steady supply for consumers and fair return on investment in the industry.

History

A Venezuelan initiative led to the setting up of OPEC after a meeting in Baghdad, Iraq, in 1960. Membership is open to any country with substantial exports of crude petroleum that shares the interests of the members.

Structure

Conference with representatives of member countries meets at least twice a year.

Board of Governors directs management and consists of one member per country, meeting at least twice a year.

Economic Commission is a specialized body designed to promote stability of oil prices.

OPEC Fund for International Development was set up in 1976 to provide aid to non-OPEC developing countries on generous terms.

Secretary-General Jan 1995– Dr. Rilwanu Lukman (Nigeria)

Past Secretaries-General

Jan 1961–Apr 1964	Fuad Rouhani (Iran)
May 1964–Apr 1965	Abdul Rahman Al-Bazzaz (Iraq)
May 1965–Dec 1966	Ashraf Lutfi (Kuwait)
Jan 1967–Dec 1967	Mohammed S. Joukhdar (Saudi Arabia)
Jan 1968–Dec 1968	Francisco R. Parra (Venezuela)
Jan 1969–Dec 1969	Elrich Sanger (Indonesia)
Jan 1970–Dec 1970	Omar El-Badri (Libya)
Jan 1971–Dec 1972	Nadim Pachachi (UAE)
Jan 1973–Dec 1974	Abderrahman Khene (Algeria)
Jan 1975–Dec 1976	M. O. Feyide (Nigeria)
Jan 1977–Dec 1978	Ali M. Jaidah (Qatar)
Jan 1979–Dec 1981	Rene G. Ortiz (Ecuador)

Jan 1981–June 1983
June 1983–July 1988
July 1988–June 1994
July 1994–Dec 1994

Marc S. Nan Nguema (Gabon)
Fadhil J. Al-Chalabi (Iraq)*
Dr. Subroto (Indonesia)
Abdalla Salem El Balri (Libya)

Members

Algeria (joined 1969)
Ecuador (joined 1973, left 1992)
Gabon (joined 1973 as associate,
   1975 as full member)
Indonesia (joined 1962)
Iran
Iraq**
Kuwait

Libya (joined 1962)
Nigeria (joined 1971)
Qatar (joined 1961)
Saudi Arabia
United Arab Emirates (joined
   1967 as Abu Dhabi)
Venezuela

Observers

Malaysia
Mexico

THE SECRETARIAT OF THE PACIFIC COMMUNITY
(formerly THE SOUTH PACIFIC COMMISSION) (SPC)

Date of Formation   Treaty, February 1947; in force, July 1948

Headquarters   Nouméa (New Caledonia)

Aims

a)   To discuss regional issues.
b)   To give training and assistance in economic, social and cultural development to countries in the region.

History

The agreement was signed in Canberra, Australia, in February 1947 by
the governments of Australia, France, the Netherlands, New Zealand,
the United Kingdom and the United States. The Netherlands withdrew
in 1962 when it ceased to administer Dutch New Guinea. Since 1947
the conference has been attended by all countries within the Commission's sphere of action.

Structure

South Pacific Conference is held annually and is the supreme decision-
making body.

---

* Acting for the secretary-general.
** Oil exports halted after 1990 by UN embargo.

Committee of Representatives meets annually before the main SPC and consists of representatives of all 27 members, each with equal voting rights.

Secretary-General
Jan 2000   Lourdes Pangelinan (Guam)

Members

American Samoa (joined 1983)
Australia
Cook Islands (joined 1980)
Fiji (joined 1971)
France
French Polynesia (joined 1983)
Guam (joined 1983)
Kiribati (joined 1983)
Marshall Islands (joined 1983)
Federated States of Micronesia
   (joined 1983)
Nauru (joined 1969)
Netherlands (withdrew 1962)
New Caledonia (joined 1983)
New Zealand
Niue (joined 1980)

Northern Mariana Islands (joined
   1983)
Palau (joined 1983)
Papua New Guinea (joined 1975)
Pitcairn Islands (joined 1983)
Solomon Islands (joined 1978)
Tokelau (joined 1983)
Tonga (joined 1983)
Tuvalu (joined 1978)
United Kingdom
United States
Vanuatu (joined 1983)
Wallis and Futuna Islands (joined
   1983)
Western Samoa (joined 1965)

UNITED NATIONS

Date of Formation   Charter, 26 June 1945; in force 24 October 1945.

Headquarters   New York (U.S.)

Aims
a) To maintain international peace and security.
b) To cooperate in establishing political, economic and social conditions under which this task can be securely achieved.

History
A four-nation conference of foreign ministers signed an agreement in Moscow on 30 October 1943 that "a general international organization . . . for the maintenance of international peace and security" was desirable. Further discussions took place at Dumbarton Oaks (Washington, D.C.) from 21 August until 7 October 1944, first among the United Kingdom, the United States and the USSR and then China, the United Kingdom and the United States. These proposals were put before the United Nations Conference on International Organization held in San Francisco between 25 April and 26 June 1945, when, after amendments, the Charter was signed. It came into force on 24 October 1945 when

China, France, the United Kingdom, the United States, the USSR and a majority of the other 45 signatories ratified the Charter. The first regular session was held in London from 10 January to 14 February 1946.

Structure

General Assembly consists of all members, each with five delegates but only one vote. It meets once a year starting on the third Tuesday in September. A special session can be called at the request of the Security Council, by the agreement of a majority of members or at the request of one member with the concurrence of the majority. The president is elected each session. Important decisions require a two-thirds majority, other decisions a simple majority of members present and voting. The Assembly has seven main committees.

Security Council is responsible for the maintenance of peace and security and can call on the armed forces of member states to help achieve that purpose. It consists of 15 members, each with one representative and one vote. China, France, the United Kingdom, the United States and Russia are permanent members. The others are elected by a two-thirds majority in the General Assembly. They serve for two years and are not immediately eligible for reelection. The Council functions continuously and its president serves for one month in alphabetical rotation. Procedural questions must be agreed on by at least nine of its members. On other matters the nine concurring votes must include the five permanent members.

Economic and Social Council is responsible for economic, social, cultural, educational, health and related matters. There are 15 specialized intergovernmental agencies, and consultation takes place with numerous international nongovernmental agencies and national organizations. It consists of 54 members elected by a two-thirds majority of the General Assembly. Eighteen are elected each year for a three-year period and can be reelected immediately. It holds two sessions a year. Its president is elected for one year and may be reelected. Decisions are made by a majority vote of those present and voting. The Council has numerous commissions and standing committees.

Trusteeship Council is responsible for the interests of territories that are not yet fully self-governing. There were formerly 11 of these Trust Territories. The members of the Council are the permanent members of the Security Council; they meet in regular session once a year and votes are by a majority of members present and voting.

International Court of Justice consists of 15 independent judges, each of a different nationality, elected by the Security Council and the General Assembly sitting independently. They meet at The Hague, Netherlands, in permanent session and serve for a nine-year term after which they may be reelected. The president and vice president are elected by the Court for three-year terms. Decisions are made by a majority of judges present, and a quorum of nine is sufficient to constitute the Court. All members of the UN are parties to the Statute of the Court. Judgments are final and without appeal.

Secretariat in New York is administered by the secretary-general, who is appointed by the General Assembly for a five-year term that can be renewed.

Secretary-General   Jan 1997   Kofi Anan (Ghana)

Past Secretaries-General

Feb 1946–Apr 1953	Trygve Lie (Norway)
Apr 1953–Sep 1961	Dag Hammarskjöld (Sweden)
Nov 1961–Dec 1971	U Thant (Burma)
Jan 1972–Dec 1981	Kurt Waldheim (Austria)
Jan 1982–Dec 1991	Javier Pérez de Cuéllar (Peru)
Jan 1992–Dec 1996	Boutros Boutros-Ghali (Egypt)

Members

Afghanistan (joined 1946)
Albania (joined 1955)
Algeria (joined 1962)
Andorra (joined 1993)
Angola (joined (1976)
Antigua and Barbuda (joined 1981)
Argentina (joined 1945)
Armenia (joined 1992)
Australia (joined 1945)
Austria (joined 1955)
Azerbaijan (joined 1992)
Bahamas (joined 1973)
Bahrain (joined 1971)
Bangladesh (joined 1974)
Barbados (joined 1966)
Belarus (joined 1945 as Byelorussian Soviet Socialist Republic)
Belgium (joined 1945)
Belize (joined 1981)
Benin (joined 1960)
Bhutan (joined 1971)
Bolivia (joined 1945)
Bosnia and Herzegovina (joined 1992)

Botswana (joined 1966)
Brazil (joined 1945)
Brunei (joined 1984)
Bulgaria (joined 1955)
Burkina Faso (joined 1960)
Burma (see Myanmar)
Burundi (joined 1962)
Byelorussia (see Belarus)
Cambodia (joined 1955)
Cameroon (joined 1960)
Canada (joined 1945)
Cape Verde (joined 1975)
Central African Republic (joined 1960)
Chad (joined 1960)
Chile (joined 1945)
China (joined 1945)
Colombia (joined 1945)
Comoros (joined 1975)
Congo, People's Republic of the (joined 1960)
Costa Rica (joined 1945)
Croatia (joined 1992)
Cuba (joined 1945)
Cyprus (joined 1960)

Czechoslovakia (joined 1945)*
Czech Republic (joined 1993)
Democratic Republic of the
   Congo (1960)
Denmark (joined 1945)
Djibouti (joined 1977)
Dominica (joined 1978)
Dominican Republic (joined
   1945)
Ecuador (joined 1945)
Egypt (joined 1945)
El Salvador (joined 1945)
Equatorial Guinea (joined 1968)
Eritrea (joined 1993)
Estonia (joined 1991)
Ethiopia (joined 1945)
Fiji (joined 1970)
Finland (joined 1955)
France (joined 1945)
Gabon (joined 1960)
The Gambia (joined 1965)
Georgia (joined 1992)
Germany (joined 1973)**
Ghana (joined 1957)
Greece (joined 1945)
Grenada (joined 1974)
Guatemala (joined 1945)
Guinea (joined 1958)
Guinea-Bissau (joined 1974)
Guyana (joined 1966)
Haiti (joined 1945)
Honduras (joined 1945)
Hungary (joined 1955)
Iceland (joined 1946)
India (joined 1945)
Indonesia (joined 1950)
Iran, Islamic Republic of (joined
   1945)
Iraq (joined 1945)
Ireland (joined 1955)

Israel (joined 1949)
Italy (joined 1955)
Ivory Coast (joined 1960)
Jamaica (joined 1962)
Japan (joined 1956)
Jordan (joined 1955)
Kazakhstan (joined 1992)
Kenya (joined 1963)
Kiribati (joined 1999)
Korea, North (joined 1991)
Korea, South (joined 1991)
Kuwait (joined 1963)
Kyrgyzstan (joined 1992)
Lao People's Democratic Republic
   (joined 1955)
Latvia (joined 1991)
Lebanon (joined 1945)
Lesotho (joined 1966)
Liberia (joined 1945)
Libyan Arab Jamahiriya (joined
   1955)
Liechtenstein (joined 1990)
Lithuania (joined 1991)
Luxembourg (joined 1945)
Macedonia (joined 1993)
Madagascar (joined 1960)
Malawi (joined 1964)
Malaysia (joined 1957)
Maldives (joined 1965)
Mali (joined 1960)
Malta (joined 1964)
Marshall Islands
   (joined 1991)
Mauritania (joined 1961)
Mauritius (joined 1968)
Mexico (joined 1945)
Micronesia, Federated States of
   (joined 1991)
Moldova (joined 1992)
Monaco (joined 1993)

---

* Czechoslovakia ceased to exist on 31 December 1992.
** As the two states of East and West Germany.

Mongolia (joined 1961)
Morocco (joined 1956)
Mozambique (joined 1975)
Myanmar (Burma) (joined 1948)
Namibia (joined 1990)
Nauru (joined 1999)
Nepal (joined 1955)
Netherlands (joined 1945)
New Zealand (joined 1945)
Nicaragua (joined 1945)
Niger (joined 1960)
Nigeria (joined 1960)
Norway (joined 1945)
Oman (joined 1971)
Pakistan (joined 1947)
Palau (joined 1994)
Panama (joined 1945)
Papua New Guinea (joined 1975)
Paraguay (joined 1945)
Peru (joined 1945)
Philippines (joined 1945)
Poland (joined 1945)
Portugal (joined 1955)
Qatar (joined 1971)
Romania (joined 1955)
Russia (replaced USSR) (1991)
Rwanda (joined 1962)
Saint Christopher and Nevis (joined 1983)
Saint Lucia (joined 1979)
Saint Vincent and the Grenadines (joined 1980)
Samoa (joined 1976)
San Marino (joined 1992)
São Tomé and Principe (joined 1975)
Saudi Arabia (joined 1945)
Senegal (joined 1960)
Seychelles (joined 1976)
Sierra Leone (joined 1961)
Singapore (joined 1965)
Slovakia (joined 1993)
Slovenia (joined 1992)

Solomon Islands (joined 1978)
Somalia (joined 1960)
South Africa (joined 1945)
Spain (joined December 1955)
Sri Lanka (joined 1955)
Sudan (joined 1956)
Suriname (joined 1975)
Swaziland (joined 1968)
Sweden (joined 1946)
Syrian Arab Republic (joined 1945)
Tajikistan (joined 1992)
Tanzania (joined 1961)
Thailand (joined 1946)
Togo (joined 1960)
Tonga (joined 1999)
Trinidad and Tobago (joined 1962)
Tunisia (joined 1956)
Turkey (joined 1945)
Turkmenistan (joined 1992)
Uganda (joined 1962)
Ukraine (formerly Ukrainian Soviet Socialist Republic) (joined 1945)
Union of Soviet Socialist Republics (1945–1991)
United Arab Emirates (joined 1971)
United Kingdom of Great Britain and Northern Ireland (joined 1945)
United States of America (joined 1945)
Uruguay (joined 1945)
Uzbekistan (joined 1992)
Vanuatu (joined 1981)
Venezuela (joined 1945)
Vietnam (joined 1977)
Yemen (joined 1947)
Yugoslavia (joined 1945)
Zambia (joined 1964)
Zimbabwe (joined 1980)

With the admission of Kiribati, Nauru and Tonga in September 1999, there are now 188 member states of the United Nations.

WARSAW PACT*

Date of Formation   Treaty, 14 May 1955; in force, 5 June 1955

Headquarters   Moscow (USSR)

Aims
a)   To safeguard the peace and security of members of the Pact.
b)   To aid with all necessary steps, including armed force, any member of the Pact who is attacked.
c)   To establish a joint command of armed forces, including joint maneuvers.

History
The Warsaw Pact was originally signed in Warsaw in 1955 after the USSR had annulled alliances with the United Kingdom and France. It was extended for a further 10 years in June 1975 and renewed for a further 20 years from April 1985. However, with the revolutions in Eastern Europe in 1989, the Warsaw Pact virtually ceased to function as a military grouping. As such countries as Hungary announced their intention to leave, the Pact began a review of its future in June 1990. Later that year its military function was abandoned. The Pact was formally ended on 1 July 1991.

Structure
Political Consultative Committee was intended to meet twice a year with rotating venue and chairmanship. In fact it met every alternate year with delegations led by first secretaries of the party.

Committee of Defense Ministers met annually.

Committee of Foreign Ministers met annually from 1976.

Military Council of national chiefs of staff met twice a year.

Commanders in Chief
1955–June 1960	Marshal I. S. Konev (USSR)
June 1960–July 1967	Marshal A. A. Grechko (USSR)
July 1967–76	Marshal I. I. Yakubovsky (USSR)
1977–July 1991	Marshal Viktor G. Kulikov (USSR)

---

* Formally ended on 1 July 1991

Members

Albania (ceased to participate in 1961 because of Stalinist and pro-Chinese attitudes; withdrew in 1968)
Bulgaria
Czechoslovakia
German Democratic Republic*
Hungary
Poland
Romania
USSR

WESTERN EUROPEAN UNION (WEU)

Date of Formation   Treaty, 23 October 1954; in force, 6 May 1955

Headquarters   London (England); Brussels (Belgium) since 1993.

Aims

a)   To coordinate defense policy and equipment of members.
b)   To collaborate in political, legal and cultural affairs.

History

On 17 March 1948 the Brussels Treaty for "collaboration in economic, social and cultural matters and for collective self-defense" was signed by Belgium, France, Luxembourg, the Netherlands and the United Kingdom. On 20 December 1950 the defense functions were transferred to NATO.

In early October 1954 the Brussels Treaty powers together with representatives of the Federal Republic of Germany, Italy, Canada and the United States met in London. The following decisions were made:

i)   The Federal Republic of Germany and Italy should be invited to accede to the Brussels Treaty.
ii)   The occupation of Western Germany should be ended.
iii)   The Federal Republic of Germany should be invited to accede to the North Atlantic Treaty.
iv)   The Federal Republic should voluntarily limit its arms production.
v)   An agency should be set up to control armaments of the seven Brussels Treaty powers.
vi)   The United Kingdom should undertake not to withdraw her four divisions from the continent against the wishes of a majority of the powers.

These decisions were ratified at a Conference of Ministers in Paris in October 1954.

---

* On 24 September 1990 East Germany formally announced its withdrawal from the Warsaw Pact.

In October 1984 a WEU meeting in Rome agreed on institutional reform and the reactivation of the Union's contribution to the North Atlantic Alliance. WEU is now (1994) being developed as the defense element of a future European Union.

Structure

Council consists of the foreign ministers or their representatives.

Assembly consists of the WEU delegates to the Consultative Assembly of the Council of Europe. It meets twice a year in Paris.

Agency for the Control of Armaments and **Standing Armaments Committee** have been set up in Paris.

The social and cultural activities were transferred to the Council of Europe on 1 June 1960.

Secretary-General   Since Nov 1999   Dr. Javier Solana Madariaga (Spain)

Past Secretaries-General

May 1955–Dec 1962	Louis Goffin (Belgium)
Dec 1962–Dec 1970	Maurice Iweins d'Eeckhoutte (Belgium)
Jan 1971–Sep 1974	Georges Heisbourg (Luxembourg)
Oct 1974–Mar 1977	F. K. von Plehwe (Acting)
Mar 1977–May 1985	Edouard Longerstaey (Belgium)
June 1985–1989	Alfred Cahen (Belgium)
1989–Nov 1999	William van Eekelen (Netherlands)

Members

Belgium	Italy	Portugal
France	Luxembourg	Spain
Germany	Netherlands	United Kingdom
Greece		

WORLD BANK (INTERNATIONAL BANK FOR RECONSTRUCTION AND DEVELOPMENT [IBRD])

Date of Formation   27 December 1945; in operation June 1946

Headquarters   Washington, D.C. (U.S.)

Aims

a) To encourage capital investment either by channeling necessary private funds or by making loans.

b) To provide funds and technical assistance to help economic development in poorer member countries.

History

The idea of a World Bank was conceived at the Bretton Woods Conference of 44 countries in July 1944. It obtains funds from

- i) capital subscribed by member countries
- ii) sales of its own securities
- iii) sales of parts of its loans
- iv) repayments
- v) net earnings

Structure

Consultative groups of aid-giving nations.

Resident missions in 33 developing countries as well as three regional missions.

Economic Development Institute is a staff college in Washington, D.C., for senior officials of member countries.

President   June 1995   James D. Wolfensdin (U.S.)

Past Presidents

18 June 1946–18 Dec 1946	Eugene Mayer (U.S.)
17 Mar 1947–30 June 1949	John J. McCloy (U.S.)
1 July 1949–31 Dec 1962	Eugene R. Black (U.S.)
1 Jan 1963–31 Mar 1968	George D. Woods (U.S.)
1 Apr 1968–30 June 1981	Robert S. McNamara (U.S.)
1 July 1981–June 1986	Alden W. Clausen (U.S.)
July 1986–July 1991	Barber Conable (U.S.)
July 1991–May 1995	Lewis Preston (U.S.)

Members

All members must be members of the International Monetary Fund (IMF). Membership in the International Development Association (IDA), the International Finance Corporation (IFC) and the Multilateral Investment Guarantee Agency (MIGA) are conditional on membership in the International Bank for Reconstruction and Development (IBRD). A fifth organization is the International Centre for the Settlement of Investment Disputes (ICSID).

At present there are 181 countries in membership with the World Bank.

WORLD CONFEDERATION OF LABOUR (WCL)

Date of Formation   1968

Headquarters   Brussels (Belgium)

Aims

Originally based on two papal encyclicals, *Rerum novarum* (1891) and *Quadragesimo anno* (1931), the WCL now includes Protestants, Buddhists and Muslims.

History

The International Federation of Christian Trade Unions originally met in 1920 and was largely Catholic. It ceased to exist in 1940 when affiliated unions in Germany and Italy were suppressed. It was reconstituted in 1945 and renamed in 1968.

Structure

Congress that meets every four years in member countries.

General Council meets annually and consists of members of Confederal Board and representatives of national and international bodies.

Confederal Board comprises 22 members elected by Congress and is responsible for general leadership.

Executive of at least 12 members elected by Congress.

There are regional offices in Latin America, Africa and Asia.

Secretary-General   Willy Thys (Belgium)

Members

Approximately 26 million workers in about 113 countries.

WORLD FEDERATION OF TRADE UNIONS (WFTU)

Date of Formation   3 October 1945

Headquarters   Prague (Czechoslovakia)*

Aims

To represent trade union organizations throughout the world.

History

The WFTU was originally set up to represent trade union organizations in more than 50 countries, both communist and noncommunist. Trade unions from the Netherlands, the United Kingdom and the United States withdrew in January 1949 because of communist domination, and by 1951 all noncommunist organizations had left, as well as the Yugoslavian Federation.

---

* The Czech government withdrew permission for the WFTU to operate from Prague in 1990. An appeal was lodged.

Structure

World Trade Union Congress meets every four years, the size of the delegation being based on the total membership of the national federations.

General Council of 134 members is the governing body and meets annually.

Bureau elected by Council controls activities between meetings. It consists of the president, general secretary and members from different continents.

General Secretary   Aleksandr Zharikov (Russia)

Members

Approximately 188 million workers from 92 national federations.

WORLD TRADE ORGANIZATION (WTO)

Date of Formation   1 January 1995

Headquarters   Geneva (Switzerland)

Aims

To supervise and liberalize world trade and resolve conflicts.

History

The WTO is the successor to the General Agreement on Tariffs and Trade (GATT), which was created in 1947 and initially intended to be replaced by a United Nations agency to be called the International Trade Organization (ITO). GATT successfully liberalized world trade over five decades, but was dissolved in 1994 during the Uruguay Round trade conference amid calls for a stronger multilateral organization to monitor trade and resolve disputes. The WTO was established with 104 countries as founding members. At the end of 1999, the WTO fell under attack for a free trade system that favors multinational corporations. Thousands of protesters shut down the Seattle conference, charging the organization with exploiting workers, destroying the environment and violating human rights. As the largest trade gathering ever held in the United States, the conference was intended to showcase the benefits of free trade, but talks soon broke down between Western and developing nations. The conference collapsed before President Clinton gained sufficient support for his plan to liberalize trade and broaden WTO's mandate.

Structure

Ministerial Conference meets every two years and appoints the director-general. General Council meets several times a year to implement the conference's policy decisions and is responsible for day to day administration. The General Council also meets as the Trade Policy Review Body and the Dispute Settlement Body. Goods Council, Services Council and Intellectual Property (TRIPS) Council report to the General Council.

Director-General   Since September 1999   Mike Moore (New Zealand)

Members

Approximately 136 members.

CHAPTER 2

HEADS OF STATE AND GOVERNMENT

AFGHANISTAN

Heads of State: King
Mohammed Zahir Shah   Nov 1933–July 1973

Heads of State: President
Mohammed Daud	July 1973–Apr 1978
Nur Mohammed Taraki	Apr 1978–Oct 1979
Hafizullah Amin	Oct 1979*–Dec 1979
Babrak Karmal	Dec 1979–Dec 1986
Mohammed Najibullah	Dec 1986**–Apr 1992***
Sibghattolah Majaddedi	April 1992–June 1992
Burhanuddin Rabbani	June 1992–Sep 1996

(Temporary government in place—Sep 1996)

Heads of Government: Prime Minister
Sidar Hashim Khan	Nov 1929–Mar 1946
Shad Mahmud Khan	Mar 1946–Sep 1953
Sardar Mohammed Daud	Sep 1953–Mar 1963
Mohammed Yusa	Mar 1963–Nov 1965
Mohammed Maiwandwal	Nov 1965–Oct 1967
Abdullah Yakta (Acting)	Oct 1967–Nov 1967
Nar Etemadi	Nov 1967–June 1971
Abdul Zahir	June 1971–Dec 1972

---

* Amin replaced Taraki as secretary-general (SG) of the People's Democratic Party of Afghanistan (PDPA) in September 1979 but did not officially become president until October 1979.

** Najibullah replaced Karmal as SG of the PDPA in May 1986 but did not officially become president until December 1986.

*** Abdul Rahim Ratif was briefly acting president in April 1992 after the fall of Najibullah. Majaddedi then became acting president for four months before handing over power to Rabbani.

Mohammed Shafeq	Dec 1972–July 1973
Mohammed Daud	July 1973–Apr 1978
Nur Mohammed Taraki	Apr 1978–Mar 1979
Hafizullah Amin	Mar 1979–Dec 1979
Babrak Karmal	Dec 1979–June 1981
Soltan Ali Keshtmand	June 1981–May 1988
Mohammed Hasan Sharq	May 1988–Feb 1989
(replaced by 20-man Supreme Military Council)	
Khaliqyar Fazal Haq	May 1990–Apr 1992
Abdul Sabbur Fareed	Apr 1992–Mar 1993
Gulbuddin Hekmatyar	Mar 1993–1994
Arsala Rahmani (acting)	1994–95
Ahmad Shah Ahmadzai (acting)	1995–96
Gulbuddin Hekmatyar	1996*

ARGENTINA

Heads of State: President

Edelmiro J Farrell	Mar 1944–June 1946
Juan Domingo Perón	June 1946–Sep 1955
Eduardo Leonardi	Sep 1955–Nov 1955
Pedro Eugenio Aramburu	Nov 1955–Mar 1958
Arturo Frondizi	Mar 1958–Mar 1962
José Maria Guido (Acting)	Mar 1962–Oct 1963
Arturo Umberto Illia	Oct 1963–June 1966
Juan Carlos Ongania	June 1966–June 1970
(8–18 June 1970, military junta in office)	
Roberto Marcelo Levingston	June 1970–Mar 1971
(22–25 Mar 1971, military junta in office)	
Alejandro Agustin Lanusse	Mar 1971–May 1973
Hector José Campora	May 1973–July 1973
Raúl Lastiri (Acting)	July 1973–Oct 1973
Juan Domingo Perón	Oct 1973–July 1974
Maria Estela Martinez de Perón**	July 1974–Sep 1975
Italo Argentino Luder (Acting)	Sep 1975–Oct 1975
Maria Estela Martinez de Perón**	Oct 1975–Mar 1976
(24–29 Mar 1976, military junta in office)	
Jorge Rafael Videla	Mar 1976–Mar 1981
Roberto Viola	Mar 1981–Dec 1981
Leopoldo Galtieri	Dec 1981–June 1982

---

* A faction of Islamic fundamentalists called Taliban seized power in September 1996. Rabbani heads the opposition alliance, and his government is still recognized by the United Nations.
** More commonly known as Isabel de Perón.

Reynaldo Bignone	July 1982–Dec 1983
Raúl Alfonsin Foulkes	Dec 1983–June 1989
Carlos Saul Menem	July 1989–Dec 1999
Fernando de la Rua	Dec 1999–

AUSTRALIA

Heads of State: Governor-General

Henry Duke of Gloucester	Jan 1945–Jan 1947
Winston J. Dugan (Acting)	Jan 1947–Mar 1947
William McKell	Mar 1947–Sep 1952
William Slim, Viscount Slim	Sep 1952–Feb 1960
William Shepherd Morrison, Viscount Dunrossil	Feb 1960–Feb 1961
Reginald Brooks (Acting)	Feb 1961–Aug 1961
William Philip Sidney, Viscount de L'Isle	Aug 1961–May 1965
Henry Abel Smith (Acting)	May 1965–Sep 1965
Richard Gardiner Casey, Baron Casey	Sep 1965–April 1969
Paul Hasluck	Apr 1969–July 1974
John Kerr	July 1974–Dec 1977
Zelman Cohen	Dec 1977–July 1982
Ninian Stephen	July 1982–Feb 1989
William George Hayden	Feb 1989–Feb 1996
William Deane	Feb 1996–

Heads of Government: Prime Minister

Francis Michael Forde (Acting)	6–13 July 1945
Joseph Benedict Chifly	July 1945–Dec 1949
Robert Gordon Menzies	Dec 1949–Jan 1966
Harold Edward Holt	Jan 1966–Dec 1967
John McEwen	Dec 1967–Jan 1968
John Grey Gorton	Jan 1968–Mar 1971
William McMahon	Mar 1971–Dec 1972
Edward Gough Whitlam	Dec 1972–Nov 1975
John Malcolm Fraser	Nov 1975–Mar 1983
Robert Hawke	Mar 1983–Dec 1991
Paul Keating	Dec 1991–Mar 1996
John Winston Howard	Mar 1996–

AUSTRIA

Heads of State: President

| Karl Renner | Dec 1945–Dec 1950 |
| Leopold Figl (Acting) | Dec 1950–May 1951 |

Theodor Körner	May 1951–Jan 1957
Julius Raab	Jan 1957–May 1957
Adolf Schärf	May 1957–Feb 1965
Josef Klaus (Acting)	Feb 1965–June 1965
Franz Jonas	June 1965–Apr 1974
Bruno Kreisky (Acting)	Apr 1974–July 1974
Rudolf Kirchschläger	July 1974–June 1986
Kurt Waldheim	June 1986–July 1992
Thomas Klestil	July 1992–

Heads of Government: Chancellor

Karl Renner	Apr 1945–Dec 1945
Leopold Figl	Dec 1945–Apr 1953
Julius Raab	Apr 1953–Apr 1961
Alfons Gorbach	Apr 1961–Apr 1964
Josef Klaus	Apr 1964–Apr 1970
Bruno Kreisky	Apr 1970–May 1983
Fred Sinowatz	May 1983–June 1986
Franz Vranitzky	June 1986–Jan 1997
Viktor Klima	Jan 1997–

BELGIUM

Heads of State: King

Leopold III*	July 1950–July 1951
Baudouin I	July 1951–July 1993
Albert	Aug 1993–

Heads of Government: Prime Minister

Hubert Pierlot	Sep 1944–Feb 1945
Achille Van Acker	Feb 1945–Aug 1945
Achille Van Acker	Aug 1945–Jan 1946
Paul-Henri Spaak	Mar 1946–Mar 1946
Achille Van Acker	Mar 1946–July 1946
Camille Huysmans	Aug 1946–Mar 1947
Paul-Henri Spaak	Mar 1947–June 1949
Gaston Eyskens	Aug 1949–June 1950
Jean Duvieusart	June 1950–Aug 1950
Joseph Pholien	Aug 1950–Jan 1952
Jean Van Houtte	Jan 1952–Apr 1954
Achille Van Acker	Apr 1954–June 1958
Gaston Eyskens	June 1958–Nov 1958
Gaston Eyskens	Nov 1958–Mar 1961

---

* From 21 September 1944 until 21 July 1950 there was a regency. Leopold III (reigning 1934–44) reassumed the throne on 22 July 1950 and abdicated on 16 July 1951.

Theo Lefevre	Apr 1961–May 1965
Pierre Harmel	July 1965–Feb 1966
Paul Vanden Boeynants	Mar 1966–Feb 1968
Gaston Eyskens	June 1968–Nov 1971
Gaston Eyskens	Jan 1972–Nov 1972
Edmond Leburton	Jan 1973–Jan 1974
Leo Tindemans	Apr 1974–June 1977
Leo Tindemans	June 1977–Oct 1978
Paul Vanden Boeynants	Nov 1978–Dec 1978
Wilfried Martens	Apr 1979–Apr 1980
Wilfried Martens	May 1980–Oct 1980
Wilfried Martens	Oct 1980–Apr 1981
Marc Eyskens	Apr 1981–Sep 1981
Wilfried Martens	Dec 1981–Nov 1985
Wilfried Martens	Nov 1985–Mar 1992
Jean-Luc Dehaene	Mar 1992–

BRAZIL

Heads of State: President

Getúlio Dornelles Vargas	Oct 1930–Oct 1945
José Linhares	Oct 1945–Jan 1946
Eurico Gaspar Dutra	Jan 1946–Jan 1951
Getúlio Dornelles Vargas	Jan 1951–Aug 1954
João Café Filho	Aug 1954–Nov 1955
Carlos Coimbra da Luz (Acting)	8–11 Nov 1955
Nereu de Oliveira Ramos (Acting)	Nov 1955–Jan 1956
Juscelino Kubitschek de Oliveira	Jan 1956–Jan 1961
Jânio da Silva Quadros	Jan 1961–Aug 1961
Pascoal Ranieri Mazzilli	Aug 1961–Sep 1961
João Belchior Marques Goulart	Sep 1961–Mar 1964
Pascoal Ranieri Mazzilli (Acting)	2–15 Apr 1964
Humberto Alencar Castelo Branco	Apr 1964–Mar 1967
Artur da Costa e Silva	Mar 1967–Oct 1969
Emilio Garrastazu	Oct 1969–Mar 1974
Ernesto Geisel	Mar 1974–Mar 1979
João Baptista de Figueiredo	Mar 1979–Mar 1985
José Sarney*	Mar 1985–Mar 1990
Fernando Collor de Mello	Mar 1990–Dec 1992
Itamar Franco**	Dec 1992–Jan 1995
Fernando Henrique Cardoso	Jan 1995–

* Sworn in on the death of president-elect Neves.
** Acting president at first during impeachment of Collor de Mello.

BULGARIA

Heads of State: Tsar

Simeon II	Aug 1943–Sep 1946

Heads of State: President
(Chairman of the Praesidium)

Vassil Kolarov (Acting)	Sep 1946–Dec 1947
Mintso Neitsev	Dec 1947–May 1950
Georgi Damyanov	May 1950–Nov 1958
Dimiter Ganev	Nov 1958–Apr 1964
Georgi Traikov	Apr 1964–July 1971
Todor Zhivkov	July 1971–Nov 1989
Petr Meladov	Nov 1989–July 1990
Zhelyu Zhelev	Aug 1990–Jan 1997
Petar Stoyanov	Jan 1997–

CANADA

Heads of State: Governor-General

Alexander, Earl of Athlone	June 1940–Apr 1946
Harold Alexander, Viscount Alexander of Tunis	Apr 1946–Feb 1952
Charles Vincent Massey	Feb 1952–Sep 1959
Georges Vanier	Sep 1959–Mar 1967
Daniel Roland Michener	Apr 1967–Jan 1974
Jules Léger	Jan 1974–Jan 1979
Edward Schreyer	Jan 1979–May 1984
Jeanne Sauvé	May 1984–Jan 1990
Ramon John Hnatyshyn	Jan 1990–Feb 1995
Romeo Le Blanc	Feb 1995–

Heads of Government: Prime Minister

William Lyon Mackenzie King	Oct 1935–Nov 1948
Louis St. Laurent	Nov 1948–June 1957
John Diefenbaker	June 1957–Apr 1963
Lester Bowles Pearson	Apr 1963–Apr 1968
Pierre Elliott Trudeau	Apr 1968–June 1979
Joseph Clark	June 1979–Feb 1980
Pierre Elliott Trudeau	Feb 1980–June 1984
John Turner	June 1984–Sep 1984
Brian Mulroney	Sep 1984–June 1993
Kim Campbell	June 1993–Nov 1993
Jean Chrétien	Nov 1993–

CHILE

Heads of State: President

Juan Antonio Ríos	Apr 1942–June 1946
Alfredo Duhalde (Acting)	June 1946–Aug 1946
Vicente Merino Bielech (Acting)	Aug 1946–Nov 1946
Gabriel González Videla	Nov 1946–Nov 1952
Carlos Ibáñez del Campo	Nov 1952–Nov 1958
Jorge Alessandri Rodriguez	Nov 1958–Nov 1963
Eduardo Frei Montalva	Nov 1963–Nov 1970
Salvador Allende Gossens	Nov 1970–Sep 1973
Augusto Pinochet Ugarte*	Sep 1973–Mar 1990
Patricio Aylwin Azócar	Mar 1990–Mar 1994
Eduardo Frei Ruiz-Tagle	Mar 1994–Jan 2000
Ricardo Lagos	Jan 2000–

CHINA

Heads of State: Chairman of the Republic**

Mao Zedong	Oct 1949–Dec 1958
Zhu De	Dec 1958–Apr 1959
Liu Shaoqi	Apr 1959–Oct 1968
Deng Piwu (Acting)	Oct 1968–Jan 1975

Under the 1982 constitution, the post of Head of State (President) was revived. Subsequent holders have been:

Li Xiannian	June 1983–Apr 1988
Yang Shangkun	Apr 1988–Apr 1993
Jiang Zemin	Apr 1993–

Chairman of Communist Party

Mao Zedong	Oct 1949–Sep 1976
Hua Guofeng	Oct 1976–June 1981
Hu Yaobang†	June 1981–Sep 1982

Prime Minister

Zhou Enlai	Oct 1949–Jan 1976
Hua Guofeng	Jan 1976–Sep 1980
Zhao Ziyang	Sep 1980–Apr 1988
Li Peng	Apr 1988–Mar 1998‡
Zhu Rongji	Mar 1998–

---

* Acting president, Sep 1973–Dec 1974.
** Office abolished in 1975.
† Until the abolition of the post in September 1982, when he became general secretary.
‡ Reappointed, March 1993.

COLOMBIA

Heads of State: President

Alberto Lleras Camargo	Aug 1945–Aug 1946
Mariano Ospina Pérez	Aug 1946–Aug 1950
Laureano Gómez	Aug 1950–June 1953
Gustavo Rojas Pinilla (military dictator)	June 1953–May 1957
Military Junta (led by Gabriel París and four others)	May 1957–Aug 1958
Alberto Lleras Camargo	Aug 1958–Aug 1962
Guillermo León Valencia	Aug 1962–Aug 1966
Carlos Lleras Restrepo	Aug 1966–Aug 1970
Misael Pastrana Borrero	Aug 1970–Aug 1974
Alfonso López Michelsen	Aug 1974–Aug 1978
Julio César Turbay Ayala	Aug 1978–Aug 1982
Belisario Betancur Cuartas	Aug 1982–Aug 1986
Virgilio Barco Vargas	Aug 1986–Aug 1990
César Gaviria Trujillo	Aug 1990–Aug 1994
Ernesto Samper Pizano	Aug 1994–Aug 1998
Andres Pastrana Arango	Aug 1998–

CONGO, DEMOCRATIC REPUBLIC OF THE (formerly ZAIRE)

Heads of Government: Governor-General (of the Belgian Congo)

Pierre Ryckmans	1934–1946
Eugène Jungers	1946–1951
Léon Petillon	1951–1958
Henri Cornelis	1958–July 1960

Heads of Government: President

Joseph Kasavubu	June 1960–Sep 1960
Joseph-Désiré Mobutu*	Aug 1961–Nov 1965
	Nov 1965–May 1997
Laurent Kabila	May 1997–

Heads of Government: Prime Minister

Patrice Lumumba	June 1960–Sep 1960
Joseph Ileo (I)**	Sep 1960

* In January 1972, Major-General Joseph Mobutu changed his name to Mobutu Sese Seko and was titled Field Marshal Mobutu Sese Seko.

** In September 1960, due to political conflict within the government, Col. Joseph-Désiré Mobutu suspended all political institutions and assumed power. He ruled with a College of Commissioners headed by Justin-Marie Bomboko.

Cyrille Adoula	Aug 1961–July 1964
Moise Tshombe	July 1964–Oct 1965
Evariste Kimba	Oct–Nov 1965
Leonard Mulamba	Nov 1965–Oct 1966
Joseph-Désiré Mobutu	Oct 1966–June 1967

President Mobutu suspended the post of prime minister for a 10-year period.

Bo-Boliko Lokonga	July 1977–Mar 1979
Nguza Karl-I-Bond	Aug 1980–Apr 1981
N'Singa Udjuu	Apr 1981–Nov 1982
Kengo Wa Dongo	Nov 1982–Oct 1986

Note: Post temporarily abolished, with powers transferred to the president. When the post was reinstated, it had no political significance until 1991, when a new prime minister, Mulumba Lukoji, was asked to form a transitional government in advance of multiparty elections. Virtual civil war existed in 1992 and 1993 as Mobutu battled against his archrival, Prime Minister Etienne Tshisekedi, whom he had appointed in September 1991 and dismissed a month later. Ethnic violence spread across the country in 1996, and Mobutu was forced into exile. In May 1997, rebel leader Laurent Desire Kabila overturned Mobutu's government and assumed power as both chief of state and head of government.

COSTA RICA
Heads of State: President

Theodoro Picado Michalski	May 1944–May 1948
José Figueres Ferrer (junta)*	May 1948–Nov 1949
Otilio Ulate Blanco	Nov 1949–Nov 1953
José Figueres Ferrer	Nov 1953–May 1958
Mario Echandi Jimenez	May 1958–May 1962
Francisco J. Orlich Bolmarchich	May 1962–May 1966
Jose Joaquin Trejos	May 1966–May 1970
Jose Figueres Ferrer	May 1970–May 1974
Daniel Oduber Quiros	May 1974–May 1978
Rodrigo Carazo Odio	May 1978–May 1982
Luis Alberto Monge	May 1982–May 1986
Oscar Arias Sanchez	May 1986–May 1990
Rafael Angel Calderón Fournier	May 1990–May 1994

---

* As leader of the junta, Figueres Ferrer was not actually president. He was, however, responsible for restoring civilian rule in 1949, and he served two subsequent terms as president.

| José María Figueres Olsen | May 1994–May 1998 |
| Miguel Angel Rodriguez | May 1998– |

CUBA
Heads of State: President

Ramón Grau San Martín	Oct 1944–Oct 1948
Carlos Prio Socarrás	Oct 1948–Mar 1952
Fulgencio Batista y Zaldívar	Mar 1952–Jan 1959
Carlos Piedra (Acting)	1–2 Jan 1959
Manuel Urrutia Lleo (Acting)	Jan 1959–July 1959
Osvaldo Dórticos Torrado	July 1959–Dec 1976
Fidel Castro Ruz*	Dec 1976–

CZECHOSLOVAKIA (until 1992)
Heads of State: President

Edvard Beneš	Feb 1945–June 1948
Klemens Gottwald	June 1948–Mar 1953
Antonín Zapotocky	Mar 1953–Nov 1957
Antonín Novotny	Nov 1957–Mar 1968
Ludvik Svoboda	Mar 1968–May 1975
Gustav Husák	May 1975–Dec 1989
Vaclav Havel	Dec 1989–July 1992**

CZECH REPUBLIC
Head of State: President

| Václav Havel | Jan 1993**– |

Head of Government: Prime Minister

Václav Klaus	Jan 1993–Nov 1997
Josef Tosovsky	Nov 1997–July 1998
Milos Zeman	July 1998–

DENMARK
Heads of State: King/Queen

Christian X	May 1912–Apr 1947
Frederick IX	Apr 1947–Jan 1972
Margarethe II	Jan 1972–

---

* Dr. Castro was prime minister from February 1959 and first secretary, Central Committee of the Communist Party, from October 1965.

** Havel resigned in July due to Slovak opposition, but was elected first president of the Czech Republic after its creation on 1 January 1993.

Heads of State: Prime Minister

Vilhelm Buhl	May 1945–Nov 1945
Knud Kristensen	Nov 1945–Nov 1947
Hans Hedtoft	Nov 1947–Oct 1950
Erik Eriksen	Oct 1950–Sep 1953
Hans Hedtoft	Sep 1953–Feb 1955
H. C. Hansen	Feb 1955–May 1957
H. C. Hansen	May 1957–Feb 1960
Viggo Kampmann	Feb 1960–Nov 1960
Viggo Kampmann	Nov 1960–Sep 1962
Jens Otto Krag	Sep 1962–Sep 1964
Jens Otto Krag	Sep 1964–Feb 1968
Hilmar Baunsgaard	Feb 1968–Oct 1971
Jens Otto Krag	Oct 1971–Oct 1972
Anker Jorgensen	Oct 1971–Dec 1973
Poul Hartling	Dec 1973–Feb 1975
Anker Jorgensen	Feb 1975–Aug 1978
Anker Jorgensen	Aug 1978–Oct 1979
Anker Jorgensen	Oct 1979–Dec 1981
Anker Jorgensen	Dec 1981–Sep 1982
Poul Schlüter	Sep 1982–Jan 1993
Poul Nyrup Rasmussen	Jan 1993–

EGYPT

Heads of State: King

Farouk	Apr 1936–July 1952
Regency for Ahmad Fuad II	July 1952–June 1953

Heads of State: President

Mohammed Neguib	June 1953–Nov 1954
Gamal Abdel Nasser	Nov 1954–Sep 1970
Anwar al-Sadat	Sep 1970–Oct 1981
Sufi Abu Talib (Acting)	Oct 1981
Hosni Mubarak	Oct 1981–

EL SALVADOR

Heads of State: President

Salvador Castarieda Castro	Mar 1945–Dec 1948
Manuel Cordoba	Dec 1948–Feb 1949
Oscar Osorio	Feb 1949–Sep 1956
José Lemus	Sep 1956–Oct 1960
Cesar Yanes Urias	Oct 1960–Jan 1961
Anibal Portillo	Jan 1961–Feb 1961

Miguel Castillo	Feb 1961–Jan 1962
Eusebio Cordon Cea	Jan 1962–July 1962
Julio Rivera Carballo	July 1962–July 1967
Fidél Sánchez Hernandez	July 1967–July 1972
Arturo Molina Barraza	July 1972–July 1977
Carlos Romero Mena	July 1977–Oct 1979
a junta led by Adolfo Majano and Jaime Gutierrez	Oct 1979–Dec 1980
José Napoleón Duarte	Dec 1980–May 1982
Alvaro Magana	May 1982–June 1984
José Napoleón Duarte	June 1984–May 1989
Alfredo Felix Cristiani Burkard	June 1989–May 1994
Armando Calderon Sol	June 1994–Mar 1999
Francisco Flores	Mar 1999–

FINLAND

Heads of State: President

Karl Mannerheim	Aug 1944–Mar 1946
Juho Paasikivi	Mar 1946–Feb 1956
Urho Kekkonen	Feb 1956–Oct 1981
Mauno Koivisto*	Oct 1981–Mar 1994
Martii Ahtisaari	Mar 1994–

Heads of Government: Prime Minister

Juho Paasikivi	Nov 1944–Mar 1946
Mauno Pekkala	Mar 1946–July 1948
Karl Fagerholm	July 1948–Mar 1950
Urho Kekkonen	Mar 1950–Nov 1953
Sakari Tuomioja	Nov 1953–May 1954
Ralf Törngren	May 1954–Oct 1954
Urho Kekkonen	Oct 1954–Mar 1956
Karl Fagerholm	Mar 1956–May 1957
Väinö Sukselainen	May 1957–Nov 1957
Rainer von Fieandt	Nov 1957–Apr 1958
Reino Kuuskoski	Apr 1958–Aug 1958
Karl Fagerholm	Aug 1958–Jan 1959
Väinö Sukselainen	Jan 1959–July 1961
Martti Miettunen	July 1961–Apr 1962
Ahti Karjalainen	Apr 1962–Dec 1963
Reino Lehto	Dec 1963–Sep 1964
Johannes Virolainen	Sep 1964–May 1966

---

* Acting president October 1981–January 1982. Elected president, 1988.

Rafael Paasio	May 1966–Mar 1968
Mauno Koivisto	Mar 1968–May 1970
Teuvo Aura	May 1970–July 1970
Ahti Karjalainen	July 1970–Oct 1971
Teuvo Aura	Oct 1971–Feb 1972
Rafael Paasio	Feb 1972–Sep 1972
Kalevi Sorsa	Sep 1972–June 1975
Keijo Liinamaa	June 1975–Nov 1975
Martti Miettunen	Nov 1975–May 1977
Kalevi Sorsa	May 1977–May 1979
Mauno Koivisto	May 1979–Jan 1982
Kalevi Sorsa	Jan 1982–Apr 1987
Harri Holkeri	Apr 1987–Mar 1991
Esko Aho	Mar 1991–Mar 1995
Paavo Lipponen	Mar 1995–

FRANCE

Heads of State: President

Vincent Auriol	Jan 1947–Jan 1954
René Coty	Jan 1954–Jan 1959
Charles de Gaulle	Jan 1959–Apr 1969
Alain Poher *per interim*	Apr 1969–June 1969
Georges Pompidou	June 1969–Apr 1974
Alain Poher *per interim*	Apr 1974–May 1974
Valéry Giscard d'Estaing	May 1974–May 1981
François Mitterrand	May 1981–May 1995
Jacques Chirac	May 1995–

Heads of Government: Prime Minister

Charles de Gaulle	Sep 1944–Jan 1946
Félix Gouin	Jan 1946–June 1946
Georges Bidault	June 1946–Nov 1946
Léon Blum	Dec 1946–Jan 1947
Paul Ramadier	Jan 1947–Nov 1947
Robert Schuman	Nov 1947–July 1948
André Marie	July 1948–Sep 1948
Robert Schuman	Sep 1948
Henri Queuille	Sep 1948–Oct 1949
Georges Bidault	Oct 1949–June 1950
Henri Queuille	July 1950
René Pleven	July 1950–Mar 1951
Henri Queuille	Mar 1951–Aug 1951
René Pleven	Aug 1951–Jan 1952

Edgar Faure	Jan 1952–Mar 1952
Antoine Pinay	Mar 1952–Jan 1953
René Mayer	Jan 1953–June 1953
Joseph Laniel	June 1953–June 1954
Pierre Mendès-France	June 1954–Feb 1955
Edgar Faure	Feb 1955–Jan 1956
Guy Mollet	Jan 1956–Nov 1957
Félix Gaillard	Nov 1957–May 1958
Pierre Pflimlin	May 1958
Charles de Gaulle	May 1958–Jan 1959
Michel Debré	Jan 1959–Apr 1962
Georges Pompidou	Apr 1962–July 1968
Jacques Maurice Couve de Murville	July 1968–June 1969
Jacques Chaban Delmas	June 1969–July 1972
Pierre Messmer	July 1972–May 1974
Jacques Chirac	May 1974–Aug 1976
Raymond Barre	Aug 1976–May 1981
Pierre Mauroy	May 1981–July 1984
Laurent Fabius	July 1984–Mar 1986
Jacques Chirac	Mar 1986–May 1988
Paul Rocard	June 1988–May 1991
Edith Cresson	May 1991–Apr 1992
Pierre Bérégovoy	Apr 1992–Mar 1993
Edouard Balladur	Mar 1993–May 1995
Alain Juppé	May 1995–June 1997
Lionel Jospin	June 1997–

GERMAN DEMOCRATIC REPUBLIC (until 1990)

Head of State: President

Wilhelm Pieck	Oct 1949–Sep 1960

Heads of Government: Chairman of the Council of State

Walter Ulbricht	Sep 1960–Aug 1973
Willi Stoph	Oct 1973–Oct 1976
Erich Honecker	Oct 1976–Oct 1989*

---

* Honecker was briefly succeeded as leader by Egon Krenz. Manfred Gerlach became interim head of state. East Germany was reunited with the rest of Germany in October 1990.

GERMANY, FEDERAL REPUBLIC OF

Heads of State: President

Theodor Heuss	Sep 1949–July 1959
Heinrich Lübke	July 1959–June 1969
Gustav Heinemann	July 1969–July 1974
Walter Scheel	July 1974–June 1979
Karl Carstens	July 1979–July 1984
Richard von Weizsäcker*	July 1984–July 1994
Roman Herzog	July 1994–May 1999
Johannes Rau	May 1999–

Heads of Government: Federal Chancellor

Konrad Adenauer	Sep 1949–Oct 1963
Ludwig Erhard	Oct 1963–Nov 1966
Kurt Georg Kiesinger	Nov 1966–Oct 1969
Willy Brandt	Oct 1969–May 1974
Walter Scheel (Acting)	May 1974
Helmut Schmidt	May 1974–Oct 1982
Helmut Kohl*	Oct 1982–Oct 1998
Gerhard Schroeder	Oct 1998–

GHANA

Heads of State: Governor-General

Charles Arden-Clarke	Mar 1957–Nov 1957
Lord Listowel (William Hare)	Nov 1957–July 1960

Heads of State: President

Kwame Nkrumah	July 1960–Feb 1966
Joseph A. Ankrah (Head, eight-man National Liberation Council [NLC])	Feb 1966–Apr 1969
Akwasi Amankwa Afrifa	Apr 1969–Aug 1969
Three-man presidential commission: Akwasi Amankwa Afrifa John W. K. Harley Albert Kwesi-Ocran	Aug 1969–Aug 1970
Edward Akufo-Addo	Aug 1970–Jan 1972
Ignatius Kutu Acheampong (Chairman, National Redemption Council, 1972–75; Chairman, Supreme Military Council [SMC], 1975–78)	Jan 1972–July 1978
Frederick W. K. Akuffo (Chairman, SMC)	July 1978–June 1979

---

* President and chancellor, respectively, of a reunited Germany after October 1990.

Jerry John Rawlings (Head, Armed Forces Revolutionary Council)	June 1979–Sep 1979
Hilla Limann	Sep 1979–Dec 1981
Jerry John Rawlings (Head, Provisional National Defense Council)	Dec 1981–

Heads of Government: Prime Minister*

Kwame Nkrumah (post abolished Feb 1966–Oct 1969)	Jan 1957–Feb 1966
Kofi Busia	Oct 1969–Jan 1972

GREECE

Heads of State: King

George II	Nov 1935–Apr 1947
Paul I	Apr 1947–Mar 1964
Constantine XIII	Mar 1964–June 1973

Heads of State: President

Giorgios Papadopoulos (Provisional)	June 1973–Nov 1973
Phaedon Gizikis	Nov 1973–Dec 1974
Mikael Stassinopoulos	Dec 1974–June 1975
Konstantinos Tsatsos	June 1975–May 1980
Konstantinos Karamanlis	May 1980–Mar 1985
Christos Sartzetakis	Mar 1985–May 1990
Konstantinos Karamanlis	May 1990–Mar 1995
Konstantinos (Kostis) Stephanopoulos	Mar 1995–

GUATEMALA

Heads of State: President

Jacobo Arbenz Guzmán	Dec 1944–Mar 1945
Juan José Arévalo	Mar 1945–Mar 1951
Jacobo Arbenz Guzmán	Mar 1951–June 1954
Carlos Diaz	June 1954
Elfego Monzon	June 1954–July 1954
Carlos Castillo Armas	July 1954–July 1957
Luiz González Lopéz	July 1957–Oct 1957
Guillermo Flores Avendaño	Oct 1957–Mar 1958
Miguel Ydígoras Fuentes	Mar 1958–Mar 1963
Enrique Peralta Azurdia	Mar 1963–July 1966
Julio César Méndez Montenegro	July 1966–July 1970

* Post abolished January 1972.

Carlos Araña Osorio	July 1970–July 1974
Kjell Eugenio Laugerud Garcia	July 1974–July 1978
Fernando Romeo Lucas García	July 1978–Mar 1982
Angel Anibal Guevara (President-elect, deposed)	Mar 1982
Governing junta—3 members: Efrain Ríos Montt Horacio Egberto Malvonado Schaad Francisco Luis Gordillo Martinez	Mar 1982–June 1982
Efrain Ríos Montt	June 1982–Aug 1983
Oscar Mejía Victores	Aug 1983–Jan 1986
Marco Vinicio Cerezo Arévalo	Jan 1986–Jan 1991
Jorge Serrano	Jan 1991–May 1993
Ramiro de León	May 1993–Jan 1996
Álvaro Arzú Irigoyen	Jan 1996–

HUNGARY

Heads of State: President

Zoltan Tildy	Feb 1946–July 1948
Arpad Szakasits	Aug 1948–Aug 1949

Heads of State: Chairman of the Presidium

Arpad Szakasits	Aug 1949–Apr 1950
Sándor Rónai	Apr 1950–Aug 1952
Istvan Dobi	Aug 1952–Apr 1967
Pál Losoncszi	Apr 1967–June 1988
Bruno Ferenc Straub	June 1988–June 1989
Imré Pozsgay	June 1989–Oct 1989

Heads of State: Acting President

Mátyás Szürös	Oct 1989*–Aug 1990
Arpad Goncz**	Aug 1990–

INDIA

Heads of State: Governor-General

Louis, 1st Earl Mountbatten	Aug 1947–June 1948
Chakravarti Rajagopalachari	June 1948–Jan 1949

---

* Elected acting president, 18 October 1989.
** Confirmed 3 August.

Heads of State: President

Rajendra Prasad	Jan 1949–May 1962
Sarvapalli Radhakrishnan	May 1962–May 1967
Zahir Hussain	May 1967–May 1969
Varahgiri Venkata Giri (Acting)	May 1969–Aug 1969
Varahgiri Venkata Giri	Aug 1969–Aug 1974
Fakhruddin Ali Ahmed	Aug 1974–Feb 1977
Basappa Danappa Jatti	Feb 1977–July 1977
Neelam Sanjiva Reddy	July 1977–July 1982
Giani Zail Singh	July 1982–July 1987
Ramaswamy Venkataraman	July 1987–July 1992
Shankar Dayal Sharma	July 1992–July 1997
Kircheril Raman Narayanan	July 1997–

Heads of Government: Prime Minister

Jawaharlal Nehru	Jan 1949–May 1964
Gulzarilal Nanda (Acting)	May 1964–June 1964
Lal Bahadur Shastri	June 1964–Jan 1966
Gulzarilal Nanda (Acting)	Jan 1966
Indira Gandhi	Jan 1966–Mar 1977
Shri Morarji Ranchodji Desai	Mar 1977–July 1979
Charan Singh	July 1979–Jan 1980
Indira Gandhi	Jan 1980–Oct 1984
Rajiv Gandhi	Oct 1984–Nov 1989
Vishwanath Pratap Singh	Nov 1989–Nov 1990
Chandra Shekhar*	Nov 1990–June 1991
P. V. Narasimha Rao	June 1991–May 1996
H. D. Deve Gowda	June 1996–Apr 1997
Inder Kumar Gujral	Apr 1997–Mar 1998
Atal Bihari Vajpayee	Mar 1998–

INDONESIA

Heads of State: President

Ahmed Sukarno	Aug 1945–Feb 1967
Suharto	Feb 1967**–May 1998†

---

* Resigned 5 March 1991. Continued in office until May 1991 elections.

** Assumed emergency executive powers March 1966, acting president February 1967–March 1968.

† Suharto resigned in May 1998, less than three months after being selected for a seventh five-year term, and announced that Vice President Habibie would assume presidency for the remainder of the term, which expires in 2003. Habibie then announced an agreement with legislative leaders to select a new president in 1999.

Bacharuddin Jusof (B. J.) Habibie May 1998–Oct 1999
Abdurrahman Wahid Oct 1999*

Heads of Government: Prime Minister

Sutan Sjahrir	Nov 1945–June 1947
Amir Sjarifuddin	July 1947–Jan 1948
Mohammed Hatta	Jan 1948–Dec 1948
Sjarifuddin Prawiraranegara	Dec 1948–May 1949
Susanto Tirtoprodjo	May 1949–July 1949
Mohammed Hatta	July 1949–Jan 1950
Halim	Jan 1950–Aug 1950
Mohammed Natsir	Sep 1950–Mar 1951
Wirjosandjojo Sukiman	Apr 1951–Feb 1952
Wilopo	Apr 1952–June 1953
Ali Sastroamidjoyo	July 1953–June 1955
Burhanuddin Harahap	Aug 1955–Mar 1956
Ali Sastroamidjoyo	Mar 1956–Mar 1957
Djuanda Kartawidjaja	Apr 1957–Nov 1963
Ahmed Sukarno	Nov 1963–Mar 1966
Suharto**	Mar 1966–Feb 1967

(post abolished Feb 1967)

IRAN

Heads of State: Shah

Mohammad Reza Pahlavi** Sep 1941–Jan 1979

Head of Provisional Government

Ayatollah Ruhollah Khomeini Head of provisional government Feb 1979, thereafter supreme religious leader and recognized as highest authority until his death on 3 June 1989. His successor was Sayed Ali Khamenei, 4 June 1989.

Heads of State: President

Abolhasan Bani-Sadr	Feb 1980–June 1981
Mohammed Ali Raja'i	July 1981–Aug 1981
Sayed Ali Khamenei	Oct 1981–June 1989

---

* Habibie dropped out of the race two hours before the 1999 elections and Muslim cleric Wahid swept the vote in the electoral assembly.
** When he left the country he had not abdicated.

Hojatolislam Ali Akbar Hashemi Rafsanjani	Aug 1989–Aug 1997
Mohammad Khatami	Aug 1997–

IRAQ

Heads of State: King

Faisal II	Apr 1939–July 1958

Heads of State: President

Muhammad Najib Rubai	July 1958–Feb 1963
Abdul Salam Mohammed Aref	Feb 1963–Apr 1966
Abdul Rahman Aref	Apr 1966–July 1968
Ahmed Hassan Bakr	July 1968–July 1979
Saddam Hussein at-Takriti*	July 1979–

IRELAND

Heads of State: President

Douglas Hyde	June 1938–June 1945
Sean T. O. Ceallaigh (O'Kelly)	June 1945–June 1959
Éamon de Valéra	June 1959–June 1973
Erskine Childers	June 1973–Nov 1974
Thomas O'Higgins (Acting)	Nov 1974–Dec 1974
Cearbhall O'Dalaigh	Dec 1974–Oct 1976
Thomas O'Higgins (Acting)	Oct 1976–Dec 1976
Padraig Ohlrighile (Patrick Hillery)	Dec 1976–Nov 1990
Mary Robinson	Nov 1990–Sep 1997
Mary McAleese	Nov 1997–

Heads of Government: Prime Minister

Éamon de Valéra	Mar 1932–Feb 1948
John Costello	Feb 1948–June 1951
Éamon de Valéra	June 1951–June 1954
John Costello	June 1954–Mar 1957
Éamon de Valéra	Mar 1957–June 1959
Seán F. Lermass	June 1959–Nov 1966
John M. Lynch	Nov 1966–Mar 1973
Liam Cosgrave	Mar 1973–July 1977
John M. Lynch	July 1977–Dec 1979
Charles J. Haughey	Dec 1979–June 1981
Garrett Fitzgerald	June 1981–Mar 1982
Charles J. Haughey	Mar 1982–Dec 1982
Garret Fitzgerald	Dec 1982–Feb 1987

---

* Declared President for Life, 1990.

Charles J. Haughey	Feb 1987–Feb 1992
Albert Reynolds	Feb 1992–Nov 1994
John Bruton	Nov 1994–June 1997
Bertie Ahern	June 1997–

ISRAEL

Heads of State: President

Chaim Azriel Weizmann (Acting)	May 1948–Feb 1949
Chaim Azriel Weizmann	Feb 1949–Nov 1952
Joseph Springzak (Acting)	Nov 1952–Dec 1952
Ishvak Ben-Zvi	Dec 1952–Apr 1963
Kadish Luz	Apr 1963–May 1963
Zalman Shazar	May 1963–May 1973
Ephraim Katzir	May 1973–May 1978
Yitzhak Navon	May 1978–May 1983
Chaim Herzog	May 1983–May 1993
Ezer Weizman	May 1993–

Heads of Government: Prime Minister

David Ben-Gurion	May 1948–Dec 1953
Moshe Sharett	Dec 1953–Nov 1955
David Ben-Gurion	Nov 1955–June 1963
Levi Eshkol	June 1963–Feb 1969
Golda Meir	Mar 1969–May 1974
Yitzhak Rabin	June 1974–June 1977
Menachem Begin	June 1977–Oct 1983
Yitzhak Shamir	Oct 1983–Sep 1984
Shimon Peres	Sep 1984–Oct 1986
Yitzhak Shamir	Oct 1986–July 1992
Yitzhak Rabin	July 1992–Nov 1995*
Shimon Peres	Nov 1995–June 1996
Benjamin Netanyahu	June 1996–May 1999**
Ehud Barak	May 1999–Dec 2000

ITALY

Heads of State: King

| Victor Emmanuel III | July 1900–May 1946 |
| Umberto II | May 1946–June 1946 |

---

* During a peace rally on 4 November 1995 Rabin was shot and killed by a Jewish extremist.

** In mid-December 1998, parliament voted to dissolve Netanyahu's government and hold elections in the spring of 1999.

Heads of State: President

Alcide de Gaspieri (Acting)	June 1946
Enrico de Nicola	June 1946–May 1948
Luigi Einaudi	May 1948–May 1955
Giovanni Gronchi	May 1955–May 1962
Antonio Segni	May 1962–Dec 1964
Giuseppe Saragat	Dec 1964–Dec 1971
Giovanni Leone	Dec 1971–June 1978
Amintore Fanfani (Acting)	June 1978–July 1978
Alessandro Pertini	July 1978–July 1985
Francesco Cossiga	July 1985–May 1992
Oscal Luigi Scalfaro	May 1992–May 1999
Carlo Ciampi	May 1999–

Heads of Government: Prime Minister

Ferruccio Parri	June 1945–Nov 1945
Alcide de Gaspieri	Dec 1945–Aug 1953
Giuseppe Pella	Aug 1953–Jan 1954
Amintore Fanfani	Jan 1954–Feb 1954
Mario Scelba	Feb 1954–June 1955
Antonio Segni	June 1955–May 1957
Adone Zoli	May 1957–June 1958
Amintore Fanfani	June 1958–Feb 1959
Antonio Segni	Feb 1959–Mar 1960
Fernando Tambroni	Mar 1960–July 1960
Amintore Fanfani	July 1960–June 1963
Giovanni Leone	June 1963–Dec 1963
Aldo Moro	Dec 1963–June 1968
Giovanni Leone	June 1968–Dec 1968
Mariano Rumor	Dec 1968–Aug 1970
Emilio Colombo	Aug 1970–Feb 1972
Giulio Andreotti	Feb 1972–July 1973
Mariano Rumor	July 1973–Nov 1974
Aldo Moro	Nov 1974–July 1976
Giulio Andreotti	July 1976–Aug 1979
Francesco Cossiga	Aug 1979–Oct 1980
A. Forlani	Oct 1980–June 1981
Giovanni Spadolini	June 1981–Dec 1982
Amintore Fanfani	Dec 1982–Aug 1983
Bettino Craxi	Aug 1983–Feb 1987
Giulio Andreotti	Feb 1987–June 1987
Giovanni Goria	July 1987–Apr 1988
Ciriaco De Mita	Apr 1988–July 1989

Giulio Andreotti	July 1989–June 1992
Giuliano Amato	June 1992–Apr 1993
Carlo Azeglio Ciampi	Apr 1993–Apr 1994
Silvio Berlusconi	Apr 1994–Dec 1994
Lamberto Dini	Jan 1995–Dec 1996
Romano Prodi	Dec 1996–Oct 1998
Massimo D'Alema	Oct 1998–

JAPAN

Head of State: Emperor

Hirohito	Dec 1926–Jan 1989
Akihito	Jan 1989–

Heads of Government: Prime Minister

Kantaro Suzuki	Apr 1945–Aug 1945
Prince Naruhiko Higashikuni	Aug 1945–Oct 1945
Kijuro Shidehara	Oct 1945–May 1946
Shigeru Yoshida	May 1946–May 1947
Tetsu Katayama	May 1947–Feb 1948
Hitoshi Ashida	Feb 1948–Oct 1948
Shigeru Yoshida	Oct 1948–Dec 1954
Ichero Hatoyama	Dec 1954–Dec 1956
Tanzan Ishibashi	Dec 1956–Feb 1957
Nobusuke Kishi	Feb 1957–July 1960
Hayato Ikeda	July 1960–Nov 1964
Eisaku Sato	Nov 1964–July 1972
Kakuei Tanaka	July 1972–Dec 1974
Takeo Miki	Dec 1974–Dec 1976
Takeo Fukuda	Dec 1976–Nov 1978
Masayoshi Ohira	Nov 1978–June 1980
Masayoshi Ito (Acting)	June 1980–July 1980
Zenko Suzuki	July 1980–Nov 1982
Yasuhiro Nakasone	Nov 1982–Nov 1987
Noboru Takeshita	Nov 1987–June 1989
Sosuke Uno	June 1989–Aug 1989
Toshiki Kaifu	Aug 1989–Oct 1991
Kiichi Miyazawa	Oct 1991–July 1993
Morihiro Hosokawa	July 1993–Apr 1994
Tsutomi Hata	Apr 1994–June 1994
Tomiichi Murayama	July 1994–Jan 1996
Ryutaro Hashimoto	Jan 1996–July 1998
Keizo Obuchi	July 1998–

KOREA, NORTH

Head of State: President

Kim II Sung	Sep 1948–July 1994
Kim Jong II	July 1994–

KOREA, SOUTH

Heads of State: President

Syngman Rhee	July1948–Apr 1960
Huh Chung (Acting)	Apr 1960–Aug 1960
Yoon Bo Sun	Aug 1960–Mar 1962
Park Chung Hee	Mar 1962–Oct 1979
Choi Kyu Hah	Oct 1979–Aug 1980
Park Choong Hoon (Acting)	Aug 1980–Sep 1980
Chun Doo Hwan	Sep 1980–Dec 1992
Kim Young Sam	Dec 1992–Feb 1998
Kim Dae Jung	Feb 1998–

MEXICO

Heads of State: President

Manuel Ávila Camacho	Dec 1940–Nov 1946
Miguel Aleman Valdés	Dec 1946–Nov 1952
Adolfo Ruiz Cortines	Dec 1952–Nov 1958
Adolpho López Mateos	Dec 1958–Nov 1964
Gustavo Diaz Ordaz	Dec 1964–Nov 1970
Luís Echeverría Alvarez	Dec 1970–Nov 1976
José López Portillo y Pacheco	Dec 1976–Nov 1982
Miguel de la Madrid Hurtado	Dec 1982–Nov 1988
Carlos Salinas de Gortari	Dec 1988–Nov 1994
Ernesto Zedillo Ponce de Leon	Dec 1994–Nov 2000*
Vincente Fox	Dec 2000

NETHERLANDS

Heads of State: Queen

Wilhelmina	Sep 1898–Sep 1948
Juliana	Nov 1948–Apr 1980
Beatrix	May 1980–

---

* To make Mexico's election system more democratic, President Zedillo discontinued the "dedazo," a practice in which the president designates his party's nominee for the upcoming election. In Mexico's first presidential primary, held in November 1999, former interior secretary Francisco Labastida, Zedillo's closest ally among those running, was the clear winner. Mexico's general presidential election was held on 2 July 2000.

Heads of Government: Prime Minister

Pieter Gerbrandy	1941–Feb 1945
Pieter Gerbrandy	Feb 1945–June 1945
Willem Schermerhorn	June 1945–July 1946
Louis Beel	July 1946–Aug 1948
Willem Drees	Aug 1948–Mar 1951
Willem Drees	Mar 1951–Sep 1952
Willem Drees	Sep 1952–Oct 1956
Willem Drees	Oct 1956–Dec 1958
Louis Beel	Dec 1958–May 1959
John de Quay	May 1959–July 1963
Victor Marijnen	July 1963–Apr 1965
Joseph Cals	Apr 1965–Nov 1966
Jelle Zijlstra	Nov 1966–Apr 1967
Petrus de Jong	Apr 1967–July 1971
Barend Biesheuvel	July 1971–July 1972
Barend Biesheuvel	July 1972–May 1973
Joop den Uyl	May 1973–Dec 1977
Andreas van Agt	Dec 1977–Sep 1981
Andreas van Agt	Sep 1981–May 1982
Andreas van Agt	May 1982–Nov 1982
Ruud Lubbers	Nov 1982–July 1986
Ruud Lubbers	July 1986–Aug 1994
Wim Kok	Aug 1994–

NICARAGUA

Heads of State: President

Anastasio Somoza Garcia	Jan 1937–May 1947
Leonardo Arguello	May 1947
Benjamin Lacayo Sacasa	May–Aug 1947
Victor Romay y Reyes	Aug 1947–May 1950
Anastasio Somoza Garcia	May 1950–Sep 1956
Luis Somoza Debayle	Sep 1956–May 1963
René Shick Gutiérrez	May 1963–Aug 1966
Lorenzo Guerrero	Aug 1966–May 1967
Anastasio Somoza Debayle	May 1967–May 1972
a three-member junta	May 1972–Dec 1974
Anastasio Somoza Debayle	Dec 1974–July 1979
Francisco Urcuyo Maliano	July 1979
a five-member junta	July 1979–Mar 1981
the junta was reduced to three, and Daniel Ortega Saavedra was appointed its coordinator	Mar 1981

Daniel Ortega Saavedra   Jan 1985–Apr 1990
Violetta Barrios de Chamorro   Apr 1990–Jan 1997
Arnoldo Aleman Lacayo   Jan 1997–

NIGERIA

Heads of State: Governor
Arthur Frederick Richards   Dec 1943–Apr 1947
John Stuart Macpherson   Feb 1948–Oct 1954

Heads of State: Governor-General
John Stuart Macpherson   Oct 1954–June 1955
James Robertson   June 1955–Nov 1960
Nnamdi Azikiwe*   Nov 1960–Oct 1963

Heads of State: President
Nnamdi Azikiwe   Oct 1963–Jan 1966
Nwafor Orizu (Acting)   Jan 1966
Johnson Aguiyi-Ironsi   Jan 1966–July 1966
Yakubu Gowon   Aug 1966–July 1975
Murtala Ramat Mohammed   July 1975–Feb 1976
Olusegun Obasanjo   Feb 1976–Oct 1979
Alhaji Shehu Shagari   Oct 1979–Dec 1983
Mohammed Buhari   Dec 1983–Aug 1985
Ibrahim Babangida   Aug 1985–Aug 1993
Ernest Shonekan   Aug 1993–Nov 1993
Gen. Sani Abacha   Nov 1993–June 1998
Abdulsalami Abubakar   June 1998–May 1999
Olusegun Obasanjo   May 1999–

Heads of Government: Prime Minister
Abubakar Tafawa Balewa   Aug 1957–Jan 1966

Military Rulers: Head of State and Commander in Chief of Armed Forces
Johnson Aguiyi-Ironsi   Jan 1966–July 1968
Yakubu Gowon   July 1968–July 1975
Murtala Ramat Muhammed   July 1975–Feb 1976
Olusegun Obasanjo   Feb 1976–Oct 1979
Mohammed Buhari   Dec 1983–Aug 1985
Ibrahim Babangida   Aug 1985–Aug 1993**

---

* President of the Republic, but not using the title between January 1966 and October 1977 nor again after December 1983.

** Presidential elections on 12 June 1993 were declared invalid, but in August Babangida agreed to step down.

| Ernest Shonekan | Aug 1993–Nov 1993 |
| Sani Abacha | Nov 1993–June 1998 |

NORWAY

Heads of State: King

Haakon VII	Nov 1905–Sep 1957
Olaf V	Sep 1957–Jan 1991
Harald V	Jan 1991–

Heads of Government: Prime Minister

Johan Nygaardsvold	1935–June 1945
Einar Gerhardsen	June 1945–Nov 1951
Oscar Torp	Nov 1951–Jan 1955
Einar Gerhardsen	Jan 1955–Aug 1963
John Lyng	Aug 1963–Sep 1963
Einar Gerhardsen	Sep 1963–Oct 1965
Per Borten	Oct 1965–Mar 1971
Trygve Bratteli	Mar 1971–Oct 1972
Lars Korvald	Oct 1972–Oct 1973
Trygve Bratteli	Oct 1973–Jan 1976
Odvar Nordli	Jan 1976–Feb 1981
Gro Harlem Brundtland	Feb 1981–Oct 1981
Kaare Willoch	Oct 1981–May 1986
Gro Harlem Brundtland	May 1986–Oct 1989
Jan Syse	Oct 1989–Nov 1990
Gro Harlem Brundtland	Nov 1990–Oct 1996
Thorbjørn Jagland	Oct 1996–Oct 1997
Kjell Magne Bondevik	Oct 1997–

PAKISTAN

Heads of State: Governor-General

Quaid-I-Azam Mohammed Ali Jinnah	Aug 1947–Sep 1948
Khwaja Naximuddin	Sep 1948–Oct 1951
Ghulam Muhammed	Oct 1951–Oct 1955
Iskander Mirza	Mar 1956–Oct 1958
Mahammed Ayub Khan	Oct 1958–Mar 1969
Agha Muhammad Yahya Khan	Mar 1969–Dec 1971
Zulfikar Ali Bhutto	Dec 1971–Aug 1973
Fazal Elahi Chaudhri	Aug 1973–Sep 1978
Mohammed Zia ul-Haq	Sep 1978–Aug 1988
Gulam Ishaq Khan	Aug 1988–July 1993*

---

* Resigned office, 18 July 1993, along with the prime minister, Nawaz Sharif.

Sardar Farooq Leghari	Nov 1993–Dec 1997
Mohammad Rafiq Tarar	Dec 1997–Oct 1999
Pervaiz Musharraf	Oct 1999–*

PHILIPPINES

Heads of State: President

Manuel Roxas y Acuna	July 1946–Apr 1948
Elpidio Quirino	Apr 1948–Jan 1954
Rámon Magsaysay	Jan 1954–Mar 1957
Carlos Polestico Garcia	Mar 1957–Dec 1961
Diosdado Macapagal	Dec 1961–Dec 1965
Ferdinand Edralin Marcos	Dec 1965–Feb 1986
Corazon Aquino	Feb 1986–June 1992
General Fidel Ramos	June 1992–June 1998
Joseph Ejereito Estrada	June 1998–

POLAND

Heads of State: President

| Boleslaw Bierut | June 1945–July 1952 |

Heads of State: Chairman of the Council of State

Aleksander Zawadski	Nov 1952–Aug 1964
Edward Ochab	Aug 1964–Apr 1968
Marshal Marian Spychalski	Apr 1968–Dec 1970
Józef Cyrankiewicz	Dec 1970–Mar 1972
Henryk Jablónski	Mar 1972–Nov 1985
Wojciech Jaruzelski	Nov 1985–July 1989

Heads of State: President

Wojciech Jaruzelski	July 1989–Dec 1990
Lech Walesa	Dec 1990–Dec 1995
Aleksander Kwasniewski	Dec 1995–

Heads of Government: First Secretary of the Politburo of the Communist Party

Wladyslaw Gomulka	Jan 1945–Sep 1948**
Boleslaw Bierut	Sep 1948–Mar 1956
Edward Ochab	Mar 1956–Oct 1956
Edward Gierek	Dec 1970–Sep 1980

---

* In a surprise military coup, General Pervaiz Musharraf overthrew the government, suspended the constitution and dissolved parliament.
** From 1956 to 1970 Gomulka was the most powerful man in Poland.

Stanislaw Kania   Sep 1980–Oct 1981
Wojciech Jaruzelski   Oct 1981–July 1989

PORTUGAL

Heads of State: President

António Oscar de Fragosa Carmona	Nov 1926–Apr 1951
António de Oliveira Salazar (Prov.)	Apr 1951–July 1951
Marshal Francisco Higino Craveiro Lopes	July 1951–Aug 1958
Américo Deus Rodrigues Tomás	Aug 1958–Apr 1974
António Sebastião Ribeiro de Spinola	Apr 1974–Sep 1974
Francisco da Costa Gomes	Oct 1974–July 1976
António Ramalho Eanes	July 1976–Mar 1986
Mário Soares	Mar 1986–*Mar 1996
Jorge Sampaio	Mar 1996–

ROMANIA

Heads of State: King

Mihail I   Sep 1940–Dec 1947

Heads of State: President

Constantin Parhon	Apr 1948–June 1952
Petru Groza	June 1952–Jan 1958
Ion Gheorghe Maurer	Jan 1958–Mar 1961
Gheorghe Gheorghiu-Dej	Mar 1961–Mar 1965
Chivu Stoica	Mar 1965–Dec 1967
Nicolae Ceausescu	Dec 1967–Dec 1989
Ion Iliescu	Dec 1989–Nov 1996
Emil Constantinescu	Nov 1996–

RUSSIAN FEDERATION

Heads of State: President**

Boris Yeltsin   June 1991–Dec 1999
Vladimir Putin   Jan 2000–

Heads of Government: Prime Minister

Boris Yeltsin	July 1991–June 1992
Yegor Gaidar	June 1992–Dec 1992
Viktor Chernomyrdin	Dec 1992–Mar 1998

---

* Elected for a second term, January 1991.
** Boris Yeltsin became the first-ever elected president on 12 June 1991 when he polled
  57.3% of the votes cast.

Sergei Kiriyenko   Mar 1998–Sep 1998
Yevgeny Primakov   Sep 1998–

SAUDI ARABIA

Heads of State: King

Abdul Aziz ibn Abdur-Rahman al-Faisal Al Sa'ud	Sep 1932–Nov 1953
Saud ibn Abdul Aziz	Nov 1953–Nov 1964
Faisal ibn Abdul Aziz	Nov 1964–Mar 1975
Khalid ibn Abdul Aziz	Mar 1975–June 1982
Fahd ibn Abdul Aziz	June 1982–*

SERBIA AND MONTENEGRO

Head of State: President

Slobodan Milosevic	Dec 1992–July 1997
Slobodan Milosevic (Yugoslavia)	July 1997–Oct 2000**
Milan Milutinovic (Serbia)	Dec 1997–
Milo Djukanovic (Montenegro)	Dec 1997–
Vojislav Kostunica (Yugoslavia)	Oct 2000–

Head of State: Prime Minister

Milan Panic	1992–93
Radoje Kontic	1993–98
Momir Bulatovic	May 1998–

SOUTH AFRICA

Heads of State: Governor-General

Nicolas Jacobus de Wet	July 1943–Jan 1946
Gideon Brand van Zyl	Jan 1946–Dec 1950
Ernest George Jansen	Jan 1951–Nov 1959
Lucas Cornelius Steyn (Acting)	Nov 1959–Jan 1960
Charles Robberts Swart	Jan 1960–May 1961

Heads of State: President

Charles Robberts Swart	May 1961–May 1967
Jozua François Naudé (Acting)	May 1967–Apr 1968
Jacobus Johannes Fouché	Apr 1968–Apr 1975

---

* Crown Prince and First Deputy Prime Minister Abdallah bin Abd al-Aziz Al Saud (half-brother to the monarch and heir to the throne since 13 June 1982) was regent from 1 January to 22 February 1996.
** Barred from running for a third term as Serbian president, Milosevic had himself inaugurated as president of Yugoslavia in July 1997.

Nicolaas Diederich	Apr 1975–Aug 1978
Marais Viljoen (Acting)	Aug 1978–Oct 1978
Balthazar John Vorster	Oct 1978–June 1979
Marais Viljoen	June 1979–Sep 1984
Pieter Willem Botha*	Sep 1984–Sep 1989
Frederik Willem de Klerk	Sep 1989–May 1994
Nelson Mandela	May 1994–June 1999
Thabo Mbeki	June 1999–

Heads of Government: Prime Minister

Jan Christian Smuts	Sep 1939–June 1948
Daniel Malan	June 1948–Nov 1954
Johannes Strijdom	Nov 1954–Aug 1958
Charles Robberts Swart (Acting)	Aug 1958–Sep 1958
Hendrik Verwoerd	Sep 1958–Sep 1966
Balthazar John Vorster	Sep 1966–Sep 1978
Pieter Willem Botha**	Sep 1978–Sep 1984

SPAIN

Head of State: Chief of State

| Francisco Franco Bahamonde | Apr 1939–Nov 1975 |

Head of State: King

| King Juan Carlos I | Nov 1975– |

Heads of Government: Prime Minister

Francisco Franco Bahamonde	Apr 1939–June 1973
Luis Carrero Blanco	June 1973–Dec 1973
Torcuato Fernández Miranda (Acting)	Dec 1973–Jan 1974
Carlos Arias Navarro	Jan 1974–July 1976
Adolfo Súarez Gonzalez	July 1976–Jan 1981
Leopoldo Calvo-Sotelo y Bustelo	Feb 1981–Dec 1982
Felipe González Márquez	Dec 1982–May 1996
José Maria Aznar Lopez	May 1996–

SWEDEN

Heads of State: King

Gustaf V	Dec 1907–Oct 1950
Gustaf VI Adolf	Oct 1950–Sep 1973
Carl XVI Gustaf	Sep 1973–

---

* Combining the post with that of prime minister.
** Post abolished and combined with that of president.

Heads of Government: Prime Minister

Tage Erlander	Oct 1946–Oct 1969
Olof Palme	Oct 1969–Oct 1976
Thorbjörn Fälldin	Oct 1976–Oct 1978
Ola Ullsten	Oct 1978–Oct 1979
Thorbjörn Fälldin	Oct 1979–Oct 1982
Olof Palme	Oct 1982–Feb 1986
Ingvar Carlsson (interim incumbency Feb–Mar 1986)	Mar 1986–Sep 1991
Carl Bildt	Oct 1991–Sep 1994
Ingvar Carlsson	Sep 1994–Mar 1996
Goran Persson	Mar 1996–

SWITZERLAND

Heads of State: President of the Confederation*

Eduard von Steiger	1945
Karl Kobelt	1946
Philipp Etter	1947
Enrico Celio	1948
Ernst Nobs	1949
Max Petitpierre	1950
Eduard von Steiger	1951
Karl Kobelt	1952
Markus Feldmann	1953
Rodolphe Rubattel	1954
Max Petitpierre	1955
Markus Feldmann	1956
Hans Streuli	1957
Thomas Holenstein	1958
Paul Chaudet	1959
Max Petitpierre	1960
Friedrich Traugott Wahlen	1961
Paul Chaudet	1962
Willy Spuehler	1963
Ludwig von Moos	1964
Hans-Peter Tschudi	1965
Hans Schaffner	1966
Roger Bonvin	1967
Willy Spuehler	1968
Ludwig von Moos	1969

---

* The president is chosen by parliament from the seven-member Federal Council for a one-year term.

Hans-Peter Tschudi	1970
Rudolf Gnaegi	1971
Nello Celio	1972
Roger Bonvin	1973
Ernst Brugger	1974
Pierre Graber	1975
Rudolf Gnaegi	1976
Kurt Furgler	1977
Willi Ritschard	1978
Hans Hurlimann	1979
Georges Andre Chevallaz	1980
Kurt Furgler	1981
Fritz Honneger	1982
Pierre Aubert	1983
Leon Schlumpf	1984
Kurt Furgler	1985
Alphons Egli	1986
Pierre Aubert	1987
Otto Stich	1988
Jean-Pascal Delamuraz	1989
Arnold Koller	1990
Flavio Cotti	1991
René Felber	1992
Adolf Ogi	1993
Otto Stich	1994
Kaspar Villiger	1995
Jean-Pascal Delamuraz	1996
Arnold Koller	1997
Flavio Cotti	1998
Ruth Dreifuss	1999

SYRIA

Heads of State: President

Sayed Shukri al Quwwatli	Jan 1944–Mar 1949
Husni Zaim	June 1949–Aug 1949
Sami Hinawi (Acting)	Aug 1949–Dec 1949
Hashem al-Atassi	Dec 1949–Dec 1951
Adib es-Shishaqli (Dictator)	Dec 1951–July 1953
Adib es-Shishaqli (President)	July 1953–Feb 1954
Hashim al-Atassi	Feb 1954–Sep 1955
Sayed Shukri al Quwwatli	Sep 1955–Feb 1958
(Union with Egypt under Egyptian head of state)	Feb 1958–Dec 1961

Nazim el-Kudsi	Dec 1961–Mar 1963
Louai Atassi	Mar 1963–July 1963
Amin el-Hafez	July 1963–Feb 1966
Nureddin Atassi	Feb 1966–Nov 1970
Ahmed Khatib	Nov 1970–Feb 1971
Hafez al-Assad	Feb 1971–June 2000
Bashar al-Assad	June 2000–

TAIWAN

Heads of State: President

Li Zongren	Dec 1949–Mar 1950
Jiang Kaishek	Mar 1950–Apr 1975
Yen Jiagan	Apr 1975–May 1978
Jiang Jinguo	May 1978–Jan 1988
Li Denghui	Jan 1988–

TURKEY

Heads of State: President

Ismet Inönü	Nov 1938–May 1950
Mahmud Celal Bayer	May 1950–May 1960
Cemal Gürsel	May 1960–Mar 1966
Sevdet Sunay	Mar 1966–Mar 1973
Fahri Korutürk	Apr 1973–Apr 1980
Ihsan Caglayangil	Apr 1980–Sep 1980
Kenan Evren	Sep 1980–Oct 1989
Turgut Özal	Oct 1989–Apr 1993
Süleyman Demirel	May 1993–

UNION OF SOVIET SOCIALIST REPUBLICS (until December 1991)

Heads of State: President

Mikhail Ivanovich Kalinin	Dec 1922–Mar 1946
Nikolai Shvernik	Mar 1946–Mar 1953
Marshal Kliment Efremovich Voroshilov	Mar 1953–May 1960
Leonid Ilich Brezhnev	May 1960–July 1962
Anastas Ivanovich Mikoyan	July 1962–Dec 1965
Nikolai Viktorovich Podgorny	Dec 1965–June 1977
Leonid Ilich Brezhnev	June 1977–Nov 1982
Yuri V. Andropov	June 1983–Feb 1984
Konstantin Ustinovich Chernenko	April 1984–Mar 1985

| Andrei Gromyko | July 1985–Sep 1988 |
| Mikhail Sergeyevich Gorbachev* | Oct 1988–Dec 1991 |

Heads of Government: General Secretary of the Communist Party (until its banning in August 1991)

Joseph Vissarionovich Stalin	Dec 1922–Mar 1953
Georgy Maksimilianovich Malenkov	Mar 1953
Nikita Sergeyevich Khrushchev	Mar 1953–Oct 1964
Leonid Ilich Brezhnev	Oct 1964–Nov 1982
Yuri Vladimirovich Andropov	June 1983–Feb 1984
Konstantin Ustinovich Chernenko	April 1984–Mar 1985
Mikhail Sergeyevich Gorbachev	Mar 1985–Aug 1991

UNITED KINGDOM

Heads of State: King/Queen

| George VI | Dec 1936–Feb 1952 |
| Elizabeth II | Feb 1952– |

Heads of Government: Prime Minister

Clement Attlee	July 1945–Oct 1951
Sir Winston Churchill	Oct 1951–Apr 1955
Sir Anthony Eden	Apr 1955–Jan 1957
(Maurice) Harold Macmillan	Jan 1957–Oct 1963
Sir Alec Douglas-Home	Oct 1963–Oct 1964
(James) Harold Wilson	Oct 1964–June 1970
Edward Heath	June 1970–Mar 1974
(James) Harold Wilson	Mar 1974–Apr 1976
(Leonard) James Callaghan	Apr 1976–May 1979
Margaret (Hilda) Thatcher	May 1979–Nov 1990
John Major	Nov 1990–May 1997
Tony Blair	May 1997–

UNITED STATES OF AMERICA

Heads of State: President

Harry S Truman	Apr 1945–Jan 1953
Dwight David Eisenhower	Jan 1953–Jan 1961
John Fitzgerald Kennedy	Jan 1961–Nov 1963
Lyndon Baines Johnson	Nov 1963–Jan 1969
Richard Milhous Nixon	Jan 1969–Aug 1974
Gerald Rudolph Ford	Aug 1974–Jan 1977

* Executive president after 1990.

James Earl Carter	Jan 1977–Jan 1981
Ronald Wilson Reagan	Jan 1981–Jan 1989
George Herbert Walker Bush	Jan 1989–Jan 1993
William Jefferson (Bill) Clinton	Jan 1993–Jan 2001
George W. Bush	Jan 2001–

VENEZUELA

Heads of State: President

Isaías Medina Angarita	May 1941–Oct 1945
Rómulo Betancourt	Oct 1945–Feb 1948
Rómulo Gallegos Freire	Feb 1948–Nov 1948
Carlos Delgado Chalbaud	Nov 1948–Nov 1950
Germán Suarez Flamerich	Nov 1950–Dec 1952
Marcos Pérez Jiménez	Dec 1952–Jan 1958
Wolfgang Larrazábal Ugueto	Jan 1958–Nov 1958
Edgard Sanabria	Nov 1958–Feb 1959
Rómulo Betancourt	Feb 1959–Mar 1964
Raúl Leoni	Mar 1964–Mar 1969
Rafael Caldera Rodriguez	Mar 1969–Mar 1974
Carlos Andrés Pérez Rodriguez	Mar 1974–Mar 1979
Luis Herréra Campins	Mar 1979–Feb 1984
Jaime Lusinchi	Feb 1984–Feb 1989
Carlos Andrés Pérez Rodriguez	Feb 1989–May 1993*
Ramon Jose Velasquez Mujica	June 1993–Dec 1993
Rafael Caldera Rodriguez	Dec 1993–Feb 1999
Hugo Chavez	Feb 1999–

VIETNAM

Heads of State: President of North Vietnam

Ho Chi Minh	Sep 1945–Sep 1969
Ton Duc Thang	Sep 1969–July 1976

Heads of State: Symbolic emperor of Vietnam, recognized in the South until 1955

Bao Dai

Heads of State: President of South Vietnam

Ngo Dinh Diem	Oct 1955–Nov 1963
Duong Van Minh	Nov 1963–Jan 1964
Nguyen Khanh	Jan 1964–Feb 1964

---

* Suspended from office. Octavio Lepage was briefly acting president until Ramon Jose Velasquez Mujica became interim president in June 1993.

Duong Van Minh	Feb 1964–Aug 1964
Nguyen Khanh	Aug 1964–Sep 1964
Duong Van Minh	Sep 1964–Oct 1964
Phan Khac Suu	Oct 1964–June 1965
Nguyen Van Thieu	June 1965–Apr 1975
Tran Van Huong	Apr 1975
Duong Van Minh	Apr 1975
Nguyen Huu Tho	Apr 1975–July 1976

Heads of State: President of (united) Vietnam

Ton Duc Thang	July 1976–Mar 1980
Nguyen Huu Tho	Apr 1980–July 1981
Truong Chinh	July 1981–Dec 1986
Nguyen Van Linh	Dec 1986–1987
Vo Chi Cong	1987–1991
Do Muoi	Aug 1991–Sep 1992
Le Duc Anh	Sep 1992–Sep 1997
Tran Duc Luong	Sep 1997–

YUGOSLAVIA

Head of State: King

| Peter II | Oct 1934–Nov 1945 |

Head of State: President of the Presidium of the National Assembly

| Ivan Ribar | Dec 1945–Jan 1953 |

Head of State: President of the Republic

| Josip Broz Tito | Jan 1953–May 1980 |

Heads of State: President of the Collective Presidency

Lazar Kolisevski	May 1980
Cvijetin Mijatovic	May 1980–May 1981
Sergej Krajger	May 1981–May 1982
Petar Stambolić	May 1982–May 1983
Mika Spiljak	May 1983–May 1984
Veselin Djuranovic	May 1984–May 1985
Radovan Vlajkovic	May 1985–May 1986
Sinan Hasani	May 1986–May 1987
Lazar Mojsov	May 1987–May 1988
Raij Dizdarevic	May 1988–May 1989
Janez Drnovsek	May 1989–May 1990
Borisav Jovic	May 1990–May 1991

Stepan Mesic*	May 1991–May 1992
Dobrica Cosic	May 1992–May 1993
Zoran Lilic	May 1993–

Heads of Government: Prime Minister

| Drago Marusic | Jan 1945–Mar 1945 |
| Josip Broz Tito | Apr 1945–Jan 1953 |

Heads of Government: President of the Federal Executive Council (Prime Minister)

Mika Spiljak	June 1963–May 1969
Mitja Ribicic	May 1969–July 1971
Djemal Bijedic	July 1971–Jan 1977
Veselin Djuranovic	Feb 1977–May 1982
Milka Planinc	May 1982–April 1986
Branko Mikulic	May 1986–Dec 1988
Anté Markovic	Jan 1989–July 1992
Milan Panic	July 1992–Dec 1992
Radoje Kontic	Dec 1992–

---

* The collective presidency virtually ceased to function as civil war loomed in Yugoslavia by mid-1991. Presidents after that date were presidents of "rump" Yugoslavia.

CHAPTER 3

LEGISLATURES AND CONSTITUTIONS

ARGENTINA—Argentine Republic

The constitution in force in 1945 was that of 1853, as amended up to 1898. It was replaced in 1949, but reestablished in 1958. It provided for a federal union of 22 provinces, one territory and a federal capital. The state was a republic with an executive president. The president made most appointments, and shared legislative power with a bicameral parliament. President and vice president were elected for a six-year term by electoral colleges, chosen by popular vote. They might not be immediately reelected.

Military coups and rule by military junta disrupted the working of the constitution in 1955–57, 1962, 1966–73 and 1976–83. During these periods the constitution was not abrogated but was kept in force insofar as it was compatible with the aims of the government.

The temporary constitution of 1949–57 was drafted to allow the then president (Perón) a second term in office and to increase the control of the central government over the national economy.

The National Congress provided by the 1853 constitution was bicameral. The House of Deputies sat for a four-year term, one-half retiring every two years. Seats were distributed by province according to population. After 1951, 10 seats were assigned to the second-largest party. Senators, 46 in number, were elected by popular vote for a nine-year term, one-third retiring every three years. Senators were nominated by the legislative bodies of each province.

Voting was obligatory for all men over 18; women were enfranchised in 1947. Proportional representation was introduced in 1963. The clergy, the regular army and those legally deprived of the franchise do not vote.

With the return to civilian rule on 10 December 1983 following presidential, congressional and municipal elections on 30 October, the 1853 constitution (with amendments up to 1898) became once more fully effective.

The 1994 elections paved the way for reform of the 1853 constitution (last reformed in 1983). President Menem pressed for a reduction of the presidential term from six years to four (with reelection for one term only), the creation of the Office of Prime Minister and a reform of the system for electing senators representing the provinces. However, in 1995, Menem was reelected to a second term and sought to change the constitution again to allow for a third term. He abandoned his bid amid opposition threats of civil disobedience and expressions of dissatisfaction from his own Peronist Party.

AUSTRALIA—Commonwealth of Australia

The original Commonwealth of Australia constitution of 1901 was still in force in 1945. It provided for a federation of six states: New South Wales, Victoria, Queensland, South Australia, Western Australia and Tasmania. The federation also included the Territory of Northern Australia and the Capital Territory.

The Federal Parliament is bicameral. The state is a constitutional monarchy; the sovereign of the United Kingdom is also sovereign of Australia and is represented there by a governor-general. The sovereign's Privy Council serves as the final court of appeal for Australian citizens. Executive power lies with the governor-general. He is advised by a Council of Ministers who are also cabinet ministers responsible to the parliament.

Each state has a governor and a parliament; all except that of Queensland are bicameral. Where state and federal law conflict, the latter prevails.

In 1945, the Capital Territory had an Advisory Council and the Northern Territory was directly ruled by the federal government. In 1947 the Northern Territory was given a Legislative Council; it received self-government in 1978. The Capital Territory received a fully elected Legislative Assembly in 1974.

The right of appeal to the Privy Council was abolished in 1986.

The constitution allows the creation of new states, and it forbids the establishment of an official religion.

The Federal Parliament has a House of Representatives and a Senate. The House has (so far as is practicable) twice as many members as the Senate. Formerly nonvoting members for the territories were given voting rights in 1966–68. Representation in both chambers is in proportion to state population. The Senate must have at least six (at present 10) senators for each original state of the Commonwealth. Since 1974 there have also been two senators for each territory. Members of the House serve a three-year term; senators serve for six years, and usually one-half submit to reelection every three years.

Bills may originate or be amended in either house, except money bills, which may originate or be amended only in the House. On other bills, disagreements between the houses are resolved by joint session or, if not resolved, can lead to dissolution.

The franchise for both houses is for everyone over 18, and voting is compulsory. British government powers to intervene in the government of Australia or its states were removed by the Australia Act of 1986.

Prime Minister Paul Keating, who served from December 1991 to March 1996, sought to move Australia toward a republican constitution. John Howard assumed leadership in 1996, but he suffered a reduced majority in the parliamentary elections of 1998. In June 1999 voters defeated a referendum to alter the constitution to establish the Commonwealth of Australia as a republic with the queen and governor-general being replaced by a president.

AUSTRIA—Republic of Austria

A provisional government was installed on 28 April 1945 (following the defeat of the German Reich, into which Austria had been incorporated in 1938). The constitution of 1920, revised in 1929, was then revived. It provided for a federal republic of nine states: Vienna, Lower Austria, Upper Austria, Salzburg, Styria, Carinthia, Tyrol, Vorarlberg and Burgenland.

The head of state is a president, elected by popular vote for a six-year term. His executive power is exercised through the chancellor and a cabinet of ministers responsible to a parliament. Legislative power lies with the people through a parliament and also through the popular initiative; petitions to the parliament can be made by 400,000 citizens who are eligible for the vote.

Total revision of the constitution must be approved by plebiscite.

Each state has an assembly elected by popular vote; the assembly then elects a governor. The legislative powers of central and state parliaments are clearly defined and separate.

The two houses are the Federal Council (Bundesrat) and National Council (Nationalrat). Nationalrat deputies are elected by universal adult suffrage. The voting age was 21 in 1945 and 20 thereafter. Candidates run in multimember constituencies; there were 165 deputies until 1971, then 183. Bundesrat members are elected for varying terms by the state assemblies; they need not be members of those assemblies but they must be eligible to be members.

Bills must pass both houses. The Bundesrat may object to a bill within eight weeks. If the Nationalrat passes it again, with half its members present, it becomes law.

Two sessions of parliament are convened every year. The government may demand extra sessions and so may one-third of the members of either house.

Austria joined the European Union on 1 January 1995, but it retains its strict constitutional neutrality and forbids foreign troops on its soil.

BELGIUM—Kingdom of Belgium

The constitution of 1831 established a limited monarchy. Legislative power is shared between the sovereign and a parliament, executive power between the sovereign and the ministers.

The legislature was reorganized in 1921 and remained in that form in 1945.

The constitution rules on the royal succession, which is in the direct male line. In default of male heirs the king may nominate his successor with parliament's consent to the choice.

The king convokes and dissolves parliament, and all his acts must be countersigned by one of his ministers.

The constitution recognizes French, Dutch and German as official languages. In 1967 and 1971 it was revised to allow the creation of three Regional and two Cultural Councils, to represent the interests of the Flemish- and French-speaking communities.

There are two houses, the Senate and the Chamber of Representatives. Members of both are elected by universal suffrage of adults over 18; women were enfranchised in March 1948. Voting is compulsory. The Chamber has a maximum of one member per 40,000 inhabitants. Members are elected on the basis of proportional representation and serve a four-year term.

The Senate has one member per 200,000 inhabitants. Some are elected indirectly by provincial councils, who each elect at least three senators. A number equal to half the number of Chamber members is then elected directly by proportional representation. Senators serve four years.

Parliament meets annually in October for a session of at least 40 days. Both houses have equal powers; both may introduce bills; and the assent of both is needed before the king may sign a bill. Money bills originate only in the Chamber.

In February 1992, legislation for the first stage of an eventual federal state was introduced in parliament. In September 1992, constitutional changes were made to devolve more power to the regions (i.e., to the parliaments of Dutch-speaking Flanders and French-speaking Wallonia). The royal power to accept or refuse prime-ministerial resignations was ended, as was the monarch's absolute right to dissolve parliament after a vote of no confidence.

In 1994, a revised constitution granted autonomy to the regions: The central government retains responsibility for foreign affairs, defense, taxation and social security, while regional governments control transportation, the environment and trade promotion, and community governments oversee education and culture. The arrangement means that Belgium essentially has six governments, each with its own legislative assembly.

BRAZIL—Federative Republic of Brazil

Brazil is a republic and a federative union of 23 states. In 1945 the then president (Vargas) had altered the 1934 constitution to give himself absolute power. He resigned in October 1945 and there was an interim period before the adoption of a new constitution in September 1946. This restored a bicameral parliament. Executive power lay with an elected president serving a five-year term as head of state; he could not seek immediate reelection. Political parties opposed to the multiparty system and to democracy were banned. In 1947 the Communist Party was declared illegal.

In 1961 most of the president's executive power was transferred to a prime minister, leading a government that was responsible to parliament. In 1963 a plebiscite restored full powers to the president, but he (Goulart) was deposed in 1964.

The new military executive ruled by a series of Institutional Acts. A parliament was provided for, but the president had power to govern without it under a new constitution of 1967; legislative bodies were suspended in 1968.

Until 1977, constitutional amendment could take place only by a two-thirds majority vote in two successive sessions of Congress; in that year an absolute majority was declared sufficient.

In October 1978 the Institutional Acts were repealed. In December 1979 new political parties were allowed. Military rule ended and a civilian president took office in 1985.

A new constitution—the eighth since independence—came into effect on 5 October 1988. Voting is compulsory for men and women between 18 and 70, and optional for those between 16 and 18 and over 70 and for illiterates. The president and vice president serve for five years and cannot seek immediate reelection. If no candidate gains 51% of the votes the two leading candidates enter a second ballot. Three senators from each state make up the 69-member Senate, which is two-thirds directly and one-third indirectly elected. Members of the Chamber of Deputies are elected by universal suffrage every four years.

Parliaments functioned normally from 1946 to 1964; they survived thereafter under military rule but without power.

The 1946 parliament was bicameral. The Chamber of Deputies had directly elected members sitting for four years; members of the Senate sat for eight. Both houses, as the National Congress, met annually. The franchise was for everyone over 18 and literate. Voting was compulsory for men and for employed women of 18 to 65, optional for unemployed women, persons over 65 and serving officers. Enlisted men and illiterates did not vote.

In 1969 Congress gained the right to overturn executive veto by a two-thirds majority vote within 45 days, but the powers of the Fifth Institutional Act remained available to the executive as a counterbalance.

Political life was renewed in 1979. The Senate was now two-thirds directly and one-third indirectly elected, and was partially renewed every four years. The Chamber of Deputies had between five and 55 seats per state, according to population.

In 1985 civil parliamentary government was fully restored and the franchise was extended to illiterates. Brazil became a federal republic under the 1988 constitution. The president and vice president are elected for a four-year term. A 1997 amendment allows them to run for consecutive terms. The National Congress maintains a bicameral structure—a Senate, whose members serve eight-year terms, and a Chamber of Deputies elected to four-year terms.

BULGARIA—Republic of Bulgaria

The constitution in force in 1945 was that of 1879 as amended in 1911. This provided for a monarchy with cabinet government, ministers being responsible to the king (who chose them) and to the National Assembly.

A republic was proclaimed in 1946. The republican constitution came into force in 1947 and was amended in 1971. It provided for a single-chamber parliament, working closely with the Bulgarian Communist Party; the party had a Central Committee electing a politburo as the state's most powerful policy-making and executive body.

The constitution did not provide for a head of state, but in practice the chairman of the Council of State functioned as such. Bulgaria was declared a unitary state.

In 1945 there was a single-chamber Sobranje (National Assembly) elected by proportional representation by men and married women over 21. There were 160 members, and each constituency had at least 20,000 electors. Members sat for four years; they had to be male, literate and over 30.

There was also a Grand Sobranje, which had twice the membership but was elected only occasionally to decide on special questions (territorial, constitutional or relating to the succession).

The 1947 republican parliament remained unicameral. Four hundred deputies serving for five years were directly elected by all citizens over 18. There was one deputy for every 20,000 inhabitants.

The Assembly elected a Council of State, which consisted of a chairman, six vice chairmen, a secretary and 17 members; all were chosen from the membership of the Assembly. There was also a Council of Ministers acting as a cabinet, with a prime minister as chairman.

In January 1990 the National Assembly instituted 21 constitutional reforms, including the abolition of the Communist Party's right to be the only governing party. This was followed in April 1990 by amendments that created an executive presidency, permitted free multiparty elections, and removed the words "socialist" and "communist" from the constitution. According to the constitution of 1991, the president is now popularly elected for a five-year term. There is a single-chamber five-year parliament with 240 seats elected by proportional representation (with a 4% threshold). The pro-Western Union of Democracy Forces (UDF) elected in 1997 pledged to work toward qualifying for membership in the European Union and NATO.

CANADA

In 1945 all the provinces except Newfoundland had joined the confederation; Newfoundland joined in 1949. In April 1999, the territory of Nunavut joined the confederation. The country was a constitutional monarchy with a governor-general representing the sovereign. Parliament consisted of the governor-general, the Senate and the House of Commons. The governor-general exercises executive power and is appointed by the sovereign on the advice of the prime minister.

The March 1867 British North America Act was amended in 1949 to reflect the addition of Newfoundland to the confederation. The act was most recently amended in 1982, when it was renamed the Constitution Act. The Official Languages Act of 1969 established English and French as dual official languages.

A constitutional link with the United Kingdom lasted until the Constitution Act of 1982. This gave the federal parliament unlimited rights to revise the constitution without reference to the United Kingdom. The 1982 constitution replaced the British North America Acts of 1867 and 1949; it contained a bill of rights and redefined ethnic, provincial and territorial rights.

There are two houses in the federal parliament: the Senate and the House of Commons. The provincial and territorial parliaments are unicameral. The federal parliament legislates on all matters not specifically reserved to provinces and territories.

Federal senators are appointed by the governor-general on the advice of the prime minister of Canada. Senators are appointed according to the following limits: Ontario and Quebec (24 senators each), Nova Scotia and New Brunswick (10 senators each), Newfoundland, Manitoba, Saskatchewan, Alberta and British Columbia (six senators each), Prince Edward Island (four senators), Yukon, the Northwest Territories and Nunavut (one senator each). They must be at least 30, and since 1965 they have been obliged to retire at 75. Members of the Commons are directly elected by universal suffrage for a maximum five-year term. The minimum voting age is 18. Seats are distributed by area according to population: Quebec has a fixed number and the others are apportioned accordingly. This system, in force in 1945, was altered in 1949 and restored in 1974. From 1949 to 1974 seats were distributed according to the population of all provinces.

The Senate acts mainly as a reviewer of legislation initiated by the Commons. Only the lower house votes on money bills.

Following two years of often acrimonious discussion, a new set of constitutional proposals was unanimously agreed on by the 10 provincial premiers and the prime minister at a meeting in August 1992. However, in the referendum of 26 October 1992 the "Charlottetown Agreement" was rejected, 54% to 46%. Six of the provinces voted against the agreement, as had Canada as a whole.

When Prime Minister Brian Mulroney retired in June 1993, the governing Progressive Conservative Party chose Defense Minister Kim Campbell as the first female prime minister in Canadian history, but not for long. Jean Chrétien of the Liberal Party was installed in the post following the national elections in October of that year and again in November 2000.

The Quebec referendum on secession was narrowly defeated in October 1995, but separatists vowed to try again. In 1997, the Reform Party replaced the Bloc Québecois as the official opposition.

CHILE—Republic of Chile

The 1925 constitution remained effective until 1973 and was nominally in force until 1981. It provided for a unitary republic with an executive presidency and a bicameral parliament. The president was directly elected by popular vote. He served for six years and was not eligible for reelection. There was no vice president except when the president needed to appoint a deputy. The president acted with a cabinet of ministers of state. They were responsible to him and they might not be members of parliament. President and cabinet might delay legislation, but parliament could ultimately overturn their veto.

In September 1973 the Marxist government of Salvador Allende was overthrown by the armed forces. Parliament was dissolved and the new president headed a junta government. Political activities were banned and a "state of siege" proclaimed, which lasted until 1978. A new constitution was approved in September 1980 providing a minimum eight-year extension for the military president (Pinochet); at the end of that extension, parliamentary government could be revived and a new president nominated by the junta.

Parliament functioned until 1973. The National Congress had a Senate and a Chamber of Deputies, both directly elected by proportional representation. Deputies sat for a four-year term, senators for eight years. Half the seats in the Senate were subject to reelection every four years. The franchise was for all literate men over 21, until 1949, when it was extended to women on the same terms.

The government submitted measures to both houses. Bills (except ones dealing with finance) might also originate in either house. A bill passed by parliament might be vetoed by the president. It could still become law if passed by a two-thirds vote of both houses.

In a plebiscite on 5 October 1988 the electorate rejected Pinochet as president. With the exception of the 1990–94 term, the president serves six years. The 1993 elections saw the reemergence of the Frei family, with Eduardo Frei Ruiz-Tagle, the candidate of a center-left coalition, winning the presidency. His father was president from 1964 to 1970.

Ricardo Lagos won the January 2000 elections by a narrow margin to become the first socialist executive in 27 years. Lagos, 61, was involved in the fight against Gen. Augusto Pinochet's dictatorship in the 1980s.

CHINA—People's Republic of China

Following civil war (from 1945) the People's Republic was proclaimed in September 1949 by the People's Political Consultative Conference. The conference inaugurated a government on 1 October 1949 and passed an Organic Law and a Common Programme. These formed the basis of the permanent constitution of 1954. It provided for a unitary, multinational republic with autonomy for national areas, which are nevertheless inalienable. All nationalities are declared equal. Society is based on state and collective ownership of the means of production. The National Congress is the only legislative body and the highest authority, but it is convened, and its laws interpreted, by its own permanent Standing Committee. There was also a State Council as executive body. The head of state was the chairman of the republic.

Effective power lay with the Central Committee of the Communist Party; this was confirmed by a new constitution adopted in 1975. It replaced the single head of state by a collective, the Standing Committee of the National People's Congress. It also directed that the proletariat should supervise the progress of the bourgeoisie. In 1978 a new constitution dropped much of this radical thought. The post of head of state was revived in 1982. In a new constitution adopted in March 1993, China embraced the principles of the "socialist market" economy.

The legislature is the National People's Congress. Deputies are elected by secret ballot for a five-year term. They sit annually, electing a Standing Committee, which then becomes the permanent legislative body. The Congress did not function during the Cultural Revolution but was revived in 1975; at the same time, the power of the party to direct the Congress in its work was reaffirmed. Under that direction the Congress has power to amend the constitution, elect state officials and remove them from office, decide the national plan and pass laws. The laws are then interpreted by the permanent Standing Committee, which in turn supervises the work of the executive.

Parties represented in Congress are the Communist Party and eight others, forming the United Front. See page 211.

A constitution adopted in 1982 restored the post of state president as head of state and constitutional amendments in 1988 allowed the renting of "land-use" rights and the formation of private companies.

In June 1989, student demonstrators calling for democratic reforms were crushed in a bloody crackdown in Beijing's Tiananmen Square. At the annual session of the National People's Congress in 1993, Communist Party leader Jiang Zemin was elected president while hard-liner Li Peng was reelected to another five-year term as prime minister. Following Deng Xiaoping's death in early 1997, Britain's 99-year lease on Hong Kong expired and, in July, the territory was returned to Chinese rule.

COLOMBIA—Republic of Colombia

From 1886 to 1991 Colombia was a unitary republic with a strong president. The president was both chief of state and head of the government. He had extensive powers of appointment and removal, power to invoke a state of siege under which he could issue decrees and suspend laws, and broad powers over foreign and economic policy. In reality, however, he was limited by the power of the various interest groups and the weakness of the state. The president was chosen by direct popular election for a four-year term. He could be reelected but could not serve consecutive terms.

The legislature was composed of two houses, the Chamber of Representatives and the Senate. It had the power of initiation, amendment and repeal of legislation, but was generally seen as reacting to executive initiatives. Members of both houses were elected on the basis of population for four-year terms and could be reelected indefinitely.

A new constitution came into effect in July 1991. It retained a directly elected president with a four-year term. The legislature continued to have two houses—a 102-member Senate and a 161-member Chamber of Representatives—but the new constitution contained articles protecting civil rights, and there was provision for the reform of the judiciary and political participation.

In 1997, a constitutional amendment that allowed for nonreactive extradition was passed, while civil unrest and intermittent guerrilla drug wars continued throughout the country.

CONGO, DEMOCRATIC REPUBLIC OF THE—(formerly Zaire)

The Colonial Charter of 1908 defined the government of the then Belgian Congo. It was last amended in 1959. Legislative power lay with the home parliament in Belgium. Executive power belonged to the king and the Belgian minister for the colonies. In the colony the king was represented by a governor-general, who was president of a consultative council. The council had 11 official members, and 54 who were not officials but represented the people. There was also an administration of central officers, provincial governors, departmental directors and a Ten-Year-Plan Commissioner. In an emergency, the governor-general received from the king the power to govern by decree.

The state became independent, as Congo, in 1960. Independence was followed by five years of war between the central government and the province of Katanga. A constitution was nevertheless drawn up in 1962, providing for a federation of 21 provinces and a central government under an elected president. The president would exercise his executive power through a prime minister and a cabinet, and would share legislative power with an elected assembly.

This was suspended in September 1963. In October 1963 the prime minister was granted full legislative powers, pending a new constitution. In November 1965 there was a military coup. General Joseph Mobutu became president, and in 1967 a plebiscite approved a new constitution, providing an executive presidency. Amendments in 1971 established a unicameral parliament and election of a president for a seven-year term. The sole political party and organ of power is the MPR (Mouvement Populaire de Ia Révolution). The Mouvement president is the president of the republic, and the party political bureau, which he appoints, is the executive. A further constitution in 1978, amended 1980, confirmed this. The structure of the state revolved around Mobuto Sese Seko (the name adopted by Mobutu in 1972 as part of a program of "national authenticity"). Head of state, and president of the only political party, he ruled with the power of an absolute king.

The single-chamber parliament set up in 1971 was the National Legislative Council. Deputies (called People's Commissioners) were directly elected. There was one per 100,000 inhabitants. Suffrage was universal. In reality, Mobutu determined the formal procedures for selecting Legislative Council members and outlined their powers and responsibilities.

Mobutu was overthrown in May 1997 by guerrilla opponent Laurent Kabila, who reclaimed the name Democratic Republic of the Congo, the country's name before Mobutu changed it to Zaire in 1971.

COSTA RICA—Republic of Costa Rica

In 1945 Costa Rica was a military dictatorship. Three years later the dictatorship was defeated and constitutional government restored.

The constitution provides for a strong parliamentary and presidential system. The president is elected for a four-year term by secret ballot and can serve only a single term. He can run again after eight years out of office. The president has broad powers to initiate social and economic programs, to appoint officials and to shape foreign policy. However, most of his decisions must be approved by the Legislative Assembly. He has the power to veto legislation, with the exception of the annual budget, but the veto can be overruled by a two-thirds majority vote in the legislature.

The Legislative Assembly is a unicameral body of 57 members elected by proportional representation. It has power over taxation, budgeting concerns and other legislation that must be passed by a simple majority. A two-thirds majority is needed to pass a constitutional amendment.

In 1994, Jose Maria Figueres Olsen of the National Liberation Party became president after proposing more government intervention in the economy. In 1998, Miguel Angel Rodriguez of the Social Christian Unity Party became president.

CUBA—Republic of Cuba

The constitution of 1940 provided for a unitary republic with an executive presidency and a bicameral parliament. The president appointed a cabinet that was responsible to parliament.

On 10 March 1952 General Fulgencio Batista took office as president and suspended the constitution. It was restored on 24 February 1955, after the Communist Party had been declared illegal. It was suspended again by the revolutionary government of Dr. Fidel Castro on 1 January 1959. Government was then by decree. In 1961 a Marxist-Leninist program was announced. The first communist constitution came into effect in February 1976. It provided for a National Assembly working with an Executive Committee, whose president is the head of state and government, and with the Committee of the Cuban Communist Party.

Under the 1940 constitution the Congress consisted of a Senate and a lower house. The Senate had nine members from each province, elected for a four-year term. The parliament did not function between 1952 and 1955, and it was abolished in 1959.

In 1976 elections were held in 169 municipal assemblies. The assemblies then elected members of 14 provincial assemblies and a new National Assembly. The current Assembly is unicameral, with 499 members. They are elected from a list representing the Communist Party, labor or producers' organizations. The Assembly appoints an executive State Council to function as a permanent body, and a Council of Ministers. The chairman of the State Council combines the functions of prime minister and president.

In 1992 the constitutional powers of the president were increased, giving him the right to declare a state of emergency, to head a national defense council and to organize the country's armed forces. Since 1993, the government has permitted limited private enterprise and raised hopes of increased religious freedom for Cubans with Pope John Paul II's visit to the country in 1998.

CZECHOSLOVAKIA—(until December 1992)

The republican constitution of 1920, held in abeyance from 1938 to 1945, became operative again in June 1945. It provided for a unitary state with the president as head of state, elected by parliament for seven years. The president had power to dissolve parliament (but not during his last six months of office) and to return bills for further consideration. Executive power lay with the government (the premier and cabinet), which had the right to put any defeated bill (other than an amendment to the constitution) to a referendum. The bicameral legislature had a lower chamber of 300 deputies directly elected by proportional representation for six years, and an upper house—the Senate—of 150 members elected for eight years. The Senate considered and might return or delay bills passed to it by the lower house.

In February 1948 communist rule was established, and in June a new constitution was introduced, creating a system similar to that of the Soviet Union. A single-chamber National Assembly, with 300 members elected for six years, elected its own presidium. This constitution was replaced in 1960 by one that was more specifically communist. The single-chamber parliament was to work with the party politburo, which would be the highest policy-making body.

Amendments added in 1968 divided the country into two equal states—the Czech Socialist Republic and the Slovak Socialist Republic—each of which has a prime minister, legislature and cabinet.

The parliament of 1945 (established 1920) had a chamber of 300 deputies directly elected by proportional representation for six years, and a Senate of 150 members elected for eight years. The Senate considered, and might return or delay, bills passed to it by the Chamber.

From 1948 to 1968 Czechoslovakia had a single-chamber National Assembly with 300 members elected for six years. The Assembly elected its own permanent presidium. After 1969 the legislature was bicameral. The upper house, the Chamber of Nations, was elected from the National Councils for the Czech and Slovak regions, respectively. Both the Czechs and the Slovaks had equal representation (75 deputies each) in this chamber. The lower house, the Chamber of the People, with 200 deputies, was nationally elected. All deputies, state and federal, sat for a five-year term. All citizens over 18 could vote. Although the constitution gave the National Assembly jurisdiction in foreign and domestic policy, in fact, it approved only measures put before it by the government.

The Communist Party's monopoly of political power was abolished by the Federal Assembly on 30 November 1989 and independent parties were legalized. In March 1990 the Assembly passed election laws allowing for free multiparty elections with proportional representation. Assembly deputies were to be elected for two-year terms. In April 1990 the state was renamed the Czech and Slovak Federative Republic.

On 25 November 1992 the Czechoslovak Federal Parliament approved (by three votes) the creation of independent Czech and Slovak states from 1 January 1993. These states are now the Czech Republic and Slovakia.

DENMARK—Kingdom of Denmark

The charter of 1915 was still in force in 1945; it provided for a monarchy with legislative power shared by king and parliament. Executive power was held by the king and exercised through his ministers. The king appointed and presided over his Council of State, and had the right to reject its decisions.

In 1953 a new constitution abolished the upper house of parliament and redefined the position of the sovereign.

The queen must be a member of the state church. She shares legislative power with the parliament and exercises executive power only through her ministers. The Council of State survives as the Cabinet, and is called the Council of State only when the queen is presiding. The Council ministers are responsible to parliament.

Before 1953 there were two houses: the Folketing (lower house) had 149 members; 117 seats were filled by direct elections following proportional representation and 31 were reserved for parties with insufficient votes to win seats. The maximum term was four years. The Landsting (upper house) had 78 members indirectly elected for an eight-year term: members were first elected from the same electoral districts as were used for the Folketing; they sat for four years and then half their number submitted to reelection.

In 1953 the Landsting was abolished. There is now a single-chamber Folketing, elected until 1978 by everyone over 21, and since 1978 by everyone over 18.

Bills may be initiated by any member, and receive three readings. If passed they may still be subject to referendum should one-third of the members request it; the prime minister decides how the referendum result should be acted upon.

EGYPT—Arab Republic of Egypt

Egypt was a unitary state and a constitutional monarchy from 1922 until 1953. The king shared executive power with a responsible government, and legislative power with a bicameral parliament. However, independence was severely limited by British influence.

An independent republic was proclaimed in June 1953. The 1923 constitution was abrogated in December 1953, and a temporary constitution gave supreme power to General Neguib and his council of ministers. The council of ministers, together with 13 army officers forming the Council of Revolution, became a joint policy-making congress.

In 1956 President Nasser introduced a new constitution: Egypt was a democratic republic and an Arab nation, with Islam as the official religion. There was a unicameral National Assembly and an executive president.

In 1958 the governments of Egypt, Syria and Yemen formed a union with one legislature and one head of state (the president of Egypt). Syria broke away from the union in September 1961 and Egypt broke the link with Yemen in December 1961. Egypt, however, retained the name of the union—United Arab Republic—until September 1971.

In 1962 a charter set out the principles of the republic as a socialist state. The Statute of the Arab Socialist Union was drawn up in the same year. This is a supplement to the constitution of 1964, which defines the socialist republic as "part of the Arab nation." The Arab Socialist Union was to be the "vanguard" for furthering socialism at all levels of administration.

A further constitution (Septmber 1971) defined Egypt as a "democratic socialist" state, with Islam as the state religion.

Parliament under the monarchy had two chambers. The lower house had indirectly elected deputies, suffrage being for all adult men. The Senate had half its members elected and half appointed.

The republican parliament is unicameral. In March 1956 women were enfranchised and voting became compulsory for men over 18.

The National People's Assembly has 454 (1994) members, all but 10 of whom are directly elected. They sit for a five-year term. Between 1962 and 1976 all candidates were from the Arab Socialist Union. Two other parties were formed before the 1976 elections, and the Union was abolished in 1980.

The Assembly nominates the president by a two-thirds majority; the choice must be confirmed by plebiscite. The president may appoint up to 10 extra Assembly members. The Assembly can empower the president to govern by decree, but only in exceptional circumstances.

In June 1990 the High Court ruled that proportional elections were unconstitutional. A 1993 referendum supported President Hosni Mubarak's bid for a third term. In addition to Mubarak's National Democratic Party, there are also 14 opposition parties and some independents in parliament.

EL SALVADOR—Republic of El Salvador

A series of military presidents and military juntas were the effective rulers until 1979. An abortive coup in March 1972 led to increased guerrilla activity against the government. In 1979 it fell and was replaced by a junta of army officers and civilians; the junta promised a democratic constitution but postponed action because of the level of violence.

A president was installed in December 1980. In March 1982 a Constituent Assembly was elected, with power to legislate and to draft a new constitution, amending (slightly) those of 1950 and 1962. The constitution came into force in December 1983. It provides for a president, holding executive power and exercising it through a Council of Ministers whom he appoints. The president is elected by popular vote for a nonrenewable term of five years. There is a one-chamber legislature. There is a Supreme Court, whose president and magistrates are elected by the legislature for renewable three-year terms.

The constitution records El Salvador's commitment to establishing a United Republic of Central America, subject to popular will.

All three postwar constitutions (1950, 1962 and 1983) have provided for a single-chamber legislative Assembly. Women received a limited franchise in 1945, and full adult suffrage for those over 18 was introduced for both sexes in 1950.

The term for members of the Assembly was two years until 1983, and is now three years. There are 60 members, elected by proportional representation.

The Assembly has the right to initiate legislation; so has the executive (the president and his chosen council) and so has the Supreme Court. If the president objects to a bill proposed by the Assembly, his objection can be overruled by a two-thirds majority vote.

Elections to the Assembly cannot take place at the same time as an election to the presidency.

The 1997 elections denied a majority to either of the two major parties, with the National Liberation Party and the right-wing ARENA party effectively splitting the Assembly.

FINLAND—Republic of Finland

The Finnish governmental system is based on the Form of Government Act of 1919 and several subsequent laws that together comprise the constitution. It is a unitary presidential-parliamentary republic.

Executive authority rests with the president, who is head of state. He has the power to appoint important executive and judicial officials, to present bills to parliament, to ratify and veto legislation and, most important, to form and dismiss governments (the State Council). These governments do not have to receive votes of confidence from parliament on formation, and the president may dismiss them even if they enjoy a parliamentary majority.

The State Council consists of a prime minister and no more than 15 ministers who prepare legislation and supervise the administration of policy. Because all ministers are considered equal and because of the power of the president, the prime minister has far less power than is true in other parliamentary systems. He leads the daily work of the State Council and is the government's spokesman in parliament but he cannot command his ministers. Although members of parliament can introduce legislation, the vast majority comes from the Council, which works with the president on the legislative program. Ministers are held legally as well as politically accountable for their actions.

Legislative power is in the hands of a 200-member unicameral parliament whose members are elected by proportional representation to four-year terms. Constitutionally there are very few limits on the power of parliament, but practically, its powers are exercised at the behest of the president and the State Council.

In 1994, Martti Ahtisaari, a Social Democrat, won the first direct presidential election, rather than being chosen by electors. Finland became a member of the European Union in January 1995, but it has not become a full member of the Western European Union.

FRANCE—French Republic

In 1945 the constitution of the Third Republic was in abeyance following the German occupation.

The constitution of the Fourth Republic came into force on 24 December 1946. The president was symbolic head of state. The bicameral legislature consisted of the National Assembly and an advisory Council of the Republic. In 1954 this Council was given power to delay legislation and to initiate bills. Executive power lay with a prime minister and his Council of Ministers. Both the Third and Fourth Republics were weak parliamentary systems characterized by unstable governments and indecisive assemblies.

The Fifth Republic was established on 4 October 1958, defining France as an indivisible and secular republic that combines the features of presidential and parliamentary government. The constitution provides for a dual executive. The president of the republic, elected by popular vote (since 1962) for a seven-year renewable term, is chief of state. The prime minister, appointed by the president but needing the confidence of the majority in the National Assembly, is head of government. A Council of Ministers, composed of the prime minister and senior members of the government chaired by the president, transacts executive business. When both the prime minister and the president have the same political orientation, the president sets the guidelines for the executive. If the orientation differs, policy is set by negotiation.

The constitution of the Fifth Republic provides for a bicameral legislature—the National Assembly, currently consisting of 577 seats, and the Senate, consisting of 321 seats. The Assembly is directly elected by majority ballot in single-member constituencies for a five-year term. (Proportional representation was used in the March 1986 elections but was abandoned thereafter.) The Senate is elected for nine years (one-third retire every three years) by an electoral college composed of Departmental Council, Territorial Assembly and Municipal Council members.

Parliament convenes for two sessions per year. No member of the government may be a member of parliament. Parliament's advice is not binding on the government nor on the president, nor does parliament determine the government's program. Parliament remains important in the Fifth Republic, but the executive is the more influential branch of government.

GERMAN DEMOCRATIC REPUBLIC—(until 1990)

The Berlin Declaration of 5 June 1945 transferred sovereignty over Germany to the governments of the United States, the United Kingdom, the USSR and France. Each government was assigned a zone of occupation in which a commander in chief would exercise control. The four commanders in chief jointly made up the Allied Control Council, which met in Berlin.

The zones controlled by the United States, the United Kingdom and France became the Federal Republic of Germany. The zone controlled by the USSR became the German Democratic Republic.

The constitution enacted on 7 October 1949 provided for a socialist state with a nonexecutive president and a strongly structured Communist Party working through a bicameral legislature: a lower house, the People's Chamber, and an upper house, the States Chamber. The latter was abolished in 1958. In 1960 the post of president was abolished and its functions transferred to that of the chairman of a newly formed Council of State.

The pre-1990 governmental structure was based on the 1968 constitution as amended in 1974. The executive was composed of two important institutions—the Council of Ministers, based on the Soviet model, and the State Council. The Council of Ministers was formally elected by the legislature; in reality, the legislature approved the selections of the Communist Party. The head of the Council was formal head of government. The chairman of the State Council was chief of state.

The 1968 constitution established a unicameral legislature, the People's Chamber. It consisted of 500 deputies directly elected for five years. Suffrage was for everyone over 18; candidates had to be 21 and normally ran as a single list. The Chamber was constitutionally "supreme state authority" although in reality political life was dominated by the Communist Party.

With reunification in 1990, the German Democratic Republic ceased to exist.

GERMANY, FEDERAL REPUBLIC OF

A constituent assembly meeting in 1948 formulated a Basic Law, which came into effect on 23 May 1949. The country comprised a federal republic of 10 states—Baden-Württemberg, Bavaria, Bremen, Hamburg, Hessen, Lower Saxony, North-Rhine–Westphalia, Rhineland-Palatinate, Saarland, Schleswig-Holstein—and West Berlin.

There was established a nonexecutive president elected for a five-year term by a special convention. Executive power lay with a chancellor and his ministers. Legislative power was vested in a Federal Assembly and Federal Council, the Assembly electing the chancellor.

The constitution defines legislation that is exclusively federal, exclusively state or concurrent.

Parliament consists of the Federal Assembly (Bundestag) and the Federal Council (Bundesrat). The Assembly, previously consisting of 496 seats, is now composed of 662 members since the unification with East Germany. The term is four years and elections are direct, by universal adult suffrage. The minimum voting age is 18. The Federal Council consists of members appointed by state governments, each state appointing members according to the number of its inhabitants. Each state has at least three votes in the Council.

Bills must pass the Assembly and are then submitted to the Council, which has a limited power of veto. A two-thirds vote of both houses is needed to amend the constitution.

The federal parliament has exclusive legislative rights over foreign affairs, federal citizenship, freedom of movement, currency, weights and measures, customs and commercial agreements, federal rail and air traffic, mail and telecommunications, copyright and crime prevention.

Major constitutional implications followed the approach of German reunification. The two German states' economic and monetary systems were unified on 1 July 1990. On 31 August 1990 East and West Germany signed a treaty covering some political and social aspects of German unity, leaving others to be decided by an all-German parliament. On 20 September both states ratified unification terms, by which East Germany would merge with the Federal Republic under Article 23 of the West German Basic Law on 3 October 1990. The Basic Law was amended to prevent future claims on former German territory now under Polish or Russian control. In December all-German elections were held for a single German parliament.

In 1996, voters in the relatively new state of Brandenburg in the east rejected a proposal to merge with Berlin. In 1998, after 16 years of rule by Christian Democrat Helmut Kohl, Germans chose centrist Social Democrat Gerhard Schroeder as chancellor.

GHANA—Republic of Ghana

Ghana became independent of Great Britain in 1957 and established a constitution calling for a parliamentary democracy designed along British lines. Three years later a republican constitution was introduced, establishing a presidential system. Subsequent elections put government in the hands of Kwame Nkrumah and his party, transforming Ghana into a de facto one-party state. This condition was formalized in 1964. The First Republic, as it was called, was toppled by a military coup in

1966. Since the coup, the country has experienced two civilian and five military regimes. Ghana is currently ruled by a civilian-military junta called the Provisional National Defense Council (PNDC), which has full executive and legislative powers. It is aided by a government composed of 32 ministers led by the PNDC coordinating secretary, who functions as prime minister. The PNDC makes all key decisions and all governmental appointments.

A new constitution was approved in a referendum on 28 April 1992. The Fourth Republic, ending 11 years of military rule, was announced on 7 January 1993. It provides for an American-style presidency, an independent judiciary and a multiparty parliament.

GREECE—Hellenic Republic

In 1945 Greece was a constitutional monarchy with a single-chamber parliament of at least 150 members. The constitution was that of 1911 as amended in 1925.

On 1 January 1952 a new constitution was promulgated, giving a parliamentary committee some legislative powers when parliament was in recess and providing for a regency if the king were absent and his heir underage. This constitution was suspended after a military coup on 21 April 1967. The monarchy was formally abolished on 1 June 1973, and a republic established, but the new republican president was overthrown by another military coup on 25 November 1973. On 25 July 1974 this military government fell, and the 1952 constitution was adapted for a republic. A new republican constitution was introduced in June 1975, following a referendum confirming preference for a unitary republic.

Under the current constitution, executive functions are divided between the president, who is head of state, and the prime minister, who is head of government. Constitutional revisions in 1986 reduced the presidential office to a largely ceremonial one. The prime minister, the leader of the party with the absolute majority or plurality in parliament, is the key political leader.

The unicameral legislature contains at least 200 deputies elected by universal adult suffrage. (The constitution provides for a maximum of 300.) The system calls for two methods of selection for parliament. Under the first method, delegates are chosen by direct universal secret ballot. The vast majority, currently 288 delegates, are selected by this method. The second method calls for the nomination of deputies by each political party. These deputies gain their seats in proportion to the seats the party won in the constituency elections. Service is for a four-year term. Ministers are not necessarily members of parliament. They have free access to debates and to speak, whether they are members or are not, but they vote only if they are members. Most legislation is introduced by government ministers, although parliament and the government have the right to do so.

GUATEMALA—Republic of Guatemala

In January 1986 Guatemala returned to an elected civilian government after more than three decades of direct or indirect rule by the armed forces. Although elections were held during these years, they were marked by fraud, and the presidency was limited to men selected by the armed forces and conservative private-interest groups.

The constitution adopted in 1985 calls for a president, elected for a five-year term, aided by a 13-member cabinet. He is commander in chief of the armed forces and head of the National Security Council. But, practically, the president's power is restricted by the military, who retain power over all matters dealing with national security and rural development. The constitution calls for a unicameral legislature of 100 deputies.

In 1993 the Guatemalan constitution seemed threatened when President Serrano declared he would rule by decree. Serrano, however, was toppled, and in 1996, a peace agreement ended the 36-year civil war.

HUNGARY—Republic of Hungary

Following the Soviet invasion at the end of World War II, a provisional and strongly communist government was installed in Hungary on 21 December 1944. A new republic was proclaimed in February 1946, and in 1949 a People's Republic with a communist view of society and economy was established. The relationship between legislature, executive and party followed the Russian model, with a single party dominating political life. In 1956 a popular revolt was violently crushed by Soviet troops. The subsequent government and party reflected the changes instituted in the aftermath of the revolt.

The executive head of state was the Presidential Council, elected by parliament. The head of the Council was the official head of state. Executive power was vested in a Council of Ministers, also elected by parliament. The prime minister, who handled administrative matters, was chief executive officer. In reality the leadership of the Communist Party developed policy and chose the executive.

Legislative power continued to reside in the 352-member National Assembly. Members were chosen for five-year terms by general election in which voting was mandatory for everyone over 18. Although there was only one party—the Communist Hungarian Socialist Workers Party—about 70% of the legislature's seats were decided between two candidates. Candidates were nominated at preelection meetings open to all voters. They had to receive one-third of the votes for nomination. To be elected, they had to gain half the votes cast.

Parliament approved a new constitution on 18 October 1989 dissolving the People's Republic, removing the right of any single party to governing powers, and instituting parliamentary democracy. The single-chamber National Assembly has 386 members, 120 elected by proportional representation. Members are elected for a four-year term. The head of state is the president of the Republic. A Hungarian Republic was proclaimed on 23 October 1989, after communists voluntarily abandoned their monopoly on power and the constitution was amended to allow a multiparty state. By 1997, Hungary experienced significant changes in the electorate's party preferences.

INDIA—Republic of India

The Government of India Act of 1935 was still in force in 1945. In 1947 the Indian Independence Act provided that the 1935 Act be retained as a provisional constitution for the new state. A new republican constitution came into force in 1950, creating a federal democratic republic with a parliamentary system of government. Under the constitution, executive authority resides in the president, who is head of state, and the prime minister, who is head of government. The president is elected to a five-year term by members of both houses of the national parliament and the lower houses of the state legislatures. He, in turn, appoints the prime minister, who must be able to command a majority in the Lok Sabha, the lower house of parliament. Because the president's role is largely symbolic, real power resides with the prime minister.

The bicameral legislature is composed of a House of the People (Lok Sabha) and a Council of States (Rajya Sabha). The House has 525 directly elected members from the states and 17 members from the territories who may be elected or appointed. As a temporary constitutional measure (which has been routinely extended), 119 seats are reserved for members of the Scheduled Castes and Scheduled Tribes, groups traditionally deprived in Indian society. Direct elections are based on universal adult suffrage. The legislative term is five years. The Council is composed of 250 members, 12 of whom are appointed by the president. The remainder are elected by the state legislatures. Members serve fixed terms, with approximately one-third retiring every two years.

Both houses have the same power over ordinary legislation; however, only the lower house can introduce money bills. The Rajya Sabha can only delay the implementation of this type of legislation.

The ruling Congress Party lost the parliamentary elections of 1996, which resulted in a period of political instability. In April 1999, the government of India virtually collapsed when the Hindu-led regime lost the parliamentary elections in the closest defeat in India's 51 years of independence. Thanks to his support of nuclear development and tough stance in the struggle with Pakistan over Kashmir, Prime Minister Vajpayee kept his post in the follow-up elections held six months later, and his 22-party National Democratic alliance won a majority of parliamentary seats.

INDONESIA—Republic of Indonesia

Indonesia's current governmental structure is based on the 1945 constitution, which provided for a president who was head of state, chief executive and commander of the armed forces. Chosen for a five-year term by the People's Consultative Assembly, he shared legislative and foreign policy powers with parliament. In 1950, the constitution was replaced with a provisional one outlining a parliamentary democracy. Nine years later the original 1945 document was reinstated.

In theory Indonesia is a unitary state with an elected legislature and a sovereign People's Consultative Assembly that elects the president. The Consultative Assembly meets only to elect the president and to outline broad policies of state. It consists of 1,380 members, two-thirds of whom are members of parliament. The others are appointed by the president or by provincial governors to represent various interests. The People's Representative Council, the legislature, is composed of 460 members elected for a five-year term. The majority are elected by proportional representation; approximately 20% are appointed by the president to represent the military, whose members cannot vote.

Despite the carefully constructed constitutional system, Indonesia is dominated by an authoritarian regime headed by a president who has the support of the armed forces. The legislature has acted only to legitimize his initiatives.

General Suharto was elected unopposed to a sixth five-year term in 1993, but he stepped down in 1998 in favor of Vice President B. J. Habibie. Habibie promised elections in 1999 but then withdrew his own candidacy days before the vote. In the nation's first democratic transfer of power, the electoral assembly chose Muslim leader Abdurrahman Wahid as president over Megawati Sukarnoputri, daughter of former president Sukarno, who held power from 1949 to 1967.

IRAN—Islamic Republic of Iran

In 1945 the 1906 constitution was still in force. Iran was a monarchy. The shah's government held executive power and theoretically shared legislative power with an elected Assembly.

Under the monarchy the shah had the right to summon or dissolve the legislature. He might return finance bills to it for further debate, but other bills, once approved by the Assembly, he had to allow. In reality, power was in the hands of the highly centralized monarchy, and the shah made most political decisions himself. Amendments in 1949 and 1957 increased the number of deputies from 136 to 200, and altered the term from two years to four. A Senate was introduced in 1950 with 60 members. Half were elected, half nominated by the shah.

The two-party system prevailed until the shah abolished it in 1975. Unrest began in 1977, and martial law was imposed in September 1978. In November 1978 a civilian government was restored, but revolution followed. The government resigned and parliament dissolved itself on 11 February 1979, by which time a provisional government had taken office (5 February) under the Ayatollah Khomeini. Actual power lay with the Ayatollah's Islamic Revolutionary Council. A constitution was drafted in March and the Islamic Republic of Iran proclaimed in April.

The December 1979 constitution provides for clerical control of all branches of government. It gives supreme authority to the state's highest religious leader, the *wali faqih*. The position of *faqih* is provided in the constitution, but is not formally part of the government, yet his powers are extensive. He appoints the highest judicial authorities, commands the armed forces and formalizes the election of the president. If the Supreme Court finds the president politically incompetent, the *faqih* can dismiss him for the good of the country. A popularly elected president acts as head of the executive and appoints ministers. He serves a four-year term. The president nominates a prime minister, who must have the confidence of the parliament.

The current legislature is the 270-member Islamic Consultative Assembly (the Majlis). Members, directly elected by those over 15 for a four-year term, are empowered to make laws and approve international agreements. All legislation, however, is passed subject to the approval of a 12-member Council of Guardians, which determines whether laws conform to Islamic principles. It is also responsible for interpreting constitutional law and supervising elections. Half the Council members are appointed by the *walifaqih* and half by the judiciary.

In 1997, moderate Mohammad Khatami beat the conservative elite to win the presidency. Khatami has supported greater social and political freedoms, putting him at odds with the supreme leader, Ayatollah Khamenei.

IRAQ—Republic of Iraq

The Organic Law of 1924 was in force until 1958. Iraq was a monarchy, with a government responsible to parliament. The king received power to dismiss the government in 1944.

In 1958 there was a revolution. The constitution of that year defined Iraq as an Islamic republic, part of the Arab nation, but offering partnership to the Iraqi Kurds of the north. There was a Sovereignty Council as executive and legislature, under the leadership of General Kassem.

In February 1963 there was a further coup, and the National Council for the Revolutionary Command took office. This Council appointed an executive president, a prime minister and a cabinet. There was another coup in November 1963 and yet another in July 1968, which installed the current regime.

The provisional constitution of May 1964 declared Iraq to be a socialist, Arab, Islamic republic. In 1970 the Revolutionary Command Council was confirmed as the supreme power; the Council elected the president and vice president. There was no independent legislature.

In 1974 a measure of autonomy was granted to the Kurds.

In 1980 the independent legislature was restored, with the election of a National Assembly.

Under the monarchy there were two houses of parliament. The Chamber of Deputies had 141 elected members; the Senate might not exceed one-quarter the number of deputies. Senators were nominated and served an eight-year term. The electoral law was amended in 1946: any Iraqi who could obtain 12 supporting signatures might be nominated for election as a deputy.

After the revolution the central executive held all legislative power. After 1970 the sole legal party was the National Progressive Front, a coalition of Ba'ath and Communist members; the Communists left the Front in 1979.

In 1980 a unicameral National Assembly was restored. Members are elected for a four-year term and there are 250 seats. Suffrage is universal. The Assembly's power is still limited by the Revolutionary Command Council.

There is also a Legislative Council of 57 members for the Kurdish community.

In 1990, Saddam Hussein was declared president for life. His attempted annexation of Kuwait as Iraq's 19th province provoked the Gulf War, which restored Kuwait's independence (see p. 304).

IRELAND

Ireland is a unitary state and a parliamentary republic. Following negotiations with Great Britain, an independent Irish Free State was established in 1921 as a dominion within the British Commonwealth. The country's name was changed to Eire under the constitution of 1937. As a dominion of Great Britain, power to accredit diplomats abroad and receive foreign diplomats was reserved to the British sovereign. These powers were given to the Irish president in the Republic of Ireland Act of 1949, which marked a complete split with Britain.

The president is the head of state. Election to the largely ceremonial post is for a term of seven years, and a president cannot serve more than two terms. The chief executive officer is the prime minister, who is responsible for the development, passage and administration of legislation. As in the British system, the prime minister must have the support of parliament.

The bicameral parliament consists of a lower house containing 166 deputies elected by the single transferable vote system of proportional representation and an upper house of 60. Membership in the upper house is gained in one of three ways: through election from various occupational panels, through election by graduates of various colleges, and through nomination by the prime minister. The houses are coequal, although if a bill is defeated in the upper house and repassed in the lower, it cannot be delayed further in the upper chamber. Most legislation is initiated by the government. The constitution can be changed only with the consent of the people at a referendum.

ISRAEL—State of Israel

The republic of Israel was proclaimed on 14 May 1948; the territory had formerly been governed by Britain under a League of Nations and United Nations mandate as Palestine.

The Transition Law was passed in 1949 and further fundamental laws were added in the following decades. These, together, form the constitution, which defines a unitary republican state, the function of the president as head of state, the parliament as legislature and the physical extent of the land of Israel.

The president is elected by parliament for five years, and may be reelected once. His executive power is limited. Since 1996, the prime minister has been indirectly elected by the people, rather than being appointed by the president.

The constitution recognizes the special status of the Jewish religion. Jewish sabbath and holy days are observed by the public services, and the rabbinical courts have jurisdiction (for the Jewish community only) in family matters. Christian and Muslim community institutions are also recognized and the relation of all religious courts to the civil courts is defined. Israel grants automatic citizenship to every Jew who desires to settle within its borders.

The Knesset is unicameral, with 120 members directly elected for a four-year term. Balloting is secret and all over 18 have the vote. The system of election is by proportional representation of a single, national constituency. Each contesting party must gain at least 1% of the votes to win seats.

Bills are initiated by the cabinet or by private members, and pass through three readings. Most legislation requires a simple majority of members present. Constitutional amendment requires a majority of the whole house.

The two strongest political parties are the nationalist Likud (Unity) Party and the peace-oriented Labor Party.

Due to growing dissatisfaction with the Middle East peace process, Israel's parliament voted in December 1998 to dissolve President Benjamin Netanyahu's government and hold elections the following spring. In May 1999, Ehud Barak of the Labor Party won the election with 56% of the vote, compared to 44% for incumbent Netanyahu of Likud.

ITALY—Italian Republic

In 1945 Italy was a constitutional monarchy. The king's executive power was exercised through ministers responsible to a bicameral parliament with which the king shared legislative power. The constitution in force was an amended form of the Fundamental Law of 1848.

A republic was formed in 1946 and a new constitution put into effect on 1 January 1948. This provided for a democratic, unitary republic with a president as head of state. The president is elected for a seven-year term by the members of parliament and three delegates from each Regional Council. He has the right to nominate the prime minister, dissolve parliament after consulting with legislative leaders, make various judicial, legislative and military appointments, and suspend the promulgation of legislation. Executive power lies with the cabinet, known as the Consiglio dei Ministri, whose president is the prime minister, the head of government. He is appointed by the president but he and his cabinet must maintain the support of parliament. Because of the proliferation of parties in Italy, no one party is able to achieve a legislative majority and so the formation of a government is based on negotiation among parties. The fall of a government does not automatically lead to new elections. Instead, party negotiations begin again.

Under the new electoral system (first used in the March 1994 elections), three-quarters of the members of each house (472 deputies and 232 senators) are elected by a majority "winner-takes-all" system. The remaining quarter of senators and deputies are still elected by the old proportional representation (PR) system. A party requires 4% of the national proportional vote to be awarded any of the PR seats. Constituencies now average 120,000 population for the Chamber of Deputies and 244,000 for the Senate.

The legislature is bicameral. The 630-member Chamber of Deputies is directly elected by all citizens over 18; deputies serve a five-year term. Representation is proportional. The 320-member Senate has at least six members for each region. Senators sit for six years. The president may nominate five senators for life.

The government is responsible to parliament, which can force it to resign by a deliberate censure motion, but not by defeating a bill. Both houses of parliament have equal legislative power.

In 1993, against a background of political scandals, and as a result of the April 1993 referendum, the Italian parliament voted to end the proportional representation system. The new legislation meant that three-quarters of the 630 deputies and 315 senators were elected by the winner-takes-all system in the 1994 elections.

In 1996, voters elected a government dominated by a center-left co-alition for the first time since the proclamation of the Italian Republic.

JAPAN

A constitution drawn up in 1947 was a revision of the 1889 Meiji constitution, thereto in force. Japan regained its sovereignty after American occupation ended in 1952, when the 1947 act came fully into effect.

Head of state is the emperor, bereft of all political power and disclaiming divine attributes. Executive power rests with the prime minister and cabinet, responsible to a bicameral parliament. The peerage was abolished, as were conscription and the standing defense forces. Women were enfranchised. Fundamental human rights were safeguarded and Japan renounced the sovereign right to make war.

The state is a unitary, secular democracy.

The Diet consists of the House of Representatives and the House of Councillors (the latter replacing a House of Peers on the abolition of the peerage). Representatives are elected by the "medium constituency," which is halfway between local and prefectural constituencies. They serve a four-year term. Seats are distributed according to population. Of councillors, half are elected by one national constituency and half by prefectural constituencies. They serve for six years, half being renewed every three. All citizens over 20 may vote. In 1991 there were 512 representatives and 252 councillors.

Bills are normally presented by the cabinet but can originate with members. For most measures the two houses are required to agree. On bills of finance or foreign treaties, if there is a difference of opinion or if the councillors fail to act within 30 days, the vote of the representatives is taken as representing the sovereign people.

KOREA, NORTH—Democratic People's Republic of Korea

Under the 1972 constitution, which replaced the 1948 Soviet-type constitution, the leading political figure is the president, who is head of the armed forces and executive head of government. The president is appointed for four-year terms by the 687-member supreme people's assembly, which is directly elected by universal suffrage. The assembly meets for brief sessions once or twice a year, its regular legislative business being carried out by a smaller permanent standing committee. The president works with and presides over a powerful policy-making and supervisory central people's committee (which is responsible to the assembly for its activities) and an administrative and executive cabinet. In practice, though, the control of the ruling party—the Korean Worker's Party—and military support are of more importance than the formalities of the constitution.

KOREA, SOUTH—Republic of Korea

As part of the postwar settlement between the United States and the Soviet Union in the Far Fast, the Korean peninsula was divided into two zones along the 38th parallel. In 1948 the southern area became the Republic of Korea with a constitution, amended to suit the purposes of various civilian and military rulers, that remains in effect.

During the First Republic, the period from 1948 to 1960 in which Syngman Rhee served as president, rule was based on a centralized presidential system in which the legislature had little power. As a result of constitutional amendments, the president was permitted to succeed himself indefinitely. Rhee was finally forced to retire in 1960 in response to outrage over his brutal methods of retaining power, and a period of democratic rule was established. Under the Second Republic, as it was called, the constitution was revised to provide for a parliamentary form of government. The military overthrew this government in 1961 and established a system that led to the dictatorial one-man rule that characterized South Korea in the 1970s. In 1972 martial law was proclaimed and the National Assembly dissolved. A new constitutional revision ratified at that time gave the president broad powers. He was commander of the armed forces, head of state and chief executive. He could declare martial law and dissolve the Assembly, which was given little power.

In 1980, further constitutional amendments were ratified. Under this constitution the president continues to have many of the powers he had previously, but he is limited in two areas. He can assume emergency powers only with the approval of the National Assembly, which can also revoke the emergency decree. He cannot dissolve parliament during its first three years, and must consult with cabinet ministers and the assembly speaker before doing so.

Under a new constitution effective from February 1988, the unicameral National Assembly has 299 members serving four-year terms. It approves legislation and can investigate executive activities. Theoretically it can also call for the impeachment of high officials. The president is directly elected for a five-year term.

In 1996–97, bribery scandals brought down several politicians, including President Chun Doo Huan. The political instability that followed helped former dissident Kim Dae Jung to become the first South Korean president ever elected from the political opposition.

MEXICO—United Mexican States

The constitution is that of 1917, amended. The country is a federal republic of 31 states (originally 29) and a federal capital district. Executive power lies with the president, who is directly elected to serve for six years. He may not be reelected.

Citizenship was originally granted to all married men who were nationals at least 18 years old, or 21 years old if unmarried but following "an honorable means of livelihood." Citizenship was extended to women on the same terms in 1953. It is now (1991) for all nationals of 18 and over having "an honorable means of livelihood."

Each state has its own constitution, an elected governor and internal autonomy. The Federal District (Mexico City) is administered by a governor whom the president appoints. Because politics on all levels is dominated by the Institutional Revolutionary Party, the government is actually highly centralized.

Congress consists of a Chamber of Deputies and a Senate. The 400 deputies are directly elected for a three-year term. Suffrage is universal; women were enfranchised in 1953.

Until 1964, Chamber seats were distributed in single-member constituencies, apportioned according to population. Since 1964 one-quarter have been filled by proportional representation from a national list. The multiparty system operates. Deputies may not be immediately reelected, nor may senators.

The Senate has 64 directly elected members, two from each state and two from the federal district. They serve a six-year term.

Congress meets annually from 1 September to 31 December. Members appoint a permanent committee of 15 deputies and 14 senators to function during the recess.

In August 1993 Congress approved a package of constitutional reforms, including changes to the Senate.

In 1997, the long-ruling Partido Revolucionario Institucional (PRI) lost control of the lower legislative house in what observers have called Mexico's most free election in history. In March 1999, President Zedillo announced that he would discontinue the practice of the "dedazo," in which the president designates his party's nominee for the upcoming election, and in November 1999, Mexico held its first presidential primary. On July 2, 2000, Vincente Fox was elected president.

NETHERLANDS—Kingdom of the Netherlands

The constitution has been amended seven times since 1945, but not significantly changed. The country is a constitutional monarchy. Executive power lies with the queen, but in fact she exercises it through a prime minister and cabinet. Legislative power is shared by queen and parliament.

There is a Council of State appointed by the queen; it consists of the queen as president, a vice president and not more than 28 members. Its function is consultative.

The royal succession is in direct line by primogeniture, and there is provision for a regency during the sovereign's minority.

The Netherlands, Aruba and the Netherlands Antilles together form a unitary kingdom; their relations are defined in a statute of 29 December 1954.

The States-General is bicameral. Until 1956 the upper chamber had 50 members and the lower, 100. Since 1956 the lower chamber has had 150 deputies, directly elected. The voting age was 23 in 1946, lowered to 21 in 1967 and 18 in 1972. The system is by proportional representation; elected candidates to the lower chamber serve for four years. The upper chamber has 75 members, elected by members of provincial parliaments for six years. Members of either chamber must be 21.

Bills are proposed by the lower house or by the government; the upper house may approve or reject them, but not amend. Parliament can amend the constitution by a bill, which must be followed by immediate dissolution; the new parliament must then produce a confirmatory two-thirds vote.

Ministers cannot be a member of parliament, but they attend sessions when policies or proposals for which they are responsible are discussed.

Parliament's legislation does not affect overseas parts of the kingdom unless this is expressly stated.

NICARAGUA—Republic of Nicaragua

Effective power lay with the Somoza family and its supporters from 1936 to 1979. The presidency of Luis Somoza Debayle (1956–62) was less despotic than that of his father; a constitution was drawn up, which came into force in 1963. It provided for a directly elected executive presidency and a bicameral legislature. The president was barred from office for the succeeding term, along with members of his family.

Luis Somoza's brother, Anastasio, was elected president in 1967. In 1971 the legislature was dissolved and the constitution abrogated. A new one came into force in 1974, allowing Anastasio Somoza to return to office after a two-year gap, and for a six-year term.

In 1979 there was a revolution and Somoza resigned. A Government of National Reconstruction took office, formed by the Sandinista National Liberation Front. The 1974 constitution was replaced by a statute of rights and by a Basic Statute, which created a Council of State; an advisory Council of Government was created in 1981.

Elections to a constituent assembly and to the presidency followed in November 1984. A new government took office under the president in January 1985. In early 1986 the country was placed under a state of emergency. A new constitution was signed in November 1986, but was immediately suspended, as the state of emergency went on. It provides for a presidential republic, the president and his chosen ministers to hold executive power. The four branches of government are the executive, legislative, electoral and judicial authorities. Political pluralism is allowed, but excludes pro-Somoza parties.

Until 1979 there was a bicameral Congress that was generally ineffective; real legislative power lay with the Somoza family and their supporters, and was enforced by the National Guard.

The 1963 constitution provided for direct elections, for universal franchise and a system of proportional representation intended to safeguard minority parties. The real power of the Congress, however, did not increase. In 1971 it voted to dissolve itself and to abrogate the 1963 constitution.

After the 1979 revolution, the new junta installed a Council of State as an interim legislature; it had 47 members (51 from May 1981). A single-chamber National Assembly was elected to replace it in November 1984. Election was direct, on the basis of universal suffrage of all over 16, and by proportional representation. There were 96 members. This body was a legislative, as well as a constituent, assembly and survives as a legislature under the 1986 constitution. In the elections of 1990, the Sandinistas lost office, but critics complained of their continuing influence on President Violetta de Chamorro's government. Conservative Arnaldo Aleman won the 1996 election over President Daniel Ortega, and launched an investigation into the previous government's possible frauds.

NIGERIA—Federal Republic of Nigeria

In 1945 Nigeria was a British dependency, consisting of a Protectorate (Northern and Southern Provinces) and a Colony (Lagos). A Legislative Council enacted laws for the Colony and Southern Provinces, and the governor administered the Northern Provinces. In 1946 a new constitution extended the Legislative Council's authority to the whole of Nigeria, and it set up regional and provincial councils as subsidiary bodies. Indirectly elected assemblies followed in 1951 and the Executive Council of the central government became a Council of Ministers.

In 1954 Nigeria became a federation of five regions: North, East, West, Lagos and Southern Cameroons (Southern Cameroons left the federation in 1961). In 1960 Nigeria became independent, retaining the monarchy and having a governor-general as head of state. In 1963 a republic was founded, but the republican constitution was suspended after a coup in January 1966. The federation was dissolved until a further coup in July 1966, when it was restored under a military government.

Military rule continued until 1979 when a civilian administration returned. The constitution then in force provided for a federation of 19 states and a capital district, with an executive, elected president. A mixed civilian-military government came into power following a coup in December 1983. It was replaced by a military council following a coup in August 1985.

In 1945 there was a Legislative Council with 30 official, 13 representative and four elected members. The Council legislated for Lagos and the Southern Provinces only until 1946. In 1951 it acquired a majority of indirectly elected members. In 1954 the federation was established, with legislation in three lists: federal, concurrent (in which federal law prevailed in case of conflict) and regional. The central parliament was much weakened.

At independence in 1960 the federal parliament had an elected House of Representatives and a Senate as revisionary body. Senators were nominated by regional governments; representatives were elected from single-member constituencies.

Parliament was dissolved by the army in 1966 and did not resume until 1979. Elections were held in 1983, but since the December 1983 coup, military councils have been the legislating bodies.

Before stepping down in 1993, General Babangida canceled 12 elections, plunging Nigeria into constitutional crisis. The military seized power that same year. Under military rule for all but 10 years since independence from Britain, the military has reneged eight times on promises to give up power, but General Abdulsalam Abubakar freed political prisoners and pledged to step aside for an elected leader by May 1999.

NORWAY—Kingdom of Norway

The country is a parliamentary monarchy and the constitution is still fundamentally that of 1814. Legislative power is vested in a bicameral parliament; executive power is vested in the king but exercised through a cabinet of ministers responsible to parliament. The king may delay but not ultimately veto legislation. He does not summon or dissolve parliament.

The royal succession is in direct male line and by primogeniture. If there is no male heir the king may propose a successor to parliament; parliament need not accept the candidate but may nominate another.

The constitution may be amended only by the two houses of parliament in joint and plenary sitting, and by a two-thirds majority vote.

The parliament (Storting) has 157 members directly elected on the basis of proportional representation. The voting age was 23 until 1949, 21 from 1949 until 1980, and now it is 18. Elected members sit for three years. Parliament meets annually in October; once assembled, the members vote a quarter of their strength to form a Lagting (second chaniber) and three-quarters to form an Odelsting (first chamber).

Questions other than legislation are normally decided by the Storting as a whole; legislation must be considered by both houses separately. They meet again as a plenary sitting to resolve differences if they disagree. The bill then needs a two-thirds majority vote.

Ministers are not members of parliament but are responsible to it. They attend sessions but do not vote. They initiate bills, all of which are proposed in the Odelsting and then sent to the Lagting.

PAKISTAN—Islamic Republic of Pakistan

The state was created in 1947 as East and West Pakistan. A Constituent Assembly was set up and was also empowered to function as a legislature under the Government of India Act of 1935. (Pakistan consisted of territories that had formerly been provinces of British India or protected states.)

Pakistan was a federation of provinces and a parliamentary monarchy, the monarch being represented by a governor-general. He was given wide executive powers. In February 1956 a republican constitution was adopted, and the governor-general replaced by a president as head of state. On 7 October 1958 the then president (who also had wide powers) abrogated the 1956 constitution and declared martial law. In 1962 a new constitution provided an executive presidency and a unicameral national assembly; it was overthrown and martial law imposed on 25 March 1969.

The provinces of the original federation had been brought together in one unit in 1955. In 1970 it was reaffirmed that Pakistan was to be a federal state, and the four provinces were restored. Also in 1970, parliamentary government was restored, but the elections of December 1970 led to civil war and the continuation of martial law. East Pakistan seceded in December 1971 and became Bangladesh.

Pakistan withdrew from the Commonwealth in 1972 and adopted a new federal, republican constitution in 1973. The president was to be a constitutional, largely ceremonial, head of an Islamic state; the prime minister would be head of a government that was responsible to a bicameral parliament. Martial law was reimposed from July 1977 until December 1985; the constitution was held in abeyance but not abrogated. Under the military government of Mohammed Zia-ul-Haq, the powers of the presidency were greatly strengthened.

A Constituent Assembly acted as parliament from 1947 until the coming into force of the 1956 constitution. In 1956 it was established that East and West Pakistan be represented in the central parliament on parity. The 1962 parliament had 75 members each from East and West, elected on the basis of limited franchise; there were also six women members elected by provincial assemblies.

In 1970 the size of the National Assembly was increased and parity abandoned; seats were distributed between East and West according to population, which gave the East a majority. This was the immediate cause of unrest and civil war.

The 1973 parliament was elected for the new state, formerly West Pakistan. It was bicameral. The new Assembly had 200 general seats and 10 reserved for women. The Senate had 63 members representing provinces, tribal areas and the capital. In 1976 a further six Assembly seats were reserved, this time for non-Muslim minorities.

No further elections were held until February 1985, when a new parliament was installed on the basis of the 1973 constitution. The president retained the final decision on legislation, but parliament was strengthened by the ending of martial law on 30 December 1985. Elections again took place in November 1988. Pakistan rejoined the Commonwealth in 1989. In July 1991 parliament approved changes to the constitution, strengthening its antiterrorist powers. Following the 1993 power struggle, elections were held in October 1993. In 1997, parliament amended the constitution to prevent a president from dismissing a government.

On 12 October 1999, a surprise military coup ousted Pakistan's government. General Pervaiz Musharraf assumed power, suspended the constitution and dissolved parliament.

POLAND—Republic of Poland

Toward the close of World War II, liberation of parts of Poland had already taken place. On 21 July 1944 a Polish Committee of National

Liberation proclaimed itself the only legal executive. The Committee became a provisional government on 31 December 1944. On 28 June 1945 a Provisional Government of National Unity was set up, based on the former body by the agreement of the Yalta Conference.

A referendum of 30 June 1946 approved the abolition of the Senate; it also approved a new program of nationalization and land reform. Poland was then a republic with a single-chamber parliament (Sejm). The parliament passed an interim constitution on 19 February 1947. This was based on the constitution of 1921 (officially in force until then) but amended to prepare for the fully communist constitution of 22 July 1952. The latter (amended 1976 and 1983) was in force until 1989. It provided for a unicameral legislature with executive power in the hands of the Council of State and, when the Sejm was not in session, the Council of Ministers.

Until 1946 there were two houses, the Diet and the Senate. The Senate was one-third nominated and two-thirds indirectly elected. There were no political parties in parliament from 1935 until 1946.

After 1946 there was a unicameral Diet (Sejm), formed as laid down in the constitution of 1921. In February 1947, after a general election, this Diet adopted the "Little Charter," which introduced a Council of State that had the power to issue decrees with the force of law and to interpret existing law when the Sejm was not in session. The Council would be elected by the Diet but would thereafter control the Diet's effectiveness. The Diet was to be summoned twice yearly, but it could empower the government to act between sessions, provided such action did not consist of imposing taxes or conscription.

After 1952 there was a Diet elected for a four-year term by all citizens over 18. There were 460 seats, each representing about 60,000 voters. All candidates had to support the policies of approved parties, forming a united front.

Round-table talks were held in February 1989 between Solidarity and the government. Fundamental changes to the constitution were proposed. These included a new office of state president, and the establishment of a new bicameral National Assembly with a newly created Senate acting as the Upper House. The Senate would not have power to initiate legislation, but would have a power of veto over the Sejm. The elections scheduled for 1989 were to be "nonconfrontational," with 65% of the seats reserved for the approved political parties. Further constitutional changes were demanded by Solidarity in 1990. These took place in November 1992, reflected in increased presidential powers, a two-chamber four-year parliament (460 seats for the Sejm, 100 for the Senate) and the removal of most vestiges of the communist constitution.

Voters approved a new constitution in May 1997 that upholds a market economy, private land ownership, personal freedoms and clear divisions of power within the branches of government.

PORTUGAL—Republic of Portugal

The constitution of 1933 remained in force until 1974. It provided for a unitary republic with a president as head of state. The president was assisted by a privy council of 10 members. Executive power lay with the cabinet; the cabinet shared legislative power with a single-chamber parliament. There was also a Corporative Chamber to which the overseas territories sent representatives. In reality, Portugal was a personalist, corporatist dictatorship controlled by Antonio Salazar from 1932 to 1968 and his successor Marcello Caetano from 1968 to 1974.

The president was at first directly elected by those citizens qualified (by literacy and prosperity) to vote. In 1959 the constitution was amended to provide for indirect presidential elections, by a college consisting of National Assembly and Corporative Chamber members, with members of municipal and overseas councils.

In 1974 a military junta, disgruntled over Portugal's colonial wars, overthrew the government and dissolved parliament. A new constitution came into force in 1976 and was revised in 1982. The president is elected by universal suffrage for a five-year term. Executive power is vested in him; he appoints the prime minister and (on the prime minister's recommendation) the cabinet. The prime minister is responsible to the president and the Assembly.

Parliament was enabled to override the junta (on nonmilitary matters) in 1976. In 1982 the junta was abolished and replaced by a Constitutional Tribunal and a Council of State, which was a nominated advisory body.

Parliament in 1945 had one house, with deputies directly elected for a four-year term. Electoral law allowed more than one list of candidates; in practice only National Union party lists were presented until 1953, when the Union in any case won all 120 seats.

The Assembly was dissolved following the revolution of 1974. The 1976 constitution provided a new assembly, unicameral, with no fewer than 240 and no more than 250 deputies, elected by proportional representation and universal adult suffrage. The voting age is 18; voters must be literate, or be paying a minimum tax and appearing on an official census.

ROMANIA—Republic of Romania

In 1945 the 1938 constitution was still in force. It provided for a monarchy in which the king shared legislative power with a bicameral legislature and executive power (after 1939) with a Principal Council. Members of the lower house were directly elected. Half the members of the upper house were elected, half nominated by the king. On 14 July 1946 the upper house was abolished and a new, unicameral Grand

National Assembly of 414 deputies instituted. Members were elected for a four-year term.

At the end of 1947 a republic was proclaimed, and a new constitution was put into force in 1948. It defined Romania as a "people's republic" with a unicameral legislature, the Grand National Assembly. The Assembly was to work with a permanent Presidium or State Council (a collective presidency) on the Russian pattern. The chairman of the Presidium was to be head of state.

In 1965 a further constitutional amendment defined Romania as a socialist republic and confirmed the basic relationship between the Communist Party, parliament and the State Council.

The presidency had been the center of political power since a 1974 constitutional amendment introducing the presidential system. The president was the head of the party, state and government; commander in chief of the armed forces; and chairman of the State Council. He could appoint and dismiss members of the government and the Supreme Court.

Members of the Grand National Assembly were elected to five-year terms by citizens 18 and over. Although legislative power was officially in its hands with the president responsible to it, in fact the legislature had only nominal power. Since 1948 all proposed laws had passed the Assembly unanimously.

Following the revolution of December 1989 and the fall of the Ceausescu regime, the National Salvation Front assumed sweeping powers pending the drafting of a new constitution. The leading role of the Communist Party was abolished by decree and multiparty elections were held (see page 244).

Under the post-communist constitution, the president is elected for a four-year term. A two-chamber parliament is elected (also for four years) by proportional representation. The Chamber of Deputies has 260 seats (plus seats for minorities); the Senate has 130 seats.

RUSSIA—Russian Federation

At the time of the collapse of the Soviet Union, the Russian constitution was a heavily amended version of the 1977 Soviet constitution (see Union of Soviet Socialist Republics). In December 1991 President Boris Yeltsin (elected on 12 June 1991) was given power by the Congress of People's Deputies to rule by decree. An attempt to cancel this power failed in April 1992. A referendum was held on 25 April 1993 to test support for the basic principles of a new constitution. President Yeltsin proposed a strengthening in presidential authority, the replacement of the Congress by a small, bicameral legislature with more power devolved to the regions, and the abolition of the office of vice president. The Supreme Soviet, the body elected by Congress members with day-to-day responsibility, proposed a weakening in presidential power, parliamentary veto over cabinet appointments and the continuation of the post of vice president. A constitutional conference opened in June 1993 but the situation remained fluid as the president and the Congress continued to disagree. The abrogation of the constitution and dissolution of the Congress of People's Deputies by Yeltsin in September 1993, and the violent suppression of dissent that followed, have not resolved the ongoing crisis. Yeltsin announced that a new constitution would be written and new parliamentary elections held before the end of 1993, followed by a presidential election at an unspecified date.

The referendum of 12 December 1993 approved the new Basic Law, replacing the 1978 constitution passed under Brezhnev. The new constitution greatly strengthens the powers of the president, who is elected for four years and can serve no more than two terms. The new powers as head of state include the right to pass decrees without reference to parliament (although they can be vetoed by a two-thirds majority); the right to declare a state of emergency (with parliamentary consent); the appointment of military commanders, diplomats and senior judges; the right to reject legislation passed by the lower house (the State Duma); and the right to call parliamentary elections. The president can be impeached after court decisions followed by a two-thirds majority in each house of parliament. There is no provision for a vice president.

Parliament consists of two chambers. The lower house, the State Duma, has 450 deputies, half elected by "winner-takes-all" and the remainder by proportional representation from party lists. The Duma approves legislation but can draft laws affecting the budget only with government consent. The upper house, the Federation Council, has 178 representatives, two from each member state of the federation. The council cannot be dissolved by the president and approves Duma legislation.

Among the constitution's provisions, which mark a decisive break with the communist past, are affirmation of the freedom of worship, speech and travel, as well as a free press. Private property is enshrined as an inalienable right and all mention of a state ideology vanished. Parliament can make constitutional changes only by a two-thirds majority in each house.

In March 1998, President Boris Yeltsin dismissed his entire government and replaced the prime minister. Yeltsin stepped down on 31 December 1999.

SAUDI ARABIA—Kingdom of Saudi Arabia

Until 1992 Saudi Arabia had no formal constitution, and the Koran was proclaimed to be the state constitution. Executive and legislative power lay with the king and the Council of Ministers. The Council had the authority to consider all questions arising in the kingdom. However, its decisions had to be referred to the king for approval. On 1 March 1992 King Fahd issued an 83-article "Basic System of Government" setting up a 60-member consultative council with the right to propose and review laws and treaties and to question ministers. The council's members are selected by the king and its powers are strictly limited to advising the ruling House of Sa'ud on such issues as the budget, defense, social and foreign policies. The council can propose and review laws and treaties but is not authorized to overrule the king or his cabinet. The council meets in secret every two weeks and members serve a four-year term. Government action not approved by the council is referred back to the king. There are also guarantees of personal freedom and protection against arbitrary search and arrest. The ruling House of Sa'ud continues to dominate political life, filling most key political positions. The king is an absolute monarch within the constraints of his family's support and the laws of Islam, which King Fahd has said continue to be the foundation of the state. In 1996, King Fahd passed authority to Crown Prince Abdullah.

SOUTH AFRICA—Republic of South Africa

In 1945 South Africa was an autonomous union within the Commonwealth, retaining the monarchy, which was represented by a governor-general as head of state. The governor-general shared legislative power with parliament and exercised executive power through a cabinet.

The union was composed of four provinces: Cape, Natal, Transvaal and Orange Free State. The government also administered South-West Africa under a mandate.

All members of parliament were of European descent. There was a Natives Representation Council until 1951. In that year the Bantu Authorities Act provided for tribal, regional and territorial authorities with some administrative and legislative powers. This followed the adoption of the separate development policy (apartheid) in 1948; the basic principle was already in practice following the Bantu Representation Act and Native Land and Trust Act of 1926.

In 1959 the Promotion of Bantu Self-Government Act provided for eight main national groups to evolve into independent political units. In 1960 the government abolished representation of Bantu-speaking nations by white members in the central parliament. The powers of national authorities were increased by the Bantu Homelands Constitution Act in 1971. The Indian and Colored (mixed black and white) communities had separate representative councils.

South Africa became a republic in 1961 with an elected president as head of state and executive power vested in a prime minister and cabinet.

The constitution (fifth amendment) bill replaced the Senate with a President's Council in 1981. In 1984 a new constitution introduced an executive presidency and a three-chamber parliament where white, Indian and Colored communities wielded legislative power.

The central parliament was bicameral until 1984. The House of Assembly was directly elected by the white community for five years. The Senate was indirectly elected, with 10 members nominated by the president. At least one senator per province was required to be knowledgeable on Colored affairs.

In 1981 the Senate was replaced by a nominated President's Council of 60 members, representing the white, Colored, Indian and Chinese communities.

In 1984 a tricameral parliament was introduced. The House of Assembly had 178 members, 166 directly and eight indirectly elected by white voters. The House of Representatives had 85 members, 80 directly and five indirectly elected by Colored voters. The House of Delegates had 45 members, 40 directly and five indirectly elected by Indian voters. All served five years. The houses elected a college to elect the president, who initiated legislation and decided inter-house disputes. He appointed a national cabinet and a Ministers' Council for each house. Each legislated for its own population group; together they legislated on national affairs.

During 1990–91, discussions took place between the government and the African National Congress (ANC) on a new political framework for South Africa. In February 1991 it was announced that the last apartheid laws were to be abolished.

In September 1991, President de Klerk unveiled his plans for a future constitution for South Africa. Although granting universal franchise, the document envisaged a complicated system of checks and balances to prevent any one party or race gaining domination. A supreme council or collective presidency would replace the existing president. Parliament would comprise two houses—one elected proportionately to the national share of the vote, the second made up of an equal number of seats from each of nine regions. The second house would be able to veto legislation and would have special powers to guard the constitution and protect minorities and regions. The proposals were immediately rejected by the ANC, but by 1993, another draft was unveiled and the climate had changed. The first non-whites entered the cabinet and the ANC approved a plan to allow minority parties to participate in the government for five years after the end of white rule.

South Africa's "interim" constitution was signed on 17 November 1993 by the negotiating parties and approved by parliament on 22 December 1993. The parliament elected by proportional representation on 27–28 April 1994 consists of a lower house, the National Assembly, and an upper house, the Senate. As well as legislating, parliament will draft and adopt a final constitution, which will come into effect in five years. The interim constitution includes a Bill of Rights and provides for a constitutional court to safeguard individual liberties and resolve disputes between the provinces and central government.

The National Assembly has 400 members, 200 of whom are drawn from a national party list and 200 from a regional list. The Senate has 90 members, 10 drawn from each of the nine provincial parliaments.

The president, who has an executive role, is drawn from the largest party. Two deputy presidents are appointed from the largest and second largest parties, that is, those that obtained at least 20% of the vote. The government is a "government of national unity," with a cabinet with a maximum of 27 members. Cabinet posts are divided proportionately among parties that received over 5% of the vote.

The nine provincial parliaments will also formulate their own regional constitutions. In addition, there is provision for the national parliament to elect a 20-strong Volkstaat Council to consider the possibility of a white Afrikaner state.

The 1994 elections gave a massive victory to Nelson Mandela and his ANC. In May 1996, after three years in the making, a post-apartheid constitution was adopted guaranteeing equal rights regardless of race. It provides for a 400-member National Assembly elected by proportional representation and a Senate comprising 10 members from each regional legislature. Mandela retired in June 1999.

SPAIN—Kingdom of Spain

The chief of the Spanish state in 1945 (Francisco Franco) had extensive powers, exercised through a single political party, which he had founded. The party worked through its own National Council, a parliament, a cabinet, a State Council and the higher courts.

On 18 July 1945 the parliament passed a bill of civil rights, and on 6 July 1947 it passed the Law of Succession. The Law provided for a king or regent, proposed by a two-thirds majority of parliament, to take power if the chief of state should die or be incapacitated.

The future reversion to monarchy was confirmed in July 1969, when Prince Don Juan Carlos de Borbón y Borbón was sworn in as General Franco's successor.

A new constitution on 29 December 1978 established a parliamentary monarchy with a bicameral parliament and an executive cabinet responsible to it.

Spain is a unitary state, but the system of regional government has some federal characteristics; there are 17 autonomous communities, each with a government and a parliament.

From 1942 until 1967 the parliament was a unicameral legislative assembly. There were no directly elected members; there were 108 indirectly elected from the Spanish and overseas provinces, with some appointed and some ex-officio members. In 1967 a further 108 members were directly elected by heads of families, wives and widows.

The constitution of 1978 established a bicameral parliament, the Cortes. The Senate has 208 members directly elected by the majority system to represent provinces and autonomous communities. The Congress of Deputies has 350 members directly elected by universal suffrage and by proportional representation.

Both houses may initiate legislation, as may the executive, the autonomous communities, and the people by popular initiative (50,000 signatures). The Senate may modify a Congress bill within two months (20 days in emergency). Congress can override Senate rejection.

The Congress elects the prime minister, who appoints a cabinet.

SWEDEN—Kingdom of Sweden

The constitution of 1809 remained in force until 1975. Sweden was a constitutional monarchy. The king held executive power, which he exercised through a Council of State headed by a prime minister. Legislative power lay with a bicameral parliament, of which all councillors of state were members.

In 1971 the upper house of parliament was abolished. In 1975 a new constitution described Sweden as a "representative and parliamentary democracy." Parliament is the central organ of power and all executive power lies with the government, which is responsible to parliament. The king is symbolic head of state and takes no part in government.

Until 1971 there were two houses. The upper house members sat for eight-year terms; they were chosen on property or income qualifications and elected, on proportional representation, by the county councils and some city electors. The lower house was elected for a four-year term. Members were directly elected on proportional representation and universal suffrage. From 1945 on the voting age was 21. All electors over 23 had the right to run, but only for their home constituencies.

The houses had equal powers in legislation, bills passing through the committee system of both. If the houses disagreed, a joint session would decide by majority vote.

In 1971 the upper house was succeeded by the Riksdag, which had 350 members elected to three-year terms. The voting age was lowered to 19 and then to 18; the age for candidates is also 18. Following continued even splits in the legislature between the socialist and nonsocialist blocs, the Riksdag was reduced to 349 members in the mid-1970s.

The 1994 elections saw the reemergence of the Social Democrats after three years of being in the opposition. Short of a majority by 13 seats in the Riksdag, they decided to establish a minority government.

SWITZERLAND—Swiss Confederation

Switzerland is a democratic federation of 26 states (cantons and half-cantons). The constitution is that of 1848, although it has been heavily revised, especially in 1874.

The political system is characterized by a high degree of cooperation; party loyalty is less important than ensuring the smooth functioning of the government. This is true despite, or perhaps because of, the government's ability to accommodate diverse ethnic and political factions.

The Federal Council, or Bundesrat, is the country's executive body, and it consists of seven members appointed individually by parliament at the beginning of a new (four-year) legislative term. The makeup of the Council generally reflects parliamentary representation, comprising two members from each of the three major parties and the seventh from a minor party. The president of the Swiss Confederation is selected from the Council to serve an annual term; the position is mainly ceremonial, and the president must still fulfill his ministerial responsibilities as a member of the Council.

The bicameral legislature is called the Federal Assembly (Bundesversammlung). It comprises a Council of State (Ständerat) with 46 members, two from each full canton, and a 200-member National Council (Nationalrat), reflecting proportional representation. Suffrage is universal for all citizens at least 20 years old.

SYRIA—Syrian Arab Republic

Independence from French rule was achieved in January 1944. There was a series of coups followed by a new constitution in September 1950. A further coup brought fresh instability, which lasted until 1954, when the 1950 constitution was revived. In February 1958 Syria merged with Egypt and Yemen to form the United Arab Republic. The union was ended by a military revolt in September 1961. A provisional government was set up, but the administration that it elected was hampered by army revolts, until in March 1963 a National Council of Revolution took control. This government was in turn overthrown by a Provisional National Leadership in February 1966. Another coup in November 1970 was followed by a government under Lieutenant General Hafez al-Assad. A provisional constitution was published and a nominated People's Council installed. Assad was sworn in as president in March 1971. The constitution was approved by plebiscite in March 1973. It confirmed the Arab Socialist Renaissance as the leading element in the government and in society. Executive power lies with the president and his ministers, legislative power with an elected assembly. Formal constitutional arrangements are misleading. The actual exercise of powers is based on personal and sectarian relationships. The president since 1971 Hafez al-Assad, who exercised extensive power, died in June 2000 and has been succeeded by his son Bashar al-Assad.

The National Assembly, having been virtually powerless, was finally dissolved in 1966. In 1971 a unicameral People's Council was appointed for a two-year term. In the 1973 constitution it was confirmed as an elected body. The Council has 195 members directly elected for a four-year term. Suffrage is for everyone over 18. There is a single list of candidates for election, that of the National Progressive Front (Ba'ath party and allies).

TURKEY—Republic of Turkey

The constitution of 1924 (amended in 1934) was still in force in 1945. Turkey was a unitary republic with a president as head of state. Islam was the official religion. All legislative and executive power lay with a unicameral legislature, the Grand National Assembly. Deputies were elected by citizens over 21 to four-year terms. Elections were indirect and on the majority system until 1946, when direct elections were introduced. Laws passed by the Assembly were sent to the president, who had the power to delay but not to veto them. The president was elected by each Assembly for a concurrent term and was considered a party office.

Following a coup on 27 May 1960 all powers of parliament were transferred to the National Unity Committee, supported by the army. The transfer was made legal by an interim constitution on 12 June 1960. A new constitution was approved by referendum on 9 July 1961. Turkey was to be a "nationalistic, democratic, secular and social republic." Legislative power returned to the bicameral legislature, which was to elect a president. A bicameral legislature was established. The lower house, the National Assembly, had 450 members elected for four-year terms. The Senate consisted of 150 members elected for six-year terms. The majority of senators were directly elected, but some were nominated by the president and some, such as past presidents, were appointed for life. All legislation originated in the Assembly or the government. The Senate had powers of revision; differences were resolved by joint session.

In contrast to earlier practice in which the president was always a member of the majority party, the new constitution provided that, once elected, the president had to resign from the Assembly and disassociate himself from party politics. He was elected for a single seven-year term. The president shared executive power with a council of ministers, composed of the prime minister and his cabinet.

On 12 September 1980 the army again overthrew the government and dissolved parliament. The military ruled through the National Security Council, which took over legislative functions. A mixed civilian-military cabinet handled day-to-day governmental business. The following year all political parties were dissolved.

A new constitution was approved in November 1982. It strengthened the presidency, giving it extensive powers of appointment and decree, and curtailed the power of the legislature. It eliminated the Senate and provided for a unicameral legislature of 400 deputies elected to five-year terms. The president can call the legislature into special sessions or dissolve it and call for new elections. He can initiate challenges to legislation, and appoints important military, judicial and governmental officials. The prime minister, the head of government, takes office only after he receives a vote of confidence on his government's program from the Assembly. New political parties were permitted in 1983.

UNION OF SOVIET SOCIALIST REPUBLICS (USSR) (until 1991)

The constitution of 1936 remained in force until 1977. The Union in 1945 had 16 constituent republics; in 1956 the status of the Karel-Finnish republic was reduced to that of an autonomous republic within the RSFSR (Russian Soviet Federated Socialist Republic). The Union was founded on communist systems of industry, property ownership, society and government.

The head of state was nonexecutive; the actual leader of the government was the general secretary of the Communist Party. However, there was no bar to the same person's holding the party and the state office.

The constitution provided for a Council of Ministers as the executive body. The legislative body was the Supreme Soviet. The Supreme Soviet elected a Presidium, which assumed all the powers of the Soviet between sessions of the latter.

Each republic had its own Supreme Soviet, Council of Ministers and Presidium. Issues reserved to the central government were defined in the constitution of 1977, which was in force until the upheaval of 1991.

The central parliament was the Supreme Soviet, which had two chambers. The Soviet of the Union had 750 members directly elected by citizens over 18, one deputy per 300,000 inhabitants. Candidates had to support the Communist Party program, even if not party members.

The Soviet of Nationalities also had 750 members directly elected to represent the national territories. There were 32 seats for each Union republic, 11 for each autonomous republic, five for each autonomous region and one for each autonomous area.

Both houses had equal legislative rights. They sat twice a year, sessions being short. The Soviet appointed the Council of Ministers to administer the law and organize the work of government. The Soviet also elected a Presidium, which acted as the highest state authority between sessions of the Soviet; it had power to convene the Soviet, to direct the work of its committees, to dissolve it and to interpret the laws it passed. The Presidium could also legislate by decree and resolution.

On 13 March 1990 the Soviet Congress of People's Deputies repealed Article 6 of the constitution, ending the Communist Party's monopoly of political power. It also strengthened the powers of the presidency, combining the posts of head of government and head of state. The president could be subject to a parliamentary veto and was prohibited from declaring a state of emergency in any of the Soviet republics without the agreement of local officials. Mikhail Gorbachev, the sole candidate, was elected president by the Congress on 15 March. The president would be chosen by popular election in 1995. In October 1990 the Supreme Soviet passed a law giving all political parties legal status equivalent to that of the Communist Party, opening the way for a multiparty democracy. At the same time the Communist Party's authority over Soviet institutions—including the armed forces, the KGB and the official trade union—was removed. The constitutional position was, however, complicated by nine of the USSR's 15 constituent republics having declared by June 1990 that their own laws had precedence over those of the central government.

The collapse of the attempted coup of 19 August 1991 transformed the constitutional situation in the Soviet Union. In a desperate attempt to hold some new form of confederation together, on 5 September 1991 the 1,900-strong Congress of People's Deputies agreed to the dramatic changes that had been proposed earlier by Gorbachev and the leaders of the republics on 2 September.

These proposals included a new Union Treaty, allowing each republic to choose its own terms for membership in the new union; the creation of an interim council of representatives of people's deputies (20 from each republic); a state council comprising the state president and heads of the republics; and a suspension of the existing Soviet Congress and Union (although deputies would retain their salaries).

Whether these often vague proposals could halt disintegration was debatable. By September 1991, the following 11 declarations of independence had been made.

Republic	Date of breakaway
Armenia	A 5-year plan
Azerbaijan	30 August 1991
Belarus	25 August 1991
Estonia	20 August 1991
Georgia	9 April 1991
Kirghizia	31 August 1991
Latvia	21 August 1991
Lithuania	11 March 1990
Moldova	27 August 1991
Ukraine	24 August 1991
Uzbekistan	31 August 1991

The process of disintegration was unstoppable. The Soviet Union ceased to exist on 31 December 1991 after the formation of the Commonwealth of Independent States (see p. 246).

UNITED KINGDOM OF GREAT BRITAIN AND NORTHERN IRELAND

There is no written constitution. The country is a constitutional monarchy and a unitary state. Legislative power lies with parliament. Executive power belongs nominally to the monarch but actually to the government, and is exercised through a cabinet of ministers responsible to parliament.

The United Kingdom government has ultimate authority throughout England, Wales, Scotland and Northern Ireland, but not in the Channel Islands nor the Isle of Man, which are dependencies of the Crown.

A separate parliament and executive for Northern Ireland (located at Stormont) functioned after 1921 with powers that were gradually increased by legislation in 1928, 1932, 1945, 1947, 1955 and 1962. Matters that never have been nor ever would be devolved from the U.K. government relate to the Crown, parliament, international relations, defense and taxation. The Northern Ireland Constitution Act of 1973 and the Northern Ireland Act of 1982 provide for a degree of devolution in government, but no such devolution operates at present (1994). Since 1974 the Northern Ireland parliament has submitted its proposals to the U.K. parliament for approval. New coalition governing arrangements between the Protestant majority and the Catholic minority are under consideration.

The queen is head of state, head of the Commonwealth and head of the established Protestant Church. She is also queen of each Commonwealth country that has retained the monarchy (16 in 2000).

United Kingdom dependent territories are administered by their own governments, but the U.K. secretary for foreign and commonwealth affairs is responsible to the U.K. parliament for that administration.

Parliament consists of a House of Commons and a House of Lords. The Commons are directly elected for a maximum five-year term; suffrage is for anyone over 18 (21 until 1970). Until 1948 business premises and universities also had a vote. The distribution of seats between constituencies is monitored by commissions required to report at least every 10 years. At the 1992 election 651 members were returned.

Members of the House of Lords (known as 'peers') consist of Lords Spiritual (senior bishops) and Lords Temporal (lay peers). Law Lords (senior judges) also sit as Lords Temporal. Members of the House of Lords are not elected. Originally, they were drawn from the various groups of senior and influential nobility in Britain, who advised the monarch throughout the country's early history. Following the House of Lords Act 1999 only 92 hereditary peers remain in the House. The majority of members are now life peers. There were 670 peers in total in March 2000.

Bills (except finance bills) may originate in either house and are given three readings. Until 1949 the Lords had power to delay legislation for two years or three sessions; this was then reduced to one year or two sessions. They may not delay finance bills, which may become law by the sovereign's assent within one month, whether the Lords have agreed to them or not.

In 1997, Scotland and Wales elected to form their own parliaments. Britain turned over its colony Hong Kong to China in July. In 1998, a widely approved referendum in both Northern Ireland and the Republic of Ireland laid the groundwork for a new form of government, but the new parliament did not operate for long before it was suspended in February 2000 due to the IRA's failure to meet disarmament deadlines. The Scottish Parliament held its first elections in 1999.

UNITED STATES OF AMERICA

The constitution of 1787 established a federal republic. By 1945 there were 48 states of the union and the capital District of Columbia. Alaska became a state in 1959, Hawaii in 1960.

The president is head of state and government. He is elected by an electoral college chosen by popular vote, and his term is four years. His executive power is exercised through a cabinet of departmental heads, whom he appoints with the consent of the Senate.

The constitution has had 26 amendments, beginning with the 10-point Bill of Rights in December 1791. Amendments since 1945 have limited the president's tenure of office to two terms (1951); granted national voting rights to the District of Columbia (1961); banned the use of the poll tax in federal elections (1964); defined presidential succession in case of presidential disability (1967); and set the voting age at 18 (1970).

The federal government has authority over national taxation, dealings with foreign powers and other national issues. Each state has its own elected governor and its own domestic legislative authority.

The Congress consists of a House of Representatives and a Senate. Representatives are elected every second year by adult suffrage, qualified in some states on grounds of residence or literacy. Seats are distributed per state according to census population. Since 1964 the population of the congressional districts has been approximately equal.

Senators, two from each state, are elected for a six-year term by popular vote; one-third are up for election every two years.

All legislation may originate in either house except for finance bills, which may originate only in the House of Representatives. The Senate may amend or reject any legislation from the House of Representatives. The Senate can also give or withhold its consent to formal treaties with foreign powers (but not to working agreements, which do not have the status of formal treaties).

Both houses work by committee. A bill passing through all committee stages and full debate in one house must then go through the same procedure in the other.

VENEZUELA—Republic of Venezuela

Venezuela is a republic and a federation (since 1864) of 20 states. There are also two federal territories and the Federal District of Caracas and 72 islands in the Caribbean. The constitution of 1936 was amended in 1945 and replaced in 1947, then amended again in 1953 and 1961.

The head of state is an executive president; legislative power belongs to a bicameral parliament. The president serves a five-year term and must be Venezuelan born and over 30. Presidential power is exercised through a cabinet; this exercise became truly democratic only after 1958. The president has a power of veto, which the parliament can ultimately overturn.

The 1961 constitution provides for a popularly elected president, National Congress, state and municipal assemblies. The states are equal and autonomous; each has an assembly and an elected governor. The Federal District and Federal Territories are administered by the president.

Congress is bicameral, consisting of a Chamber of Deputies and a Senate. Deputies were originally elected by municipal councils; direct election was introduced in 1945. Seats are distributed according to population. At present (1994) there is one deputy per 50,000 inhabitants.

Two senators are elected for each state and for the Federal District. Senators must be 30, deputies 21. Voting is compulsory for everyone 18 and over, and the system follows proportional representation. The high proportion of illiterates is not barred from the franchise; voting is by colored card.

The second term of President Betancourt (1959–64) restored independence to parliament and confirmed the principle of popular election in the 1961 constitution. The Congress term coincides with that of the presidency. Congress is essentially a vetoing agency. It initiates policy only when the president's party is in the minority.

VIETNAM—Socialist Republic of Vietnam

In 1945, at the end of the Japanese occupation, the communist Viet Minh League set up a republic in the north and promulgated a constitution the following year. In 1945–46, the French returned to the south and recognized the north as a "free state within the Indochinese Federation." The Viet Minh continued a war for total independence, culminating in the siege of Dien Bien Phu in 1954. A cease-fire agreement signed in Geneva that year provisionally partitioned the country, pending general elections to bring about unification. The elections were never held.

The north became the Democratic Republic of Vietnam, and in 1960 adopted a constitution defining the nation as a socialist, democratic, people's republic led by the workers. The head of state was an executive president. A unicameral legislature, the National Assembly, was drawn from a one-party list. The Assembly had a permanent Standing Committee empowered to interpret all laws and to govern by decree.

The south became the Republic of Vietnam and in 1956 adopted a constitution providing for an elected, executive presidency and an elected National Assembly. This Assembly was not elected until September 1963 and was dissolved that November. A bicameral assembly was first elected in 1967. The House of Representatives sat for a four-year term, the Senate for six.

The Vietnam War ended in victory for the north, and the two states were united in 1976 under the 1960 northern constitution. In 1980 a new constitution was promulgated for a united Vietnam. It describes Vietnam as a proletarian dictatorship and places executive and administrative power in the Council of Ministers. A Council of State serves as a "collective presidency" with both ceremonial and oversight functions.

Legislative and constitutional authority belong to the National Assembly of 496 deputies popularly elected from a one-party list. Under the constitution the Assembly has the highest formal authority to make laws, amend the constitution and choose the members of the two councils. In reality the Assembly's authority is extremely limited and its sessions serve mainly to ratify party policy. According to the constitution, the Communist Party is the only force leading the state, and the government's primary responsibility is to give concrete form to its policies.

In April 1992 the Vietnamese National Assembly unanimously approved a new constitution. This mainly reflected the country's moves to a free-market economy.

YUGOSLAVIA—Federal Republic of Yugoslavia

Yugoslavia's postwar constitution was promulgated on 11 November 1945. The constitution that it developed came into force on 31 January 1946. It provided for a federal republic composed of six states (Serbia, Croatia, Slovenia, Bosnia and Herzegovina, Macedonia, and Montenegro) and established a president as head of state with legislative authority in a bicameral parliament.

The constitution ratified in 1953 stipulated that all power belonged to the people and was to be exercised through a hierarchy of self-governing committees and assemblies, of which the most important was the Council of Producers. This was the lower house of the bicameral legislature. The Federal Chamber was the upper house. Deputies to the Council of Producers were elected by the economically active population. Federal Council deputies were, in part, directly elected on the basis of universal adult suffrage and in part indirectly elected by state, provincial and regional councils. The head of state was the president.

In 1963 the country became a socialist federal republic, comprising the original states and "two socialist autonomous provinces." The Council of Producers was replaced by the Council of Working Committees representing workers in different fields. The Federal Chamber of 70 members was delegated by the states and provinces. All deputies served four-year terms.

The constitution of 1974 emphasized the hierarchy of people's assemblies as the main organ of policy and decision making, with the federal parliament at the head of the system. A collective state presidency was introduced; the annual president of this group acts as head of state.

Until his death in 1980, Josip Broz Tito was the dominant political force in the nation, holding both the office of president of the republic and president of the Communist Party. Both offices were abolished upon his death, and later the executive branch of government consisted of a collective presidency of nine members, the Presidium, which included the head of state, and the Federal Executive Council, which was the collective head of government. Constitutionally, the Presidium had the authority to command the armed forces, propose policies, appoint to high judicial and military posts and promulgate laws.

Since 1974 the bicameral legislature—the Assembly of the Socialist Federal Republic of Yugoslavia—has been composed of the Federal Chamber, elected by members of commune assemblies within the republics and provinces, and the Chamber of Republics and Provinces, composed of delegates elected by republican and provincial assemblies.

In contrast to the legislatures in most communist countries, the Assembly was an active participant in governmental affairs.

Against a background of increasing demands for secession, in December 1989 a constitutional change gave the central government more power to deal with unrest. Constitutional changes in the constituent republics (especially Slovenia) increased the likelihood that the country would fall apart.

During 1991, this happened as Slovenia and Croatia declared independence and a bloody and destructive civil war broke out. This subsequently spread to Bosnia (see p. 292) and became a three-way struggle among Croatians, Serbs and Bosnians, as the Croats and Serbs attempted to annex most of Bosnia, and the Bosnians fought to remain an independent multinational state.

On 27 April 1992 Serbia and Montenegro proclaimed a "new" federal Yugoslavia with its own constitution. On 20 July 1992 the European Community refused to accept this as the legal successor.

In 1996–97, President Slobodan Milosevic refused to recognize opposition victories in local elections. Constitutionally barred from another term as president of Serbia, Milosevic became president of the Federal Republic of Yugoslavia in July 1997. In May 1998, Montenegro elected Milosevic-opponent Milo Djukanovic as president. In September 2000, Yugoslavia elected opposition leader Vojislav Kostunica as president by a wide margin. Kostunica took effective control following Milosevic's downfall in October 2000.

CHAPTER 4
TREATIES, ALLIANCES AND DIPLOMATIC AGREEMENTS

This chapter is arranged alphabetically by country. The chapter does not attempt to include the multitude of cultural, educational or commercial treaties. These, indeed, would occupy a large volume in themselves. It is confined to major diplomatic and military agreements of *political* significance.

AFGHANISTAN

4 Jan 1950	Treaty of peace and friendship with **India**
18 Dec 1955	Ten-year extension to 1931 treaty of neutrality and nonaggression with **Soviet Union** (extended further on 6 August 1965 and 10 December 1975)
27 Aug 1960	Treaty of friendship and nonaggression with **China**
24 Nov 1963	Boundary treaty with **China**
5 Dec 1978	Treaty of friendship, cooperation and good-neighborliness with **Soviet Union**
4 Apr 1980	Agreement with **Soviet Union** formalizing presence of Soviet troops in Afghanistan
25 June 1981	Treaty of friendship with **Czechoslovakia**
23 May 1982	Treaty of friendship with **East Germany**
14 May 1988	Geneva accord with **Pakistan** guaranteed by United States and Soviet Union, for noninterference in each other's affairs

ALGERIA

18 Mar 1962	Cease-fire and terms for independence agreed on with **France** at Evian
15 Jan 1969	Treaty of cooperation with **Morocco**
10 Apr 1969	Treaty of solidarity with **Libya**
6 Jan 1970	Twenty-year treaty of brotherhood, good-neighborliness and cooperation with **Tunisia**

8 Apr 1976	Agreement for increased regional cooperation with **Libya** and **Niger**
5 Jan 1983	Border demarcation agreement with **Niger**
20 Mar 1983	Twenty-year treaty of friendship and concord with **Tunisia** (**Mauritania** acceded later in 1983)
27 Mar 1983	Cooperation agreement with **Libya**
8 May 1983	Border demarcation agreement with **Mali**
15 Feb 1989	Treaty creating Arab Maghreb Union signed with **Libya, Mauritania, Morocco** and **Tunisia**

ANGOLA

15 Jan 1975	Agreement on independence from **Portugal**
8 Oct 1976	Treaty of friendship with **Soviet Union**
20 Nov 1976	Agreement with **Mozambique, Tanzania** and **Zambia** for a joint defense strategy
15 Dec 1976	Cooperation agreement with **Cape Verde**
26 June 1978	Three-year friendship and cooperation treaty with **Portugal**
17 Oct 1978	Framework agreements on cooperation and normalization of relations with **Zambia**
22 Oct 1978	Treaty of friendship and cooperation with **Bulgaria**
19 Feb 1979	Twenty-year treaty of friendship and cooperation with **East Germany**
14 Apr 1979	Treaty of friendship and cooperation with **Romania**
10 May 1979	Agreement with **Zambia** for creation of a joint security force
12 Oct 1979	Nonaggression pact with **Zaïre** and **Zambia**
19 Oct 1981	Treaty of friendship and cooperation with **North Korea**
16 Feb 1984	Lusaka accord with **South Africa**
9 Feb 1985	Agreement on defense and security with **Zaïre**
31 May 1992	Estoril Accord signed with UNITA in an attempt to end civil war (see p. 313)

ARGENTINA

10 May 1964	Agreement with **United States** for military assistance program
5 May 1970	Agreement with **United States** on armed forces cooperative projects
5 Apr 1972	Agreement with **Chile** to settle disputes by negotiation or arbitration (abrogated by Argentina on 21 Jan 1982)

19 Nov 1973	Agreement with **Uruguay** ending dispute over navigation rights in the River Plate
15 Sep 1982	Agreement with **Chile** to extend 1972 pact
23 Jan 1984	Treaty of peace and friendship with **Chile**
29 Nov 1984	Treaty with **Chile** for the settlement of the Beagle Channel dispute
5 May 1987	Nuclear cooperation agreement with **Iran**
Feb 1990	Diplomatic relations resumed with **Great Britain**
Mar 1991	Mercosur Agreement signed with **Brazil, Paraguay, and Uruguay**

AUSTRALIA

13 May 1947	Agreement with **Great Britain** for construction of Woomera rocket-testing range
20 Feb 1951	Mutual defense assistance agreement with **United States**
1 Sep 1951	Pacific Security Treaty with **United States** and **New Zealand** (ANZUS Pact)
13 Sep 1953	Agreement with **Great Britain** to share cost of maintaining Woomera range
8 Sep 1954	South-East Asia Collective Defense Treaty
4 Apr 1955	Agreement with **Great Britain** on a new atomic testing ground at Maralinga
12 July 1957	Agreement with **United States** for cooperation in use of atomic energy for mutual defense purposes
23 Aug 1960	Agreement with **United States** on a mutual weapons development program
9 May 1963	Agreement with **United States** on establishment of a naval communications station in Australia
16 June 1966	Australia joins the Asian and Pacific Council
9 Dec 1966	Agreement with **United States** on establishment of a joint space research facility
28 Aug 1969	Memorandum of understanding with **New Zealand** on joint defense planning and arms purchase
10 Nov 1969	Agreement with **United States** relating to the establishment of a joint defense space communications station in Australia
7 June 1970	Agreement with **New Zealand** to standardize defense equipment
9 Jan 1971	Agreement with **Great Britain, New Zealand, Malaysia** and **Singapore** on five-power arrangements for defense of Malaysia and Singapore

10 Jan 1974	Agreement with **United States** on joint operation of the U.S. naval communications station at North-West Cape
16 June 1976	Treaty of friendship and cooperation with **Japan**
20 Sep 1977	Agreement with **United States** on establishing in southwest Australia an OMEGA navigating facility
22 Nov 1988	Accord with **United States** on continued use of joint defense facilities in Australia
Feb 1994	Australia recognizes independence of **Macedonia**

BELGIUM

17 Mar 1948	Brussels Treaty with **Great Britain, France, Luxembourg** and the **Netherlands**
4 Apr 1949	North Atlantic Treaty
27 Jan 1950	Military assistance agreement with **United States**
12 Nov 1952	Agreement with **Great Britain** on the establishment of a military base in the Campine region
30 Mar 1953	Agreement with **Great Britain** and **Canada** on the stationing of Canadian forces in Belgium
23 Oct 1954	Paris agreements on creation of Western European Union
25 July 1959	Agreement with **France** and **Luxembourg** on cooperation for internal defense
22 Apr 1960	Agreement with **United States** on a weapons production program
17 May 1960	Agreement with **United States** on cooperation in use of atomic energy for mutual defense purposes
1 Aug 1975	Final Act of the Helsinki Conference on security and cooperation in Europe
28 Mar 1976	General cooperation agreement with **Zaïre** (abrogated by Zaïre on 13 January 1989)
19 June 1990	Treaty abolishing all internal borders signed with **France, West Germany, Netherlands** and **Luxembourg**
Dec 1991	Maastricht Treaty on European unity agreed to
1 Nov 1993	Maastricht Treaty takes effect, creating the European Union

BRAZIL

15 Mar 1952	Military assistance agreement with **United States** (terminated by Brazil 11 March 1978)
5 Apr 1955	Military services agreement with **Great Britain**

20 Sep 1955	Agreement with **United States** on continuation of joint military and defense commissions
27 Jan 1967	Agreement with **United States** governing the use of American-supplied armaments
17 Aug 1977	Agreement with **Bolivia** for friendship and cooperation
1 June 1983	Agreement with **Suriname** on military and economic assistance
6 Feb 1984	Military and economic cooperation agreements with **United States**
14 Oct 1984	Five-year military cooperation agreement with **Saudi Arabia**
Mar 1991	Mercosur Agreement signed with **Argentina, Paraguay** and **Uruguay**

BULGARIA

10 Feb 1947	Peace treaty with the Allied powers
27 Nov 1947	Twenty-year treaty of friendship and cooperation with **Yugoslavia** (abrogated by Bulgaria on 1 Oct 1949)
16 Dec 1947	Twenty-year treaty of friendship and cooperation with **Albania**
16 Jan 1948	Twenty-year treaty of friendship and cooperation with **Romania**
16 Mar 1948	Treaty of friendship, cooperation and mutual assistance with **Soviet Union**
23 Apr 1948	Twenty-year treaty of friendship and cooperation with **Czechoslovakia**
29 May 1948	Twenty-year treaty of friendship and cooperation with **Poland**
19 July 1948	Twenty-year treaty of friendship and cooperation with **Hungary**
14 May 1955	Warsaw Pact
9 Apr 1964	Treaty of friendship and cooperation with **Yemen Republic**
6 Apr 1967	Treaty of friendship and mutual assistance with **Poland**
12 May 1967	Treaty of friendship and mutual assistance with **Soviet Union**
23 July 1967	Treaty of friendship and mutual assistance with **Mongolia**
7 Sep 1967	Treaty of friendship and mutual assistance with **East Germany**
26 Apr 1968	Twenty-year treaty of friendship and cooperation with **Czechoslovakia**

10 July 1969	Twenty-year treaty of friendship and cooperation with **Hungary**
19 Nov 1970	Twenty-year treaty of friendship and cooperation with **Romania**
1 Aug 1975	Final Act of the Helsinki Conference on security and cooperation in **Europe**
5 May 1977	Treaty of friendship and cooperation with **Mongolia**
14 Sep 1977	Treaty of friendship and cooperation with **East Germany**
22 Oct 1978	Treaty of friendship and cooperation with **Angola**
1 Oct 1979	Treaty of friendship and cooperation with **Vietnam**
4 Oct 1979	Treaty of friendship and cooperation with **Laos**
16 Oct 1981	Agreement on mutual military cooperation with **Tanzania**
11 Nov 1981	Treaty of friendship and cooperation with **South Yemen**
Jan 1983	Treaty of friendship and cooperation with **Libya**
1984	Treaty of friendship and cooperation with **North Korea**
30 Apr 1985	Twenty-year treaty of friendship and cooperation with **Syria**
1990	Diplomatic relations established with **South Korea**

CANADA

4 Apr 1949	North Atlantic Treaty
1 Aug 1951	Agreement with **United States** on extension and coordination of the continental radar defense system
25 May 1952	Agreement with **France** on exchange of defense-science information
30 Mar 1953	Agreement with **Great Britain** and **Belgium** on transit and stationing of Canadian forces in Belgium
23 Oct 1954	Paris Agreements
19 Apr 1955	Agreement with **France** relating to the convention on foreign forces stationed in Germany of 1952 (further agreement on 26 Jan 1956)
5 May 1955	Agreement with **United States** for establishment and operation of a distant early-warning system
22 June 1955	Agreement with **NATO** partners on atomic cooperation
17 Sep 1956	Agreement with **West Germany** on training German aircrews in Canada (further agreement 10 Dec 1956)

13 Apr 1957   Agreement with the **Netherlands** on extension of NATO aircrew training program

17 Apr 1957   Agreement with **Denmark** on aircrew training for NATO (renewed 25 Mar 1960, extended 30 June 1964)

12 May 1958   Agreement with **United States** on the organization and operation of the North American Air Defense Command (NORAD) (extended 30 March 1968, 12 May 1973, 8 May 1975, 12 May 1980 and 11 Mar 1981)

20 June 1958   Agreement on establishment, maintenance and operation by **United States** of aerial refueling facilities in Canada

2 Sep 1958   Agreement with **United States** providing for establishment of a Canadian–U.S. committee on joint defense

1 May 1959   Agreement with **United States** on establishment, maintenance and operation of short-range tactical air navigation facilities in Canada

13 July 1959   Agreement with **United States** on establishment of a ballistic missile early-warning system

24 May 1960   Agreement with **Norway** on exchange of information on defense

12 June 1961   Agreement with **United States** on air defense cooperation and a defense production sharing program

27 Sep 1961   Agreement with **United States** on extension and strengthening of the continental air defense system

25 May 1962   Agreement with **France** on exchange of defense-science information

18 July 1962   Agreement with **Greece** on exchange of defense-science information

23 July 1962   Declaration on neutrality of **Laos** at Geneva

16 Aug 1963   Agreement with **United States** on availability of nuclear warheads for Canadian forces

15 Nov 1963   Agreement with **United States** establishing a joint civil emergency planning committee

30 June 1964   Agreement with **Norway** on the continuation of Canada's NATO air training program

19 May 1971   Agreement with **Soviet Union** for consultation on foreign affairs

1 Aug 1975   Final Act of the Helsinki Conference on security and cooperation in Europe

11 Apr 1977   Memorandum of understanding with **United States** concerning a regional operations control center

5 Oct 1978	Memorandum of understanding with **United States** concerning a NAVSTAR global positioning system
1 Feb 1979	Memorandum of understanding with **United States** concerning coordination of research and development work
14 Dec 1979	Agreement on cooperation for development with **Bangladesh**
25 Oct 1982	Agreement with **United States** on cruise missile tests in Alberta
18 Mar 1985	Agreement with **United States** for a new chain of ground radar stations across Canadian Arctic and northern Alaska to be known as North Warning System
20 Mar 1986	Agreement with **United States** for five-year extension of North American Air Defense System
2 Jan 1988	Agreement with **United States** eliminating trade and tariff barriers
13 Aug 1992	North American Free Trade Association (NAFTA) agreement with **United States** and **Mexico**
1 Jan 1994	North American Free Trade Agreement (NAFTA) takes effect, eliminating restrictions on the flow of goods, services and investment between the **United States,** Canada and **Mexico**

CHILE

9 Apr 1952	Military assistance agreement with **United States**
31 July 1954	Military service agreement with **Great Britain**
5 Apr 1972	Agreement with **Argentina** to settle disputes by negotiation or arbitration (abrogated by **Argentina** on 21 Jan 1982)
15 Sep 1982	Agreement with **Argentina** to extend 1972 pact
23 Jan 1984	Treaty of peace and friendship with **Argentina**
29 Nov 1984	Treaty with **Argentina** for the settlement of the Beagle Channel dispute

CHINA

23 May 1951	Agreement with **Tibet** regarding that country's autonomy
21 July 1954	Geneva declaration on Indochina
25 Dec 1955	Treaty of friendship with **East Germany**
27 Aug 1957	Treaty of friendship with **Czechoslovakia**
6 May 1959	Treaty of friendship with **Hungary**
28 Jan 1960	Treaty of friendship and nonaggression with **Burma**

21 Mar 1960	Border agreement with **Nepal**
28 Apr 1960	Treaty of peace and friendship with **Nepal**
31 May 1960	Treaty of friendship and mutual economic aid with **Mongolia**
27 Aug 1960	Treaty of friendship and nonaggression with **Afghanistan**
13 Sep 1960	Treaty of friendship with **Guinea**
1 Oct 1960	Border agreement with **Burma**
19 Dec 1960	Treaty of friendship and nonaggression with **Cambodia**
1 Apr 1961	Treaty of friendship with **Indonesia**
11 July 1961	Treaty of friendship, cooperation and mutual assistance with **North Korea**
18 Aug 1961	Treaty of friendship with **Ghana**
5 Oct 1961	Border agreement with **Nepal**
23 July 1962	Declaration on neutrality of **Laos** at Geneva
26 Dec 1962	Border agreement with **Mongolia**
2 Mar 1963	Border agreement with **Pakistan**
24 Nov 1963	Border agreement with **Afghanistan**
9 June 1964	Treaty of friendship with **Yemen Republic**
2 Oct 1964	Treaty of friendship with **Congo**
3 Nov 1964	Treaty of friendship with **Mali**
20 Feb 1965	Treaty of friendship with **Tanzania**
26 Mar 1965	Border agreement with **Pakistan**
7 July 1965	Treaty of friendship and good-neighborly relations with **North Vietnam**
8 Aug 1969	Agreement with **Soviet Union** on the navigation of the Amur and Ussuri rivers
15 Nov 1969	Agreement with **Tanzania** and **Zambia** to build the Tan-Zam railway.
20 Apr 1976	Military aid protocol with **Egypt**
12 Aug 1978	Treaty of peace and friendship with **Japan**
17 Sep 1980	Treaty for the normalization of relations with **United States**
19 Dec 1984	Agreement with **Great Britain** on the future of Hong Kong
7 Apr 1985	Military cooperation agreement with **Italy**
13 Apr 1987	Agreement with **Portugal** on the return of Macao in 1999
July 1990	**Saudi Arabia** recognizes China
Aug 1990	**Indonesia** and China establish relations
Oct 1990	**Singapore** and China establish relations
Apr 1991	China and **Taiwan** officially end "state of war" between the two countries

Nov 1991	China and Vietnam restore diplomatic relations
24 Aug 1992	Diplomatic relations established with South Korea and Israel
10 Sep 1992	Comprehensive trade agreement with United States
7 Sep 1993	Border peace deal with India signed, reducing troop numbers along border and establishing a cease-fire line
Apr 1994	China and Kazakhstan sign border agreement
6 June 1996	China agrees to world ban on atomic testing
5 Oct 1998	China signs international accord to improve human rights

CONGO

15 Aug 1960	Cooperation and mutual defense agreement with France
2 Oct 1964	Treaty of friendship with China
4 Feb 1968	Union of Central African States formed with Chad and Central African Republic
1 Jan 1974	Cooperation agreement with France
13 May 1981	Twenty-year treaty of friendship and cooperation with Soviet Union

CONGO, DEMOCRATIC REPUBLIC OF (formerly Zaïre)

19 July 1963	Military assistance agreement with United States
30 Aug 1966	Mutual security pact with Burundi and Rwanda (reaffirmed on 12 June 1974)
May 1974	Military cooperation agreement with France
28 Mar 1976	General cooperation agreement with Belgium (abrogated by Zaïre on 13 January 1989)
12 Oct 1977	Nonaggression pact with Angola and Zambia
7 Feb 1980	Technical military cooperation agreement with Egypt
19 Mar 1980	Treaty of friendship and cooperation with Romania
20 Jan 1983	Military cooperation agreements with Israel
9 Feb 1985	Agreement on defense and security with Angola
9 July 1985	Military cooperation agreement with Chad

CUBA

2 Sep 1947	Inter-American Treaty of Reciprocal Assistance (Cuba withdrew on 29 March 1960)
1 June 1980	Twenty-five-year treaty of friendship and cooperation with East Germany

Oct 1982	Twenty-five-year treaty of friendship and cooperation with **Vietnam**
27 July 1993	Virtual normalization of telephone links with **United States**
4 Jan 1999	**United States** agrees to ease restrictions on Cuba

CZECHOSLOVAKIA (until 1992)

9 May 1946	Twenty-year treaty of friendship and cooperation with **Yugoslavia** (abrogated by Czechoslovakia on 4 Oct 1949)
10 Mar 1947	Twenty-year treaty of friendship and cooperation with **Poland**
23 Apr 1948	Twenty-year treaty of friendship and cooperation with **Bulgaria**
21 July 1948	Twenty-year treaty of friendship and cooperation with **Romania**
16 Apr 1949	Twenty-year treaty of friendship and cooperation with **Hungary**
14 May 1955	Warsaw Pact
27 Aug 1957	Treaty of friendship with **China**
27 Nov 1960	Treaty of friendship and cooperation with **Cambodia**
20 May 1964	Treaty of friendship and cooperation with **Yemen Republic**
1 Mar 1967	Treaty of friendship and mutual assistance with **Poland**
17 Mar 1967	Treaty of friendship and mutual assistance with **East Germany**
26 Apr 1968	Treaty of friendship and cooperation with **Bulgaria**
14 June 1968	Treaty of friendship and cooperation with **Hungary**
16 Aug 1968	Treaty of friendship and cooperation with **Romania**
16 Oct 1968	Treaty with **Soviet Union** on temporary stationing of Soviet forces in Czechoslovakia
6 May 1970	Twenty-year treaty of friendship and cooperation with **Soviet Union**
11 Dec 1973	Treaty for the normalization of relations with **West Germany**
1 Aug 1975	Final Act of the Helsinki Conference on security and cooperation in Europe
3 Oct 1977	Treaty of friendship, cooperation and mutual assistance with **East Germany**
3 Dec 1978	Treaty of friendship and cooperation with **Ethiopia**
17 Feb 1980	Treaty of friendship and cooperation with **Laos**

25 June 1981	Treaty of friendship and cooperation with **Afghanistan**
Sep 1981	Treaty of friendship and cooperation with **South Yemen**
13 Sep 1981	Treaty of friendship and cooperation with **Ethiopia**
21 Oct 1981	Treaty of friendship with **Mozambique**
17 May 1982	Cooperation agreement with **Zambia**
9 Sep 1982	Treaty of friendship and cooperation with **Libya**
27 Feb 1990	Agreement with **Soviet Union** for withdrawal of Soviet forces by July 1991
1991	Treaty of friendship with **Germany**
26 Aug 1992	**Czech** and **Slovak** republics announce their formal separation into independent states as of 1 Jan 1993, dissolving the 74-year-old federation
12 Mar 1999	Czech Republic, **Poland** and **Hungary** join NATO

DENMARK

4 Apr 1949	North Atlantic Treaty
27 Jan 1950	Mutual defense assistance agreement with **United States**
20 Jan 1955	Military service agreement with **Great Britain**
8 Oct 1956	Agreement with **Great Britain** relating to the status of forces in NATO
17 Apr 1957	Agreement with **Canada** on aircrew training
12 Apr 1960	Agreement with **United States** on a weapons production program
1 Aug 1975	Final Act of the Helsinki Conference on security and cooperation in Europe
Dec 1991	Maastricht Treaty on European union (rejected by referendum, accepted in second referendum)
Dec 1993	Denmark recognizes independence of **Macedonia**
1 Nov 1993	Maastricht Treaty takes effect, creating the European Union

EGYPT

22 Mar 1945	Pact of Union of Arab States with **Iraq, Lebanon, Saudi Arabia, Syria, Transjordan** and **Yemen**
17 June 1950	Collective Security Pact with **Saudi Arabia, Syria, Lebanon** and **Yemen**
Oct 1954	Treaty with **Great Britain** for withdrawal of British forces from Canal Zone
27 Sep 1955	Armaments agreement with **Czechoslovakia**
1 Feb 1958	Union with **Syria** to form the United Arab Republic (dissolved in 1961)

26 May 1964	Agreement with **Iraq** for the establishment of a joint presidency council and military command
24 Aug 1965	Agreement with **Saudi Arabia** for a cease-fire in Yemen
4 Nov 1966	Defense agreement with **Syria**
30 May 1967	Defense pact with **Jordan** (joined by **Iraq** on 4 June 1967)
30 Aug 1967	Agreement with **Saudi Arabia** regarding Yemen
5 Nov 1970	Agreement on political federation with **Libya** and **Sudan** (joined by Syria on 26 Nov 1970)
16 Mar 1971	Agreement for united military command with **Syria**
27 May 1971	Fifteen-year treaty of friendship with **Soviet Union** (abrogated by Egypt on 15 Mar 1976)
20 Aug 1971	Agreement for Federation of Arab Republics with **Syria** and **Libya**
22 Feb 1973	Treaty of friendship with **Chad**
11 Nov 1973	Agreement with **Israel** on a cease-fire line
18 Jan 1974	Agreement with **Israel** for the disengagement of forces on the Suez Canal
2 Feb 1974	Agreement with **Sudan** for the coordination of their political and economic strategies
14 June 1974	Declaration of cooperation and friendship with **United States**
4 Sep 1975	Agreement with **Israel** for Israeli withdrawal in Sinai and establishment of a buffer zone
13 Oct 1975	Agreement with **United States** on the establishment of an early-warning system in the Sinai
20 Apr 1976	Military aid protocol with **China**
15 July 1976	Defense agreement with **Sudan**
21 Dec 1976	Agreement with **Syria** on formation of a unified political command (joined by **Sudan** on 28 Feb 1977)
Jan 1977	Defense agreement with **Sudan** of 1976 activated
29 Apr 1977	Military cooperation agreement with **France**
17 Sep 1978	Camp David agreements with **Israel** for conclusion of peace treaty and overall Middle East settlement
26 Mar 1979	Peace treaty with **Israel**
7 Feb 1980	Technical military cooperation agreement with **Zaïre**
10 July 1981	Agreement with **Israel** and **United States** on formation of an international peace-keeping force for the Sinai
6 Aug 1981	Five-year defense agreement with **United States**
19 Jan 1982	Agreement with **Israel** on withdrawal from Sinai
12 Oct 1982	Charter of political and economic integration with **Sudan** and close coordination of foreign policy, security and development

| 15 Feb 1989 | Formation of Arab Cooperation Council with **Iraq, Jordan** and **North Yemen** |

ETHIOPIA

22 May 1953	Mutual defense assistance agreement with **United States**
14 May 1954	Agreement with **United States** on military bases
July 1963	Defense agreement with **Kenya**
5 Sep 1968	Agreement with **Somalia** to end subversive activity
9 June 1970	Treaty with **Kenya** delimiting their border
6 May 1977	Cooperation agreements with **Soviet Union**
20 Nov 1978	Twenty-year treaty of friendship and cooperation with **Soviet Union**
3 Dec 1978	Treaty of friendship and cooperation with **Czechoslovakia**
31 Jan 1979	Treaty of friendship and cooperation with **Kenya**
31 May 1979	Protocol for military cooperation with **East Germany**
15 Nov 1979	Twenty-year treaty of friendship and cooperation with **East Germany**
2 Dec 1979	Fifteen-year treaty of friendship and cooperation with **South Yemen**
12 Dec 1979	Treaty of friendship and cooperation with **Poland**
21 Mar 1981	Treaty of friendship and cooperation with **Djibouti**
19 Aug 1981	Treaty of friendship and cooperation with **Libya** and **South Yemen**
13 Sep 1981	Treaty of friendship and cooperation with **Czechoslovakia**
25 Apr 1993	Referendum in Ethiopia confirms independence of **Eritrea**

FRANCE

4 Mar 1947	Dunkirk treaty with **Great Britain**
17 Mar 1948	Brussels treaty for collective military aid and economic and social cooperation
19 Apr 1948	Agreement with **Great Britain** on military air transit
4 Apr 1949	North Atlantic Treaty
21 Dec 1949	Military service agreement with **Great Britain**
27 Jan 1950	Mutual defense assistance agreement with **United States**
23 Oct 1950	Agreement with **Great Britain, United States** and **West Germany** on defense materials
23 Dec 1950	Agreement with **Cambodia, Laos, Vietnam** and **United States** for mutual defense assistance in Indochina
6 Mar 1952	Military service agreement with **Great Britain**

26 May 1952	Convention on relations with **Great Britain, United States** and **West Germany**
21 July 1954	Geneva Declaration on the problem of restoring peace in Indochina.
8 Sep 1954	South-East Asia Collective Defense Treaty
23 Oct 1954	Paris agreements for formation of Western European Union
19 Apr 1955	Agreement with **Canada** concerning the convention on foreign forces stationed in Germany (further agreement 26 Jan 1956)
27 Oct 1956	Treaty with **West Germany** for its incorporation of the Saar
7 May 1959	Agreement with **United States** for cooperation in the use of atomic energy for mutual defense purposes
25 July 1959	Agreement with **Belgium** and **Luxembourg** on cooperation for internal defense
22 June 1960	Mutual defense agreements with **Mali** and **Senegal**
27 June 1960	Mutual defense agreement with **Madagascar**
11 Aug 1960	Mutual defense agreement with **Chad**
13 Aug 1960	Mutual defense agreement with **Central African Republic**
15 Aug 1960	Mutual defense agreement with **Congo**
17 Aug 1960	Mutual defense agreement with **Gabon**
19 Sep 1960	Agreement with **United States** on a weapons production program
25 Oct 1960	Agreement with **West Germany** on logistics and training for German forces
13 Nov 1960	Mutual defense agreement with **Cameroon**
24 Apr 1961	Mutual defense agreements with **Ivory Coast, Dahomey, Upper Volta** and **Niger**
19 June 1961	Mutual defense agreement with **Mauritania**
27 July 1961	Agreement with **United States** for cooperation in the use of atomic energy for mutual defense purposes (revised agreement 1 August 1985)
18 Mar 1962	Cease-fire and terms for independence agreed on with **Algeria** at Evian
25 May 1962	Agreement with **Canada** on exchange of defense-science information
23 July 1962	Declaration on the neutrality of **Laos** at Geneva
22 Jan 1963	Treaty of cooperation with **West Germany**
10 July 1963	Mutual defense agreement with **Togo**
9 Apr 1964	Agreement with **Portugal** for the establishment of a French tracking station for ballistic missiles in the Azores

1 May 1964	Mutual defense agreement with **Chad**
9 Nov 1966	Agreement with **Soviet Union** on establishment of a "Hot Line"
22 June 1970	Five-year military cooperation agreement with **Spain**
3 Sep 1971	Agreement on Berlin with **Great Britain, Soviet Union** and **United States**
29 Oct 1971	Agreement on principles of cooperation with **Soviet Union**
5 Nov 1972	Agreement with **Great Britain, Soviet Union** and **United States** on maintenance of four-power rights and responsibilities in Germany
4 June 1973	Cooperation agreement with **Madagascar**
1 Jan 1974	Cooperation agreement with **Congo**
12 Feb 1974	Cooperation agreement with **Gabon**
21 Feb 1974	Cooperation agreement with **Cameroon**
29 Mar 1974	Treaty of friendship and cooperation with **Senegal**
May 1974	Military cooperation agreement with **Zaïre**
23 Feb 1975	Cooperation agreement with **Benin**
20 June 1975	Declaration on principles of friendly cooperation with **Poland**
1 Aug 1975	Final Act of the Helsinki Conference on security and cooperation in Europe
6 Mar 1976	Cooperation agreement with **Chad**
23 Mar 1976	Cooperation agreement with **Togo**
16 July 1976	Exchange of letters with **Soviet Union** on prevention of nuclear war
29 Apr 1977	Military cooperation agreement with **Egypt**
22 June 1977	Declaration with **Soviet Union** on nonproliferation of nuclear weapons
27 June 1977	Treaty of friendship and cooperation with **Djibouti**
10 Nov 1978	Treaty of friendship and cooperation with the **Comoros**
28 Apr 1979	Agreement with **Soviet Union** for cooperation to promote peace and détente
17 Sep 1980	Military cooperation agreement with **Sudan**
17 Sep 1984	Agreement with Libya on mutual withdrawal of troops from **Chad**
Apr 1985	Agreement with **Portugal** to extend French use of missile-tracking station in the Azores for 12 years
12 Feb 1986	Channel fixed-link treaty signed with **Great Britain**
19 June 1990	Treaty abolishing all internal borders signed with **Belgium, West Germany, Netherlands** and **Luxembourg**

12 Sep 1990	Treaty on the Final Settlement with Respect to Germany, signed with **East Germany, West Germany, Great Britain, United States** and **Soviet Union**
Dec 1991	Maastricht Treaty on European union
Feb 1992	Solidarity Pact signed with **Russia**
Dec 1993	France recognizes independence of **Macedonia**
29 Jan 1996	France announces end to nuclear tests

GERMANY, EAST (until 1990)

7 June 1950	Agreement with **Poland** on the Oder-Neisse frontier
14 May 1955	Warsaw Pact
20 Sept 1955	Treaty by which **Soviet Union** recognized East Germany as a sovereign state
25 Dec 1955	Ten-year treaty of friendship with **China**
12 Mar 1957	Treaty with **Soviet Union** on stationing of Soviet troops
22 Aug 1957	Treaty of friendship and cooperation with **Mongolia**
17 May 1964	Treaty of friendship and cooperation with **Tanzania**
12 June 1964	Twenty-year treaty of friendship and mutual assistance with **Soviet Union**
15 Mar 1967	Twenty-year treaty of friendship and mutual assistance with **Poland**
17 Mar 1967	Twenty-year treaty of friendship and mutual assistance with **Czechoslovakia**
18 May 1967	Twenty-year treaty of friendship and mutual assistance with **Hungary**
7 Sep 1967	Twenty-year treaty of friendship and mutual assistance with **Bulgaria**
12 Sep 1968	Treaty of friendship and cooperation with **Mongolia**
20 Dec 1971	Agreement with **West Germany** on traffic to **West Berlin**
12 May 1972	Twenty-year treaty of friendship with **Romania**
26 May 1972	Agreement with **West Germany** on questions of traffic
21 Dec 1972	Agreement with **West Germany** on the basis of relations between the two countries
1 Aug 1975	Final Act of the Helsinki Conference on security and cooperation in Europe
7 Oct 1975	Twenty-five-year treaty of friendship, cooperation and mutual assistance with **Soviet Union**
24 Mar 1977	Treaty of friendship and cooperation with **Hungary**
6 May 1977	Treaty of friendship and cooperation with **Mongolia**
22 May 1977	Treaty of friendship and cooperation with **Poland**
14 Sep 1977	Treaty of friendship and cooperation with **Bulgaria**

3 Oct 1977	Treaty of friendship, cooperation and mutual assistance with **Czechoslovakia**
4 Dec 1977	Treaty of friendship and cooperation with **Vietnam**
19 Feb 1979	Twenty-year treaty of friendship and cooperation with **Angola**
24 Feb 1979	Twenty-year treaty of friendship and cooperation with **Mozambique**
26 May 1979	Protocol for military cooperation with **Mozambique**
31 May 1979	Protocol for military cooperation with **Ethiopia**
15 Nov 1979	Twenty-year treaty of friendship and cooperation with **Ethiopia**
17 Nov 1979	Twenty-year treaty of friendship and cooperation with **South Yemen**
1 June 1980	Twenty-five-year treaty of friendship and cooperation with **Cuba**
23 May 1982	Treaty of friendship and cooperation with **Afghanistan**
22 Sep 1982	Treaty of friendship and cooperation with **Laos**
1984	Treaty of friendship and cooperation with **North Korea**
7 Sep 1987	Cooperation accords with **West Germany** on technology and the environment
18 May 1990	Treaty with **West Germany**, establishing a monetary, economic and social union
31 Aug 1990	Treaty with **West Germany**, establishing political and social terms for reunification, and Berlin as the capital of the united Germany
12 Sep 1990	Treaty on the Final Settlement with Respect to Germany signed with **West Germany, France, Great Britain, United States** and **Soviet Union**
24 Sep 1990	East Germany formally withdraws from the Warsaw Pact

GERMANY (WEST GERMANY until 1990)

26 May 1952	Agreement on relations with **Great Britain, France** and **United States** (amended by Paris agreements of 23 October 1954)
7 July 1952	Treaty of friendship with **Saudi Arabia**
9 Sep 1952	Agreement with **Great Britain** on bases in Germany (further agreements October 1954 and May 1957)
23 Oct 1954	Paris agreements
5 May 1955	West Germany joins NATO
30 June 1955	Mutual defense assistance agreement with **United States**

17 Sep 1956	Agreement with **Canada** on training German aircrews in Canada (further agreement 10 December 1956)
27 Oct 1956	Treaty with **France** for incorporation of the Saar into West Germany
12 Dec 1956	Agreements with **United States** on training of German army and navy personnel
11 Apr 1957	Agreement with **Great Britain** relating to the convention on foreign forces stationed in Germany
7 June 1957	Agreement with **Great Britain** on maintenance costs of British forces in Germany (further agreements 3 October 1958 and 28 April 1967)
10 July 1957	Agreement with the **Netherlands** on cost of maintenance of British forces
5 May 1959	Agreement with **United States** for cooperation in use of atomic energy for mutual defense purposes
27 May 1960	Agreement with **United States** relating to a weapons production program
25 Oct 1960	Agreement with **France** on logistics and training of German forces
22 Jan 1963	Cooperation agreement with **France**
12 Aug 1970	Treaty with **Soviet Union** renouncing the use of force
7 Dec 1970	Agreement with **Poland** on Oder-Neisse boundary and normalization of relations
18 Mar 1971	Five-year agreement with **Great Britain** on troop-support costs
10 Dec 1971	Agreement with **United States** on maintenance costs of U.S. forces in Europe
21 Dec 1971	Accord with **East Germany** on transit to West Berlin
26 May 1972	Treaty with **East Germany** on the basis of relations between the two Germanies
11 Dec 1973	Treaty with **Czechoslovakia** for the normalization of relations
25 Apr 1974	Agreement with **United States** on troop-support costs
19 Sep 1974	Declaration on normalization of relations with **Finland**
1 Aug 1975	Final Act of the Helsinki Conference on security and cooperation in Europe
1 June 1977	Treaty of cooperation and friendly relations with **Tonga**
29 June 1977	Cooperation agreement with **Romania**
18 Oct 1977	Agreement with **Great Britain** to end payments to offset British foreign exchange costs of stationing troops in West Germany
17 Oct 1978	Memorandum of understanding with **United States** concerning principles governing mutual cooperation for defense equipment

15 Apr 1982	Wartime host-nation support agreement with **United States**
22 July 1986	Accords for cooperation in science and technology with the **Soviet Union**
22 Apr 1987	Nuclear energy cooperation pact with **Soviet Union**
7 Sep 1987	Cooperation accords with **East Germany** on technology and the environment
18 May 1990	Treaty with **East Germany**, establishing a monetary, economic and social union
19 June 1990	Treaty abolishing all internal borders signed with **Belgium, France, Netherlands** and **Luxembourg**
31 Aug 1990	Treaty with **East Germany**, establishing political and social terms for reunification, and Berlin as the capital of the united Germany
12 Sep 1990	Treaty on the Final Settlement with Respect to Germany signed with **East Germany, France, Great Britain, United States** and **Soviet Union**
13 Sep 1990	Treaty with **Soviet Union** of good-neighborliness, partnership and cooperation
June 1991	Treaty of friendship with **Poland**
Dec 1991	Maastricht Treaty on European union
Dec 1993	Germany recognizes independence of **Macedonia**

GHANA

18 Aug 1961	Treaty of friendship with **Soviet Union**
3 Mar 1964	Defense agreement with **Great Britain**
10 Dec 1984	Cooperation agreement with **Benin, Nigeria** and **Togo**
19 Dec 1984	Military training agreement with **Great Britain**

GREECE

20 June 1947	Military assistance agreement with **United States**
21 Feb 1949	Agreement with **United States** on use of certain Greek islands for training exercises by U.S. Mediterranean fleet
18 Feb 1952	North Atlantic Treaty
12 Oct 1953	Agreement with **United States** concerning military facilities
7 Sep 1956	Agreement with **United States** concerning status of U.S. forces in Greece
19 Feb 1959	Agreement on future of Cyprus with **Great Britain, Turkey** and Cypriot communities
6 May 1959	Agreement with **United States** for cooperation in the use of atomic energy for mutual defense purposes

15 Feb 1960	Agreement with **United States** on a weapons production program
18 July 1962	Agreement with **Canada** on the exchange of defense-science information
15 June 1971	Agreement with **Romania** to respect the inviolability of each other's frontiers
1 Aug 1975	Final Act of the Helsinki Conference on security and cooperation in Europe
15 Apr 1976	Four-year defense cooperation agreement with **United States**
30 Aug 1979	Exchange of notes with **United States** on the grant of defense articles and services under the military assistance program
2 Sep 1983	Defense agreement with **Great Britain**
9 Sep 1983	Five-year defense and economic cooperation agreement with **United States**
10 Nov 1986	Defense industrial cooperation agreement with **United States**
8 July 1990	Defense cooperation agreement with **United States**
Dec 1991	Maastricht Treaty on European union
Jan 2000	Greece and **Turkey** sign series of agreements four years after their countries came close to entering war over tiny Aegean island. Accords cover range of areas including commerce, immigration and the environment

HUNGARY

10 Feb 1947	Peace treaty with the Allied powers
8 Dec 1947	Twenty-year treaty of friendship and cooperation with **Yugoslavia** (abrogated by Hungary on 30 September 1949)
24 Jan 1948	Twenty-year treaty of friendship and cooperation with **Romania**
18 Feb 1948	Treaty of friendship, cooperation and mutual assistance with **Soviet Union**
19 July 1948	Twenty-year treaty of friendship and cooperation with **Bulgaria**
16 Apr 1949	Twenty-year treaty of friendship and cooperation with **Czechoslovakia**
14 May 1955	Warsaw Pact
27 May 1957	Treaty with **Soviet Union** on stationing of forces in **Hungary**
6 May 1959	Treaty of friendship with **China**
20 May 1964	Treaty of friendship and cooperation with **Yemen Republic**

18 May 1967	Twenty-year treaty of friendship and mutual assistance with **East Germany**
7 Sep 1967	Twenty-year treaty of friendship and mutual assistance with **Soviet Union**
16 May 1968	Twenty-year treaty of friendship and mutual assistance with **Poland**
14 June 1968	Twenty-year treaty of friendship and mutual assistance with **Czechoslovakia**
10 July 1969	Twenty-year treaty of friendship and mutual assistance with **Bulgaria**
24 Feb 1972	Twenty-year treaty of friendship and mutual assistance with **Romania**
1 Aug 1975	Final Act of the Helsinki conference on security and cooperation in Europe
24 Mar 1977	Treaty of friendship and cooperation with **East Germany**
5 Nov 1981	Treaty of friendship and cooperation with **South Yemen**
Feb 1990	Agreement with the **Vatican** to resume diplomatic relations
10 Mar 1990	Agreement with **Soviet Union** for withdrawal of Soviet troops by July 1991
12 Mar 1999	**Czech Republic, Poland,** and Hungary join NATO

INDIA

8 Aug 1949	Treaty of peace and friendship with **Bhutan**
4 Jan 1950	Treaty of peace and friendship with **Afghanistan**
31 July 1950	Treaty of peace and friendship with **Nepal**
5 Dec 1950	Treaty with **Sikkim** for her continuation as an internally autonomous protectorate of **India**
11 July 1952	Treaty of peace and friendship with **Philippines**
29 Apr 1954	Nonaggression treaty with **China**
28 Feb 1956	Five-year agreement with **Indonesia** on mutual aid between air forces
3 Dec 1958	Naval cooperation agreement with **Indonesia**
3 June 1960	Agreement with **Indonesia** for military cooperation and mutual assistance in developing armies
19 Sep 1960	Indus Waters Treaty with **Pakistan,** settling dispute over allocation of waters of the Indus River System
23 July 1962	Declaration on the neutrality of **Laos** at Geneva
27 Nov 1962	Agreement for supply of arms by **Great Britain** only for defense against Chinese aggression
13 Jan 1965	Military assistance agreement with **United States**

10 Jan 1966	Declaration of conference with **Pakistan** at Tashkent on the restoration of "normal and peaceful relations"
19 Mar 1967	Border demarcation agreement with **Burma**
9 Aug 1971	Twenty-year treaty of peace, friendship and cooperation with **Soviet Union**
19 Mar 1972	Twenty-five-year defense agreement with **Bangladesh**
3 July 1972	Peace treaty with **Pakistan** signed at Simla
11 Dec 1972	Agreement with **Pakistan** defining "line of control" in Kashmir area
28 Aug 1973	Agreement with **Pakistan** on repatriation of prisoners of war
24 Sep 1974	Agreement with **Portugal** over Goa and other former Portuguese Indian territories
29 July 1987	Accord with **Sri Lanka** on future of its Tamil population
1992	Establishment of diplomatic relations with **Baltic states, Armenia, Georgia, Ukraine** and **Israel**
28 Jan 1993	Treaty of friendship and cooperation with **Russia**
7 Sep 1993	Border peace deal with **China** signed, reducing troop numbers and establishing a cease-fire line
22 Nov 1993	Diplomatic relations with **South Africa** reestablished

INDONESIA

15 Aug 1950	Agreement with **United States** for a program of military assistance
17 Apr 1959	Treaty of friendship with **Malaysia**
1 Apr 1961	Treaty of friendship with **China**
16 Aug 1962	Agreement with the **Netherlands** on Western New Guinea
5 Aug 1963	Manila Declaration concerning formation of confederation with **Malaya** and **Philippines**
8 Aug 1967	Association of South-East Asian Nations
17 Mar 1970	Treaty of friendship with **Malaysia**
18 Aug 1970	Exchange of notes with **United States** on furnishing of combat equipment to Indonesia
15 Feb 1972	Agreement with **Philippines** on military cooperation
4 Apr 1972	Agreement with **Singapore** on status and supervision of Straits of Malacca
6 Apr 1972	Agreement with **Malaysia** on closer antiguerrilla cooperation in border areas (revised agreement 3 December 1984)

11 Mar 1975	Border cooperation and control agreements with Philippines
25 Feb 1982	Maritime treaty with **Malaysia**
Aug 1990	Diplomatic relations restored with **China**

IRAN

23 May 1950	Mutual defense assistance agreement with **United States**
3 Nov 1955	Baghdad Pact
5 Mar 1959	Cooperation agreement with **United States**
4 Mar 1975	Five-year economic and military aid agreement with **United States**
13 June 1975	Reconciliation treaty with **Iraq** (abrogated by Iraq on 17 September 1980)
12 Apr 1982	Political and economic cooperation agreement with **South Yemen**
12 Dec 1986	Economic cooperation agreement with **Soviet Union**
5 May 1987	Nuclear cooperation agreement with **Argentina**
14 Oct 1990	Agreement with **Iraq** to restore diplomatic relations
24 Mar 1991	Diplomatic relations with **Saudi Arabia** restored
1992	Embassies established in **Azerbaijan, Tajikistan** and **Turkmenistan**
Feb 1994	Agreement on military and nuclear cooperation with North Korea

IRAQ

24 Feb 1955	Baghdad Pact with **Turkey**
26 May 1964	Agreement with **Egypt** for the establishment of a joint presidency council and military command
4 June 1967	Defense pact with **Egypt** and **Jordan**
30 July 1969	Defense pact with **Syria**
9 Apr 1972	Fifteen-year treaty of friendship and cooperation with **Soviet Union**
13 June 1975	Reconciliation treaty with **Iran** (abrogated by Iraq on 17 September 1980)
26 Oct 1978	National Charter for joint action agreed on with **Syria** (abandoned in 1979)
26 Dec 1981	Boundary agreement with **Saudi Arabia**
15 Feb 1989	Formation of Arab Cooperation Council with **Egypt, Jordan** and **North Yemen**
27 Mar 1989	Nonaggression pact with **Saudi Arabia**
14 Oct 1990	Agreement with **Iran** to restore diplomatic relations

27–28 Feb 1991	Cease-fire with Allies after Gulf War (following invasion of Kuwait)
19 July 1993	Iraq accepts UN weapons monitoring

ISRAEL

23 July 1952	Mutual defense assistance agreement with **United States**
11 Nov 1973	Agreement with **Egypt** on a cease-fire line
18 Jan 1974	Agreement with **Egypt** for disengagement of forces on the Suez Canal
5 June 1974	Agreement with **Syria** for disengagement of forces on the Golan Heights
1 Sep 1975	Agreement with **United States** concerning the establishment of an early-warning system in Sinai
4 Sep 1975	Agreement with **Egypt** for an Israeli withdrawal in Sinai and the establishment of a buffer zone
17 Sep 1978	Camp David agreements with **Egypt** for conclusion of peace treaty and overall Middle East settlement
26 Mar 1979	Peace treaty with **Egypt**
10 July 1981	Agreement with **Egypt** and **United States** on a peace-keeping force for Sinai
30 Nov 1981	Strategic cooperation agreement with **United States** to deter threats to peace and security in the Middle East
19 Jan 1982	Agreement with **Egypt** on withdrawal from Sinai
20 Jan 1983	Five-year military cooperation agreement with **Zaïre**
17 May 1983	Accord with **Lebanon** on withdrawal of Israeli forces (not effective)
14 Dec 1987	Ten-year special military trade status agreement with **United States**
18 Oct 1991	Diplomatic relations established with **Soviet Union**
May 1992	Diplomatic relations established with **Nigeria**
1992	Diplomatic relations established with **India**
9 Sep 1993	Israel recognizes **Palestine Liberation Organization**, followed by historic peace accord in Washington
30 Dec 1993	Israel and the **Vatican** agree to establish diplomatic relations (full agreement June 1994)
4 May 1994	Israel and the **PLO** sign agreement on limited self-rule for Gaza and Jericho
24 Sep 1995	Israel and Palestine agree on transferring West Bank to Arabs
16 Jan 1997	Hebron agreement signed; Israel gives up large part of West Bank city of Hebron to **Palestine**

23 Oct 1998	Wynes Mill Agreement between Israel and **Palestine** moves Middle East peace talks forward
4 Sep 1999	Israeli prime minister Ehud Barak and **PLO** leader Yasir Arafat announce peace accord
17 Jan 2000	Israel and **Syria** postpone peace talks

ITALY

5 Sep 1946	Agreement with **Austria** on South Tyrol
10 Feb 1947	Peace treaty with the Allied powers
4 Apr 1949	North Atlantic Treaty
27 Jan 1950	Mutual defense assistance agreement with **United States**
5 Oct 1954	Agreement with **Yugoslavia** on status of Trieste
23 Oct 1954	Paris agreements for creation of Western European Union
30 Mar 1959	Agreement with **United States** on equipping Italian armed forces with intermediate-range ballistic missiles
7 July 1960	Agreement with **United States** on a weapons-production program
1 Aug 1975	Final Act of the Helsinki Conference on security and cooperation in Europe
1 Oct 1975	Treaty of Osimo with **Yugoslavia** finalizing their border around Trieste
11 Sep 1978	Memorandum of understanding with **United States** concerning the principles governing mutual cooperation for defense equipment
15 Sep 1980	Agreement with **Malta** on the island's neutrality
7 Apr 1985	Military cooperation agreement with **China**
Dec 1991	Maastricht Treaty on European union
June 1992	Agreement with **Austria** over autonomy for Trentino–Alto Adige (South Tyrol) ending 32-year dispute
1 Nov 1993	Maastricht Treaty takes effect, creating the European Union

JAPAN

8 Sep 1951	Peace treaty with the Allied powers
8 Mar 1954	Mutual defense assistance agreement with **United States**
20 Jan 1958	Reparations agreement with **Indonesia**
13 May 1959	Reparations agreement with **South Vietnam**
19 Jan 1960	Treaty of mutual cooperation and security with **United States**

9 Dec 1960	Treaty of friendship, commerce and navigation with **Philippines**
22 June 1965	Treaty on basic relations with **South Korea**
16 June 1966	Japan joins the Asian and Pacific Council
5 Apr 1968	Agreement with **United States** for the return to Japan of Bonin and Volcano Islands, together with Rosario, Parece and Marcus Islands
17 June 1971	Agreement with **United States** for transfer of sovereignty over Ryukyu Islands
16 June 1976	Treaty of friendship and cooperation with **Australia**
10 Aug 1977	Agreement to promote political, economic and cultural cooperation with **Malaysia**
12 Aug 1978	Treaty of peace and friendship with **China**
10 May 1979	Revised treaty of friendship, commerce and navigation with **Philippines**
26 Dec 1984	Agreement with **United States** on a joint military operational plan
24 Sep 1990	Agreement with **South Korea** settling differences arising from World War II
Jan 1992	Diplomatic relations established with **South Africa**
6 Nov 1992	Normalization of economic ties with **Vietnam**

JORDAN

29 Aug 1962	Agreements with **Saudi Arabia** on military, political and economic cooperation
30 May 1967	Defense pact with **Egypt** (joined by **Iraq** on 4 June 1967)
18 June 1974	Declaration on military cooperation with **United States**
12 June 1975	Agreement with **Syria** for coordination of military, political, economic and cultural policies
19 Feb 1976	Agreement for mutual cooperation with **Syria**
23 Feb 1977	Exchange of notes with **United States** on the furnishing of defense articles and services
27 Aug 1979	Exchange of notes with **United States** on the grant of defense articles and services under the military assistance program
15 Feb 1989	Formation of Arab Cooperation Council with **Iraq, Egypt** and **North Yemen**

KAMPUCHEA (CAMBODIA)

23 Dec 1950	Agreement with **France, Laos, Vietnam** and **United States** for mutual defense assistance in Indochina
21 July 1954	Geneva Agreements on Indochina

27 Nov 1960	Treaty of friendship and cooperation with **Czechoslovakia**
19 Dec 1960	Treaty of friendship and cooperation with **China**
23 July 1962	Declaration on the neutrality of **Laos** at Geneva
28 May 1978	Treaty of friendship and cooperation with **Romania**
18 Feb 1979	Treaty of peace, friendship and cooperation with **Vietnam**
7 July 1982	Agreement with **Vietnam** defining territorial waters
20 July 1983	Border treaty with **Vietnam**
23 Oct 1991	Peace agreement signed in Paris designed to end 13-year civil war. United Nations is mandated to supervise the peace and prepare for elections in 1993
Mar 1994	Diplomatic relations established with the **Vatican**

KENYA

6 May 1964	Defense agreement with **Great Britain**
28 Oct 1967	Declaration of Arusha ending border war with **Somalia**
9 June 1970	Border treaty with **Ethiopia**
31 Jan 1979	Treaty of friendship and cooperation with **Ethiopia**
26 June 1980	Military cooperation and aid agreement with **United States**
29 June 1981	Cooperation agreement with **Somalia**
2 Dec 1984	Border security agreement with **Somalia**

KOREA, NORTH

27 July 1953	Panmunjom armistice
6 July 1961	Treaty of friendship, cooperation and mutual assistance with **Soviet Union**
11 July 1961	Treaty of friendship, cooperation and mutual assistance with **China**
9 Nov 1979	Twenty-year treaty of friendship and cooperation with **Guinea-Bissau**
12 Oct 1980	Twenty-year treaty of friendship and cooperation with **Guinea**
12 Oct 1980	Ten-year treaty of friendship and cooperation with **Zimbabwe**
19 Oct 1981	Treaty of friendship and cooperation with **Angola**
1984	Treaty of peace and friendship with **East Germany**
1984	Treaty of peace and friendship with **Bulgaria**
11 Oct 1984	Treaty of friendship and cooperation with **South Yemen**

24 Oct 1984	Agreement with **Nigeria** on establishment of joint defense program
17 Sep 1991	North Korea takes seat at United Nations
12 Dec 1991	Draft nonaggression pact with **South Korea** agreed on
1991	Restoration of diplomatic relations with **Thailand.** Trade agreements with **Indonesia** and **Malaysia**
1992	Establishment of diplomatic relations with **Philippines**
Feb 1994	Agreement on military and nuclear cooperation with **Iran**

KOREA, SOUTH

26 Jan 1950	Mutual defense assistance agreement with **United States**
27 July 1953	Panmunjom armistice
1 Oct 1953	Mutual defense treaty with the **United States**
22 June 1965	Treaty on basic relations with **Japan**
16 June 1966	Member of Asian and **Pacific Council**
2 July 1981	Military and economic cooperation agreements with **Singapore**
1990	Diplomatic relations established with **Bulgaria, Czechoslovakia, Mongolia** and **Romania**
17 Sep 1991	South Korea takes seat at United Nations
12 Dec 1991	Draft nonaggression pact with **North Korea** agreed on
1 Jan 1992	Pact with **North Korea** banning nuclear weapons from Korean peninsula
24 Aug 1992	Diplomatic relations established with **China**
22 Nov 1992	Diplomatic relations with **Vietnam** established

LAOS

23 Dec 1950	Mutual defense assistance agreement with **United States, France, Cambodia** and **Vietnam**
31 Dec 1951	Agreement with **United States** on economic and military aid
21 July 1954	Geneva Agreements on Indochina
23 July 1962	Declaration on the neutrality of **Laos** at Geneva
21 Feb 1973	Peace treaty with the Pathet Lao insurgents
18 July 1977	Twenty-five-year treaty of friendship with **Vietnam**
4 Oct 1979	Treaty of friendship and cooperation with **Bulgaria**
8 Dec 1979	Treaty of friendship and cooperation with **Mongolia**
17 Feb 1980	Treaty of friendship and cooperation with **Czechoslovakia**
22 Sep 1982	Twenty-five-year treaty of friendship and cooperation with **East Germany**

LIBYA

29 July 1953	Twenty-year treaty of friendship and alliance with **Great Britain**
9 Sep 1954	Agreement with **United States** on military bases
30 June 1957	Military assistance agreement with **United States**
10 Apr 1969	Treaty of solidarity with **Algeria**
13 Dec 1969	Agreement with **Great Britain** for British withdrawal from Libyan bases
5 Nov 1970	Agreement on political federation with **Egypt** and **Sudan**
20 Aug 1971	Agreement with **Egypt** and **Syria** to establish Federation of Arab Republics
24 Aug 1973	Ten-year treaty of friendship and cooperation with **Burundi**
12 Jan 1974	Agreement for merger with **Tunisia** (not implemented)
9 Mar 1974	Defense and security treaty with **Niger**
29 Oct 1975	Treaty of friendship and cooperation with **Cameroon**
Dec 1975	Defense agreement with **Algeria**
5 Jan 1976	Treaty of mutual defense and assistance with **Togo**
8 Apr 1976	Agreement for increased regional cooperation with **Algeria** and **Niger**
17 Mar 1980	Defense pact with **Malta**
15 June 1980	Treaty of friendship with **Chad**
10 Oct 1980	Formation with **Syria** of the "Arab Masses State"
19 Aug 1981	Trilateral treaty of friendship and cooperation with **Ethiopia** and **South Yemen**
9 Sep 1982	Treaty of friendship and cooperation with **Czechoslovakia**
24 Jan 1983	Treaty of friendship and cooperation with **Romania**
Jan 1983	Treaty of friendship and cooperation with **Bulgaria**
27 Mar 1983	Cooperation agreement with **Algeria**
13 Aug 1984	Treaty of federation with **Morocco** (abrogated by Morocco on 29 August 1986)
17 Sep 1984	Agreement with **France** on mutual withdrawal of troops from Chad
18 Nov 1984	Five-year treaty of security and economic cooperation with **Malta**
22 May 1988	Economic and social cooperation pact with **Tunisia**
15 Feb 1989	Treaty creating Arab Maghreb Union signed with **Algeria, Tunisia, Mauritania** and **Morocco**
31 Aug 1989	Agreement with **Chad**, referring dispute over Aouzou Strip to international arbitration
31 Aug 1990	Agreement for integration with **Sudan**

MALAYSIA

12 Oct 1957	Treaty of defense and mutual assistance with **Great Britain**
17 Apr 1959	Treaty of friendship with **Indonesia**
31 July 1961	Association of South-East Asia formed with **Thailand** and **Philippines** (dissolved 29 August 1967)
5 Aug 1963	Manila Declaration concerning formation of confederation with **Indonesia** and **Philippines**
1 June 1966	Agreement with **Indonesia** ending "confrontation"
16 June 1966	Member of Asian and Pacific Council
8 Aug 1967	Member of Association of South-East Asian Nations (further treaty on 24 February 1976)
11 Nov 1969	Agreement with **Thailand** to establish a joint command to combat insurgents on their border
7 Mar 1970	Agreement with **Thailand** for military cooperation against insurgents operating on their border
17 Mar 1970	Treaty of friendship with **Indonesia**
9 Jan 1971	Agreement with **Great Britain, Australia, New Zealand** and **Singapore** on five-power arrangements for defense of Malaysia and Singapore
6 Apr 1972	Agreement with **Indonesia** on closer antiguerrilla cooperation
4 Mar 1977	Agreement with **Thailand** for combined operations against communist guerrillas
10 Aug 1977	Agreement with **Japan** to promote political, economic and cultural cooperation
25 Feb 1982	Maritime treaty with **Indonesia**
June 1983	Agreement with **Thailand** on combined operations against guerrillas
3 Dec 1984	Revised security accord with **Indonesia**
1991	Trade agreement with **North Korea**

MEXICO

1 Jan 1994	North American Free Trade Agreement (NAFTA) takes effect, eliminating restrictions on the flow of goods, services and investment between the **United States, Canada** and Mexico

MOZAMBIQUE

7 Sep 1974	Agreement on independence from **Portugal**
7 Sep 1975	Cooperation agreement with **Tanzania**
Oct 1975	Cooperation agreement with **Portugal**

20 Nov 1976	Agreement with **Angola, Tanzania** and **Zambia** for a joint defense strategy
31 Mar 1977	Treaty of friendship with **Soviet Union**
24 Feb 1979	Twenty-year treaty of friendship and cooperation with **East Germany**
20 Apr 1979	Treaty of friendship and cooperation with **Romania**
26 May 1979	Protocol for military cooperation with **East Germany**
23 May 1980	Military cooperation agreement with **Zimbabwe**
21 Oct 1981	Treaty of friendship with **Czechoslovakia**
15 Feb 1982	Military and economic cooperation agreement with **Tanzania**
16 Mar 1984	Nkomati Accord (nonaggression pact) with **South Africa**
23 Oct 1984	Defense and security cooperation agreement with **Malawi**
4 Oct 1992	Formal signature of peace treaty with Renamo (Mozambique National Resistance) ending civil war (preliminary accord reached in August)

NETHERLANDS

17 Mar 1948	Brussels Treaty
4 Apr 1949	North Atlantic Treaty
27 Jan 1950	Mutual defense assistance agreement with **United States**
13 Aug 1954	Agreement with **United States** on stationing of U.S. armed forces in the Netherlands
23 Oct 1954	Paris agreements for creation of Western European Union
13 June 1956	Paris agreement with **Great Britain** on the convention on foreign forces stationed in Germany
13 Apr 1957	Agreement with **Canada** on extension of NATO air-crew training program
10 July 1957	Agreement with **West Germany** on cost of maintenance of Dutch forces in the Federal Republic
6 May 1959	Agreement with **United States** on cooperation in the use of atomic energy for defense purposes
24 Mar 1960	Agreement with **United States** on a weapons-production program
1 Aug 1975	Final Act of the Helsinki Conference on security and cooperation in Europe
24 Aug 1978	Memorandum of understanding with **United States** concerning principles governing mutual cooperation for defense equipment

4 Nov 1985	Agreement with **United States** on deployment of cruise missiles
19 June 1990	Treaty abolishing all internal borders signed with **Belgium, France, West Germany** and **Luxembourg**
11 Dec 1991	Maastricht Treaty on European union
16 Dec 1993	The Netherlands recognizes independence of **Macedonia**

NEW ZEALAND

1 Sep 1951	Pacific Security Treaty (ANZUS Pact) with **United States** and **Australia**
19 June 1952	Mutual defense assistance agreement with **United States**
8 Sep 1954	South-East Asia Collective Defense Treaty
16 June 1966	Member of the Asian and Pacific Council
28 Aug 1969	Memorandum of understanding with **Australia** on joint defense planning and arms purchase
9 Jan 1971	Agreement with **Great Britain, Australia, Malaysia** and **Singapore** on five-power arrangements for defense of Malaysia and Singapore
26 Feb 1982	Memorandum of understanding with **United States** setting out procedures for providing New Zealand with logistic support in event of emergency

NIGERIA

20 Nov 1960	Defense agreement with **Great Britain** (abrogated by joint decision on 21 January 1962)
11 Dec 1972	Treaty of friendship, cooperation and mutual assistance with **Chad**
3 Mar 1973	Treaty of cooperation and mutual assistance with **Mali**
5 June 1981	Cooperation agreement with **Somalia**
24 Oct 1984	Agreement with **North Korea** on the establishment of joint defense programs
10 Dec 1984	Cooperation agreements with **Ghana, Benin** and **Togo**
May 1992	Diplomatic relations established with **Israel**

NORWAY

4 Apr 1949	North Atlantic Treaty
27 Jan 1950	Mutual defense assistance agreement with **United States**
30 Oct 1957	Agreement with **West Germany** on delivery of armament spare parts

13 Feb 1960	Agreement with **United States** on a weapons production program
24 May 1960	Agreement with **Canada** on the exchange of defense information
1 Aug 1975	Final Act of the Helsinki Conference on security and cooperation in Europe
16 Jan 1981	Agreement with **United States** on stockpiling of military equipment for a U.S. marine brigade in Norway

PAKISTAN

30 Aug 1950	Treaty of friendship with **Syria**
25 June 1952	Treaty of peace and friendship with **Burma**
2 Apr 1954	Treaty of friendly cooperation with **Turkey**
8 Sep 1954	South-East Asia Collective Defense Treaty
23 Sep 1955	Pakistan joined the Baghdad Pact
8 July 1957	Treaty of friendship with **Spain**
28 Aug 1958	Treaty of friendship with **Thailand**
5 Mar 1959	Treaty of defense and cooperation with **United States**
19 Sep 1960	Indus Waters Treaty with **India**, settling dispute over allocation of the waters of the Indus River System
2 Mar 1963	Border treaty with **China**
21 July 1964	Regional cooperation for development initiated by **Iran** and **Turkey**
26 Mar 1965	Border treaty with **China**
10 Jan 1966	Declaration of conference with **India** at Tashkent on restoration of "normal and peaceful relations"
3 July 1972	Peace treaty with **India** agreed to at Simla
11 Dec 1972	Agreement with **India** defining the "line of control" in Kashmir area
28 Aug 1973	Agreement with **India** on repatriation of prisoners of war
14 May 1988	Geneva accord with **Afghanistan,** guaranteed by **United States** and **Soviet Union,** for noninterference in each other's affairs

PHILIPPINES

14 Mar 1947	Agreement with **United States** concerning military bases
11 July 1952	Treaty of peace and amity with **India**
30 Aug 1951	Mutual defense treaty with **United States**
26 June 1953	Military assistance agreement with **United States**
8 Sep 1954	South-East Asia Collective Defense Treaty
27 Apr 1955	Military assistance agreement with **United States**

15 May 1958	Agreement with **United States** for establishment of a Mutual Defense Board
9 Dec 1960	Treaty of friendship, trade and navigation with **Japan**
31 July 1961	Association of South-East Asia formed with **Malaya** and **Thailand** (dissolved 29 August 1967)
5 Aug 1963	Manila Declaration concerning formation of confederation with **Malaya** and **Indonesia**
16 June 1966	Member of Asian and Pacific Council
8 Aug 1967	Member of Association of South-East Asian Nations
15 Feb 1972	Agreement on military cooperation with **Indonesia**
11 Mar 1975	Border cooperation and control agreements with **Indonesia**
6 Jan 1979	Agreement with **United States** for continued use of bases
10 May 1979	Revised treaty of friendship, trade and navigation with **Japan**
1 June 1983	Agreement with **United States** for continued use of bases
27 Aug 1991	Further agreement with **United States** over future of naval bases
1992	Diplomatic relations established with **North Korea**
24 Nov 1992	U.S. forces turn over the Subic Bay naval base to the Philippines, ending nearly a century of American military presence

POLAND

21 Apr 1945	Treaty of friendship, cooperation and mutual assistance with **Soviet Union**
18 Mar 1946	Twenty-year treaty of friendship and cooperation with **Yugoslavia** (abrogated by Poland on 9 September 1949)
10 Mar 1947	Twenty-year treaty of friendship and cooperation with **Czechoslovakia**
29 May 1948	Twenty-year treaty of friendship and cooperation with **Bulgaria**
26 Jan 1949	Twenty-year treaty of friendship and cooperation with **Romania**
7 June 1950	Agreement with **East Germany** on the Oder-Neisse frontier
14 May 1955	Warsaw Pact
17 Dec 1956	Treaty with **Soviet Union** on stationing of Soviet troops in Poland
23 July 1962	Declaration on the neutrality of **Laos** at Geneva

8 Apr 1965	Treaty of friendship and mutual assistance with **Soviet Union**
1 Mar 1967	Treaty of friendship and mutual assistance with **Czechoslovakia**
15 Mar 1967	Treaty of friendship and mutual assistance with **East Germany**
6 Apr 1967	Treaty of friendship and mutual assistance with **Bulgaria**
16 May 1968	Treaty of friendship and mutual assistance with **Hungary**
12 Nov 1970	Treaty of friendship and mutual assistance with **Romania**
7 Dec 1970	Agreement for the normalization of relations with **West Germany**
20 June 1975	Declaration on the principles of friendly cooperation with **France**
1 Aug 1975	Final Act of the Helsinki Conference on security and cooperation in Europe
28 May 1977	Treaty of friendship and cooperation with **East Germany**
12 Dec 1979	Treaty of friendship and cooperation with **Ethiopia**
July 1989	Agreement with the **Vatican** to resume diplomatic relations
12 Mar 1999	**Czech Republic,** Poland and **Hungary** join NATO

PORTUGAL

4 Apr 1949	North Atlantic Treaty
5 Jan 1951	Mutual defense assistance agreement with **United States**
6 Sep 1951	Agreement with **United States** defining grant of facilities in the Azores
26 Sep 1960	Agreement with **United States** on a weapons production program
9 Apr 1964	Agreement with **France** on setting up a French tracking station for ballistic missiles in the Azores
9 Dec 1971	Agreement with **United States** for the use of Azores base until February 1974
26 Aug 1974	Agreement for independence of **Guinea-Bissau**
7 Sep 1974	Agreement for independence of **Mozambique**
28 Sep 1974	Agreement with **India** over Goa and other former Portuguese Indian territories
15 Jan 1975	Agreement for independence of **Angola**

5 July 1975	Friendship and cooperation agreement with **Cape Verde**
1 Aug 1975	Final Act of the Helsinki Conference on security and cooperation in Europe
Oct 1975	General cooperation agreement with **Mozambique**
22 Nov 1977	Friendship and cooperation treaty with **Spain**
Jan 1978	Cooperation agreements with **Guinea-Bissau**
26 June 1978	Three-year friendship and cooperation agreement with **Angola**
28 Mar 1979	Memorandum of understanding with **United States** concerning principles governing mutual cooperation in defense equipment
18 June 1979	Agreement with **United States** for use of Azores base until February 1983
27 Aug 1979	Exchange of notes with **United States** concerning grant of defense articles and services under the military assistance program
13 Dec 1983	Agreement with **United States** for use of military base in Azores for further seven years
Apr 1985	Agreement with **France** to extend French missile-tracking station in the Azores for 12 years
13 Apr 1987	Agreement with **China** on the return of Macao in 1999
Dec 1991	Maastricht Treaty on European union
1 Nov 1993	Maastricht Treaty takes effect, creating the European Union

ROMANIA

10 Feb 1947	Peace treaty with the Allied powers
19 Dec 1947	Twenty-year treaty of friendship and cooperation with **Yugoslavia** (abrogated by Romania on 2 October 1949)
16 Jan 1948	Twenty-year treaty of friendship and cooperation with **Bulgaria**
24 Jan 1948	Twenty-year treaty of friendship and cooperation with **Hungary**
4 Feb 1948	Treaty of friendship, cooperation and mutual assistance with **Soviet Union**
21 July 1948	Twenty-year treaty of friendship and cooperation with **Czechoslovakia**
26 Jan 1949	Twenty-year treaty of friendship and cooperation with **Poland**

14 May 1955	Warsaw Pact
15 Apr 1957	Treaty with **Soviet Union** on stationing of Soviet troops in Romania
16 Aug 1968	Treaty of friendship and mutual assistance with **Czechoslovakia**
7 July 1970	Treaty of friendship and mutual assistance with **Soviet Union**
12 Nov 1970	Treaty of friendship and mutual assistance with **Poland**
19 Nov 1970	Treaty of friendship and mutual assistance with **Bulgaria**
15 June 1971	Agreement with **Greece** to respect frontiers
24 Feb 1972	Treaty of friendship and mutual assistance with **Hungary**
12 May 1972	Treaty of friendship and mutual assistance with **East Germany**
1 Aug 1975	Final Act of the Helsinki Conference on security and cooperation in Europe
29 June 1977	Cooperation agreement with **West Germany**
28 May 1978	Treaty of friendship and cooperation with **Kampuchea**
11 Apr 1979	Treaty of friendship and cooperation with **Gabon**
14 Apr 1979	Treaty of friendship and cooperation with **Angola**
17 Apr 1979	Treaty of friendship and cooperation with **Zambia**
20 Apr 1979	Treaty of friendship and cooperation with **Mozambique**
23 Apr 1979	Treaty of friendship and cooperation with **Burundi**
25 Apr 1979	Treaty of friendship and cooperation with **Sudan**
19 Mar 1980	Treaty of friendship and cooperation with **Zaïre**
24 Jan 1983	Treaty of friendship and cooperation with **Libya**
17 June 1983	Treaty of friendship and cooperation with **Mongolia**

RUSSIA

7 Feb 1992	Solidarity pact signed with **France**
3 Aug 1992	Agreement with **Ukraine** on division of Black Sea fleet
Sep 1992	Agreement with **Lithuania** for withdrawal of Russian troops
9 Nov 1992	Friendship treaty signed with **Great Britain**
1 Jan 1993	START II agreement between Boris Yeltsin and President Bush signed
28 Jan 1993	Treaty of friendship with **India**
30 April 1993	Treaty with **Latvia** on withdrawal of remaining Russian troops

18 June 1993	Further attempt to agree with **Ukraine** over division of Black Sea fleet
25 Aug 1993	Treaty on trade and energy with **Poland**. Russia apologizes for Katyn massacre
8 Sep 1993	Agreement with **United States** to increase military cooperation
13 Sep 1993	Agreement on anti-crime pact with **Italy**
21 June 1994	Agreement with **NATO** on Partnership for Peace
27 May 1996	Peace treaty signed to end war in **Chechnya**
12 May 1997	Russian president Yeltsin signs **Chechnya** peace treaty

SAUDI ARABIA

22 Mar 1945	Pact of the Union of Arab States (Arab League)
17 June 1950	Collective security pact with **Egypt, Syria, Lebanon** and **Yemen**
7 July 1952	Treaty of friendship with **West Germany**
27 June 1953	Agreement with **United States** for providing a military assistance advisory group
29 Aug 1962	Cooperation agreement with **Jordan**
24 Aug 1965	Agreement with **Egypt** for a cease-fire in the Yemen
30 Aug 1967	Agreement with **Egypt** on the Yemen
8 June 1974	Military and economic cooperation agreement with **United States**
19 July 1976	Gulf Organization for Development
27 Feb 1977	Exchange of notes with **United States** concerning the U.S. military training mission
4 Feb 1981	Gulf Co-operation Council
20 Dec 1981	Security agreement with **Bahrain**
26 Dec 1981	Boundary agreement with **Iraq**
9 Feb 1982	Joint military commission established with **United States**
14 Oct 1984	Five-year military cooperation agreement with **Brazil**
27 Mar 1989	Nonaggression pact with **Iraq**
24 Mar 1991	Diplomatic relations with **Iran** resumed
20 Dec 1992	Settlement of border dispute with **Qatar**

SERBIA

21 Nov 1995	**Bosnia,** Serbia and **Croatia** sign the Dayton Peace Accord to end the war in Bosnia
12 Oct 1998	NATO, on verge of air strikes, reaches settlement with Milosevic on Kosovo
9 June 1999	Serbs sign agreement to pull troops out of **Kosovo** after 11 weeks of NATO air attacks

SOMALIA

28 Oct 1967	Declaration of Arusha ending border war with **Kenya**
5 Sep 1968	Agreement with **Ethiopia** to end subversive activity
11 July 1974	Treaty of friendship and cooperation with **Soviet Union** (abrogated by Somalia on 13 November 1977)
29 Apr 1978	Exchange of notes with **United States** concerning furnishing of defense articles and services
22 Aug 1980	Military facilities agreement with **United States**
5 June 1981	Cooperation agreement with **Nigeria**
29 June 1981	Cooperation agreement with **Kenya**
2 Dec 1984	Border security agreement with **Kenya**

SOUTH AFRICA*

9 Nov 1951	Mutual defense assistance agreement with **United States**
4 July 1955	Simonstown naval cooperation agreement with **Great Britain** (revised January 1957; terminated 16 June 1975)
16 Feb 1984	Lusaka Accord with **Angola**
16 Mar 1984	Nkomati Accord with **Mozambique**
1992	South Africa signs nuclear nonproliferation treaty
Oct 1993	Diplomatic relations established with **Jordan** and **Swaziland**; end of UN economic sanctions
22 Nov 1993	Diplomatic relations with **India** reestablished

SPAIN

26 Sep 1953	Mutual defense assistance agreement with **United States**
22 June 1970	Five-year military cooperation agreement with **France**
6 Aug 1970	Treaty of friendship and cooperation with **United States,** extending use of U.S. bases in Spain until 1975
9 July 1974	Declaration with **United States** on principles of continued defense cooperation
1 Aug 1975	Final Act of the Helsinki Conference on security and cooperation in Europe

---

* South Africa also concluded agreements recognizing the "independence" of Transkei (1976), Bophuthatswana (1977), Venda (1979) and Ciskei (1981). Their independence was not recognized internationally.

5 Oct 1975	Agreement with **United States** on maintenance of U.S. bases and increased military aid
14 Nov 1975	Agreement with **Morocco** and **Mauritania** concerning the Western Sahara
24 Jan 1976	Treaty of friendship and cooperation with **United States**
12 May 1977	Agreement with **United States** on setting up combined military coordinating and planning staff
22 Nov 1977	Treaty of friendship and cooperation with **Portugal**
26 Sep 1981	Military cooperation agreement with **Equatorial Guinea**
30 May 1982	Spain becomes a member of NATO
28 Sep 1988	Eight-year pact with **United States,** providing it with three military bases
Dec 1991	Maastricht Treaty on European union
1 Nov 1993	Maastricht Treaty takes effect, creating the European Union

SUDAN

9 Jan 1956	Adherence to the Arab League
5 Nov 1970	Agreement on political federation with **Libya** and **Egypt** (joined by Iraq on 26 November 1970)
27 Mar 1972	Peace agreement between the government and Anyanya rebels
28 June 1972	Mutual defense and trade agreements with **Uganda**
2 Feb 1974	Agreement with **Egypt** on the coordination of political and economic strategies
15 July 1976	Twenty-five-year defense agreement with **Egypt**
Jan 1977	Defense agreement with **Egypt** of 1976 activated
28 Feb 1977	Defense agreement with **Egypt** and **Syria**
25 Apr 1979	Treaty of friendship and cooperation with **Romania**
17 Sep 1980	Military cooperation agreement with **France**
12 Oct 1982	Charter of political and economic integration with **Egypt** and close coordination of foreign policy, security and development
31 Aug 1990	Agreement for integration with **Libya**

SYRIA

22 Mar 1945	Pact of the Union of Arab States (Arab League)
17 June 1950	Collective security pact with **Egypt, Lebanon, Saudi Arabia** and **Yemen**
1 Feb 1958	Union with **Egypt** to form the United Arab Republic (dissolved 1961)

4 Nov 1966	Defense agreement with **Egypt**
30 July 1969	Defense pact with **Iraq**
26 Nov 1970	Syria joins **Libya, Sudan** and **Egypt** in proposed political federation
16 Mar 1971	Agreement with **Egypt** for a united military command
20 Aug 1971	Agreement for creation of Federation of Arab Republics with **Egypt** and **Libya**
14 May 1972	Military cooperation agreement with **Soviet Union**
5 June 1974	Agreement with **Israel** for disengagement of forces on the Golan Heights
12 June 1975	Agreement with **Jordan** for coordination of military, political, economic and cultural policies
19 Feb 1976	Economic and mutual cooperation pact with **Jordan**
21 Dec 1976	Agreement with **Egypt** on formation of a unified political command (joined by **Sudan** on 28 February 1977)
26 Oct 1978	National Charter for joint action with **Iraq** (abandoned in 1979)
8 Oct 1980	Twenty-year treaty of friendship and cooperation with **Soviet Union**
10 Oct 1980	Formation with **Libya** of the "Arab Masses State"
30 Apr 1985	Twenty-year treaty of friendship and cooperation with **Bulgaria**
17 Jan 2000	**Israel** and Syria postpone peace talks

TANZANIA

20 Feb 1965	Treaty of friendship with **China**
15 Nov 1969	Agreement with **China** and **Zambia** for building of Tan-Zam railway
6 May 1970	Agreement with **China** on a naval base at Dar es Salaam
5 Oct 1972	Peace treaty with **Uganda**
7 Sep 1975	Cooperation agreement with **Mozambique**
20 Nov 1976	Agreement with **Angola, Mozambique** and **Zambia** for a joint defense strategy
5 Dec 1980	Treaty of friendship and cooperation with **Zimbabwe**
16 Oct 1981	Agreement on mutual military cooperation with **Bulgaria**
15 Feb 1982	Military and economic cooperation agreement with **Mozambique**

THAILAND

1 Jan 1946	Peace treaty with **Great Britain** and **India**
17 Oct 1950	Military assistance agreement with **United States**

8 Sep 1954	South-East Asia Collective Defense Treaty
31 July 1961	Formation with **Malaya** and **Philippines** of Association of South-East Asia (dissolved on 29 August 1967)
6 Mar 1962	Declaration with **United States** on support against aggression
23 July 1962	Declaration on neutrality of **Laos** at Geneva
16 June 1966	Member of Asian and Pacific Council
8 Aug 1967	Member of Association of South-East Asian Nations
7 Mar 1970	Agreement with **Malaysia** for combined operations against insurgents on their border
4 Mar 1977	Agreement with **Malaysia** for joint operations against insurgents
June 1983	Agreement with **Malaysia** for joint operations against guerrillas

TURKEY

12 July 1947	Military assistance agreement with **United States**
18 Feb 1952	Adherence to North Atlantic Treaty
2 Apr 1954	Agreement with **Pakistan** on friendly cooperation
23 June 1954	Agreement with **United States** on implementation of NATO agreement on status of forces
28 Oct 1959	Agreement with **United States** regarding introduction of modern weapons into defense forces in Turkey
2 Mar 1960	Agreement with **United States** on a weapons production program
3 July 1964	Regional Cooperation for Development pact formed with **Iran** and **Pakistan**
3 July 1969	Agreement with **United States** on use of American bases (abrogated by Turkey on 25 July 1975)
1 Aug 1975	Final Act of the Helsinki Conference on security and cooperation in Europe
26 Mar 1976	Agreement with **United States** for reopening American bases
25 June 1978	Treaty of friendship and cooperation with **Soviet Union**
31 Aug 1979	Exchange of notes with **United States** for reopening American bases
30 Mar 1980	Defense cooperation agreement with **United States**
29 Nov 1982	Agreement with **United States** on use of Turkish airfields
12 Dec 1986	Defense and economic cooperation agreement with **United States**

16 Mar 1987   Defense and economic cooperation agreement with
              United States
Jan 2000   **Greece** and Turkey sign series of agreements four years
              after their countries came close to war over tiny
              Aegean island. Accords cover range of areas includ-
              ing commerce, immigration and the environment

UNION OF SOVIET SOCIALIST REPUBLICS (until 1991)

11 Apr 1945   Treaty of friendship, cooperation and mutual assis-
              tance with **Yugoslavia** (abrogated by Soviet Union
              on 28 September 1949)
21 Apr 1945   Treaty of friendship, cooperation and mutual assis-
              tance with **Poland**
27 Feb 1946   Treaty of friendship and mutual assistance with
              Mongolia
4 Feb 1948   Treaty of friendship, cooperation and mutual assis-
              tance with **Romania**
18 Feb 1948   Treaty of friendship, cooperation and mutual assis-
              tance with **Hungary**
18 Mar 1948   Treaty of friendship, cooperation and mutual assis-
              tance with **Bulgaria**
6 Apr 1948   Mutual assistance pact with **Finland** (extended 19 Sep-
              tember 1955, 20 July 1970 and 6 June 1983)
14 Feb 1950   Treaty of friendship, alliance and mutual assistance
              with **China**
21 July 1954 Geneva Declaration on Indochina
12 Oct 1954   Agreement on political cooperation with **China**
14 May 1955   Warsaw Pact
20 Sep 1955   Treaty recognizing **East Germany** as a sovereign state
18 Dec 1955   Ten-year extension of 1931 treaty of neutrality and
              nonaggression with **Afghanistan** (further extensions
              6 August 1965 and 10 December 1975)
17 Dec 1956   Agreement with **Poland** on stationing of Soviet troops
12 Mar 1957   Agreement with **East Germany** on stationing of Soviet
              troops
15 Apr 1957   Agreement with **Romania** on stationing of Soviet
              troops
17 Apr 1957   Agreement with **Albania** on political cooperation and
              economic aid
27 May 1957   Agreement with **Hungary** on stationing of Soviet
              troops
6 July 1961   Treaty of friendship, cooperation and mutual assis-
              tance with **North Korea**

23 July 1962	Declaration on the neutrality of **Laos** at Geneva
20 June 1963	Memorandum of understanding with **United States** for establishment of a "Hot Line"
20 Apr 1964	Agreement with **United States** on reduction of fissionable materials production
12 June 1964	Treaty of friendship and mutual assistance with **East Germany**
8 Apr 1965	Treaty of friendship and mutual assistance with **Poland**
15 Jan 1966	Treaty of friendship, cooperation and mutual assistance with **Mongolia**
9 Nov 1966	Agreement with **France** on establishment of a "Hot Line"
12 May 1967	Treaty of friendship and mutual assistance with **Bulgaria**
25 Aug 1967	Agreement with **Great Britain** on establishment of a "Hot Line"
7 Sep 1967	Treaty of friendship and mutual assistance with **Hungary**
16 Oct 1968	Treaty with **Czechoslovakia** on temporary stationing of Soviet forces
8 Aug 1969	Agreement with **China** on the navigation of the Amur and Ussuri rivers
6 May 1970	Treaty of friendship and mutual assistance with **Czechoslovakia**
7 July 1970	Treaty of friendship and mutual assistance with **Romania**
12 Aug 1970	Treaty with **West Germany** renouncing the use of force
27 May 1971	Treaty of friendship with **Egypt** (abrogated by Egypt on 15 March 1976)
9 Aug 1971	Treaty of peace, friendship and cooperation with **India**
3 Sep 1971	Agreement with **United States, Great Britain** and **France** on Berlin
30 Sep 1971	Agreements with **United States** on modernizing the "Hot Line" and reducing the risk of nuclear accidents
29 Oct 1971	Agreement on principles of cooperation with **France**
9 Apr 1972	Fifteen-year treaty of friendship and cooperation with **Iraq**
14 May 1972	Military cooperation agreement with **Syria**
25 May 1972	Agreement with **United States** on prevention of incidents on and over the high seas
26 May 1972	SALT anti-ballistic missile agreement with **United States** and interim agreement on limitation of strategic arms

29 May 1972	Agreement with **United States** on the basic principles of relations between the two countries
5 Nov 1972	Agreement with **United States, Great Britain** and **France** on the maintenance of four-power rights and responsibilities in Germany
22 May 1973	Protocol agreement with **United States** on prevention of incidents on and over the high seas
21 June 1973	Agreement with **United States** on the basic principles of negotiations on the further limitation of strategic offensive arms
22 June 1973	Agreement with **United States** on the prevention of nuclear war
3 July 1974	Protocol to the SALT ABM agreement with **United States** limiting ABM deployment to a single area
3 July 1974	Threshold test-ban treaty with **United States**
11 July 1974	Fifteen-year treaty of friendship and cooperation with **Somalia** (abrogated by Somalia on 13 November 1977)
17 Feb 1975	Declaration with **Great Britain** on the nonproliferation of nuclear weapons
1 Aug 1975	Final Act of the Helsinki Conference on peace and security in Europe
7 Oct 1975	Twenty-five-year treaty of friendship, cooperation and mutual assistance with **East Germany**
28 May 1976	Treaty with **United States** on peaceful nuclear explosions
16 July 1976	Exchange of letters with **France** on prevention of accidental nuclear war
8 Oct 1976	Twenty-year treaty of friendship and cooperation with **Angola**
20 Oct 1976	Agreement with **Mongolia** for closer cooperation
31 Mar 1977	Twenty-year treaty of friendship and cooperation with **Mozambique**
22 June 1977	Declaration with **France** on nonproliferation of nuclear weapons
10 Oct 1977	Agreement with **Great Britain** on prevention of accidental nuclear war
25 June 1978	Treaty of friendship and cooperation with **Turkey**
3 Nov 1978	Twenty-five-year treaty of friendship and cooperation with **Vietnam**
20 Nov 1978	Twenty-year treaty of friendship and cooperation with **Ethiopia**
5 Dec 1978	Treaty of friendship, good-neighborliness and cooperation with **Afghanistan**

28 Apr 1979	Agreement with **France** to promote peace and détente
18 June 1979	SALT II agreement with **United States** on limitation of strategic offensive arms (unratified by United States)
25 Oct 1979	Twenty-year treaty of friendship and cooperation with **South Yemen**
8 Oct 1980	Twenty-year treaty of friendship and cooperation with **Syria**
13 May 1981	Twenty-year treaty of friendship and cooperation with the **Congo**
17 July 1984	Agreement with **United States** to expand and improve the "Hot Line"
9 Oct 1984	Treaty of friendship and cooperation with **North Yemen**
6 Feb 1986	Five-year economic and industrial cooperation agreement with **Great Britain**
31 Mar 1986	Cooperation agreements with **Great Britain**
24 Apr 1986	Cooperation agreement with **Britain** on energy conservation and development
22 July 1986	Accords for cooperation in science and technology with **West Germany**
12 Dec 1986	Economic cooperation agreement with **Iran**
22 Apr 1987	Nuclear energy cooperation pact with **West Germany**
27 Feb 1990	Agreement with **Czechoslovakia** for withdrawal of Soviet forces by July 1991
10 Mar 1990	Agreement with **Hungary** for withdrawal of Soviet forces by July 1991
12 Sep 1990	Treaty on the Final Settlement with Respect to Germany signed with **East Germany, West Germany, France, Great Britain** and **United States**
13 Sep 1990	Treaty with **West Germany** for good-neighborliness, partnership and cooperation
6 Sep 1991	Soviet Union recognizes independence of Baltic states (**Estonia, Latvia, Lithuania**)
18 Oct 1991	Establishment of diplomatic relations with **Israel**

UNITED KINGDOM OF GREAT BRITAIN AND NORTHERN IRELAND

22 Mar 1946	Treaty with **Jordan**
4 Mar 1947	Treaty of Dunkirk: 50-year alliance with **France**
13 May 1947	Agreement with **Australia** for construction of Woomera rocket-testing range

28 Aug 1947	Defense agreement with **Burma** (abrogated by Burma on 3 January 1953)
27 Oct 1947	Agreement with **Chile** regarding military services (ended on 29 September 1959)
9 Nov 1947	Agreement with **Nepal** on employment of Gurkha trooops in the British army
11 Nov 1947	Defense agreement with **Ceylon**
15 Mar 1948	Twenty-year mutual defense treaty with **Jordan** (ended 14 March 1957)
17 Mar 1948	Treaty of Brussels
19 Apr 1948	Agreements with **France** regarding military facilities and air transit
12 Nov 1948	Defense agreement between Great Britain (acting on behalf of Fiji) and **New Zealand**
4 Apr 1949	North Atlantic Treaty
21 Dec 1949	Military service agreement with **France**
27 Jan 1950	Mutual defense assistance agreement with **United States**
21 July 1950	Agreement with **United States** on a long-range proving ground for guided missiles in the Bahamas
23 Oct 1950	Agreement with **United States, France** and **West Germany** on defense materials
30 Oct 1950	Treaty of peace and friendship with **Nepal**
15 Jan 1952	Agreement with **United States** extending the Bahamas long-range proving ground by additional sites in the Turks and Caicos Islands
6 Mar 1952	Military service agreement with **France**
26 May 1952	Convention on relations between **Great Britain, France, United States** and **West Germany**
3 July 1952	Agreement with **Ethiopia** on provision of facilities for military aircraft
9 Sep 1952	Agreement with **West Germany** on British bases (further agreements October 1954 and May 1957)
12 Nov 1952	Agreement with **Belgium** on establishment of a military base at Campine
1 Jan 1953	Agreement with **Maldive Islands** by which Great Britain retains the right to establish and maintain defense facilities
13 Mar 1953	Agreement with **Ethiopia** on provision of facilities at Asmara for British military aircraft
30 Mar 1953	Agreement with **Canada** and **Belgium** on transit and stationing of Canadian forces in Belgium
29 July 1953	Treaty of friendship and alliance with **Libya**
13 Sep 1953	Agreement with **Australia** to share the cost of maintaining the Woomera range

8 June 1954	Agreement with **United States** on a special program of facilities assistance for mutual defense purposes
21 July 1954	Geneva declarations on Indochina
31 July 1954	Military service agreement with **Chile**
8 Sep 1954	South-East Asia Collective Defense Treaty
23 Oct 1954	Paris agreements for creation of Western European Union
20 Jan 1955	Military service agreement with **Denmark**
4 Apr 1955	Britain joins the Baghdad Pact
4 Apr 1955	Agreement with **Australia** on a new atomic-testing ground to be known as Maralinga
5 Apr 1955	Military services agreement with **Brazil**
15 May 1955	Austrian State Treaty signed with **United States, Soviet Union, France** and **Austria**
15 June 1955	Agreement with **United States** on cooperation regarding atomic information for mutual defense purposes
4 July 1955	Simonstown naval cooperation agreement with **South Africa** (revised January 1967; ended 16 June 1975)
25 June 1956	Agreements with **United States** extending Bahamas long-range proving ground by additional sites in St. Lucia and Ascension Island (further agreements 25 August 1959, 7 July 1965 and 17 July 1967)
3 Jan 1957	Agreement with **Maldive Islands** on reestablishment of wartime airfield on Gan
4 Jan 1957	Agreement with **United States** on civil aviation and long-range proving grounds for guided missiles in the West Indies
1 Apr 1957	Agreement with **United States** extending Bahamas long-range proving ground to include island of Great Exuma
11 Apr 1957	Agreement with **West Germany** relating to the convention of 1952 on foreign forces stationed in Germany
7 June 1957	Agreement with **West Germany** on maintenance cost of British forces stationed in Germany (further agreements 3 October 1958 and 28 April 1967)
13 June 1957	Agreement with the **Netherlands** relating to convention of 1952 on foreign forces stationed in Germany
12 Oct 1957	Treaty of defense and mutual assistance with **Malaya**
22 Feb 1958	Agreement with **United States** on supply of intermediate-range ballistic missiles
3 July 1958	Agreement with **United States** on cooperation on uses of atomic energy for mutual defense purposes
25 July 1958	Agreement with **Muscat** and **Oman** for military and economic assistance
25 Aug 1958	Treaty of friendship with **Tonga**

11 Feb 1959	Treaty of friendship and protection with **Federation of Arab Emirates of the South**
19 Feb 1959	Agreements on Cyprus with **Greece, Turkey** and representatives of Greek and Turkish **Cypriots**
7 May 1959	Agreement with **United States** enabling Great Britain to purchase component parts of American atomic weapons and weapons systems, other than warheads, and allowing mutual transfer of nuclear materials
14 Feb 1960	Agreement with **Maldive Islands** granting Great Britain use of Gan airfield for 30 years retrospectively from December 1956 (confirmed under independence agreement of 26 July 1965)
15 Feb 1960	Agreement with **United States** on establishment and operation of a ballistic missile early-warning station at Fylingdales Moor
24 June 1960	Agreement with **United States** on the establishment in the Bahamas of a long-range aid-to-navigation station
7 July 1960	Treaty with **Cyprus** regarding British bases
1 Nov 1960	Agreement with **United States** to provide facilities for U.S. Polaris nuclear submarines at Holy Loch
20 Nov 1960	Defense agreement with **Nigeria** (abrogated by joint decision on 21 January 1962)
19 June 1961	Defense agreement with **Kuwait** (ended on 13 April 1968)
18 July 1961	Agreement with **United States** setting up a missile defense alarm system in the United Kingdom
29 June 1962	Agreement with **United States** on a weapons production program
23 July 1962	Declaration on neutrality of **Laos** at Geneva
27 Nov 1962	Agreement with **India** for supply of arms to be used against China only
6 Apr 1963	Agreement with **United States** on terms of sale of up to 100 Polaris missiles to Great Britain
3 Mar 1964	Defense agreement with **Uganda**
6 Mar 1964	Defense agreement with **Kenya**
21 Sep 1964	Ten-year defense agreement with **Malta** (abrogated by Malta on 30 June 1971)
31 Mar 1965	Agreement with **Jamaica** on training and development for her armed forces
17 Feb 1966	Settlement of territorial dispute with **Venezuela**
30 Dec 1966	Agreement with **United States** on availability of certain Indian Ocean islands for defense purposes

1 Apr 1967	Agreement with **United States** on joint use of British Indian Ocean Territory for defense purposes
25 Aug 1967	Agreement with **Soviet Union** for establishment of a "Hot Line"
12 Mar 1968	Defense agreement with **Mauritius**
15 Dec 1970	Agreement with **United States** to start work in 1971 on a naval communications station on the Indian Ocean island of Diego Garcia
9 Jan 1971	Agreement with **Australia, New Zealand, Malaysia** and **Singapore** on five-power arrangements for defense of Malaysia and Singapore
18 Mar 1971	Agreement with **West Germany** on troop-support costs
15 Aug 1971	Treaty of friendship with **Bahrain**
1 Sep 1971	Treaty of friendship with **Qatar**
3 Sep 1971	Agreement with **United States, Soviet Union** and **France** on Berlin
23 Nov 1971	Defense agreement with **Brunei**
2 Dec 1971	Treaty of friendship with **Union of Arab Emirates**
26 Mar 1972	Seven-year agreement with **Malta** and NATO on use of Maltese military facilities
5 Nov 1972	Agreement with **United States, France** and **Soviet Union** on maintenance of four-power rights and responsibilities in Germany
30 Mar 1973	Exchange of notes with **United States** on expanded use of Ascension Island
5 Feb 1974	Agreement with **United States** to expand military facilities at Indian Ocean base of Diego Garcia
17 Feb 1975	Declaration with **Soviet Union** on nonproliferation of nuclear weapons
1 Aug 1975	Final Act of the Helsinki Conference on security and cooperation in Europe
24 Sep 1975	Memorandum of understanding with **United States** on principles for defense equipment
25 Feb 1976	Exchange of notes with **United States** on an American naval support facility on Diego Garcia
10 Oct 1977	Agreement with **Soviet Union** on prevention of accidental nuclear war
18 Oct 1977	Agreement with **West Germany** to end after 1980 payments to offset British foreign exchange costs of stationing troops in Germany
14 Dec 1977	Agreement with **United States** on defense areas and facilities in Antigua
7 Jan 1979	Independence agreement with **Brunei**

12 Dec 1979	Agreement with **United States** on defense areas in the Turks and Caicos Islands
21 Dec 1979	Lancaster House agreements with representatives of Popular Front and Salisbury on future of **Zimbabwe**
2 Sep 1983	Defense agreement with **Greece**
17 Aug 1984	Military training agreement with **Uganda**
19 Dec 1984	Agreement with **China** on the future of Hong Kong
15 Nov 1985	Hillsborough agreement with **Irish Republic** on government of Northern Ireland
6 Feb 1986	Five-year economic and industrial cooperation agreement with **Soviet Union**
12 Feb 1986	Channel fixed-link treaty signed with **France**
24 Apr 1986	Cooperation agreement with **Soviet Union** on energy conservation and development
31 Mar 1987	Cooperation agreements with **Soviet Union**
Feb 1990	Agreement to restore diplomatic relations with **Argentina**
12 Sep 1990	Treaty on the Final Settlement with Respect to Germany signed with **East Germany, West Germany, France, United States** and **Soviet Union**
1991	Resumption of diplomatic relations with **Albania** and **Iran**
Dec 1991	Maastricht Treaty on European union (not ratified by parliament until 2 August 1993)
May 1992	Agreement with **Vietnam** on repatriation of up to 52,000 "boat people" from Hong Kong
9 Nov 1992	Friendship treaty signed with **Russia**
May 1993	Great Britain recognizes independence of **Eritrea**
Dec 1993	Great Britain recognizes independence of **Macedonia**
May 1994	Great Britain lifts 12-year-old arms embargo against **Israel**
20 May 1993	British Commons approves European unity pact
1 Nov 1993	Maastricht Treaty takes effect, creating the European Union
31 Aug 1994	IRA declares cease-fire in Northern Ireland
10 Apr 1998	Landmark peace settlement, the Good Friday Accord, reached in **Northern Ireland**
2 Dec 1999	New **Northern Ireland** government begins self-rule for first time in 25 years

UNITED STATES OF AMERICA

14 Mar 1947	Agreement with **Philippines** concerning U.S. military bases
3 Sep 1947	Agreement with **China** relating to the presence of U.S. armed forces

21 Feb 1949	Agreement with **Greece** on use of certain Greek islands for training exercises by U.S. Mediterranean fleet
4 Apr 1949	North Atlantic Treaty
26 Jan 1950	Mutual defense assistance agreement with **South Korea**
27 Jan 1950	Mutual defense assistance agreements under the North Atlantic Treaty with **Belgium, Great Britain, Denmark, France, Italy, Luxembourg,** the **Netherlands** and **Norway**
23 May 1950	Mutual defense assistance agreement with **Iran**
21 July 1950	Agreement with **Great Britain** concerning a long-range proving ground for guided missiles in the Bahamas
15 Aug 1950	Agreement with **Indonesia** for a program of military assistance
5 Jan 1951	Mutual defense assistance agreement with **Portugal**
20 Feb 1951	Mutual defense assistance agreement with **Australia**
27 Apr 1951	Agreement with **Denmark** concerning the defense of Greenland
5 May 1951	Defense agreement with **Iceland**
1 Aug 1951	Agreement with **Canada** relating to the extension and coordination of the continental radar defense system
30 Aug 1951	Security treaty for mutual defense with **Philippines**
1 Sep 1951	Pacific Security Treaty with **Australia** and **New Zealand** (ANZUS Pact)
6 Sep 1951	Defense agreement with **Portugal**
8 Sep 1951	Security treaty with **Japan**
9 Nov 1951	Mutual defense assistance agreement with **South Africa**
19 Nov 1951	Mutual defense assistance agreement with **Liberia**
20 Feb 1952	Military assistance agreement with **Ecuador**
22 Feb 1952	Military assistance agreement with **Peru**
15 Mar 1952	Military assistance agreement with **Brazil** (terminated by Brazil 11 March 1978)
9 Apr 1952	Military assistance agreement with **Chile**
17 Apr 1952	Military assistance agreement with **Colombia**
19 June 1952	Mutual defense assistance agreement with **New Zealand**
30 June 1952	Military assistance agreement with **Uruguay**
23 July 1952	Mutual defense assistance agreement with **Israel**
2 Mar 1953	Agreement with **Great Britain** concerning a long-range proving ground for guided missiles in the Bahamas
22 May 1953	Mutual defense assistance agreement with **Ethiopia**
27 June 1953	Agreement with **Saudi Arabia** for provision of a military assistance advisory group
5 July 1953	Agreement on military assistance with **Philippines**
27 July 1953	Panmunjom armistice in Korea

26 Sep 1953	Mutual defense assistance agreement with **Spain** (extended 26 September 1963)
1 Oct 1953	Mutual defense treaty with **South Korea**
12 Oct 1953	Agreement with **Greece** concerning military facilities
8 Mar 1954	Mutual defense assistance agreement with **Japan**
23 Apr 1954	Military assistance agreement with **Nicaragua**
14 May 1954	Agreement with **Ethiopia** on military bases
19 May 1954	Mutual defense assistance agreement with **Pakistan**
20 May 1954	Military assistance agreement with **Honduras**
23 June 1954	Agreement with **Turkey** concerning the implementation of NATO agreement on status of forces
21 July 1954	Geneva agreements on Indochina
8 Sep 1954	South-East Asia Collective Defense Treaty
9 Sep 1954	Agreement with **Libya** on military bases
23 Oct 1954	Paris agreements
16 Nov 1954	Agreement with the **Netherlands** on the stationing of U.S. troops
2 Dec 1954	Mutual defense treaty with **Nationalist China**
14 Dec 1954	Agreement with the **Netherlands** establishing an air defense technical center
28 Jan 1955	Military assistance agreement with **Haiti**
27 Apr 1955	Military assistance agreement with **Philippines**
5 May 1955	Agreement with **Canada** on establishment and operation of a distant early-warning system
18 June 1955	Military assistance agreement with **Guatemala**
30 June 1955	Mutual defense assistance agreement with **West Germany**
20 Sep 1955	Agreement with **Brazil** for continuation of joint military and defense commissions
20 Sep 1955	Agreement with **Colombia** on military advisors
26 Apr 1956	Agreement with **Honduras** on military advisors
25 June 1956	Agreement with **Great Britain** relating to the extension of the Bahamas long-range proving ground by the establishment of additional sites on Ascension Island
7 Sep 1956	Agreement with **Greece** on the status of U.S. forces
6 Dec 1956	Agreement with **Iceland** on the presence of defense forces in the country
12 Dec 1956	Agreement with **West Germany** on the training of German army and naval personnel
9 Feb 1957	Agreement with **Nicaragua** on military advisers
1 Apr 1957	Agreement with **Great Britain** concerning a long-range proving ground for guided missiles in the Bahamas
6 June 1957	Military assistance agreement with **Lebanon**
30 June 1957	Military assistance agreement with **Libya**

22 Feb 1958	Agreement with **Great Britain** for supply by United States of intermediate-range ballistic missiles
22 Apr 1958	Military assistance agreement with **Bolivia**
12 May 1958	Agreement with **Canada** on the organization and operation of the North American Air Defense Command (NORAD) (extended 30 March 1968, 12 May 1973, 8 May 1975, 12 May 1980 and 11 March 1981)
15 May 1958	Agreement with **Philippines** for the establishment of a mutual defense board
20 June 1958	Agreement with **Canada** relating to the establishment, maintenance and operation by United States of overall refueling facilities in Canada
28 July 1958	Adherence to Baghdad Pact
2 Sep 1958	Agreement with **Canada** for establishing a committee on joint defense
5 Mar 1959	Agreement for cooperation with **Turkey**
5 Mar 1959	Agreement for cooperation with **Iran**
5 Mar 1959	Agreement for cooperation with **Pakistan**
1 May 1959	Agreement with **Canada** relating to the establishment, maintenance and operation of short-range tactical air navigation facilities in Canada
8 July 1959	Agreement with **Liberia** on military cooperation.
13 July 1959	Agreement with **Canada** on the establishment of a ballistic missile early-warning system
25 Aug 1959	Agreement with **Great Britain** relating to the extension of the Bahamas long-range proving ground by the establishment of additional sites on Ascension Island
28 Oct 1959	Agreement with **Turkey** on the introduction of modern weapons into the NATO defense forces in Turkey
19 Jan 1960	Treaty of mutual cooperation and security with **Japan**
13 Feb 1960	Agreement with **Norway** on a weapons production program
15 Feb 1960	Agreement with **Greece** on a weapons production program
15 Feb 1960	Agreement with **Great Britain** relating to the establishment and operation of a ballistic missile early-warning station at Fylingdales Moor
2 Mar 1960	Agreement with **Turkey** on a weapons-production program
24 Mar 1960	Agreement with the **Netherlands** on a weapons-production program
27 May 1960	Agreement with **West Germany** on a weapons-production program

24 June 1960	Agreement with **Great Britain** concerning the establishment of a long-range aid-to-navigation station in the Bahamas
7 July 1960	Agreement with **Italy** on a weapons-production program
23 Aug 1960	Agreement with **Australia** on a mutual weapons development program
19 Sep 1960	Agreement with **France** on a weapons-production program
26 Sep 1960	Agreement with **Portugal** on a weapons-production program
2 Dec 1960	Agreement with **Denmark** on the defense of Greenland
31 Jan 1961	Agreement with **Norway** on a shipbuilding program for the Norwegian navy
3 Apr 1961	Agreement with **Colombia** relating to the furnishing of military equipment, materials and services
20 May 1961	Military assistance agreement with **Mali**
12 June 1961	Agreement with **Canada** for improving the air defense of the Canada–U.S. region of NATO
18 July 1961	Agreement with **Great Britain** for the setting up of a missile defense alarm station
27 July 1961	Agreement with **France** for cooperation in the use of atomic energy for mutual defense purposes
27 Sep 1961	Agreement with **Canada** on the extension and strengthening of the continental air-defense system
8 Mar 1962	Military assistance agreement with **Dominican Republic**
13 Apr 1962	Agreement with **El Salvador** on furnishing defense equipment and services to contribute to internal security
26 Apr 1962	Agreement with **Bolivia** on furnishing defense equipment and services
23 May 1962	Agreement with **Panama** on furnishing defense equipment and services
13 June 1962	Agreement with **Dahomey** on furnishing military equipment, materials and services to help assure security and independence
14 June 1962	Agreement with **Niger** on furnishing military equipment, materials and services to help assure security and independence
18 June 1962	Agreement with **Costa Rica** on furnishing defense equipment and services
29 June 1962	Agreement with **Great Britain** relating to a weapons-production program

20 July 1962	Agreement with **Senegal** on furnishing military equipment, materials and services
23 July 1962	Geneva declaration on the neutrality of **Laos**
2 Aug 1962	Agreement with **Guatemala** on furnishing defense equipment and services
25 Aug 1962	Military assistance agreement with **Paraguay**
24 Oct 1962	Military assistance agreement with **Honduras**
20 Dec 1962	Agreement with **Peru** on furnishing defense equipment and services
6 Apr 1963	Agreement with **Great Britain** on purchase of Polaris missiles
9 May 1963	Agreement with **Australia** relating to the establishment of a U.S. naval communications station
6 June 1963	Agreement with **Jamaica** on furnishing defense equipment and services
20 June 1963	Memorandum of understanding with **Soviet Union** on establishment of a "Hot Line"
19 July 1963	Military assistance agreement with **Congo**
15 Nov 1963	Agreement with **Canada** establishing a joint civil emergency planning committee
10 Feb 1964	Military assistance agreement with **Paraguay**
20 Apr 1964	Statement with **Soviet Union** on reduction of fissionable materials production
10 May 1964	Agreement with **Argentina** relating to a military assistance program
13 Jan 1965	Military assistance agreement with **India**
29 June 1965	Military assistance agreement with **Guinea**
11 Apr 1966	Military assistance agreement with **Paraguay**
26 May 1966	Agreement with **Guyana** on the future use of Atkinson Field
9 Dec 1966	Agreement with **Australia** on the establishment of a joint defense space research facility
30 Dec 1966	Agreement with **Great Britain** on the availability of certain Indian Ocean islands for defense purposes
1 Apr 1967	Agreement with **Great Britain** on the joint use of the British Indian Ocean Territory for defense purposes
5 Apr 1968	Agreement with **Japan** for return of Bonin and Volcano Islands, together with Rosario, Parece and Marcus Islands
3 July 1969	Agreement with **Turkey** on U.S. bases
10 Nov 1969	Agreement with **Australia** on the establishment of a joint defense space communications station
5 May 1970	Agreement with **Argentina** on armed forces cooperative projects

6 Aug 1970	Treaty of friendship and cooperation with **Spain**
19 Aug 1970	Exchange of notes with **Indonesia** on furnishing of combat equipment
17 June 1971	Agreement with **Japan** on transfer of sovereignty over the Ryukyu Islands
3 Sep 1971	Agreement with **Great Britain, France** and **Soviet Union** on Berlin
30 Sep 1971	Agreements with **Soviet Union** on modernization of the "Hot Line" and prevention of nuclear accidents
9 Dec 1971	Agreement with **Portugal** on the use of the Azores base until February 1974
10 Dec 1971	Agreement with **West Germany** on the maintenance costs of U.S. forces in Europe
23 Dec 1971	Agreement with **Bahrain** to establish a permanent U.S. naval facility
25 May 1972	Agreement with **Soviet Union** on prevention of incidents on and over the high seas
26 May 1972	SALT ABM agreement with **Soviet Union** and interim agreement on limitation of strategic arms
29 May 1972	Agreement with **Soviet Union** on basic principles of relations between the two countries
5 Nov 1972	Agreement with **Great Britain, France** and **Soviet Union** on maintenance of four-power rights and responsibilities in Germany
27 Jan 1973	Agreement to end the war and restore peace in Vietnam with **North** and **South Vietnam** and the **South Vietnamese Provisional Revolutionary Government**
30 Mar 1973	Exchange of notes with **Great Britain** for the expanded use of Ascension Island
22 May 1973	Protocol to agreement with **Soviet Union** on prevention of incidents on and over the high seas
21 June 1973	Agreement with **Soviet Union** on basic principles of negotiation on the further limitation of strategic offensive arms
22 June 1973	Agreement with **Soviet Union** on prevention of nuclear war
10 Jan 1974	Agreement with **Australia** on joint operation of the U.S. naval communications station at North-West Cape
25 Apr 1974	Agreement with **West Germany** on troop support costs
8 June 1974	Agreement with **Saudi Arabia** on cooperation in economics, technology, industry and defense
14 June 1974	Declaration on cooperation and friendship with **Egypt**
18 June 1974	Declaration with **Jordan** on military cooperation

3 July 1974	Protocol to SALT ABM agreement with **Soviet Union** limiting ABM deployment to one area
3 July 1974	Threshold test-ban treaty with **Soviet Union**
9 July 1974	Declaration of principles of continued defense cooperation with **Spain**
22 Oct 1974	Exchange of notes with **Iceland** on continuation of 1951 defense agreement
25 Oct 1974	Exchange of notes with **Tunisia** on a program of grants for military equipment and materials
4 Mar 1975	Five-year economic and military aid agreement with **Iran**
1 Aug 1975	Final Act of the Helsinki Conference on security and cooperation in Europe
1 Sep 1975	Agreement with **Israel** concerning an early-warning system in Sinai
24 Sep 1975	Memorandum of understanding with **Great Britain** on principles governing cooperation in research and development, production and procurement of defense equipment
5 Oct 1975	Five-year agreement with **Spain** on U.S. bases and increased military aid
13 Oct 1975	Agreement with **Egypt** concerning establishment of an early-warning system in Sinai
24 Jan 1976	Treaty of friendship and cooperation with **Spain**
25 Feb 1976	Exchange of notes with **Great Britain** on a U.S. naval support facility in Diego Garcia
26 Mar 1976	Agreement with **Turkey** on reopening of U.S. bases
15 Apr 1976	Military and naval cooperation agreement with **Greece**
28 May 1976	Treaty with **Soviet Union** on peaceful nuclear explosions
Feb 1977	Exchange of notes with **Jordan** on furnishing of defense articles and services
27 Feb 1977	Exchange of notes with **Saudi Arabia** on military training mission
11 Apr 1977	Memorandum of understanding with **Canada** on a regional operations control center
12 May 1977	Agreement with **Spain** on setting up a combined military coordinating and planning staff
7 Sep 1977	Basic treaty and neutrality with **Panama,** settling future of Panama Canal
7 Sep 1977	General security of information agreement with **France**
7 Sep 1977	General security of information agreement with **West Germany**

20 Sep 1977   Agreement with **Australia** on establishment of an OMEGA navigating facility in southwest Australia

14 Dec 1977   Agreement with **Great Britain** on U.S. defense areas and facilities in Antigua

29 Apr 1978   Exchange of notes with **Somalia** on furnishing defense articles and services

19 May 1978   Memorandum of understanding with **Norway** on principles governing mutual cooperation in the research and development, procurement and logistical support of defense equipment

24 Aug 1978   Memorandum of understanding with the **Netherlands** on principles governing mutual cooperation in the research and development, procurement and logistical support of defense equipment

7 Sep 1978   Exchange of notes with **Panama** for economic and military cooperation

11 Sep 1978   Memorandum of understanding with **Italy** on principles governing mutual cooperation in the research and development, procurement and logistical support of defense equipment

5 Oct 1978   Memorandum of understanding with **Canada** concerning NAVSTAR global positioning system

17 Oct 1978   Memorandum of understanding with **West Germany** on principles governing mutual cooperation in the research and development, procurement and logistical support of defense equipment

6 Jan 1979   Agreement with **Philippines** on use of bases

1 Feb 1979   Memorandum of understanding with **Canada** on coordination of cooperative research and development

28 Mar 1979   Memorandum of understanding with **Portugal** on principles governing mutual cooperation in the research and development, procurement and logistical support of defense equipment

18 June 1979   Agreement with **Portugal** for use of Azores base until February 1983

18 June 1979   SALT II agreement with **Soviet Union** on limitation of strategic offensive arms (unratified by United States)

27 Aug 1979   Exchange of notes with **Portugal** on the grant of defense articles and services under the military assistance program

27 Aug 1979   Exchange of notes with **Jordan** concerning the grant of defense articles and services under the military assistance program

30 Aug 1979	Exchange of notes with **Greece** concerning the grant of defense articles and services under the military assistance program
31 Aug 1979	Exchange of notes with **Turkey** concerning the grant of defense articles and services under the military assistance program
12 Dec 1979	Agreement with **Great Britain** on U.S. defense areas in the Turks and Caicos Islands
30 Mar 1980	Defense cooperation agreement with **Turkey**
4 June 1980	Exchange of notes with **Oman** for security and trade cooperation
26 June 1980	Military cooperation and aid agreement with **Kenya**
22 Aug 1980	Military facilities agreement with **Somalia**
17 Sep 1980	Agreement for normalization of relations with **China**
16 Jan 1981	Agreement with **Norway** on stockpiling of military equipment for a U.S. marine brigade in Norway
10 July 1981	Agreement with **Israel** and **Egypt** on formation of an international peace-keeping force to patrol the Sinai after Israel's withdrawal
6 Aug 1981	Five-year defense pact with **Egypt**
30 Nov 1981	Strategic cooperation agreement with **Israel** to deter threats to peace and security in the Middle East
9 Feb 1982	Joint military commission with **Saudi Arabia**
26 Feb 1982	Memorandum of understanding with **New Zealand** setting out procedures for providing New Zealand with logistic support in event of emergency
15 Apr 1982	Wartime host nation support agreement with **West Germany**
27 May 1982	Agreement with **Morocco** on use of air bases in event of a Middle East crisis
25 Oct 1982	Agreement with **Canada** on cruise missile tests in Alberta
29 Nov 1982	Agreement with **Turkey** for use of Turkish airfields
1 June 1983	Agreement with **Philippines** for continued use of bases
9 Sep 1983	Defense and economic cooperation agreements with **Greece**
13 Dec 1983	Agreement with **Portugal** for continued use of military facilities in the Azores
6 Feb 1984	Military and economic cooperation agreements with **Brazil**
17 July 1984	Agreement with **Soviet Union** to expand and improve the "Hot Line"
26 Dec 1984	Agreement with **Japan** for joint military operational plan

18 Mar 1985	Agreement with **Canada** for new chain of ground radar stations across Canadian Arctic and northern Alaska to be known as North Warning System
1 Aug 1985	Revised version of 1961 bilateral nuclear defense cooperation agreement with **France**
4 Nov 1985	Agreement with the **Netherlands** on deployment of cruise missiles
20 Mar 1986	Agreement with **Canada** for five-year extension of North American Air Defense system
10 Nov 1986	Defense industrial cooperation agreement with **Greece**
12 Dec 1986	Defense and economic cooperation agreement with **Turkey**
16 Mar 1987	Defense and economic cooperation agreement with **Turkey**
14 Dec 1987	Ten-year special military trade status agreement with **Israel**
2 Jan 1988	Agreement with **Canada** eliminating trade and tariff barriers
28 Sep 1988	Eight-year pact with **Spain,** providing United States with three military bases
22 Nov 1988	Accord with **Australia** on continued use of joint defense facilities in Australia
8 July 1990	Defense cooperation agreement with **Greece**
12 Sep 1990	Treaty on the Final Settlement with Respect to Germany signed with **East Germany, West Germany, France, Great Britain** and **Soviet Union**
27 Aug 1991	Agreement with **Philippines** over U.S. bases
2 Sep 1991	Independence of Baltic states (**Estonia, Latvia, Lithuania**) recognized
Sep 1991	Defense pact signed with **Kuwait**
13 Aug 1992	North American Free Trade Association (NAFTA) agreement with **Canada** and **Mexico**
10 Sep 1992	Comprehensive trade agreement signed with **China**
14 Dec 1992	Easing of economic embargo on **Vietnam**
1 Jan 1993	START II agreement signed with President Yeltsin of **Russia**
19 May 1993	United States recognizes government of President Eduardo dos Santos of **Angola**
23 July 1993	Virtual normalization of U.S. telephone links with **Cuba**
27 July 1993	Agreement with **Ukraine** over dismantling of nuclear missiles on Ukrainian territory
8 Sep 1993	Agreement to increase military cooperation with **Russia**
Feb 1994	Independence of **Macedonia** recognized

May 1994	Agreement to open diplomatic liaison offices with **Vietnam**
31 July 1991	U.S. president Bush and **Soviet Union** prime minister Gorbachev negotiate a strategic arms reduction treaty calling for additional reductions in U.S. and Soviet nuclear arsenals and on-site inspections
1 Feb 1992	U.S. president Bush and **Russian** prime minister Yeltsin announce a formal end to the cold war after the disintegration of the Soviet Union.
1 Oct 1992	Senate ratifies second Strategic Arms Limitation Treaty (START II), which calls for cutting nuclear warheads in the United States and **Russia** by two-thirds by 2003. Bush and Yeltsin sign the treaty the following year
1 Jan 1994	North American Free Trade Agreement (NAFTA) takes effect, eliminating restrictions on the flow of goods, services and investment between the United States, **Canada** and **Mexico**
26 Jan 1996	Senate ratifies major arms reduction treaty
4 Jan 1999	United States agrees to ease restrictions on **Cuba**

VIETNAM

23 Dec 1950	Agreement for mutual defense assistance in Indochina with **France, Cambodia, Laos** and **United States**
21 July 1954	Geneva Agreements on Indochina
30 Nov 1961	Treaty of amity with **United States** (South Vietnam)
23 July 1962	Declaration on the neutrality of **Laos** at Geneva
7 July 1965	Treaty of friendship and good-neighborly relations with **China** (North Vietnam)
16 June 1966	South Vietnam joins Asian and Pacific Council
27 Jan 1973	Agreement to end the war and restore peace in Vietnam between **United States, North Vietnam, South Vietnam** and **South Vietnam Provisional Revolutionary Government**
18 July 1977	Twenty-five-year treaty of friendship with **Laos**
4 Dec 1977	Treaty of friendship and cooperation with **East Germany**
3 Nov 1978	Twenty-five-year treaty of friendship and cooperation with **Soviet Union**
18 Feb 1979	Treaty of peace, friendship and cooperation with **Kampuchea**
3 Dec 1979	Twenty-five-year treaty of friendship and cooperation with **Mongolia**
7 July 1982	Agreement with **Kampuchea** defining territorial waters

20 July 1983	Border treaty with **Kampuchea**
5 Nov 1991	Diplomatic relations established with **China**
1 May 1992	Agreement with **Great Britain** on repatriation of up to 52,000 "boat people"

YUGOSLAVIA (until 1991)

11 Apr 1945	Treaty of friendship, cooperation and mutual assistance with **Soviet Union** (abrogated by Soviet Union on 28 September 1949)
18 Mar 1946	Twenty-year treaty of friendship and cooperation with **Poland** (abrogated by Poland on 9 September 1949)
9 May 1946	Twenty-year treaty of friendship and cooperation with **Czechoslovakia** (abrogated by Czechoslovakia on 4 October 1949)
10 July 1946	Twenty-year treaty of friendship and cooperation with **Albania** (abrogated by Yugoslavia on 13 November 1949)
27 Nov 1947	Twenty-year treaty of friendship and cooperation with **Bulgaria** (abrogated by Bulgaria on 1 October 1949)
8 Dec 1947	Twenty-year treaty of friendship and cooperation with **Hungary** (abrogated by Hungary on 30 September 1949)
19 Dec 1947	Twenty-year treaty of friendship and cooperation with **Romania** (abrogated by Romania on 2 October 1949)
5 Oct 1954	Agreement with **Italy** on status of Trieste
1 Aug 1975	Final Act of the Helsinki Conference on security and cooperation in Europe
1 Oct 1975	Treaty of Osimo with **Italy** finalizing their border around Trieste
17 Apr 1992	**United States** recognizes three former Yugoslav republics
22 Sep 1992	**United Nations** expels Serbian-dominated Yugoslavia

ZAMBIA

15 Nov 1969	Agreement with **China** and **Tanzania** on building Tan-Zam railway
20 Nov 1976	Agreement with **Angola, Mozambique** and **Tanzania** for a joint defense strategy
17 Oct 1978	Framework agreements on cooperation and normalization of relations with **Angola**

17 Apr 1979   Treaty of friendship and cooperation with **Romania**
12 Oct 1979   Nonaggression pact with **Angola** and **Zaïre**
17 May 1982   Cooperation agreement with **Czechoslovakia**

ZIMBABWE

21 Dec 1979   Lancaster House agreements with **Great Britain** on the future of Zimbabwe
23 May 1980   Military cooperation agreement with **Mozambique**
12 Oct 1980   Ten-year treaty of friendship and cooperation with **North Korea**
5 Dec 1980   Treaty of friendship and cooperation with **Tanzania**

CHAPTER 5
POLITICAL PARTIES

AFGHANISTAN

Until the fall of the communist regime in 1992, the sole official party was the Communist People's Democratic Party of Afghanistan (PDPA), which came into power with the coup d'etat of 27 April 1978 and which was under Soviet control after 27 December 1979. In June 1990, it was renamed the Fatherland Party.

On 27 September 1996, the Afghan Government was displaced by the Islamic Taliban movement; Afghanistan has no functioning government at this time, and the country remains divided among fighting factions. The main groups (with their leaders) are:

Taliban   The Religious Students Movement led by Mohammed Omar, a radical Islamic fundamentalist. Controls the capital of Kabul and approximately two-thirds of the country, including the predominately ethnic Pashtun areas in southern Afghanistan.

Jamiat-i-Islami   Islamic Society led by Burhanuddin Rabbani and Ahmad Shah Masood, moderates. An opposition force with a stronghold in the ethnically diverse north.

United Islamic Front for the Salvation of Afghanistan   Led by Abdul Dostam of the National Islamic Movement, Jumbesh-i-Melli Islami.

Hezb-i-Wahadat-Akbari   (led by Mohammad Akbari)   and **Hezb-I-Wahadat Khalili** (led by Abdul Karim Khalili) Factions of the Islamic Unity Party.

Other smaller parties are:

Hezb-i-Islami-Gulbuddin   Led by Gulbuddin Hekmatyar, a radical Islamic fundamentalist. This faction of the Islamic Party is believed to be one of the best-armed and best-organized groups.

Hezb-i-Islami-Khalis   Breakaway faction of Mr. Hekmatyar's group led by Younus Khalis, a Muslim fundamentalist cleric.

Ittehad-e-Islami   The Islamic Union for the Liberation of Afghanistan led by Abdul Rasul Sayyaf. Closely aligned to the militant Muslim Brotherhood and heavily financed by Saudi Arabia's radical Islamic groups.

Harakat-e-Inquilab-e-Islami   Islamic Revolutionary Movement led by Muhammad Nabi Muhammadi, a moderate Sunni Muslim cleric.

Mahaz-i-Milli-Islami   National Islamic Front led by Sayed Ahamad Gailani, a spiritual leader of Afghanistan's mystic Sufi Islamic sect.

Jabha-i-Najat-i-Milli Afghanistan   Afghanistan National Liberation Front, led by Sibghatullah Mojadidi, former professor of Islamic philosophy.

Harakat-e-Islami   Islamic Movement led by Mohammed Mohseni, a smaller Shi'a-dominated group based in Pakistan.

ALBANIA

Following antigovernment demonstrations in December 1990, Albania's ruling Party of Labor announced its abandonment of Stalinism, the legalization of political parties, and free elections to the People's Assembly.

Socialist Party of Albania (SPA)   Formerly the Albanian Communist Party (formed in 1941); renamed the Party of Labor of Albania (PLA) in 1948. Until 1990 the PLA was the only legal political party. The party took the name Socialist Party of Albania in 1991 and is committed to democratic socialism and a free-market economy. The SPA won 101 seats and 53% of the vote in the June 1997 People's Assembly elections.

Democratic Party of Albania (DPA)   Formed in December 1990, the DPA advocates free-market economics within a parliamentary democratic system. The party took 27 seats and 25% of the vote in the People's Assembly in the March 1997 election.

Social Democratic Party (SDA)   The SDA was formed in 1990 and has a platform of gradual economic reform. The party took eight seats and 2.5% of the vote in the June 1997 election.

Union for Human Rights   Formed in 1992, the Union for Human Rights won four seats and 3% of the vote for the People's Assembly in June 1997.

Albanian Republican Party (ARP)   The ARP, which was formed in 1991, took two seats and 2% of the vote in the June 1997 election.

Among other parties are the National Front, Movement of Legality Party, Christian Democratic Party and the Democratic Alliance. Independents took three seats in the June 1997 election.

ARGENTINA

From 1976 to late 1983 Argentina was ruled by a series of military governments. This period was ended following the defeat of Argentina by Great Britain in the Falklands (Malvinas) war. Elections were held in October 1983.

Justicialist Party (PJ)   The PJ has its origins in the Peronist movement. Founded by Lieutenant General Juan Domingo Perón, this was an extreme nationalist and populist movement, which split into two factions in 1974 after the general's death. The dominant faction is that of the Officialists (Oficialistas), led by Jose Maria Vernet. In 1997, the Peronists won 39% of the vote.

Intransigent Party (PI)   Led by Oscar Alende, it is a socialist party that developed from a left-wing faction of the UCR. It refused to cooperate with the military government or the Peronists.

Movement for Integration and Development (MID)   Another breakaway faction from the UCR; wants to defuse the destabilizing potential of Peronism by integrating it into mainstream political life. It advocates policies of foreign investment and increased industrialization.

A third-party faction was formed in 1985, the reformist Frente Renovador, Justicia, Democracia y Participación. In May 1989 one of its leaders, Carlos Menem, was elected Argentine president.

Radical Civic Union (UCR)   Founded in 1890, a major party of the moderate democratic left. Traditionally an opposition party and one opposed to military intervention in politics, the party is led by Fernando de la Rua. It advocates policies of protectionism and economic nationalism and seeks to pursue an independent foreign policy.

Union of the Democratic Center (UCD)   Founded in 1980 as a coalition of eight center parties.

Among other parties are the right-wing Alianza Federal (formed 1983), the left-wing Frente de Izquierda Popular, Front for a Country in Solidarity (FREPASO), the Partido Comunista de Argentina (founded 1918), the Partido Democrata Cristiano (founded 1954), the Trotskyist Partido Obrero (founded 1982), the Partido Socialista Popular (founded 1982), Grupo de 8 (founded 1990 by dissident members of the Partido Justicialista) and Modin (Movimiento por la Dignidad y la Independencia) (founded 1991, right-wing).

AUSTRALIA

Liberal Party (LP)   Founded in 1945, the party has been in office, in coalition with the National Country Party, for most of the postwar period (1947–72 and 1972–80). It is the major right-of-center party in Australia and is committed to free enterprise. Since 1949, there has been a coalition between the Liberal Party and the National Party. Faced with a split in the National Party, the Liberal leader, John Howard, refused to renegotiate the coalition in April 1987, but differences were settled in the course of the campaign. After losing four successive bids, the Liberal-National Party was successful in October 1998, taking 80% of the House vote, 35% of the Senate vote and seating Howard as prime minister.

National Party (NP)   Established in 1916 as the Country Party, it is a free-enterprise party appealing to the rural population. It has rarely attracted more than 10% of the popular vote, but it has been an indispensable junior partner of the Liberal Party, which has relied on its support to form governments. This historic link was jeopardized in April 1987 after a split between the Queensland branch of the party led by Sir John Bjelke-Petersen and the southern establishment. Once the coalition was restored, the Liberal-National Party won the October 1998 election and National leader Timothy Andrew Fischer became deputy prime minister.

Australian Labour Party (ALP)   Founded as the political arm of the trade union movement in the 1890s, the ALP had been in office for much of the forties (1941–49). The party has been in opposition for much of the postwar period; it has recently held office in the early 1970s and early 1980s. The party is roughly divided into an orthodox socialist left wing in the party organization and trade unions, and a right-wing parliamentary party. A Labour Party administration was controversially dismissed by the governor-general in 1975, and lost the subsequent general election. However, Labour won four successive victories, including former prime minister Paul Keating. In the October 1998 election, under Kim Beazley, Labour took 67% of the House vote and 29% of the Senate vote.

Australian Democratic Labour Party (ADLP)   Founded in 1955 by breakaway Labour Party members as an anticommunist party, its support has declined steadily from a peak of 9.4% in 1958 and is now negligible.

Other Australian parties include the Communist Party of Australia (founded 1920) and the Australia Party (founded 1966), both of which have attracted very little electoral support. The Australian Democratic

Party, founded in 1977 by an ex-Liberal minister, has had slightly more success. There is also a Green Party.

AUSTRIA

Socialist Party of Austria (SPO)   The Social Democratic Workers' Party was founded in 1888. Following its prohibition in 1934, a splinter group, the Revolutionary Socialists, broke away. The two groups were reunited as the Socialist Party of Austria (SPO) after World War II. A moderate social democratic party, the SPO obtained an absolute majority in parliament in 1970 under the leadership of Bruno Kreisky, and remained in power for 13 years before losing its majority and forming a "small coalition" with the FPO *(q.v.)*. Its support is disproportionately concentrated in Vienna. It took the name Social Democratic Party in 1991. In the December 1995 National Council election, SPO won 38% of the vote.

Austrian People's Party (OVP)   Founded in 1945, the OVP is the major conservative party in Austria and the postwar successor to the clerical Christian Social Party. The party ruled in coalition with the SPO from 1945 to 1965 and alone from 1966 to 1970. The core of its support comes from the urban middle classes and farmers. Although not a party member, Dr. Kurt Waldheim was sponsored by the OVP in his controversial 1986 presidential election campaign. Waldheim was elected despite evidence of complicity in war crimes, only to find himself diplomatically isolated. In April 1987 he was entered on a list of suspected war criminals by the United States, which effectively prevented his entry into the United States as a private citizen. OVP took 28% of the vote in the December 1995 election.

Freedom Party of Austria (FPO)   Established in 1955, FPO is in part the successor to prewar German nationalist parties, and more immediately to the League of Independents, which drew support from former National Socialists (Nazis). It is structured on a federal basis, and regional parties enjoy a great deal of autonomy. There is particular tension between a more liberal Viennese wing and a more nationalist wing based largely in Carinthia. The party first came to power in 1983 as the junior coalition partner of the SPO. In 1986 the leader of the extreme rightwing Carinthian party was elected national leader, precipitating the breakup of the ruling SPO–FPO coalition and fresh elections in November of that year. Following the election, in which it doubled its share of the popular vote, the party was again excluded from power by the formation of an SPO–OVP grand coalition. It polled 22% of the vote in the 1995 election.

United Greens of Austria (VGO)/The Alternative List of Austria
The Green movement in Austria is considerably more conservative and

middle class than its German counterpart. It runs a joint list in elections with the so-called "alternatives," who are more radical. The two parties first entered a provincial diet in Vorarlberg in 1984 and first entered parliament in 1986 with nine members. Its most prominent public personality, Frieda Meissner-Blau, campaigned for the presidency against Kurt Waldheim in 1986. The Green Alternative List polled 4.6% of the votes in 1995.

Communist Party of Austria (KPO)   Formed after World War I, the KPO has failed to attract significant electoral support. Its popularity increased during World War II, but support receded after 1945. Its remaining strength lies in the trade unions. It was last represented in parliament in 1959, and on the Vienna City Council in 1969.

There is also, among other parties, an extreme right-wing grouping, the National Democratic Party of Austria (NDP).

BELGIUM

Christian Social Party/Christian People's Party (PSC/CVP)
Founded in 1945 as the postwar successor to the former Catholic Party, the PSC/CVP is now technically nondenominational and appeals to all sections of society. However, it upholds the position of the Roman Catholic Church and draws support from Catholic trade unions. Since the 1960s the Flemish wing has effectively constituted a separate party, Christelijke Volkspartij (CVP). In the May 1995 elections for the Chamber of Deputies, CVP took 17% of the vote and PSC took 8%.

Belgian Socialist Party (PSB)   Established in 1885, an orthodox socialist party with strong support in the Walloon industrial centers and the trade union movement. It split from the Flemish wing in 1978. The Flemish party was reestablished as an independent party, Belgische Socialistiche Partij (BSP), and both are affiliated with the Socialist International.

Communist Party (PCB/KPB)   Founded in 1921. The party joined a government coalition in the 1940s but has attracted very little support since then. It changed its name in 1990 to the Union of Belgian Communists.

Freedom and Progress Party (PLP/PVV)   Liberal party founded in 1961 as a successor to the old Liberal Party. Originally resistant to federalism, it is conservative, and favors free enterprise and control of public spending. It stresses issues dealing with farmers and industrial workers. The Flemish wing (PVV) has effectively been a separate party since 1970.

Flemish Party (Vlaams Blok)   The party was founded in 1979 as successor to the Flemish People's Party and the Flemish National Party by Flemish nationalists opposed to concessions made by the Volksunie while in office. It attracted over 7% of the vote in the 1995 Chamber elections.

Francophone Democratic Front (FDF)　Alliance of several small Walloon parties founded in 1964.

People's Union (Volksunie)　A Flemish nationalist party founded in 1954, its aim is a federal structure for Belgium. It is a successor to the Front Party, founded in 1918 with the aim to divide Belgium by setting up a separate Flemish state. It attracted nearly 5% of the vote in 1995.

Liberal Reform Party (PRL)　Founded in 1961 out of the old Liberal Party, it avoided a linguistic split until the founding of the PVV by a breakaway Flemish-speaking faction. Led by Louis Michel, it is a conservative party that advocates economic liberalism.

Walloon Party (PW)　The Parti Wallon was founded in 1985 by the amalgamation of the Rassemblement Wallon (founded 1968) with two other Walloon groupings.

National Front (FN)　A right-wing extremist nationalist party founded in 1988.

Other Belgian parties include the Party of German-Speaking Belgians, based in Eupen; the pro-Chinese Marxist-Leninist Communist Party of Belgium; and the Belgian Labor Party, which is an anti-Soviet Marxist-Leninist party; Agalev, the Flemish community Ecologist Party; Ecolo, the French-speaking Ecologist Party; and the former United Feminist Party (PFU), a feminist, pacifist, republican party formed in 1972. It changed its name in 1990 to Feminist Humanist Party.

BRAZIL

From 1965 to 1986 Brazil was under military rule. The first free congressional and gubernatorial elections were held on 15 November 1986.

National Parliamentary Movement (MNP)　Founded in 1991 by a grouping of 11 of the 19 parties in Congress; advocates a parliamentary system.

Brazilian Communist Parry (PCB)　Founded in 1947, the PCB was a pro-Moscow party. It was originally banned by the government.

Democratic Labor Party (PDT)　A social-democratic party, originally called the Brazilian Labor Party (PTB), it advocates policies of full employment, land reform and redistribution of income. Party leaders are Leonel da Moura Brizola (president) and Carmen Cynira (general secretary).

Party of the Brazilian Democratic Movement (PMDB) The Brazilian Democratic Movement (MDB) was established by the government in 1965 as an opposition party. Its successor, the PMDB, was founded in 1980 by centrist members of the MDB after the dissolution of the latter in 1979. Essentially Christian Democratic in outlook, the party includes members from almost the entire political spectrum. The party won a majority in both houses in the first free elections in 1986, and also won 21 of 23 governorships. Its initial support came mainly from the urban middle classes, intellectuals and workers. Its policies include restructuring of the economy, assistance for the disadvantaged sections of society and redistribution of income. It is strongly committed to democracy. PMDB won 27 Senate seats and 82 Chamber seats in the October 1998 election.

Party of Brazilian Social Democracy (PSDB) Founded in 1988, a center-left breakaway from the PMDB. PSDB won 16 Senate seats and 99 Chamber seats in the October 1998 election.

Social Democratic Party (PDS) Essentially a conservative Christian-Democratic party, founded in 1980 by the military government as a successor to the pro-government National Renovation Alliance (ARENA). The PDS was one of the two parties allowed to operate during the military dictatorship. Despite the deliberate complexity of electoral procedure designed to improve its chances in the general election of 1982, it failed to achieve an absolute majority over the opposition parties. Despite liberalization aimed at attracting electoral support from the increasingly significant new urban middle class, its support still lies largely in rural areas.

Party of the Workers (PT) Founded in 1980, and associated with the independent trade union movement, the PT is Brazil's first independent labor party. A left-wing party, it advocates job creation, redistribution of income and the guaranteeing of civil and political liberties. The PT won seven Senate seats and 68 Chamber seats in the October 1998 election.

Party of National Reconstruction (PRN) A right-wing party formed in 1988. Its candidate won the 1989 presidential election in the second round with 53% of the vote.

Among other parties are the Liberal Party (PL) and the Green Party (PV).

BULGARIA

Bulgaria was effectively a one-party state until 1989. The Fatherland Front, which included the Bulgarian Communist Party and the Bulgarian Agrarian Party, attracted more than 99% of the vote. Antigovernment demonstrations in 1989 forced the Fatherland Front to relinquish sole governing power and to allow the formation of other parties. The first free elections in 58 years were held on 10 and 17 June 1990.

Bulgarian Agrarian Party (BAP)   The BAP was founded in 1899 as a mass peasant party. Some members refused to cooperate with the communists in the Fatherland Front of 1944 and formed an independent agrarian party, which effectively ceased to exist after the establishment of communist rule in 1947. The BAP had 99 seats in the 400-member National Assembly in 1986.

Bulgarian Communist Party (BCP)   Formed in 1891 as the Bulgarian Social Democratic Party, from which it split in 1919, it formed part of the broad-based Fatherland Front, which took power in 1944 with the backing of the USSR, and subsequently came to dominate the organization. It had 276 members in the 400-seat National Assembly in 1986. In 1989, it changed its name to Bulgarian Socialist Party *(q.v.)*.

Bulgarian Socialist Party (BSP)   The former Bulgarian Communist Party changed its name following antigovernment demonstrations that led to constitutional reforms in 1989. In the June 1990 Grand National Assembly elections the BSP won 211 of the 400 seats, and in April 1998 BSP won 22% of the vote.

Union of Democratic Forces (UDF)   The main opposition grouping, an alliance of 16 parties formed in 1989. The UDF includes the Ecoglasnost Independent Association, Citizens' Initiative Movement and Bulgarian Workers' Social Democratic Party (United) among its component organizations. The UDF won 144 National Assembly seats in the 1990 elections, and 52% of the vote in 1997.

Among other parties in what remains a fluid situation are the Agrarian Party (which had been absorbed into the Fatherland Front in 1947); and the Movement for Rights and Freedom (MRF), an ethnic Turkish minority party that took 23 seats in the 1990 elections.

CANADA

Canadian Alliance   Formed in January 2000 by a merger of the Reform Party and elements of the Progressive Conservative Party, the Canadian Reform Conservative Alliance, or Canadian Alliance, makes up the opposition in the parliament. The party adopts conservative positions on social and economic issues. In the 2000 elections the Alliance gained eight more seats than its predecessor Reform Party did in 1997. (See below.)

Liberal Party   Founded in 1867, it is one of Canada's two major parties, historically associated with free trade and social reform policies. Its most notable postwar leader has been Pierre Trudeau, under whose direction it developed progressive welfare and foreign policies and dominated postwar Canadian politics. The party suffered a loss of support in the 1980s but won a parliamentary majority in the election of 1993, which brought Prime Minister Jean Chrétien into power. In the June 1997 House of Commons elections, the Liberal Party won 38% of the vote. The November 2000 election resulted in a further Liberal victory.

Progressive Conservative Party (PC) Founded in 1854, its policies differ little from those of the Liberals, but greater emphasis is placed on the free market, and its foreign policy is more nationalist and pro-Commonwealth. Under the leadership of Brian Mulroney, the PC won elections in 1984 and 1988, and aligned Canada more closely with the United States under the conservative administrations of Presidents Reagan and Bush. In 1993 the party suffered the worst defeat in its history as its parliamentary representation was reduced to only two seats. The PC bounced back in 1997, winning 20 seats, but fared worse in 2000, winning only 12 seats.

New Democratic Party A democratic socialist party founded in 1961 as successor to the Cooperative Commonwealth Federation (founded 1933). As the CCF, the labor movement's political representation had seen its electoral support decline. Since 1961 it has steadily increased, and the NDP had consistently attracted 20% of the vote since the 1980s, but its popularity dropped to 11% in 1997.

Social Credit Party Founded in 1935, it attracts little support nationally, but was the governing party of Alberta from 1935 to 1971, and of British Columbia from 1952 to 1972. The equivalent party in Quebec is the Ralliement des Creditistes.

Reform Party of Canada Founded in 1987 (and with some 60,000 members in 1992), the party advocates increased power for the federal government and opposes bilingualism. The Reform Party won 60 seats and 19% of the vote in 1997.

Parti Quebecois This provincial Quebec separatist party with a social democratic orientation was founded in 1968. The Bloc Quebecois won 44 seats and 11% of the vote in 1997.

Other parties include the Communist Party of Canada, and a pro-Chinese Workers' Communist Party (Marxist-Leninist) of Canada. There are also the Green Party of Canada (formed in 1983) and the Equality Party, representing English speakers in Quebec (formed in 1989).

CHILE

After 1973, Chile was governed by a right-wing military junta. Political parties were allowed to function once more in March 1987, when all except Marxist parties were legalized. A constitutional amendment in July 1989 revoked the ban on Marxist parties. In 1988, 16 political parties and opposition groups had united under the title Comando por el No to oppose the government's nominee for the presidency in a referendum held on 5 October 1988. This became the CPD and put forward Patricio Aylwin Azócar for the 14 December 1989 presidential election.

Unidad Popular　This coalition of communists, Marxist socialists and leftist radicals came together in 1969 and helped to elect Salvador Allende in 1970. It participated in his government until Allende was overthrown by the military in 1973.

Christian Democratic Party (PDC)　A Catholic party with an "officialist" and a leftist wing. The party gained support from the radicals from 1952 until it lost power to Allende in 1970. It was tolerated by the junta until 1977. In March 1994, PDC candidate Eduardo Frei Ruiz-Tagle was elected president.

Radical Party　A non-Marxist center-left party, the strongest political force in Chile before the rise of the Christian Democrats. It formed a common front with socialists and communists in 1970.

Communist Party　Legal between 1958 and 1973, its power base lay in the trade union movement. It became part of Unidad Popular in 1970.

Socialist Party　More militant than the Communist Party, it was also a member of Unidad Popular. Salvador Allende was leader of the traditionalist wing. The party had pro-Castro tendencies. On 16 January 2000, Ricardo Lagos became the first socialist president in 27 years. Lagos, 61, was involved in the fight against Gen. Augusto Pinochet's dictatorship in the 1980s.

Concertatión de los Partidos de la Democracia (CPD)　An alliance that emerged from the Comando por el No grouping to support a single center-left presidential candidate. Its candidate won 55.2% of the vote in the December 1989 presidential election, and 58% in March 1994. The alliance includes the Party for Democracy (PPD) headed by Sergio Bitar, the Radical Social Democratic Party (PRSD) headed by Anselmo Sule and the Christian Democratic Party (PDC) headed by Enrique Krauss.

Union for the Progress of Chile (UPP)　Consists mainly of two parties: National Renewal (RN) headed by Alberto Espina, and Independent Democratic Union (UDI) headed by Pablo Longueira. The alliance won 36% of the vote in the December 1997 Chamber of Deputies election.

Chile 2000's main party is Progressive Center-Center Union (UCCP) headed by Francisco Javier Errazuriz. Chile 2000 took only one seat in the 1997 Senate election.

Among other parties are the right-wing Avanzada Nacional; the center-left Intransigencia Democratica; the Christian left Izquierda Cristiana; and the Movimiento de Accion Popular Unitaria (MAPU), a Marxist party formed in 1989.

Note: The political party situation remains in flux, with new alliances constantly being formed.

CHINA

China is effectively a one-party state dominated by the Communist Party. Nevertheless, eight minor parties also exist and join with the Communist Party in government.

Communist Party of China Founded in 1921, the Communist Party came to power in 1949 under the leadership of Mao Zedong following years of civil war. For a number of years Communist China was dependent on the USSR, but from the mid-1950s Mao set out to develop a specifically Chinese communism. The Soviet Union withdrew its technical support in 1960, and relations between the two countries have remained strained since then. Internal conflicts within the party came to a head during the Cultural Revolution, which began in 1966, and during which a number of leading party members were removed. Following Mao's death in 1976, radical and moderate elements within the party again came into conflict, and the moderates emerged victorious.

There are eight minority parties, consisting mainly of intellectuals. They are the following:

Revolutionary Committee of the Kuomintang (founded 1948)
China Democratic League (founded 1944)
China Democratic National Construction Association (founded 1945)
China Association for Promoting Democracy (founded 1945)
Chinese Peasants' and Workers' Democratic Party (founded 1947)
China Zhi Gong Dang (founded 1947)
Jin San Society (founded 1946)
Taiwan Democratic Self-Government League (founded 1947)

Although China's economy and society are in rapid change, the Communist Party's monolithic hold on power remains intact.

COLOMBIA

Liberal Party   Formed by followers of Francisco de Paula Santander, Colombia's first vice president, in the 19th century, it is one of Colombia's two major parties. The Liberals dominated Colombian politics in the 1970s and early 1980s, and were in power from 1930 to 1946 and from 1974 to 1982. In March 1986 the Liberals won the congressional elections and in May their candidate, Dr. Virgiho Barco Vargas, was elected president with 58% of the vote. They easily won the October 1991 election with 86 seats in the House of Representatives, but their popularity slipped back to 50% and 51 seats in the March 1998 Senate elections under Liberal Party leader Horaero Serpa.

Conservative Party   Colombia's second major party, it was founded by followers of Simon Bolivar, Colombia's first president. It was in power from 1946 to 1953, and was in office after 1982, when the Conservative presidential candidate, Dr. Belisano Betancourt Cuartas, won a clear victory over his Liberal opponent with 49.5% of the vote. It was defeated in 1986. Under the leadership of Omar Yepes Alzate, the Conservative Party won 24% of the vote in 1998 Senate elections.

National Front   Following increasingly violent civil conflict *(La violencia)*, a military coup in 1953 brought General Gustavo Rojas Pinilla to power. He in turn was overthrown by the military backed by both the Liberal and Conservative parties in 1957. The two parties then agreed to alternate in office under a system (National Front) that operated until 1974, when competitive elections were restored.

Democratic Alliance (ADM-19)   is a coalition of small leftist parties and dissident liberals and conservatives. Begun as a left-wing urban guerrilla group, Movement of 19 April (M-19) became a political party in October 1989. It is now Alianza Democratica (ADM-19), an alliance of center-left groups that won 15 seats in the October 1991 elections.

Patriotic Union (UP)   is a legal political party formed by the Revolutionary Armed Forces of Colombia (FARC) and the Colombian Communist Party (PCC).

COSTA RICA

National Liberation Party (Partido Liberación Nacional; PLN) Formed in 1951 as an outgrowth of the 1948 revolution and dominated by the charismatic José Maria Figueres Olsen, the PLN advocates a pro-United States foreign policy, anticommunism, and public spending, especially on health care and education. It has contributed greatly to the country's political stability. PLN won 23 seats and 35% of the vote in the February 1998 elections for the Legislative Assembly.

United Christian Socialist Party (Partido Unidad Social Cristiana; PUSC)   The successor to the prerevolutionary Unity Party, the recent PUSC comprises both conservative and liberal (Christian Democrat) factions. PUSC's candidate, Miguel Angel Rodríguez, won the presidency with 47% of the vote in May 1998. The party took 27 seats and 41% of the vote in the 1998 Legislative Assembly elections.

People United (Pueblo Unido)   A coalition of leftist parties, People United won only limited representation in the 1986 and 1998 elections.

Costa Rica is mainly a two-party system, with the PUSC and PLN garnering the majority of votes. Numerous small parties share less than 25% of the population's support, including: National Integration Party (PIN); National Independent Party (PNI); National Christian Alliance Party (ANC); Democratic Force Party (PFD); Libertarian Movement Party (PML); Costa Rican Renovation Party (PRC); New Democratic Party (PDN); and the National Rescue Party (PRN).

CUBA

Communist Party of Cuba (PCC)   The PCC is heir to the Cuban Revolutionary Party, founded in 1892. The first Cuban Marxist-Leninist party was founded in 1925, and became the Popular Socialist Party (PSP) in 1943. Following an unsuccessful uprising against the Batista regime in 1953, Fidel Castro and a group of others, including Che Guevara, established themselves as the center of a popular antigovernment movement from 1956, and finally overthrew the regime in 1958. The PSP played little part in the revolution, but came together with Castro's 26 July Movement to form the Integrated Revolutionary Organizations (OCI), immediate predecessor of the United Party of the Cuban Socialist Revolution, which in 1965 changed its name to Communist Party of Cuba. The party has had close relations with both the Communist Party of the Soviet Union and the Non-Aligned Movement.

Cuba remained apparently unaffected by the changes in the communist world, and particularly those in its ally the USSR, with Castro denouncing *glasnost* and *perestroika*. Nonetheless, a Party for Human Rights (PDH) was formed in 1988. With the collapse of the Soviet Union, Cuba suffered severe economic recession, but the Communist Party remains in control.

CZECHOSLOVAKIA (until 31 December 1992)

Until 1989 Czechoslovakia was effectively a one-party state dominated by the Communist Party of Czechoslovakia. The regime fell in a "Velvet

Revolution," parties were formed, and free elections were held on 8/9 June 1990. The Communist Party won 47 seats with 13.6% of the vote. On 31 December 1992 Czechoslovakia ceased to exist when, in the so-called Velvet Divorce, Slovakia and the Czech Republic became independent states.

Communist Party of Czechoslovakia (KSC)   In the 1946 elections the party, founded in 1921, became the largest in the industrial western provinces of Bohemia and Moravia, and second largest in Slovakia. The country was ruled by a National Front government under communist leader Klemens Gottwald until 1948, when the KSC seized power. Attempts in 1968 by a new central committee under Alexander Dubcek to liberalize the system were prevented by a Soviet invasion. From 1969 the party was consistently pro-Soviet, and was at first reluctant to back Mikhail Gorbachev's campaign for *glasnost* (openness) and *perestroika* (restructuring) until the Soviet leader's visit to Prague in 1987.

Communist Party of Slovakia (KSS)   The Slovakian division of the KSC, the KSS had its own congress and central committee.

Civic Forum   A Czech party formed in November 1989 by a coalition of human rights and opposition organizations, Civic Forum advocated a return to parliamentary democracy. In the June 1990 elections it won on a joint ticket with Public Against Violence, gaining 6.3% of the vote and 170 of the 300 legislature seats. In February 1991 the party split into a moderate and a radical wing.

Public Against Violence   Formed in 1989 as the sister party to Civic Forum in Slovakia.

Christian Democratic Union   A conservative coalition formed in 1989 by the People's Party and the Czech and Slovak Christian Democratic parties, it took 11.6% of the vote and 43 seats in the 1990 elections. Prior to 1989, a National Front list was presented, which also contained members of other, minor parties. These included the Czechoslovak People's Party, a Roman Catholic party; the Czechoslovak Socialist Party; and two Slovak parties, the Slovak Freedom Party and the Slovak Reconstruction Party.

DENMARK

Social Democratic Party   Founded in 1871, the party is supported mainly by industrial and farm workers. It has consistently polled the largest proportion of votes in elections and has been in office for much of the postwar period, but often in coalition or as a minority government. Leaders in recent years have included Jens Otto Krag and Anker Jørgensen, who formed six administrations in the seventies and early eighties. A coalition led by the Social Democrats broke down in 1981 and was followed by a Social Democratic minority government. This, too, fell, in September 1982. The party is a staunch supporter of human rights and civil liberties. It is in favor of NATO, the EEC and Nordic cooperation. The party is affiliated to the Socialist International. Social Democrat Poul Nyrup Rasmussen became prime minister in January 1993.

Liberal Party (Venstre) A moderate liberal party founded in 1870 as the Agrarian Party, its support has declined since 1945, and it was over-taken as Denmark's second largest party by the Conservative Party in the late seventies. It is opposed to state intervention, high taxation and high public spending. It favors decentralization and participatory de-mocracy. The party is currently a member of the ruling coalition. In the March 1998 parliament elections, the Liberal Party won 43 seats, second only to the Social Democrats with 65.

Radical Liberal Party (Radikale Venstre) Founded in 1905, the party attracts small landowners and urban professionals. It favors a mixed economy, and has a marked internationalist outlook. The party has never been strong in the postwar period, although its support increased temporarily in the late sixties and early seventies.

Conservative People's Party Founded in 1916, the party represents business and industrial interests, and pursues free market economic policies. It has improved its electoral appeal in the late 1970s and 1980s, and is the largest party in the center-right coalition that governed Denmark after 1982.

Socialist People's Party (SI) Its formation in 1958 by Aksel Larsen, chairman of the Danish Communist Party, and other former communists constituted an important first step in the development of Eurocommunism. It has attracted left-wing protest votes and its electoral support has rivaled that of the Venstre in recent years. The party favors unilateral disarmament and opposes NATO and the EU. It supports Danish membership in the Nordic Council.

Other parties include the Progress Party (founded 1972); the Center Democrats (founded 1973), a right-wing splinter group of social democrats favoring social-liberal cooperation and a mixed economy, and currently a member of the ruling coalition; the Christian People's Party (founded 1970), an "anti-permissive" party, otherwise liberal on economic and foreign policy issues; the Progress Party, a party founded to campaign for the abolition of income tax and for drastically reduced public spending; the Left Socialists (Venstresocialisterne, founded 1967); and the Communist Party (founded 1919), which had close links with the Communist Party of the Soviet Union. The Greens were formed in 1983.

EGYPT

Egypt has a limited party system, with the National Democratic Party (NDP) as the dominant party. The formation of political parties must be approved by the government.

Muslim Brotherhood Formed in 1928, this Muslim fundamentalist party, which advocates basing the state on adherence to Islamic law, is officially illegal.

National Democratic Party (NDP) Successor to the Arab Socialist Party, the NDP is strongest of the three parties that replaced the Arab Socialist Union (ASU) in 1977. A center party supporting the government, it was in turn superseded by the NDP. The party describes itself as a democratic socialist party that recognizes Islam as an important element in the state. The party dominates Egyptian politics with leader Hosni Mubarak serving as president since 1981.

National Progressive Unionist Party Founded in 1976, the party emerged from the left wing of the ASU. It supports nationalization and support for the Palestinians, and opposes a rapprochement with Israel.

Socialist Labor Party (SLP) Reestablished in 1978, the party has its origins in a Socialist Party of the 1930s. It supports greater political freedom and an extension of civil and political liberties.

Socialist Liberal Party (LSP) Founded in 1976 by right-wingers in the ASU, the party constituted an opposition to President Anwar al-Sadat.

Other legally constituted political parties include the New Wafd Party, the National Progressive Unionist Party, and the Socialist Labor Party, which are represented in government, and the Socialist Liberal Party and the Umma Party, which are excluded from power.

EL SALVADOR

National Republican Alliance (ARENA) Founded in 1981, the rightist ARENA party's fortunes were closely linked to those of its controversial, charismatic leader, the late major Roberto D'Aubuisson. Through 1984 the party maintained power despite, or perhaps through, its alleged use of intimidation and abuses of human rights. However, D'Aubuisson's defeat in the 1985 presidential election indicated his loss of U.S. support. In 1994 the party's candidate for president was elected in a runoff. ARENA won 35% of the vote in the March 1997 elections for the Legislative Assembly.

Christian Democratic Party (PDC)   Formed in 1960 and eventually the major opposition party to PCN, the PDC, with its leftist coalition partners, was defrauded of the presidency in the 1972 and 1977 elections, events that led to the 1979 coup. With the restoration of civilian government in 1980, PDC's leader José Napoleón Duarte was called in from exile to serve as president, at first by appointment and then, in 1985, by election.

Party of National Reconciliation (PCN)   The official government party from 1969 to 1979, the PCN gained a reputation for corruption and abuse of power. In the elections of the 1980s it has run a distant third behind the PDC and ARENA.

Farabundo Martí National Liberation Front (FMLN)   Emerged as a close second to ARENA in the March 1997 election, FMLN won 34% of the popular vote in the Legislative Assembly. The party is headed by general coordinator Facundo Guardado.

Other parties include the Democratic Convergence (CD), the Popular Labor Party (PPL), the Liberal Democratic Party (PLD), and the Social Christian Union (USC), formed by the union of the Social Christian Renovation Party (PRSC) and the Unity Movement (MU).

FINLAND

Finland has a multiparty system that accommodates unusually diverse positions. Elections were last held 21 March 1999 (next to be held March 2003).

Center Party   Finland's leading nonsocialist party, the Center Party was originally called the Agrarian Union (1906), reflecting its early orientation; however, with the postwar decline in the farming population, it has sought a broader, moderate democratic platform, favoring small enterprise and a neutral foreign policy. The Center Party won 23% of the vote in March 1999 parliamentary elections.

Finnish Christian League   Founded in 1958 as the voice of the Lutheran pietist tradition, the party has moved from a moderate to a relatively far right position. It calls for the restoration of "basic values"—that is, family and religion—and draws support from devout Lutherans and the clergy. The Finnish Christian League took just 4% of the vote in the 1999 parliamentary elections.

Finnish People's Democratic League (SKDL)   Founded in 1944 as a merger of the Finnish Communist Party (SKP) and other groups, the SKDL (or Leftist Alliance) advocates a broad leftist platform, including expanded state enterprises, worker participation in management, and employment reforms. Its popularity has declined drastically since the late 1970s; however, the SKP, fairly autonomous within the larger organization and concerned with longer range goals, has maintained its strength, taking 10% of the vote in the 1999 elections.

Finnish Rural Party   A 1956 offshoot of the Agrarian (Center) Party, the Rural Party claims to represent those who have been neglected by the political system. Its platform embraces both socialist and nonsocialist policies. Successes in the 1983 elections may signal a transition from opposition to governing party.

Finnish Social Democratic Party (SDP)   Founded in 1899 as the voice of the labor movement, the SDP has advocated moderate, reformist social democracy since the 1920s. It has maintained its ties with the unions, but it now draws mainly white-collar, middle-class support. SDP won 23% of the vote in 1999.

National Coalition Party   Founded in 1918 as a party of the far right, the National Coalition Party has recently endorsed more moderate policies, making it the most popular conservative party in Finnish history and the primary voice of the anti-Soviet, pro-Western opposition. The National Coalition won 21% of the vote in the 1999 elections.

Swedish People's Party   Founded in 1906 to pursue the interests of the Swedish-speaking elite, the party has a moderate conservative stance. As changing demographics and ideologies have obviated its original function, its popularity has dwindled. The Swedish People's Party took just 5% of the vote in 1999.

Among many other parties are the Finnish Pensioners' Party (formed in 1986); the Green Association (formed in 1988); the Communist Workers' Party (formed in 1989); and the Constitutional Party of the Right (POP, formed in 1973).

FRANCE

Center of Social Democrats   A Christian Democratic party favoring a mixed economy, it superseded the centrist Centre Democrate et Progrès, founded by followers of Georges Pompidou in 1973, and the Centre Democrate. Both supported Giscard d'Estaing before merging in 1976. This Centrist Union took 52 seats in the September 1998 Senate elections.

Communist Party (PCF)   Founded in 1920, the party's success and support has been largely in local government and the trade unions. The party has adopted a Eurocommunist stance since the 1970s, subscribed to a United Left program with the PS until 1977, and subsequently joined the Socialists in government under Pierre Mauroy between 1981 and 1984. Support declined sharply in the 1980s. It won 23 seats in the 1993 elections, and 16 Senate seats in September 1998.

Democratic Socialist Movement (MDS)   Founded in 1973 in opposition to the Socialist-Communist common program, the party favors centrist cooperation and has supported the Mouvement Reformateur and the Federation of Reformers. It has attracted little electoral support.

National Front   Formed in 1972 by Jean-Marie Le Pen, a former Poujadist deputy, the National Front is an extreme right-wing party with neo-Fascist tendencies. In the 1980s it dramatically increased its support on an anti-immigrant platform and was still a potent force in the 1990s.

Union of Democrats for the Republic (UDR)   Founded in 1967 as successor to the Gaullist Union for the New Republic (UNR) of 1958, it hoped to form a vehicle for Gaullist policies that would outlive de Gaulle.

Rassemblement pour la Republique (RPR)   The RPR was formed as a successor to the UDR following tensions between the Gaullist and Giscardian wings and the resignation of Jacques Chirac in 1976. It was the largest party in parliament after the 1993 elections with 247 seats, but dropped back to 99 seats in 1998.

National Federation of Independent Republicans (RI)   A non-Gaullist conservative party founded in 1966 by Valéry Giscard d'Estaing, it participated in coalition governments throughout the 1960s and 1970s.

Radical Party (RRRS)   Founded in 1901, the RRRS participated in government in the Fourth Republic. It is a radical and anticlerical party, but more conservative than the PS. It supports the EU and NATO. Along with the Republican Party it has been part of the UDF since 1978.

Socialist Party (PS)   Founded 1905 as the Section Française de l'Internationale Ouvrière (SF10), it became the Parti Socialiste in 1969. In opposition throughout the Fifth Republic, it came to power in the parliamentary elections of 1981, which followed François Mitterrand's victory in the presidential election. Its policies are moderate left-of-center. It suffered a humiliating collapse in 1993, winning only 54 seats, but bounced back slightly with 78 seats in 1998.

Unified Socialist Party (PSU)   Founded in 1960 as successor to the Parti Socialiste Autonome and two other small groups, the PSU is a left-socialist party; it has campaigned with the autogestion movement in recent years, in support of worker participation in management of industrial enterprises.

Union pour la Democratie Francaise (UDI)   Formed in 1978 to unite the non-Gaullist "majority" candidates, it won 213 seats in the 1993 elections.

Other parties include the Ecologists (founded 1977); the Democratic Center, a center-left party formed from former sections of the Mouvement Republicain Populaire, the Democratic Assembly, the National Center of Independents and the former Democratic Center; the Anarchist Combat Organization; and the Anarchist Federation. A Green Party was formed in France in 1984.

GERMAN DEMOCRATIC REPUBLIC (until 1990)

Until 1989 East Germany was effectively a one-party state dominated by the Socialist Unity Party (SED). The National Front, comprising the SED and a number of minor parties, nominated all candidates. The communist regime fell in 1989 and East Germany held its first free elections in March 1990. In October 1990 East Germany united with West Germany. All-German elections were held in December 1990.

Christian Democrat Union (CDU)   Emerging in 1989 as the sister party of the West German conservative CDU, it participated in the March 1990 East German elections as part of an "Alliance for Germany," taking 164 seats with 40.9% of the vote.

German Social Union (DSU)   Formed in 1989 by 12 opposition and center-right groups as the sister party of the Bavarian Christian Social Union, it was part of the "Alliance for Germany" in the March 1990 East German elections, winning 25 seats with 6.3% of the vote.

Democratic Awakening (DA)   A Christian party formed in 1989, it took part in the March 1990 East German elections with the "Alliance for Germany" and took four seats with 0.9% of the vote.

Social Democratic Party (SPD)   Sister party of the West German SPD. Re-formed in 1989 with the collapse of the SED, in which it had been merged with the Communists, the SPD won 87 seats with 21.8% of the vote in the March 1990 East German elections.

Party of Democratic Socialism (PDS)   Formed in 1989 as the successor to the Communist Party, it won 16.3% of the vote and 65 seats in the March 1990 East German elections.

Among other parties that emerged in 1989 and participated in the March 1990 East German elections were the Green Party, Democratic Farmers, Alliance of Free Democrats, and Alliance '90.

GERMANY, FEDERAL REPUBLIC OF

East and West Germany were united in October 1990. The first elections for an all-German parliament were held on 2 December 1990.

Christian Democratic Union (CDU) Founded in 1945 as the postwar successor to the Catholic Center Party, the CDU is West Germany's major conservative party and is now nondenominational. Its most notable postwar leader was Konrad Adenauer. A CDU/CSU-FDP coalition held office under the chancellorship of Dr. Helmut Kohl from 1982 to 1998. In the December 1990 all-German elections, the CDU was returned as the leading party with 36.7% of the vote, taking 239 seats. But the CDU/CSU coalition slipped back to second place in September 1998, claiming 35% of the vote and 245 seats. Kohl resigned as honorary chairman in January 2000 amid criticism of so-called secret donations while he was the chancellor in the 1990s.

Christian Social Union (CSU) The Bavarian wing of the CDU, this party is, nevertheless, autonomous. Under the leadership of Franz Josef Strauss, prime minister of Bavaria, it was somewhat to the right of the national party, which does not campaign in the province. Allied with the East German DSU, the CSU won 51 seats in the December 1990 all-German elections with 7.1% of the vote.

Social Democratic Party of Germany (SPD) Reestablished in 1945 as successor to the prewar SPD founded in the 19th century, the party pursues moderate social democrat policies. Its notable leaders have included Willy Brandt, originator of *Ostpolitik*, which normalized relations with East Germany, and Helmut Schmidt. The party's support lies largely among the industrial working class and in the conurbations, large towns and industrialized states. The SPD took 33.5% of the vote and 239 seats in the December 1990 all-German elections. In September 1998, SPD, under the leadership of Gerhard Schröder, beat out CDU/CSU as the leading party, winning 41% of the vote and 298 seats in the Federal Assembly.

Free Democratic Party (FDP) Politically to the right of center and economically liberal, the FDP has always had a very limited base of electoral support. Nevertheless, the party has been the junior member in both social-liberal and conservative-liberal coalitions in the 1970s and 1980s, and increased its support in the 1987 election. In 1998, the party took 6% of the vote and 43 seats.

National Democratic Party of Germany (NPD)   An extreme right-wing party founded in 1964, the NPD is arguably neo-Nazi but has managed to evade prosecution. It achieved an upsurge of support in the late 1960s, and it managed to get members elected in local elections, but never gained the necessary 5% to enter parliament.

Greens   Founded in the 1970s as a radical ecologist party also campaigning for grass-roots democracy and against the superpowers and international power blocs, it first entered a regional diet in Bremen in 1979 and parliament in 1983. Support for the Greens fell away in the December 1990 all-German elections, with the party taking 3.9% of the vote but failing to win any seats. But a combination of Alliance '90 and the Greens in East Germany won eight seats with 1.2% of the vote. In May 1991, the Greens split into a radical faction and a more conservative faction. Alliance '90/Greens won 7% of the vote and 47 seats in the 1998 elections.

German Communist Party   The KPD, Germany's original Communist Party, was outlawed by the CDU/CSU government of Konrad Adenauer in 1956. A new Communist Party (DKP) was founded in 1968.

Republican Party   A right-wing nationalist party founded in 1983, the Republicans took 2.1% of the vote in the December 1990 all-German elections. Support for the Republicans, and a variety of neo-Nazi groups, surged in the early 1990s.

Party of Democratic Socialism (PDS)   The successor party to the East German Communist Party, the PDS took 17 seats with 2.4% of the vote in 1990, and 36 seats with 5% of the vote in 1998.

Among other parties are the right-wing Ecological Democratic Party (ODP) and the Women's Party (FP). The center-right Association of Free Citizens was founded in 1993 by Manfred Brunner.

GHANA

Political parties were prohibited under the present government, the fifth military regime since Ghana achieved independence in 1957. The three civilian governments tended toward an informal two-party system, divided along urban-populist and rural-elite lines. All political parties were once more proscribed in December 1981. There remain a number in exile, and these include the Campaign for Democracy, the Dawn Group and the New Democratic Movement (both socialist), and the Ghana Democratic Movement.

In the April 1992 referendum, a multiparty constitution was approved. The National Democratic Party of President Jerry Rawlings won sweeping victories (189 of 200 seats) in the December parliamentary elections, defeating the opposition New Patriotic Party. Rawlings was reelected with 57% of the vote in December 1996.

GREECE

Greece was ruled by a military junta between 1967 and 1975. The principal pre-1967 parties were as follows:

Center Union (EK) A center-left formation led by George Papandreou.

National Radical Union (ERE) A center-right formation led by Konstantinos Karamanlis.

Liberal Democratic Center (FIK) A splinter group of the Center Union.

United Democratic Left An organization representing the interests of the Communist Party, which was outlawed.

The post-1975 parties include:

Pan-Hellenic Socialist Movement (PASOK) Founded in 1974 and led by Andreas Papandreou, the party came in third in the first democratic elections in 1974. It went on to become the party of government after the 1981 election and retained power in 1985. After a period in opposition, it returned to power in 1993, and claimed 162 seats in the September 1996 parliamentary elections.

New Democracy Moderate conservative party founded in 1974 by Karamanlis, and effectively a successor to ERE. In the first democratic elections for 10 years (1974), it gained over half the vote and two-thirds of the seats in parliament. Since then it has lost power (1981) and support to PASOK. It subsequently returned to power before losing again in 1993. NDE won 108 seats with 38% of the vote in the 1996 elections.

Communist Party of Greece-Exterior (KKE) Founded in 1918, the party was illegal for much of the period between then and 1974. It was an orthodox pro-Soviet party attracting about 10% of the vote. There is also a KKE-Fsoterikon (interior) that broke away from the party on the issue of support for the Soviet Union, whose leadership the new party did not recognize. It now attracts little popular support.

Progressive Party A right-wing party founded in 1955 and reestablished in 1979.

Ecologist Alternative This environmental party won a seat in the 1989 general election, retaining it in the 1990 election.

Political Spring   Formed in 1993 by former foreign minister Antonis Samaras to "break the mold" of Greek politics. It won 10 seats (4.8%) in 1993, but failed to garner 3% of the vote in 1996.

GUATEMALA

Christian Democrats of Guatemala (DCG)   The target of death squads in the late 1970s and early 1980s, the DCG survived to see its leader, Marco Vinicio Cerezo Arevalo, become Guatemala's first civilian president in over 30 years. The party is considered moderate leftist and draws support from organized labor and the middle class. DCG took only four seats in the November 1995 congressional elections.

Union of the National Center (UCN)   Although it fared poorly in the 1985 runoff election, the UCN represents the possibility of a moderate conservative party in a country long dominated by rightist extremists. The UCN candidate, Jorge Capio, was defeated in the second round of the 1991 presidential election, gaining 30% of the vote.

Institutional Democratic Party (PID)   Founded in 1965, the PID became the political vehicle of the military clique that ruled from 1970 to 1982, during which period it gained support largely through intimidation and by forming coalitions. Since 1982 it has declined, but continues to wield some power through alliance with the MLN.

National Liberation Movement (MLN)   The product of a 1954 coup, the MLN is violently anticommunist, drawing support from rural landowners and small farmers. Its fortunes have declined since the late 1970s. MLN took only one seat in the 1995 elections.

Revolutionary Party (PR)   Founded in 1944 and the party of government until the 1954 coup, the PR shifted to the far right in the 1970s, temporarily gaining power but destroying its long-term credibility.

Solidarity Action Movement (MAS)   A conservative party whose candidate, Jorge Serrano, won the second round of the 1991 presidential election with 68.3% of the vote after building an alliance with nine parties ranging from the extreme right to the center.

National Advancement Party (PAN)   Headed by Raphael Barrios Flores, PAN's presidential candidate, Alvaro Enrique Arzu Irigoyen, won the presidency in a runoff election with 51.2% of the vote in January 1996, beating out Jorge Portillo Cabrera of the FRG with 48.8%. PAN also took 45 seats in 1995.

Guatemalan Republican Front (FRG)   In 1995, the FRG, headed by Efrain Rios Montt, emerged as the second-largest party, winning 21 seats in Congress.

Other parties include: Social Democratic Party (PSD) led by Sergio Flores Cruz; Democratic Union (UD) led by Jose Chea Urruela; New Guatemalan Democratic Front (FDNG) led by Rafael Arriaga Martinez; and Guatemalan National Revolutionary Union (URNG) led by Jorge Soto.

HUNGARY

Until 1989 Hungary was effectively a one-party state. The Hungarian Socialist Workers' Party dominated the Patriotic People's Front, of which all candidates had to be supporters. Hungary underwent fundamental political and constitutional changes in 1989. Political parties outside the HSWP were legalized in October 1989. Free elections for the National Assembly were held on 25 March 1990, with a second round on 8 April.

Hungarian Socialist Workers' Party (HSWP) Founded in 1948 as a successor to the prewar Hungarian Communist Party (founded 1918), between 1946 and 1948 the Communists gradually eliminated the other parties, and the left-wing Social Democrats joined with them in June of that year to form the United Workers' Party.

The party leader, Matyas Rákosi, remained in power until the death of Stalin in 1953, when he was replaced as prime minister by Imre Nagy, who instituted economic reforms. Two years later Nagy was dismissed, and in 1956 Rákosi himself was forced to resign as party leader. The crisis of 1956 arose from a conflict between Rákosi's hardline, Soviet-backed successor, Ernest Gero, and Nagy, who returned as prime minister. Gero's successor as party leader, János Kádár, at first supported Nagy's policies of withdrawal from the Warsaw Pact, free elections and permanent neutrality, but went over to the Soviets. Following the suppression of all opposition by the USSR, Nagy was executed and Kádár confirmed as leader. The party itself was reconstituted as the Hungarian Socialist Workers' Party.

However, under Kadar's leadership Hungary pursued more liberal economic and social policies than the other members of the Eastern bloc. In 1988, Kadar was replaced. The HSWP dissolved itself at its October 1989 congress and reemerged as the Hungarian Socialist Party. (A small section of the HSWP re-formed as a new HSWP.)

Hungarian Democratic Forum (HDF) A center-right party formed in 1988, HDF was legalized in 1989. It advocated gradual privatization of the economy and negotiations on the future of the Warsaw Pact. In the 1990 elections HDF emerged as the clear winner with 42.74% of the popular vote, taking 165 out of the 394 National Assembly seats. By early 1991 popular disappointment with the economy and slow progress toward lessening central control led to a significant loss of support.

HDF won 17 seats with just 2.8% of the vote in May 1998 National Assembly elections.

Alliance of Free Democrats (SzDSz)   Formed in 1989, the liberal SzDSz stands for rapid privatization and a market economy, and it called for a negotiated withdrawal from the Warsaw Pact. It emerged as the second-largest party in the 1990 elections, with 23.83% of the vote and 92 seats. In 1998, the party dropped back to fourth place, winning 24 seats with 7.9% of the vote.

Independent Smallholders' Party (FKgP)   The FKgP was founded in 1988 and legalized in 1989. It supports privatization and restoration to the original owners of land confiscated by the communist regime in 1947. The party obtained 13.8% of the vote and 48 seats in the 1998 elections. It forms part of the center alliance with the HDF.

Hungarian Socialist Party (HSP)   Successor party to the HSWP, formed in October 1989. It advocates a mixed economy on Scandinavian lines. The HSP won 33 National Assembly seats with 8.54% of the vote in the 1990 elections, but won 134 seats with 32% of the vote in 1998.

Christian Democratic People's Party   Legalized in 1989, the party won 21 sets in the 1990 elections with 5.44% support, but failed to win 3% of the vote in 1998. It supported the HDF as part of a center alliance.

Social Democrat Party   Formed in 1890, absorbed into the Communist Party in 1948, and revived in 1988, the Social Democrats were legalized as a separate party in 1989.

League of Young Democrats (FIDESZ)   Formed in 1989, FIDESZ allied with the Alliance of Free Democrats in the 1990 elections, winning 21 seats with 5.44% of the vote. In 1998, it emerged as the second-largest party, winning 148 seats with 28.2% of the vote.

Among other parties are Agrarian Alliance, which won one seat in the 1990 elections. Representatives of national minorities in Hungary were guaranteed one seat each in the National Assembly.

INDIA

Indian National Congress (I)   The party was founded in 1978 by supporters of Indira Gandhi after her failure to win the leadership of the Congress Party following the election victory of the Janata in 1977. Mrs. Gandhi was returned to power in 1980 with an overwhelming majority for Congress I and its allies. Following Mrs. Gandhi's assassination in 1984, her son, Rajiv Gandhi, replaced her as leader and prime minister of India and won a landslide election victory. Since then, however, the party's record in regional elections has been dismal. In 1987 it was defeated in West Bengal and Kerala, and was routed in state elections in Haryana, where the opposition alliance of Lok Dal and Bharatiya Janata parties won 85% of all seats. The state is in the northern Hindi-speaking region, a Congress stronghold. Congress won 193 out of 525 Lok Sabha (lower house) seats in the November 1989 general election but, although it remained the largest single party, lost power. In the March 1990 state elections, Congress lost control of a number of its traditional strongholds. After the assassination of Rajiv Gandhi during the 1991 election campaign P. V. Narasimha Rao became leader of the party. The party won 141 seats in the People's Assembly in the March 1998 elections, and Sonia Gandhi is currently the party's president.

Indian National Congress The historic ruling party of India, founded in 1885, its members included Mahatma Gandhi and Jawaharlal Nehru. The party governed India from independence until 1977; between 1975 and 1977 it ruled by emergency decree. From 1978 to 1980 it joined the Janata Party in a coalition government. The party has reaffirmed its support for democratic socialism, secularism and nonalignment.

Bharatiya Janata Party (BJP) Founded in 1977 by the four largest opposition parties—the Indian National Congress (Organization), which broke away from the National Congress in 1964; the Bharatiya Lok Dal; the Bharatiya Jan Sangh, or Indian People's Union; and the Socialist Party—it merged with the Congress for Democracy. Internal divisions subsequently arose. In 1980 the Janata Party and its allies gained 33 out of 542 seats in parliament to Congress (I)'s 375, but lost support in 1984. The BJP won 88 seats in the November 1989 general election as an influential part of a united anti-Congress National Front. It went on to make impressive gains in the 1990 state elections on a wave of right-wing Hindu nationalist revivalism. In 1998, it emerged as the largest political party, winning 178 seats in the People's Assembly. In April 1999, the government of India virtually collapsed following losses by the Hindu nationalist-led regime, 269–270, in the closest parliamentary defeat in India's 51 years of independence. In the October 1999 elections that followed, Prime Minister Atal Bihari Vajpayee kept his post and his 22-party National Democratic Alliance won a majority of parliamentary seats.

Communist Party of India (CPI) Founded in 1920, its activities were prohibited by the British. A pro-Soviet party, it campaigns as part of a left-front coalition dominated by the Communist Party of India (Marxist), which split from the party in 1964. There have recently been left-front governments dominated by the CPI (Marxist) in West Bengal and Tripura.

People's Party (Lok Dal)   Founded in 1979 by the Janata Party (secular), the Socialist Group and others, it campaigns for a system of land-ownership based on small property owners.

People's Party (Janata Dal)   Formed in 1988 by a merger of other parties, it stands for nonalignment and the eradication of poverty, unemployment and extremes of wealth. The party led an anti-Congress National Front at the November 1989 general election, and the People's Party leader, V. P. Singh, became prime minister. In November 1990 over 50 People's Party MPs defected to Janata Dal (Socialist), forcing Singh's resignation from office.

INDONESIA

Development Unity Party (PPP)   In 1973 the government forced the four Muslim parties to merge in the PPP. Although internal divisions remain, the party survives as the somewhat defused and divided representative of Indonesian Muslim interests, and as the principal opposition to the government.

Golkar   The official party of President Suharto's New Order government since 1969, Golkar was essentially the political arm of the government bureaucracy, devised to dominate political institutions and undermine significant opposition. It is markedly pro-Western and anti-communist, and moderately supportive of Third World economic development. When Suharto stepped down in May 1998 after 32 years of authoritarian rule, Vice President B. J Habibie took over the presidency.

Indonesian Democracy Party (PDI)   Like the PPP, the PDI is the result of a forced 1973 fusion of not particularly compatible groups, among them the once-powerful Indonesian Nationalist Party. Together they were reduced to a minor political power until 7 June 1999, on the occasion of Indonesia's first free parliamentary election since 1955, when the ruling Golkar Party took a back seat to the Indonesian Democracy Party-Struggle (PDI-P), led by Megawati Sukarnoputri, the daughter of Sukarno, Indonesia's first president. She had been the head of the PDI in 1994 until Suharto had her removed. Sukarnoputri was named vice president in October 1999.

National Awakening Party   Led by Muslim cleric Abdurrahman Wahid, the National Awakening Party took third place behind the Golkar Party and PDI-P in the June 1999 parliamentary elections, winning just 12% of the vote. But in October Wahid swept the presidential elections when Golkar Party's incumbent B.J. Habibie stepped down hours before the election and the electoral assembly chose Wahid over Sukarnoputri. Rioting ensued, and Wahid, commonly known as Gus Dur, quickly appointed Sukarnoputri vice president.

Note: On 22 August 1991 General Dharsono announced the formation of a "Forum for the Purification of the People's Sovereignty," bringing together various strands of the opposition.

IRAN

Under the shah Iran had a limited constitutional system.

New Iran Party   Founded in 1963 by the Progressive Center, a group of civil servants and businessmen, it was the majority party in parliament in the 1960s.

People's Party   Founded in 1957, it promoted agricultural and labor-reform policies.

Pan-Iran Party   A nationalist party founded in 1965.

After the overthrow of the shah in 1979 an Islamic Republic was declared.

Islamic Republican Party   Founded in 1978 as the political organization of the Ayatollah Khomeini, its policy is to maintain the Islamic Republic. The party dissolved itself in June 1987, claiming to have achieved its intentions.

Muslim People's Republican Party   A moderate religious party opposed to theocratic dictatorship, founded in 1979. Two of its leaders were executed in 1980 for allegedly taking part in a rebellion in the northwest.

People's Party   Founded in 1920, it had its origins in the Iranian Social Democratic Party of 1904. As the Communist Party of Iran it was banned in 1931. It reemerged as the Tudeh in 1941, was banned again in 1949, and operated illegally under the shah. The party was essentially a pro-Soviet communist party.

Liberation Movement   Formed in 1961, Nelzat-Azadi, which stands for an Islamic approach to human rights, is now the only officially recognized party.

Other parties include the Kurdish Democratic Party of Iran, the Azerbaijan Democratic Party, the reconstituted Pan-Iranist Party, the secular liberal Radical Party and the Sunni minority Muslim Union Party.

Among left-wing groupings are the Communist Party of Iran (founded 1983 and opposed to the Tudeh), the militant Marxist "People's Fighters" and the Mujaheddin-e-Khalq ("People's Holy Warriors").

Among resistance opposition groups in exile are the National Council of Resistance for Liberty and Independence (formed by Mehdi Bazargan in 1986) and the Paris-based National Resistance Movement of Dr. Bakhtiar.

Since President Mohammad Khatami's election in May 1997, several political parties have been licensed, including: Executives of Construction, Islamic Iran Solidarity Party, and Islamic Partnership Front. Other important political groupings are: Tehran Militant Clergy Association, Militant Clerics Association and Islamic Coalition Association.

IRAQ

Iraq is effectively a one-party state.

Ba'ath Arab Socialist Party   Founded in 1947, the party was a member of the National Front that overthrew the monarchy in 1958 and the Kassem dictatorship in 1963. Since 1968, when it overthrew the Aref dictatorship, it has been the ruling political force in Iraq. It is left-wing, anti-imperialist, and supports foreign liberation movements. Anti-Zionist and against rapprochement between Israel and Egypt and between Israel and other neighboring states, it supports the Palestinians.

Other parties include the Iraqi Communist Party (founded 1934), the National Progressive Front (founded 1973) and a number of Kurdish parties.

IRELAND

Fianna Fáil   Currently (in coalition with Labour) the ruling party of Ireland, Fianna Fáil ("Soldiers of Destiny") was founded in 1926 as successor to those groups that rejected the Act of Settlement. It has consistently attracted the largest proportion of votes (40–50%) and been the largest party in parliament. It is a right-of-center republican party, supporting the peaceful unification of Ireland.

Fine Gael   Founded in 1933 from Cumann na nGaedheal, which accepted partition and dominion status in 1921, it is a center Christian Democratic party, the second strongest during the postwar period, and has governed in coalition with the Labour Party.

Labour Party   Founded in 1912, it is a moderate democratic-socialist party. Support has fluctuated (8–15%) since 1945. It has been the junior partner of Fine Gael in coalitions.

Sinn Féin (the Workers' Party)   The party was founded in 1905 to end British occupation and then bring about a democratic socialist republic in Ireland.

Progressive Democrats   Formed in 1985 by a breakaway group from Fianna Fáil, the party proposes constitutional and tax reform, the clear separation of church and state, support for private enterprise, and a peaceful solution in Northern Ireland. It gained 11% of votes and 14 Dáil seats in the 1987 election. This fell to 5% and six seats in 1989, and just four seats in 1997.

Green Party   Formerly the Ecology Party, the Greens won their first seat in the Dáil in 1989, and raised that to two seats in 1997.

Other parties include the Irish Republican Socialist Party (founded 1974), the Communist Party of Ireland (founded 1933) and the Socialist Party (founded 1970).

ISRAEL

Israel Labor Party   Founded in 1968 by the merger of the traditional Labor Party with a number of other factions, the party is a democratic-socialist and Zionist party. It consistently attracted by far the largest proportion of electoral support from independence until 1977, when it was overtaken by the Likud. During that period it led the ruling coalitions and had the largest representation in the Knesset. The party has strong links with the trade unions; it favors compromise as a means to peace with the Arabs, and promotes policies of collective endeavor such as the *kibbutzim*. The party was returned to power in the 1992 elections and won the majority of seats (34) in the Knesset in 1996. Ehud Barak of the Labor Party won the spring 1999 presidential election with 55.9% of the vote, against 43.9% for incumbent Benjamin Netanyahu of Likud.

Likud   The Likud is the major right-of-center political force in Israeli politics. It was established in 1973 as a merger of three groups: the Gahal, a group of Zionist revisionists under Menachem Begin, together with the Liberal Party; the La'am, a group of right-wingers and nationalists; and Hillel Seidel, an independent politician. In 1977 it was joined by a group headed by Ariel Sharon. It is a right-wing grouping opposing government intervention in the economy and supporting the incorporation of all of the former Palestine Mandate into Israel, including Gaza and the West Bank. Following an inconclusive election result in 1984 (Labor 44 and Likud 41 out of a total 120 seats in the Knesset), Labor leader Shimon Peres formed a national unity government, with the Likud's Yitzhak Shamir as deputy prime minister. These roles were to be reversed after 25 months. The 1988 elections produced a similar deadlock, but in the June 1992 elections Labor won a clear victory. Likud won 32 seats in the Knesset in May 1996 parliamentary elections.

Other parties include the Civil Rights Movement (founded 1973), which campaigns for women's rights and supports a moderate foreign policy; the Democratic Movement (founded 1976), which opposes the religious establishment; the Independent Liberal Party (founded 1965), which supports a mixed economy and a moderate foreign policy; the Liberal Party of Israel (founded 1961); the National Religious Party (founded 1956), a Zionist and religious party that participated in the Likud coalition of 1977; the New Communist Party (founded 1965), which supports self-determination for the Palestinians; and Agudat Israel, which supports the enforcement of strict observance of Jewish law. Meretz is an alliance of Ratz, Shinui and the United Workers' Party. It formed part of the 1992 coalition government with Labor. The Arab Democratic Party, formed in 1988 when it won a seat in the Knesset, supports the aims of the Palestinian Liberation Organization. It now (1994) has two seats. Homeland, also formed in 1988, is a right-wing nationalist party that advocates the expulsion of Palestinians from the occupied West Bank and Gaza.

ITALY

Christian Democratic Party (DC)   Founded in 1943 as the successor to the pre-Fascist Partito Popolare, the party has participated in all Italian governments since 1945, and has been the dominant force in Italian politics. Its electoral support has declined steadily since the 1940s, when it was associated with the name of Alcide de Gasperi. It is a moderate conservative party uniting a number of factions and attempting to appeal to all classes. The 1987 election showed an increase in support for the party of 0.9% over 1983, but in 1992, after revelations of nearly universal corruption, support slumped to 29.7%. In 1993 it renamed itself the Italian Popular Party. Under the Olive Tree alliance of PPI, Greens and Democrats of the Left, the grouping won 157 seats in the Senate and 284 seats in the Chamber of Deputies in April 1996 elections.

Communist Party (PCI)   Founded in 1921, the PCI was Italy's second-largest party and the largest communist party in Western Europe, with electoral support around 30% in the late 1970s and 1980s. It advocated nationalization and agrarian reform, development of the south, reform of government and an independent foreign policy. Following Togliatti's development of the concept of "polycentrism" in world communism, it was relatively independent of Moscow. In 1983, the party won sympathy votes following the death of its popular leader, Enrico Berlinguer, but the 1987 election marked a decline of 3.5% in support for the party. In 1991, it changed its name to the Democratic Party of the Left (q.v.).

Socialist Party (PSI)   Founded in 1892 as the party of the Italian labor movement, the PSI is now a center-left party that participated in government in the 1960s and that led one of Italy's most stable postwar governments under Prime Minister Bettino Craxi from 1983 to April 1987. The success of Craxi's premiership led to an increase in popular support over the years, and particularly during the 1987 election, but, riddled by scandal, the party's support collapsed in 1992 to just 13.6%.

Italian Social Democratic Party   The party was formed by a minority of socialists who broke with the PSI in 1947 over the issue of collaboration with the Communists, favored by PSI leader Pietro Nenni and the majority of the party. Temporarily reunited with the PSI between 1966 and 1969, it broke away again on the same issue. Relatively conservative, it advocates a mixed economy and is a strong supporter of NATO.

Republican Party (PRI)   Established in 1894, the PRI is now a moderately left-liberal party founded on the doctrines of Giuseppe Mazzini. It has relatively little electoral support (4.4% in 1992), but has intermittently joined coalition governments throughout the postwar period.

Italian Social Movement-National Right (MSI-DN)   Founded in 1946, this extreme right-wing party with neo-Fascist tendencies and members attracted an average 5% to 7% of the popular vote (5.4% in 1992, a loss of 0.6% since 1987). Its support is strongest in the south of Italy, and particularly in Naples. It became the National Alliance in 1993, contesting the 1994 election with the Forza Italia. Under the Freedom Alliance with Forza Italia, Christian Democratic Center and the Democratic Union for the Republic, the grouping took 116 seats in the Senate and 246 seats in the Chamber of Deputies in 1996.

National Democracy (DN)   The DN is a splinter group that broke away from the Italian Social Movement in 1977 in order to dissociate itself from neo-Fascism.

Greens   Formed in 1987, the Greens gained 2.5% of the vote and 13 Chamber of Deputies seats in 1987 and one Senate seat with 2% support. In 1992, they gained 2.8% of the vote and 16 seats in the Chamber of Deputies.

Forza Italia   The right-wing party formed by Silvio Berlusconi to fight the 1994 elections. Anti-immigrant, pro-market forces and populist, it gathered much of the old Christian Democratic vote.

Anti-Mafia Party (La Rete)   This party won 13 seats and 1.9% of the vote in 1992. It was founded in 1991 to contest regional elections in Sicily.

Northern League This party represents the rising populist force of northern Italy. It won 55 seats and 8.7% of the vote in 1992. The party is anti-Rome, anti-Mafia, anti-immigrant and anti-tax. It is led by Umberto Bossi. It formed out of the 1994 Berlusconi alliance.

Democratic Party of the Left Formed in February 1991, this party is the successor to the former Italian Communist Party. Led by Achille Occhetto, it is seeking to find a new identity after the collapse of communism in the Eastern bloc.

Communist Refoundation The hard-line core of the old Communist Party that refused to join the PDS when it abandoned Marxism in 1991.

Popular Party Successor to the discredited Christian Democrats, it lost greatly in the 1994 elections.

Postwar Italy has seen a number of minority and regional parties, including the Liberal Party, the Radical Party, the South Tyrol People's Party and the Monarchist Party.

JAPAN

Liberal Democratic Party (LDP) Founded in 1955 through a merger of the Liberal and Democratic parties, it is a conservative party with an industry-oriented economic program and a pro-American foreign policy. The Liberal Democratic Party was in power from 1955 to 1993, when, weakened because of continuing corruption scandals, it lost power to a coalition of opposition parties, although it remains the largest party in parliament. It is now (2000) led by Keizo Obuchi.

Japan Socialist Party (JSP) Founded in 1946, the party joined a coalition government in 1947–48. It is a democratic socialist party committed to nonalignment. It is Japan's second-largest party, but its support has declined steadily as Japan's multiparty system has developed. The JSP became the first Japanese party to be led by a woman, Takako Doi, who was elected leader in 1986. Although failing to capitalize fully on Liberal Democratic weakness in the February 1990 elections, the JSP took 25% of the popular vote and appeared to be threatening the Liberal Democrats' dominance in postwar politics.

Democratic Socialist Party (SDP) Founded in 1960 by former right-wing members of the Japan Socialist Party as a non-Marxist social democratic alternative, it has never attracted more than 10% of the vote.

Democratic Party of Japan (DPJ) After the legislative elections of October 1996, the DPJ was formed by former members of the SDP, and in April 1998 was joined by three additional parties, which had formed after the New Frontier Party disbanded.

Japan Communist Party (JCP)   Founded in 1922, the JCP is not recognized by China. Relations with the Soviet Union's Communist Party were severed in 1964 and restored in the late 1970s. Its electoral support rose to a peak of about 10% in the seventies; since then it has declined slightly, winning 26 seats in the House of Representatives in October 1996 and 23 seats in the House of Councillors in July 1998.

Clean Government Party (Komeito)   Founded in 1964 as the political arm of the Buddhist lay movement, it is a center-left party that advocates a reformist coalition to challenge the ruling Liberal Democrats. It attracts about 10% of the popular vote. In November 1998, the New Peace Party and Komei merged to form Komeito.

New Liberal Club   A splinter group of the Liberal Democratic Party, founded in 1976, when it attracted 4.2% of the vote. Since then its support has declined.

KOREA, SOUTH

After the legislative election of April 1996, the following parties disbanded:

The New Korea Democratic Party (NKDP)   Restoration of political rights allowed for the 1985 formation of the NKDP, which has absorbed smaller antigovernment forces to emerge as a significant opposition party. NKDP disbanded following the April 1996 legislative elections.

Democratic Justice Party (DJP)   DJP was founded in November 1980. The party has had limited success in raising the standard of living. The precarious relations with North Korea are its chief foreign policy concern.

Democratic Liberal Party   This party was formed in 1990 through the merger of the Democratic Justice Party, the New Democratic Republican Party (which had been formed in 1987), and the Reunification Democratic Party (formed in 1981).

The current parties and their leaders include:

National Congress for New Politics (NCNP)   The party's candidate, Kim Dae-jung, was elected president of South Korea in February 1998 with 40% of the vote. In August of that year, NCNP merged with the New People's Party (NPP).

Grand National Party (GNP)   Headed by Cho Sun, the GNP holds the majority of seats (137) in the National Assembly or Kukhoe as of February 1999.

United Liberal Democrats (ULD)   Headed by Pak Tae-chun, ULD holds 53 seats in the Kukhoe.

MEXICO

Institutional Revolutionary Party (PRI)   Founded in 1929 as the Partido National Revolucionario, it has dominated Mexican politics from its inception. It is a moderate left-of-center party with some conservative elements. The party's candidate, Ernesto Zedillo Ponce de León, won the presidency in December 1994 with 50% of the vote, and it consistently holds the majority of legislative seats: In July 1997, PRI took 77 seats in the Senate and 237 in the Chamber of Deputies. To make Mexico's election system more democratic, President Zedillo announced in March 1999 that he would discontinue the practice of the "dedazo," in which the president designates his party's nominee for the upcoming election. In Mexico's first presidential primary, held in November 1999, former interior secretary Francisco Labastida, Zedillo's closest ally among those running, was the clear winner. Mexico's general presidential election is scheduled for 2 July 2000.

National Action Party (PAN)   Founded in 1939 and led by Pablo Emiho Madero, the PAN is the major right-of-center party. It is pro-clerical, opposes state intervention in the economy, and appeals to the urban middle class and business interests. PAN's candidate, Diego Fernandez de Cevallos, won nearly 27% of the vote in the 1994 presidential elections. The party won 33 Senate seats and 120 Chamber of Deputies seats in July 1997.

Socialist Workers' Party (PST)   A Marxist-Leninist party founded in 1973, it advocates free trade unions, nationalization of foreign companies and banks, government control of basic industries and national resources, and a state monopoly in foreign trade.

Unified Socialist Party of Mexico (PSUM)   Founded in 1981 by the merger of five left-wing parties, the PSUM is Marxist in outlook.

Popular Socialist Party (PPS)   Founded in 1948, the PPS is Marxist-Leninist in outlook. It is opposed to American influence. It is supported by intellectuals and students, and to a certain extent by workers. Its leadership is more communist than its rank and file.

Democratic Revolutionary Party (PRD)   A center-left party formed in 1989 by the merger of parts of Corriente Democratica (CD) and the

Partido Mexicana Socialista (PMS). PRD's candidate, Cuauhtemoc Cardenas Solorzano, won 17% of the vote in the 1994 presidential elections. The party won 15 Senate seats and 127 Chamber seats in 1997.

Other parties include the Mexican Green Ecologist Party (PVEM) led by Jorge Gonzalez Torres; the Workers Party (PT), led by Alberto Anaya Gutierrez; Communist Party (founded 1919); the Revolutionary Socialist Party (founded 1976); and the Mexican People's Party (founded 1977), which have campaigned as a united front in elections; the Popular Socialist Party (founded 1948); the Authentic Party of the Mexican Revolution, founded in 1954 by a breakaway group from the PRI; the Mexican Democratic Party (founded 1971); and the liberal Unification and Progress (UPAC), formed in 1978.

THE NETHERLANDS

The Christian Democratic Appeal (CDA) The CDA was formed in 1980 as an amalgamation of the three main religious parties, which had roots going back to the beginnings of the Dutch party system in the early 19th century but had suffered a decline in the 1970s. The party advocates application of Christian principles to political affairs and is considered to have a centrist orientation. Drawing support from all social classes but especially from smaller towns and rural areas, the CDA has traditionally been the largest party in the Netherlands, but in the last legislative elections, other parties won more seats in the Chambers.

Labor Party (PvdA) Founded in 1946, the party sought to revise its Marxist origins so as to accommodate a broader liberal constituency, although the leadership that came into power in the late 1960s reaffirmed its commitment to such key policies as European unification, pacifism and opposition to economic austerity programs. The PvdA is the best-financed and most efficient of the Netherlands' parties, although it depends on a coalition with the larger CDA for political clout. PvdA currently holds the majority of seats in the Second Chamber, winning 45 seats with 30% of the vote in May 1998.

People's Party for Freedom and Democracy (VVD) A secular party with a predominantly conservative platform, the VVD was formed in 1948 as a successor to the old Dutch Liberal Party. Its advocacy of free enterprise and limited government economic intervention is coupled with a relatively liberal stance on such issues as social security and worker participation in profits and management. Mainly upper class and middle class in its constituency, the VVD doubled its membership in the 1970s. VVD currently holds the majority of seats in the First Chamber, winning 23 seats in June 1995.

Among other parties are Democrats '66 (D66); the Green Left; the Political Reformed Party (SGP), a Calvinist grouping; the Reformed Political Association (GPV); and the right-wing nationalist Center Democrats (CD). Each of these won minor representation in the 1989 elections. There is also a Communist Party of the Netherlands (CPN), currently seeking a change of name and identity. An extreme right-wing party, the Nederlands Blok, was founded in 1992 by associates of Hans Janmaat.

NICARAGUA

Sandinista National Liberation Front (FSLN)   Founded in 1961 as an anti-Somoza guerrilla organization, the FSLN was the major force behind the 1979 revolution. The party has a populist, Marxist orientation, focused on raising living standards, socializing the economy, increasing lower-class participation in government, and resisting United States intervention Although FSLN austerity measures have proved unpopular, the 1984 election confirmed its status as the governing party until 1990.

National Opposition Union (UNO)   This is an anti-Sandinista alliance of 14 parties that emerged in 1987–88. In the February 1990 National Assembly elections, UNO won 51 out of 92 seats, defeating the FSLN. Its candidate, Violetta Barrios de Chamorro, was elected president with 54.7% of the vote.

Liberal Alliance   The current ruling party consists of a coalition of political parties, including the right-wing Liberal Constitutionalist Party (PLC) and the Independent Liberal Party for National Unity (PLIUN), the central-right Neo-Liberal Party (PALI) and the center-left Central American Unionist Party (PUCA). In January 1997, the Liberal Alliance's candidate, Arnoldo Aleman Lacayo, won the presidency with 51% of the vote.

Other parties include: On the political right, Nicaraguan Party of the Christian Road (PCCN), Conservative National Party (PNC), Nationalist Liberal Party (PLN); on the center right, Nicaraguan Resistance Party (PRN), Independent Liberal Party (PLI), National Project (PRONAL), Conservative Action Movement (MAC); on the center left: Sandinista Renovation Movement (MRS), Social Democratic Party (PSD), Social Christian Party (PSC), Movement for Revolutionary Unity (MUR), Unity Alliance (AU), Conservative Party of Nicaragua (PCN), National Democratic Party (PND), Nicaraguan Democratic Movement (MDN).

NIGERIA

Nigeria's party system was suspended from 1983 to 1989. The principal pre-1983 parties were:

National Party of Nigeria (NPN) Formed in 1978 as a coalition party, the NPN's wealth and multiethnic base allowed it to dominate the political scene in ethnically divided Nigeria. Its position was centrist, which was also true of Nigeria's other major parties.

Nigerian People's Party (NPP) Founded as a coalition of smaller groups, the NPP initially suffered from factionalism; however, it gained some power as a coalition partner to the NPN prior to the 1983 elections. It sustained considerable losses in those elections.

Unity Party of Nigeria Formed in 1979, the Unity Party had widespread appeal, which eroded under suspicions that the party was a stronghold of the Yoruba ethnic group. Its poor showing in the 1983 elections indicated that even this Yoruba support had declined.

The ban on political parties was lifted in May 1989 and by July, 12 parties had been formed. In October 1989 Nigeria's president ordered their dissolution and announced that the Armed Forces Revolutionary Council was forming two parties, which it would support financially. These were a right-of-center National Republican Convention and a left-of-center Social Democratic Party. The main opposition alliance was the Campaign for Democracy, founded in November 1991 by 25 human rights organizations. Political parties were again allowed to form in July 1998, but just three parties were registered by the Provisional Ruling Council for participation in local, state and national elections:

People's Democratic Party (PDP) Headed by Soloman Lar, the PDP holds a majority of seats in the Senate (61) and House of Representatives (206), following the February 1999 elections. The National Assembly was suspended by the military government following a takeover in November 1993, but a new civilian government was elected in February 1999.

All People's Party (APP) Headed by Mahmud Waziri, the APP won 24 seats in the Senate and 74 seats in the House in 1999.

Alliance for Democracy (AD) Headed by Ayo Adebanjo, AD won 20 seats in the Senate and 68 seats in the House in 1999.

NORWAY

Norwegian Labor Party (DNA) Founded in 1887, the DNA is a democratic socialist party affiliated with the Socialist International. It is

Norway's largest party, usually attracting more than 40% of the vote. The party governed Norway from 1945 to 1963 and for much of the 1970s, and formed two administrations in the 1980s. It returned to power in the 1993 elections and continued to win with a majority of 65 seats and 35% of the vote in the September 1997 parliamentary elections.

Conservative Party (Hoyre)   Founded in 1884, the Hoyre is Norway's major right-of-center party. Until 1977 its share of the vote fluctuated between 15% and 20%. Since then its popularity has increased considerably, and in 1997, it trails the Labor Party with 23 seats and 14% of the vote.

Center Party   Founded in 1920, the Center Party is a nonsocialist agrarian-based party. It is committed to the welfare state and supports a mixed economy. It won 31 seats in the 1993 elections on an anti-Europe platform, but dropped back to 11 seats with 8% of the vote in 1997.

Christian People's Party   Founded in 1933, this is a centrist Christian Democratic party.

Liberal Party (Venstre)   Founded in 1884, its support has declined steadily since 1945. In the 1970s and 1980s it won less than 5% of the vote, and in 1997 took just six seats.

Other parties include the Socialist People's Party (founded 1961), which merged into the Socialist Left Party in 1975; the Communist Party (founded 1923) and the Workers' Communist Party (Marxist-Leninist, founded 1975); the right-wing Progressive Party; and the Lappish People's Party. A Green Environmentalist Party was formed in 1988, and a socialist environmental grouping, Local Candidates for the Environment and Solidarity, was organized in 1989.

PAKISTAN

Pakistan was ruled by a military government after 1977, and political parties were prohibited until 1986. Political parties had to apply for registration, and President Zia ul-Haq retained the power of veto over the legalization of a party. Before 1977, constitutional government with democratic parties had been sporadic. Among the former parties were the following:

Pakistan Muslim League (PML/N)   Founded in 1962 as the successor to Muhammad Ah Jinnah's All-India Muslim League, it was the dominant and governing party until 1969. In the 1997 elections, PML/N won the majority of seats in both the Senate (30) and the National Assembly (137). On 12 October 1999, the military deposed Prime

Minister Nawaz Sharif because of discontent over the Kashmir crisis. Gen. Pervez Musharraf suspended the constitution and assumed control.

Pakistan People's Party (PPP) Founded in 1967, this was the left-wing socialist party of Zulfikar Ah Bhutto. As prime minister, Bhutto took Pakistan out of the Commonwealth in the 1970s when certain members recognized Bangladesh (formerly East Pakistan). He was deposed by the army in 1977 and executed in 1979. Parliamentary democracy was restored in October 1988 following the death of President Zia, and a general election was held in November. Mr. Bhutto's daughter, Benazir Bhutto, became prime minister following the PPP's victory in the November 1988 elections. Her government was defeated in elections held in 1990, succeeded to power again in 1993, and dropped back to second-place status in 1997, winning 17 seats in the Senate and 18 seats in the National Assembly. Bhutto continued to lead the PPP, while a spin-off opposition group, Pakistan People's Party/Shaheed Bhutto (PPP/SB) is run by Ghinva Bhutto.

Islamic Democratic Alliance (IDA) A coalition of nine right-wing nationalist and religious parties united by opposition to the Pakistan People's Party and advocacy of a more Islamic state. The IDA won power in the 1990 general election.

Other parties include: Balochistan National Movement/Mengal Group (BNM/M); Jamiat-al-Hadith (JAH); Jamhoori Watan Party (JWP); Baluch National Party (BNP); Muhajir Quami Mahal (formed in 1986), a party of Muslim immigrants in Pakistan; the socialist Awami National Party, the result of the merger of several parties in 1986; and Jamiahil Ulema-e-Eslam, a Sunni Muslim party formed in 1950.

PHILIPPINES

Laban Ng Masang Pilipino or Struggle of the Filipino Masses (LAMP) Joseph Estrada, the titular head of the LAMP party, won the presidency in May 1998. The party is practically run by Eduardo Cojuango and Edgardo Angara. LAMP holds 12 Senate seats and 135 House seats as of the May 1998 legislative elections.

Lakas Headed by Raul Manglapus, Lakas's candidate Gloria Macapagal-Arroyo lost the presidential election in 1998, but was appointed vice president. The party won five Senate seats and 37 House seats.

New Society Movement (KBL) The KBL was established in 1978 as the official political party of President Ferdinand E. Marcos. Marcos and his wife, Imelda, continued to lead it after their 1986 exile.

United Democratic Organization (UNIDO) UNIDO, formed in 1981, was a coalition of anti-Marcos political groups, including President Corazon Aquino's Laban and Vice President Salvador Laurel's United Democratic Opposition. UNIDO sought to restore civil rights and political freedom, and to reconstruct the Philippines' battered economic and social foundations.

Social Democratic Party (SDP)   Francisco Tatad, a former information minister in Marcos's government, founded SDP in 1981. The party supports state ownership of key economic enterprises and a pro-U.S. foreign policy.

Filipino Democratic Party   A pro-Aquino party formed in 1988 by the merger of People's Struggle (formed in 1987), the People's Power movement, and a conservative faction of the Filipino Democratic Party.

Nacionalista Party   Originally founded in 1907, this party was revived in 1988 by Mrs. Aquino's right-wing opponents. It absorbed UNIDO.

Besides these major parties, other political organizations have played significant roles on the political scene. Three posed significant challenges to the Aquino government: the Muslim leftist Moro National Liberation Front, and the two communist parties. The Liberal Party (LP), the People's Reform Party (PRP) and Aksyon Democratiko or Democratic Action Party did not win significant support in the 1998 elections.

POLAND

Until 1989 Poland was effectively a one-party state dominated by the Polish United Workers' Party. In June 1989, Solidarity and other opposition groups were allowed to contest elections for the Sejm and the Senate.

Polish United Workers' Party   Founded in 1948 through the union of the Polish Workers' Party (successor to the prewar Communist Party of Poland) and the Polish Socialist Party. The party cooperated with the Democratic Party, a non-Marxist intellectuals' party, and the United Peasants' Party, which represented the interests of small farmers and agricultural workers, within the National Unity Front.

Social Democracy of the Republic of Poland (SDRP)   Formed in 1990 as a result of the dissolution of the Polish United Workers' Party. The post-communist version of the party is known as the Democratic Left Alliance or Social Democracy of Poland (SLD) and headed by Leszek Miller. After emerging victorious in the last elections, the Alliance dropped back to second-place status in 1997, winning 27% of the vote to claim 164 seats in the Sejm and 28 seats in the Senate.

Solidarity   This labor union/populist movement formed an electoral wing named the Solidarity Citizens' Committee to contest the 1989 elections. The post-Solidarity version of the party is known as the Solidarity Electoral Action Social Movement (AWS), and in 1997, the party won the majority of the popular vote (34%), taking 201 seats in the Senate and 200 in the Sejm.

Polish Peasant Party-Solidarity   The rural electoral wing of Solidarity, formed in 1989 to contest elections.

Polish Peasant Party-Odrodzenie   Founded in 1989 to replace the United Peasants' Party, which had been formed in 1949 as part of the communist-dominated National Unity Front.

A plethora of small parties has emerged in recent elections. Post-Solidarity parties include: Freedom Union (UW), a merger of the Democratic Union and the Liberal Democratic Congress; the Christian-National Union (ZCHN); the Center Alliance Party (PC); the Peasant Alliance (PL); Union of Labor (LP), and the Conservative Party (PK). Noncommunist, non-Solidarity parties include the Movement for the Reconstruction of Poland (ROP); Confederation for an Independent Poland (KPN); German Minority (MN); and the Union of Real Politics (UPR).

PORTUGAL

From 1926 until 1974 Portugal was a military dictatorship. António de Oliveira Salazar was replaced as prime minister in 1968, but it was not until the revolution of 1974 that parliamentary democracy was restored.

Socialist Party (PSP)   Founded in 1973 as successor to a tradition dating back to 1875, the PSP is a democratic socialist party affiliated with the Socialist International. It was by far the largest party in the first democratic elections in 1975, and in 1976 Dr. Mario Soares, the Socialist leader, became prime minister. It subsequently lost support and was defeated in 1979. Following an alliance with minor parties, it was again the strongest party in 1983, gaining 101 seats. However, it lost heavily in the 1985 election, and had only 57 seats in the subsequent parliament. Party leader Mario Soares was elected president with a narrow margin in 1986, and Jorge Sampaio was elected president by a wider margin in 1996. The PSP won 112 seats with 44% of the vote in the Assembly elections of October 1995.

Social Democratic Party (PSD)   Founded in 1974, the PSD is a reformist social democratic party and a partner with the Center Democratic Party in the Democratic Alliance. It was the second-largest party in 1975, 1976 and 1983. Following the election of Cavaco Silva to the leadership in May 1985, the party withdrew from the ruling coalition. In the subsequent election it won 88 seats, and formed a government with the consent of the two smaller right-wing parties.

Democratic Renewal Party Founded in 1985 by followers of Dr. Antonio Ramalho Eanes, it won 45 seats in the 1985 general election.

Communist Party Founded in 1921 and legalized in 1974, the Marxist-Leninist party has attracted 15% to 20% of the vote in free elections since 1975. The party's electoral support declined in the 1980s. It participated in the 1986 election in alliance with elements of the Portuguese Democratic Movement, the Greens, and left independents.

Center Democratic Party (CDS) This is a center party in the Christian-Democratic tradition, founded in 1974. The party's president, Diogo Freitas do Amaral, was appointed to the council of state that year under the newly established democracy. In 1979 and 1980 the party formed the Democratic Alliance with the Social Democrats. Campaigning alone it has failed to attract more than 20% of the vote. Its support fell badly in the 1985 election, when it won only 22 seats. The party is now known as the Popular Party (PP), but the coalition won just 15 seats with 9% of the vote in the 1995 elections.

Other parties include the Popular Democratic Union, an extreme left-wing party founded in 1974; the National Front, an extreme right-wing party formed in 1980; and the right-wing Christian Democratic Party.

ROMANIA

Until 1989 Romania was effectively a one-party state dominated by the Romanian Communist Party, technically part of the Socialist Unity Front. The communist regime was overthrown in December 1989 and the dictator Nicolae Ceausescu was executed. Provisional power was taken by a 145-strong National Salvation Front, which ruled by decree. Political parties were legalized, and in February 1990 the NSF offered to share power with other parties. Presidential and legislative elections were held in May 1990.

Romanian Communist Party (PCR) Founded in 1921, the party campaigned with others in a People's Democratic Front (PDF) after 1944. Following its union with the Social Democratic Party in 1947, it changed its name to Romanian Workers' Party. Unsympathetic social democrats and other noncommunists were subsequently excluded from the PDF. The party was led by Nicolae Ceausescu from 1965 to 1989.

The small Socialist Labor Party now claims the mantle of the former communists.

National Salvation Front (NSF)   This party is a center-left grouping formed in 1989 to advance political democratization. The NSF formed a provisional government until the May 1990 elections, in which its presidential candidate, Ion Iliescu, was elected with 85.07% of the vote. The NSF won 263 out of the 387 National Assembly seats. Iliescu has now joined with the Party of Social Democracy in Romania.

Party of Social Democracy in Romania (PDSR)   Iliescu lost the November 1996 presidential election to Emil Constantinescu 46% to 54%, and his party also took second-place status to the CDR. PDSR won 41 Senate seats and 91 Chamber seats with roughly 22% of the vote in each election.

National Liberal Party (NLP)   This party was founded in 1869, banned in 1947, and revived in 1989. It advocated privatization of the economy and parliamentary democracy. The NLP won 29 National Assembly seats with 6.4% of the popular vote in the 1990 elections. Its presidential candidate was the runner-up with 10% of the vote. NLP failed to gain representation in the 1996 election.

Hungarian Democratic Union of Romania (HDUR)   Founded in 1989, HDUR represents the interests of Romania's Hungarian minority population. The HDUR was elected to 29 seats with 7.2% of the vote in the 1990 elections, and 11 seats with 6.8% of the vote in 1996.

Christian Democratic National Peasants' Party (CDNPP) Formed in 1990 by a merger of the previously banned National Peasant Party and the Christian Democratic Party. It is a center-right party supporting parliamentary democracy and a market economy. It took 2.6% of the vote and 12 seats in the 1990 National Assembly elections. To increase voting strength, CDNPP united with the National Liberal Party to form the bulk of an alliance known as the Democratic Convention (CDR). The party earned the majority of votes in the November 1996 elections, winning 53 seats in the Senate with 31% of the vote, and 122 seats in the Chamber of Deputies with 30% of the vote.

Union of Social Democrats (USD)   Headed by Petre Roman, this is an alliance of the Democratic Party and the Romanian Social Democratic Party. USD won 23 Senate seats and 53 Chamber seats with roughly 13% of the vote in 1996 elections.

Other small parties that failed to gain representation in the most recent election include the Socialist Labor Party, the Socialist Party and the National Liberal Alliance, a coalition of the Civic Alliance Party and the Liberal Party '93.

RUSSIA

With the Soviet Union splintering, Boris Yeltsin was elected president of Russia in June 1991, taking 57% of the total vote. The final collapse came following the attempted coup of August 1991, after which a Commonwealth of Independent States (CIS) emerged, with Russia as the dominant member of a group initially comprising 11 of the 15 former states of the USSR. A large number of noncommunist parties had emerged in 1988–91 (the most prominent of which was Democratic Russia), and more were formed following the collapse of Soviet communism in 1991. Yeltsin resigned on 31 December 1999, and Vladimir Putin became the acting president. One of Putin's first acts was to grant Yeltsin immunity from prosecution for alleged corruption and financial misconduct.

Communist Party of the Soviet Union (CPSU)   The ruling party from 1917 to 1991. The Russian Social Democratic Labor Party was founded in 1898. Lenin's Bolsheviks ("majoritarians") broke away in 1903, becoming a separate party in 1912. The Bolsheviks seized power during the October 1917 Revolution. The CPSU's last general secretary, Mikhail Gorbachev, resigned from the party following the abortive August 1991 coup mounted by party conservatives. A Russian Communist Party was formed in June 1990 but was outlawed following the coup. The party was re-legalized in November 1992, and won 157 seats in the State Duma with 22% of the vote in the December 1995 elections.

Democratic Party in Russia   Formed in 1990 by members of the Democratic Platform wing of the CPSU and the Moscow Society of Electors, the party is moderately conservative and advocates a united Russia.

People's Party of Free Russia   Formed in 1990 as the Democratic Party of Communists of Russia as part of the former CPSU.

People's Party of Russia   A liberal democratic party formed in 1991.

Republican Party of the Russian Federation   Formed in 1990 from members of the Democratic Platform grouping in the CPSU, the party is committed to a mixed economy and the unity of Russia.

Russian Christian-Democratic Movement   Formed in 1990, the movement advocates the restoration of the monarchy and parliamentary democracy.

In 1995, 43 political organizations qualified to run candidates on the Duma party list ballot, and that number was expected to grow to 150 for the 1999 elections. The most recent choices included:

Liberal Democratic Party Extreme-right, nationalist and anti-Semitic. Led by Vladimir Zhirinovsky. The party won 51 seats with 11% of the vote.

Our Home is Russia Earned 55 seats with 10% of the vote. Led by Prime Minister Viktor Chernomyrdin, the center-right OHR was supported by Yeltsin and perceived as supporting his economic reforms.

Yabloko (Apple) Bloc The Yavlinsky-led bloc emphasizes slower, more considered reforms. Won 45 seats with 7% of the vote.

Agrarian Party Anti-reform. Favors collective and state farms and wants strict controls on private land ownership. Earned 20 seats.

Russia's Democratic Choice The main pro-government, pro-Yeltsin party led by Yegor Gaidar, the architect of the Yeltsin economic reforms. It is committed to reduce state involvement in economic management. The party won nine seats in the Duma.

Other parties not listed above but holding seats in the Duma are Power to the People; Congress of Russian Communities; and Forward Russia! Women of Russia, which has a distinct feminist stance. The green movement is represented by Kedr (Cedar) (the Constructive Ecological Movement).

SAUDI ARABIA

The Saudi government is dominated by the royal House of Sa'ud, and political opposition is not tolerated. However, several groups, although not organized parties, could be considered potential alternatives to the status quo. Muslim fanaticism (the November 1979 attack on Mecca's Great Mosque) has threatened Saudi moderation in the past and could do so again in the future; the Shi'a minority is especially discontented and subject to Iranian and other radical influences. In addition, the military, loyal to the monarchy, could turn against it, and the labor force, much of which is foreign, could be a catalyst for change. The royal family itself occasionally evoked the possibility of a consultative council, which could lead to a more representative form of government. In 1993 a consultative council was granted, consisting of 90 members and a chairman appointed by the monarch for four-year terms. However, political parties are still not allowed.

SOUTH AFRICA

National Party (NP)   The major postwar force in South African politics, the NP was formed in 1914 by Afrikaners opposed to reconciliation with the British population, and, although cooperation between these white ethnic groups has developed, Afrikaners continue to dominate the party. Since the late 1970s, the NP's leadership has promoted very limited interracial cooperation in South African politics, reflected in the 1983 constitution; however, although the Colored and Indian minorities did gain some participatory rights, power still resided with the whites and the NP remained an exclusively white party until the 1990s. Despite NP's claims for reform and denial of apartheid, the prospects for South Africa's black majority remained bleak until the advent of President F. W. de Klerk and the reforms of 1990–91. The Nationalists have since adjusted to political life in an ANC-dominated country. The party is known as the New National Party, and it won 82 seats in the National Assembly with 20% of the vote in the April 1994 elections.

Progressive Federal Party (PFP)   A merger of smaller parties, the PFP emerged in the 1977 election as the largest and most liberal white opposition party to the NP. It advocates universal suffrage and an end to racial discrimination, and opposed the 1983 constitution's exclusion of blacks. The PFP has recently opened its membership to all races. (See Democratic Party, below.)

Conservative Party   Formed in 1982, the party was organized by right-wing members of the Nationalist Party expelled for their disagreement with the abandonment of classical apartheid. It was led by Andries Treurnicht.

Democratic Party   This party was created in 1989 by the merger of the Independent Party and the Progressive Federal Party. Supported largely by white liberals of British origin, the party advocates the dismantling of apartheid, a gradual transition to one person–one vote, and a market economy. The party earned less than 2% of the vote in 1994.

Afrikaner Resistance Movement (AWB)   A neo-Nazi white supremacist paramilitary organization founded in 1973 and led by Eugene TerreBlanche, this party was reputedly strongly supported among white security forces.

African National Congress (ANC)   Formed in 1912, banned in 1960, and legalized in 1989, this is the most popular political organization representing black interests. It advocates cooperation with the left and liberals to end apartheid, and opened its membership to all races in 1985. Led by Nelson Mandela, the ANC became the dominant force in the new South Africa after its triumph in the 1994 elections, winning

252 seats with 63% of the vote. Mandela retired as president in June 1999, and was replaced by ANC member Thabo Mbeki.

Azanian Peoples' Organization (AZAPO) Founded in 1978, AZAPO does not accept white members and advocates a democratic socialist Azania (South Africa).

Inkatha (Inkatha Freedom Party) Led by Chief Mangosuthu Buthelezi, this is the party of the Zulus and is the archrival of the African National Congress. Advocates a strongly federal South Africa. The party earned 43 seats with 11% of the vote in 1994.

Freedom Front The extreme right-wing white party led by Constand Viljoen, which campaigns for a Boer *Volkstaat*. The Freedom Front earned nine seats with 2% of the vote in 1994.

In addition to the above, smaller parties include the extreme right-wing Reconstituted National Party (formed in 1969); the Pan-Africanist Congress (PAC); the South African Communist Party; and the United Democratic Front (UDA), a colored and Indian anti-apartheid party founded in 1983.

SPAIN

Spain was a dictatorship under the personal rule of General Francisco Franco from 1936 until his death in 1975. Political parties were legalized in 1977.

Spanish Socialist Workers' Party (PSOE) Founded in 1879, the ruling PSOE is a moderate democratic socialist party affiliated to the Socialist International. The party was the strongest in the Spanish parliament in the 1980s, attracting 46.5% of the vote in 1982 and 44.1% in 1986. Mid-term local and European parliament elections in 1987 showed some loss of support for the party, but it retained its hold on power (with minor parties) in 1993. In the March 1996 elections, PSOE won 96 Senate seats and 38% of the vote, coming in second to the Popular Party.

Democratic Coalition This is an alliance formed in 1978 from various right-wing parties, including the Popular Alliance, a conservative party founded in 1976. It attracted only 6.5% of the vote in 1979 and supported the UCD government (1979–82). In the 1982 and 1986 elections it attracted much of the UCD's right-of-center support.

Popular Alliance (AP) Founded in 1976, and once the main Spanish opposition party, the AP is conservative in outlook, favoring free enterprise, public order, family values and national unity. Now part of Popular Party or Partido Popular (PD), the party triumphed in the 1996 elections, winning 132 seats and 39% of the vote.

Popular Democratic Party   Founded in 1982 by right-wing members of the UCD, it is a Christian-Democratic party.

Convergence and Union (CiU)   Founded in 1979, the CiU is a regional party based in Barcelona, and is the ruling party in Catalonia.

Communist Party (PCE)   Founded in 1920 and legalized in 1977, it has traditionally had a close relationship with the Italian Communist Party, and shared the latter's Eurocommunist outlook and independence from Moscow. Since 1980 it has lost support to the PSOE.

Democratic and Social Center   A center-right party founded in 1982 by former prime minister Adolfo Suarez Gonzalez.

Union of the Democratic Center (UCD)   Founded in 1977 as a coalition of several center parties, it attracted a third of the popular vote in the 1970s, but was eclipsed as the major nonsocialist party by the Democratic Coalition.

Basque Nationalist Left (PNV)   Founded in 1893, the PNV is a regional party based in Bilbao. It is against the use of violence to achieve its aims and opposed to the terrorist activities of ETA.

Partido Popular (D)   Formerly Alianza Popular, this center-right party was formed by a merger with Christian Democracy and Popular Democracy.

National Front (UN)   An extremist right-wing party formed in 1986.

SWEDEN

Social Democratic Labor Party (SAP)   Founded in 1880, the SAP is a democratic socialist party affiliated with the Socialist International. It advocates a nonaligned foreign policy. Except for the period 1976–82, it has been in office either as senior coalition partner or (since 1982) alone. Since 1945 it has attracted more than 40% of the vote, but in the September 1998 elections, SAP's popularity dropped to 37%.

Communist Left Party (VPK)   Founded in 1917, it was renamed Communist Left Party in 1967 after the secession of pro-Chinese elements, and is now known simply as the Left Party. As a Eurocommunist party, it attracted about 5% of the vote, but in the 1998 elections the Left Party earned 12% of the vote.

Center Party   Formed from a coalition of two smaller moderate parties in 1922, it is relatively progressive and advocates a social market economy and decentralization. It is strongly opposed to nuclear power. Its electoral support has fluctuated between 10% and 25% and, under Thorbjörn Fälldin, it was the senior partner in three of the four center-right coalitions of the late seventies and early eighties. Under Lennart Daleus, the Center Party won just 5% of the 1998 vote.

Liberal Party Founded in 1902, it advocates traditional liberal policies, including a free-market economy, and emphasizes equality between men and women and international cooperation and development. The main opposition party in the 1950s, it is now the smallest nonsocialist party. Its electoral support has fluctuated between 10% and 25%, except in 1982 when it fell sharply to 5.9%, and in 1998 when it received just 4.9%.

Moderate Party Founded in 1904 as the Conservative Party, it is an antisocialist party advocating a free-market economy. Its electoral performance has improved in recent years (21.3% in 1985 and 22.7% in 1998).

Green Ecology Party (MpG) The MpG won 1.5% of the vote in the 1985 elections, increasing this to 5.5% in the 1988 elections, when it gained 20 seats. In 1998, the Greens got 16 seats with 4.5% of the vote.

SWITZERLAND

Christian Democratic People's Party of Switzerland (CVP) The major conservative party, the CVP advocates individual rights against state intervention, and the maintenance of autonomous associations (religious, educational and political). Founded in 1912, the CVP has from its origins counted on small businessmen, artisans and workers and devout Catholics for support. CVP won 16 seats in the Council of States and 34 in the National Council in the December 1998 elections.

Radical Free Democratic Party (FDP) Originally called the Free Democrats and then the Motherland Party, FDP took the lead in the December 1998 elections, winning 17 seats in the Council of States and 45 in the National Council.

Swiss People's Party (SVP) Led by Ueli Maurer, SVP won just five Council of States seats and 34 National Council seats in 1998.

Social Democratic Party (SPS) Formed by a merger of the Populist Party, a left-of-center grouping that won 117 seats in the 1983 general election to become the second-largest party in parliament, and the Social Democratic Populist Party. Led by Ursula Koch, SPS won five seats in the Council of States, but 54 in the National Council in 1998.

Other small parties include the Liberal Party, the Alliance of Independents' Party, the Worker's Party and the Green Party.

UNION OF SOVIET SOCIALIST REPUBLICS (until 1991)

The former Soviet Union was effectively a one-party state until the end of the 1980s. The right to nominate candidates in elections was restricted to the Communist Party of the Soviet Union (CPSU). The results of a confused referendum held in March 1991 suggested that the majority of constituent republics wanted greater decentralization of power, if not outright independence. A proposed new "Union Treaty" was abandoned in the wake of the August 1991 coup, and the USSR ceased to exist in December 1991. See entry for Russia (p. 246) for developments since December 1991.

UNITED KINGDOM

Conservative and Unionist Party   The modern party was established around 1830 as successor to the Tory Party. It is a center-right party representing agricultural and business interests. One of the two major British political parties, it has dominated the country's politics for most of the 20th century, and since 1945 has been in office three times (1951–64, 1970–74, and from 1979). Under the leadership of Margaret Thatcher it moved quite significantly to the right. In the 1987 general election the Conservative Party was returned to office for the third successive time under Mrs. Thatcher's leadership. However, its large majority in the House of Commons was achieved on its lowest share of the popular vote and in the face of heavy Conservative losses in Scotland and Wales. In December 1990 Mrs. Thatcher was dramatically replaced as leader by John Major because of the party's growing unpopularity over a range of issues, including particularly Britain's future in Europe and the poll tax. Under Major, the Conservatives won a historic (if somewhat unexpected) fourth term in office, only to see a dramatic slump in their electoral support after the April 1992 election. In May 1997, the Conservatives won 31% of the vote.

Labour Party   Founded in 1900, the Labour Party is a democratic socialist party affiliated with the Socialist International. Essentially a reformist party representing organized labor and the working class, its right wing is concentrated in the parliamentary party and trade union movement, and its left wing in the party organization. It has been in office three times since 1945 (1945–51, 1964–70, and 1974–79). The 1987 election saw some revival from its crushing defeats in 1979 and 1983.

After 1987 the Labour Party benefited from Mrs. Thatcher's personal unpopularity and from the apparent increase in political coherence that followed a two-year policy review, but it failed again in the 1992 election, its fourth successive election defeat. In 1997, Prime Minister Tony Blair took the Labour Party to victory, winning 418 seats in the House of Commons with 45% of the vote.

Liberal Party   Successor to the 18th-century Whigs, the Liberal Party has been superseded by the Labour Party as the main non-Conservative Party in the 20th century. From 1981 to 1988, it cooperated with the Social Democratic Party in an electoral alliance that served to revive its electoral fortunes, although insufficiently for it to gain a corresponding number of seats in parliament. The party merged with the Social Democrats in March 1988.

Social and Liberal Democrats   Formed in March 1988 from a merger of the Liberal Party and the majority of the Social Democratic Party (except Owen's supporters), the first elected leader of the new party (from August 1988) was Paddy Ashdown. Popularly known as the Liberal Democrats, the party won 20 seats in 1992 and held firm to third place in the 1997 elections, with 46 seats and 17% of the vote.

Social Democratic Party (SDP)   Founded in 1981 by four dissident right-wing members of the Labour Party, it subsequently cooperated with the Liberal Party in an electoral alliance. Despite its origins, the SDP was politically to the right of the Liberal Party. The 1987 election confirmed the failure of the Liberal–SDP Alliance to win a significant number of seats in parliament. In July 1987 the SDP voted to open negotiations to merge with the Liberal Party. Its leader, David Owen, resigned in protest. The SDP merged with the Liberals in March 1988.

Green Party   Successor to the Ecology Party. In the 1989 European elections it polled more votes than the Liberal Democrats. Membership (1993) is estimated at less than 14,000. It failed to win any seats in the 1992 election.

Regional Parties

The Scottish National Party (SNP), formed in 1928, had its greatest success in the 1970s. In 1974 it polled some 30% of the Scottish vote. Plaid Cymru, the Welsh nationalist party, was founded in 1925. Its strongest support is in rural Wales. Both parties are represented in parliament. Blair produced constitutional reform that partially decentralized the United Kingdom, leading to the formation of separate parliaments in Wales and Scotland by 1999.

Other parties include the extreme right National Front, the electorally insignificant Communist Party of Great Britain (renamed Democratic Left in 1991) and the left-wing Socialist Workers Party.

Northern Ireland

The parties of the mainland of Great Britain do not formally organize in Northern Ireland. On 2 December 1999 Britain transferred governing power to the Northern Irish parliament with the promise that the IRA would disarm their illegal weapons. However, Sinn Fein had not complied with the disarmament requirement by the deadline, and the parliament was suspended on 12 February 2000.

Official Unionist Party (OUP)   Founded in 1898 to represent those—mainly Protestant—citizens of Northern Ireland who seek to maintain the union with Great Britain, the party followed the whip of the Conservative Party in the House of Commons until 1974.

Ulster Democratic Unionist Party (DUP)   Formed in 1969 by dissident unionists led by Ian Paisley, it remains the smaller of the two unionist parties.

Social Democratic and Labour Party (SDLP)   Founded in 1970 by members of other parties, it is a left-of-center party and the principal party representing the interests of Roman Catholics. It is against sectarianism and violence.

Sinn Fein   Sinn Fein has in recent years put forward candidates in Northern Ireland elections with some success. The party won one seat in the Commons, which it retained in 1987, but the MP, Gerry Adams, refused to take up his place at Westminster and lost his seat in 1992. Adams still heads Sinn Fein. In 1999, Adams and Martin McGuinness, another Sinn Fein member, received seats in Northern Ireland's long-awaited but ultimately short-lived four-party, 12-member parliament.

Alliance Party of Northern Ireland   A center party founded in 1970 to overcome sectarian differences in Northern Ireland, it has had some success in local government and in Northern Ireland Assembly elections. It has no seats at Westminster.

UNITED STATES OF AMERICA

Democratic Party   Founded in 1800, the Democratic Party is one of the two traditional governing parties in the United States. Since 1932, the party has been essentially a coalition of liberals, conservative Southern Democrats, and others. For this reason it can be called a center-left party only with some qualification. It has attracted the support of industrial unions and intellectuals and has given much attention to civil rights and welfare. However, its position in the 1980s as the majority party at many levels rested on the unreliable support of Southern conservatives and their constituencies. In 1992 and again in 1996, under Bill Clinton, a Southern centrist, the Democrats won the presidency again, having lost three successive elections (in 1980, 1984 and 1988).

Republican Party   Founded in 1854 by opponents of slavery, the Republican Party is the more conservative of the two major parties. For much of the postwar period, the Republicans, despite success in presidential elections, have been in a minority in both houses of Congress. That situation reversed itself in the 1990s, after the Republicans lost the presidency but gained a majority of the House and Senate. The party won the presidential elections of 1980, 1984, 1988 and 2000. However, under George Bush and then Bob Dole, it lost in 1992 and 1996.

The support attracted by socialist parties in the United States is negligible. Parties to the left of the Democrats include the Communist Party of the USA (founded 1919), many of whose leading members were arrested on various charges in the late 1940s and early 1950s; the Social Party of America, founded in 1874; and the pro-Chinese U.S. Communist Party (Marxist-Leninist).

A feature of both the 1992 and 1996 presidential elections was the strong showing of the "populist" independent, Ross Perot, who won support from disillusioned Republicans and some Democrats.

VENEZUELA

Postwar Venezuelan democracy can be said to have begun with the end of the dictatorship of Perez Jimenez in 1958.

Democratic Action Party (AD)   Founded in 1936 as the National Democratic Party, Acción Democratica is the major center-left party in Venezuela, and now the country's ruling party. It is social democratic in outlook and seeks to further cooperation within the Third World and between North and South. AD won the majority of votes in the December 1998 elections, earning 16 Senate seats and 53 seats in the Chamber of Deputies.

Christian Social Party (COPEl)   The major center-right party of Venezuela, founded in 1946, it is a party in the conservative Christian-Democratic tradition, but with a strong commitment to social welfare and popular measures such as agrarian reform. The party improved its electoral appeal significantly during the 1970s, and was the government party until 1983. In 1998, COPEI took second place with 14 Senate seats and 51 Chamber of Deputies seats.

Movement Toward Socialism (MAS)   Formed in 1971 by Communist Party dissidents, it is Eurocommunist in its outlook, favoring an adaptation of socialism to the specific needs of Venezuela. MAS won just three seats in the Senate and 22 in the Chamber of Deputies in 1998.

Democratic Republican Union (URD)   A center-left party founded in 1946, it was the country's second-largest party in the 1950s, but it has lost support in recent years.

Radical Cause or La Causa (LCR)   Led by Lucas Matheus, La Causa gained support in 1998, increasing its seats in the Chamber of Deputies from three to 40 and adding nine Senate seats.

Among other parties are the Movement of the Revolutionary Left (MIR), which allied with MAS in the 1988 elections, winning three out of 49 Senate seats and 18 seats in the 201-seat Chamber of Deputies; the National Convergence, which won five Senate seats and 18 Chamber of Deputies seats in 1998.

VIETNAM

Vietnam won independence from France in 1954, when it was divided at the 17th parallel. Since the end of the Vietnam war in 1975, when the country was reunited, it has been dominated by the Communist Party of Vietnam.

Communist Party of Vietnam   The party was founded in 1930 as the Communist Party of Indochina by Ho Chi Minh, who led the communist-dominated Viet Minh guerrilla movement against the Japanese from 1941. In 1954, following the end of the war against the French and the division of the country into separate states (which was to have been for a period of two years only), Ho Chi Minh became the prime minister and president of North Vietnam. Originally neutral in Sino-Soviet relations, the party has been pro-Soviet since the mid-1970s. A crisis of confidence within the party led to the announcement of limited policy and personnel changes in 1986, when Nguyen Van Linh was elected general secretary. Linh, a reformer who admired Hungary, praised the Chinese community and discouraged the harassment of intellectuals. In June 1991, amid sweeping changes to the leadership, Do Muoi (the prime minister) took over as general secretary. Technocrats were given promotion to rescue the economy. In September 1997, Tran Duc Luong was elected president with 92% of the vote and Phan Van Khai was appointed prime minister.

YUGOSLAVIA (until 1991)

Until 1990 Yugoslavia was effectively a one-party state dominated by the League of Communists of Yugoslavia, which controlled the Socialist Alliance of the Working People of Yugoslavia. A multiparty system was introduced in 1990 and many new national and regional parties were either formed or (where they had previously existed) legalized. There were demands from many of the federation's constituent republics for independence. In 1991, Slovenia and Croatia declared independence. Fighting erupted between Croats and Serbs. Later, Bosnia was engulfed by war. The current federation is the third state to call itself by the name Yugoslavia, officially the Federal Republic of Yugoslavia. Serbia and Montenegro have elected their own leaders, but they have not been recognized by the international community as the successor state of Yugoslavia.

ZAIRE/CONGO

Popular Movement of the Revolution (MPR)   Founded in 1967, the MPR was the only legal political party until January 1991 and approved all candidates elected to the National Executive Council. There was no formal division between party and state institutions, and the domination of the party by Joseph Mobutu (Mobutu Sese Seko) led to a doctrine known as "Mobutism." The country's first multiparty presidential and legislative elections had been scheduled for May 1997 but were not held because Laurent Desire Kabila overthrew the Mobutu government and seized control of the country. The party may be replaced by the Union for the Republic (UPR).

Alliance of Democratic Forces for the Liberation of Congo-Zaire (AFDL)   President Kabila assumed power in March 1997, changing the name of the country back to the Congo. He originally announced a two-year timetable for political reform, but has since postponed elections until all foreign military forces attempting his overthrow had withdrawn from the country. Kabila has banned all political party activity indefinitely.

Other parties have included Union for Democracy and Social Progress, Congolese Rally for Democracy, Democratic Social Christian Party, Union of Federalists and Independent Republicans, and the Unified Lumumbast Party.

CHAPTER 6

ELECTIONS

**ARGENTINA
LEGISLATIVE ELECTIONS (SEATS IN CHAMBER OF DEPUTIES)***

From 1976 to 1983 Argentina was ruled by a series of military dictatorships. The first elections after the handover of power by the military were the simultaneous presidential and congressional elections of October 1983.

Date of Election	AR	A	PD	PJ	UCR	Others	Total
1983				111	129	14	254
1987				105	117	32	254*
1989							254
1991				119	85	50	254
1993				103	84	72	259
1995			2	134	69	52	277
1997	3	111	3	119		20	256
1999	9	63	2	50			124

ABBREVIATIONS
AR   Action for the Republic   PJ   Justicialist Party
A   Alliance   UCR Radical Civic Union
PD   Democratic Party

* Half of the seats are filled every two years.

**AUSTRALIA
LEGISLATIVE ELECTIONS (HOUSE OF REPRESENTATIVES)**

Date of Election	ALP	LP	N/CP	AD	DLP	I
28 Sep 1946	43	17	12			2*
			Coalition LP–CP			
10 Dec 1949	47		55–19			1
28 Apr 1951	52		52–17			
29 May 1954	57		47–17			
10 Dec 1955	47		57–18			
22 Nov 1958	45		58–19			

AUSTRALIA
LEGISLATIVE ELECTIONS (HOUSE OF REPRESENTATIVES) (CONT.)

Date of Election	ALP	LP	N/CP	AD	DLP	I
9 Dec 1961	60		45–17			
30 Nov 1963	50		52–20			
26 Nov 1966	41		61–21			
25 Oct 1969	59		46–20			1
2 Dec 1972	67		38–20			
18 May 1974	66		40–22			
13 Dec 1975	36		68–23			
2 Dec 1977	38		67–19			
18 Oct 1980	51		54–20			
1 Dec 1984	82		45–21			
11 July 1987	86		43–19			
24 Mar 1990	78		55–14			1
13 Mar 1993	80		49–16			2
1996	49		76–18			
1998	66		64–16			

ABBREVIATIONS

ALP	Australian Labor Party	AD	Australian Democratic Party
LP	Liberal Party	DLP	Democratic Labor Party
N/CP	National Party (since the 1970s known as Country Party)	I	Independent

* And others.

Sources: 1946–1980. *Supplement to World Elections On File:* 1984, *Political Handbook of the World.* (See Source List for complete citations.)

AUSTRALIA
LEGISLATIVE ELECTIONS (SENATE)

Date of Election	ALP	LP	N/CP	AD	DLP	I
21 Sept 1946	33	2	1 Coalition LP–CP			
10 Dec 1949	34		26			
28 Apr 1951	28		32			
8 May 1953	29		31			
10 Dec 1955	27		30		2	1*
22 Nov 1958	26		32		2	
9 Dec 1961	27		31		1	1
5 Dec 1964	28		29		2	1
24 Nov 1967	27		28		4	1
21 Nov 1970	26		26		5	3
18 May 1974	29		29			2*
13 Dec 1975	27		35			2
10 Dec 1977	26		35	2		1
18 Oct 1980	27		31	5		1
1 Dec 1984	34	28	5	7		2*

AUSTRALIA
LEGISLATIVE ELECTIONS (SENATE) (CONT.)

Date of Election	ALP	LP	N/CP	AD	DLP	I
11 July 1987	33	28	6	7		2
24 Mar 1990	32	29	4	8		3
13 Mar 1993	30	30	6	7		3
1996	30	29	6	7		4*
1998	29	31	3	9		4*

ABBREVIATIONS
ALP   Australian Labor Party
LP   Liberal Party
N/CP   National Party (since the 1970s known as Country Party)

AD   Australian Democratic Party
DLP   Democratic Labor Party
I   Independent

* And others.

Sources: Political Handbook of the World; Europa Yearbook; Political Systems and Parties; The Political Reference Almanac, 1999–2000. (See Source List for complete citations.)

AUSTRIA
LEGISLATIVE ELECTIONS (SEATS IN PARLIAMENT)

Date of Election	ÖVP	SPÖ	FPÖ*	KPÖ	Others	Total
25 Oct 1945	85	76		4		165
9 Oct 1949	77	67	16	5		165
22 Feb 1953	74	73	14	4		165
13 May 1956	82	74	6	3		165
10 May 1959	79	78	8			165
18 Nov 1962	81	76	8			165
6 Mar 1966	85	74	6			165
1 Mar 1970	79	81	5			165
10 Oct 1971	80	93	10			183
5 Oct 1975	80	93	10			183
6 May 1979	77	95	11			183
24 Apr 1983	81	90	12			183
23 Nov 1986	76	80	18		9**	183
7 Oct 1990	60	80	33		10**	183
1995	53	71	40		19	183
1999	52	65	52		14	183

ABBREVIATIONS
ÖVP   Österreichische Volkspartei / Austrian People's Party
SPÖ   Sozialistische Partei Österreichs / Socialist Party of Austria (renamed Social Democratic Party in 1991)
FPÖ   Freiheitliche Partei Österreichs / Freedom Party of Austria
VdU   Verein der Unabhängigen / League of Independents
KPÖ   Kommunistische Partei Österreichs / Communist Party of Austria

* VdU until 1959.

** Green/Alternative combined list.

BELGIUM
LEGISLATIVE ELECTIONS (SEATS IN PARLIAMENT)*

Date of Election	CVP	PS	PVV	PCB	Others	Total
17 Feb 1946	92	69	17	23	1	202
29 June 1949	105	66	29	12		212
4 June 1950	108	77	20	7		212
11 Apr 1954	95	86	25	4	2	212
1 June 1958	104	84	21	2	1	212
26 Mar 1961	96	84	20	5	7	212
23 May 1965	77	64	48	6	17	212
31 Mar 1968	69	59	47	5	32	212
7 Nov 1971	67	61	34	5	45	212
10 Mar 1974	72	59	30	4	47	212
17 Apr 1977	56	24	17	2	113	212
17 Dec 1978	57	25	22	4	104	212
8 Nov 1981	43	18	28	2	121	212
13 Oct 1985	49	20	22	0	121	212
13 Dec 1987	43	40	25	0	104	212
24 Nov 1991	39	35	26	0	112**	212
1995	29	21	21		100	150
1999	22	14	23		91	150

ABBREVIATIONS
CVP (PSC)   Christian People's Party   PVV   Freedom and Progress Party
PS (SP)   Socialist Party   PCB   Belgium Socialist Party

* Elections to the lower chamber (Chamber of Representatives). The Belgian Senate is also directly elected.
** Including 20 PRL (Liberals), 18 PSC (Christian Socialists) and 12 for the neo-Fascist Flemish Bloc.

BRAZIL
PRESIDENTIAL ELECTIONS*

Date of Election	Candidate	Party	Vote (#)	Vote (%)
1945	Enrico Dutra	PSD	3,251,507	52.4
	Eduardo Gomes	UDN	2,039,341	32.9
	Yeddo Fíuza	PCdoB	569,818	9.2
1950	Getúlio Vargas	PTB	3,849,040	46.6
	Eduardo Gomes	UDN	2,342,384	28.4
	Cristiano Machado	PSD	1,697,193	20.6
	Null vote		356,906	4.3
1955	Juscelino Kubitschek	PSD	3,077,411	33.8
	Juarez Távora	UDN	2,610,462	28.7
	Adhemar de Barros	PSP	2,222,725	24.4
	Plínio Salgado	PRP	714,379	7.9
	Null vote		472,037	5.2
1960	Jânio Quadros	UDN	5,636,623	44.8
	Henrique Lott	PSD/PTB	3,846,825	30.6
	Adhemar de Barros	PSP	2,195,709	17.4
	Null vote		907,197	7.2

BRAZIL
PRESIDENTIAL ELECTIONS* (CONT.)

Date of Election	Candidate	Party	Vote (#)	Vote (%)
1989**	Fernando Collor de Mello	PNR	35,089,998	53.0
(17 Dec)	Luiz Inacio Lula da Silva	PT	31,076,364	47.0
1998	Fernando Henrique Cardoso	PSDB	35,936,916	53.1
	Luiz Inacio Lula da Silva	PT	21,475,330	31.7
	Civo Gomes	PPS	7,426,232	11

ABBREVIATIONS
PSD   Partido Social Democratico / Social Democratic Party
UDN   Uniao Democratica Nacional / National Democratic Union
PCdoB   Partido Comunista do Brasil / Communist Party of Brazil
PTB   Partido Trabalhista Brasileiro / Brazilian Labor Party
PSB   Partido Socialista Brasileiro / Brazilian Socialist Party
PSP   Partido Social Progressivo / Social Progressive Party
PRP   Partido de Representacao Popular / Popular Representation Party

* Presidents from 1965 until 1989 were indirectly elected. Only candidates who received more than 1% of the vote are listed.

** Second ballot. No candidate achieved an overall majority on first ballot.

Source: *Brazil: Politics in a Patrimonial Society.* (See Source List for complete citation.)

BRAZIL
LEGISLATIVE ELECTIONS (SENATE)

Date of Election	PMDB	UDN	PSD	PTB	PSP	PR	PFL	PDT	PT	PDC	Other
1950		13	30	7	5	4					4
1954		13	23	16	3	4					4
1958		15	21	20	1	1					5
1962		17	23	18	2				1	2	3
1966*		46		20							
1970		59		7							
1974		46		20							
1978		42		25							
			PDS								
1982	21		46	1				1			
1986	44		5	1			16	2		1	3
1994	22		10	5			19	6		5	9
1998	27		16	1			20	2		7	18

ABBREVIATIONS

PMDB   Partido do Movimento Democratico Brasileiro / Party of the Brazilian Democratic Movement
UDN   Uniao Democratica Nacional / National Democratic Union
PSD   Partido Social Democratico / Social Democratic Party
PTB   Partido Trabalhista Brasileiro / Brazilian Labor Party
PSP   Partido Social Progressivo / Social Progressive Party
PR   Partido Republicano / Republican Party
PFL   Partido da Frente Liberal / Liberal Front Party
PDT   Partido Democratico Trabalhista / Democratic Labor Party

BRAZIL
LEGISLATIVE ELECTIONS (SENATE) (CONT.)

PT   Partido dos Trabalhadores / Party of the Workers
PDC   Partido Democratico Cristao / Christian Democrat Party
PDS   Partido Democratico Social / Social Democratic Party (a descendant of ARENA and distinct from the old
        PSD)

* The Institutional Act of 1965 dissolved the existing political parties and established a new, two-party system made up of
  an official government party and one opposition group.

Sources: *Political Handbook of the World; Europa Yearbook; Brazil: Politics in a Patrimonial Society.* (See Source List for
        complete citations.)

BRAZIL
LEGISLATIVE ELECTIONS (CHAMBER OF DEPUTIES)

Date of Election	PMDB	UDN	PSD	PTB	PSP	PR	PFL	PDT	PT	PDC	Other
1945*		85	173	23	7	12					20
1950		76	108	61	26	11					22
1954		74	114	60	28	18					32
1958		71	116	70	28	16					41
1962		96	122	97	23	13				18	35
		ARENA		**MDB**							
1966**		269		140							
1970		223		87							
1974		198		166							
1978		231		189							
		PSDB		**PTB**	**PPB**	**PRN**					
1982	200		235	13				23	8		
1986	259		36	19			115	24	19	3	12
1990	109		40	33		41	92	46	34	21	87
1994	107	64		31		1	88	33	49		38
1998	82	99		31	60		106	25	58		34

ABBREVIATIONS
PMDB   Partido do Movimento Democratico Brasileiro / Party of the Brazilian Democratic Movement
UDN   Uniao Democratica Nacional / National Democratic Union
PSD   Partido Social Democratico / Social Democratic Party
PTB   Partido Trabalhista Brasileiro / Brazilian Labor Party
PSP   Partido Social Progressivo / Social Progressive Party
PR   Partido Republicano / Republican Party
PFL   Partido da Frente Liberal / Liberal Front Party
PDT   Partido Democratico Trabalhista / Democratic Labor Party
PT   Partido dos Trabalhadores / Party of the Workers

BRAZIL
LEGISLATIVE ELECTIONS (CHAMBER OF DEPUTIES) (CONT.)

PDC   Partido Democratica Cristao / Christian Democrat Party
ARENA   Alianca Renovadora Nacional / National Renovating Alliance
MDB   Movimento Democratico Brasileiro / Brazilian Democratic Movement
PSDB   Partido da Social Democracia Brasileiro / Brazilian Social Democratic Party
PPB   Partido Progressista Brasileiro / Brazilian Progressive Party
PRN   Partido da Reconstrucao Nacional / National Reconstruction Party

* Totals for Constituent Assembly: Deputies *and* Senators. The 20 seats in "Other" include 15 for the Brazilian Communist Party.

** The Institutional Act of 1965 dissolved the existing political parties and established a new, two-party system made up of an official government party and one opposition group.

Sources: *Political Handbook of the World; Europa Yearbook; Keesing's Contemporary Archives; Brazil: Politics in a Patrimonial Society.* (See Source List for complete citations.)

CANADA
LEGISLATIVE ELECTIONS (SEATS IN PARLIAMENT)

Date of Election	Lib	Con	CCF	CA	SCP	New Dem	BQ	Rall	Others	Total
11 June 1945	125	67	28		13				12	245
27 June 1949	193	41	13		10				5	262
10 Aug 1953	171	51	23		15				5	265
10 June 1957	105	112	25		19				4	265
31 Mar 1958	49	208	8							265
18 June 1962	100	116			30	19				265
8 Apr 1963	129	95			24	17				265
18 Nov 1965	131	97			5	21		9	2	265
25 June 1968	155	72				22		14	1	264
30 Oct 1972	109	107			15	31			2	264
8 July 1974	141	95			11	16			1	264
22 May 1979	114	136			6	26				282
18 Feb 1980	147	103			32					282
4 Sep 1984	40	211				30			1	282
21 Nov 1988	82	170				43				295
25 Oct 1993	177	2				9			107*	
1997	155	20				21			105*	301
2000	173	12		66		13	37			301

ABBREVIATIONS
Lib   Liberal Party of Canada
Con   Conservative Party (Progressive Conservative Party from 1974)
CCF   Cooperative Commonwealth Federation
SCP   Social Credit Party of Canada
New Dem   New Democratic Party
Rall   Ralliement
CA   Canadian Reform Conservative Alliance (Canadian Alliance)
BQ   Bloc Québécois

* Includes Reform Party 52; Bloc Quebecois 54; Independent 1.

CHILE
LEGISLATIVE ELECTIONS (SENATE)*

Parties

Date of Election	Rightists					Leftists						
	Lib	TrCon	Con	LibPr	Agr	AuSo	Rad	Soc	Com	Fal	Dem	Agr
1945	10		10	1	2	2	12	2	5		1	
1949	12	6	2	1			13	3	2	2	1	3

Parties

	PCU	PDC	PDN	PR	PN	PS	PSP	PCC	PL	Other	Ind
1953	6			10		2	4		11	12	
1957	6	3	4	10		8			8	(1 vac)	5
1961	4	4		13		7		4	10	3	
1965		12		10	5	4	5	5		7	
1969		23		8	5	4		7		(1 vac)	2
1973		19		2	8	7		9	5		

Parties

	PDC	UDI	RN	PS	PPD	UCCP	UPC	Other
1989	13	2	11		4			8
1993	13	3	11	5	2	1		4
1997	14	9	7	4	2	1	1	

ABBREVIATIONS

Lib	Liberals	Oth	Other
TrCon	Traditionalist Conservatives	PCU	Partido Conservativa Unido / United Conservative Party
Con	Conservatives	PDN	Partido Democrata Nacional / National Democratic Party
LibPr	Liberal Progressives	PN	Partido Nacional / National Party
Agr	Agrarians	PSP	Partido Socialista Popular / Popular Socialist Party
AuSo	Authentic Socialists	PCC	Partido Comunista de Chile / Communist Party of Chile
Rad	Radicals	RN	Renovacion Nacional / National Renovation
Soc	Socialists	UDI	Union Democrata Independiente / Independent Democratic Union
Com	Communists		
Fal	Falangists	PPD	Partido por la Democracia / Party for Democracy
Dem	Democrats	UPC	Union por Chile / Union for Chile
Agr	Agrarians	PRSD	Partido Radical Socialdemocrata / Social-Democratic Radical Party
Ind	Independent		
Vac	Vacancy	UCCP	Union de Centro Centro Progresista / Center Center Union
PR	Partido Radical / Radical Party	PDC	Partido Democrata Cristiano / Christian Democratic Party
PL	Partido Liberal / Liberal Party	PS	Partido Socialista de Chile / Socialist Party of Chile

* From 1973 to 1989, Chile was ruled by a military junta. In the 1989 Senate elections the Christian Democrats took 13 seats, their allies a further 9 and various right-wingers (PRN, 11 and UDI, 5) took 16.

Sources: *Political Handbook of the World; Europa Yearbook.* (See Source List for complete citations.)

CHILE
LEGISLATIVE ELECTIONS (CHAMBER OF DEPUTIES)

Date of Election*	Parties												
	Rightists						Leftists						
	Lib	TrCon	Con	LibPr	Agr	Oth	Rad	Soc	Com	Fal	Dem	Agr	Oth
1945	34		36		3	1	40	6	15	4	8		
1949	33	21	10	2		3	41			3	6	14	12

	Parties											
	PCU	ALP	PDC	PDN	PR	PN	PS	PSP	PCC	PL	Oth	Ind
1953	16	25			20		7	21		22	36	
1957	22		23	11	39		9		6	32	1	2
1961	17		23	12	39		12		16			
1965			81		19	9	9	6	18	28	5	
1969			55		24	34	15		22			
1973			50		5	34	28		25		8	

	Parties								
	PDC	RN	UDI	PPD	PS	UPC	PRSD	Oth	Ind
1989	38	29	11	17	7		5	16	
1993	37	29	15	15	15		2	7	
1997	39	23	17	17	11	6	4	2	2

ABBREVIATIONS

Lib	Liberals	PCU	Partido Conservativa Unido / United Conservative Party
TrCon	Traditionalist Conservatives	PDC	Partido Democrata Cristiano / Christian Democrat Party
Con	Conservatives	PDN	Partido Democrata Nacional / National Democratic Party
LibPr	Liberal Progressives	PR	Partido Radical / Radical Party
Agr	Agrarians	PN	Partido Nacional / National Party
Rad	Radicals	PS	Partido Socialista de Chile / Socialist Party of Chile
Soc	Socialists	PSP	Partido Socialista Popular / Popular Socialist Party
Com	Communists	PCC	Partido Comunista de Chile / Communist Party of Chile
Fal	Falangists	PL	Partido Liberal / Liberal Party
Dem	Democrats	RN	Renovacion Nacional / National Renovation
Agr	Agrarians	UDI	Union Democrata Independiente / Independent Democratic Union
Oth	Other	PPD	Partido por la Democracia / Party for Democracy
Ind	Independent	UPC	Union por Chile / Union for Chile
Vac	Vacancy	PRSD	Partido Radical Socialdemocrata / Social-Democratic Radical Party

* From 1973 to 1989, Chile was ruled by a military junta. In the election to the Chamber of Deputies on 14 December 1989, the Christian Democrats took 39 seats; National Renovation, 29; PPD, 16; UDI, 11; and Center Right Independents, 11. The Socialists (PSP) took 7; the Radical Party, 5; and there were 5 others.

Sources: *Political Handbook of the World; Europa Yearbook.* (See Source List for complete citations.)

CHILE
PRESIDENTIAL ELECTIONS*

Year	Candidate	Party	Vote	Vote (%)
1946	Gabriel González Videla	L:Rad/Com/Au Soc	191,351	40.2
	Eduardo Cruz Coke	Con	141,134	29.7
	Fernando Allesandri Rodriguez	Lib	129,092	27.2
1952	Carlos Ibáñez del Campo	Ind	432,920	46.8
	Arturo Matte	R:Con/Lib	252,648	27.8
	Pedro E. Alfonso	C:Rad	183,878	19.9
	Salvador Allende Gossens	L:Soc	51,984	5.5
1958	Jorge Alessandri Rodriguez	R:Con/Lib	386,192	31.6
	Salvador Allende Gossens	L:Soc/Com	354,300	28.9
	Eduardo Frei Montalva	C:CD	254,323	20.7
	Luis Bossay	C:Rad	189,182	15.6
	Antonio Zamorano	Ind Left	41,224	3.3
1964	Eduardo Frei Montalva	C-R:CD/Con Lib	1,404,809	56.1
	Salvador Allende Gossens	L:Soc/Com	975,210	38.9
	Julio Duran Neumann	C-R:Rad	124,764	5.0
1970	Salvador Allende Gossens	L:Soc/Com	1,075,616	36.6
	Jorge Alessandri Rodriguez	R:Ind/Nat	1,036,278	35.2
	Radomiro Tomic	C:CD	824,849	28.1
1989	Patricio Aylwin Azocar	C:L	3,850,000	55.2
	Hernan Büchi Buc	R:Dem/Prog	2,052,000	29.4
	Francisco Javier Errázuriz	Ind	1,077,000	15.4
1993	Eduardo Frei Ruiz-Tagle	PDC	4,008,654	58.0
	Arturo Alessandri Besa	UPP	1,685,584	24.4
	Others (4)		1,216,349	17.6
First Round	Ricardo Lagos	PPD	3,383,334	48
12 Dec 1999	Joaquin Infante	ApC	3,352,192	47.5
	Gladys Marin	PCC	225,224	3.2
	Others		93,741	1.3
Second Round	Ricardo Lagos	PPD	3,677,968	51.3
16 Jan 2000	Joaquin Lavin	ApC	3,490,561	48.7

ABBREVIATIONS

Au Soc	Authentic Socialist	Com	Communist
I	Independent	CD	Christian Democrat
R	Right	Nat	National
C	Center	PPD	Partido por la Democracia (Party for Democracy, coalition of Socialist,
L	Left		Christian Democrat and Radical Parties)
Con	Conservative	ApC	Alianza por Chile (Alliance for Chile, coalition of Democratic Union and
Lib	Liberal		National Renovation Parties)
Rad	Radical	PCC	Communist Party of Chile
Soc	Socialist	PDC	Partido Democrata Cristiano / Christian Democratic Party
		UPP	Democracia y Progresso / Democracy and Progress

* After the 1973 military coup, no presidential elections took place until 14 December 1989.

Sources: *Political Systems and Parties; Keesing's Contemporary Archives.* (See Source List for complete citations.)

DENMARK
LEGISLATIVE ELECTIONS (SEATS IN PARLIAMENT)*

Date of Election	Soc Dems	Libs	Cons	Comms	Others	Total
30 Oct 1945	48	38	26	18	18	148
28 Oct 1947	57	49	17	9	16	148
5 Sept 1950	59	32	27	7	24	149
21 April 1953	61	33	26	7	22	149
22 Sept 1953	74	42	30	8	21	175
14 May 1957	70	45	30	6	24	175
15 Nov 1960	76	38	32		29	175
22 Sep 1964	76	38	36		25	175
22 Nov 1966	69	35	34		37	175
23 Jan 1968	62	34	37		42	175
21 Sep 1971	70	30	31		44	175
4 Dec 1973	46	22	16	6	85	175
9 Jan 1975	53	42	10	7	63	175
15 Feb 1977	65	21	15	7	67	175
23 Oct 1977	68	22	22		63	175
8 Dec 1981	59	20	26		70	175
10 Jan 1984	56	22	42		55	175
8 Sep 1987	54	19	38		64	175
10 May 1988	55	22	25		63	175
12 Dec 1990	69	29	30		47	175
1994	62	42	27		48	179
1998	63	42	16		58	179

ABBREVIATIONS
Soc Dems   Social Democrats
Libs   Liberals
Cons   Conservatives
Comms   Communists

* The Assembly consists of 179 seats. Greenland and the Faroe Islands each have two deputies.

EGYPT
LEGISLATIVE ELECTIONS (PEOPLE'S ASSEMBLY)

Date of Election	National Democratic Party	New Wafd Party	Socialist Labor Party	Liberals	Independents	Appointed
May 1984	396	58	4			10
Apr 1987	360	34	55	2	7	10
Nov 1990	Elections boycotted by all the major opposition parties. The National Democratic Party won 270 seats, with 80 more Independents who were NDP members.					
1995	415				16	10

FRANCE
LEGISLATIVE ELECTIONS (SEATS IN CHAMBER OF DEPUTIES)

Date of Election	CP	PS	RS	PRM*	C/M	G	P	Others	Total
21 Oct 1945	148	134	35	141	62			2	522
2 June 1946	146	115	39	160	62				522
10 Nov 1946	166	90	55	158	70			5	544
17 June 1951	97	94	77	82	87	107	51		544
2 Jan 1956	147	88	73	71	95	16		3	544
23 Nov 1958	10	44	44	57	133	198			465
18 Nov 1962	41		208		84	229			465
5 Mar 1967	72	117		45		232		4	470
23 June 1968	33	57		31		349			470

Date of Election	CP	PS	UDR	IR	Ref	CDP	NF	Others	Total
4 & 11 Mar 1973	73	102	183	55	34	30		13	490

Date of Election	CP	PS/LR	UDF	RPR	RPR/UDF	NF	Others	Total
12 & 19 Mar 1973	86	103	124	154			14	481
14 & 21 June 1981	44	285	65	85			12	491
16 Mar 1986	35	206	53	76	147	35	23	575
5 & 12 June 1988	27	206(PS)			271	1		575

Date of Election	CP	PS	UDF	RPR	RPR/UDF	NF	Others	Total
21 & 28 Mar 1993	23	54	213	247	—	—	40	577
1997	38	247	108	134	—	—	56	583

ABBREVIATIONS

CP	Communist Party	RS	Radical Socialists
PS	Socialist Party	LR	Left Radicals
G	Gaullists	P	Poujadists
IR	Independent Republicans	Ref	Reformists
C/M	Conservatives and Moderates	UDR	Union of Democrats for the Republic
PRM	Popular Republican Movement	NF	National Front
CDP	Centre Démocratie et Progrès	RPR	Rassemblement pour la République
UDF	Union for French Democracy		

* From 1967 Democratic Center.

GERMANY
LEGISLATIVE ELECTIONS (SEATS IN PARLIAMENT)

Date of Election	CDU/CSU	SPD	FDP	Greens	Others	Total
14 Aug 1949	139	131	52		80	402
6 Sep 1953	244	151	48		44	487
15 Sep 1957	270	169	41		17	497
17 Sep 1961	242	190	67			499
19 Sep 1965	245	202	49			496

GERMANY
LEGISLATIVE ELECTIONS (SEATS IN PARLIAMENT) (CONT.)

Date of Election	CDU/CSU	SPD	FDP	Greens	Others	Total
28 Sep 1969	242	224	30			496
19 Nov 1972	225	230	41			496
3 Oct 1976	243	214	39			496
5 Oct 1980	226	218	53			497
6 Mar 1983	244	193	34	27		498
25 Jan 1987	223	186	46	42		497

Following German reunification in October 1990, the first elections for the all-German parliament were held on 2 December 1990. The outcome was:

	1990	1994	1998
CDU	239	244	198
CSU*	51	50	47
FDP	79	47	44
(Coalition)	372		
SPD	239		
PDS	17	30	35
Alliance 90/Greens	8	49	47
Greens			
Republicans			
Others**			
	636	420	371

ABBREVIATIONS
CDU   Christlichdemokratische Union / Christian Democratic Union (outside Bavaria)
CSU   Christlichsoziale Union / Christian Social Union (in Bavaria)
SPD   Sozialdemokratische Partei Deutschlands / Social Democratic Party of Germany
FDP   Freidemokratische Partei / Free Democratic Party

* DSU in East Germany.
** 16 parties in all.

GREECE
LEGISLATIVE ELECTIONS (SEATS IN PARLIAMENT)

1946	Nationalist (& allies), 206; National Political Union, 68; Liberals, 48
1950	Populists, 62; Liberals, 56; National Progressive Union, 45; Papandreou Group, 35
1951	Hellenic Party, 114; National Progressive Union, 74; Liberals, 57
1952	Hellenic Party, 247; National Progressive Union and Liberals, 51
1956	National Radical Union, 165; Democratic Union, 132
1958	National Radical Union, 171; United Democratic Left, 79; Liberals, 36
1961	National Radical Union, 176; Progressives and Center Union, 100; Pan-Democratic Agrarian Front (i.e., United Left), 24
1963	Center Union, 138; National Radical Union, 132; Pan-Democratic Agrarian Front, 28
1964	Center Union, 171; Progressive and National Radical Union, 107; United Left, 22
1974	New Democracy, 220; Center Union, 60; Panhellenic Socialist Union (Pasok), 12; Communists and United Left, 8

GREECE
LEGISLATIVE ELECTIONS (SEATS IN PARLIAMENT) (CONT.)

1977	New Democracy, 172; Pasok, 93; Democratic Center Union, 15; Communists (KKE), 11; others, 9
1981	Pasok, 172; New Democracy, 115; Communists (KKE), 13
1985	Pasok, 161; New Democracy, 126; Communists (both wings), 13
1989 (June)	New Democracy, 145; Pasok, 125; Left Coalition, 28; others; 2
1989 (Nov)	New Democracy, 148; Pasok, 128; Left Coalition, 21; Ecologist Alternative, 1; others, 2
1990 (Apr)	New Democracy, 150; Pasok, 123; Left Coalition, 19; Ecologist Alternative, 1; others, 6
1993 (Oct)	Pasok, 170; New Democracy, 111; Political Spring, 10; Greek Communist Party (KKE), 9; others, 0
1997	Pasok, 162; New Democracy, 108; Greek Communist Party (KKE), 11; Left Coalition, 10; Democratic Social Movement, 9
2000	Pasok, 157; New Democracy, 126; Greek Communist Party, 11; Left Coalition, 6

INDIA
LEGISLATIVE ELECTIONS (SEATS IN PARLIAMENT)

Date of Election	Cong	Comm	Soc	PSP	JS	Sw	DMK	CD	J	Other	Total
1952	362	27	12		3						489
1957	369	27		21	4					73	494
Feb 1962	361	29			14	18				72	494
Feb 1967	282	42			35	44	25			90	518
Mar 1971	366	48			22	8	23			51	518
Mar 1977	153	29					19	28	271	40	540

Date of Election	Cong	Cong (I)*	LF**	LD	J*	Vacancies	Other	Total
Jan 1980	13	374	54	41	34	19	9	544

Date of Election	Cong	Cong (I)*	Comm	J	Telegu Desam	Other	Total
Dec 1984		413	22	13	30	64	542

Date of Election	Cong	Com	Soc	PSP	JS	Sw	DMK	BJP***	J	Other	Total
Nov 1989****	192	51						88	141	53	525
June 1991	227	48					11	119	55	53	513 (+32 vacant)
1996	141	32	17				17	162		172	541

INDIA
LEGISLATIVE ELECTIONS (SEATS IN PARLIAMENT) (CONT.)

Date of Election	Cong	Com	Soc	PSP	JS	Sw	DMK	BJP***	J	Other	Total
1998	141	32	20				6	179		167	545
1999	113	32	26				12	182		172	537

ABBREVIATIONS

Cong	Congress	Soc	Socialists
Comm	Communists	PSP	Praja Samadavadi Party
JS	Jan Sangh		(People's Socialist Party)
J	Janata	Sw	Swatantra
DMK	Dravida Munnetra Kazhagam	CD	Congress for Democracy
LF	Left Front	LD	Lok Dal

* And allies.

** Including Communists.

*** BJP=Bharatiya Janata Party (Hindu nationalist).

**** Only 525 seats contested, the others to be filled later.

INDONESIA

Since independence, Indonesia has developed no tradition of truly free elections. Golkar has been the dominant force in the political life of the country for over two decades. The following table gives summary results since 1977:

2 May 1977	Golkar	232
	Indonesian Democratic Party	29
	United Development Party	99
	Total (of elective seats)	360
4 May 1982	Golkar	246
	Indonesian Democratic Party	24
	United Development Party	94
	Total (of elective seats)	364
23 Apr 1987	Golkar	299
	Indonesian Democratic Party	40
	United Development Party	61
	Total (of elective seats)	400
9 June 1992	Golkar*	282
	United Development Party	62
	Indonesian Democratic Party	56
	Total (of elective seats)	400
1997	Golkar	325
	United Devel. Party	89
	IDP	11
	Total (of elective seats)	425

* Golkar won all 27 provinces.

ISRAEL
LEGISLATIVE ELECTION (SEATS IN KNESSET)

Date of Election	Lab	UWP	R	FP	GZ	UL	Lib	Gah	Lik	Others	Total
25 Jan 1949	46	19	16	14						25	120
30 July 1951	45	15	15	8	20					17	120
26 July 1955	40	10	17	15	13	9				16	120
3 July 1959	47	7	18	17		9				22	120
15 Aug 1961	50	9	18	17			17			9	120
2 Nov 1965	63		17					26		14	120
28 Oct 1969	56		18					26		20	120
31 Dec 1973	51		10						39	20	120
17 May 1977	32		12						43	33	120
30 June 1981	47		6						48	19	120
23 July 1984	44								41	35	120
1 Nov 1988	39		18						40	23*	120
3 June 1992	44								32	44**	120
1996	34		9						22	54	119
1999	26***		5						19	70****	120

ABBREVIATIONS
Lab	Labor	GZ	General Zionists
UWP	United Workers' Party	UL	Unity of Labor
R	United Religious Front (1949)	Lib	Liberals
	Religious groupings (1951–69)	Gah	Gahal
	National Religious Party (1973–81)	Lik	Likud
FP	Freedom Party		

* Including 6 Arab bloc, 7 Rightists, 5 Citizens Rights' Movement, 3 Mapam and 2 Shinui (Liberal-Center).

** Including 12 Meretz, 8 Tsomet, 6 Shas, 6 National Religious Party, 4 United Torah, 3 Moledet, 2 Hadash and 2 Arab Democratic Party.

*** Including 2 Gesher and 1 Meimad

**** Including 17 Shas, 10 Meretz, 6 Yisrael Ba'aliyah, 6 Shinui-Mifleget Merkaz, 6 ha-Merkaz, 5 Hamiflage Hadati Leumit, 5 Yahadut Ha' Torah, 5 United Arab List, 4 National Union, 3 Democratic Front for Race and Equality, 4 Our Home Israel, 2 National Democratic Alliance, 2 One Nation.

ITALY
LEGISLATIVE ELECTIONS (CHAMBER OF DEPUTIES)

Date of Election	U	PL	LN	RC	PPI	PCI	PSI	PA	AN	C
1946					207	104	115			
1948					305	131	52		6	
1953					263	143	75		29	
1958					273	140	84		24	
1963					260	166	87		27	
1968					266	177	91		24	
1972					267	179	61		56	
1976					263	227	57		35	
1979					262	221	62		30	
1983					225	198	73		42	
1987					234	177	94		35	

ITALY
LEGISLATIVE ELECTIONS (CHAMBER OF DEPUTIES) (CONT.)

Date of Election	U	PL	LN	RC	PPI	PCI	PSI	PA	AN	C
1992			55	35	206	107	92		34	
1994		366						213		46
1996	284	246	59	35						

ABBREVIATIONS
U   L'Ulivo / Olive Tree
PL   Polo Liberta / Freedom Alliance
LN   Lega Nord / Nothern League
RC   Rifondazione Communista / Communist Refoundation
PPI   Partito Popolare Italiano / Italian Popular Party (formerly the Christian Democratic Party, rena-med 1993)
PCI   Partido Communista Italiano / Italian Communist Party (renamed Democratic Party of the Left in 1991)
PSI   Partido Socialista Italiano / Italian Socialist Party
PA   Progressive Alliance (included the Democratic Party of the Left, La Rete, Greens, and Socialists)
AN   Alleanza Nazionale / National Alliance (formerly the Italian Social Movement, renamed in 1993)
C   Center (included the Popular Party and the Pact for Italy)

ITALY
LEGISLATIVE ELECTIONS (SENATE)

Date of Election	U	PL	LN	RC	PPI	PCI	PSI	AN
1948					151	68	41	6
1953					110	51	28	9
1958					121	56	37	8
1963					132	81	47	17
1968					266	87	46	11
1972					135	94	33	26
1976					135	116	29	15
1979					138	109	32	13
1983					120	107	38	18
1987					124	99	38	16
1992			25	20	107	64	49	16
1994								46
1996	157	116	27					

ABBREVIATIONS
U   L'Ulivo / Olive Tree
PL   Polo Liberta / Freedom Alliance
LN   Lega Nord / Nothern League
RC   Rifondazione Communista / Communist Refoundation
PPI   Partito Popolare Italiano / Italian Popular Party (formerly the Christian Democratic Party, rena-med 1993)
PCI   Partido Communista Italiano / Italian Communist Party (renamed Democratic Party of the Left in 1991)
PSI   Partido Socialista Italiano / Italian Socialist Party
AN   Alleanza Nazionale / National Alliance (formenrly the Italian Social Movement, renamed in 1993)

JAPAN
LEGISLATIVE ELECTIONS—HOUSE OF REPRESENTATIVES

Date of Election	LDP	NFP	DP	JCP	SDP	CGP	DSP	JRP	JNP
1946				5	92				
1947				4	143				
1949				35	48				
1952					111				
1953				1	138				
1955				2	156				
1958	287			1	166				
1960	296			3	145		17		
1963	283			5	144		23		
1967	277			5	140	25	30		
1969	288			14	90	47	31		
1972	271			38	118	29	19		
1976	249			17	123	55	29		
1979	248			39	107	57	35		
1980	286			29	107	33	32		
1983	258			27	113	59	38		
1986	304			27	86	57	26		
1990	275			16	136	45	14		
1993	223			15	70	51	15	55	30
1996	239	156	52	26	15				
2000	233		127	20	19	31			

ABBREVIATIONS
LDP   Liberal Democratic Party / Jiyuminshuto
NFP   New Frontier Party / Shinshinto
DP   Democratic Party / Minshuto
JCP   Japan Communist Party / Nihon Kyosanto
SDP   Social Democratic Party / Shakai Minshuto (formerly the Japan Socialist Party)
CGP   Clean Government Party / Komeito
DSP   Democratic Socialist Party / Minshu Shakaito
JRP   Japan Renewal Party / Shinseito
JNP   Japan New Party

NETHERLANDS
LEGISLATIVE ELECTIONS (SEATS IN PARLIAMENT)

Date of Election	KV (CDA)	PvdA	ARP	VVD	Others	Total
17 May 1946	32	29	13	6	20	100
7 July 1948	32	27	13	8	20	100
25 June 1952	30	30	12	9	19	100
13 June 1956	49	50	15	13	23	150
12 Mar 1959	49	48	14	19	20	150
15 May 1963	50	43	13	16	28	150
15 Feb 1967	42	37	15	17	39	150
28 Mar 1971	35	39	13	16	47	150
29 Nov 1972	27	43	14	22	44	150
25 May 1977	49	53		28	20	150

NETHERLANDS
LEGISLATIVE ELECTIONS (SEATS IN PARLIAMENT) (CONT.)

Date of Election	KV (CDA)	PvdA	ARP	VVD	Others	Total
26 May 1981	48	44		26	32	150
8 Sep 1982	45	47		36	22	150
21 May 1986	54	52		27	17	150
6 Sep 1989	54	49		22	25	150
3 May 1994	34	37		31	48*	150
1998	29	45		38	38*	150

ABBREVIATIONS
KV   Catholic People's Party (Christian Democratic Appeal from 1977)
PvdA   Labor Party
ARP   Anti-Revolutionary Party
VVD   People's Party for Freedom and Democracy

* "Others" includes 24 Democrats.

NORWAY
LEGISLATIVE ELECTIONS (SEATS IN PARLIAMENT)

Date of Election	Lab	Con	Lib	CP	A(C)	Others	Total
8 Oct 1945	76	25	20	8	10	11	150
10 Oct 1949	85	23	21	9	12		150
12 Oct 1953	77	27	15	14	14	3	150
7 Oct 1957	78	29	15	12	15	1	150
11 Sep 1961	74	29	14	15	16	2	150
12 Sep 1965	68	31	18	13	18	2	150
7 Sep 1969	74	13	13	14	20	16	150
9 Sep 1973	62	29	2	20	21	21	155
11 Sep 1977	76	41	2	22	12	2	155
13 Sep 1981	66	53	2	16	10	8	155
8 Sep 1985	71	50		16	12	8	157
11 Sep 1989	63	37		14	11	40	165
13 Sep 1993	67	28	1	13	31	25	165
1997	65	23	6	25	11	41	171

ABBREVIATIONS
Lab   Labor   CP   Christian People's Party
Con   Conservative   A(C)   Agrarian (Center)
Lib   Liberal

PORTUGAL
LEGISLATIVE ELECTIONS (SEATS IN PARLIAMENT)

The following elections have taken place since the coup of April 1974. Prior to that date, under the Salazar regime, only government candidates were elected.

Date of Election	PSD	PDP	PCP (PS)	CDS	DM	DA	Others	Total
Apr 1975	115	80	30	16	5		1	247
Apr 1976	107	73	40	42			1	263

PORTUGAL
LEGISLATIVE ELECTIONS (SEATS IN PARLIAMENT) (CONT.)

Date of Election	PSD	PDP	PCP (PS)	CDS	DM	DA		Others	Total
Dec 1979	73		47			118		8	246
Oct 1980						DC	PRD		
April 1983	101		44			30		0	250
Oct 1985	88		57	39		22	44	0	250
July 1987	146		59	20		4	7	14	250
Oct 1991	135		72	5				18*	230
1995	88		112					30	230
1999	81		115					32	230

ABBREVIATIONS

PSP	Socialists	DM	Democratic Movement
PDP	Democratic Party	DA	Democratic Alliance
PCP	Communist Party	DC	Democratic Center
CDS	Social Democratic Center	PRD	Party of Democratic Renewal

* Communists (CDU) and their left-wing allies, 17; National Solidarity Party, 1.

RUSSIA
PRESIDENTIAL ELECTIONS

The first free presidential elections in the history of Russia were held on 12 June 1991.

Date	Candidates	Party	Vote	Vote (%)
1991	Boris Yeltsin		45,552,041	57.3
	Nikolai Ryzhkov		13,395,335	16.9
	Vladimir Zhirinovsky	LDPR	6,211,007	7.8
	Others		8,148,357	10.3
1996	Boris Yeltsin		26,665,495	35.3
	Gennady Zyuganov	KPRF	24,211,686	32
	Aleksandr Lebed	KRO	10,974,736	14.5
	Grigory Yavlinsky	JABLOKO	5,550,752	7.3
	Vladimir Zhirinovsky	LDPR	4,311,479	5.7
Runoff 7/3/1996	Boris Yeltsin		40,202,349	53.8
	Gennady Zyuganov		30,104,589	40.3
2000	Vladimir Putin		39,740,434	53
	Gennady Zyuganov	KPRF	21,928,471	29.2
	Grigory Yavlinsky	JABLOKO	4,351,452	5.8
	Aman Tuleyev		2,217,361	3
	Vladimir Zhirinovsky	LDPR	2,026,513	2.7

ABBREVIATIONS

LDPR	Liberal Democratic Party of Russia / Liberal'no-demokratikeskaja Partija Rossii
KPRF	Communist Party of the Russian Federation / Kommunistikeskaja Parttija Rossijskoi Federacii
KRO	Congress of Russian Communities / Kongress russkich obshkin
JABLOKO	Appeal / Jabloko

RUSSIA
LEGISLATIVE ELECTIONS

Nationwide elections for Russia's parliament were held on 12 December 1993.

Date of Election	KPRF	LDPR	NDR	JABLOKO	APR	DVR	KRO	VN	Ind
1993	32	59		20	21	40			
1995	157	51	55	45	20	9	5	9	78
1999	113	17	7	21					

ABBREVIATIONS
KPRF	Communist Party of the Russian Federation / Kommunistikeskaja Partija Rossijskoi Federacii
LDPR	Liberal Democratic Party of Russia / Liberal'no-demokratikeskaja Partija Rossii
NDR	Our Home Is Russia / Nash dom—Rossija
JABLOKO	Appeal / Jabloko
APR	Agrarian Party of Russia / Agramaja Partija Rossii
DVR	Russia's Democratic Choice Party / Demokratikeskii Vybor Rossii
KRO	Congress of Russian Communities / Kongress russkich obshkin
VN	Power to the People! / Vlast' Narodu!
Ind	Independent

SOUTH AFRICA

The first all-race elections in the history of South Africa (dubbed the "Liberation Election" by the African National Congress) were held on 27–28 April 1994.

These multiracial elections heralded the advent of majority rule in South Africa. The outcome of the vote, which although declared free and fair, was marred by many irregularities.

Date of Election	ANC	DP	IFP	NNP	UDM	ACDP	FF	PAC
1994	252	7	43	82			9	5
1999	157	51	55	45	14	6	3	3

ABBREVIATIONS:
ANC	African National Congress	UDM	United Democratic Movement
DP	Democratic Party	ACDP	African Christian Democratic Party
IFP	Inkatha Freedom Party	FF	Freedom Front
NNP	New National Party	PAC	Pan Africanist Congress

SPAIN
LEGISLATIVE ELECTIONS (SEATS IN PARLIAMENT)

Date of Election	UCD	PSOE	PCE	CD	CU	PNV	PP	Others	Total
1977	165	118	20	16	11	8		12	350
1979	168	121	23	9	8	7		14	350

SPAIN
LEGISLATIVE ELECTIONS (SEATS IN PARLIAMENT) (CONT.)

Date of Election	UCD	PSOE	PCE	CD	CU	PNV	PP	Others	Total
1982	12	202*			12	8	106*	10	350
1986	19	184	7		18	6	105	11	350
1989	14	175	18*		18	5	106	14	350
1993		159	18		17	5	141	17**	340
1996		141			16	5	156	48	350
2000		125			15	7	183	20	350

ABBREVIATIONS
UCD   Union of the Democratic Center (1986 = Democratic and Social Center)
PSOE Socialists
CU   Convergence and Unity
PNV   Basque Nationalist Left
PP   Popular Party
CD   Party of the Democratic Coalition
PCE   Communists

* With allies.
** Catalan.

SWEDEN
LEGISLATIVE ELECTIONS (SEATS IN PARLIAMENT)

Date of Election	Mod	A/C	F	SD	Comm	Others	Greens	Total
19 Sep 1948	23	30	57	112	8	0	0	230
21 Sep 1952	31	26	58	110	5	0	0	230
26 Sep 1956	42	19	58	106	6	0	0	231
1 June 1958	45	32	38	111	5	0	0	231
18 Sep 1960	39	34	40	114	5	0	0	232
20 Sep 1964	33	36	43	113	8	0	0	233
15 Sep 1968	29	37	32	125	3	7	0	233
20 Sep 1970	41	71	58	163	17	0	0	350
16 Sep 1973	90	51	34	156	19	0	0	350
19 Sep 1976	86	55	39	152	17	0	0	349
16 Sep 1979	73	64	38	154	20	0	0	349
19 Sep 1982	86	56	21	166	20	0	0	349
15 Sep 1985	76	44	51	159	19	0	0	349
18 Sep 1988	66	42	44	156	21	0	20	349
15 Sep 1991		170		138	16	25*	0	349
1994	80	27	26	162	22	14	18	349
1998	92	18	17	131	43	42	16	349

ABBREVIATIONS
Mod   Moderates (formerly Conservatives)   SD   Social Democrats
A/C   Agrarian / Center   Comm Communists
F   Folkspartiet (Liberals)

* New Democracy Party.

TURKEY
LEGISLATIVE ELECTIONS (SEATS IN PARLIAMENT)

Date of Election	DP	RPP	NP	JP	NAP	NTP	NSP	Others
1946	64	64						6
1950	396	68	1					7
1954	505	31						6
1957	424	178						8
1961		173		158	54	65		–
1965		134	31	240		19		26
1969		143		265				51
1973		185		149			48	68
1977		213		189	16		24	8

Following a military coup in 1980, no more democratic elections were held. In the election of 1983 only three parties were allowed to take part.

Date of Election	RP	DYP*	ANAP	DSP	CHP*	SHP*	FP*	MHP
1983		71	212			117		
1987		59	292			99		
1991	62	178	115	7		8		
1995	158	135	132	75	50			
1999		85	86	136			111	129

ABBREVIATIONS

DP	Democratic Party	DYP	True Path Party (merged with National Democracy Party in 1985)
RPP	Republican People's Party		
NP	Nation Party	ANAP	Motherland Party
JP	Justice Party	DSP	Democratic Left Party
NAP	Nationalist Action Party	CHP	Republican People's Party (merged with SHP in 1985)
NTP	New Turkey Party	SHP	Social Democrat Populist Party (resulting from a merger of the Populist Party and SODEP in 1985)
NSP	National Salvation Party		
RP	Welfare Party	FP	Virtue Party (formerly the Welfare Party)
		MHP	Nationalist Movement Party

UNITED KINGDOM
LEGISLATIVE ELECTIONS (SEATS IN PARLIAMENT)

Date of Election	Cons	Labour	Liberal	SNP	PC	Others	Total
5 July 1945	213	393	12			22	640
23 Feb 1950	298	315	9			3	625
25 Oct 1951	321	295	6			3	625
26 May 1955	344	277	6			3	630
8 Oct 1959	365	258	6			1	630
15 Oct 1964	304	317	9				630
31 Mar 1966	253	363	12			2	630
18 June 1970	330	287	6	1		6	630
28 Feb 1974	297	301	14	7	2	14	635
10 Oct 1974	277	319	13	11	3	12	635

UNITED KINGDOM
LEGISLATIVE ELECTIONS (SEATS IN PARLIAMENT) (CONT.)

Date of Election	Cons	Labour	Liberal	SNP	PC	Others	Total
3 May 1979	339	269	11	2	2	12	635
9 June 1983	397	209	23*	2	2	17	650
11 June 1987	376	229	22*	3	3	17	650
9 April 1992	336	271	20*	3	4	17	651
1997	165	419	46			29	659

ABBREVIATIONS
Cons   Conservative Party
SNP   Scottish National Party
PC   Plaid Cymru

* Includes the Social Democrats. In 1992 the figures are for the Liberal Democrats.

UNITED STATES
PRESIDENTIAL ELECTIONS

Date	Candidates* (President & V. President)	Party	Popular Vote (#)	Popular Vote (%)	Electoral Vote
1948	Harry S Truman Alben W. Barkley	D	24,179,345	49.6	303
	Thomas E. Dewey Earl Warren	R	21,991,291	45.1	189
	J. Strom Thurmond Fielding Wright	SR	1,176,125		39
1952	Dwight D. Eisenhower Richard M. Nixon	R	33,936,234	55.1	442
	Adlai E. Stevenson John Sparkman	D	27,314,992	44.4	89
1956	Dwight D. Eisenhower Richard M. Nixon	R	35,590,472	57.4	457
	Adlai E. Stevenson Estes Kefauver	D	26,022,752	42.0	73**
1960	John F. Kennedy Lyndon B. Johnson	D	34,226,157	49.7	303
	Richard M. Nixon Henry Cabot Lodge, Jr.	R	34,108,157	49.5	219***
1964	Lyndon B. Johnson Hubert H. Humphrey	D	43,129,566	61.1	486
	Barry Goldwater William E. Miller	R	27,178,188	38.5	52
1968	Richard M. Nixon Spiro T. Agnew	R	31,785,480	43.4	301
	Hubert H. Humphrey Edmund Muskie	D	31,275,166	42.7	191
	George C. Wallace Curtis E. LeMay	AI	9,906,473	13.5	46

UNITED STATES
PRESIDENTIAL ELECTIONS (CONT.)

Date	Candidates* (President & V. President)	Party	Popular Vote (#)	Popular Vote (%)	Electoral Vote
1972	Richard M. Nixon Spiro T. Agnew	R	47,169,911	60.7	520
	George McGovern R. Sargent Shriver	D	29,170,383	37.5	17****
1976	Jimmy Carter Walter Mondale	D	40,830,763	50.1	297
	Gerald Ford Robert Dole	R	39,147,793	48.0	240†
1980	Ronald Reagan George H. W. Bush	R	43,904,153	50.7	489
	Jimmy Carter Walter F. Mondale	D	35,483,883	41.0	49
	John B. Anderson Patrick J. Lucey	I	5,720,060	6.6	
	Edward E. Clark David Koch	L	921,299	1.1	
1984	Ronald Reagan George H. W. Bush	R	54,455,075	58.8	525
	Walter F. Mondale Geraldine A. Ferraro	D	37,577,185	40.6	13
1988	George H. W. Bush James Danforth Quayle	R	48,886,097	53.4	426
	Michael S. Dukakis Lloyd Millard Bentsen	D	41,809,074	45.6	111
	Others	I	899,522	1.0	1
1992	William Jefferson (Bill) Clinton Albert Gore	D	43,728,275	43.2	370
	George H. W. Bush James Danforth Quayle	R	38,167,416	37.7	168
	Ross Perot James Stockdale	I	19,237,247	19.0	—
1996	William Jefferson (Bill) Clinton	D	45,628,667	48.9	
	Robert J. (Bob) Dole	R	37,869,435	40.6	
	Ross Perot	I	7,874,283	8.4	
2000	Albert Gore	D	50,158,094	48	267
	George W. Bush	R	49,820,518	48	271
	Ralph Nader	GR }	3,835,594 }	4	0
	Patrick Buchanan	REF			0

ABBREVIATIONS

R	Republican Party	I	Independent
D	Democratic Party	L	Libertarian
SR	States' Rights Party ("Dixiecrats")	REF	Reform Party
AI	American Independent Party	GR	Green Party

* Only candidates who received greater than 1% of the popular vote are listed.

** One Alabama elector cast his vote for Walter B. Jones and Herman Talmadge.

*** Sen. Harry F. Byrd of Virginia received 15 electoral votes.

**** The Libertarian candidate John Hospers received one electoral vote.

† One Washington elector cast a vote for Ronald Reagan.

Sources: *America Votes; Congressional Quarterly Guide to US Elections.* (See Source List for complete citations).

UNITED STATES
LEGISLATIVE ELECTIONS (SENATE)

Date of Election	D	R	I	C
1946	45	51		
1948	54	42		
1950	48	47	1	
1952	47	48	1	
1954	48	47	1	
1956	49	47		
1958	64	34		
1960	64	36		
1962	67	33		
1964	68	32		
1966	64	36		
1968	58	42		
1970	54	44	1	1
1972	56	42	1	1
1974	61	37	1	1
1976	61	38	1	
1978	58	41	1	
1980	46	53	1	
1982	46	54		
1984	47	53		
1986	55	45		
1988	55	45		
1990	56	44		
1992	57	43		
1994	48	52		
1996	45	55		
1998	45	55		
2000	50	50		

ABBREVIATIONS
D   Democratic Party   I   Independent
R   Republican Party   C   Conservative

Source: *Congressional Quarterly Guide to U.S. Elections.* (See Source List for complete citation.)

UNITED STATES
LEGISLATIVE ELECTIONS (HOUSE OF REPRESENTATIVES)

Date of Election	D	R	Oth	V
1946	188	246	1	
1948	263	171	1	
1950	234	199	2	
1952	213	221	1	
1954	232	203		2
1956	234	201		
1958	283	154		
1960	263	174		
1962	258	176	1	

UNITED STATES
LEGISLATIVE ELECTIONS (HOUSE OF REPRESENTATIVES) (CONT.)

Date of Election	D	R	Oth	V
1964	295	140		
1966	248	187		
1968	243	192		
1970	255	180		
1972	243	192		
1974	291	144		
1976	292	143		
1978	277	158		
1980	243	192		
1982	269	166		
1984	253	182		
1986	258	177		
1988	260	175		
1990	267	167	1	
1992	258	176	1	
1994	204	230	1	
1996	207	226	1	
1998	211	223	1	
2000	211	220	2	

ABBREVIATIONS
D   Democratic Party   Oth   Other
R   Republican Party   V   Vacancies

Source: *Congressional Quarterly Guide to U.S. Elections.* (See Source List for complete citation.)

VENEZUELA
LEGISLATIVE ELECTIONS (SENATE)

Date of Election	AD	COPEI	MAS	MEP	CCN	URD	FDN	FDP	I & O
1947	38	4				1			3
1958*	23	6				8			6
1963	22	8				5	3		7
1968	19	16		5	4	3	1	2	2
1973	29	14	2	2	1	1			
1978	23	22	2						
1983	27	16	2						
1988	23	22	3						1
1993	16	14							

Date of Election	AD	COPEI	CN	CR	I & O
1998	17	7	10 2	9	20

ABBREVIATIONS
AD   Accion Democratica / Democratic Action
COPEI   Partido Social-Cristiano/Comite Organizado Pro Elecciones Independientes / Christian Social
        Party
CN   Convergencia Nacional (coalition includes MAS and MIR)
CR   Causa Radical
MIR   Movimiento de Izquierda Revolucionaria
MAS   Movimiento al Socialismo / Movement toward Socialism

VENEZUELA
LEGISLATIVE ELECTIONS (SENATE) (CONT.)

MEP   Movimiento Electoral del Pueblo / People's Electoral Movement
CCN   Cruzada Civica Nacionalista / Nationalist Civic Crusade
URD   Union Republicana Democratica / Democratic Republican Union
FDN   Frente Democratica Nacional / Democratic National Front
FDP   Fuerza Popular Democratica / Popular Democratic Force
I & O   Independents and Others

* A military coup took place in 1948 and the legislature was dissolved. The overthrow of a dictatorship in place
in 1958 led to the reinstatement of the democratic electoral process.

Sources: *Political Handbook of the World; Chronicle of Parliamentary Elections; Europa World Year Book,*
Venezuelan Embassy, Washington, D.C. (See Source List for complete citations.)

VENEZUELA
LEGISLATIVE ELECTIONS (CHAMBER OF DEPUTIES)

Date of Election	AD	COPEI	MAS		MEP	CCN	URD	FDN	FDP	I & O
1947	83	16					4			7
				AD-Op						
1958*	30	19			28		34		1	21
1963	65	40					17	12		37
1968	66	59			25	2	18	4	10	11
1973	102	64	9		8	7	5		2	6
1978	88	88	11		3					9
1983	109	60	10		3		8			10
1988	97	67	18							19
1993	55	54								
			CN		**CR**					
1998	55	27	50	17	40					66

ABBREVIATIONS
AD   Accion Democratica / Democratic Action
COPEI   Partido Social-Cristiano/Comite Organizado Pro Elecciones Independientes / Christian Social
Party
MAS   Movimiento al Socialismo / Movement toward Socialism
CN   Convergencia Nacional (coalition includes MAS and MIR)
CR   Causa Radical
MIR   Movimiento de Izquierda Revolucionaria
MEP   Movimiento Electoral del Pueblo / People's Electoral Movement
CCN   Cruzada Civica Nacionalista / Nationalist Civic Crusade
URD   Union Republicana Democratica / Democratic Republican Union
FDN   Frente Democratica Nacional / Democratic National Front
FDP   Fuerza Popular Democratica / Popular Democratic Force
I & O   Independents and Others
AD-Op   Accion Democratica en oposicion / Democratic Action—Opposition

* A military coup took place in 1948 and the legislature was dissolved. The overthrow of a dictatorship in place
in 1958 led to the reinstatement of democratic electoral process.

Sources: *Political Handbook of the World; Chronicle of Parliamentary Elections; Europa World Year Book;*
Venezuelan Embassy, Washington, D.C. (See Source List for complete citations.)

VENEZUELA
PRESIDENTIAL ELECTIONS

Year	Candidate	Party	Vote	Vote (%)
1947	Rómulo Gallegos	AD	871,752	74.3
	Rafael Caldera	COPEI	262,204	22.4
	Gustavo Machado	PCV	38,587	3.3
1958	Rómulo Betancourt	AD	1,284,092	49.2
	Wolfgang Larrazabal	I (URD)	903,479	34.6
	Rafael Caldera Rodriguez	COPEI	423,262	16.2
1963	Raúl Leoni	AD	957,574	32.8
	Rafael Caldera Rodriguez	COPEI	589,177	20.2
	Jovito Villalba	URD	510,975	17.5
	Arturo Usler Pietri	I	469,363	16.1
	Wolfgang Larrazabal	FDP	275,325	9.4
	Raúl Ramos Gimenez	AD (Op)	66,880	2.3
1968	Rafael Caldera Rodriguez	COPEI	1,083,712	29.1
	Gonzalo Barrios	AD	1,050,806	28.2
	Miguel Angel Burelli	URD, FDP, FDN	826,758	22.2
	Luis Beltran Prieto	MEP	719,461	19.3
1973	Carlos Andrés Pérez Rodriguez	AD	2,130,743	48.7
	Lorenzo Fernandez	COPEI	1,605,628	36.7
	Jesus Angel Paz Galarraga	NF	221,827	5.1
	Jose Vicente Rangel	MAS	186,255	4.3
	Jovito Villalba	URD	134,478	3.1
1978	Luis Herréra Campins	COPEI	2,469,042	46.6
	Luis Pinerua Ordaz	AD	2,295,052	43.3
	Jose Vincente Rangel	MAS	272,595	5.2
	Diego Arria Salicetti	I	90,379	1.7
	Luis Alberto Prieto	MEP	58,723	1.1
1983	Jaime Lusinchi	AD	3,733,220	57.2
	Rafael Caldera Rodriguez	COPEI	2,271,269	34.8
	Teodoro Petkoff	MAS	274,197	4.2
	Jose Vicente Rangel	NA	219,368	3.4
1988*	Carlos Andrés Pérez Rodriguez	AD	3,880,000	54.6
	Edvardo Fernandez	COPEI	2,970,000	40.0
	Teodoro Petkoff	MAS	200,480	2.7
1993	Rafael Caldera Rodríguez	CN	1,710, 722	30.5
	Claudio Fermín	AD	1,325,287	23.6
	Oswaldo Alvarez Paz	COPEI	1,276, 506	22.7
	Andrés Velázquez	CR	1,232,653	21.9
	Others		71,531	1.3
1998	Hugo Chaves	MVR	3,673,685	56.5
	Henrique Salas	PRVZL	2,613,161	39.5

ABBREVIATIONS
AD   Accion Democratica / Democratic Action
COPEI   Partido Social-Cristiano/Comite Organizado Pro Elecciones Independientes / Christian Social
        Party

VENEZUELA
PRESIDENTIAL ELECTIONS (CONT.)

CN	Convergencia Nacional (coalition includes MAS and MIR)
CR	Causa Radical
MIR	Movimiento de Izquierda Revolucionaria
PCV	Partido Comunista Venezolana/Venezuelan Communist Party
I	Independent
URD	Union Republicana Democratica / Democratic Republican Union
FDP	Fuerza Popular Democratica / Popular Democratic Force
FDN	Frente Democratica Nacional / Democratic National Front
MEP	Movimiento Electoral del Pueblo / People's Electoral Movement
NF	Nueva Fuerza / New Force
MAS	Movimiento al Socialismo / Movement toward Socialism
PRVZL	Proyecto Veuezuela

* In addition to the three leading candidates, there were 17 other parties contesting the elections.

Sources: *Statistical Abstract of Latin America; Keesing's Contemporary Archives; Europa World Year Book;* Venezuelan Embassy, Washington, D.C. (See Source List for complete citations.)

SOURCE LIST

Chronicle of Parliamentary Elections. Geneva: International Center for Parliamentary Documentation, 1966/67.

Congressional Quarterly Guide to U.S. Elections. Washington, D.C.: Congressional Quarterly, 1985.

Europa Year Book. London: Europa Publications, 1959–   .

Keesing's Contemporary Archives. London: Keesing's Limited.

1984 Political Handbook of the World. New York: McGraw-Hill, 1984.

Roett, Riordan. *Brazil: Politics in a Patrimonial Society.* New York: Praeger, 1984.

Statistical Abstracts of Latin America. Los Angeles: University of California, 1955.

Supplement to World Elections On File (1946–80). New York: Facts On File Publications, 1980.

The Political Reference Almanac 1999–2000 (ed. Anthony Quain). Arlington, Va.: Keynote Publishing, 1999.

World Elections since 1945 (ed. Ian Gorvin). London: Longman Reference, 1991.

CHAPTER 7

THE VIOLENT WORLD

INTERNATIONAL CONFLICTS, COLONIAL WARS AND CIVIL STRIFE SINCE 1945

EUROPE

Greece, Civil War, 1946–49

Combatants   Greek national army versus communist partisans of the Democratic Army of Greece.

Key dates   The Greek Communist Party made the decision to renew the armed struggle on 12 February 1946, and fighting began on Mount Olympus on 30 March 1946. The communists' wartime National Popular Liberation Army (ELAS) was renamed the Democratic Army of Greece in December 1946. The communist guerrillas, supported by Albania, Yugoslavia and Bulgaria, were initially successful. On 29 December 1947 their leader, Markos Vafiades, proclaimed a provisional republic in the mountains of northern Greece. But large quantities of aid sent from the United States after the proclamation of the Truman Doctrine on 12 March 1947 enabled government forces to take the offensive on 19 June 1948. Yugoslavia ceased to support the partisans after its expulsion from the Cominform on 28 June 1948. Mount Grammos, a rebel stronghold, was declared cleared by government troops on 28 August 1949. The Greek communist broadcasting station announced the end of hostilities on 16 October 1949.

Casualties   Greek armed forces: 12,777 killed, 37,732 wounded and 4,527 missing; communist forces: 38,000 killed and 40,000 taken prisoner.

East Germany, Workers' Uprising, 1953

Combatants   East German workers versus security police (with Soviet support).

Key dates Demonstrations by building workers in East Berlin on 16 June 1953 spread to a number of factories the following day. More than 300 places in East Germany were affected, including major towns such as Magdeburg, Jena, Görlitz and Brandenburg. The disorders were suppressed by security police, and curfew and martial law restrictions remained in force until 12 July 1953.

Casualties 21 civilians killed and 187 injured; four police killed and 191 injured.

Poland, Workers' Uprising, 1956

Combatants Polish workers versus security forces.

Key dates A revolt of workers seeking better conditions broke out in Poznan on 28 June 1956. It was suppressed by the security forces.

Casualties 53 dead (including nine soldiers) and 300 injured.

Hungary, National Uprising, 1956

Combatants Hungarian civil population and armed forces versus Soviet armed forces.

Key dates Student demonstrations in Budapest on 23 October 1956 led to a general uprising against the government of Ernö Gerö. On 27 October Soviet troops were withdrawn from Budapest. On 1 November 1956 Imre Nagy, the new prime minister, announced Hungary's withdrawal from the Warsaw Pact and asked the United Nations to recognize its neutrality. Soviet reinforcements surrounded Budapest and entered the city early on 4 November. Resistance ended on 14 November 1956.

Casualties 3,000 Hungarians and 669 Russians killed.

Czechoslovakia, Soviet Invasion, 1968

Combatants Czech civilian demonstrators versus Soviet, Polish, Hungarian, Bulgarian and East German armed forces.

Key dates During the night of 20/21 August 1968 some 250,000 Soviet troops, accompanied by token contingents from Poland, Hungary, Bulgaria and East Germany, crossed the Czech frontier and occupied Prague and other leading cities to reverse the liberalizing reforms of Alexander Dubček's government. The Czech army was ordered to offer no resistance, but there were extensive civilian demonstrations against the occupying forces.

Casualties 70 Czechs killed and 1,000 wounded.

Northern Ireland, Civil Insurgency, 1969–continuing

Combatants   U.K. security forces versus Provisional Irish Republican Army versus Loyalist paramilitary groups.

Key dates   In 1969 long-standing sectarian animosity between the Catholic and Protestant communities in Northern Ireland degenerated into violent conflict, sparked by the campaign for Catholic civil rights. British troops were deployed in Londonderry on 14 August 1969 and Belfast on 15 August at the request of the government of Northern Ireland. The first British soldier to be killed was shot by an IRA sniper in Belfast on 6 February 1971. At the peak in August 1972 there were 21,500 British soldiers in Northern Ireland. Currently (1994), 12 regular infantry battalions support the Royal Ulster Constabulary. On 27 August 1992 the conflict claimed its 3,000th death, a total that included 600 British soldiers. The conflict reached a new intensity in 1993. On 31 August 1994 the IRA declared a cease-fire that lasted for 17 months, but dissolved in February 1996. Starting on 6 October 1997, after three years of negotiations, representatives of eight of the 10 major Northern Irish political parties participated in formal peace talks that lasted for 19 months. Two groups, the Protestant Ulster Party and the Sinn Fein, the political arm of the IRA, were temporarily suspended for continued violence. On 10 April 1998 Northern Ireland reached a landmark peace settlement called the Good Friday Accord, which calls for Protestants to give the Republic of Ireland a voice in Northern Irish affairs, and for Catholics to suspend the goal of a united Ireland. Despite the deaths of three Catholic boys in July 1998 during the traditional Protestant marches, Catholic and Protestant leaders were given the Nobel Peace Prize as an incentive to lasting peace. On 2 December 1999 Britain transferred governing power to the Northern Irish parliament with the promise that the IRA would disarm its illegal weapons. However, Sinn Féin had not complied by the deadline, and the parliament was suspended on 12 February 2000.

Casualties   In all, over 3,000 dead and 35,000 injured.

Soviet Union (and its successor states after 31 December 1991), 1988–continuing

Combatants   Security forces and ethnic/nationalist groupings.

Key dates   During the final days of the Soviet Union, ethnic clashes were already developing. For example, rioting between Armenians and Azerbaijanis, sparked by a dispute over control of the Nagorno-Karabakh region, began on 20 February 1988. In Uzbekistan, fighting between Uzbeks and Meskhetian Turks began on 4 June 1989. The armed forces also moved against nationalist movements in Georgia, Moldova, Azerbaijan and the Baltic Republics. After the collapse of the Soviet Union, serious conflicts developed in the following areas:

Azerbaijan/Armenia Nagorno-Karabakh is a Christian Armenian enclave surrounded by Muslim Azerbaijani territory. The Karabakh forces secured a land corridor to Armenia. What began as guerrilla clashes escalated into full-scale war across the Caucasus, with modern weapons supplied by former Soviet troops.

Chechnya The southern republic accelerated its drive for independence in 1994 and Russian troops fought a costly two-year war against the Chechens. A cease-fire was arranged in June 1996, and the war formally ended with a peace treaty in May 1997. Islamic militants in Dagestan, a neighboring republic, announced a holy war against Russia in August 1999, and Russia retaliated by launching air strikes and sending ground troops into Chechnya. In December, the Kremlin ordered evacuation of the capital of Grozny and 215,000 Chechen refugees fled the region, but 10,000 to 40,000 residents were trapped in the city, afraid to leave amid the gunfire. On 6 February 2000, Russian troops captured Grozny, and the fighting continues.

Georgia The Abkhazia region near the Black Sea began agitating for independence, and in January 1992 Georgian tanks were sent to repress the demands. Bombing and guerrilla warfare around the Abkhazian capital of Sukhumi caused thousands of refugees to flee. Georgia accused Russian troop units deployed in the area of being pro-Abkhazian and called for a UN peacekeeping force. Meanwhile, there were clashes in South Ossetia when Georgia abolished the area's autonomy.

Moldova In 1989 the government of Moldova suggested future integration with Romania and adopted laws discriminating against Russians and Ukrainians in the Trans-Dniestra region. The region proclaimed itself an autonomous republic. In fighting between the rebels and the Moldovan militia, Russia and the Ukraine were accused of actively supporting the secessionist movement.

Russia The Ingush, a people deported by Stalin in the 1940s but allowed to return to North Ossetia by Khrushchev, claimed land in a border area. There were clashes with the majority population and Russia dispatched paratroops to separate the combatants.

Tajikistan There was civil war after an opposition coalition of Islamic militants from the south of the Central Asian republic and supporters of democracy ousted the communist leader, Rakhmon Nabiyev, and held power for 10 weeks. They faced communists supporting former president Nabiyev and city dwellers from the north, together with mountain tribesmen from the south. Russian troops, acting on behalf of the Commonwealth of Independent States, crushed the opposition takeover. Thousands fled as refugees into Afghanistan.

Casualties   No statistics available.

Romania, Revolution and Civil War, 1989

Combatants   Romanian people versus armed forces and secret police ("Securitate").

Key dates   On 17 December 1989 Romanian security forces fired on protesters in the city of Timisoara. Fighting spread to Bucharest and other major cities. The army changed sides on 22 December, supporting the popular uprising against the Ceausescu regime. Ceausescu and his wife were executed by firing squad on 25 December having been found guilty of genocide by a military court.

Casualties   Some 4,000 dead, mainly civilians.

Yugoslavia, Civil War in the (former), 1991–continuing

Combatants   Serb militants, Croat nationalists, and Bosnian Muslims.

Key dates   The conflict falls into two stages. With the collapse of communist regimes in Eastern Europe after 1989, central authority in Yugoslavia also began to be threatened. Secessionist tendencies were strongest in Slovenia and Croatia. There had been long-standing and bitter hatred between Serbs and Croats. During World War II, Croatia had seen the installation of a puppet Fascist regime, eventually defeated with the help of Yugoslav partisans. In 1991, both Slovenia (the most westernized republic, bordering on Austria) and Croatia declared independence. Fighting between Serbs and Croats intensified, particularly around Serbian enclaves (such as Krajina, Osijek and Vukovar) within Croatia. By the end of August 1991, an estimated 500 lives had been lost. Repeated cease-fire attempts failed, and in September Croatia and Serbia were at war. A UN-sponsored cease-fire took effect on 2 January 1992 and the European Community recognized the independence of Croatia and Slovenia on 15 January. The arrival of UN peacekeepers in Croatia in February ended the Croatian phase of the war.

On 29 February 1992, Muslim leaders in Bosnia-Herzegovina declared independence. Bosnian Serbs and the Serbian leadership in Belgrade rejected this, and war began on 6 April with the opening of the siege of the capital Sarajevo. Serbs were accused of "ethnic cleansing" to secure territorial domination, and a UN trade embargo was imposed on Serbia on 31 May. Peace talks in Geneva, mediated by Lord Owen and Cyrus Vance, began on 26 August, and proposals to divide Bosnia on ethnic lines were presented on 28 October, to be accepted by Croats and Muslims but rejected by Serbs. On 16 November a UN naval blockade was mounted against Serbia and Montenegro. Fighting continued as a further peace conference was held in Geneva on 22–23 January 1993. Serbs attacking Muslim enclaves took Srebrenica on 18 April. As fighting continued, with an estimated 40–50,000 killed and millions made refugees, numerous peace plans failed. The Bosnian Serb onslaught against Goradze (a UN safe haven) in April 1994 brought an intensification of the conflict, with the UN forces made to look impotent.

In November 1995, Bosnia, Serbia and Croatia signed the Dayton Peace Accord to end the war in Bosnia.

In March 1998, a guerrilla war broke out in the southern Yugoslavian province of Kosovo, and proof of civilian killings forced NATO to intervene for the first time ever in the dealings of a sovereign nation with its own people. Peace talks failed and in March 1999, NATO launched air strikes on Serbian targets. Some 850,000 Kosovo refugees fled to neighboring regions as Milosevic continued his campaign of ethnic cleansing. On 3 June 1999, Serbia agreed to end the 11-week war and signed a UN–approved peace agreement with NATO. In February 2000, fighting again broke out between Serbs and Albanians in Kosovo, and NATO peacekeepers struggled to contain the violence.

Casualties   No reliable statistics available, but by the end of 1993 one source gave 148,000 persons dead or missing (including 16,500 children).

MIDDLE EAST AND NORTH AFRICA

Palestine, Guerrilla Warfare, 1946–48

Combatants   British security forces versus Haganah, Irgun Zvai Leumi and Lohmey Herut Israel.

Key dates   Guerrilla warfare broke out after World War II, waged against British forces and the Arab population by Jewish Zionists seeking to speed the creation of an independent Jewish state. On 22 July 1946 the King David Hotel in Jerusalem, housing the British headquarters, was blown up with the loss of 91 lives. On 15 May 1948, Great Britain surrendered its mandate over Palestine and withdrew its armed forces. The Zionists proclaimed Israel a sovereign Jewish state.

Casualties   British army losses were 223 killed and 478 wounded; no casualty statistics are available for other combatants.

Israel, War of Independence, 1948–49

Combatants   Israeli Defense Forces versus armed forces of Egypt, Jordan, Syria, Iraq and Lebanon.

Key dates   Israel was invaded by the armies of its Arab neighbors on the day the British mandate ended, 15 May 1948. After initial Arab gains, Israel counterattacked successfully, enlarging its national territory. Only the British-trained Arab Legion of Jordan offered effective opposition. Separate armistices were agreed to with Egypt (23 February 1949), Jordan (3 April 1949) and Syria (20 July 1949).

Casualties   Of Israelis, 6,000 were killed and 15,000 wounded; Arab states suffered 15,000 dead and 25,000 wounded. Approximately 750,000 Palestinians were permanently exiled.

Tunisia, War of Independence, 1952–56

Combatants   French armed forces versus Tunisian nationalists.

Key dates   In February 1952 Habib Bourguiba and other leaders of the New Constitution Party were arrested, and the ensuing disorders led to the introduction of martial law. In the countryside the Tunisian nationalists waged a guerrilla campaign, while in the towns there were terrorist outrages by nationalists and by the "Red Hand," a secret settler organization. Preoccupied with the Algerian revolt, France granted Tunisia independence on 20 March 1956.

Casualties   No statistics available.

Morocco, War of Independence, 1953–56

Combatants   French armed forces versus Moroccan nationalists.

Key dates   Nationalist agitation grew when Sultan Muhammad V was forced into exile on 20 August 1953 after refusing to cooperate with the French authorities. The Army of National Liberation, composed of Berber tribesmen who had seen service with the French army during World War II and the First Indochina War, began a large-scale guerrilla campaign in 1955. The Sultan returned on 5 November 1955, and a Franco-Moroccan declaration on 2 March 1956 ended the French protectorate and established the independence of Morocco.

Casualties   No statistics available.

Algeria, War of Independence, 1954–62

Combatants   French armed forces versus Algerian nationalists versus French settlers' Organisation Armée Secrète (OAS).

Key dates   Algerian nationalists staged attacks on French military and civilian targets on 1 November 1954. In August 1956 the guerrilla groups formed the Armée de Libération Nationale. The French army conducted a brutal counterinsurgency campaign, which, while effective, alienated its supporters. On 13 May 1956 criticism of army methods led the commander in chief in Algeria, General Massu, to refuse to recognize the government of France. General de Gaulle, returned to power in France on 1 June 1958, set a course for Algerian self-determination. A mutiny by the French army in Algeria, led by generals Challe and Salan, began on 22 April 1961, but was suppressed. Despite terrorism by French settlers of the OAS, peace talks began at Evian-les-Bains in May 1961, and a cease-fire was agreed to on 18 March 1962. Algeria was declared independent on 3 July 1962.

Casualties   French forces: 17,456 dead; French settlers: 2,788 dead; an estimated 1 million Algerians died.

Cyprus, State of Emergency, 1955–59

Combatants   National Organization of Cypriot Fighters (EOKA) versus British security forces and Turkish Cypriots.

Key dates   Agitation for union with Greece (Enosis) led in April 1955 to the start of a campaign of terrorism and guerrilla warfare by EOKA, the militant wing of the Enosis movement. A state of emergency was declared on 27 November 1955. Archbishop Makarios of Cyprus was deported to the Seychelles on 9 March 1956. A cease-fire came into effect on 13 March 1959, and the state of emergency was lifted on 4 December 1959. Cyprus became an independent republic on 16 August 1960.

Casualties   British losses: 142 dead and 684 wounded; Greek Cypriot: 278 dead and 295 wounded; Turkish Cypriot: 84 dead and 258 wounded.

Egypt, Suez Crisis, 1956

Combatants   Israel, France and Great Britain versus Egypt.

Key dates   Egypt nationalized the Suez Canal on 26 July 1956. After secret talks with Great Britain and France, Israel invaded Sinai on 29 October 1956. When Egypt rejected a cease-fire ultimatum by France and Britain, their air forces began to attack Egyptian air bases on 31 October. On 5 November British and French forces invaded the Canal Zone. Pressure from the United Nations and world opinion forced a cease-fire at midnight on 6/7 November 1956.

Casualties   Great Britain: 22 killed and 97 wounded; France: 10 killed and 33 wounded; Israel: 189 killed and 900 wounded; Egypt: 1,650 killed, 5,000 wounded, 6,000 missing.

Morocco, Ifni Incident, 1957

Combatants   Moroccan irregulars versus Spanish armed forces.

Key dates   On 23 November 1957, some 1,200 Moroccan irregulars attacked the Spanish-held territory of Ifni. The Spanish garrison was strengthened and Madrid announced that order had been restored on 8 December 1957.

Casualties   61 Spanish killed and 128 wounded; no statistics available for Moroccan forces.

Lebanon, Civil War, 1958

Combatants   Maronite Christians (with United States support) versus Muslim rebels.

Key dates   Civil war broke out in Lebanon in April 1958 between the pro-Western government of President Chamoun, dominated by Maronite Christians, and pro-Nasserite Muslims. Following the overthrow of the Iraqi monarchy in an army coup on 14 July 1958, President Chamoun appealed for aid, and on 15 July U.S. troops landed in Beirut. On 23 September 1958 the neutralist General Chehab took over from President Chamoun. The last U.S. troops were withdrawn from Lebanon on 25 October 1958.

Casualties   No statistics available.

Tunisia, Conflict with France, 1958–61

Combatants   French armed forces versus Tunisian armed forces.

Key dates   On 8 February 1958 the French air force bombed the Tunisian town of Sakiet, killing 79 people, in retaliation for Tunisian assistance to the Algerian rebels. Clashes took place as Tunisia demanded the evacuation of French bases. On 17 June 1958 the French agreed to withdraw from all bases except Bizerte. On 5 July 1961 Tunisia made a formal claim to the French Bizerte base and imposed a blockade on 17 July. France sent reinforcements, which occupied the town of Bizerte in heavy fighting on 19–22 July. An agreement for the withdrawal of French troops from the town was signed on 29 September 1961, and the French base was evacuated by 15 October 1963.

Casualties   French: 21 dead; Tunisians: 1,300 dead, mainly civilians, in the 1961 clash.

Revolt of the Kurds, 1961–continuing

Combatants   Iraqi armed forces versus Kurdish rebels.

Key dates   The Kurdish minority in northeast Iraq, led by General Mustafa Barzani, rose in revolt in March 1961 after the failure of negotiations on autonomy with General Kassem's regime. The Kurdish militia, the Pesh Merga ("Forward to Death"), fought a prolonged campaign, growing in strength up to 1974, thanks to support from Iran. Then on 13 June 1975 Iran and Iraq signed the Algiers Pact, by which Iran agreed to stop its supplies and close its borders to the Kurds. In the 1980s Kurds in Iran and Turkey also took up arms against their respective governments, particularly during the Iran–Iraq War. Iraq began to use chemical weapons against Kurdish civilians in March 1988; gas bombs were dropped on 70 Kurdish villages on 25 August 1988.

In 1991, taking advantage of Iraq's preoccupation with the Gulf War, Kurdish rebels seized most of Iraqi Kurdistan, taking such cities as Arbil, Dahuk and Kirkuk. After the Gulf War cease-fire, Saddam Hussain turned his armies against them. The Kurdish refugee flight provoked a world outcry, and Allied forces established "safe havens" along the border with Turkey.

Casualties   No statistics available.

North Yemen, Civil War, 1962–70

Combatants   Royalists (supported by Saudi Arabia) versus republicans (supported by Egypt).

Key dates   The royal government of North Yemen was overthrown in an army coup led by Colonel Sallal on 26 September 1962. A civil war began, in which the republican regime was supported by up to 70,000 Egyptian troops and the royalist tribesmen were assisted by arms supplies and technicians from Saudi Arabia. Egypt's defeat in the Six-Day War in 1967 led to an agreement with Saudi Arabia for a disengagement of forces from North Yemen, signed at a meeting of Arab heads of state in Khartoum on 31 August 1967. Sporadic fighting continued until Saudi Arabian mediation secured the formation of a coalition government on 23 May 1970.

Casualties   No statistics available.

Algeria, Border Conflict with Morocco, 1963

Combatants   Moroccan forces versus Algerian forces.

Key dates   A series of border clashes between Moroccan and Algerian forces in the Atlas Mountains took place in September and October 1963. Ethiopia and Mali mediated a cease-fire on 30 October 1963, and an agreement for the establishment of a demilitarized zone was signed on 20 February 1964.

Casualties   No statistics available.

Cyprus, Civil War, 1963–68

Combatants   Greek Cypriots (supported by Greece) versus Turkish Cypriots (supported by Turkey).

Key dates   President Makarios's proposals for constitutional reform led to fighting between Greek and Turkish Cypriots on 21 December 1963. There was a cease-fire on 25 December. A UN peacekeeping force was established in Cyprus on 27 March 1964. On 7–9 August 1964 Turkish planes attacked Greek Cypriot positions on the northwest coast in retaliation for attacks on Turkish Cypriots. There was renewed fighting between Turkish and Greek communities in 1967. A settlement was reached after mediation by the UN and the United States on 3 December 1967, and the withdrawal of Greek regulars from Cyprus, and the demobilization of Turkish forces held in readiness to invade, was completed by 16 January 1968.

Casualties   No statistics available.

South Arabian Federation, Civil War, 1963–67

Combatants   British armed forces and South Arabian federal army versus National Liberation Front (NLF) versus Front for the Liberation of Occupied South Yemen (FLOSY) (with Egyptian and North Yemeni support).

Key dates   After the creation of the South Arabian Federation in January 1963, British troops were involved in suppressing internal disorders in Aden and in fighting in the Radfan area north of Aden against rebel tribesmen supported by Egypt and North Yemen. At a constitutional conference in London in June 1964, agreement was reached for the independence of the Federation by 1968. Civil war developed between two rival nationalist movements: FLOSY and NLF. When Egyptian support for FLOSY ended after the Six-Day War in 1967, the NLF, with the backing of the federal army, won control of the country. The withdrawal of British troops began on 25 August 1967 and was completed on 29 November.

Casualties   92 British soldiers killed and 500 wounded; in Aden, 18 British civilians killed and 58 wounded; no statistics are available for other combatants.

Oman, War in the Dhofar, 1965–75

Combatants   Sultan's armed forces (with British, Iranian, Jordanian and Saudi Arabian support) versus Popular Front for the Liberation of Oman (supported by Iraq and South Yemen).

Key dates Civil war broke out in 1965 between the sultan's armed forces and dissident tribesmen in the Dhofar, who had won control of most of the region by 1970. On 23 July 1970 Sultan Said bin Taimur was deposed by his son, Qaboos, who greatly strengthened the armed forces. With foreign assistance, including an Iranian expeditionary force of 2,000 men, the revolt was suppressed, and the sultan officially declared the war ended on 11 December 1975.

Casualties No statistics available.

Israel, Six-Day War, 1967

Combatants Israel versus Egypt, Jordan, Syria and Iraq.

Key dates Israel decided on a preemptive strike following Egypt's request for the withdrawal of the UN peacekeeping force from Sinai on 16 May, the closure of the Gulf of Aqaba to Israeli shipping on 22 May and the signature of an Egyptian–Jordanian defense pact on 30 May.

On 5 June 1967 Israel launched devastating air attacks on Egyptian air bases. Israeli forces then invaded Sinai and reached the Suez Canal on 7 June. By nightfall on 7 June, Jordan had been defeated and Jerusalem and the West Bank were in Israeli hands. On 9 June, Israeli troops attacked Syria and occupied the Golan Heights. A cease-fire was agreed to on 10 June 1967.

Casualties Israel: 983 killed and 4,517 wounded; Arab states: 4,000 dead and 6,000 wounded.

South Yemen, Conflicts with Saudi Arabia and Rebel Exiles, 1969–72

Combatants South Yemen armed forces versus rebel exiles (supported by Saudi Arabia and North Yemen).

Key dates An unsuccessful attempt by the new left-wing government in South Yemen to assert a claim to disputed border territory led to clashes with Saudi Arabia in November 1969. Saudi Arabia provided training and a base at ash-Sharawrah for South Yemeni exiles, organized into an "Army of Deliverance," which raided South Yemen. In 1972 fighting spread to the border between North and South Yemen. In August 1972 South Yemeni exiles in the north formed a United National Front of South Yemen. Their forces, supplied by Saudi Arabia, mounted attacks on 26 September 1972, which brought full-scale fighting. Arab mediation brought agreement between North and South Yemen in Cairo on 28 October 1972 to meet for discussions on a merger of the two countries.

Casualties No statistics available.

Jordan, Civil War, 1970–71

Combatants   Jordanian armed forces versus Palestine Liberation Organization (PLO) and Syrian armed forces.

Key dates   After serious clashes between Palestinian guerrillas and the Jordanian army, King Hussein declared martial law on 16 September 1970. Civil war broke out in Amman on 19 September as the army attacked the Palestinian refugee camps. Some 250 Syrian tanks entered Jordan in support of the Palestinians, but suffered losses in Jordanian air strikes and withdrew on 23 September 1970. A cease-fire was agreed to on 25 September 1970. Further heavy fighting took place early in 1971 and the PLO guerrillas withdrew from Amman on 13 April. Their expulsion from Jordan was completed by 18 July 1971.

Casualties   No statistics available.

Israel, Yom Kippur War, 1973

Combatants   Israeli armed forces versus armed forces of Egypt and Syria, with contingents of Jordanians, Moroccans, Saudi Arabians and Iraqis.

Key dates   On 6 October 1973 Egyptian forces crossed the Suez Canal, overwhelming Israel's Bar-Lev defense line in a well-planned surprise attack. Syrian forces attacked the Golan Heights, but initial gains were surrendered by 12 October. In a daring counterstroke on 15 October 1973, Israeli forces crossed to the west bank of the Suez Canal and encircled the Egyptian Third Army. A cease-fire became effective on 24 October 1973.

Casualties   Israel: 2,812 killed and 7,500 wounded; Egypt: 5,000 killed, 12,000 wounded and 8,000 taken prisoner or missing; Syria: 3,000 killed, 6,000 wounded and 500 taken prisoner or missing; other Arab losses: 340 killed and 1,000 wounded.

Cyprus, Turkish Invasion, 1974

Combatants   Greek Cypriots and Greek armed forces (one battalion stationed on Cyprus) versus Turkish Cypriots and Turkish armed forces.

Key dates   On 15 July 1974 Archbishop Makarios was deposed as president in a coup by the National Guard, and replaced by Nikos Sampson, a former National Organization of Greek Cypriot Fighters (EOKA) gunman. Fighting broke out between Greek and Turkish Cypriots. On 20 July 1974 Turkish forces invaded northern Cyprus. Sampson resigned on 23 July and a military standstill was agreed to on 30 July. Turkish forces renewed their advance on 14 August 1974. When a new cease-fire came into effect on 16 August the Turks controlled more than a third of the island.

Casualties   No statistics available.

Western Sahara, Polisario Insurgency, 1975–91

Combatants   Moroccan and Mauritanian armed forces (supported by France) versus the Popular Front for the Liberation of Saguia el-Hamra and Rio de Oro (Polisario; supported by Algeria and Libya).

Key dates   The Spanish colony of Western Sahara was claimed by both Morocco and Mauritania, while there was also an independence movement, the Polisario, formed in 1973 and supported by Algeria. On 6 November 1975 King Hassan of Morocco sent 350,000 unarmed Moroccans in a "Green March" into the Western Sahara. They were recalled after three days, but agreement was reached in Madrid on 14 November 1975 for a Spanish withdrawal and joint administration of the territory after 28 February 1976 by Morocco and Mauritania. Their armed forces came into conflict with the Polisario, which proclaimed the Saharan Arab Democratic Republic. The Polisario concentrated on Mauritanian targets, mounting a daring raid on the capital, Nouakchott, on 7 June 1976. Morocco and Mauritania formed a joint military command on 13 May 1977, and Mauritania received support from the French air force. On 5 August 1979 Mauritania came to terms with Polisario, but Morocco moved to occupy the whole of the Western Sahara. Libya recognized the Polisario in April 1980. In 1984 Morocco built a 1,600-mile defensive wall from the Moroccan town of Zag to Dakhla on the Atlantic coast, protecting the economically important north of the territory and creating an effective stalemate. Despite acceptance of a UN cease-fire plan by both sides on 30 August 1988, the political future of the Western Sahara had not been settled by 1991, and Polisario attacks on the Hassan Wall continued. Fighting flared again in August 1991 around Tifariti, prior to the arrival of a UN force. A cease-fire was agreed to in September 1991 after 16 years of civil war.

Casualties   Over 10,000 dead.

Lebanon, Civil War and Invasions, 1975–continuing

Combatants   Civil strife between the Lebanese army, Christian Phalangist militia, Muslim militia and Palestinians, with intervention by Syrian and Israeli armed forces.

Key dates   Tensions between the Christian and Muslim communities in Lebanon were exacerbated by the influx of Palestinian guerrillas expelled from Jordan in 1971. A state of civil war existed after a massacre of Palestinians by Phalangist gunmen on 13 April 1975. Syrian forces were drawn into the conflict on 1 June 1976. A cease-fire was agreed to on 17 October 1976, backed by an Arab Deterrent Force consisting mainly of Syrian troops, but fighting soon resumed. Palestinian raids into Israel led to an Israeli incursion into Lebanon from 15 March to 13 June 1978. Israel launched a full-scale invasion of Lebanon on 6 June 1982 and forced a Palestinian evacuation from Beirut, beginning on 22 August 1982. An agreement between Israel and the Lebanese government on 17 May 1983 proved a dead letter, but Israel withdrew its forces from Lebanon during 1985. Fighting between the various factions continued unabated. Eventually, Syrian forces occupied West Beirut in strength on 22 February 1987 to separate the warring militias. A bloody new phase in the conflict began in March 1989 when the Maronite Christian general, Michel Aoun, launched a "war of liberation" against Syria. This lasted until 13 October 1990, when Aoun sought sanctuary in the French embassy in Beirut, and went into exile in France. Peace has prevailed since 1991 and reconstruction has begun, but the low-grade war between Israeli troops and the extremist Hezbollah guerrillas continued for years. In June 1999, Israel bombed southern Lebanon in its most severe attack in years. Israel's prime minister has promised to withdraw troops and make peace with Syria, which controls the guerrillas.

Casualties   150,000 dead.

Libya, Conflict with Egypt, 1977

Combatants   Libyan armed forces versus Egyptian armed forces.

Key dates   Strained relations and border incidents led Egypt to mount a limited punitive action against Libya on 21 July 1977 in the shape of an armed incursion and air attacks on the major Libyan air base at Al Adem. A cease-fire was agreed to, through the mediation of Yasir Arafat, chairman of the PLO, and others, on 24 July 1977.

Casualties   No statistics available.

Iran, Gulf War with Iraq, 1980–88

Combatants   Iraqi armed forces versus Iranian armed forces.

Key dates   Hoping to exploit the instability of Iran after the fall of the shah, Iraq abrogated the Algiers Pact of 1975, by which it had been forced to accept joint control of the Shatt al-Arab waterway, and invaded Iran on 12 September 1980. Khorramshahr fell on 13 October 1980, but the Iranian government did not collapse, and its armed forces began to counterattack successfully. Each side bombed the other's oil installations and attacked international shipping in the Gulf. Iran rejected Iraq's cease-fire overtures as the military stalemate deepened. On 9 January 1987 Iran launched a major offensive—code-named Karbala-5–with the aim of capturing Basra. The Iranians advanced some distance toward their objective, while suffering heavy casualties. In 1987 and 1988 Iraq made major advances. Iran accepted the UN cease-fire resolution on 18 July 1988, and a cease-fire came into effect on 20 August. Following the invasion of Kuwait, Iraq offered to accept Iran's terms for a comprehensive peace settlement on 14 August 1990.

Casualties   Iran: 600,000 dead and 800,000 wounded; Iraq: 400,000 dead.

Turkey, Kurdish Insurgency, 1984–continuing

Combatants   Turkish armed forces against Kurd nationalists (PKK).

Key dates   The Kurdish Workers Party (PKK) was formed in 1974 and in 1984 its military wing, the People's Army for the Liberation of Kurdistan, began armed action against the Turkish government. Fighting intensified in 1989–90, with urban guerrilla attacks and assassinations. In August–October 1991 the government attacked alleged PKK camps in northern Iraq but offered increased autonomy to Kurdish areas. The left-wing Devrimci Sol (Revolutionary Left) has also carried out a campaign of bombings and assassinations, with over 30 attacks in 1991. In 1993 the government heightened its action in the Kurdish areas bordering Iraq.

Casualties   No statistics available.

Israel, Palestinian Uprising ("Intifada"), 1987–continuing

Combatants   Israeli security forces versus Palestinians.

Key dates   Widespread unrest in the Gaza Strip and the West Bank developed into a full-scale uprising on 9 December 1987. The conflict was rekindled in 1990 by the killing of seven laborers from Gaza on 20 May by an apparently deranged Israeli civilian, and the shooting on 8 October of 17 Arabs at the Temple Mount in Jerusalem by Israeli security forces. Faced with increasing militancy from the Hamas (*q.v.*, Chapter 10) fundamentalist group, Israel responded by deporting 417 Palestinians to southern Lebanon on 17 December 1992. Meanwhile, the 1,000th Palestinian to die in the Intifada was killed on 27 January 1993.

The Intifada was at least temporarily put on hold after the mutual recognition and preliminary agreement between Israel and the PLO in September 1993, but the Hebron Massacre of 25 February 1994 has led to renewed violence.

In January 1997 the Hebron agreement called for the withdrawal of Israeli troops from the city, but peace negotiations were undermined when new Jewish settlements were contructed on the West Bank. Hamas suicide bombers claimed the lives of at least 20 Israeli civilians. An October 1998 peace agreement yielded some compromise, but the fighting continued off and on while Prime Minister Benjamin Netanyahu's government floundered and finally lost in the 1999 elections to Ehud Barak. In September 1999 Israel moved ahead with the Wye accord and ceded more territory to the Palestinians, but peace talks broke down again at the beginning of 2000, when both sides failed to agree on which additional areas would go to the Palestinians.

Casualties   1,200 Arabs and 100 Israelis dead by January 1994.

Gulf War, 1990–91

Combatants   Iraq versus Coalition Forces
Land contingents: Argentina, Bangladesh, Czechoslovakia, Egypt, France, Gulf Cooperation Council states (Bahrain, Kuwait, Oman, Qatar, Saudi Arabia, and United Arab Emirates), Honduras, Niger, Pakistan, Morocco, Senegal, Syria, United Kingdom and United States.
Naval contingents: Argentina, Australia, Belgium, Great Britain, Canada, Denmark, France, Greece, Gulf Cooperation Council states, Italy, Netherlands, Norway, Portugal, Soviet Union, Spain, United States.

Key dates   Iraq invaded Kuwait on 2 August 1990; UN Resolution 660, condemning the invasion and calling for immediate and unconditional withdrawal, was passed the same day. The United States ordered naval forces to the Gulf on 3 August, and sent troops to Saudi Arabia on 7 August (Operation "Desert Shield"). UN Resolution 661, imposing economic sanctions on Iraq, was passed on 6 August. On 8 August Iraq announced the annexation of Kuwait. On 29 November UN Resolution 678 sanctioned the use of force if Iraq had not withdrawn by 15 January 1991. On 6 December Saddam Hussein announced that all foreigners detained in Iraq would be released. The Allied air offensive against Iraq ("Operation Desert Storm") began shortly before midnight GMT on 16 January. The first Iraqi Scud missiles struck Israel on 18 January, but the attacks failed to bring Israel into the war. The Iraqi army launched a surprise attack on 29 January, capturing the town of Khafji. The Allied ground offensive began on 24 February. Kuwait City was entered by the Allies on 26 February. With Kuwait liberated and the Iraqi army defeated, President Bush ordered a cease-fire, which went into effect at 8 A.M. local time on 28 February. Under the terms of the cease-fire agreement, Iraq had to agree to destroy all its nuclear, chemical and ballistic weapons. Saddam Hussein did not comply, despite strict UN economic sanctions, and several military skirmishes between Iraq and the United States have occurred throughout 1997–98. On 16 December 1998 the United States and Britain began four days of air strikes, and have continued the sustained, low-level warfare with almost daily bombings of Iraqi targets within the no-fly zones that were established in the 1991 cease-fire agreement.

Casualties   Iraq: 150,000 estimated dead (including civilians), and 200,000 missing or captured. Coalition Forces: 166 killed, 207 wounded, and 106 missing or captured.

Yemen, Civil War, 1994

Combatants   Armed forces controlled by President Ali Abdullah Salih (the leader of the formerly conservative north) and Vice President Ali Salem al-Baidh (the leader of the formerly Marxist south).

Key dates   North and South Yemen united into one state in May 1990. Following elections, Mr. al-Baidh refused in August 1993 to be sworn in as vice president and boycotted the capital. The armed forces were not merged, but sections were garrisoned in one another's territories. The north refused a southern demand for the return of its forces in early 1994. On 4 May northern forces attacked and routed elements of locally based southern forces and began an advance to link up with their own troops in the south. The south responded on 5 May with air and missile attacks on the northern capital, San'a, with northern aircraft bombing Aden in retaliation. On 17 May northern troops seized part of the al-Anad base, a key stronghold commanding approaches to Aden. North Yemen called a three-day truce on 20 May but fighting for control of al-Anad resumed on 21 May as Mr. al-Baidh announced the establishment of a breakaway Democratic Republic of Yemen, with a quarter of the population of the formerly united Yemen. On 1 June northern forces moved closer to besieged Aden and defied a 2 June UN Security Council demand for a cease-fire. The leaders of South Yemen fled into exile on 7 July as northern forces closed in.

Casualties   No statistics available.

AFRICA SOUTH OF THE SAHARA

Madagascar, Nationalist Revolt, 1947

Combatants   Mouvement Démocratique de la Rénovation Malagache versus French security forces.

Key dates   A nationalist insurrection against French rule began on 29 March 1947. After several bloody encounters, French forces regained control by the end of July 1947.

Casualties   At least 11,000 dead.

Kenya, Mau Mau Insurgency, 1952–60

Combatants   Mau Mau guerrillas versus British security forces.

Key dates   Growing violence by Mau Mau, a Kikuyu-based secret society, led the British authorities to declare a state of emergency on 20 October 1952. Jomo Kenyatta, later to be the first prime minister of independent Kenya, was sentenced to seven years in prison for Mau Mau activities on 20 October 1953. Murders and attacks on farms of white settlers and on Africans who did not support Mau Mau were countered by a British military campaign in which the insurgents were driven into the remote mountain area of western Kenya. The insurgency was under control by October 1956, though the state of emergency was not lifted until 12 January 1960.

Casualties   11,000 Mau Mau dead; from the security forces there were 534 Africans killed and 465 wounded; 63 British were killed and 102 wounded; civilian dead numbered 1,817 Africans, 32 Europeans and 26 Asians.

Sudan, Civil War, 1955–continuing

Combatants   Government forces representing the Arab Muslim north of Sudan versus rebels from the Christian or animist black African south.

Key dates   The conflict began in 1955 with riots in Yambio in July and mutinies by southern troops in August. The Anya Nya rebels, demanding secession for southern Sudan, began a guerrilla campaign in 1963. Peace talks between the insurgents and the government began in Addis Ababa in February 1972. A cease-fire went into effect on 12 March 1972 and the south was granted a measure of autonomy. However, a mutiny of southern troops in May 1983 and opposition to President Nimeiri's imposition of Islamic law on the country in September 1983 led to renewed civil war. The Sudan People's Liberation Army was formed under Colonel John Garang, and President Nimeiri declared a state of emergency on 29 April 1984. Nimeiri was overthrown by a military coup on 6 April 1985, but subsequent governments failed to end the civil war, and fighting intensified in 1990. A cease-fire was declared on 20 March 1993 in anticipation of peace talks. On 20 August 1998 U.S. cruise missiles destroyed a pharmaceutical plant that allegedly manufactured chemical weapons and was financed by the wealthy Islamic militant, Osama bin Laden, rumored to be responsible for several terrorist actions on American soil.

Casualties   An estimated 1 million people have died in battle or from famine and disease resulting from war.

Congo (Zaïre), Civil War, 1960–67

Combatants   Congo National Army and United Nations Force versus Katangese secessionists.

Key dates   Belgium granted independence to the Congo (formerly Zaïre) on 30 June 1960. Widespread disorder followed. The army mutinied, and on 11 July 1960 Moise Tshombe declared the rich mining province of Katanga an independent state. The prime minister of the Congo, Patrice Lumumba, appealed to the United Nations, and the establishment of a peacekeeping force was approved by the Security Council on 14 July 1960. On 14 September 1960 the army chief of staff, Colonel Mobutu, seized power. Lumumba was seized by Mobutu's troops, handed over to the Katangese and murdered on 9 February 1961. For the next two years, periods of armed conflict and negotiation (during which Dag Hammarskjöld, UN secretary-general, was killed in a plane crash on 18 September 1961) failed to solve the Congo's problems. Katanga's secession eventually ended when a UN offensive in December 1962 forced Tshombe into exile on 15 January 1963. The last UN forces left the Congo on 30 June 1964. Violence continued until November 1967, when a revolt by mercenaries in the eastern provinces, which had begun on 5 July, was finally suppressed.

Casualties   No statistics available.

South Africa, Liberation Struggle, 1961–94

Combatants   South African armed forces and supporters against the African National Congress.

Key dates   The African National Congress (ANC) began low-key armed resistance against the white-dominated apartheid state in 1961 through its military wing, Umkhonto we Sizwe ("Spear of the Nation"). This was suspended in August 1990 as discussions began on the form of a post-apartheid South Africa. As negotiations continued, there was evidence that the government—indirectly by using the Zulu Inkatha movement and other anti-ANC groups, and directly with the security forces—was continuing to attempt to weaken the ANC by violence. Over 3,500 people were killed in political violence in 1990 and over 2,500 in 1991, largely in clashes in black townships. In July 1991 the

ANC announced that it would maintain its military wing for self-defense until a democratic constitution had been instituted.

In November 1993, a new majority-rule constitution was approved by leaders of the ruling National Party, the ANC and other black and white political parties. Multiracial elections were scheduled for April 1994. The violence, however, did not end, forcing a state of emergency to be declared in Natal in April 1994. The elections took place as scheduled, and as expected, were won by the ANC.

Casualties   Over 10,000 dead by 1994.

Angola, War of Independence, 1961–75

Combatants   Nationalist insurgents versus Portuguese armed forces.

Key dates   The liberation struggle began in Portuguese Angola on 3 February 1961 when insurgents attempted to free political prisoners in Luanda. The risings were suppressed with great bloodshed, but a guerrilla campaign developed, and by 1974 Portugal was maintaining an army in Angola of 25,000 white and 38,000 locally enlisted troops. After the coup in Portugal on 25 April 1974, negotiations began, and on 15 January 1975 the Portuguese agreed to Angolan independence. As rival liberation groups fought for control of the country (see p. 313), the independence of Angola was proclaimed on 11 November 1975.

Casualties   No statistics available.

Kenya, Border Conflict with Somalia, 1963–67

Combatants   Kenyans versus Somalis.

Key dates   The 1960 independence constitution of the Somali Democratic Republic contained a commitment to recover its "lost territories," which included the northern frontier district of Kenya. Serious border clashes between the Kenyans and Somalis began in March 1963, and diplomatic relations were broken off in December. Sporadic fighting continued until the two countries agreed to end the dispute with the Declaration of Arusha on 28 October 1967.

Casualties   No statistics available.

Guinea-Bissau, War of Independence, 1963–74

Combatants   African Party for the Independence of Guinea and Cape Verde (PAIGC) versus Portuguese armed forces.

Key dates   Armed resistance to Portuguese rule was launched by PAIGC in 1963. PAIGC proclaimed the independence of the republic on 24 September 1973. Following the coup d'état in Lisbon on 25 April

1974, led by General Antonio de Spinola (who had been governor and commander in chief in Guinea), the Portuguese recognized the independence of Guinea on 10 September 1974.

Casualties   No statistics available.

Ethiopia, Conflict in Eritrea and Tigray, 1963–91

Combatants   Ethiopian armed forces (with Cuban and Soviet support) versus Eritrean and Tigrean separatists.

Key dates   Eritrea was integrated into the Ethiopian Empire on 14 November 1962, and a separatist movement, the Eritrean Liberation Front, took up arms the following year. Taking advantage of the instability caused by the overthrow of Emperor Haile Selassie on 12 September 1974, separatist guerrillas succeeded in taking control of most of Eritrea except the capital, Asmara, by the end of 1977. The conclusion of the Ogaden War in March 1978 (see p. 314) enabled the Ethiopian army, with Cuban and Soviet assistance, to launch a major counteroffensive in Eritrea on 15 May 1978. Warfare continued in the 1980s, and the Ethiopian government was also faced with a guerrilla campaign in Tigray Province by the Tigrean People's Liberation Army. Following guerrilla successes and an attempted coup against him on 18 May 1989, President Mengistu offered talks with the two separatist movements. Talks took place, but no agreement on an end to the conflict had been reached by the beginning of 1991. Guerrilla success increased in early 1991, leading to the flight of Mengistu on 21 May. Addis Ababa fell on 28 May. Eritrea subsequently proclaimed its independence, which was confirmed by referendum in 1993.

Casualties   No statistics available.

Ethiopia, Invasion by Somalia, 1964

Combatants   Ethiopian armed forces versus Somalis.

Key dates   After a series of border clashes, Somali armed forces crossed into Ethiopia on 7 February 1964 to assert the Somali Republic's claim to the Ogaden desert region. The Organization of African Unity called for an end to hostilities, and on 30 March 1964 President Abboud of Sudan secured a cease-fire based on the original boundary.

Casualties   No statistics available.

Mozambique, War of Independence, 1964–74

Combatants   Front for the Liberation of Mozambique (FRELIMO) versus Portuguese armed forces.

Key dates   FRELIMO launched its first attacks on 25 September 1964, and gradually took control of large areas of the countryside. By 1974 Portugal was forced to maintain an army in Mozambique of 24,000 white and 20,000 locally enlisted troops. After the coup in Portugal of 25 April 1974, negotiations were opened with FRELIMO. Despite a violent revolt by white settlers in Lourenço Marques on 3 September 1974, a cease-fire agreement was signed on 7 September 1974 and Mozambique officially became independent on 25 June 1975.

Casualties   No statistics available.

Rhodesia, War of Independence, 1965–79

Combatants   Rhodesian security forces versus Zimbabwe People's Revolutionary Army (ZIPRA) and Zimbabwe African National Liberation Army (ZANLA).

Key dates   Black nationalist guerrilla activity in Southern Rhodesia grew after the unilateral declaration of independence by Ian Smith's white minority regime on 11 November 1965. Two guerrilla forces were operating: ZIPRA, the military wing of Joshua Nkomo's Zimbabwe African People's Union, based in Zambia and recruiting from the Ndebele peoples; and ZANLA, the military wing of Robert Mugabe's Zimbabwe African National Union, based in Mozambique and recruiting from the Shona peoples. These two groupings united to form the Patriotic Front on 9 October 1976. A settlement for an end to the conflict based on a new constitution was reached at the conclusion of a conference at Lancaster House, London, on 15 December 1979. Zimbabwe became an independent republic on 18 April 1980.

Casualties   12,000 killed (est.).

Chad, Civil War and Conflict with Libya, 1965–88

Combatants   Chad armed forces versus Front de Libération Nationale (FROLINAT); Forces Armées Populaires (FAP) versus Forces Armées du Nord (FAN); with military intervention by France, Libya and Zaïre.

Key dates   The civil war in Chad originated in the mid-1960s as a conflict between the French-backed government of President Tombalbaye and a number of separatist factions in the Muslim north of the country, grouped into the Front de Libération Nationale and supported by Libya. By the mid-1970s FROLINAT controlled three-quarters of the country. On 6 February 1978 the head of state, General Malloum, who had overthrown President Tombalbaye in 1975, announced a cease-fire with FROLINAT. Conflict then developed between two factions in FROLINAT: FAN, under Hissène Habré, and the more militant FAP, under

Goukouni Oueddei, backed by Libya. Habré's army defeated FAP and captured the capital, N'Djamena, on 7 June 1982. Fighting resumed in 1983 when FAP and Libyan troops advanced and took the strategically important town of Faya-Largeau on 24 June. Habré appealed for foreign assistance, and troops were sent by Zaïre on 3 July and by France on 14 August. The Libyan advance was halted, and France and Libya signed a withdrawal agreement on 17 September 1984. Libyan troops remained in the north of Chad, however, and created a de facto partition of the country until Goukouni Oueddei was shot and wounded in an argument with Libyan troops, and his men changed sides in 1986. A united Chadian force mounted a surprise attack and captured the Libyan air base at Ouadi Doum in March 1987, forcing the Libyans to evacuate most of the territory they had occupied. The Organization of African Unity negotiated a cease-fire on 13 September 1987, and Chad and Libya resumed diplomatic relations on 3 October 1988.

Casualties   No statistics available.

Namibia, War of Independence, 1966–90

Combatants   South African defense forces versus South West Africa People's Organization (SWAPO).

Key dates   Namibia was mandated to South Africa by the League of Nations on 17 December 1920. South Africa refused to recognize the South West Africa People's Organization, which was designated the "sole authentic representative of the Namibian people" by the United Nations in 1973. SWAPO launched a guerrilla campaign in October 1966, and this was stepped up in 1978 from bases in Angola and Zambia. Following talks between South Africa, Angola, Cuba and the United States in 1988, implementation of a UN plan for Namibia's transition to independence began on 1 April 1989. Namibia became independent on 21 March 1990.

Casualties   No statistics available.

Nigeria, Civil War, 1967–70

Combatants   Nigerian federal forces versus Biafran secessionists.

Key dates   On 30 May 1967 the military governor of the Eastern Region of Nigeria, Colonel Ojukwu, declared the Ibo homeland an independent sovereign state under the name of the Republic of Biafra. Troops of the Nigerian federal army attacked across the northern border of Biafra on 7 July 1967. The Biafrans invaded the neighboring Mid-West Region on 9 August 1967. The federal army recaptured Biafra on 22 September 1967, and Port Harcourt fell on 20 May 1968. Supply shortages and starvation finally led to the collapse of Biafran resistance after a four-pronged federal attack in December 1969. The Biafran army surrendered on 15 January 1970.

Casualties   Total civilian and military dead estimated at 600,000.

Burundi, Civil War, 1972–73–continuing

Combatants   Hutu versus Tutsi (with Zaïrean support).

Key dates   On 29 April 1972 guerrillas from the majority Hutu tribe in Burundi attacked the ruling Tutsi minority, killing between 5,000 and 15,000 in an abortive coup. The Burundi armed forces, under Tutsi command, retaliated with assistance from Zaïre, and by the end of May 1972 the death toll amongst the Hutu had risen to an estimated 200,000. Refugees poured into neighboring states. On 10 May 1973 Hutu rebels from Rwanda and Tanzania invaded Burundi. The Burundi army in response crossed into Tanzania on 29 June and killed 10 people. President Mobutu of Zaïre mediated an accord between the presidents of Tanzania and Burundi on 21 July 1973. Further conflict erupted in 1986 and 1991. In 1993 Burundi's first democratically elected president and the first Hutu to assume power was killed during a coup, and the second Hutu president was killed the following April, when a plane carrying him and the Rwandan president was shot down. The civil war flared anew, with Hutu youth gangs massacring Tutsi civilians, and the Tutsi-controlled army retaliating by killing Hutus. In July 1996, six nations devised a proposal to send troops into Burundi to maintain peace, but the Tutsi army overthrew the Hutu government and installed its own president. Nelson Mandela was appointed the new mediator for the civil war in early 2000.

Casualties   Over 200,000.

Uganda, Rebel Invasion, 1972

Combatants   Ugandan armed forces versus Ugandan exiles.

Key dates   On 17 September 1972 some 1,000 armed supporters of ex-president Milton Obote, who had been overthrown by General Amin in January 1971, invaded Uganda from Tanzania. The guerrillas were easily repulsed, and the Ugandan air force bombed the Tanzanian towns of Bukoba and Mwanza in reprisal. The Organization of African Unity and the Somali foreign minister mediated a peace agreement between Uganda and Tanzania, which was signed on 5 October 1972.

Casualties   No statistics available.

Angola, Civil War, 1975–continuing

Combatants Popular Movement for the Liberation of Angola (MPLA) and Cuban troops versus National Front for the Liberation of Angola (FNLA), National Union for the Total Independence of Angola (UNITA) and South African defense forces.

Key dates The three rival liberation movements signed an agreement with Portugal on 15 January 1976 regarding Angolan independence, but were soon engaged in a civil war for control of the country. Major fighting between the MPLA and FNLA broke out in the capital, Luanda, on 27 March 1975. During July 1975 the MPLA gained control of Luanda. In the ensuing conflict the Marxist MPLA received aid from the Soviet Union and was supported by some 15,000 Cuban troops, while the FNLA/UNITA alignment received supplies from the United States, via Zaïre, and South African military support from October 1975. When independence was declared on 11 November 1975, FNLA/UNITA established a rival government in Huambo. The MPLA drove FNLA forces into Zaïre and captured Huambo on 8 February 1976. The United States had halted its aid to FNLA/UNITA on 27 January 1976. The Organization of African Unity recognized the MPLA government on 11 February 1976, and South Africa announced the withdrawal of its forces on 25 March 1976. UNITA continued to wage a guerrilla campaign in Angola with aid from South Africa in the 1980s. A situation of stalemate led to negotiations, and on 22 June 1989 the Angolan president, Eduardo Dos Santos, and Dr. Jonas Savimbi, the leader of UNITA, agreed on a cease-fire. This broke down, and fighting continued in 1990. The conflict appeared settled by the 1991 Estoril Accord, but subsequently resumed. In mid-1993 it was claiming an estimated 1,000 lives per day. Peace talks had collapsed on 1 March 1993 when UNITA failed to attend. Between 1994 and 1998, when the United Nations oversaw the Lusaka peace accord, there was relative peace in Angola, except for aiding rebels to overthrow the leaders of both the Republic of Congo and the Democratic Republic of the Congo. In 1997, a coalition government with UNITA was implemented, but Savimbi violated the accord by mobilizing his army and retaking territory. The government suspended coalition rule in September 1998 and the country resumed civil war. UNITA gained control of 70% of the country in the first six months of 1999, and both sides continue to plant land mines and attack civilians. The UN has since pulled out of Angola amid criticism that both sides refuse to work toward peace.

Casualties An estimated 400,000 deaths.

Mozambique, Civil War, 1976–92

Combatants   Mozambique armed forces versus Mozambique National Resistance Movement (with Rhodesian and South African support).

Key dates   From 1976 on, Rhodesia fostered a guerrilla campaign by anti-FRELIMO dissidents in Mozambique, which was harboring Robert Mugabe's ZANLA (see p. 310). After 1980 South Africa took over the support of the MNRM as part of its policy of "destabilizing" its neighbors. The MNRM concentrated on sabotage and guerrilla raids on communications, power lines and foreign-aided development projects. Mozambique and South Africa signed a nonaggression pact, the Nkomati Accord, on 16 March 1984, but MNRM activity continued. The possibility of peace emerged in 1990, with talks between the government and MNRM in Rome in July. A peace accord was signed on 7 August 1992 and a formal signature of peace ended the war in October 1992.

Casualties   No statistics available, but 200,000 casualties estimated by 1991.

Zaïre, Rebel Invasions from Angola, 1977–78

Combatants   Zaïre armed forces (with Moroccan, French and Belgian support) versus Congolese National Liberation Front (with Cuban support).

Key dates   On 8 March 1977 Zaïre's Shaba province (formerly Katanga) was invaded from Angola by some 2,000 insurgents claiming to be members of the Congolese National Liberation Front. President Mobutu accused Cuban troops of leading the invasion and appealed for African support on 2 April 1977. On 10 April French transport aircraft carried 1,500 Moroccan troops to Zaïre and they helped the Zaïre army to repel the invasion. On 11 May 1978 a second invasion from Angola by some 3,000 rebels took place. French and Belgian paratroopers were sent to Kolwezi to rescue European hostages on 19 May 1978 and the invaders were dispersed. Zaïre and Angola signed a nonaggression pact on 12 October 1979.

Casualties   No statistics available.

Ethiopia, Conflict in the Ogaden, 1977–78

Combatants   Ethiopian armed forces (with Cuban and Soviet support) versus Western Somali Liberation Front and Somali armed forces.

Key dates   The turmoil in Ethiopia after the overthrow of Emperor Haile Selassie on 12 September 1974 led the Somali Republic to pursue its claim to the Ogaden by fostering a guerrilla movement in the area, the Western Somali Liberation Front. A Somali-backed offensive in 1977 gave the guerrillas control of the southern desert area, and an attack launched against Harar on 23 November 1977 narrowly failed. However, with Cuban and Soviet support, Ethiopia launched a counteroffensive on 7 February 1978 and recovered control of the Ogaden. On 9 March 1978 Somalia announced the withdrawal of its forces from the Ogaden.

Casualties   9,000 dead.

Uganda, Conflict with Tanzania, 1978–79

Combatants   Ugandan armed forces (with Libyan support) versus Tanzanian armed forces and Ugandan National Liberation Front.

Key dates   On 27 October 1978 Uganda invaded Tanzania and occupied some 700 square miles of Tanzanian territory known as the Kagera salient. A Tanzanian counteroffensive on 12 November 1978 ejected the Ugandans from the salient. In January 1979, Tanzanian forces, with armed Ugandan exiles, advanced into Uganda. Kampala fell on 11 April 1979 and President Amin fled the country.

Casualties   4,000 dead.

Somalia, Civil War, 1981–continuing

Combatants   Somali armed forces versus Somali National Movement and other rebels.

Key dates   The Somali National Movement began attacks in northern Somalia in 1981 in an attempt to overthrow President Siad Barre. Fighting intensified when larger forces were deployed on 27 May 1988 to create bases in the north. The country's second city, Hargeisa, fell to the rebels on 31 May. It was subsequently retaken by government forces, but fighting continued. A second rebel group, the Somali Patriotic Movement (SPM), was formed in the south in 1989, and a third, the United Somalia Congress (USC), in 1990. The three groups began cooperating against the government in August 1990. Mogadishu, the capital, fell to USC forces in January 1991 and Siad Barre fled. USC leader Ali Madhi Muhammad was declared interim president of Somalia, but this was not accepted by the other groups and fighting continued. Ali Madhi was confirmed as president in August 1991, but a USC faction under Muhammad Farrah Aidid continued opposition. Following difficulties in distributing food aid, a U.S.–led United Nations force landed in Somalia in December 1991. In January 1993 the 14 main political groupings reached a peace agreement, but UN forces continued clashing with individual factions, particularly the forces of General Aidid. Clashes continued through the year. The last U.S. peacekeepers left on 25 March 1994.

Since the breakaway nation, Somaliland Republic, claimed independence in 1991, several warlords have set up their own ministates, including Puntland and Jubaland. In 1999, Somali warlord Aidid allied himself with Eritrea in its war with Ethiopia, causing the conflict to move into Somalia.

Casualties   No statistics available.

Liberia, Civil War, 1989–93

Combatants   Liberian armed forces versus rebels of the National Patriotic Front of Liberia.

Key dates   The insurrection against the government of President Doe began on 24 December 1989, with military action by National Patriotic Front guerrillas, who had infiltrated from the Ivory Coast under the leadership of Charles Taylor. President Doe was killed on 11 September 1990, after being wounded and captured by a splinter group of rebels led by Prince Yormie Johnson. Despite the presence of a peacekeeping force, established under the auspices of the Economic Community of West African States, fighting continued between Prince Johnson's men, the National Patriotic Front and forces formerly loyal to President Doe. Despite a cease-fire agreement at the end of 1990, there was continued violence, with the appearance of a Sierra Leone-based United Liberation Movement for Democracy (Ulimo) and NPFL clashes with the peacekeeping force. In July 1993 a new peace accord was made between the government, the NPLF and Ulimo.

Casualties   Over 30,000 dead.

Rwanda, Civil War, 1990–continuing

Combatants   Rwandan armed forces versus Patriotic Front rebels.

Key dates   On 30 September 1990 Rwanda was invaded by Ugandan-based rebels of the Rwandan Patriotic Front (RPF), seeking to overthrow the government. French and Belgian troops intervened on 4 October and Zaïre also sent forces to support President Juvenal Habyarimana. As RPF forces were broken into small units, fighting died down in November 1990, only to flare up again in mid-1991. In July 1992 there was a cease-fire as negotiations took place between the government and the RPF. Renewed fighting occurred in 1993. On 6 April 1994 the president of Rwanda, Juvenal Habyarimana, died with the Burundi president in a rocket attack on their aircraft. Following his death, rebel RPF forces advanced on the capital Kigali from the north, forcing the self-proclaimed president Theodore Sindikubwado's government to move to Gitarama. Mass killings of Tutsis by the government militia and Hutu death squads began and by 7 May an estimated 200,000 Tutsis had died while thousands more had become refugees. On 16 May RPF forces cut a second crucial road out of Kigali. On 17 May the United States blocked the expansion of a small UN peace force. There were reports that RPF troops were slaughtering Hutu civilians. On 21 May the RPF rejected a UN planned cease-fire at Kigali Airport to allow delivery of food and medicines and the following day seized the airport and an army barracks in the capital. A short truce on 23 May was broken and 500,000 were now estimated to have died. As the RPF tightened its hold on Kigali, it capured Gitarama on 13 June, forcing the government and officials to flee. On 15 June France threatened military intervention with European and African allies if the massacre of civilians did not stop. This took place in June 1994. In July Kigali fell to the rebels.

In September 1998, a UN tribunal sentenced Rwanda's former prime minister Jean Kambanda to life in prison for his part in the 1994 killings, becoming the first person in history to be convicted for genocide.

Casualties An estimated 800,000 Tutsis were slaughtered during the 1994 civil war. No other statistics available.

ASIA

Indonesia, War of Independence, 1945–49

Combatants Indonesian People's Army versus Dutch, British and Indian armed forces.

Key dates The independence of the Republic of Indonesia (formerly Netherlands East Indies) was proclaimed by the nationalist leaders, Sukarno and Hatta, on 17 August 1945. British, Indian and Dutch troops began to arrive on 29 September 1945. British troops captured the rebel capital of Surabaya on 29 November 1945. The Dutch recognized the Indonesian Republic (comprising Java, Sumatra and Madura) on 13 November 1946. The withdrawal of British troops was completed on 30 November 1946. A nationalist uprising on West Java on 4 May 1947 led to Dutch military action in Java on 20 July 1947. A truce arranged under UN auspices on 17 January 1948 broke down, and the Dutch occupied the rebel capital, Jogjakarta, on 19 December 1948. International opposition and guerrilla warfare led to the Dutch decision to withdraw and to the independence of Indonesia on 27 December 1949.

Casualties   Indonesians: 80,000 killed and wounded; Dutch: 25,000 killed and wounded; British and Indian: 556 killed and 1,393 wounded.

China, Civil War, 1945–49

Combatants   Communists versus Nationalists.

Key dates   Civil war between the Nationalist government under Jiang Kaishek and the Communist forces led by Mao Zedong resumed after the defeat of Japan in August 1945. Through the mediation of General George C. Marshall, a truce was arranged on 14 January 1946. It broke down and American supplies to the Nationalists were halted on 29 July 1946. A Nationalist offensive in Shensi took the Communist capital, Yenan, on 19 March 1947, but it was retaken in April 1948. As communist forces advanced, Beijing fell on 22 January 1949, Nanjing on 22 April 1949 and Shanghai on 27 May 1949. Mao Zedong proclaimed the People's Republic of China on 1 October 1949. The Nationalists withdrew to Taiwan on 7 December 1949.

Casualties   No statistics available.

Philippines, Hukbalahap Insurgency, 1946–54

Combatants   Philippines armed forces versus Hukbalahap (Huk) insurgents.

Key dates   When the Philippines became independent on 4 July 1946, the wartime communist Anti-Japanese People's Liberation Army, or Hukbalahaps, waged a guerrilla campaign against the government of the republic. By 1950 the Hukbalahaps, with an army of 15,000 men and support of the peasantry, had established control over central Luzon. However, with American backing, a new defense secretary, Rámon Magsaysay, revitalized the Philippine armed forces. Counterinsurgency operations, together with a program of land reform and the resettlement of dissidents, meant that by 1954 the revolt had come to an end. The Hukbalahap leader, Luis Taruc, surrendered on 17 May 1954.

Casualties   No statistics available.

Vietnam, First Indochina War, 1946–54

Combatants   French armed forces versus Viet Minh insurgents.

Key dates   Following the surrender of Japan, Ho Chi Minh proclaimed the Democratic Republic of Vietnam at Hanoi on 2 September 1945. French and British forces regained control in Saigon, and after negotiations French troops entered Hanoi on 16 March 1946. After French naval forces shelled the Vietnamese quarter of Haiphong on 23 November 1946, an abortive Viet Minh uprising took place in Hanoi on 19 December 1946. Guerrilla warfare grew into full-scale conflict between the French and the Viet Minh forces under General Giap. On 20 November 1953 the French established a forward base at Dien Bien Phu to lure the Viet Minh into a set-piece battle, but the garrison of 15,000 men was overwhelmed on 7 May 1954. An agreement for a cease-fire, temporary division of the country at latitude 17°N and unification following nationwide elections in 1956 was signed at the Geneva Conference on 27 July 1954.

Casualties   No statistics available.

India, Kashmir Conflict with Pakistan, 1947–continuing

Combatants   Kashmir and Indian armed forces versus Muslim insurgents and Pakistani armed forces.

Key dates   A rebellion by the Muslim majority in Kashmir led the Hindu maharajah to accede to the Indian Union, and Indian troops were flown into Kashmir on 27 October 1947. Pakistan sent aid to the Muslim Azad ("free") Kashmir irregulars, and Pakistani army units crossed into Kashmir in March 1948. An undeclared state of war between India and Pakistan continued until UN mediation brought about a cease-fire on 1 January 1949. India formally annexed Kashmir on 26 January 1957. The conflict in Kashmir still continues. Over 35,000 are reported killed by Indian troops since 1988. India and Pakistan both tested nuclear weapons in 1998 and nuclear-capable ballistic missiles in 1999, reportedly inspired by the continued dispute over Kashmir. India controls two-thirds of the Himalayan region, its only state that is predominantly Muslim. India blamed Pakistan for sending soldiers across the so-called Line of Control that divides Kashmir between India and Pakistan, and Pakistan countered that the guerrillas are independent freedom fighters. On 26 May 1999 India launched air strikes and later sent in ground troops against Islamic guerrilla forces in Kashmir. In August, Pakistan was forced to withdraw.

Casualties   No statistics available.

Burma (Myanmar), Civil War, 1948–continuing

Combatants   Burmese armed forces versus communists, ethnic minorities, People's Volunteer Organization, Mujahids and Kuomintang refugees.

Key dates   In the year after gaining independence on 4 January 1948 the Burmese government faced armed opposition from a wide range of dissident groups: the communists, themselves divided into the White Flag

Stalinists and the Red Flag Trotskyites; a private army of wartime "old comrades" known as the People's Volunteer Organization, who made common cause with army mutineers; ethnic minorities seeking autonomy, such as the Mons and Karens; and bands of Muslim terrorists, Mujahids, in the north of Arakan. By 12 March 1949, when Mandalay fell to the Karen National Defense Organization and the communists, most of Burma was in rebel hands. But the rebels were disunited, and Mandalay was retaken by government forces on 24 April 1949. The rebel capital, Toungoo, was captured on 19 March 1950. The government held the initiative and was able to deal with a new threat posed by Chinese Nationalist refugees in the eastern Shan states. An offensive in November 1954 reduced the Mujahid menace, and Operation "Final Victory" was launched against the Karens on 21 January 1955. Outbreaks of fighting have occurred since 1955, but never on the scale of the early years of independence. The Burmese army mounted a major offensive against the Karens in 1988–89, but despite the ruling junta's tight grip, it has been unable to subdue the insurgency in the south as the Karens continue to push for an independent homeland.

The civilian government was overthrown in September 1988 by a military junta, and when elections were held in May 1990, the State Law and Order Restoration Council (SLORC) refused to recognize the results. In 1991, Aun San Suu Kyi, the leader of the opposition and daughter of assassinated general Aung San, who was revered as the father of Burmese independence, was awarded the Nobel Peace Prize, but remained under house arrest from 1989 to 10 July 1995. In September 1998 Suu Kyi declared that opposition politicians would act as the country's parliament that was never allowed to convene and denounced the ruling junta as illegitimate. The government retaliated with demonstrations calling for the deportation of Suu Kyi.

Casualties   No statistics available.

Malaya, Communist Insurgency, 1948–60

Combatants   Commonwealth armed forces versus "Malayan Races Liberation Army."

Key dates   The Federation of Malaya was proclaimed on 1 February 1948. Communist guerrilla activity began, and a state of emergency was declared on 16 June 1948. In April 1950 General Sir Harold Briggs was appointed to coordinate anti-communist operations. He inaugurated the Briggs Plan for settling Chinese squatters in new villages to cut them off from the insurgents. General Sir Gerald Templer became high commissioner and director of military operations on 15 January 1952, and a new offensive was launched on 7 February 1952. British authorities announced that the Communist Party's high command in Malaya had withdrawn to Sumatra on 8 February 1954. The emergency was officially ended on 31 July 1960.

Casualties   Commonwealth: 2,384 killed and 2,400 wounded; Communist forces: 6,705 killed, 1,286 wounded and 2,696 captured; civilian casualties numbered 4,668.

Indonesia, Civil War, 1950–62

Combatants   Indonesian armed forces versus Darul Islam, South Moluccan guerrillas and dissident Indonesian army colonels.

Key dates   In 1950 prolonged guerrilla campaigns began by a fanatical Muslim sect, Darul Islam, and by the South Moluccans, who proclaimed their independence on 26 April 1950. In 1957, objections to Javanese domination of Indonesian affairs and suspicion of Dr. Sukarno's left-wing policies led the military commanders in Borneo, Sumatra and Celebes to refuse to acknowledge the authority of the cabinet. A Revolutionary Government of the Indonesian Republic was proclaimed on 15 February 1958. The authorities took military action against the right-wing rebels, capturing their headquarters at Bukittingi on 5 May 1958, and their capital, Menado, on 26 June 1958. The rebel movement finally collapsed when an amnesty was offered on 31 July 1961, and the civilian leaders surrendered. Opposition from Darul Islam was also suppressed by 1962.

Casualties   No statistics available.

Korean War, 1950–53

Combatants   North Korean and Chinese armed forces versus South Korean armed forces and UN command, comprising combat troops from the United States, Australia, Belgium, Great Britain, Canada, Colombia, Ethiopia, France, Greece, Luxembourg, Netherlands, New Zealand, Philippines and Thailand, and medical units from India, Italy, Norway and Sweden.

Key dates   North Korean troops invaded the south on 25 June 1950. The United Nations decided to intervene following an emergency session of the Security Council, which was being boycotted by the Soviet Union. The first U.S. troops landed at Pusan airport on 1 July 1950. General MacArthur mounted an amphibious landing at Inchon on 15 September 1950, and Seoul was recaptured on 26 September. The advance of the UN forces into North Korea on 1 October 1950 led to the entry of China into the war on 25 November 1950. Seoul fell to the Chinese on 4 January 1951, but was retaken by UN forces on 14 March 1951. General MacArthur was relieved of his command on 11 April 1951 after expressing his desire to expand the war into China. Truce talks began on 10 July 1951, and an armistice was finally signed at Panmunjom on 27 July 1953.

Casualties   South Korea: 47,000 dead, 183,000 wounded and 70,000 missing or taken prisoner; United States: 33,699 dead, 103,284 wounded in action and 13,000 missing or taken prisoner (of whom 5,000 returned); other members of UN Command: 3,194 dead, 11,297 wounded and 2,769 missing or taken prisoner; China: 900,000 dead or wounded; North Korea: 520,000 dead or wounded.

Nationalist China, Bombardment by People's Republic of China, 1950–62

Combatants   Nationalist Chinese (with United States' support) versus Communist Chinese.

Key dates   When the defeated Chinese Nationalist forces took refuge on Taiwan on 7 December 1949, they also retained strong garrisons on Quemoy, Matsu and the Tachen Islands, only a few miles offshore. Communist artillery carried out heavy bombardments of Quemoy. On 6 February 1955 the U.S. Seventh Fleet began the evacuation of 25,000 troops and 17,000 civilians from the Tachen Islands in the face of mounting communist threats. Heavy shelling of Quemoy resumed on 23 August 1958, but threats of invasion were countered by an American military buildup. Sporadic shelling continued until 1962.

Casualties   No statistics available.

Tibet, Chinese Annexation, 1950–59

Combatants   Tibetan nationalists versus Chinese armed forces.

Key dates   The Chinese invaded across the eastern frontier of Tibet on 7 October 1950. An agreement was signed on 23 May 1951 giving China control of Tibet's affairs, and Chinese troops entered Lhasa in September 1951. The Dalai Lama remained as a figurehead ruler, but there was widespread guerrilla activity against the Chinese forces of occupation. The last serious resistance came in 1959. On 10 March 1959 an uprising took place in Lhasa, but it was suppressed by Chinese tanks, and on 30 March the Dalai Lama fled to asylum in India.

Casualties   No statistics available.

Laos, Civil War, 1959–75

Combatants   Civil war between royalist-neutralists, rightists and the communist Pathet Lao (with involvement by the United States, Thailand and North and South Vietnam).

Key dates   The arrest of Prince Souphanouvong and other leaders of the communist Pathet Lao on 28 July 1959 marked the end of attempts at coalition government and the beginning of a three-way conflict between neutralists under Premier Prince Souvanna Phouma, rightists under General Nosavan, and the Pathet Lao. International efforts to find a settlement led to a cease-fire on 3 May 1961 and recognition for the neutrality of Laos at a conference in Geneva on 23 July 1962. But fighting resumed in Laos, with growing involvement by North Vietnam, Thailand and the United States. The South Vietnamese army attacked Laos on 8 February 1971 to disrupt the Ho Chi Minh trail. A new cease-fire agreement was reached on 21 February 1973, and a coalition government formed in 1974. But communist victories in Vietnam and Cambodia in April 1975 opened the door to a takeover by the Pathet Lao in Laos. The Pathet Lao declared Vientiane liberated on 23 August 1975, and Laos was proclaimed the Lao People's Democratic Republic on 2 December 1975, with Prince Souphanouvong as president.

Casualties   No statistics available.

Vietnam, Second Indochina War, 1959–75

Combatants   South Vietnamese armed forces (supported by United States, South Korea, Australia, New Zealand, Thailand and Philippines) versus North Vietnamese armed forces and Viet Cong guerrillas.

Key dates   Following the temporary division of Vietnam at the Geneva Conference in 1954, Ngo Dinh Diem became president of South Vietnam and secured American support for his refusal to abide by the treaty by holding elections and reuniting with the north in 1956. His government became increasingly authoritarian and repressive, and unrest grew. The communists in South Vietnam (the Viet Cong) built up their strength and launched their first attack on the South Vietnamese armed forces on 8 July 1959 near Bien Hoa, killing two American advisors. A state of emergency was proclaimed in the south on 19 October 1961. After alleged North Vietnamese attacks on American warships in international waters, the U.S. Congress passed the Gulf of Tonkin resolution on 7 August 1964, giving President Johnson wide military powers in South Vietnam. The sustained bombing of North Vietnam by U.S. aircraft ("Operation Rolling Thunder") began on 7 February 1965. The first American combat troops landed at Da Nang on 8 March 1965 and engaged the Viet Cong on 15 June. On 30 January 1968 communist forces launched their Tet offensive with heavy attacks on Saigon, Hué and 30 provincial capitals. On 31 March 1968 President Johnson announced the end of the bombing of the north, and on 13 May 1968 peace discussions began in Paris. On 25 January 1969 these discussions were transformed into a formal conference. American and South Vietnamese troops invaded Cambodia in 1970, and the South Vietnamese made an incursion into Laos in 1971. A new communist offensive against the south began on 30 March 1972, and this led to a resumption of American bombing of the north on 6 April. The last American ground combat units were withdrawn on 11 August 1972. American bombing was halted on 15 January 1973, and a peace agreement was signed in Paris on 27 January. In 1975 a North Vietnamese offensive, which began on 6 January, overran the south, and Saigon was occupied on 30 April.

Casualties   (1964–73) United States: 47,239 killed in action, 10,446 noncombat deaths, 152,303 wounded and 695 missing; South Vietnamese armed forces: 183,528 dead and 500,000 wounded; South Korea: 4,407 dead; Australia: 492 dead; New Zealand: 35 dead; Thailand: 351 dead; North Vietnamese armed forces and Viet Cong: 950,000 dead.

Brunei, Pro-Indonesian Revolt, 1962

Combatants   Brunei armed forces (with British support) versus Brunei People's Party rebels.

Key dates   On 8 December 1962 A. M. Azahari, leader of the Brunei People's Party, staged a revolt in opposition to the idea that Brunei should join the federation of Malaysia. British and Gurkha troops were flown in from Singapore, and the rebellion was suppressed by 17 December 1962.

Casualties   No statistics available.

India, Himalayan Conflict with China, 1962

Combatants   Indian armed forces versus Chinese armed forces.

Key dates   After a series of incidents in the disputed border areas, Chinese forces attacked on 20 October 1962 and drove the Indian forces back on the northeast frontier and in the Ladakh region. India declared a state of emergency on 26 October 1962, and launched an unsuccessful counteroffensive on 14 November 1962. On 21 November the Chinese announced that they would cease fire all along the border and withdraw 12.5 miles behind the line of actual control that existed on 7 November 1959.

Casualties Indian losses: 1,383 killed, 1,696 missing and 3,968 captured; no Chinese casualty statistics available.

Indonesia, Conflict on Irian Jaya, 1962–continuing

Combatants Dutch armed forces versus Indonesian armed forces; Indonesian armed forces versus Free Papua Movement guerrillas.

Key dates Following a clash between Indonesian and Dutch naval forces on 15 January 1962, President Sukarno ordered military mobilization and sent armed units into West New Guinea. In a settlement negotiated through the United Nations, the Dutch agreed on 15 August 1962 to hand over Western New Guinea, which was incorporated into Indonesia as Irian Barat on 1 May 1963. The Free Papua Movement, opposed to Indonesian control and desiring unification with Papua New Guinea, undertook small-scale guerrilla operations. Fighting in 1984 led to the movement of over 11,000 refugees to Papua New Guinea. Irian Jaya saw rioting and violence in 1999, as did other areas, particularly East Timor.

Casualties No statistics available.

Malaysia, Confrontation with Indonesia, 1963–66

Combatants Malaysian Federation (with Commonwealth support) versus Indonesian armed forces.

Key dates When the Federation of Malaysia was established on 16 September 1963, President Sukarno of Indonesia announced a policy of "confrontation" on the grounds that it was "neocolonialist." A campaign of propaganda, sabotage and guerrilla raids from Indonesia into Sarawak and Sabah followed. After Sukarno had handed over power to General Suharto on 12 March 1966, "confrontation" came to an end with a peace agreement signed in Bangkok on 1 June 1966.

Casualties Commonwealth forces: 114 killed and 181 wounded; Indonesia: 590 killed, 222 wounded and 771 captured.

India, Conflict with Pakistan, 1965

Combatants Indian armed forces versus Pakistani armed forces and Muslim irregulars.

Key dates Border clashes took place in the Rann of Kutch in April 1965, but a cease-fire agreement came into effect on 1 July. More serious fighting in Kashmir and the Punjab began on 5 August 1965, when Muslim irregulars invaded east Kashmir. The Indian army contained these incursions, but on 1 September 1965 Pakistani regular forces crossed the frontier. India launched a three-pronged attack toward La-hore on 6 September. As a military stalemate developed, the UN Security Council called for a cease-fire, which came into effect on 23 September 1965.

Casualties Indian losses: 2,212 killed, 7,636 wounded and 1,500 missing; no Pakistani casualty statistics available.

Indonesia, Attempted Communist Coup, 1965 (followed by virtual civil war)

Combatants Indonesian government forces versus PKI (Communist Party of Indonesia) with support from rebel military commanders.

Key dates An attempted coup by the "30th September Movement," apparently led by Colonel Untung, was launched on 1 October 1965. Details remain very obscure. The coup was crushed in Jakarta (but only after six loyalist generals were murdered). However, in parts of Java the communists took control (the city of Jogjakarta in central Java was briefly seized). Fighting was subsequently reported in north Sumatra, Celebes and Kalimantan (Borneo). Bloody attacks on the population continued into 1966 in central Java, especially around Jogjakarta, Su-rakarta and Semarang. The massacres left an estimated 500,000 dead as the government regained control.

Casualties Up to 500,000 "communists" (including many ethnic Chi-nese).

Philippines, Communist and Muslim Insurgencies, 1968–continuing

Combatants Philippine armed forces versus New People's Army and Bangsa Moro Army (Army of the Moro Nation).

Key dates The Hukbalahap insurgency had faded by the mid-1950s, but in December 1968 a congress of reestablishment was held on Luzon, which reconstituted the Communist Party. Its New People's Army (NPA) began a guerrilla campaign. The government also faced armed opposi-tion from Muslim separatists of the Moro National Liberation Front (MNLF) on Mindanao. President Marcos declared martial law on 23 September 1972. A cease-fire with the MNLF was announced on 22 December 1976 after talks held in Libya, but fighting continued. Presi-dent Aquino signed a 60-day truce with the NPA on 27 November 1986, but fighting resumed when it expired in 1987. In 1996, as MNLF con-tinued to fight for an Islamic homeland, the group reached an agreement with the government for more political autonomy and an administrative body was established with the former rebel chief as its head to oversee development of Mindanao. Clashes continued between the army and the Moro Islamic Liberation Front, but peace talks were ongoing in 1998.

Casualties   No statistics available.

China, Border Conflict with Soviet Union, 1969

Combatants   Chinese armed forces versus Soviet armed forces.

Key dates   Long-standing Sino-Soviet border disputes erupted into serious fighting on Damansky Island in the Ussuri River on 2 March 1969. Each side blamed the other for the clash, in which 31 Soviet frontier guards were killed. The fighting spread farther west to the border between Sinkiang and Kazakhstan. On 11 September 1969 the Soviet prime minister, Alexei Kosygin, who was returning from the funeral of Ho Chi Minh in Hanoi, stopped briefly at Beijing airport for a meeting with Zhou Enlai. Talks were arranged and tension on the border subsided.

Casualties   No statistics available.

Kampuchea, Civil War, 1970–75

Combatants   Kampuchean, South Vietnamese and United States armed forces versus Khmer Rouge, North Vietnamese and Viet Cong.

Key dates   On 18 March 1970, Lieutenant General Lon Nol ousted the head of state, Prince Norodom Sihanouk, who was out of the country. Sihanouk allied himself with his former enemies, the Marxist Khmer Rouge, to form the National United Front of Cambodia. Lon Nol appealed for aid on 14 April 1970, and on 29 April, U.S. and South Vietnamese troops mounted an incursion into Kampuchea to attack North Vietnamese Viet Cong and Khmer Rouge forces. The last U.S. troops withdrew on 29 June 1970. The communists took control of the countryside, and in 1975 cut supply routes to the capital, Phnom Penh. Lon Nol left the country on 1 April 1975 and the Khmer Rouge occupied Phnom Penh on 17 April.

Casualties   No statistics available.

Bangladesh, War of Independence, 1971

Combatants   Pakistani armed forces and *razakar* irregulars versus Mukti Bahini and Indian armed forces.

Key dates   Elections in December 1970 resulted in a landslide victory in East Pakistan for the Awami League. On 26 March 1971 Sheikh Mujibur Rahman, the head of the League, proclaimed East Pakistan an independent republic under the name of Bangladesh. He was arrested, and West Pakistani troops and locally raised irregulars, *razakars*, put down large-scale resistance by 10 May 1971. Awami League fighters, the Mukti Bahini, began a guerrilla campaign, and clashes grew between India and Pakistan as millions of refugees fled into India. President Yahya Khan declared a state of emergency in Pakistan on 23 November 1971. On 3 December 1971 the Pakistani air force launched surprise attacks on Indian airfields. On 4 December some 160,000 Indian troops invaded East Pakistan. Pakistani forces in East Pakistan surrendered on 16 December 1971, and a general cease-fire came into effect the following day.

Casualties   India: 3,037 killed, 7,300 wounded and 1,561 captured and missing; Pakistan: 7,982 killed, 9,547 wounded and 85,000 captured and missing, including 15,000 wounded.

Sri Lanka, JVP Revolt, 1971

Combatants   Sri Lankan security forces versus Janata Vimukti Peramuna (People's Liberation Front).

Key dates   A state of emergency was declared in Sri Lanka on 16 March 1971 following the disclosure of a plot to overthrow the government by the ultra-left JVP. An abortive uprising began on 5 April 1971, but by May some 4,000 rebels were in custody and resistance had ceased.

Casualties   1,200 killed, including 60 members of the security forces.

East Timor, Civil War and Indonesian Annexation, 1975– continuing

Combatants   Timor Democratic Union (UDT) versus Revolutionary Front for the Independence of Timor (FRETILIN), with intervention by Indonesian armed forces.

Key dates   In June 1975 Portugal announced its intention of holding independence elections in its colony of East Timor. On 11 August 1975 the moderate UDT, which favored continuing links with Portugal, attempted to stage a coup, but by 20 August civil war had broken out with the communist group FRETILIN. As increasing numbers of refugees fled into Indonesian West Timor, Indonesian troops entered East Timor on 7 December 1975 to forestall a left-wing takeover. By 28 December the Indonesians were in control, and East Timor was officially integrated into Indonesia on 17 July 1976. This annexation was not recognized by the international community. In 1996, two East Timorese resistance activists received the Nobel Peace Prize. In 1999, several areas of Indonesia saw rioting and violence, particularly in East Timor. A referendum on independence was announced in February, only to be followed by heightened fighting between separatist guerrillas and pro-Indonesian paramilitary forces. A UN–sponsored referendum was twice rescheduled because of violence, but on August 30, 79% of the population voted to secede. In retaliation, pro-Indonesian militias massacred civilians and drove a third of the population out of the region. UN peacekeeping forces entered the region on 12 September 1999.

Casualties More than 200,000 Timorese are reported to have died from famine, disease and fighting since the annexation.

Sri Lanka, Communal Strife, 1977–continuing

Combatants Sri Lankan armed forces and Indian Peacekeeping Force (IPKF) versus Tamil separatists and JVP (see page 328).

Key dates Tension between the Tamil minority and the Sinhalese majority in Sri Lanka led to rioting in the northern town of Jaffna, beginning on 14 August 1977, in which 125 people died. The situation grew more serious in the 1980s. Acts of terrorism by the Tamil Liberation Tigers provoked violence by the army against the Tamil community. A state of emergency was declared on 4 June 1981. Sir Lanka signed an accord with India on 29 July 1987, regarding a Tamil homeland, and an IPKF was set up on Sri Lanka. Hostilities took place between the IPKF and Tamil separatists. The JVP objected to the Indian presence, and began a guerrilla campaign against the government. India withdrew its last troops on 24 March 1990. Civil strife continued in 1991. In 1993, President Ranasinghe Premadasa was assassinated by a Tamil rebel who strapped explosives to himself and detonated them. As terrorist attacks on civilians continued, the new president extended the state of emergency to the entire country. Three days after President Kumaratunga's reelection in December 1999, she was wounded by a suicide bomber.

Casualties Over 60,000 deaths.

Kampuchea (Cambodia), Vietnamese Invasion and Civil War, 1978–continuing

Combatants Vietnamese armed forces and Kampuchean troops of the Heng Samrin government versus Khmer Rouge, Khmer People's National Liberation Front and guerrillas loyal to Prince Sihanouk.

Key dates After a series of clashes on the border, Vietnamese forces and Kampuchean rebels launched an invasion of Kampuchea on 25 December 1978. The capital Phnom Penh was occupied on 7 January 1979, and a People's Republic of Kampuchea, with Heng Samrin as president, was proclaimed. Guerrilla operations against the Vietnamese occupying forces were carried out by three groups: the Khmer Rouge, guerrillas loyal to the former head of state, Prince Sihanouk, and the noncommunist Khmer People's National Liberation Front. The three groups formed a unified military command on 14 March 1989, with Prince Sihanouk as head, but the Khmer Rouge as the dominant partner. Vietnam completed the withdrawal of its forces from Kampuchea on 26 September 1989. Civil war continued, with the Khmer Rouge making significant advances. A new cease-fire agreement was signed on 27 August 1991, but it remained to be seen if it would be effective. Despite elections in 1993, there has been continuing fighting between government troops and Khmer Rouge guerrillas. In March 1994, government troops captured the headquarters of Pol Pot at Pailin in western Cambodia. A serious split emerged in the Khmer Rouge in August 1996 when a number of military divisions sought peace with the Cambodian government. In July 1997 Cambodia slipped toward civil war as Hun Sen ousted Prince Norodom Ranariddh. In November 1997 Khmer Rouge guerrillas were claiming significant military gains against Hun Sen's government, and refugees continued to flee to Thailand. At the time of Pol Pot's death in April 1998, a force of between 300 to 2,000 Khmer Rouge guerrillas was still holding out against government troops on the Cambodian border. In March 1998 the armed forces of Hun Sen's government advanced into Anlong Veng, the last major stronghold of the Khmer Rouge's resistance forces. Several thousand Khmer Rouge guerrillas were reported to have defected, leaving around 2,000 fighters under the control of Ta Mok, the Khmer Rouge leader since 1997. By December 1998 the Khmer Rouge organization was reduced to a remnant of 200 fighters.

Casualties   No statistics available.

Afghanistan, Soviet Occupation and Civil War, 1979– continuing

Combatants   Soviet and Afghan government forces versus Mujaheddin guerrillas.

Key dates   The instability of the Soviet-backed regime and growing resistance to the reforms led to a full-scale Soviet invasion of Afghanistan on 27 December 1979. A new government was installed under Babrak Karmal, but a very considerable Soviet military presence had to be maintained in the country to combat the Mujaheddin guerrillas. Following Babrak Karmal's resignation on 4 May 1986, his successor, Major General Najibullah, announced a six-month cease-fire on 15 January 1987, but this was rejected by the Mujaheddin. Withdrawal of Soviet forces from Afghanistan began on 15 May 1988, and was completed on 15 February 1989. Divisions within the Mujaheddin and an effective performance by the Afghan army meant that President Najibullah remained in power, and civil war continued into the 1990s. However, in April 1992, Najibullah was overthrown. Renewed civil war in Afghanistan raged as 1993 opened. Beginning on 19 January, fighting had claimed 3,000 lives by February 1993 in a struggle between the government of President Burhanuddin Rabbani and the Hezb-i-Islami of Gulbuddin Hekmatyar. Intermittent fighting continued into 1994 between Rabbani's forces and those of General Abdul Rashid Dostam.

In September 1996, a group of Islamic students calling themselves the Taliban seized control of the capital of Kabul and imposed harsh fundamentalist laws, including stoning for adultery and severing hands for theft. By fall 1998, the Taliban controlled 90% of the country. In May 1998, UN–sponsored peace talks among the warring factions broke down, and on August 20, U.S. cruise missiles struck a terrorism training complex in Afghanistan believed to have been financed by Islamic terrorist Osama bin Laden. In 1999, fighting continued between the Taliban and opposition forces. The opposition alliance headed by former president Rabbani is still recognized as the legitimate government by the United Nations.

Casualties   Official casualty figures for the Soviet armed forces were 15,000 killed and 37,000 wounded. No statistics available for Afghan losses.

Vietnam, Chinese Invasion, 1979

Combatants   Vietnamese armed forces versus Chinese armed forces.

Key dates   Chinese forces launched an invasion of Vietnam on 17 February 1979 in retaliation for Vietnam's intervention in Kampuchea (see p. 329). Following the fall of the provincial capital, Lang Son, on 3 March 1979, the Chinese government announced that it had accomplished its aims, and the withdrawal of its forces was completed by 16 March 1979.

Casualties   20,000 dead.

LATIN AMERICA

Costa Rica, Civil War, 1948

Combatants   Costa Rican armed forces and communist militia versus National Liberation Party forces.

Key dates   Civil war broke out in March 1948 when President Teodoro Picado attempted to annul the elections. He allowed the communists to organize a 2,000-strong militia to support the regular army. But the forces of the National Liberation Party, led by Colonel José Figueres, gradually took control of the country and entered the capital, San José, on 24 April 1948. President Picado resigned and the regular army was disbanded.

Casualties   No statistics available.

Costa Rica, Rebel Invasion, 1948

Combatants   Costa Rican Civil Guard versus armed exiles.

Key dates   On 10 December 1948 Costa Rica was invaded from Nicaragua by 1,000 armed supporters of the ex-president, Calderon Guardia. The town of La Cruz fell, but the rebels had been driven out by 17 December 1948.

Casualties   No statistics available.

Cuba, Guerrilla Insurgency, 1953–59

Combatants   Cuban armed forces versus communist guerrillas.

Key dates   An attempted uprising led by Fidel Castro in Santiago and Bayamo on 26 July 1953 was suppressed. Castro was imprisoned but granted an amnesty in May 1955. He led an unsuccessful landing in Oriente Province on 30 November 1955, but commenced a successful guerrilla campaign based in the Sierra Maestra. Castro launched a final offensive in October 1958, and General Batista fled the country on 1 January 1959.

Casualties   No statistics available.

Guatemala, Rebel Invasion, 1954

Combatants   Guatemalan armed forces versus "Army of Liberation."

Key dates   An Army of Liberation, composed of Guatemalan exiles and supported by the U.S. Central Intelligence Agency, invaded Guatemala from Honduras and Nicaragua on 18 June 1954. The left-wing government of President Arbenz was overthrown by 27 June and the leader of the exiles, Colonel Carlos Castillo Armas, was declared president on 8 July 1954.

Casualties   No statistics available.

Costa Rica, Rebel Invasion, 1954

Combatants   Costa Rican Civil Guard versus armed exiles.

Key dates   On 25 July 1954 Costa Rican exiles based in Nicaragua crossed the border, but were repelled. A Nicaraguan plane was hit and both sides mobilized on the border, but the United States sent planes to Costa Rica to deter further Nicaraguan action.

Casualties   No statistics available.

Costa Rica, Rebel Invasion, 1955

Combatants   Costa Rican Civil Guard versus armed exiles.

Key dates   On 11 January 1955 a 500-strong force of rebels invaded from Nicaragua. After an 11-day campaign and pressure brought to bear on the Nicaraguan government through the council of the Organization of American States, the invaders were driven out.

Casualties   No statistics available.

Honduras, Border Conflict with Nicaragua, 1957

Combatants   Honduran armed forces versus Nicaraguan armed forces.

Key dates   On 18 April 1957 Nicaraguan troops crossed the Coco River and invaded Honduras to seize disputed border territory. Honduras recaptured the town of Morocon on 1 May. The Organization of American States arranged a cease-fire and withdrawal of forces on 6 May 1957.

Casualties   No statistics available.

Cuba, Bay of Pigs Invasion, 1961

Combatants   Cuban armed forces versus anti-Castro exiles.

Key dates   Some 1,500 anti-Castro exiles landed in the Bay of Pigs on 17 April 1961, in an operation sponsored by the U.S. Central Intelligence Agency. The invasion was defeated after three days' fighting when the expected anti-Castro uprising failed to take place.

Casualties   Cuban armed forces suffered 87 dead and 250 wounded; 1,240 invaders were captured.

Guatemala, Guerrilla Insurgency, 1961–1996

Combatants   Guatemalan armed forces versus Fuerzas Armadas Rebeldes.

Key dates   Guerrilla warfare began soon after the revolt against the government of President Ydigoras Fuentes on 13 November 1960 by junior army officers who objected to the presence of American-sponsored training camps for Cuban exiles. The rebels were defeated, but soon launched a guerrilla campaign. In the late 1960s they allied with the Guatemalan Communist Party to form the Fuerzas Armadas Rebeldes (Insurgent Armed Forces), a name later changed to the Guerrilla Army of the Poor. American special forces assisted in government operations against the insurgents, who were forced to switch their attacks from the countryside to the cities for a time. Retaliation by right-wing death squads resulted in thousands of deaths on both sides. In 1977 the United States halted military aid to Guatemala over human-rights violations, but the embargo was lifted on 17 January 1983. A state of siege was introduced on 1 July 1982. Violence subsided in 1985, flared again in 1990–91 and then appeared to end with a negotiated agreement. But in 1993 there was renewed fighting in the Ixcan area of northern Guatemala. When Jorge Serrano Elías attempted to dissolve Congress and the Supreme Court, the military deposed him and instead allowed the inauguration of de Leon Carpio, the former attorney general of human rights. In December 1996, a peace agreement ended 36 years of civil war, the longest in Latin American history.

Casualties   Over 150,000 deaths, 50,000 missing.

Dominican Republic, Civil War, 1965

Combatants   Dominican "Constitutionalists" versus "Loyalists," with intervention by the United States and the Organization of American States.

Key dates   Civil war broke out on 24 April 1965 between the Constitutionalists, supporting former president Bosch, and the Loyalist forces of President Reid Cabral. On 28 April 1965, 400 U.S. marines were sent in to prevent a left-wing takeover, and during the next month a further 24,000 American troops were landed. A cease-fire was signed on 6 May and at the end of May an Inter-American Peacekeeping Force, comprising units from the United States, Honduras, Nicaragua, Costa Rica, Brazil and El Salvador, under the auspices of the Organization of American States, was formed to keep the warring factions apart.

Casualties   No statistics available.

Honduras, Soccer War with El Salvador, 1969

Combatants   Honduran armed forces versus El Salvadorean armed forces.

Key dates   Hostilities were sparked off by the harassing of a visiting Honduran soccer team in San Salvador (in retaliation for the treatment of the Salvadoran team in Honduras) and the victory of El Salvador over Honduras in a World Cup soccer match on 15 June 1969. The underlying cause was the presence of some 300,000 Salvadoran workers living, many illegally, in Honduras. Riots led to the deaths of two Salvadorans and the expulsion of 11,000 others. In response the Salvadoran army crossed the border at several points on 14 July 1969. Honduras accepted an Organization of American States (OAS) cease-fire call on 16 July but El Salvador continued fighting. The OAS formally branded El Salvador as the aggressor and voted to impose sanctions on 29 July. El Salvador began to withdraw on 30 July and this was completed by 5 August 1969.

Casualties   About 2,000 killed in total.

Nicaragua, Civil War, 1978–90

Combatants   National Guard versus Sandinista National Liberation Front (FSLN); Sandinista forces versus "contras" and Democratic Revolutionary Front.

Key dates   Civil war was precipitated by the murder of President Anastasio Somoza's leading opponent, newspaper editor Pedro Joaquin Chamorro, on 10 January 1978. The FSLN made steady advances, and Somoza finally fled the country on 17 July 1979. Civil war continued as the Sandinista government faced two military threats: the first, the Democratic Revolutionary Front, a group of rebels led by dissident Sandinist Eden Pastora, mounted raids from its base in Costa Rica; the second, the Nicaraguan Democratic Front or "contras," was a force of ex-National Guardsmen who operated from their exile in Honduras and who received extensive American aid until the U.S. Congress halted funding on 25 June 1984. The Sandinista regime declared a state of emergency in May 1982, but disunity among its enemies enabled it to function despite the guerrilla threat. On 8 August 1987 leaders of the five Central American countries, including Nicaragua, met in Guatemala City to sign a peace accord calling for the democratization of Nicaragua and for contra–Sandinista negotiations. A 60-day cease-fire was announced in Sapoa on 23 March 1988; subsequently the U.S. Congress reinstated "humanitarian" aid to the contras as a further incentive to peace. Violence in the run-up to the 1990 elections led President Ortega to end the cease-fire on 1 November 1989. The Sandinista government was defeated in the elections held in February 1990. The military chief of the contras, Israel Galeano, and 100 of his soldiers handed in their weapons to UN forces on 27 June 1990, formally marking the end of their guerrilla campaign.

Casualties   10,000 deaths in the anti-Somoza struggle, a further 10,000 in the "contra" war.

El Salvador, Guerrilla Insurgency, 1979–92

Combatants　Salvadoran armed forces versus Farabundo Martí National Liberation Front.

Key dates　Guerrilla activity by the left-wing Farabundo Martí National Liberation Front intensified after 1979. Conflict between the 40,000-strong Salvadoran army, backed by the United States, and 9,000 Liberation Front guerrillas reached a stalemate by the end of 1986. Following the election of Alfredo Cristiani of the right-wing Republican Nationalist Alliance as president in March 1989, talks took place with the rebels in Mexico City in September. These broke down, and a guerrilla offensive launched on 11 November 1989 brought some of the worst fighting of the decade. A UN cease-fire was negotiated on 31 December 1991. On 1 February 1992, the UN–negotiated truce went into effect, formally ending 12 years of civil war.

Casualties　An estimated 75,000 deaths by the end of 1991.

Peru, Guerrilla Warfare, 1980–1999

Combatants　Peruvian armed forces and right-wing death squads versus guerrillas of the Sendero Luminosa, and the Tupac Amaru urban terrorist movement.

Key dates　The campaign against the government by the Maoist guerrilla movement Sendero Luminoso ("Shining Path") began in May 1980, and continued throughout the decade. Despite the arrest of its leader, Shining Path violence continued, and in January 1995, fighting flared again along part of the disputed border with Ecuador. In December 1996, Tupac Amaru rebels seized a diplomatic compound of the Japanese ambassador's residence in Lima and held 72 hostages for nearly four months. In May 1999, the presidents of Ecuador and Peru signed a treaty ending their nearly 60-year border dispute.

Casualties　Estimated 25,000 dead from all sides, 1980–94.

Argentina, Falkland Islands Conflict with United Kingdom, 1982

Combatants　Argentinian armed forces versus British task force.

Key dates　Argentina invaded the Falkland Islands on 2 April 1982. The first ships of the British task force sailed from Portsmouth on 5 April. South Georgia Island was recaptured on 25 April. The Argentinian cruiser *General Belgrano* was sunk on 2 May 1982. British forces established a bridgehead at San Carlos on East Falkland Island on 21 May. The Argentinians surrendered at Port Stanley on 14 June 1982.

Casualties   255 members of the British task force were killed and 777 wounded. Argentine casualties: statistics not available.

Grenada, Invasion by United States, 1983

Combatants   Grenadian People's Revolutionary Army (with Cuban support) versus U.S. armed forces and contingents from Jamaica, Barbados, Dominica, Antigua, St. Lucia and St. Vincent.

Key dates   On 19 October 1983 the army took control in Grenada after a power struggle led to the murder of Prime Minister Maurice Bishop. On 21 October the Organization of Eastern Caribbean States appealed to the United States to intervene and on 25 October U.S. marines and airborne troops invaded Grenada, together with token contingents from six Caribbean countries. Resistance from the Grenadian army and 700 Cuban construction workers with paramilitary training was overcome and order restored by 27 October 1983.

Casualties   42 U.S. servicemen killed; 59 Grenadian and Cuban personnel killed.

Panama, Invasion by United States, 1989

Combatants   United States armed forces versus Panamanian armed forces and President Noriega's "Dignity Battalions."

Key dates   President Noriega of Panama declared that a state of war existed between his country and the United States on 15 December 1989. An off-duty U.S. marine, Lieutenant Robert Paz, was killed at a roadblock on 16 December. American forces began the invasion of Panama, code-named Operation Just Cause, on 20 December. Fighting ended on 31 December. President Noriega took refuge in the Vatican embassy in Panama City, but gave himself up to U.S. forces on 3 January 1990.

Casualties   26 U.S. servicemen killed and 323 wounded; 314 members of the Panamanian defense forces and an unknown number of civilians killed.

UNITED NATIONS PEACEKEEPING OPERATIONS

UNSCOB: United Nations Special Commission in the Balkans, 1947–54

Established by the UN General Assembly in October 1947 to investigate and offer mediation on Greece's complaints of border violations by its neighbors. Replaced in 1952 by a subcommission of the UN Peace Observation Commission. The UN presence in Greece ended in August 1954.

Participants: Belgium, Brazil, China, France, Great Britain, Mexico, Netherlands, United States.

UNTSO: United Nations Truce Supervision Organization for Israel's Borders, 1949–continuing

Grew out of the UN Truce Commission established in April 1948 and given separate recognition by the Security Council in August 1949 to supervise the armistices agreed on between Israel and its Arab neighbors earlier in 1949.

UNTSO has assisted with UNDOF on the Golan Heights in the Israel-Syria sector and UNIFIL in the Israel-Lebanon sector, and was also present in the Egypt-Israel sector in the Sinai.

Participants: Argentina, Australia, Austria, Belgium, Canada, Chile, China, Denmark, Estonia, Finland, France, Ireland, Italy, Netherlands, New Zealand, Norway, Russia, Slovak Republic, Slovenia, Sweden, United States.

UNMOGIP: United Nations Military Observer Group for India and Pakistan, 1949–continuing

Established to supervise the cease-fire of January 1949 between India and Pakistan in Kashmir.

The military authorities of India have lodged no complaints since January 1972 and have restricted UN observers on the Indian side of the Line of Control. They continue to provide accommodation, transport and other facilities to UNMOGIP.

Participants: Belgium, Chile, Denmark, Ecuador, Finland, Italy, New Zealand, Norway, Republic of Korea, Sweden, Uruguay.

UNCI: United Nations Commission for Indonesia, 1949–51

Established in January 1949 to supervise the truce between the Republic of Indonesia and the Netherlands. The UN mission was disbanded after the transfer of full sovereignty to Indonesia.

Participants: Australia, Belgium, China, France, Great Britain, United States.

UNEF: United Nations Emergency Force, Egypt-Israel Border, 1956–67

Established in November 1956 to supervise the cease-fire between Egypt and Israel following the Suez Crisis.

Participants: Brazil, Canada, Colombia, Denmark, Finland, India, Indonesia, Norway, Sweden, Yugoslavia.

UNOGIL: United Nations Observer Group in Lebanon, 1958
Established at Lebanon's request in July 1958 after Lebanon accused the United Arab Republic of interference in its affairs; withdrawn in December.

Participants: Afghanistan, Argentina, Burma, Canada, Chile, Denmark, Ecuador, Finland, India, Indonesia, Ireland, Italy, Nepal, Netherlands, New Zealand, Norway, Peru, Portugal, Sri Lanka, Sweden, Thailand.

UNCO: United Nations Congo Operation, 1960–64
Established to maintain law, order and essential services in the Congo at the request of the central government after independence. UN forces reached a maximum strength of 19,825 men in July 1961. The last UN troops left on 30 June 1964.

Participants: Argentina, Australia, Brazil, Burma, Canada, Congo, Denmark, Ecuador, Ethiopia, Ghana, Greece, Guinea, India, Indonesia, Iran, Ireland, Italy, Liberia, Malaya, Mali, Morocco, Netherlands, New Zealand, Nigeria, Norway, Pakistan, Philippines, Sierra Leone, Sri Lanka, Sudan, Sweden, Tunisia, UAR, Yugoslavia.

UNTEA–UNSF: United Nations Temporary Executive Authority-Security Force, West Irian, 1962–63
Established in September 1962 to administer West New Guinea (West Irian) until Indonesia took over full sovereignty from the Netherlands in May 1963.

Participants: Canada, Pakistan, United States (with 21 observers being provided before the arrival of UNTEA–UNSF by Brazil, India, Ireland, Nigeria, Sri Lanka and Sweden).

UNYOM: United Nations Yemen Observation Mission, 1963–64
Established to supervise the disengagement of royalist and republican factions in the civil war. The mission was withdrawn in September 1964 after reporting that compliance with the disengagement was minimal.

Participants: Canada, Denmark, Ghana, India, Italy, Netherlands, Norway, Pakistan, Sweden, Yugoslavia.

UNFICYP: United Nations Force in Cyprus, 1964–continuing
Established in March 1964 to keep the peace between the Greek and Turkish Cypriot communities.

Following a de facto cease-fire, which came into effect on 16 August 1974, UNFICYP has maintained a buffer zone between the lines of the Cyprus National Guard and of the Turkish forces. In the absence of a political settlement to the Cyprus problem, UNFICYP continues its presence on the island.

Participants: Argentina, Australia, Austria, Canada, Finland, Hungary, India, Ireland, Netherlands, Slovenia, United Kingdom.

UNIPOM: United Nations India-Pakistan Observation Mission, 1965–66
Established in September 1965 to supervise the cease-fire between India and Pakistan. Disbanded on completion of its mission in March 1966.

Participants: Australia, Belgium, Brazil, Burma, Canada, Chile, Denmark, Ethiopia, Finland, Ireland, Italy, Nepal, Netherlands, New Zealand, Nigeria, Norway, Sri Lanka, Sweden, Uruguay, Venezuela.

UNEF: United Nations Emergency Force, Egypt-Israel Border, 1973–79
Established to supervise truce following the Yom Kippur War in October 1973. Its mandate ended with the signing of an Egyptian–Israeli peace treaty in 1979.

Participants: Australia, Austria, Canada, Finland, Ghana, Indonesia, Ireland, Nepal, Panama, Peru, Poland, Senegal, Sweden.

UNDOF: United Nations Disengagement Observer Force, Syria-Israel Border, 1974–continuing
Established in May 1974 to supervise the disengagement of Israeli and Syrian forces on the Golan Heights.

Participants: Austria, Canada, Japan, Poland, Slovak Republic.

UNIFIL: United Nations Interim Force in Lebanon, 1978–continuing
Established in March 1978 to confirm the Israeli withdrawal from southern Lebanon and assist the Lebanese government in restoring law and order.

UNIFIL has been prevented from fully implementing its mandate because Israel has maintained its occupation of south Lebanon, where the Israeli forces are attacked by resistance groups. UNIFIL strives to protect the inhabitants of the area from the fighting.

Participants: Fiji, Finland, France, Ghana, India, Ireland, Italy, Nepal, Poland.

ONUCA: United Nations Observer Group in Central America, 1989–92

ONUCA was established in 1989 for the on-site verification of the security arrangements contained in the Guatemala Agreement (Esquipulas II) of 7 August 1987. These include the ending of aid to irregular forces and ending use of the territory of a state for attacking others. In March 1990 the mission was expanded to include taking delivery of and destroying arms and ammunition of the Nicaraguan Resistance as they demobilized. ONUCA operated in El Salvador, Honduras and Nicaragua. Mission completed on 16 January 1992 and resources transferred to ONUSAL.

ONUSAL: United Nations Observer Mission in El Salvador, 1991–95

ONUSAL became operational in July 1991 to monitor agreements concluded between the government and the FMLN. A peace agreement was signed between the government and the FMLN in January 1992 under which both sides would report their full strength of troops and weapons to ONUSAL, which would also dispose of FMLN weapons as they were handed over during demobilization. The UN disbanded ONUCA and transferred its manpower and equipment to ONUSAL. ONUSAL is to monitor the cease-fire (military observers), monitor human rights violations (civilian observers) and establish a police force on democratic lines.

After the armed conflict had been formally brought to an end in December 1992, ONUSAL verified that elections were carried out successfully in March and April 1994. After ONUSAL completed its mandate on 30 April 1995, a small group of United Nations civilian personnel—known as the United Nations Mission in El Salvador (MINUSAL)—remained in El Salvador to verify implementation of the outstanding points of the agreements.

Participants: Observers from Brazil, Chile, Colombia, Guyana, Italy, Mexico, Spain and Venezuela.

UNIKOM: United Nations Iraq/Kuwait Observer Mission, 1991–continuing

Established in April 1991 following the recapture of Kuwait from Iraq by Coalition Forces. Its mandate is to monitor the Khor Abdullah and a demilitarized zone (DMZ) extending 10 km (6.2 miles) into Iraq and 5 km (3.1 miles) into Kuwait from the agreed-on boundary between the two (Iraq/Kuwait Restoration of Friendly Relations, Recognition and Related Matters dated 4 October 1963). In February 1993 the Security Council adopted a resolution to strengthen UNIKOM, replacing the unarmed observer mission with a 750-strong military force.

Participants: Units from Canada (Engineers), Chile (Air Wing), Denmark (Administrative Staff), Norway (Medical). Observers from Argentina, Austria, Bangladesh, Canada, China, Denmark, Fiji, Finland, France, Ghana, Greece, Hungary, India, Indonesia, Ireland, Italy, Kenya, Malaysia, Nigeria, Norway, Pakistan, Poland, Romania, Russia, Senegal, Singapore, Sweden, Thailand, Turkey, United Kingdom, Uruguay, United States, Venezuela.

MINURSO: United Nations Mission for the Referendum in Western Sahara, 1991–continuing

Established in April 1991 to supervise a referendum to choose between independence and integration into Morocco. A transitional period would begin with the coming into effect of a cease-fire and end when the referendum results were announced. Although a cease-fire went into effect on 6 September 1991, the transitional period did not begin since the UN had been unable to complete its registration of eligible voters. It is now apparent that, despite earlier agreements, substantial areas of difference between the two sides remain. MINURSO is therefore currently restricted to verifying the cease-fire.

Participants: Australia (signals), Canada (movement control), Switzerland (civilian medical). Observers from Argentina, Australia, Austria, Bangladesh, Canada, China, Egypt, France, Ghana, Greece, Guinea, Ireland, Italy, Kenya, Malaysia, Nigeria, Pakistan, Peru, Poland, Russia, Tunisia, United Kingdom, United States, Venezuela.

UNAVEM II: United Nations Angola Verification Mission II, 1991–95

Established June 1991 to verify the cease-fire as set out in the Peace Accords, agreed to by the government of Angola and UNITA, and to monitor the Angolan police as set out in the Protocol of Estoril. Despite the United Nations verification that the elections—held in September

1992—had been free and fair, their results were contested by UNITA. After renewed fighting in October 1992 between the government and UNITA forces, UNAVEM II's mandate was adjusted in order to help the two sides reach agreement for completing the peace process and implement cease-fires. Following the signing of the Lusaka Protocol, UNAVEM II verified the initial stages of the peace agreement. In February 1995, the Security Council set up a new mission—UNAVEM III—to monitor and verify the implementation of the Protocol.

Participants: Observers from Algeria, Argentina, Brazil, Canada, Congo, Czechoslovakia, Egypt, Guinea-Bissau, Hungary, India, Ireland, Jordan, Malaysia, Morocco, Netherlands, Nigeria, Norway, Senegal, Singapore, Spain, Sweden, Yugoslavia, Zimbabwe.

UNTAC: United Nations Transitional Authority in Cambodia, 1992–September 1993
Established following the signing of the Cambodia peace settlement of 23 October 1991, the force became operational on 15 March 1992. It was to supervise the preparation of elections due in May 1993 and ensure that the conditions of the peace settlement were not violated.

Participants: Infantry battalions from Bangladesh, Bulgaria, France, Ghana, India, Indonesia, Malaysia, Netherlands, Pakistan, Tunisia and Uruguay. Military observers from Algeria, Argentina, Austria, Bangladesh, Belgium, Bulgaria, Cameroon, China, France, Ghana, India, Indonesia, Ireland, Malaysia, New Zealand, Pakistan, Poland, Russia, Senegal, Tunisia, United Kingdom and United States.

UNPROFOR: United Nations Protection Force, 1992–95
Established in March 1992, UNPROFOR, which includes military, police and civilian components, was initially deployed in three "United Nations Protected Areas" (UNPAs) in Croatia to create the conditions of peace and security required to permit the negotiation of an overall political settlement of the Yugoslav crisis. Its activities were subsequently extended to Bosnia Herzegovina, including the supply of relief food convoys and the protection of the Muslim "safe havens" (see p. 292–93). By mid-1993 there were over 24,000 UN troops in former Yugoslavia, with France contributing 5,800 men. The role of UNPROFOR became increasingly difficult in 1994 as it tried to defend such "safe havens" as Goradze. NATO air power had to be called in.

In 1994 and 1995, UNPROFOR monitored a cease-fire agreement signed by the Bosnian government and Bosnian Croat forces, and between the Bosnian government and Bosnian Serb forces. On 31 March

1995, the Security Council decided to restructure UNPROFOR, replacing it with three separate but interlinked peacekeeping operations.

Participants: Argentina, Bangladesh, Belgium, Brazil, Canada, Colombia, Czech Republic, Denmark, Egypt, Finland, France, Ghana, Indonesia, Ireland, Jordan, Kenya, Lithuania, Malaysia, Nepal, Netherlands, New Zealand, Nigeria, Norway, Pakistan, Poland, Portugal, Russian Federation, Slovak Republic, Spain, Sweden, Switzerland, Tunisia, Turkey, Ukraine, United Kingdom, United States, Venezuela.

UNOSOM I: United Nations Operation in Somalia, 1992–93

The UN Security Council adopted Resolution 733 on 23 January 1992, calling on all parties to cease hostilities and imposing a general and complete embargo on the delivery of arms and military equipment to Somalia. Following the visit of a UN team to Mogadishu, the Security Council, but its Resolution 751 on 21 April 1992, decided to establish an operation to monitor the cease-fire and to provide protection for relief supply convoys. In August 1992, UNOSOM I's mandate was enlarged to protect humanitarian convoys and distribution centers. In December 1992, after the situation in Somalia further deteriorated, the Security Council authorized Member States to form the United Task Force (UNI-TAF) to establish a safe environment for the delivery of humanitarian assistance. In March 1993, UNOSOM I was replaced with UNOSOM II.

UNOSOM II: United Nations Operation in Somalia, 1993–95

Established to take over from the Unified Task Force (UNITAF)—a multinational force, organized and led by the United States, which, in December 1992, had been authorized by the Security Council to use "all necessary means" to establish a secure environment for humanitarian relief operations in Somalia. UNOSOM II's responsibilities included preventing resumption of violence, seizing unauthorized small arms, maintaining security at transportation areas, continuing mine-clearing, and assisting in repatriation of refugees in Somalia. Several violent outbreaks occurred throughout 1992 and 1993 as General Mohamad Fahrah Aidid, a militia warlord who objected to UN control of the airport, shelled ships carrying food, hijacked vehicles and looted convoys and warehouses. UN troops returned fire in an attempt to maintain the flow of humanitarian aid. On 5 June 1993, Aidid ambushed UN troops, killing 22 and wounding 54. The militia dragged American bodies through the streets, causing an about-face in America's willingness to participate in relief efforts. Peace talks on an interim government collapsed in

March 1994 and the last of the U.S. troops left later that month, leaving 19,000 UN troops behind. The Security Council revised UNOSOM II's mandate to exclude the use of coercive methods and UNOSOM II was withdrawn in early March 1995.

UNOMOZ: United Nations Operation in Mozambique, 1992–94

On 16 December 1992 the Security Council approved the establishment of the United Nations Operation in Mozambique (UNOMOZ), which remained in place until 31 October 1993. The UN force monitored the cease-fire reached in October 1992 between the formerly Marxist government of President Joaquim Chissano and rebels of the Mozambique National Resistance. They began to oversee disbanding the military forces of both sides, help organize the elections and do humanitarian work.

After successful presidential and legislative elections in October 1994, and the installation of Mozambique's new parliament and the inauguration of the president of Mozambique in early December, UNOMOZ's mandate formally came to an end at midnight on 9 December 1994. The mission was formally liquidated at the end of January 1995.

Participants: Argentina, Australia, Austria, Bangladesh, Botswana, Brazil, Canada, Cape Verde, China, Czech Republic, Egypt, Ghana, Guinea Bissau, Guyana, Hungary, India, Indonesia, Italy, Japan, Jordan, Malaysia, Nepal, Netherlands, New Zealand, Nigeria, Pakistan, Portugal, Russian Federation, Spain, Sri Lanka, Sweden, Togo, United States, Uruguay, Zambia.

UNOMUR: United Nations Observer Mission Uganda-Rwanda, 1993–94

In June 1993, the Security Council established UNOMUR to monitor the border between Uganda and Rwanda and verify that no lethal weapons or military ammunitions were coming across it. UNOMUR was unable to implement its mandate because of tragic events in April 1994, but helped build confidence following the Arusha Peace Agreement until UNOMIR took over. UNOMUR was officially closed on 21 September 1994.

UNAMIR: United Nations Assistance Mission for Rwanda, 1993–96

In October 1993 the Security Council established UNAMIR to implement the Arusha peace agreement signed by the Rwandese parties on 4 August 1993. UNAMIR's mandate was: to ensure security of the capital city of Kigali; monitor the cease-fire agreement, including establishment of an expanded demilitarized zone and demobilization procedures; monitor security during the final period of the transitional government leading up to elections; assist with mine-clearance; and assist in the coordination of humanitarian assistance activities in conjunction with relief operations. After renewed fighting in April 1994, the mandate of UNAMIR was adjusted so that it could act as an intermediary between the warring Rwandese parties in an attempt to secure agreement to a cease-fire, assist in the resumption of humanitarian relief operations and monitor the safety and security of civilians who sought refuge with UNAMIR. Following the cease-fire and the installation of the new government, the tasks of UNAMIR were adjusted to ensure stability in the northwestern and southwestern regions of Rwanda; to encourage the return of the displaced population; and to provide security for humanitarian assistance operations. UNAMIR also contributed to the security of human rights officers and assisted in training a new, integrated police force. In December 1995, the Security Council further adjusted UNAMIR's mandate to focus primarily on facilitating the safe and voluntary return of refugees. UNAMIR's mandate came to an end on 8 March 1996. The withdrawal of the mission was completed in April.

Participants: Argentina, Australia, Austria, Bangladesh, Canada, Chad, Congo, Djibouti, Ethiopia, Fiji, Ghana, Guinea, Guinea-Bissau, India, Jordan, Malawi, Mali, Niger, Nigeria, Poland, Russian Federation, Senegal, Tunisia, United Kingdom, Uruguay, Zambia, Zimbabwe.

UNOMIL: United Nations Observer Mission in Liberia, 1993–97

On 22 September 1993 the Security Council established UNOMIL to support the peace agreement of the Economic Community of West African States (ECOWAS) and the Liberian National Transitional Government; to investigate allegations of cease-fire violations; to monitor disarmament and observance of the arms embargo; to assist in the demobilization of combatants; to support humanitarian assistance activities; and to verify the election process.

Participants: Austria, Bangladesh, Belgium, Brazil, China, Congo, Czech Republic, Egypt, Guinea-Bissau, Hungary, India, Jordan, Kenya, Malaysia, Nepal, Netherlands, Pakistan, Poland, Russian Federation, Slovak Republic, Sweden, Uruguay.

UNMIH: United Nations Mission in Haiti, 1993–96

UNMIH was originally established to implement provisions of the Governors Island Agreement signed by the Haitian parties on 3 July 1993. In 1993, UNMIH's mandate was to assist in modernizing the armed forces of Haiti and establishing a new police force. However, due to noncooperation of the Haitian military authorities, UNMIH could not be fully deployed at that time. In October 1994, UNMIH's mandate was revised to assist the newly restored Haitian Constitutional Government in training the Haitian armed forces, creating a separate police force, and establishing free legislative elections. Elections were held in 1995, and the transfer of power to the new president took place on 7 February 1996. UNMIH's mandate was extended for the final period until the end of June 1996.

UNOMIG: United Nations Observer Mission in Georgia, 1993–continuing

On 24 August 1993 the Security Council established UNOMIG to verify compliance with the 27 July 1993 cease-fire agreement between Georgia and the Abkhaz authorities. After UNOMIG's original mandate was invalidated by the resumed fighting in Abkhazia in September 1993, the mission was given an interim mandate to maintain contacts with both sides of the conflict and with the Russian military contingents. Following an additional cease-fire agreement in May 1994, UNOMIG's mandate was expanded to verify that troops and heavy military equipment do not remain in or reenter the security zone and to monitor the withdrawal of Georgian troops from the Kodori Valley to places beyond the frontiers of Abkhazia. In 1996 the Council established a human rights office in Sukhumi.

Participants: Albania, Austria, Bangladesh, Czech Republic, Denmark, Egypt, France, Germany, Greece, Hungary, Indonesia, Jordan, Pakistan, Poland, Republic of Korea, Russia, Sweden, Switzerland, Turkey, United Kingdom, United States, Uruguay.

UNASOG: United Nations Aouzou Strip Observer Group, May–June 1994

Established to verify the withdrawal of the Libyan administration and forces from the Aouzou Strip. UNASOG accomplished its mandate after both sides—the Republic of Chad and the Libyan Arab Jamahiriya—declared withdrawal to be complete.

UNMOT: United Nations Organization Mission of Observers in Tajikistan, 1994–continuing

UNMOT was established in 1994 to monitor the cease-fire agreement between the government of Tajikistan and the United Tajik opposition. In 1997, both parties signed a peace agreement and UNMOT's mandate was expanded to help monitor its implementation.

Participants: Austria, Bangladesh, Bulgaria, Czech Republic, Denmark, Jordan, Nepal, Nigeria, Poland, Uruguay.

UNAVEM III: United Nations Angola Verification Mission III, 1995–97

Established to assist in restoring peace between Angola and UNITA following the 1991 signing of the Lusaka protocol. UNAVEM III's mandate was to provide mediation to the Angolan parties, supervise disengagement of forces, verify withdrawal of UNITA forces, supervise collection of armaments, monitor neutrality of Angolan police, facilitate humanitarian activities, participate in mine-clearance attempts and ensure that presidential elections were freely held.

Participants: Bangladesh, Brazil, Bulgaria, Congo, Egypt, France, Guinea-Bissau, Hungary, India, Jordan, Kenya, Malaysia, Mali, Namibia, Netherlands, New Zealand, Nigeria, Norway, Pakistan, Poland, Portugal, Romania, Russian Federation, Senegal, Slovak Republic, Sweden, Tanzania, Ukraine, Uruguay, Zambia.

UNPREDEP: United Nations Preventive Deployment Force, 1995–99

Established on 31 March 1995 to replace UNPROFOR in the former Yugoslav Republic of Macedonia, the mandate of UNPREDEP remained essentially the same: to monitor and report any developments in the border areas that could undermine stability in the former Yugoslav Republic of Macedonia. Effective 1 February 1996, following the termination of the mandates of UNCRO and UNPROFOR, UNPREDEP became an independent mission that operated 24 permanent observation posts along a 420-kilometer stretch on the Macedonian side of the border with the Federal Republic of Yugoslavia and Albania. The mission was extended several times to continue deterring threats and preventing clashes and to monitor any illicit arms flows. UNPREDEP came to an end on 28 February 1999, due to the veto of China, a permanent member of the Security Council.

Participants: Argentina, Bangladesh, Belgium, Brazil, Canada, Czech Republic, Denmark, Egypt, Finland, Ghana, Indonesia, Ireland, Jordan, Kenya, Nepal, New Zealand, Nigeria, Norway, Pakistan, Poland, Portugal, Russian Federation, Sweden, Switzerland, Turkey, Ukraine, United States.

UNMIBH: United Nations Mission in Boznia and Herzegovina, 1995–continuing

On 21 December 1995 the Security Council established an International Police Task Force (IPTF) within the territory of Bosnia and Herzegovina and a United Nations Civilian Office (UNCO). It was initially authorized for one year as outlined in the peace agreement signed by the leaders of Bosnia and Herzegovina, Croatia and the Federal Republic of Yugoslavia (Serbia and Montenegro) on 14 December 1995. UNMIBH combines IPTF and UNCO and cooperates with the NATO-led Multinational Implementation Force (IFOR) and the Multinational Stabilization Force (SFOR) to ensure compliance with the peace agreement and to advance the UN goals of policing, monitoring, humanitarian relief, de-mining and economic reconstruction.

Participants: Argentina, Austria, Bangladesh, Bulgaria, Canada, Chile, Denmark, Egypt, Estonia, Fiji, Finland, France, Germany, Ghana, Greece, Hungary, Iceland, India, Indonesia, Ireland, Italy, Jordan, Kenya, Lithuania, Malaysia, Nepal, Netherlands, Nigeria, Norway, Pakistan, Poland, Portugal, Romania, Russian Federation, Senegal, Spain, Sweden, Switzerland, Thailand, Tunisia, Turkey, Ukraine, United Kingdom and United States.

UNCRO: United Nations Confidence Restoration Operation, 1995–96

Established on 31 March 1995 to replace UNPROFOR in Croatia, UNCRO's troops and observers were deployed in Serb-controlled Western Slavonia, the Krajina region and Eastern Slavonia. Observers were also stationed in the Prevlaka peninsula. The new mandate included verifying the terms of the 1994 cease-fire agreement, facilitating the delivery of international humanitarian assistance to Bosnia and Herzegovina through the territory of Croatia, and monitoring the demilitarization of the Prevlaka peninsula. UNCRO monitored military personnel, equipment, supplies and weapons crossing over the international borders between Croatia and Bosnia and Herzegovina, and Croatia and the Federal Republic of Yugoslavia (Serbia and Montenegro). Croatia's reintegration by force of Western Slavonia and the Krajina region in May and August 1995 effectively eliminated the need for United Nations troops in those areas and their withdrawal was initiated. However, in Eastern Slavonia—the last Serb-controlled territory in Croatia—the mandate of UNCRO remained essentially unchanged until the Croatia government and the Croatian Serb leadership agreed to negotiate. UN–sponsored talks resulted in the Basic Agreement on the Region of Eastern Slavonia, Baranja and Western Sirmium on 12 November 1995, which provided for that region's peaceful integration into Croatia. UNCRO was terminated on 15 January 1996.

UNTAES: United Nations Transitional Administration in Eastern Slavonia, Baranja and Western Sirmium, 1996–98

At the request of the Basic Agreement on the Region of Eastern Slavonia, Baranja and Western Sirmium, which provides for the peaceful integration of that region into Croatia, the Security Council established UNTAES to govern the region during the transition and to authorize an international force to maintain peace. The military component supervised demilitarization, monitored the safe return of refugees and contributed to peace and security in the region. The civilian component established and trained a temporary police force, monitored treatment of prisoners and organized elections and certified the results.

Participants: Argentina, Austria, Bangladesh, Belgium, Brazil, Czech Republic, Denmark, Egypt, Fiji, Finland, Ghana, Indonesia, Ireland, Jordan, Kenya, Lithuania, Nepal, Netherlands, New Zealand, Nigeria, Norway, Pakistan, Poland, Russian Federation, Slovak Republic, Sweden, Switzerland, Tunisia, Ukraine, United States.

UNSIMH: United Nations Support Mission in Haiti, 1996–97

UNSIMH was established in July 1996 to assist the government of Haiti in establishing and training an effective national police force.

UNMOP: United Nations Mission of Observers in Prevlaka, 1996–continuing

United Nations military observers had been deployed in the Prevlaka peninsula since October 1992, when the Security Council authorized UNPROFOR to assume responsibility for monitoring the demilitarization of that area. Following the restructuring of UNPROFOR in March 1995, those functions were carried out by UNCRO, which was terminated in January 1996. The Security Council then authorized UN military observers to continue monitoring the demilitarization of the peninsula for a period of three months, to be extended for an additional three months if the secretary-general reported that it would decrease tension in the region. UNMOP became an independent mission on 1 February 1996, and its mandate has continuously been extended so that the mission can continue monitoring the demilitarization of the Prevlaka peninsula.

MINUGUA: United Nations Verification Mission in Guatemala, January to May 1997

On 20 January 1997 MINUGUA was established as a civilian and humanitarian mission to verify the cease-fire between the government of Guatemala and the Unidad Revolucionaria Nacional Guatemalteca (URNG), which was signed at Oslo on 4 December 1996. The duties included observing formal cessation of hostilities, separation of forces, and demobilization of URNG combatants. The mandate lasted three months.

Participants: Argentina, Australia, Austria, Brazil, Canada, Colombia, Ecuador, Germany, Italy, Norway, Russian Federation, Singapore, Spain, Sweden, Ukraine, United States, Uruguay and Venezuela.

UNTMIH: United Nations Transition Mission in Haiti, August–November 1997

UNTMIH's mandate was to assist in the training of the Haitian National Police (HNP) in crowd control, rapid reaction force and palace security. Tasks of UNTMIH's military security element included ensuring safety and freedom of movement of UN personnel.

Participants: Argentina, Benin, Canada, France, India, Mali, Niger, Pakistan, Senegal, Togo, Tunisia, United States.

MONUA: United Nations Mission of Observers in Angola, 1997–99

On 30 June 1997 the Security Council established MONUA to assist the Angolan parties in consolidating peace and national reconciliation, establish stability and aid in rehabilitation of the country. MONUA's tasks included working toward demobilization, incorporating ex-combatants of UNITA into the Angolan Armed Forces (FAA) and the Angolan National Police (ANP), and disarming the civilian population. The mandate was extended on several occasions before liquidation.

Participants: Bangladesh, Bolivia, Brazil, Egypt, Ghana, India, Jordan, Pakistan, Poland, Portugal, Romania, Russian Federation, Senegal, Uruguay, Zambia, Zimbabwe.

MIPONUH: United Nations Civilian Police Mission in Haiti, 1997–2000

In December 1997 the Security Council established MIPONUH to assist in training the Haitian National Police with special emphasis on assistance at the supervisory level and on training specialized police units. MIPONUH completed its mandate on 15 March 2000 and was succeeded by the new International Civilian Support Mission in Haiti (MICAH). Its mandate is to consolidate the results achieved by MIPONUH and its predecessor missions and further promote human rights.

Participants: Argentina, Benin, Canada, France, India, Mali, Niger, Senegal, Togo, Tunisia, United States.

UNPSG: United Nations Civilian Police Support Group, January to October 1998

On 16 January 1998 the Security Council established UNPSG to take over policing tasks from the United Nations Transitional Administration for Eastern Slavonia, Baranja and Western Sirmium after the UNTAES mission's mandate expiration. The mandate was to continue monitoring the Croatian police in the Danube region, particularly the return of displaced persons, for a single nine-month period ending on 15 October 1998.

Participants: Argentina, Austria, Denmark, Egypt, Fiji, Finland, Indonesia, Ireland, Jordan, Kenya, Lithuania, Norway, Poland, Russian Federation, Sweden, Switzerland, Ukraine, United States.

UNOMSIL: United Nations Mission of Observers in Sierra Leone, 1998–99

On 13 July 1998 the Security Council established UNOMSIL to monitor the military and security situation in Sierra Leone, supervise disarmament and demobilization of former combatants in secure areas of the country, and advise the government and local police on internationally accepted standards of policing in democratic societies. The mission ended in October 1999, when UNAMSIL took over.

Participants: Bangladesh, Croatia, the Czech Republic, Denmark, Egypt, France, India, Indonesia, Jordan, Kenya, Kyrgyzstan, Malaysia, Nepal, New Zealand, Norway, Pakistan, Russian Federation, Sweden, Thailand, the United Republic of Tanzania, United Kingdom, Uruguay, Zambia.

MINURCA: United Nations Mission in the Central African Republic, 1998–2000

In April 1998, the Security Council set up MINURCA to maintain security and stability in Bangui. The mission was meant to supervise the final disposal of weapons and to give legal or technical advice on elections.

Participants: Benin, Burkina Faso, Cameroon, Canada, Chad, Côte d'Ivoire, Egypt, France, Gabon, Mali, Portugal, Senegal, Togo, Tunisia.

UNMIK: United Nations Interim Administration Mission in Kosovo, 1999–continuing

On 10 June 1999 the Security Council established an interim international civilian administration in Kosovo so that citizens there could enjoy substantial autonomy. After NATO suspended its air operations following the withdrawal of security forces of the Federal Republic of Yugoslavia from Kosovo, the mission became known as UNMIK.

UNTAET: United Nations Transitional Administration in East Timor, 1999–continuing

On 30 August 1999 the people of East Timor voted for independence from Portugal. UNTAET was established to administer the territory and exercise legislative and executive authority during the transition period.

Participants: Argentina, Australia, Austria, Bangladesh, Bolivia, Brazil, Canada, China, Denmark, Egypt, Fiji, France, Gambia, Ghana, Ireland, Jordan, Kenya, Korea (Republic of), Malaysia, Mozambique, Nepal, New Zealand, Niger, Norway, Pakistan, Papua New Guinea, Philippines, Portugal, Russian Federation, Senegal, Singapore, Spain, Sri Lanka, Sweden, Thailand, Turkey, United Kingdom, United States, Uruguay, Zambia, Zimbabwe.

UNAMSIL: United Nations Mission in Sierra Leone, 1999–continuing

On 22 October 1999 UNAMSIL was established to implement the Lome Peace Agreement and to assist in the disarmament, demobilization and reintegration plan. On 7 February 2000 the Security Council revised the mandate and increased its size to: monitor adherence to the cease-fire agreement; provide security at key locations and government buildings (particularly in Freetown and at Lungi airport); facilitate the free flow of people, goods and humanitarian assistance; provide security at all sites of the disarmament, demobilization and reintegration program; assist the Sierra Leone law enforcement authorities; and to guard weapons, ammunition and other military equipment collected from warring parties and assist in their disposal or destruction.

Participants: Bangladesh, Bolivia, Canada, Croatia, Czech Republic, Denmark, Egypt, France, Gambia, Ghana, India, Indonesia, Jordan, Kenya, Kyrgyzstan, Malaysia, Namibia, Nepal, New Zealand, Nigeria, Norway, Pakistan, Russian Federation, Slovakia, Sweden, Thailand, United Republic of Tanzania, United Kingdom, Uruguay, Zambia.

MONUC: United Nations Organization Mission in the Democratic Republic of the Congo, 1999–continuing

The Democratic Republic of the Congo and five regional states signed the Lusaka cease-fire agreement in July 1999. MONUC was established on 30 November 1999 to supervise the disarmament of all armed groups and the orderly withdrawal of all foreign forces, obtain release of all prisoners of war, and carry out emergency mine-deployment actions.

Participants: Algeria, Bangladesh, Benin, Bolivia, Canada, Egypt, France, Ghana, India, Italy, Kenya, Libya, Mali, Nepal, Pakistan, Poland, Romania, Russian Federation, South Africa, Sweden, United Kingdom, United Republic of Tanzania, Uruguay, Zambia.

MAJOR ACTS OF TERRORISM 1968–2000

1968   23 July   **Air Piracy:** An Israeli El Al Boeing 707, en route from Rome to Tel Aviv, is hijacked over Italy by three members of the Popular Front for the Liberation of Palestine (PFLP) and forced to fly to Algiers. The Algerian government releases the hostages in groups, the last on 31 August, and lets the plane go on 1 September.

28 Aug   **Guatemala:** John G. Mein, U.S. ambassador to Guatemala, is killed by gunmen in Guatemala City.

12 Oct   **Brazil:** Captain Charles R. Chandler of the U.S. Army is killed by two gunmen as he leaves his home in São Paulo.

22 Nov **Israel:** A car bomb explosion in the Jewish sector of Jerusalem kills 12.

26 Dec **Greece:** Two Palestinians attack an Israeli El Al Boeing 707 at Athens airport with grenades and small arms, killing one passenger.

28 Dec **Lebanon:** Israeli commandos take over Beirut airport and destroy 13 civilian aircraft belonging to three Arab airlines.

1969 18 Feb **Switzerland:** Four Arab gunmen attack an Israeli El Al Boeing 720 at Zurich airport, injuring six passengers and crew.

18 July **Great Britain:** Bombs planted by Palestinians explode in Marks and Spencer store in London.

29 Aug **Air Piracy:** A U.S. Trans World Airlines Boeing 707, en route from Rome to Athens and Tel Aviv, is hijacked by two PFLP terrorists and forced to fly to Damascus. The plane is destroyed by a bomb after landing. Two Israeli passengers held as hostages are exchanged on December 5 for 13 Syrian prisoners in Israel.

4 Sep **Brazil:** Charles Elbrick, U.S. ambassador, kidnapped in Rio de Janeiro. He is released when 15 prisoners are flown out to Mexico.

12 Dec **Italy:** Bomb explosion in the National Bank of Agriculture in Milan kills 16 and injures 90.

1970 10 Feb **West Germany:** Grenade attack by three Arabs on a bus at Munich airport kills one Israeli and wounds 11 other people.

31 Mar **Guatemala:** Count Karl von Spreti, West German ambassador to Guatemala, kidnapped in Guatemala City and found dead on 5 April.

29 May **Argentina:** Lieutenant General Pedro Aramburu, a former provisional president of Argentina, is kidnapped from his home by four men and found shot on 16 July.

31 July **Uruguay:** Two diplomats are kidnapped by Tupamaros guerrillas in Montevideo. Dan Mitrione of the U.S. Agency for International Development is found shot on 10 August. Aloysio Gomide, Brazilian vice consul, is released on 21 February 1971 after a ransom is paid by his family.

6 Sep **Air Piracy:** PFLP terrorists seize three planes en route to New York—a Swissair DC-8 from Zurich, a TWA Boeing 707 from Frankfurt and a Pan Amer-

ican World Airways 747 from Amsterdam. An attempt to seize a fourth plane, an El Al Boeing 707, fails when a hijacker is shot dead by security guards. The Swissair and TWA planes are flown to Dawson's Field in the Jordanian desert. The Pan Am plane is flown to Beirut and then on to Cairo, where it is evacuated and blown up. A further plane, a BOAC VC10, en route from Bombay to London, is hijacked on 9 September and flown to Dawson's Field. The three planes are destroyed on 12 September. The hostages are freed during the remainder of September as part of a deal for the release of Arab terrorists held in Europe.

	5 Oct	**Canada:** James Cross, a British diplomat, is kidnapped by French-Canadian separatists in Montreal. He is released on 3 December 1970 in return for safe conduct to Cuba for hijackers.
	10 Oct	**Canada:** Pierre Laporte, Quebec Labor minister, is seized by separatists in Montreal and found dead on 18 October.
	1 Dec	**Spain:** Eugen Beihl, West German honorary consul, is kidnapped from his home in San Sebastian by Basque nationalists. He is released on 25 December on condition that death sentences on six Basques on trial at Burgos be commuted to imprisonment.
1971	8 Jan	**Uruguay:** Geoffrey Jackson, the British ambassador, is kidnapped by Tupamaros guerrillas in Montevideo. He is released on 9 September three days after the escape of 106 Tupamaros from prison.
	14 Mar	**Netherlands:** Fuel tanks in Rotterdam are blown up by Palestinians and French sympathizers.
	7 Apr	**Sweden:** Vladimir Rolovic, Yugoslav ambassador to Sweden, is shot in Stockholm by two Croatians and dies on 15 April.
	17 May	**Turkey:** Ephraim Elrom, Israeli consul-general in Istanbul, is kidnapped by Turkish People's Liberation Army and found dead on 23 May.
	27 July	**France:** Palestinian bomb attack on Jordanian embassy, Paris.
	21 Aug	**Philippines:** Ten are killed and 74 are wounded by terrorist grenades at a preelection rally of opposition Liberal Party in Manila.
	28 Nov	**Egypt:** Wasif Tell, Jordanian prime minister, is assassinated in Cairo by Black September guerrillas.

1972

15 Dec **Great Britain:** Zaid Rifai, Jordanian ambassador in London, is wounded when shots are fired at his car by Black September guerrillas.

16 Dec **Switzerland:** Parcel bomb attempt on the life of Ibrahim Zreikat, Jordanian ambassador to Switzerland, injures two policemen in Geneva.

6 Feb **Netherlands:** Two gas-processing plants in Rotterdam are blown up by Black September guerrillas.

6 Feb **West Germany:** Five Jordanians are killed in Cologne by Black September.

8 Feb **West Germany:** A factory making electric generators for Israeli aircraft is damaged in Hamburg.

21 Feb **Air Piracy:** A West German Lufthansa jumbo jet en route from New Delhi to Athens is hijacked by five PFLP terrorists and diverted to Aden. The passengers are released, and the 16 crew are freed on 23 February when the West Germans pay a $5 million ransom.

22 Feb **Great Britain:** A Provisional IRA bomb attack on the Officers' Mess of the Parachute Regiment in Aldershot kills seven.

18 Mar **Canada:** Bomb explosion in a supermarket in Toronto kills two.

21 Mar **Argentina:** Oberdan Sallustro, Fiat executive president in Argentina, is kidnapped in Buenos Aires by Ejercito Revolucionario Popular (ERP), and shot dead on 10 April, as police surround the kidnappers' hideout.

27 Mar **Turkey:** One Canadian and two British NATO radar technicians are kidnapped in Ankara by the Turkish People's Liberation Army and murdered when police discover the kidnappers' hideout. Ten terrorists are killed by police.

8 May **Air Piracy:** A Belgian Sabena Airlines plane en route from Vienna to Tel Aviv is hijacked by four Black September terrorists and diverted to Lod airport, Tel Aviv. Israeli paratroopers disguised as mechanics enter the plane, shoot dead two hijackers and wound a third on 9 May.

11 May **West Germany:** Bombs explode at headquarters of the Fifth U.S. Army Corps in Frankfurt, killing Colonel Paul Bloomquist and wounding 13 others.

31 May	**Israel:** Three Japanese Red Army terrorists attack passengers at Lod airport near Tel Aviv, killing 26 and wounding 76 others.
8 July	**Lebanon:** Ghassan Kanafani, a leader of the Popular Front for the Liberation of Palestine, is killed, together with his niece, by a car bomb in Beirut.
21 July	**Northern Ireland:** Nine are killed in Belfast in a coordinated series of at least 20 bombings by the Provisional IRA.
5 Sep	**West Germany:** Black September terrorists seize the Israeli quarters at the Olympic Games village in Munich. Two Israeli athletes are killed initially and a further nine hostages, five terrorists and a policeman die in a shoot-out at the airport.
19 Sep	**Great Britain:** Dr. Arni Shachori, counsellor for agricultural affairs at the Israeli embassy in London, is killed by a letter bomb sent from Amsterdam by Black September.
29 Oct	**Air Piracy:** A Lufthansa Boeing 727 en route from Beirut to Ankara is hijacked by two Black September terrorists and forced to fly to Munich. Without landing, it returns to Zagreb in Yugoslavia and circles the airport until a smaller plane carrying three Arabs held for the Munich massacre arrives. The three terrorists then board the hijacked aircraft and fly to Tripoli in Libya.
8 Dec	**France:** Mahmoud Hamshari, PLO representative in Paris, is killed by an electronically triggered bomb attached to his phone by Israeli agents.
1973 1 Mar	**Egypt:** The Saudi Arabian embassy in Khartoum is seized by Black September during a party for an American, George C. Moore. The Belgian chargé d'affaires, Guy Eid, the U.S. ambassador, Cleo Noel, and Moore are killed.
8 Mar	**Great Britain:** Car bombs in London outside the Old Bailey and the Army Recruiting Office off Trafalgar Square kill one man and injure some 200 others.
10 Apr	**Lebanon:** Israeli commandos attack the homes of Palestinian guerrillas in Beirut, killing 17.
17 May	**Italy:** Four are killed and over 40 injured in a grenade explosion at the entrance to police headquarters in Milan.
28 June	**France:** Mohammed Boudia, a top Arab terrorist, is killed by a car bomb planted in his car in Paris.

1 July **United States:** Colonel Yosef Alon, Israeli military attaché in Washington, is shot dead outside his home.

20 July **Air Piracy:** A Japan Air Lines 747, en route from Amsterdam to Tokyo, is hijacked by three PFLP and one Japanese Red Army terrorist. A woman hijacker accidentally kills herself with a grenade. The plane lands at Dubai and is then flown to Benghazi, Libya, on 24 July. The plane is evacuated and then blown up.

5 Aug **Greece:** At Athens, Palestinians kill five and wound over 50 in a machine-gun and grenade attack on passengers disembarked from a TWA flight from Tel Aviv.

28 Sep **Austria:** Palestinian guerrillas seize three Soviet Jewish emigrants on a Moscow-Vienna train, releasing them when Austrian chancellor Bruno Kreisky agrees to close facilities for emigrants awaiting transfer to Israel at Schönau Castle.

22 Nov **Argentina:** John A. Swint, general manager of a subsidiary of Ford Motor, Argentina, is killed with two bodyguards in Cordoba by terrorists of the Peronist Armed Forces.

6 Dec **Argentina:** Victor Samuelson, an American manager with Esso, Argentina, is kidnapped in Buenos Aires by the ERP. He is released on 29 April 1974 after payment of a $14.2 million ransom.

18 Dec **Great Britain:** Two IRA car bombs and a parcel bomb injure some 60 people in London.

20 Dec **Spain:** Spanish premier Luis Carrero Blanco is killed when Basque terrorists explode a bomb beneath his car in Madrid.

31 Dec **Great Britain:** Edward Sieff, president of Marks and Spencer, survives assassination attempt at his home in London by Carlos, the Venezuelan terrorist.

1974 3 Feb **Great Britain:** An IRA suitcase bomb hidden in the luggage compartment of a bus traveling through Yorkshire with soldiers and their families kills 11 and wounds 14.

5 Feb **United States:** Patty Hearst, 19-year-old granddaughter of newspaper magnate William Randolph Hearst, is kidnapped in Berkeley, California, by members of the Symbionese Liberation Army, who demand that her father provide millions of dollars

to feed the poor. On 3 April the kidnappers release a tape in which Patty announces she has joined the SLA. She is finally arrested in San Francisco on 18 September 1975, after allegedly taking part in a bank robbery and other operations. Although claiming she had acted under duress, she is sentenced to two years' imprisonment.

11 Apr   **Israel:** Three Arab guerrillas enter the town of Kiryat Shmona and kill 18 people in an apartment block. The terrorists are killed when explosives they are carrying are set off.

15 May   **Israel:** Three Palestinian commandos attack the village of Maalot, killing 25 people, mainly students. Israeli jets attack targets in southern Lebanon in retaliation the following day.

17 May   **Ireland:** Car bombs explode in Dublin and Monaghan, killing 30 and injuring some 200 others.

28 May   **Italy:** Bomb explosion at anti-Fascist rally in Brescia kills seven and injures 93.

13 June   **Israel:** Three women are killed in a Palestinian raid on Shamir, a northern Israeli kibbutz.

17 June   **Italy:** Bomb planted by Italian neo-Fascist group, the Black Order, on Rome–Munich train explodes between Florence and Bologna, killing 12 people.

24 June   **Israel:** Three people are killed in a Palestinian guerrilla attack on the town of Nahariya, near the Lebanese border.

15 July   **Argentina:** Arturo Roig, former interior minister of Argentina, is shot dead in Buenos Aires.

17 July   **Great Britain:** IRA bomb explosion in the armory of the Tower of London kills one tourist and injures 36.

30 Aug   **Japan:** Bomb explosion in front of the Mitsubishi Heavy Industries building in Tokyo kills eight and wounds over 300.

13 Sep   **Netherlands:** Three Japanese Red Army terrorists seize 11 hostages at the French embassy in The Hague. They secure the release of a comrade, Yukata Furuya, from a French prison, and the four are flown to Damascus, Syria.

19 Nov   **Israel:** Four are killed in a guerrilla raid on an apartment building in the northern town of Bein Shean, near the Jordanian border.

1975   26 Feb   **Argentina:** John P. Egan, U.S. honorary consul in Cordoba, is kidnapped by Montoneros guerrillas and murdered when the government refuses to negotiate for his release.

       27 Feb   **West Germany:** Peter Lorenz, chairman of the West Berlin Christian Democratic Union, is kidnapped. He is set free on 4 March when the government releases five Baader-Meinhof terrorists.

       5 Mar   **Israel:** Eight Palestinian guerrillas attack a shorefront hotel in Tel Aviv, killing 11.

       24 Apr   **Sweden:** Six Red Army Faction members occupy the West German embassy in Stockholm and demand the release of 26 Baader-Meinhof terrorists. They blow up the embassy as police prepare to attack, then surrender.

       4 July   **Israel:** Palestinian bomb explodes in Zion Square, Jerusalem, killing 14 and wounding some 80 others.

       4 Aug   **Malaysia:** Five Japanese Red Army guerrillas attack the American and Swedish embassies in Kuala Lumpur. The terrorists and four hostages are flown to Libya.

       5 Sep   **Great Britain:** Two are killed and 63 injured by an IRA bomb at the London Hilton Hotel.

       3 Oct   **Ireland:** Tiede Herrema, a Dutch industrialist, is kidnapped in Limerick in an attempt to secure the release of three IRA prisoners. He is freed on 7 November when police surround the kidnappers' hideout at Monastervin.

       22 Oct   **Austria:** Danis Tunaligil, Turkish ambassador, is shot dead at his embassy in Vienna by three terrorists.

       24 Oct   **France:** Ismail Erez, Turkish ambassador in Paris, and his chauffeur are killed by two gunmen.

       13 Nov   **Israel:** Six are killed and 42 wounded by bomb blast near Zion Square, Jerusalem.

       27 Nov   **Great Britain:** Ross McWhirter, editor of the *Guinness Book of Records,* is shot dead by the IRA at his north London home after he establishes a reward fund for information leading to the arrest of terrorists.

       2 Dec   **Netherlands:** South Moluccan terrorists demanding independence from Indonesia for their homeland seize a train near Beilin in the Netherlands, killing

two people and holding 50 hostages. The six terrorists surrender on 14 December.

4 Dec **Netherlands:** South Moluccans seize the Indonesian consulate in Amsterdam. One hostage is killed, but terrorists surrender on 19 December.

12 Dec **Great Britain:** Four IRA gunmen surrender after six-day siege in a flat in Balcombe Street in central London.

21 Dec **Austria:** The headquarters of OPEC in Vienna is seized by Palestinian and Baader-Meinhof terrorists led by "Carlos," the Venezuelan terrorist chief.

23 Dec **Greece:** Richard S. Welch, CIA station chief, is murdered by terrorists in Athens.

29 Dec **United States:** Eleven people are killed and 70 injured when a bomb explodes in a baggage-claim area at LaGuardia Airport, New York.

1976 4 Jan **Northern Ireland:** Five Catholics are murdered in Belfast.

5 Jan **Northern Ireland:** Ten Protestant workmen are shot dead by the IRA in Belfast.

16 June **Lebanon:** Francis E. Meloy, U.S. ambassador to Lebanon, and Robert O. Waring, his economic advisor, are kidnapped and killed, along with their Lebanese driver, in Beirut.

27 June **Air Piracy:** Palestinian and Baader-Meinhof terrorists hijack an Air France A300B airbus en route from Tel Aviv to Paris, shortly after it leaves Athens. The terrorists force the plane to fly to Entebbe in Uganda, where they demand the release of 53 prisoners from jails in Israel, Kenya, West Germany, Switzerland and France. On 3 July some 200 Israeli commandos, transported in three C130 Hercules aircraft, make a surprise assault on Entebbe and rescue the hostages. All seven hijackers and 20 Ugandan troops are killed, together with three hostages and an Israeli officer, Lieutenant Colonel Netanyahu. An Israeli woman, Mrs. Dora Bloch, who had been moved to a Kampala hospital, is believed to have been murdered.

21 July **Ireland:** Christopher Ewart-Biggs, British ambassador in Ireland, and his secretary, Judith Cooke, are killed by an IRA land mine as he is driving near his home in Dublin.

11 Aug	**Turkey:** Two Palestinian terrorists kill four and wound over 30 passengers waiting to board an El Al plane at Yesilkoy airport, Istanbul.
20 Aug	**Argentina:** Forty-seven people are killed by right-wing death squads in two suburbs of Buenos Aires.
28 Oct	**Northern Ireland:** Maire Drumm, former vice president of the Provisional Sinn Fein, is shot dead in a Belfast hospital, while recuperating from cataract treatment, by members of the Ulster Volunteer Force, a Protestant paramilitary group.
17 Nov	**Jordan:** Four Palestinians attack the Intercontinental Hotel in Amman, but are overrun by Jordanian troops. Three terrorists and five others are killed.
1977 7 Apr	**West Germany:** Siegfried Buback, chief federal prosecutor, together with his driver and bodyguard, are shot dead in their car in Karlsruhe by Baader-Meinhof terrorists.
10 Apr	**Great Britain:** Palestinian terrorists assassinate the former Yemeni prime minister, Abdullah al-Hejiri, his wife and the minister at the Yemeni embassy in London.
23 May	**Netherlands:** South Moluccans seize a train at Assen and a school at Bovinsmilde. The siege at the school ends on 27 May. Two hostages and six terrorists are killed in an army attempt to rescue train hostages on 11 June.
30 July	**West Germany:** Jurgen Ponto, chairman of the Dresdner Bank, is shot and killed at his home near Frankfurt.
5 Sep	**West Germany:** Hans-Martin Schleyer, president of the Federation of German Employers Associations, is kidnapped in Cologne by terrorists, who kill his driver and three of his police guards. The kidnappers demand the release of 11 left-wing terrorists. Schleyer's body is found in the trunk of a car in Mulhouse, France, on 19 October.
28 Sep	**Air Piracy:** A Japan Air Lines DC-8 en route from Paris to Tokyo is hijacked by five Japanese Red Army terrorists off Bombay and forced to land at Dacca in Bangladesh. The aircraft is eventually flown to Algiers, after stops at Kuwait and Damascus. The passengers are then set free in return for the release of six prisoners in Japan and a ransom of $6 million.

	11 Oct	**Yemen:** Colonel Ibrahim al-Hamdi, president of Yemen, and his brother, Abdullah Mohammed al-Hamdi, are assassinated in San'a.
	13 Oct	**Air Piracy:** A Lufthansa Boeing 737 en route from Majorca to Frankfurt is hijacked by four Arab terrorists, who take the aircraft to Rome, Cyprus, Bahrain, Dubai and Aden, where they shoot dead the pilot, Jürgen Schumann. Finally the plane lands at Mogadishu in Somalia, where it is stormed by German commandos on 17 October. Three terrorists are killed and 86 passengers are released.
	7 Dec	**Egypt:** David Holden, Middle East expert of *The Sunday Times* (London), is murdered in Cairo.
1978	4 Jan	**Great Britain:** Said Hammami, representative of the PLO in London, is shot dead in his office by Palestinians opposed to Yasir Arafat's policy of negotiating with Israel.
	14 Feb	**Israel:** Two are killed and 35 wounded when a bomb explodes on a crowded bus in Jerusalem.
	17 Feb	**Northern Ireland:** Twelve are killed and 30 injured in an IRA firebomb explosion at the Le Mon House restaurant in Belfast.
	18 Feb	**Cyprus:** Two Palestinian gunmen murder Yusuf el Sebai, editor of Cairo's daily newspaper, *Al Ahram*, and seize 30 hostages at the Hilton Hotel in Nicosia. Terrorists fly out in a Cyprus Airways plane but are refused landing rights elsewhere and return to Larnaca airport. Egyptian troops attempt to seize terrorists on 19 February, but 15 of the 74 commandos die in a gun battle with the Cyprus National Guard and PLO.
	10 Mar	**Italy:** Judge Rosario Berardi is murdered by Red Brigades in Rome.
	11 Mar	**Israel:** Palestinian terrorists kill 35 people on a bus traveling between Haifa and Tel Aviv.
	13 Mar	**Netherlands:** South Moluccans seize a government building in Assen, killing one man and taking 71 hostages. Marines storm the building on 14 March and capture the terrorists; five hostages are wounded.
	16 Mar	**Italy:** Aldo Moro, former Italian premier, is kidnapped in Rome by the Red Brigades, who kill five bodyguards. His body is found in a stolen car in the center of Rome on 10 May.

20 May **France:** Three Arabs open fire on passengers waiting to board an El Al flight at Orly Airport. One policeman and the three terrorists are killed.

15 June **Kuwait:** Ali Yasin, representative of the PLO, is murdered by Black June terrorists.

9 July **Great Britain:** General al-Naif, former premier of Iraq, is assassinated outside the Intercontinental Hotel in London.

31 July **France:** Gunmen invade the Iraqi embassy in Paris, taking hostages. They surrender, but an attempted ambush by the Iraqi secret service as they leave the building results in the deaths of a French police inspector and an Iraqi diplomat.

3 Aug **France:** Ezzedine Kalak, PLO representative, and his deputy, Hamad Adnan, are killed by Black June terrorists at the Arab League office in Paris.

6 Aug **Pakistan:** Gunmen attack the PLO office in Islamabad, killing three PLO members and a police guard.

6 Aug **Zimbabwe:** An explosion in a crowded store in Harare kills 11 and injures 76.

13 Aug **Lebanon:** Bombing of headquarters of PLO in Beirut kills 150.

19 Aug **Iran:** Some 430 people are killed by Muslim arsonists in a crowded theater in Abadan.

20 Aug **Great Britain:** An attack on an El Al aircrew bus outside the Europa Hotel in London leaves one stewardess dead and nine injured.

22 Aug **Nicaragua:** Twenty-five Sandinista guerrillas seize the National Palace in Managua, killing six people and holding a thousand hostage. The guerrillas fly to Panama on 24 August with 59 released prisoners and a $500,000 ransom.

11 Sep **Great Britain:** Georgi Markov, a Bulgarian exile working for the BBC, is murdered by an injection of a powerful poison in a London street.

1979 29 Jan **Italy:** Emilio Alessandri, public prosecutor, is assassinated by Red Brigades in Milan.

14 Feb **Afghanistan:** Adolph Dubs, U.S. ambassador, is kidnapped by Muslim extremists and dies, together with the four kidnappers, when Afghan police storm the room in the Kabul Hotel where he is held.

22 Mar **Netherlands:** Sir Richard Sykes, British ambassador, is shot at the door of his residence in The Hague by the Provisional IRA.

30 Mar	**Great Britain:** Airey Neave, Conservative MP for Abingdon and opposition spokesman on Northern Ireland, is killed by an IRA bomb in his car as he leaves the House of Commons garage in London.
16 June	**Syria:** Sixty-three cadets are killed and 23 wounded by the Muslim Brotherhood at a military academy in Aleppo.
25 June	**Belgium:** An attempt on the life of General Alexander Haig, Supreme Commander Allied Forces in Europe, fails when a bomb in a culvert near Mons explodes just after his car has passed.
13 July	**Turkey:** Palestinians seize the Egyptian embassy in Ankara. Two Turkish policemen and an Egyptian hostage die.
27 Aug	**Northern Ireland:** Eighteen British soldiers are killed by a remote-controlled bomb at Warrenpoint, County Down.
27 Aug	**Ireland:** Lord Mountbatten, together with his grandson, Nicholas Knatchbull, Lady Brabourne and a local boy, Paul Maxwell, are killed when an IRA bomb blows up their fishing boat off the coast of County Sligo.
21 Sep	**Italy:** Carlo Ghiglieno, a Fiat executive, is murdered by Red Brigades in Turin.
4 Nov	**Iran:** United States embassy in Tehran is seized by Iranian militants and 90 hostages are taken, including 60 Americans.
20 Nov	**Saudi Arabia:** Some 300 Muslim extremists invade the Grand Mosque in Mecca. Fighting to evict them continues until 4 December and leaves 161 dead.
14 Dec	**Turkey:** Three American civilians employed by the Boeing Aircraft Company and a U.S. Army sergeant are shot while waiting for a bus in Florya, near Istanbul, by the Marxist-Leninist Armed Propaganda Squad.
15 Dec	**Cyprus:** Ibrahim Ali Aziz, PLO head of guerrilla operations in the occupied West Bank, and Ali Salem Ahmed, second secretary of the PLO diplomatic mission, are shot dead in Nicosia.
1980 31 Jan	**Guatemala:** Thirty-five people are killed when police storm the Spanish embassy in Guatemala City, where guerrillas held the ambassador and other diplomats hostage.
29 Feb	**Colombia:** Terrorists seize the embassy of the Dominican Republic in Bogotá and take 60 hostages;

the terrorists fly to Cuba with 12 hostages on 27 April.

24 Mar **El Salvador:** Oscar Romero, Roman Catholic archbishop of San Salvador, is shot dead by four gunmen in a hospital chapel. During a gun battle at his funeral on 30 March, 39 people are killed.

7 Apr **Israel:** Five Palestinians are killed by Israeli commandos after taking hostages in a kibbutz near the Lebanese border; two Israeli civilians die.

30 Apr **Great Britain:** Gunmen demanding the release of political prisoners in Iran seize the Iranian embassy in London and kill two hostages. The Special Armed Services storm the embassy on 5 May; five terrorists are killed and one is arrested.

19 July **Turkey:** Nihat Erin, former prime minister, is assassinated in Istanbul.

21 July **France:** Salah al-Din Bitar, former prime minister of Syria, is assassinated in Paris.

2 Aug **Italy:** Eighty-four are killed and 200 injured in a bomb explosion at Bologna's central railway station.

26 Sep **West Germany:** Twelve are killed and 300 wounded in a bomb explosion at the Munich beer festival.

3 Oct **France:** Bomb explodes outside a synagogue in Paris, killing four.

3 Oct **Spain:** Basque terrorists shoot dead three policemen, and three civil guards the following day.

31 Dec **Kenya:** Sixteen die in a bomb explosion at the Norfolk Hotel, Nairobi, owned by a family of Jewish origin.

1981 21 Jan **Northern Ireland:** Sir Norman Strange, former Stormont Speaker, and his son are shot dead by the IRA at their home in South Armagh.

2 Mar **Air Piracy:** A Pakistan International Airlines Boeing 720 on an internal flight from Karachi to Peshawar is hijacked by three Al-Zulfikar terrorists and forced to land at Kabul in Afghanistan. A Pakistani diplomat, Tariq Rahim, is shot dead. The aircraft is flown to Damascus, where the hostages are set free on 14 March in return for the release of 55 prisoners in Pakistan.

28 Mar **Air Piracy:** An internal Indonesian flight is hijacked by five armed men and forced to fly to Bangkok, Thailand. On 30 March the aircraft is stormed by Indonesian and Thai commandos, who kill four of the hijackers and release the hostages.

	13 May	**Italy:** Pope John Paul II is shot and badly wounded by a Turkish terrorist, Mehmet Ali Agca.
	19 May	**Northern Ireland:** Five soldiers die in a land-mine explosion in South Armagh.
	19 Oct	**Great Britain:** An IRA nail-bomb attack on a bus carrying Irish Guards in London kills two passers-by and wounds 35 people.
	28 Nov	**Syria:** A car bomb planted by the Muslim Brotherhood kills 64 people in Damascus.
	17 Dec	**Italy:** Brigadier General James Dozier, NATO deputy chief of staff, is kidnapped by Red Brigade terrorists but freed by an Italian antiterrorist squad on 28 January 1982.
1982	30 Mar	**France:** Six are killed and 15 wounded by a bomb explosion on a Paris–Toulouse train.
	3 June	**Great Britain:** Shlomo Argov, Israeli ambassador, is shot and critically wounded in London.
	20 July	**Great Britain:** Eleven soldiers are killed and over 50 people injured by IRA bombs in Hyde Park and beneath the bandstand in Regent's Park.
	7 Aug	**Turkey:** Eleven are killed in an attack by Armenian terrorists at Ankara airport.
	9 Aug	**Paris:** Six die and 22 are injured in a gun attack on a Jewish restaurant.
	6 Dec	**Northern Ireland:** Seventeen people, including 11 soldiers, are killed in an explosion at a public house in Ballykelly.
1983	18 Apr	**Lebanon:** Bomb attack on the American embassy in Beirut leaves some 60 dead and 120 injured.
	20 May	**South Africa:** Car bomb explosion in central Pretoria kills 18.
	15 July	**France:** Bomb planted by Armenian terrorists at Orly Airport, Paris, kills seven and injures 50.
	27 July	**Portugal:** Armenian terrorists seize the Turkish embassy in Lisbon. When commandos storm the embassy, five Armenians and the wife of the Turkish chargé d'affaires are killed.
	9 Oct	**Burma:** Bomb explosion in Rangoon kills 21 people, including four South Korean ministers on an official visit.
	23 Oct	**Lebanon:** Suicide truck-bomb attacks on the U.S. marine headquarters and French paratroop barracks in Beirut kill 241 Americans and 58 French.

	4 Nov	**Lebanon:** Sixty are killed in a suicide bombing of Israeli military headquarters in Tyre.
	17 Dec	**Great Britain:** Six are killed and 90 injured by an IRA car bomb outside the Harrods store in London.
1984	15 Feb	**Italy:** Leamon Hunt, director-general of the Sinai multinational peacekeeping force, is assassinated by Red Brigade terrorists in Rome.
	17 Apr	**Great Britain:** Policewoman Yvonne Fletcher is killed by shots fired from the Libyan People's Bureau in London at anti-Qadaffi demonstrators; Libyan diplomats are expelled after a 10-day siege.
	31 July	**Air Piracy:** An Air France Boeing 737 en route from Frankfurt to Paris is hijacked by three armed men and forced to fly to Tehran. The hijackers demand the release of five terrorists jailed in France for the attempted murder of Dr. Chapour Bakhtiar in 1980. The French government refuses to comply with the demands of the hijackers, who surrender to the Iranians on 2 August.
	2 Aug	**India:** A bomb explosion at Madras airport kills 29 people.
	23 Aug	**Iran:** A bomb planted near Tehran's central railway station kills at least 17 and injures 300.
	20 Sep	**Lebanon:** A truck-bomb attack on the American embassy in Beirut kills nine people.
	12 Oct	**Great Britain:** An IRA bomb planted in the Grand Hotel, Brighton, where Prime Minister Margaret Thatcher and members of her cabinet are staying for the Conservative Party Conference, kills five people and injures 32.
	3 Dec	**Air Piracy:** A Kuwaiti airliner bound for Karachi is hijacked by Shiite terrorists demanding the release of 13 Shiite Muslims imprisoned in Kuwait. The aircraft is taken to Tehran, where two officials of the American Agency for Development are shot dead. Iranian security forces disguised as cleaners enter the aircraft on 9 December, releasing the remaining passengers and capturing the hijackers.
	23 Dec	**Italy:** A bomb explosion on a train near Florence kills 15 passengers.
1985	28 Feb	**Northern Ireland** Eight policemen and one civilian are killed in an IRA mortar attack on Newry police station.

12 Apr   **Spain:** Eighteen die and 82 are injured in a bomb explosion in Madrid; responsibility is claimed by Shia Muslim extremists.

14 June   **Air Piracy:** An American Trans World Airlines jet en route from Athens to Rome is hijacked by Lebanese Shiite terrorists attempting to secure the release of Shiite prisoners in Israel. The aircraft is diverted to Beirut and twice flown to Algiers. In Beirut an American passenger, U.S. Navy diver Robert D. Stethem, is killed and a further 39 Americans are transferred to the control of the Shiite militia, Amal. On 24 June Israel releases a number of Shiite prisoners, and on 30 June the American passengers are set free. The remaining Shiite prisoners are freed by Israel in July, August and September.

19 June   **West Germany:** Three are killed and 42 injured in a bomb attack at Frankfurt airport.

24 July   **Burma:** Some 70 people are killed when a mine explodes under a passenger train traveling from Rangoon to Mandalay.

25 Sep   **Cyprus:** One British and two Arab gunmen kill three Israelis on board a yacht in Larnaca harbor after demanding the release of Palestinians held in Israel.

30 Sep   **Lebanon:** Four Russian diplomats are kidnapped in West Beirut; one of them is later found murdered, while the others are released.

7 Oct   **Italy:** Palestinians hijack an Italian cruise liner, *Achille Lauro*, in the Mediterranean and murder an invalid American passenger. The hijackers surrender in Egypt on 9 October. American jets intercept the aircraft taking the hijackers to Tunis on 10 October and force it to land in Sicily, where the Italian authorities arrest them.

6 Nov   **Colombia:** M-19 Movement guerrillas seize the Palace of Justice in Bogotá and hold senior judges hostage. When troops storm the building the next day, all the guerrillas, 12 judges and 50 others die.

23 Nov   **Air Piracy:** An Egypt Air plane, en route from Athens to Cairo, is hijacked by five members of a PLO splinter group, Egypt's Revolution, and forced to land at Luqa airport, Malta. An American woman passenger is murdered by the terrorists, and some 60 people die when Egyptian commandos storm the aircraft on 24 November.

	27 Dec	**Italy:** An Arab terrorist attack at Rome airport kills 14 people.
	27 Dec	**Austria:** An Arab terrorist attack at Vienna airport kills three.
1986	28 Feb	**Sweden:** Prime Minister Olof Palme is shot dead by an unknown assassin in a Stockholm street.
	5 Apr	**West Germany:** An explosion in a West Berlin discotheque kills a U.S. serviceman and a Turkish woman, and injures 200 people.
	25 Apr	**Spain:** A bomb explosion in Madrid kills five members of the Civil Guard.
	31 May	**Sri Lanka:** At the end of a month of violence, a bomb planted by Tamil extremists on a Colombo-bound train kills eight passengers.
	14 July	**Spain:** Eleven Civil Guards are killed and more than 50 injured by a car bomb detonated by Basque separatists in Madrid.
	5 Sep	**Air Piracy:** Four Arab terrorists seize an American Pan Am Boeing 747 at Karachi airport in Pakistan and demand to be flown to Cyprus, intending to secure the release of three men imprisoned for the murder of Israelis at Larnaca harbor in September 1985. The crew escapes, but some 20 people are killed when the hijackers open fire, believing that a commando assault on the plane is in progress.
	6 Sep	**Turkey:** Twenty-one worshipers at a synagogue in Istanbul are killed by machine-gun and hand grenade by two terrorists, who themselves die in the explosions.
	7 Sep	**Chile:** An unsuccessful attempt on the life of President Pinochet leaves five bodyguards dead.
	14 Sep	**South Korea:** A bomb blast at Seoul's Kimpo Airport kills five and wounds 26 people.
	15 Oct	**Israel:** One person is killed and 70 are injured in a grenade attack on army recruits and their relatives taking part in a ceremony at the Wailing Wall in Jerusalem.
	25 Oct	**Spain:** Provincial military governor General Rafael Garrido Gil, his wife and son are killed by a bomb placed in their car by a motorcyclist in San Sebastian.
	17 Nov	**France:** Georges Besse, chairman of the state-owned Renault car company, is shot dead by Action Directe terrorists in Paris.

1987   20 Mar   **Ialy:** Terrorists shoot dead a senior air force general, Licio Giorgieri, in Rome.

23 Mar   **West Germany:** An IRA bomb at the U.K. military base at Rheindalen injures 31.

17 Apr   **Sri Lanka:** Tamil separatists ambush three buses and two trucks near Trincomalee, killing 120.

21 Apr   **Sri Lanka:** A bomb explosion in Colombo kills over 100.

25 Apr   **Northern Ireland:** Lord Justice Maurice Gibson and his wife are killed by a car bomb as they cross from Eire into Northern Ireland at Killen.

1 June   **Lebanon:** Premier Rashid Karami is killed by a bomb planted in his helicopter.

19 June   **Spain:** A bomb planted by Basque separatists in the underground parking garage of a department store in Barcelona kills 19.

6 July   **India:** Sikh militants kill 40 Hindu bus passengers in the Punjab. A further 32 are killed in the neighboring state of Haryana on 7 July.

14 July   **Pakistan:** Two bomb explosions in Karachi, blamed on Afghan agents, kill 70.

24 July   **Air Piracy:** Air Afrique DC-10, on flight from Brazzaville to Bangui, hijacked to Geneva by a Lebanese Shiite, Hussain Ali Hariri, demanding release of a Lebanese held in West Germany. Swiss security forces storm the aircraft and capture the hijacker. One French passenger killed.

30 July   **South Africa:** Bomb explosion near military barracks in Johannesburg injures 68 people.

18 Aug   **Sri Lanka:** Grenade attack in the parliament fails to assassinate the president, but kills one member of parliament and injures 15.

8 Nov   **Northern Ireland:** Bomb explosion at Remembrance Day service at Enniskillen kills 11 and injures 31.

9 Nov   **Sri Lanka:** Tamil separatist bombing in Colombo kills 32, injures over 100.

29 Nov   **Air Piracy:** A bomb on a Korean plane kills all 116 passengers.

11 Dec   **Spain:** Basque separatist bomb in Saragossa kills 12.

1988   14 Feb   **Cyprus:** Three PLO officials killed in a car bomb explosion in Limassol.

19 Feb   **Namibia:** Bomb attack kills 14.

7 Mar   **Israel:** Three Palestinians, who hijacked a bus in the Negev, are killed by Israeli troops; three bus passengers die.

8 Mar **Air Piracy:** Five of the 11 hijackers of an Aeroflot plane are killed when Soviet security forces storm the plane at Leningrad.

16 Mar **Northern Ireland:** Three killed and 50 injured in a grenade and pistol attack by a loyalist gunman at the funeral of three IRA men killed by the Special Armed Services in Gibraltar on 6 March.

5 Apr **Air Piracy:** Kuwaiti airliner, en route from Bangkok to Kuwait, hijacked to Iran by gunmen demanding the release of 17 terrorists imprisoned in Kuwait. The plane was ordered to Cyprus, where two passengers were killed, then on to Algiers, where the remaining hostages were released on 20 April in return for safe passage for the hijackers.

14 Apr **Italy:** Five killed by bomb at the U.S. Navy Club in Naples.

16 Apr **Italy:** Senator Robert Ruffilli murdered by Red Brigade terrorists.

16 Apr **Tunisia:** Khalid Wazir (Abu Jihad), second-in-command of the PLO, assassinated in Tunis.

23 Apr **Lebanon:** Car bomb in Tripoli kills 69 and injures over 100.

1 May **Netherlands:** Three off-duty British soldiers die in two IRA attacks.

1 May **Sri Lanka:** More than 26 bus passengers killed by a land mine.

15 June **Northern Ireland:** Six soldiers killed when their van is blown up by the IRA at Lisburn.

28 June **Greece:** U.S. naval attaché, Captain William E. Nordeen, killed by anti-NATO terrorists in Athens.

11 July **Greece:** Terrorist attack on cruise ship *City of Poros* kills 11.

1 Aug **Great Britain:** One soldier killed and nine injured by an IRA bomb at army barracks in North London.

17 Aug **Pakistan:** President Zia killed by a bomb planted on his aircraft, together with more than 30 others, including the U.S. ambassador, Arnold L. Raphel.

20 Aug **Northern Ireland:** Eight British soldiers killed when their bus is blown up by the IRA near Omagh.

30 Oct **Israel:** Gasoline bomb attack by Palestinians in Jericho kills 4.

21 Dec **Air Piracy:** Pan Am Boeing 747, flying from London to New York, is blown up over Scotland, killing 259 passengers and crew, and 11 residents of Lockerbie.

1989 17 Mar **Lebanon:** Car bomb in Beirut kills 12.

	13 Apr	**Sri Lanka:** 45 killed in Tamil bombing in Trincomalee.
	7 Sep	**West Germany:** Heidi Hazell, German wife of a British soldier, shot by the IRA in Dortmund.
	19 Sep	**Air Piracy:** DC-10 airliner of the French Union de Transport Aerien crashes in Niger following a bomb explosion on board, killing 171.
	22 Sep	**Great Britain:** IRA bomb attack on Royal Marines' barracks at Deal in Kent kills 11 bandsmen.
	22 Nov	**Lebanon:** New president of Lebanon, Rene Mouawad, killed by a car bomb.
	30 Nov	**West Germany:** Red Army Faction car bomb kills Alfred Herrhausen, chief executive of the Deutsche Bank, at Bad Homburg near Frankfurt.
	6 Dec	**Colombia:** Bomb planted at the security and intelligence agency by drug traffickers kills 50.
1990	2 Jan	**Northern Ireland:** Loyalist killed by car bomb in East Belfast.
	20 Jan	**Northern Ireland:** IRA bomb kills boy during "Bloody Sunday" anniversary march.
	4 Feb	**Israel:** Nine dead in attack on tourist bus near Ismalia. Many wounded.
	20 Feb	**Great Britain:** Bomb explodes in army vehicle in Leicester, injuring 3.
	28 Mar	**Peru:** Maoist guerrillas use car bombs and assassination to disrupt presidential and congressional election.
	3 Apr	**India:** Bomb planted by Sikh separatists kills 32 and injures 50 in Punjab.
	4 Apr	**Northern Ireland:** Huge IRA bomb near Downpatrick kills 4 UDR soldiers.
	11 Apr	**Great Britain:** Teeside Customs seizes parts of suspected "supergun" destined for Iraq. Trucks carrying suspected parts later seized in Greece and Turkey.
	June	**Great Britain:** IRA bomb damages home of Lord McAlpine, ex-treasurer of the Conservative Party. Later the same month, IRA bombs Carlton Club in London's West End.
	30 July	**Great Britain:** Conservative MP Ian Gow assassinated by IRA car bombs at his Sussex home.
	Aug	**Great Britain:** Attempt by IRA to murder Lord Armstrong (former head of the Civil Service) and, later, Lieutenant-General Sir Anthony Farrar-Hockley.

	Sep	**Great Britain:** Sir Peter Terry, former governor of Gibraltar, shot and wounded by IRA.
1991	7 Feb	**Great Britain:** IRA mortar bomb attack on British cabinet at 10 Downing Street.
	17 Feb	**Colombia:** Bomb at Medellin kills 22 and injures 140.
	18 Feb	**Great Britain:** IRA bombs Paddington and Victoria railroad stations, London. All London rail terminals temporarily closed.
	2 Mar	**Sri Lanka:** Ranjan Wijeratne, deputy minister of defense, killed by car bomb.
	21 May	**India:** Leader of the Congress (I) Party, Rajiv Gandhi, is assassinated near Madras in a bomb attack during an election rally.
	15 June	**India:** Sikh terrorists in Punjab kill 74 in attack on two passenger trains.
	8 Aug	**France:** Former Iranian prime minister Shahpour Bakhtiar and his secretary assassinated in Paris by Iranian agents.
	2 Nov	**Northern Ireland:** IRA bombs Musgrave Park Hospital, Belfast; two British soldiers killed.
	25 Dec	**Turkey:** Clothing store in Istanbul firebombed by Kurdish terrorists, killing 11.
1992	5 Feb	**Northern Ireland:** Five Catholics killed in Belfast betting shop. British government begins review of Protestant Ulster Defence Association (UDA) activities. UDA proscribed in August.
	16 Feb	**Lebanon:** Sheikh Abbas Mussawi (leader of pro-Iranian Hezbollah), his wife, son and bodyguards assassinated in Israeli raid.
	17 Mar	**Argentina:** Israeli embassy in Buenos Aires bombed; 29 people killed and 252 wounded. The Iranian-backed Islamic Jihad claims responsibility.
	10 Apr	**Great Britain:** IRA bombs Baltic Exchange building in City of London; three dead, 80 injured.
	23 May	**Italy:** Assassination of senior Italian judge in continuing Mafia campaign.
	29 June	**Algeria:** President Mohamed Boudiaf of Algeria assassinated; presumed to be the work of Muslim fundamentalists.
	17 July	**Peru:** "Shining Path" car bomb kills 18 in Lima.
	21 Aug	**Germany:** Neo-Nazis launch five night attacks on hostels of asylum-seekers in Rostock and elsewhere.
	28 Aug	**Algeria:** Bomb kills nine and injures 128 at Algiers airport.

Oct   **Sri Lanka:** Death toll of 164 after Tamil rebels massacre four mainly Muslim villages in the north-central district of Polonnaruwa. Worst massacre since 140 Muslims killed at Katankudy in August 1990.

Nov   **Germany:** Continuing neo-Nazi violence. Three Turks burned to death in Mölln.

14 Nov   **Northern Ireland:** IRA "Bookmaker's Shop Massacre" in North Belfast. Three killed, 12 injured. IRA bombing also devastates center of Coleraine.

1993   30 Jan   **Colombia:** Massive car bomb kills 11, injures scores more. Believed to be the work of drug baron Pablo Escobar.

26 Feb   **United States:** Seven dead, 1,000 injured (some seriously) in car bomb explosion in World Trade Center, New York.

26 Feb   **Great Britain:** IRA bombs gas works in Warrington.

12 Mar   **India:** Three hundred dead, over 1,300 injured by coordinated series of bombings in heart of Bombay.

16 Mar   **India:** Eighty dead in bombings in congested Bow Bazaar area of Calcutta.

20 Mar   **Great Britain:** IRA strikes again at Warrington.

10 Apr   **South Africa:** Leading ANC figure Chris Hani assassinated by right-wing extremist.

24 Apr   **Great Britain:** City of London bombed by IRA for second time (in Bishopsgate), leaving one dead, 36 injured.

1 May   **Sri Lanka:** President Premadasa assassinated by Tamil Tiger suicide bomber.

27 May   **Italy:** Uffizi gallery in Florence devastated by bomb.

29 May   **Germany:** Five Turks killed at Solingen after arson attacks by neo-Nazis.

2 July   **Turkey:** Forty people die in hotel in Sivas set ablaze by Muslim fundamentalists in protest against Salman Rushdie's *Satanic Verses*. Translator of part of the book staying at the hotel.

July   **Turkey:** Coordinated attacks by PKK guerrillas in 28 cities across Europe and at seaside resort of Antalya.

25 July   **South Africa:** Twelve killed when hooded gunmen attack churchgoers at St. James Church, Kenilworth (a Cape Town suburb). Possibly the work of APLA (Azanian People's Liberation Army).

28 July **Italy:** Terrorist bombs leave five dead in Milan, 20 injured in Rome.

8 Sep **South Africa:** Nineteen dead and 22 injured in shooting at Wadeville industrial zone, east of Johannesburg.

21 Sep **Israel:** Assassination of PLO peace advocate Mohammed Hashem Abu Shaaban.

22 Sep **South Africa:** "Day of terror" as 31 die on day parliament debates formation of Transitional Council.

23 Oct **Northern Ireland:** IRA bomb kills 10, injures 56, in attack on UDA headquarters in Shankhill Road, West Belfast.

30 Oct **Northern Ireland:** Seven killed as loyalist gunmen attack Rising Sun pub, Greysteel.

30 Dec **South Africa:** Four die as black gunmen attack Heidelberg restaurant in Observatory, white Cape Town suburb.

1994 6 Apr **Rwanda:** Assassination of presidents of Rwanda and Burundi in missile attack on their plane.

6 Apr **Israel:** Suicide attack on school bus by Hamas organization in Afula (in revenge for Hebron massacre). Seven dead, 50 injured.

13 Apr **Israel:** Second revenge attack by Hamas on commuter bus at Hadera, central Israel. Six dead, 25 wounded.

24 Apr **South Africa:** Nine dead, 90 injured in car bomb near ANC headquarters in central Johannesburg.

27 Apr **South Africa:** Widespread bombings by right-wing extremists as first multiracial elections begin.

18 July **Argentina:** Bombing of a Jewish cultural center in Buenos Aires. 100 dead.

1995 19 Apr **United States:** Car bomb blows up Oklahoma City federal building. 168 dead.

4 Nov **Israel:** Prime Minister Yitzhak Rabin assassinated by Jewish extremist at peace rally.

1996 1 Feb **Sri Lanka:** Suidide bombing leaves at least 73 dead.

4 Mar **Israel:** Suicide bombing leaves 59 dead.

25 June **Saudi Arabia:** Truck bomb explodes at U.S. base. 19 dead.

25 July **United States:** Bomb explodes at Summer Olympic Games in Atlanta.

10 Nov **Russia:** Bomb explodes in cemetery. 13 dead.

1997 4 Sep **Israel:** Hamas suicide bombers claim the lives of more than 20 Israeli civilians.

	17 Nov	**Egypt:** Islamic militants kill 62 at Luxor tourist site.
	22 Dec	**Mexico:** Gunmen raid Indian village. 45 dead.
1998	7 Aug	**Kenya:** U.S. embassies in Kenya and Tanzania bombed; Islamic extremist Osama bin Laden believed to have been responsible.
	20 Aug	**Afghanistan:** U.S. cruise missiles hit suspected terrorist bases in Sudan and Afghanistan.
	1 Nov	**Saudi Arabia:** Osama bin Laden reported to have plotted terrorist attacks on U.S. targets in Persian Gulf.
1999	5 Apr	**Netherlands:** Two Libyan suspects tried on charges of planting bomb that blew up Pan Am Flight 103 over Scotland in 1988, killing 270 people.
	12 Oct	**Burundi:** Humanitarian convoy seized by rebels. Two UN workers and seven others dead.
	13 Oct	**Russia:** Gunmen take six UN employees and their interpreter hostage in Georgia.
	27 Oct	**Armenia:** Gunmen attack parliament in session, killing prime minister and six others.
	12 Nov	**Pakistan:** U.S. and UN buildings targeted in rocket attack allegedly coordinated as retaliation for sanctions against Afghanistan for its failure to turn over Osama bin Laden.
	25 Dec	**India:** Muslim terrorists hijack Indian Airlines jet with 189 on board.
	Feb	**Lebanon:** Hezbollah guerrillas and Israeli forces battle as Israelis prepare to withdraw from Lebanon.
2000	12 Aug	**Russia:** Bomb explodes near Moscow's Pushkin Square, killing eight. Some Russian officials blame Chechen separatists for the attack.
	12 Oct	**Yemen:** The U.S. Navy missile destroyer U.S.S. *Cole* is damaged in a terrorist attack while refueling in Aden. Seventeen sailors are killed; 39 are wounded.

CHAPTER 8

THE NUCLEAR AGE

CHRONOLOGY OF THE NUCLEAR ERA

1942	June	Manhattan Project: The U.S. Army Corps of Engineers establishes the Manhattan Engineer District to administer work on the production of an atomic bomb.
	2 Dec	The first nuclear chain reaction takes place at the University of Chicago, a breakthrough on the road to the creation of an atomic bomb.
1945	16 July	The first successful explosion of an experimental atomic device takes place at Alamogordo, New Mexico.
	6 Aug	U.S. Air Force B-29 bomber, *Enola Gay*, drops the first atomic bomb, nicknamed "Little Boy," on the Japanese city of Hiroshima.
	9 Aug	A second atomic bomb, nicknamed "Fat Man," is dropped on Nagasaki.
1946	24 Jan	The United Nations General Assembly passes a resolution to establish an Atomic Energy Commission.
	14 June	At the first meeting of the Atomic Energy Commission the United States delegate, Bernard M. Baruch, puts forward a plan by which the United States would surrender its atomic weapons and reveal the secrets of controlling atomic energy to an international control agency. The Baruch Plan is rejected by the Soviet Union.
	1 July	The United States carries out the first nuclear test in peacetime at Bikini Atoll in the Marshall Islands.
	1 Aug	President Truman signs the Atomic Energy Act, restricting exchange of information with other nations on atomic energy, thus ending cooperation

between the United States and Great Britain in the development of nuclear weapons.

1949   29 Aug   The Soviet Union explodes an atomic bomb, ending the American monopoly of nuclear weapons.

1952   11 Jan   The UN Atomic Energy Commission is abolished and the Disarmament Commission is established in its place.

        3 Oct   Great Britain tests its first atomic bomb.

        1 Nov   The United States explodes the first hydrogen device at Eniwetok lagoon in the Marshall Islands.

1953   12 Aug   The Soviet Union tests its first hydrogen bomb in Siberia.

        8 Dec   Atoms for Peace: President Eisenhower announces a plan at the UN General Assembly for a pool of fissile material to be available for peaceful purposes.

1954   12 Jan   Massive Retaliation: in the aftermath of the Korean War, John Foster Dulles, U.S. secretary of state, announces that "local defenses must be reinforced by the further deterrent of massive retaliatory power" and that "the way to deter aggression is for free communities to be willing and able to respond vigorously at places and with weapons of our own choosing." In other words, aggression by a proxy, such as North Korea, might be met by a nuclear attack on the Soviet Union.

        30 Sep   The USS *Nautilus*, the first American atomic-powered submarine, is commissioned.

1955   21 July   At the Geneva summit, President Eisenhower puts forward his "open skies" proposal for mutual aerial photography of each other's territory by the Soviet Union and the United States as a step toward disarmament.

1957   29 July   The UN International Atomic Energy Agency is established to promote the safe use of atomic energy for peaceful purposes.

        15 Aug   The first British hydrogen bomb is exploded near Christmas Island.

        26 Aug   The Soviet Union announces the successful launch of an intercontinental ballistic missile.

        2 Oct   Adam Rapacki, foreign minister of Poland, proposes in a speech to the UN General Assembly the creation of a nuclear-free zone in central Europe. The plan is rejected by NATO on the grounds that

nuclear weapons are essential to offset Soviet superiority in conventional forces.

1958   17 Feb   The first meeting of Great Britain's Campaign for Nuclear Disarmament is held in London.

1959   7 Sep   The Ten-Power Committee on Disarmament, comprising representatives from Great Britain, Canada, France, Italy, the United States, Bulgaria, Czechoslovakia, Poland, Romania and the Soviet Union, is established.

1 Dec   The treaty for the peaceful use of Antarctica opens for signature in Washington.

1960   13 Feb   France explodes its first atomic device in the Sahara.

20 July   A Polaris missile from the USS *George Washington* is successfully fired underwater for the first time.

15 Nov   The first Polaris nuclear submarine, USS *George Washington*, becomes operational.

16–18 Dec   The United States offers five submarines with 80 Polaris missiles to create a NATO Multilateral Nuclear Force at the NATO ministerial meeting in Paris.

1962   14 Mar   The first meeting in Geneva of the Eighteen Nation Disarmament Committee, the former Ten-Power Committee with the addition of Brazil, Burma, Egypt, Ethiopia, India, Mexico, Nigeria and Sweden, is held.

16 June   U.S secretary of defense Robert McNamara announces in a speech at the University of Michigan, Ann Arbor, a new strategy of "flexible response" to replace that of "massive retaliation."

22–28 Oct   Cuban Missile Crisis: President Kennedy announces on 22 October that aerial reconnaissance has established that offensive missile sites are being constructed by the Soviet Union in Cuba and that a naval and air "quarantine" is being imposed until the sites are dismantled. On 28 October Mr. Khrushchev agrees to remove the missiles from Cuba in return for an American guarantee not to invade.

18–20 Dec   President Kennedy meets Prime Minister Harold Macmillan at Nassau in the Bahamas and agrees to make U.S. Polaris missiles available to Great Britain for use with British warheads.

1963	5 Apr	A "Hot Line" agreement is reached between the United States and the Soviet Union.
	5 Aug	The Partial Test-Ban Treaty, outlawing nuclear tests in the atmosphere and outer space and under water, is concluded.
1964	16 Oct	The first Chinese atomic explosion takes place at Lop Nor in Sinkiang Province.
1965	18 Feb	Secretary of Defense Robert McNamara announces that the United States would rely on threat of "assured destruction" to deter a Soviet attack.
1966	14 Dec	NATO establishes the Nuclear Defense Affairs Committee (all members except France, Iceland and Luxembourg) and the Nuclear Planning Group (all members except France and Iceland).
1967	27 Jan	A treaty banning nuclear weapons in outer space is opened for signature in London, Moscow and Washington.
	14 Feb	The Treaty of Tlatelolco, prohibiting nuclear weapons in Latin America, is opened for signature in Mexico City.
	17 June	The first Chinese hydrogen bomb test is carried out.
	14 Dec	NATO adopts a strategy of "flexible response," based on maintaining the capability of threatening a balanced and flexible range of responses, conventional and nuclear, to all levels of aggression.
1968	1 July	The Nonproliferation Treaty is opened for signature in London, Moscow and Washington (see p. 473).
	25 Aug	France explodes its first hydrogen bomb.
1969	14 Mar	President Nixon announces the decision to deploy a ballistic missile defense system, "Safeguard," primarily to defend ICBM sites.
	26 Aug	Eight new members join the 18-nation Disarmament Committee, which is renamed the Conference of the Committee on Disarmament. Five additional members join on 1 January 1975.
	17 Nov	Preparatory negotiations on Strategic Arms Limitation Talks (SALT) between the United States and the Soviet Union begin in Helsinki.
1970	16 Apr	Strategic Arms Limitation Talks are opened in Vienna.
	3 Aug	The first successful underwater launch of a Poseidon missile is accomplished from the USS *James Madison*.

1971	11 Feb	The Sea-bed Treaty prohibiting the emplacement of nuclear weapons on the sea-bed is opened for signature in London, Moscow and Washington.
1972	26 May	SALT I antiballistic missile agreement and five-year interim agreement on the limitation of strategic arms is signed by the United States and the Soviet Union (see p. 481).
1973	30 Oct	Mutual and Balanced Force Reduction talks between NATO and the Warsaw Pact begin in Vienna.
1974	10 Jan	U.S. secretary of defense James Schlesinger announces a new doctrine of "limited strategic strike options" in the event of a nuclear war, in which a broad spectrum of deterrence would be available before the resort to large-scale strategic strikes.
	18 May	India explodes its first atomic device at Pokharan in the Rajasthan desert.
	3 July	A Protocol to the U.S.–Soviet SALT ABM agreement, limiting ABM deployment to a single area, is agreed to.
	3 July	A U.S.–Soviet Threshold Test-Ban Treaty is signed, limiting underground nuclear tests.
	24 Nov	The Vladivostok Accord between the United States and the Soviet Union, setting out the framework for future negotiations on controlling the strategic arms race, is reached.
1976	28 May	A U.S.–Soviet Treaty restricting nuclear explosions for peaceful purposes is ratified.
1977	7 July	The United States announces that it has tested an Enhanced Radiation Weapon or "neutron bomb."
1978	7 Apr	President Carter announces the postponement of a decision on the production and deployment of the neutron bomb.
1979	28 Mar	A major nuclear accident in the United States at Three Mile Island, near Harrisburg, Pennsylvania, results in thousands of gallons of radioactive water and a plume of radioactive gas being released.
	18 June	A SALT II agreement is signed by the United States and Soviet Union, restricting numbers of strategic offensive weapons. The United States withholds ratification of the treaty following the Soviet invasion of Afghanistan in December 1979 (see p. 330).
	12 Dec	NATO announces its intention to modernize its long-range theater nuclear systems by the deploy-

ment of 464 ground-launched cruise missiles and 108 Pershing II medium-range ballistic missiles in Europe.

1980   25 July   President Carter signs Presidential Directive 59, emphasizing the possibility of flexible, controlled re-

NUCLEAR ARSENALS: STRATEGIC DELIVERY SYSTEMS OF THE SUPERPOWERS 1960–96

	United States			Soviet Union/Russia		
	ICBM	SLBM	LRB	ICBM	SLBM	LRB
1960	18	32	450	35	na	na
1961	63	96	600	50	na	na
1962	294	144	630	75	na	na
1963	424	224	630	100	100	na
1964	834	416	630	200	120	na
1965	854	496	630	270	120	na
1966	904	592	600	300	125	na
1967	1054	656	540	460	130	155
1968	1054	656	480	800	130	155
1969	1054	656	450	1050	130	150
1970	1054	656	405	1300	160	140
1971	1054	656	360	1510	280	140
1972	1054	656	390	1530	560	140
1973	1054	656	397	1575	628	140
1974	1054	656	397	1618	720	140
1975	1054	656	397	1527	784	135
1976	1054	656	387	1477	845	135
1977	1054	656	373	1350	909	135
1978	1054	656	366	1400	1028	135
1979	1054	656	365	1398	1028	156
1980	1054	656	338	1398	1028	156
1981	1052	576	316	1398	989	150
1982	1052	520	316	1398	989	150
1983	1045	568	272	1398	980	143
1984	1037	592	241	1398	981	143
1985	1030	616	324	1398	966	165
1988	1000	640	396	1382	922	155
1990	1000	592	311	1356	930	162
1991	550	480	287	1006	832	100
1992	550	488	190	950	628	112
1993	550	336	191	898	520	113
1994	580	360	194	818	456	113
1995	575	384	179	771	440	113
1996	575	408	179	755	440	113

Source: Natural Resources Defense Council
na   no statistics available
ICBM   Intercontinental Ballistic Missiles
SLBM   Submarine-Launched Ballistic Missiles
LRB   Long-Range Bombers

taliation against a range of military and political targets in a prolonged nuclear war.

22 Aug   The U.S. Department of Defense announces its intention to build an Advanced Technology, or "stealth," bomber with a greatly reduced radar detectability.

1981   7 June   In Operation Babylon, Israeli F-16 aircraft drop 16 tons of explosives on Iraq's Osirak nuclear plant on the grounds that Iraq is manufacturing offensive nuclear weapons.

1993   5 Oct   China breaks nuclear test moratorium.

1995   5 Sep   France explodes nuclear device in Pacific; wide protests ensue.

1998   11, 13 May   India sets off five nuclear tests despite worldwide disapproval.

29, 30 May   Pakistan stages five nuclear tests in response to India's.

1999   2 April   China launches long-range missile.

11 April   India launches nuclear ballistic missile.

14 April   Pakistan fires new and improved version of nuclear ballistic missile.

ARMS CONTROL: Bilateral Agreements

1963   20 June   U.S.-Soviet memorandum of understanding regarding the establishment of a direct communications link (Hot Line) for use in time of emergency.

1964   20 April   Statements by the United States and the USSR agreeing to the reduction of fissionable materials production.

1966   9 Nov   French-Soviet agreement on the establishment of a direct communications link (Hot Line).

1967   25 Aug   British-Soviet agreement on the establishment of a direct communications link (Hot Line).

1971   30 Sep   U.S.-Soviet Hot Line modernization agreement.

30 Sep   U.S.-Soviet nuclear accidents agreement, including notification of unauthorized detonation of nuclear weapons and advance warning of planned missile launches extending beyond the national territory.

1972   25 May   U.S.-Soviet agreement on the prevention of incidents involving naval vessels on the high seas and the flight of military aircraft over the high seas.

26 May   U.S.-Soviet SALT antiballistic missile agreement, limiting deployment of ABM systems to two areas in each

country, with no more than 100 launchers and 100 interceptor missiles in each deployment area.

26 May   U.S.-Soviet SALT interim agreement on limitation of strategic arms. In September 1977 the United States and the USSR state that although the interim agreement is due to expire on 3 October 1977, they intend to refrain from any actions incompatible with its provisions.

29 May   U.S.-Soviet agreement on the basic principles of relations between the two countries, including doing their utmost to avoid military confrontations and to prevent the outbreak of nuclear war.

21 Dec   U.S.-Soviet memorandum of understanding regarding the establishment of a Standing Consultative Commission to promote objectives and implementation of nuclear accidents agreement of 1971 and SALT agreements of 1972.

1973   22 May   Protocol to U.S.-Soviet agreement on the prevention of incidents on and over the high seas, regarding simulating attacks on or hazarding navigation of nonmilitary vessels.

30 May   Protocol establishing governing procedures and regulations for U.S.-Soviet Standing Consultative Commission.

21 June   U.S.-Soviet agreement on the basic principles of negotiations on the further limitation of strategic offensive arms.

22 June   U.S.-Soviet agreement on the prevention of nuclear war.

1974   3 July   Protocol to the U.S.-Soviet SALT ABM agreement limiting ABM deployment to a single area.

3 July   U.S.-Soviet Threshold Test-Ban Treaty prohibiting underground weapons tests of any devices having a yield exceeding 150 kilotons, and agreeing to limit number of underground nuclear-weapons tests to a minimum.

24 Nov   U.S.-Soviet statement that a new agreement on the limitation of strategic offensive arms will incorporate the relevant provisions of the Interim Agreement of 1972 and cover the period from October 1977 to December 1985.

1975   17 Feb   British-Soviet declaration on the nonproliferation of nuclear weapons, stating common concern that nuclear materials should be carefully protected at all times.

1976   28 May   U.S.-Soviet treaty on peaceful nuclear explosions, prohibiting the carrying out of individual underground explosions for peaceful purposes having a yield exceeding 150 kilotons or group explosions exceeding 1,500 kilotons.

	16 July	French-Soviet exchange of letters on the prevention of the accidental or unauthorized use of nuclear weapons.
1977	22 June	French-Soviet declaration on the nonproliferation of nuclear weapons.
	10 Oct	British-Soviet agreement on the prevention of an accidental outbreak of nuclear war.
1979	18 June	U.S.-Soviet treaty on the limitation of strategic offensive arms (SALT II agreement). The treaty establishes a ceiling of 2,400 on all types of strategic delivery vehicles, to be reduced to 2,250 by the end of 1981. Of these, a limit of 1,320 is to be imposed on the combined total of missiles equipped with multiple independently targetable reentry vehicles (MIRVs) and bombers carrying long-range cruise missiles. Moreover, of these only 1,200 can be MIRVed strategic missiles and there is a further sublimit of 820 on launchers of MIRVed intercontinental ballistic missiles. The U.S. Congress refuses to ratify the agreement following the Soviet invasion of Afghanistan in December 1979.
1984	17 July	U.S.-Soviet agreement to expand and improve the operation of the Hot Line.
1987	8 Dec	U.S.-Soviet treaty on the elimination of intermediate nuclear forces (INF) signed in Washington.
1991	30 July	U.S.-Soviet START agreement (see page 485). Not yet ratified by U.S. Senate.
1993	1 Jan	START II agreement between President Bush and President Yeltsin (see page 486).
1996	26 Jan	U.S. Senate ratifies START II.
	29 Jan	France announces end to nuclear tests.
1999	13 Oct	Senate rejects 1996 nuclear test-ban treaty; international leaders scold United States.

ARMS CONTROL: Multilateral Agreements

1925   GENEVA PROTOCOL
Signed in Geneva: 17 June 1925
Entered into force: 8 February 1928
Parties as of 1 January 1992: 130
Protocol prohibits the use in war of asphyxiating, poisonous or other gases, and bacteriological methods of warfare.

1959   ANTARCTIC TREATY
Signed in Washington: 1 December 1959
Entered into force: 23 June 1961
Parties as of 1 January 1992: 40
Treaty declares the Antarctic an area to be used exclusively for peaceful purposes.

1963   PARTIAL TEST-BAN TREATY
Signed in Moscow: 5 August 1963
Entered into force: 10 October 1963
Parties as of 1 January 1992: 119
Treaty bans nuclear-weapon tests in the atmosphere, in outer space and under water.

1967   OUTER SPACE TREATY
Signed in London, Moscow and Washington: 27 January 1967
Entered into force: 10 October 1967
Parties as of 1 January 1992: 92
Treaty prohibits the placing in orbit around the Earth of any objects carrying nuclear weapons or any other kinds of weapons of mass destruction, the installation of such weapons on celestial bodies or the stationing of them in outer space.

1967   TREATY OF TLATELOLCO
Signed in Mexico City: 14 February 1967
Entered into force: 22 April 1968
Parties as of 1 January 1992—to Treaty: 23
—to Additional Protocol I: 3
—to Additional Protocol II: 5
Treaty prohibits nuclear weapons in Latin America. Under Additional Protocol I, states having responsibility for territories within Latin America undertake to respect the treaty; under Additional Protocol II, nuclear-weapon states undertake to respect the treaty and not to use or threaten to use nuclear weapons against parties to it.

1968   NONPROLIFERATION TREATY
Signed in London, Moscow and Washington: 1 July 1968
Entered into force: 5 March 1970
Parties as of 1 January 1992—to Treaty: 146
—to Safeguards Agreement: 88
Treaty prohibits nuclear-weapon states from transferring or assisting in manufacture of nuclear weapons and prohibits non-nuclear-weapon states from acquiring or manufacturing them. Non-nuclear-weapon states undertake to conclude safeguards agreements with the International Atomic Energy Agency to prevent diversion of nuclear energy from peaceful uses to nuclear weapons.

1971 SEA-BED TREATY
Signed in London, Moscow and Washington: 11 February 1971
Entered into force: 18 May 1972
Parties as of 1 January 1992: 85
Treaty prohibits emplacement of nuclear weapons and other weapons of mass destruction on the sea-bed or in the subsoil thereof.

1972 BIOLOGICAL WEAPONS CONVENTION
Signed in London, Moscow and Washington: 10 April 1972
Entered into force: 26 March 1975
Parties as of 1 January 1992: 118
Convention prohibits development, production and stockpiling of biological and toxin weapons, and states that destruction of existing stocks should take place not later than nine months after the entry into force of the convention.

1977 ENVIRONMENTAL MODIFICATION (ENMOD) CONVENTION
Signed in Geneva: 18 May 1977
Entered into force: 5 October 1978
Parties as of 1 January 1992: 54
Convention prohibits military or any other hostile use of environmental modification techniques having widespread, long-lasting or severe effects.

1981 "INHUMANE WEAPONS" CONVENTION
Signed in New York: 10 April 1981
Entered into force: 2 December 1983
Parties as of 1 January 1992: 31
The convention prohibits or restricts use of certain conventional weapons that may be deemed to be excessively injurious or to have indiscriminate effects, e.g., mines, booby-traps and incendiary weapons.

1985 SOUTH PACIFIC NUCLEAR FREE ZONE TREATY
Signed in Rarotonga, Cook Islands: 6 August 1985
Entered into force: 11 December 1986
Parties as of 1 January 1992: 11
The treaty prohibits manufacture or acquisition by other means of any nuclear explosive devices, as well as the possession or control over such devices, by the parties anywhere inside or outside the South Pacific area.

1990 CONFERENCE ON SECURITY AND COOPERATION IN EUROPE (CSCE)
See page 450.

1993 CHEMICAL WEAPONS CONVENTION
Opened for signature: 13 January 1993

Entered into force: 29 April 1996
Parties: 165 signatories, 93 ratifications
Convention prohibits the production, acquisition, retention or use of chemical weapons.

1996   COMPREHENSIVE NUCLEAR TEST BAN TREATY (CTBT)
Opened for signature: 24 September 1996.
Enters into force: (See below)
Parties as of March 2000: 154 signed, 51 ratified
The treaty will ban any nuclear-weapon test explosion or any other nuclear explosion (i.e., true zero yield). To enter into force, all 44 states that were members of the UN Conference on Disarmament as of 18 June 1996 must deposit their instruments of ratification. Three of these states (India, Pakistan and North Korea) have not yet signed the treaty.

ARMS CONTROL: ADHERENTS TO MULTILATERAL AGREEMENTS

	Geneva Protocol	Antarctic Treaty	Partial Test-Ban Treaty	Outer Space Treaty	Treaty of Tlatelolco	Non-Proliferation Treaty	Sea-Bed Treaty	Biological Weapons Convention	Enmod Convention	"Inhumane Weapons" Convention	Treaty of Rarotonga	Comprehensive Test Ban Treaty	Chemical Weapons Convention
AFGHANISTAN	1986		1964	1988		1970 SA	1971	1975	1985				(1993)
ALBANIA	1989					1990						(1996)	1994
ALGERIA	1992		(1963)			1995	1992		1991			(1996)	1995
ANGOLA	1990					1996						(1996)	
ANTIGUA AND BARBUDA	1989		1988	1988	1983	1985	1988		1988			(1997)	
ARGENTINA	1969	1961	1986	1969	(1967)		1983	1979	1987			1998	1995
AUSTRALIA	1930	1961	1963	1967		1973 SA	1973	1977	1984	1983	1986	1998	1994
AUSTRIA	1928	1987	1964	1968		1969 SA	1972	1973	1990	1983		1998	1995
BAHAMAS	1973		1976	1976	1977	1976	1989	1986				(1996)	(1994)
BAHRAIN	1988					1988		1988					1997
BANGLADESH	1989		1985	1986		1979 SA		1985	1979			(1996)	1997
BARBADOS	1976				1969	1980							
BELGIUM	1928	1960	1966	1968 / 1973		1975 SA	1972	1973 / 1979	1982			1999	1997
BELIZE					(1992)	1985		1986					
BENIN	1986		1964	1986		1972	1986	1975	1986	1989		(1996)	(1993)
BHUTAN	1979		1978			1985		1978					(1997)
BOLIVIA	1985		1965	(1967)	1969	1970	(1971)	1975	(1977)			1999	(1993)
BOTSWANA	1962		1968	(1967)		1969	1972	1991					
BRAZIL	1970	1975	1964	1969	1968		1988	1973	1984 / 1984			1998	1996
BRUNEI DARUS-SALAM						1985						(1997)	(1993)
BULGARIA	1934	1978	1963	1967		1969 SA	1971	1972	1978	1982		1999	1994
BURKINA FASO	1971		(1963)	1968		1970		1991				(1996)	(1993)
BURMA (MYANMAR)	1948		1963	1970			(1971)						
BURUNDI			(1963)	(1967)			(1971)						(1993)
BYELORUSSIA	1970		1963	1967		1971	1971	(1972) / 1975	1978	1982		(1996)	

ARMS CONTROL: ADHERENTS TO MULTILATERAL AGREEMENTS (CONT.)

	Geneva Protocol	Antarctic Treaty	Partial Test-Ban Treaty	Outer Space Treaty	Treaty of Tlatelolco	Non-Proliferation Treaty	Sea-Bed Treaty	Biological Weapons Convention	Enmod Convention	"Inhumane Weapons" Convention	Treaty of Rarotonga	Comprehensive Test Ban Treaty	Chemical Weapons Convention
CAMEROON	1989		(1963)	(1967)		1969	(1971)						1996
CANADA	1930	1988	1964	1967		1969	1972	1972	1981			1998	1995
CAPE VERDE			1979			1979 SA	1979						(1993)
CENTRAL AFRICAN REPUBLIC	1970		1964	(1967)		1970	1981	1977 (1972)	1979			(1996)	(1993)
CHAD			1965			1971							(1994)
CHILE	1935	1961	1965	1981	1974	1995		1980				(1996)	1996
CHINA	1929	1983		1983	PII 1974	1992		1984				(1996)	1997
COLOMBIA		1989	1985	(1967)	1972 SA	1986	1991	1983	1994	1982	1989	(1996)	(1993)
CONGO (Rep. of)						1978	1978	1978				(1996)	(1993)
COSTA RICA			1967		1969 SA	1970 SA	(1971)	1973				1996	1996
CUBA	1966	1984	1965	1977			1977	1976	1978	1987			1997
CYPRUS	1966	1962	1965	1972		1970 SA	1971	1973	1978	1988		(1996)	(1993)
CZECH REPUBLIC	1938		1963	1967		1969 SA	1972	1973	1993	1982		1997	(1993)
DENMARK	1930	1965	1964	1967		1969 SA	1971	1973	1978	1982		1998	1995
DOMINICA	1978			1978	(1989)	1984 SA							
DOMINICAN REPUBLIC	1970		1964	1968	1968 SA	1971 SA	1972	1973	1992			(1996)	(1993)
ECUADOR	1970	1987	1964	1969	1969 SA	1969 SA		1975		1982		(1996)	1995
EGYPT	1928		1964	1967		1981 SA		(1972)	1982			(1996)	
EL SALVADOR	(1925)		1964	1969	1968 SA	1972 SA		(1972)				1998	1995
EQUATORIAL GUINEA	1989		1989	1989		1984	(1971)	1989				(1996)	1997
ESTONIA	1931		(1963)			1992						1999	(1993)
ETHIOPIA	1935			(1967)		1970 SA	1977	1975	(1977)			(1996)	1996

ARMS CONTROL: ADHERENTS TO MULTILATERAL AGREEMENTS (CONT.)

	Geneva Protocol	Antarctic Treaty	Partial Test-Ban Treaty	Outer Space Treaty	Treaty of Tlatelolco	Non-Proliferation Treaty	Sea-Bed Treaty	Biological Weapons Convention	Enmod Convention	"Inhumane Weapons" Convention	Treaty of Rarotonga	Comprehensive Test Ban Treaty	Chemical Weapons Convention
FIJI	1973					1972 SA		1973			1985	1996	1993
FINLAND	1929	1984	1964	1967		1969 SA	1971	1974	1978	1982		1999	1995
FRANCE	1926	1960		1970	PI; PII 1974	1992 SA		1984		1988		1998	1995
GABON	1966		1964			1974		(1972)					
GAMBIA			1965	(1967)		1975 SA	(1971)	(1972)				(1996)	(1993)
GERMANY, EAST	1929	1974	1963	1967		1969 SA	1971	1972	1978	1982			
GERMANY	1929	1979	1964	1971		1975 SA	1975	1983	1983			1998	1994
GREECE	1931	1987	1963	1971		1970 SA	(1971)	1975	1983			1999	1994
GRENADA	1989				1975	1975 SA		1986					(1997)
GUATEMALA	1983		1964	1974	1970 SA	1970 SA	(1977)	1973	1988	1983		1998	(1993)
GUINEA	1989		1976	1976		1985 SA	(1971)					(1996)	1997
GUINEA-BISSAU				(1967)		1976	1976	1976				(1997)	(1993)
GUYANA			(1963)	(1967)		1993		(1973)					
HAITI					1969	1970		(1972)				(1996)	1993
HOLY SEE (VATICAN CITY)	1966					1971 SA			(1977)			(1996)	(1993)
HONDURAS	1952		1964	(1967)	1968 SA	1973 SA	1971	1979				(1996)	(1993)
HUNGARY	1967	1984	1963	1967		1969 SA	1971	1972	1978	1982		1999	1996
ICELAND			1964	1968		1969 SA	1972	1973	(1977)			(1996)	1997
INDIA	1930	1983	1963	1982			1973	1974	1978	1984			1996
INDONESIA	1971		1964	(1967)		1979 SA		(1972)				(1996)	(1993)
IRAN	1929		1964	(1967)		1970 SA	1971	1973	(1977)			(1996)	(1993)

ARMS CONTROL: ADHERENTS TO MULTILATERAL AGREEMENTS (CONT.)

	Geneva Protocol	Antarctic Treaty	Partial Test-Ban Treaty	Outer Space Treaty	Treaty of Tlatelolco	Non-Proliferation Treaty	Sea-Bed Treaty	Biological Weapons Convention	Enmod Convention	"Inhumane Weapons" Convention	Treaty of Rarotonga	Comprehensive Test Ban Treaty	Chemical Weapons Convention
IRAQ	1931		1964	1968		1969 SA	1972	1991	(1977)				
IRELAND	1930		1963	1968		1968 SA	1971	1972	1982			1999	1996
ISRAEL	1969		1964	1977								(1996)	(1993)
ITALY	1928	1981	1964	1972		1975 SA	1974	1975	1981			1999	1995
IVORY COAST	1970		1965			1973 SA	1972	(1972)					
JAMAICA	1970		1991	1970	1969 SA	1970 SA	(1971)	1975				(1996)	(1997)
JAPAN	1970	1960	1964	1967		1976 SA	1971	1982	1982	1982		1997	1995
JORDAN	1977		1964	(1967)		1970 SA	1971	1975				1998	
KAMPUCHEA	1983					1972	(1972)						
KENYA	1970		1965	1984		1970		1983				(1996)	1997
KIRIBATI						1985		1976			1986		
KOREA, NORTH	1989	1987	1964	1967		1985		1987	1984				
KOREA, SOUTH	1989	1986	1964			1975 SA	1987	1987	1986	1983		1999	(1993)
KUWAIT	1971		1965	1972		1989	1971	1972	1980			(1996)	1997
LAOS	1989		1965	1972		1970	1992	1973	1978			(1997)	1997
LATVIA	1931					1992						(1996)	1996
LEBANON	1969		1965	1969		1970 SA	(1971)	1975	(1977)			(1996)	1996
LESOTHO	1972			(1967)		1970 SA	1973	1977				1999	1994
LIBERIA	1927		1964			1970		(1972)				(1996)	(1993)
LIBYA	1971		1968	1968		1975 SA	(1971)	1982	(1977)				
LIECHTENSTEIN	1991					1978 SA	1991			1989		(1996)	(1993)
LITHUANIA	1932					1991		1991				(1996)	(1993)

ARMS CONTROL: ADHERENTS TO MULTILATERAL AGREEMENTS (CONT.)

	Geneva Protocol	Antarctic Treaty	Partial Test-Ban Treaty	Outer Space Treaty	Treaty of Tlatelolco	Non-Proliferation Treaty	Sea-Bed Treaty	Biological Weapons Convention	Enmod Convention	"Inhumane Weapons" Convention	Treaty of Rarotonga	Comprehensive Test Ban Treaty	Chemical Weapons Convention
LUXEMBOURG	1936		1965	(1967)		1975 SA	1982	1976	(1977)			1999	1997
MADAGASCAR	1967		1965	1968		1970 SA	(1971)	(1972)				(1996)	(1993)
MALAWI	1970		1964			1986		(1972)				(1996)	(1993)
MALAYSIA	1970		1964	(1967)		1970 SA	1972	1991	1978			(1998)	(1993)
MALDIVES	1966					1970 SA						(1997)	1994
MALI	1966		(1963)	1968		1970	(1971)	(1972)				1999	1997
MALTA	1970		1964			1970	1971	1975				(1996)	1997
MAURITANIA			1964									(1996)	(1993)
MAURITIUS	1970		1969	1969		1969 SA	1971	1972	1992				1993
MEXICO	1932		1963	1968	1967	1969 SA	1984	1974		1982		1999	1994
MONACO	1967					1995						1998	1995
MONGOLIA	1968		1963	1967		1969 SA	1971	1972	1978	1982		1997	1995
MOROCCO	1970		1966	1967		1970 SA	1971	(1972)	(1977)			(1996)	1995
NAURU						1982 SA					1987		(1993)
NEPAL	1969		1964	1967		1970 SA	1971	(1972)				(1996)	(1993)
NETHERLANDS	1930	1967	1964	1969	PI 1971	1975 SA	1976	1981	1983	1987		1999	1995
NEW ZEALAND	1930	1960	1963	1968		1969 SA	1972	1972	1984		1986	1999	1996
NICARAGUA	(1925)		1965	(1967)	1968 SA	1973 SA	1973	1975	(1977)			(1996)	(1993)
NIGER	1967		1964	1967				1972				(1996)	1997
NIGERIA	1968		1967	1967		1968	1971	1973	1993	(1982)		(1996)	(1993)

ARMS CONTROL: ADHERENTS TO MULTILATERAL AGREEMENTS (CONT.)

	Geneva Protocol	Antarctic Treaty	Partial Test-Ban Treaty	Outer Space Treaty	Treaty of Tlatelolco	Non-Proliferation Treaty	Sea-Bed Treaty	Biological Weapons Convention	Enmod Convention	"Inhumane Weapons" Convention	Treaty of Rarotonga	Comprehensive Test Ban Treaty	Chemical Weapons Convention
NORWAY	1932	1960	1963	1963		1969 SA	1971	1973	1979	1983		1999	1994
PAKISTAN	1960		1988	1968				1974		1985			(1993)
PANAMA	1970		1966	(1967)	1971 SA	1977	1974	1974	1986				
PAPUA NEW GUINEA	1981	1981	1980	1980		1982 SA		1980	1980		1989	(1996)	1996
PARAGUAY	1933		(1963)		1969 SA	1970 SA	(1971)	1976				(1996)	1994
PERU	1985	1981	1964	1979	1969 SA	1970 SA		1985				1997	1995
PHILIPPINES	1973		1965	(1967)		1972 SA		1973				(1996)	1996
POLAND	1929	1961	1963	1968		1969 SA	1971	1973	1978	1983		1999	1995
PORTUGAL	1930		(1963)			1977 SA	1975	1975	(1977)			(1996)	1996
QATAR	1976					1989	1974	1975				1997	(1993)
ROMANIA	1929	1971	1963	1968		1970 SA	1972	1979	1983	(1982)		(1996)	1995
RUSSIAN FEDERATION	1928	1960	1963	1967	1979	1970 SA	1972	1975	1978	1982	1988	(1996)	
RWANDA	1964		1963	(1967)		1975		1975	1993				(1993)
SAINT LUCIA	1988					1979	1975		1979				(1993)
SAINT VINCENT AND THE GRENADINES			1964	1968		1984		1975					
SAMOA			1965			1975 SA					1986		
SÃO TOMÉ AN PRINCIPE						1983	1979	1979	1979			(1996)	
SAUDI ARABIA	1971		1964	1976		1988	1972	1972					1996
SENEGAL	1977					1970 SA	(1971)	1975				1999	1997

ARMS CONTROL: ADHERENTS TO MULTILATERAL AGREEMENTS (CONT.)

	Geneva Protocol	Antarctic Treaty	Partial Test-Ban Treaty	Outer Space Treaty	Treaty of Tlatelolco	Non-Proliferation Treaty	Sea-Bed Treaty	Biological Weapons Convention	Enmod Convention	"Inhumane Weapons" Convention	Treaty of Rarotonga	Comprehensive Test Ban Treaty	Chemical Weapons Convention
SEYCHELLES	1976			1978		1985	1985	1979				(1996)	1993
SIERRA LEONE	1967		1964	1967		1975	1985	1976	(1978)				(1993)
SINGAPORE	1965		1968	1976		1976	1976	1975				(1999)	1997
SLOVAK REPUBLIC						1993	1991					1998	1995
SLOVENIA						1992 SA	1992					1999	1997
SOLOMON ISLANDS	1978					1981	1987	1987	1981		1989	(1996)	
SOMALIA	1930		(1963)	(1967)		1970		1972					
SOUTH AFRICA	1930	1960	1963	1968		1991	1973	1975				1999	1995
SPAIN	1929	1982	1964	1968		1987	1987	1979	1978			1998	1994
SRI LANKA	1954		1964	1986		1979 SA		1986	1978			(1996)	1994
SUDAN	1980		1966			1973 SA	(1971)						
SURINAME	1975				1977	1976 SA						(1997)	1997
SWAZILAND	1991		1969			1969 SA	1971					(1996)	1997
SWEDEN	1930	1984	1963	1967		1970 SA	1972	1976	1984	1982		1998	1993
SWITZERLAND	1932	1990	1964	1969		1977 SA	1976	1976	1988	1982		1999	
SYRIA	1968		1964	1968		1969	1972	(1972)					
TAIWAN	1929		1964	1970		1970	(1971)	1973	(1977)				
TANZANIA	1963		1964					(1972)					
THAILAND	1931		1963	1968		1972 SA		1975				(1996)	(1993)
TOGO	1971		1964	1989		1970	1971	1976				(1996)	1997
TONGA	1971		1971	1971		1971		1976					
TRINIDAD AND TOBAGO	1970		1964	(1967)	1970	(1968)							
TUNISIA	1967		1965	1968		1970	1971	1973	1978	1987		(1996)	1997
TURKEY	1929		1965	1968		1980 SA	1972	1974	(1977)	(1982)		(1996)	1997

ARMS CONTROL: ADHERENTS TO MULTILATERAL AGREEMENTS (CONT.)

	Geneva Protocol	Antarctic Treaty	Partial Test-Ban Treaty	Outer Space Treaty	Treaty of Tlatelolco	Non-Proliferation Treaty	Sea-Bed Treaty	Biological Weapons Convention	Enmod Convention	"Inhumane Weapons" Convention	Treaty of Rarotonga	Comprehensive Test Ban Treaty	Chemical Weapons Convention
TUVALU	1978										1986	(1996)	(1993)
UGANDA	1965		1964	1968		1982	1971		(1977)			(1996)	(1993)
UKRAINE			1963	1967		1994	1972	1975	1978	1982			
USSR	1928	1960	1963	1967	PII 1979	1970	1972	1975	1978	1982	1988 P2 P3	(1996)	(1993)
UNITED ARAB EMIRATES						1995	(1972)	(1972)					
UNITED KING-DOM	1930	1960	1963	1969	PI 1969 PII 1969	1968 SA	1972	1975	1978	(1982)		1998	1996
UNITED STATES	1975	1960	1963	1967	PI 1987 PII 1971	1970 SA	1972	1975	1980			(1996)	1997
URUGUAY	1977	1980	1969	1970	1968 SA	1970 SA	(1971)	1981	1993			(1996)	1994
VENEZUELA	1928		1965	1970	1970 SA	1975 SA		1978				(1997)	(1993)
VIETNAM	1980			1980		1982	1980	1980	1980			(1996)	(1993)
YEMEN	1986		1979	1979		1979	1979	1979	1977			(1996)	(1993)
YUGOSLAVIA	1929		1964	(1967)		1970 SA	1973	1973		1983			(1993)
ZAÏRE (DEM REP OF CONGO)			1965	(1967)		1970 SA		1977	(1978)			(1996)	
ZAMBIA			1965	1973		1991	1972						(1993)
ZIMBABWE						1991		1990				(1996)	1997

KEY:

Dates are those of ratification, or, if in parentheses, of signature where ratification has not taken place.

SA: Adherence to Safeguards Agreement of the Non-Proliferation Treaty (see p. 388).

P I & P II: Adherence to Protocol I and Protocol II of the Treaty of Tlatelolco (see p. 388).

NUCLEAR EXPLOSIONS SINCE 1945

Year	U.S. a	u	USSR a	u	U.K. a	u	FRANCE a	u	CHINA a	u	INDIA a	u	Total
1945	3	0											3
1946	1	1											2
1947	0	0											0
1948	3	0											3
1949	0	0	1	0									1
1950	0	0	0	0									0
1951	15	1	2	0									18
1952	10	0	0	0	1	0							11
1953	11	0	2	0	2	0							15
1954	6	0	2	0	0	0							8
1955	16	2	4	0	0	0							22
1956	18	0	7	0	6	0							31
1957	27	5	13	0	7	0							52
1958	61	16	26	0	5	0							108
1959	0	0	0	0	0	0							0
1960	0	0	0	0	0	0	3	0					3
1961	0	10	30	2	0	0	1	1					44
1962	37	59	41	1	0	2	0	1					141
1963	4	43	0	0	0	0	0	3					50
1964	0	29	0	6	0	1	0	3	1	0			40
1965	0	29	0	9	0	1	0	4	1	0			44
1966	0	40	0	15	0	0	5	1	3	0			64
1967	0	29	0	15	0	0	3	0	2	0			49
1968	0	39	0	13	0	0	5	0	1	0			58
1969	0	29	0	15	0	0	0	0	1	1			46
1970	0	33	0	12	0	0	8	0	1	0			54
1971	0	15	0	19	0	0	5	0	1	0			40
1972	0	15	0	22	0	0	3	0	2	0			42
1973	0	14	0	14	0	0	5	0	1	0			34
1974	0	12	0	19	0	1	7	0	1	0	0	1	41
1975	0	17	0	15	0	0	0	2	0	1	0	0	35
1976	0	15	0	17	0	1	0	3	3	1	0	0	40
1977	0	12	0	18	0	0	0	6	1	0	0	0	37
1978	0	16	0	27	0	2	0	7	2	1	0	0	55
1979	0	15	0	29	0	1	0	9	0	0	0	0	54
1980	0	14	0	21	0	3	0	11	1	0	0	0	50
1981	0	16	0	21	0	1	0	11	0	0	0	0	49
1982	0	18	0	31	0	1	0	5	0	0	0	0	55
1983	0	17	0	27	0	1	0	7	0	1	0	0	53
1984	0	17	0	27	0	2	0	7	0	2	0	0	55
1985	0	15	0	7	0	1	0	8	0	0	0	0	31
1986	0	14	0	0	0	1	0	8	0	0	0	0	23
1987	0	14	0	23	0	1	0	8	0	1	0	0	47
1988	0	14	0	17	0	0	0	8	0	1	0	0	40
1989	0	11	0	7	0	1	0	8	0	0	0	0	27
1990	0	8	0	1	0	1	0	6	0	2	0	0	18
1991	0	7	0	0	0	1	0	6	0	0	0	0	14
1992	0	6	0	0	0	0	0	0	0	2	0	0	8
1993	0	0	0	0	0	0	0	0	0	1	0	0	1
1994	0	0	0	0	0	0	0	0	0	2	0	0	2

NUCLEAR EXPLOSIONS SINCE 1945 (CONT.)

Year	U.S. a	U.S. u	USSR a	USSR u	U.K. a	U.K. u	FRANCE a	FRANCE u	CHINA a	CHINA u	INDIA a	INDIA u	Total
1995	0	0	0	0	0	0	0	5	0	2	0	0	7
1996	0	0	0	0	0	0	0	1	0	2	0	0	3

Source: 1992–1996 Natural Resources Defense Council.

Note: A further 33 Soviet atmospheric tests were conducted in the period 1949–58, for which specific dates are not available.

The most current official data is from 1996; however, in 1998 India conducted five nuclear tests, and Pakistan responded with several nuclear tests of its own. In 1999, both countries tested nuclear-capable ballistic missiles.

a = atmospheric

u = underground/underwater

CHAPTER 9

POPULATION AND URBANIZATION

Parentheses indicate estimates.

AFGHANISTAN		
	Total Population	**Population Percentage of Population Urban**
1950	8,420,000	5.8
1955	9,125,000	
1960	10,016,000	8.0
1965	11,115,000	
1970	12,457,000	11.0
1975	14,038,000	13.1
1980	14,607,000	15.6
1985	14,636,000	18.5
1990	16,500,000	21.0
1998	24,792,375	20.0

Sources: *World Population Prospects: Estimates and Projections as Assessed in 1982* (New York: United Nations, 1982).

John Paxton, ed., *The Statesman's Year-Book, 1989–90,* 126th ed. (New York: St. Martin's Press, 1989).

Brian Hunter, ed., *The Statesman's Year-Book, 1993–94,* 130th ed. (New York: St. Martin's Press, 1993).

Source for total pop/urban %: *World Almanac and Book of Facts 1999* (Mahwah, N.J.: World Almanac Books, 1998).

	1948	**1964**	**1973**	**1982**	**1990**	**1993**
			Cities (in thousands)			
Kabul	154	400	318	1,127	(2,000)	1,142
Herat			108	156		177
Kandahar (Quandahar)		119	140	198		225

Source: *U.N. Demographic Yearbook 1960, 1964, 1974.*

Source for city populations: *Time Almanac 1999* (Boston: Information Please LLC, 1998).

ARGENTINA

	Total Population	Population Percentage of Population Urban
1947	15,894,000	62.5
1960	20,011,000	73.8
1970	23,362,000	78.4
1975	(26,050,000)	(80.7)
1980	(27,947,000)	(82.9)
1983	(29,627,000)	
1991	32,370,000	(83.0)
1998	36,265,463	88.0

	_____		Cities (in thousands)				
	1947	**1960**	**1970**	**1980***	**1983**	**1991**	**1995**
Buenos Aires	4,603	(7,000)	8,925	9,927			11,931
Bahía Blanca	113	150	175	221			
Córdoba	370	589	799	982		1,180	
La Plata	207	330	506	560			
Mar del Plata	115	142	300	407			
Mendoza	212	109	471	597			
Rosario	468	672	811	955	950		
San Juan	82	107	224	290			
San Miguel de Tucuman	194	288	368	497			
Santa Fe	169	260	245	287			

* Last official census.

AUSTRALIA

	Total Population	Population Percentage of Population Urban
1947	7,561,000	68.9
1961	10,508,000	82.1
1971	12,756,000	85.6
1981	14,574,000	86.0 (1976)
1984	15,540,000	
1992	17,414,000	85.4 (1986)
1998	18,613,087	85.0

In 1976, the total population of 13,548,000 included 144,400 aborigines. At the 1986 census the total was 227,000.

			Cities (in thousands)				
	1954	**1966**	**1973**	**1981**	**1987**	**1991**	**1994**
Canberra	28	100	185	197	289	279	279
Adelaide	484	727	868	900	1,013	1,024	1,076
Brisbane	502	719	911	958	1,215	1,327	786
Geelong		105	127	132	149	153	
Greater Wollongong	91	163	206	211	234	239	

AUSTRALIA (CONT.)

| | Cities (in thousands) | | | | | | |
	1954	1966	1973	1981	1987	1991	1994
Hobart	95	119	158	162	180	182	
Melbourne	1,524	2,108	2,584	2,604	2,964	3,154	3,198
Newcastle	178	234	358	363	419	433	
Perth	349	499	739	806	1,083	1,143	1,239
Sydney	1,863	2,445	2,874	3,022	3,531	3,699	3,739

AUSTRIA

	Total Population	Population Percentage of Population Urban
1951	6,934,000	49.2
1961	7,074,000	(30.9) (1960)
1971	7,456,000	51.9
1981	7,555,000	54.9
1983	(7,549,000)	65.0
1988	(7,596,000)	
1991	7,812,000	57.7 (1990)
1998	8,133,611	64.0

| | Cities (in thousands) | | | | | | |
	1951	1961	1971	1981	1984	1991	1995
Vienna	1,766	1,628	1,615	1,516	1,531	1,533	
Graz	226	237	249	243	243	232	237
Innsbruck		101	105	116	117	115	118
Linz	185	196	203	198	199	203	203
Salzburg	103	108	129	138	139	144	144

BELGIUM

	Total Population	Population Percentage of Population Urban
1947	8,512,000	62.7
1961	9,190,000	
1970	9,651,000	(86.8) (1968)
1981	9,849,000	(94.6) (1975)
1983	(9,856,000)	
1987	(9,875,000)	(95.0) (1983)

BELGIUM (CONT.)

	Total Population	Population Percentage of Population Urban
1992	(10,002,000)	(96.9) (1990)
1998	10,174,992	97.0

Cities (in thousands)

	1947	1966	1971	1981	1984	1988	1992	1994
Brussels	956	1,075	1,075	997	982	970	950	949
Antwerp		662	672	186		476	466	476
Bruges			118	118	118	118	117	117
Charleroi		280	214	222	213	209	207	207
Ghent	228	233	225	239		232	230	230
La Louviere			113			76	77	
Liège	425	450	440	214	203	200	196	
Namur				102	102	103	104	

BRAZIL

	Total Population	Population Percentage of Population Urban
1950	51,976,000	36.2
1960	79,967,000	46.3
1970	92,342,000	55.9
1980	118,675,000	67.7
1983	(129,766,000)	(81.1) (1982)
1989	147,404,000	75.0 (1989)
1991	146,154,000	(76.9) (1990)
1998	169,806,557	79.0

Cities (in thousands)

	1950	1960	1970	1980	1991	1995
Belo Horizonte	339	(583)	1,228	1,442	2,049	2,600
Curitiba	138	(258)	584	844	1,290	
Fortaleza	205	(405)	829	645	1,758	
Goiania	40	(105)	363	703	921	
Manaus	90	(184)	284	613	1,010	
Pôrto Alegre	375	(553) (1959)	870	1,109	1,263	3,000
Recife	512	(765) (1959)	1,046	1,184	1,290	2,901
Rio de Janeiro	2,303	(3,124) (1959)	4,252	5,093	5,336	5,473
Salvador	389	(571) (1959)	1,005	1,496	2,056	2,600
São Paulo	2,017	(3,674)	5,870	7,034	9,480	9,394

BULGARIA

	Total Population	Population Percentage of Population Urban
1956	7,614,000	33.6
1965	8,228,000	46.5
1975	8,730,000	(58.7)
1983	(8,939,000)	(64.6)
1985	8,942,000	65.2
1988	8,973,000	66.0
1992	8,472,000	(70.3) (1990)
1998	8,240,426	69.0

				Cities (in thousands)			
	1956	1966	1975	1982	1987	1990	1994
Sofia	665	810	967	(1,064)	1,128	1,141	1,114
Burgas		108	144	(171)	198	205	198
Pleven			108	(130)	134	138	
Plovdiv	162	226	300	(355)	357	379	345
Ruse		132	160	(174)	190	192	170
Stara Zagora			122	(138)	156	165	
Varna	120	184	253	(293)	306	315	307

CANADA

	Total Population	Population Percentage of Population Urban
1951	14,009,000	62.9
1961	18,238,000	
1971	21,568,000	76.1
1981	24,343,000	75.7
1983	(24,907,000)	(76.0)
1986	25,354,000	76.3
1991	27,297,000	76.6
1998	30,675,398	77.0

				Cities (in thousands)*			
	1956	1966	1974	1983	1986	1991	1996
Ottawa	345	495	626	(738)	819	921	1,010
Calgary	200	331	444	(635)	671	754	822
Edmonton	251	401	529	(698)	785	840	863
Hamilton	328	449	520	(548)	557	600	624
Montreal	1,621	2,437	2,798	(2,862)	2,921	3,127	3,327
Quebec	310	413	499	(580)	603	646	672
St. Catharine's			311	(304)	343	365	
Toronto	1,358	2,158	2,741	(3,067)	3,427	3,893	4,264
Vancouver	665	892	1,137	(1,311)	1,381	1,603	1,832
Winnipeg	409	509	570	601	623	652	667

* Census Metropolitan Areas.

CHILE

	Total Population	Population Percentage of Population Urban
1952	5,993,000	60.2
1960	7,374,000	68.2
1970	8,885,000	76.0
1980	(11,104,000)	(81.1)
1982	(11,275,440)	(82.5)
1988	(12,683,000)	
1992	13,232,000	(85.6) (1990)
1998	14,787,781	84.0

			Cities (in thousands)			
	1955	1966	1975	1983	1987	1993
Santiago	(1,539)	2,314	3,263	(4,132)	(4,858)	4,628
Antofagasta	62	117	150	(170)	(205)	
Chillán	(1952) 53		102	(124)	(149)	
Concepción	(1952) (143)	178	500	(210)	(294)	318
Rancagua	40		108	(142)	(172)	
Talca	(1952) 55		115	(138)	(164)	
Talcahuano	(1952) 55	102	184	(213)	(231)	257
Temuco	(1952) 51		138	(165)	(218)	263
Valparaíso	(1952) (248)	280	592	(268)*	(278)*	302
Vina del Mar	(97)	138	229	(299)	(297)	319

* City area only.

CHINA

	Total Population	Population Percentage of Population Urban
1953	590,195,000	(13.5) (1955)
1965	(700,000,000)	20.1 (1970)
1975	(933,000,000)	
1982	1,008,000,000	
1990	1,134,000,000	21.4
1993	(1,180,000,000)	
1998	1,236,914,658	29.0

		Cities (in thousands)		
	1953	1970	1984	1993
Beijing (Peking)	4,010 (1957)	(7,570)	9,452	11,414

CHINA (CONT.)

	Cities (in thousands)			
	1953	1970	1984	1993
Chengdu	(1,107)		8,540	
Huaiyin	287		8,956	
Nantong	260		7,427	
Shanghai	6,900 (1957)	(10,820)	12,048	
Shantou	280		7,895	
Tianjin		(4,280)	7,989	5,000
Weifang	145		7,845	
Yangzhou	180		8,677	

COLOMBIA

	Total Population	Population Percentage of Population Urban
1950	11,597,000	37.1
1955	13,390,000	
1960	15,538,000	48.2
1965	18,114,000	
1970	20,803,000	57.2
1975	23,177,000	60.8
1980	25,794,000	64.2
1985	28,714,000	67.4
1992	(33,391,000)	70.3 (1990)
1998	38,580,949	73.0

Sources: *World Population Prospects: Estimates and Projections as Assessed in 1982* (New York: United Nations, 1982).

John Paxton, ed. *The Statesman's Year-Book, 1989–90,* 126th ed. (New York: St. Martin's Press, 1989).

	Cities (in thousands)					
	1951	1964	1973	1985	1992	1995
Bogotá	648	1,681	2,836	4,185	4,820	5,026
Barranquilla	280	521	690	920	1,018	1,064
Bucaramanga	112	251	316	364	349	
Cali	284	813	968	1,397	1,624	1,719
Cartagena	129	198	309	560	688	747
Medellín	358	777	1,112	1,506	1,581	1,621

Sources: *U.N. Demographic Yearbook 1960, 1964, 1974.*

John Paxton, ed., *The Statesman's Year-Book, 1989–90,* 126th ed. (New York: St. Martin's Press, 1989).

Brian Hunter, ed., *The Statesman's Year-Book, 1993–94,* 130th ed. (New York: St. Martin's Press, 1993).

CONGO, DEMOCRATIC REPUBLIC OF THE (FORMERLY ZAÏRE)

	Total Population	Population Percentage of Population Urban
1947	10,805,000	15.8
1958	12,769,000	
1970	21,637,000	21.6
1980	(26,377,000)	(34.2)
1984	29,671,000	44.0
1989	(32,600,000)	
1991	(38,545,000)	
1997	47,440,362	43.0

	Cities (in thousands)				
	1955/6	1966	1974	1984	1997
Kinshasa	290	508	2,008	2,654	
Bukavu	31		182	171	
Kananga				291	
Kikwit	13		150	147	338
Kisangani	56	150	311	283	
Lubumbashi	157	233	404	543	
Matadi	70		144	145	
Mbandaka	31		134	125	
Mbuji-Mayi			337	423	

COSTA RICA

	Total Population	Population Percentage of Population Urban
1950	858,000	33.5
1955	1,024,000	
1960	1,236,000	36.6
1965	1,482,000	
1970	1,732,000	39.7
1975	1,965,000	41.3
1980	2,279,000	43.4
1985	2,600,000	45.9
1989	2,887,000	
1991	(3,029,000)	47.0
1998	3,604,642	50.0

Source: World Population Prospects: Estimates and Projections as Assessed in 1982 (New York: United Nations, 1982).

	Cities (in thousands)				
	1950	1963	1973	1984	1994
San José	87	102	215	285	316

Sources: U.N. Demographic Yearbook 1960, 1964, 1974.
John Paxton, ed., The Statesman's Year-Book, 1989–90, 126th ed. (New York: St. Martin's Press, 1989).
Brian Hunter, ed., The Statesman's Year-Book, 1993–94, 130th ed. (New York: St. Martin's Press, 1993).

CUBA

	Total Population	Population Percentage of Population Urban
1950	5,858,000	49.4
1955	6,426,000	
1960	7,029,000	54.9
1965	7,808,000	
1970	8,572,000	60.2
1975	9,332,000	64.2
1980	9,732,000	68.1
1986	10,240,000	71.8
1991	10,700,000	
1998	11,050,729	76.0

Sources: *World Population Prospects: Estimates and Projections as Assessed in 1982* (New York: United Nations, 1982).
John Paxton, ed., *The Statesman's Year-Book, 1989–90,* 126th ed. (New York: St. Martin's Press, 1989).
Brian Hunter, ed., *The Statesman's Year-Book, 1993–94,* 130th ed. (New York: St. Martin's Press, 1993).

	Cities (in thousands)					
	1953	1962	1970	1983	1986	1994
Havana	785	978	1,009	1,972	(2,015)	2,241
Camagüey	110	162	198	254	(261)	294
Guantánamo			129	171	(174)	208
Holguín			132	192	(195)	242
Santa Clara		106	130	176	(178)	205
Santiago de Cuba	163	220	278	353	(359)	440

Sources: *U.N. Demographic Yearbook 1960, 1964, 1974.*
John Paxton, ed., *The Statesman's Year-Book, 1989–90,* 126th ed. (New York: St. Martin's Press, 1989).
Brian Hunter, ed., *The Statesman's Year-Book, 1993–94,* 130th ed. (New York: St. Martin's Press, 1993).

CZECHOSLOVAKIA (UNTIL 1992)

	Total Population	Population Percentage of Population Urban
1950	12,338,000	51.2
1961	13,746,000	47.6
1970	14,345,000	55.5
1980	15,283,000	(66.7) (1974)
1983	(15,415,000)	
1989	15,624,000	68.6 (1990)
1998	10,286,470	66.0

	Cities (in thousands)						
	1950	1965	1974	1980	1984	1989	1994
Prague	932	1,023	1,096	1,182	(1,186)	1,211	1,216
Bratislava	193	268	329	380	(401)	435	
Brno	285	328	344	371	(381)	390	390
Košice		102	166	202	(214)	232	

CZECHOSLOVAKIA (UNTIL 1992) (CONT.)

Cities (in thousands)

	1950	1965	1974	1980	1984	1989	1994
Olomouc				102	(104)	107	106
Ostrava	189	263	292	322	(324)	331	326
Plzeň	124	140	154	171	(174)	175	172

DENMARK

	Total Population	Population Percentage of Population Urban
1950	4,281,000	67.3
1960	4,585,000	47.2
1970	4,938,000	66.9
1980	(5,123,000)	(82.6) (1976)
1985	5,111,000	
1989	5,130,000	
1992	5,160,000	86.4 (1990)
1998	5,333,617	85.0

Cities (in thousands)

	1955	1965	1976	1989	1992
Copenhagen	1,227	1,378		1,339	1,339
Ålborg			(155)	154	157
Århus	166	187	(246)	259	268
Odense	121	133	(168)	175	179

EGYPT

	Total Population	Population Percentage of Population Urban
1947	18,967,000	30.1
1957	22,997,000	35.8
1966	30,076,000	39.8
1976	36,626,000	43.4
1980	42,289,000	44.2
1985	46,694,000	
1989	50,740,000	
1992	56,000,000	
1998	66,050,004	45.0

EGYPT (CONT.)

				Cities (in thousands)					
	1947	1957	1966	1976	1981	1986	1990	1992	1994
Cairo	2,091	2,877	4,220	5,074	5,650	6,325	6,452		6,849
Alexandria	919	1,278	1,081	2,318	2,576	2,893	3,170	3,382	
Assyut	90	106	154	214		291			
El-Mahalla El-Kubra	116	157	225	292		385			
Giza	66	209	571	1,230		1,671	2,156	2,144	
Mansura	102	136	191	259		358			
Port Said	178	213	283	263	348	382	461		
Suez	107	163	264	194	224	265	392		
Zagaziq	81	110	151	203		274			

EL SALVADOR

	Total Population	Population Percentage of Population Urban
1950	1,940,000	36.5
1955	2,218,000	
1960	2,574,000	38.3
1965	3,005,000	
1970	3,582,000	39.4
1975	4,143,000	39.9
1980	4,797,000	41.1
1987	5,009,000	
1992	5,050,000	
1998	5,752,067	45.0

Sources: *World Population Prospects: Estimates and Projections as Assessed in 1982* (New York: United Nations, 1982).
John Paxton, ed., *The Statesman's Year-Book, 1989–90,* 126th ed. (New York: St. Martin's Press, 1989).
Brian Hunter, ed., *The Statesman's Year-Book, 1993–94,* 130th ed. (New York: St. Martin's Press, 1993).

			Cities (in thousands)			
	1950	1963	1971	1985	1992	1993
San Salvador	162	281	336	972	1,522	972

Source: *U.N. Demographic Yearbook 1960, 1964, 1974.*

FINLAND

	Total Population	Population Percentage of Population Urban
1950	4,009,000	32.0
1955	4,235,000	
1960	4,430,000	38.1
1965	4,564,000	
1970	4,606,000	50.3
1975	4,711,000	56.6
1980	4,787,000	59.8
1985	4,875,000	—
1989	4,954,000	61.8
1991	5,029,000	67.9 (1990)
1998	5,149,242	64.0

Sources: *World Population Prospects: Estimates and Projections as Assessed in 1982* (New York: United Nations, 1982).
John Paxton, ed., *The Statesman's Year-Book, 1989–90,* 126th ed. (New York: St. Martin's Press, 1989).
Brian Hunter, ed., *The Statesman's Year-Book, 1993–94,* 130th ed. (New York: St. Martin's Press, 1993).

	1950	1963	1973	Cities (in thousands) 1983	1989	1991	1995
Helsinki	369	482	510	484	490	498	516
Tampere	101	135	164	167	171	174	179
Turku	102	133	161	163	160	159	162

Source: *U.N. Demographic Yearbook 1960, 1964, 1974.*

FRANCE

	Total Population	Population Percentage of Population Urban
1954	42,844,000	55.9
1968	(48,919,000) (1965)	70.0
1975	52,544,000	73.0
1984	54,748,000	73.4 (1982)
1989	56,184,000	
1992	57,456,000	74.1 (1990)
1998	58,804,944	74.0

	1954	1968	Cities (in thousands) 1975	1982	1990	1995
Paris	4,823		8,613	8,510	9,060	9,469
Bordeaux	416	555	622	628	685	201
Grenoble	147	332	395	392	400	
Lille	359	881	944	935	950	
Lyons				1,170	1,262	415

FRANCE (CONT.)

	1954	1968	Cities (in thousands) 1975	1982	1990	1995
Marseilles	661	964	1,077	1,080	1,087	801
Nantes	242	394	462	465	492	245
Nice	244	393	440	449	476	342
Toulon	141	340	389	410	438	
Toulouse	269	440	521	523	608	359

GERMANY

Prior to October 1990, Germany was divided into two states (German Democratic Republic and Federal Republic of Germany).

	Total Population
1991	79,753,200

GERMAN DEMOCRATIC REPUBLIC

	Total Population	Population Percentage of Population Urban
1950	17,199,000	68.8
1964	15,940,000	72.9
1971	17,068,000	73.8
1981	16,706,000	(76.2) (1980)
1984	16,660,000	(76.6) (1983)
1988	16,674,000	(76.8) (1988)
1998	82,079,454	87.0

	1955	1966	Cities (in thousands) 1975	1984	1988	1997
Berlin	(1,150)	1,071	1,094	1,197	1,284	3,478
Dresden	(497)	507	508	520	518	
Erfurt	(188)	192	203	215	220	
Halle	(290)	276	239	236	236	
Karl Marx Stadt	(290)	295	304	317	312	
Leipzig	(614)	596	569	555	545	
Magdeburg	(261)	268	277	289	291	
Potsdam	(118)	111	118	138	143	
Rostock	(150)	185	212	242	254	

GERMANY, FEDERAL REPUBLIC OF

	Total Population	Population Percentage of Population Urban
1950	47,696,000	71.1
1961	53,977,000	
1970	60,651,000	
1984	61,675,000	
1988	61,241,700	81.3 (1990)

	Cities (in thousands)*					
	1956	1966	1974	1984	1987	1997
Berlin	(2,195)	2,197 (1961)	2,048	1,852	2,016	
Bremen	(512)	599	584	536	533	551
Cologne	(718)	861	832	932	928	963
Dortmund	(611)	657	632	585	584	602
Düsseldorf	(659)	698	629	571	563	573
Essen	(702)	721	674	629	623	620
Frankfurt am Main	(626)	685	663	605	619	656
Hamburg	(1,760)	1,851	1,752	1,600	1,594	1,704
Munich	(975)	1,231	1,337	1,277	1,189	1,251
Stuttgart	(605)	630	625	563	552	592

* Bonn, capital of the Federal Republic until reunification, had a population of 276,500 in 1987.

GHANA

	Total Population	Population Percentage of Population Urban
1950	4,242,000	14.5
1955	5,405,000	
1960	6,772,000	23.3
1965	7,786,000	
1970	8,614,000	29.1
1975	9,800,000	32.3
1980	11,457,000	35.9
1985	13,478,000	39.6
1988	(13,800,000)	
1991	15,510,000	33.0
1998	18,497,206	36.0

Source: *World Population Prospects: Estimates and Projections as Assessed in 1982* (New York: United Nations, 1982).

	Cities (in thousands)				
	1948	1960	1970	1984	1988
Accra	136	338	564	867	949
Kumasi		181	260	376	385

Sources: *U.N. Demographic Yearbook 1960, 1964, 1974.*
John Paxton, ed., *The Statesman's Year-Book, 1989–90*, 126th ed. (New York: St. Martin's Press, 1989).
Brian Hunter, ed., *The Statesman's Year-Book, 1993–94*, 130th ed. (New York: St. Martin's Press, 1993).

GREECE

	Total Population	Population Percentage of Population Urban
1951	7,633,000	36.8
1961	8,389,000	43.3
1971	8,769,000	64.8
1981	9,740,000	69.7
1983	(9,846,000)	
1987	(9,990,000	
1991	10,264,000	
1998	10,662,138	59.0

	Cities (in thousands)				
	1951	**1961**	**1971**	**1981**	**1991**
Athens	1,379	1,853	2,101	3,027	3,000
Patras		102	121	154	155
Piraeus	186	184	439	196	170
Peristéri			118	141	
Thessalonica		378	557	706	720

GUATEMALA

	Total Population	Population Percentage of Population Urban
1950	2,962,000	30.5
1955	3,423,000	
1960	3,966,000	33.0
1965	4,615,000	
1970	5,353,000	35.7
1975	6,243,000	37.0
1980	7,262,000	38.9
1985	8,403,000	41.4
1992	9,740,000	39.0
1998	12,007,580	39.0

Sources: *World Population Prospects: Estimates and Projections as Assessed in 1982* (New York: United Nations, 1982).
John Paxton, ed., *The Statesman's Year-Book, 1989–90,* 126th ed. (New York: St. Martin's Press, 1989).

	Cities (in thousands)					
	1950	**1963**	**1973**	**1979**	**1989**	**1994**
Guatemala City	284	439	707	793	2,000	1,150

Sources: *U.N. Demographic Yearbook 1960, 1964, 1974.*
John Paxton, ed., *The Statesman's Year-Book, 1989–90,* 126th ed. (New York: St. Martin's Press, 1989).
Brian Hunter, ed., *The Statesman's Year-Book, 1993–94,* 130th ed. (New York: St. Martin's Press, 1993).

HUNGARY

	Total Population	Population Percentage of Population Urban
1949	9,205,000	36.5
1960	9,961,000	39.7
1970	10,322,000	45.2
1980	10,709,000	53.2
1985	(10,657,000)	(54.3) (1982)
1989	10,590,000	60.0
1992	10,335,000	62.1
1998	10,208,127	65.0

			Cities (in thousands)			
	1956	1966	1974	1985	1989	1995
Budapest	(1,850)	1,960	2,051	(2,071)	2,115	2,009
Debrecen	(130)	150	180	(209)	220	210
Gyor			115	(128)	132	
Miskolc	(150)	173	195	(212)	208	182
Nyíregyháza				(116)	119	
Pécs	(110)	136	160	(175)	183	163
Szeged		117	166	(179)	189	169
Székesféhervár				(110)	114	

INDIA

	Total Population	Population Percentage of Population Urban
1951	356,879,000	17.3
1961	435,512,000	18.0
1971	548,160,000	19.9
1981	685,185,000	23.3
1985	748,000,000	
1991	846,300,000	24.7
1998	984,003,683	27.0

			Cities (in thousands)			
	1951	1961	1971	1981	1991	1996
Ahmedabad	794	1,206	1,742	2,515	2,873	4,776
Bangalore	779	1,207	1,654	2,914	2,651	4,807
Bombay	2,839	4,152	5,971	8,227	9,990	
Calcutta	4,578	4,405	7,031	9,166	10,916	12,118
Delhi	1,384	2,359	3,647	5,714	7,175	10,298
Kanpur	705	971	1,275	1,688	1,958	
Lucknow	497	656	814	1,007	1,592	
Madras	1,416	1,729	3,170	4,277	3,795	5,361
Nagpur	449	690	930	1,298	1,622	
Poona (Pune)	345	737	1,135	1,685	1,560	

INDONESIA

	Total Population	Population Percentage of Population Urban
1950	79,538,000	12.4
1955	86,552,000	
1960	96,194,000	14.6
1965	107,041,000	
1970	120,280,000	17.1
1975	135,666,000	19.4
1980	147,490,000	22.2
1985	164,887,000	25.3
1992	183,000,000	28.8 (1990)
1998	212,941,810	36.0

Sources: *World Population Prospects: Estimates and Projections as Assessed in 1982* (New York: United Nations, 1982).
John Paxton, ed., *The Statesman's Year-Book, 1989–90,* 126th ed. (New York: St. Martin's Press, 1989).
Brian Hunter, ed., *The Statesman's Year-Book, 1993–94,* 130th ed. (New York: St. Martin's Press, 1993).

	Cities (in thousands)					
	1955	1961	1971	1980	1990	1995
Jakarta	1,865	2,907	4,576	6,503		9,161
Bandung	833	973	1,202	1,463	2,027	
Malang	280	341	422	512		
Medan	308	479	636	1,379	1,686	
Palembang	285	475	583	787		
Semarang	371	503	647	1,027	1,005	
Surabaja	929	1,008	1,556	2,028	2,421	
Ujung Pandang				709		

Sources: *U.N. Demographic Yearbook 1960, 1964, 1974.*
John Paxton, ed., *The Statesman's Year-Book, 1989–90,* 126th ed. (New York: St. Martin's Press, 1989).
Brian Hunter, ed., *The Statesman's Year-Book, 1993–94,* 130th ed. (New York: St. Martin's Press, 1993).

IRAN

	Total Population	Population Percentage of Population Urban
1956	18,955,000	30.1
1966	25,785,000	39.1
1976	33,708,000	(44.0) (1975)
1985	44,220,000	(50.2) (1982)
1989	(54,000,000)	
1991	58,100,000	54.9 (1990)
1998	68,959,931	60.0

	Cities (in thousands)				
	1956	1966	1976	1986	1991
Tehran	1,512	2,695	4,589	6,043	6,451
Abadan	226	271	308		

IRAN (CONT.)

			Cities (in thousands)		
	1956	1966	1976	1986	1991
Ahwaz	120	207	340	580	
Esfahan	255	424	842	986	
Kermanshah	125	188	336		
Mashhad	242	409	743	1,464	1,500
Qom	96	134	247	543	
Orumiyeh	68	110	165	301	
Tabriz	290	405	715	971	1,090
Shiraz	171	269	448	848	

IRAQ

	Total Population	Population Percentage of Population Urban
1947	4,816,000	33.8
1957	6,317,000	37.3
1965	8,047,000	51.1
1977	12,000,000	63.7
1983	(14,654,000)	
1988	(17,060,000)	
1990	17,856,000	74.2
1998	21,722,287	75.0

			Cities (in thousands)		
	1957	1965	1985	1987	1995
Baghdad	656	1,657	(4,648)		4,478
Basra	165	311	(617)	406	
Hilla	121	111	(215)		
Kirkuk		184	(208)	419	
Mosul	180	264	(571)	664	
Najaf		136	(243)		

Sources: *World Population Prospects: Estimates and Projections as Assessed in 1982* (New York: United Nations, 1982).
John Paxton, ed., *The Statesman's Year-Book, 1989–90,* 126th ed. (New York: St. Martin's Press, 1989).
Brian Hunter, ed., *The Statesman's Year-Book, 1993–94,* 130th ed. (New York: St. Martin's Press, 1993).

IRELAND

	Total Population	Population Percentage of Population Urban
1950	2,969,000	41.1
1955	2,921,000	
1960	2,834,000	45.8
1965	2,876,000	
1970	2,954,000	51.7

IRELAND (CONT.)

	Total Population	Population Percentage of Population Urban
1975	3,206,000	53.6
1980	3,401,000	55.3
1985	3,595,000	57.0
1992	3,550,000	
1998	3,619,480	58.0

	Cities (in thousands)						
	1946	**1951**	**1961**	**1971**	**1981**	**1986***	**1991**
Dublin	506	522	537	566	525	921	1,057
Cork	76	75	78	128	136	174	293

Sources: *U.N. Demographic Yearbook 1960, 1964, 1974.*
John Paxton, ed., *The Statesman's Year-Book, 1989–90,* 126th ed. (New York: St. Martin's Press, 1989).
Brian Hunter, ed., *The Statesman's Year-Book, 1993–94,* 130th ed. (New York: St. Martin's Press, 1993).

* Includes Dún Laoghaire.

ISRAEL

	Total Population*	Population Percentage of Population Urban
1950	(1,748,000)	(71.7) (1951)
1961	2,183,000	77.9
1972	3,148,000	85.3
1983	4,037,600	(86.8) (1982)
1992	5,170,000	91.6 (1990)
1998	5,643,966	91.0

* These figures exclude the Occupied Territories of the West Bank and the Gaza Strip.

	Cities (in thousands)					
	1955	**1965**	**1972**	**1982**	**1988**	**1993**
Jerusalem	(156)	192	314	(424)	493	551
Bat Yam	16	53	100	(135)	133	
Beer Sheva	20	65	84	(113)	113	
Haifa	(158)	205	336	(382)	227	250
Holon	31	70	98	(135)	146	
Netanya	31	55	71	(102)		
Petah Tiawa	45	69	92	(124)		
Ramat Gan	56	103	118	(118)	116	
Tel Aviv	(364)	392	1,091	(1,305)		356

ITALY

	Total Population	Population Percentage of Population Urban
1951	47,159,000	
1961	49,904,000	47.7
1971	53,745,000	
1981	56,224,000	
1985	57,115,000	
1991	56,411,000	
1998	56,782,748	67.0

	Cities (in thousands)					
	1951	1965	1975	1985	1989	1994
Rome	1,652	2,485	2,868	2,832	2,816	2,693
Bari	268	332	376	367	357	355
Bologna	341	482	491	439	422	395
Catania	300	392	399	376	371	372
Florence	375	455	466	433	417	461
Genoa	688	845	806	735	714	707
Milan	1,274	1,670	1,731	1,530	1,464	1,561
Naples	1,011	1,228	1,224	1,204	1,203	1,204
Palermo	491	628	663	719	731	695
Turin	719	1,112	1,202	1,042	1,012	953

JAPAN

	Total Population	Population Percentage of Population Urban
1950	83,200,000	37.5
1960	93,419,000	
1970	103,720,000	72.1
1980	117,060,000	76.2
1985	(120,482,000)	
1988	(122,780,000)	
1991	(124,043,000)	77.0 (1990)
1998	125,931,533	78.0

	Cities (in thousands)						
	1955	1966	1975	1985	1988	1990	1995
Tokyo	7,867	11,005	11,663	8,389	8,156	8,163	7,996
Fukuoka	544	778	1,000	1,158	1,157	1,237	1,263
Kawasaki	445	856	1,020	1,080	1,114	1,174	1,196
Kitakyushu		1,047	1,060	1,062	1,035	1,026	

JAPAN (CONT.)

	1955	1966	1975	1985	1988	1990	1995
				Cities (in thousands)			
Kobe	979	1,228	1,360	1,409	1,427	1,477	1,501
Kyoto	1,204	1,379	1,460	1,490	1,419	1,416	1,456
Nagoya	1,337	1,954	2,080	2,114	2,100	2,155	2,162
Osaka	2,547	3,133	2,780	2,632	2,544	2,642	2,602
Sapporo	427	815	1,240	1,531	1,582	1,672	1,719
Yokohama	1,144	1,860	2,620	2,956	3,122	3,220	3,276

KOREA, SOUTH

	Total Population	Population Percentage of Population Urban
1950	20,357,000	21.4
1955	21,422,000	
1960	25,003,000	27.7
1965	28,530,000	
1970	31,923,000	40.7
1975	35,281,000	48.0
1980	38,124,000	56.9
1985	40,872,000	65.3
1991	43,268,000	74.4 (1990)
1998	46,416,796	83.0

Sources: *World Population Prospects: Estimates and Projections as Assessed in 1982* (New York: United Nations, 1982).
John Paxton, ed., *The Statesman's Year-Book, 1989–90,* 126th ed. (New York: St. Martin's Press, 1989).
Brian Hunter, ed., *The Statesman's Year-Book, 1993–94,* 130th ed. (New York: St. Martin's Press, 1993).

	1949	1962	1970	1980	1985	1990	1995
			Cities (in thousands)				
Seoul	1,446	2,983	5,433	8,364	9,646	10,628	10,776
Inchon (Incheon)	266	430	634	1,084	1,387	1,818	2,308
Kwangchu (Gwangju)	139	313	494	728	906	1,145	
Pusan (Busan)	474	1,271	1,842	3,160	3,517	3,798	3,814
Taegu (Daegu)	314	717	1,064	1,605	2,031	2,229	2,449
Taejon (Daejeon)	127	269	407	652	866	1,062	

Sources: *U.N. Demographic Yearbook 1960, 1964, 1974.*
John Paxton, ed., *The Statesman's Year-Book, 1989–90,* 126th ed. (New York: St. Martin's Press, 1989).
Brian Hunter, ed., *The Statesman's Year-Book, 1993–94,* 130th ed. (New York: St. Martin's Press, 1993).

MEXICO

	Total Population	Population Percentage of Population Urban
1950	25,791,000	42.6
1960	34,923,000	50.7
1970	48,225,000	58.7
1980	66,846,000	66.0 (1979)
1983	(75,103,000)	
1989	84,280,000	66.3 (1988)
1992	(84,439,000)	72.6 (1991)
1998	98,552,776	74.0

			Cities (in thousands)			
	1950	1960	1970	1980	1990	1995
Mexico City*	2,335	2,698	7,315	12,932	13,636	16,908 (1996)
Ciudad Juárez	123	(256) (1958)	436	567	798	
Guadalajara*	377	734 (1958)	1,195	2,244	2,847	2,178
Mexicali	65	172	390	510	602	

* Includes metropolitan area.

NETHERLANDS

	Total Population	Population Percentage of Population Urban
1947	9,625,000	54.6
1960	11,462,000	80.0
1971	13,061,000	(78.0) (1970)
1985	14,454,000	(88.4) (1980)
1989	14,805,240	
1992	15,129,150	
1998	15,731,112	89.0

			Cities (in thousands)				
	1955	1966	1974	1985	1989	1992	1994
Amsterdam	(864)	1,044	996	998	1,038	1,080	724
Arnhem	(116)	262	278	293	299	306	
Eindhoven	(152)	315	352	375	382	388	196
Enschede	(115)	223	238	245	250	253	
Groningen	(141)	196	203	207	206	208	
Haarlem	(166)	239	234	215	214	214	
Nijmegen	(118)	192	211	236	242	246	
Rotterdam	(712)	1,048	1,036	1,021	1,040	1,060	598
The Hague	(597)	743	682	672	684	693	445
Utrecht	(244)	434	462	504	526	539	234

NICARAGUA

	Total Population	Population Percentage of Population Urban
1950	1,098,000	34.9
1955	1,277,000	
1960	1,493,000	39.6
1965	1,750,000	
1971	1,878,000	47.0
1975	2,408,000	51.3
1980	2,771,000	55.5
1985	3,272,000	59.4
1991	3,870,000	59.7
1998	4,583,379	63.0

Sources: *World Population Prospects: Estimates and Projections as Assessed in 1982* (New York: United Nations, 1982).
John Paxton, ed., *The Statesman's Year-Book, 1989–90,* 126th ed. (New York: St. Martin's Press, 1989).
Brian Hunter, ed., *The Statesman's Year-Book, 1993–94,* 130th ed. (New York: St. Martin's Press, 1993).

	Cities (in thousands)					
	1950	**1963**	**1971**	**1979**	**1985**	**1992**
Managua	109	235	399	608	682	974

Sources: *U.N. Demographic Yearbook 1960, 1964, 1974.*
John Paxton, ed., *The Statesman's Year-Book, 1989–90,* 126th ed. (New York: St. Martin's Press, 1989).
Brian Hunter, ed., *The Statesman's Year-Book, 1993–94,* 130th ed. (New York: St. Martin's Press, 1993).

NIGERIA

	Total Population	Population (all figures are estimates) Percentage of Population Urban
1953	30,418,000	10.2
1963*	55,670,000	16.1
1975	74,870,000	
1991	88,500,000	
1998	110,532,242	40.0

	Cities (in thousands)					
	1952	**1963***	**1975**	**1983**	**1995**	**1996**
Lagos	272	665	1,061	1,097		1,518
Abeokuta	84	187	253	309		
Ibadan	459	627	847	1,060	1,365	
Ilesha	72	166	224	273		
Ilorin	41	209	282	344		
Kano	130	295	399	487	657	
Ogbomosho	140	343	432	527	712	
Oshogbo	123	209	282	345		
Port Harcourt	71	178	242	296		
Zaria	54	166	224	274		

* These figures later repudiated by the government. The figures for 1975 and 1983 must be treated with extreme caution.

NORWAY

	Total Population	Population Percentage of Population Urban
1950	3,279,000	32.2
1960	3,591,000	32.1
1970	3,874,000	42.4
1980	4,091,000	70.7
1991	4,274,000	
1998	4,419,955	73.0

				Cities (in thousands)			
	1950	1960	1970	1980	1985	1990	1995
Oslo	506	581	645	643	447	459	483
Bergen	144	152	182	181	207	213	222
Drammen		50	56	57	51	52	
Stavanger		70	79	91	94	98	103
Trondheim		93	112	128	134	138	143

PAKISTAN

	Total Population	Population Percentage of Population Urban
1951	75,842,000*	10.4
1961	93,832,000	13.1
1972	64,980,000	25.5
1981	84,250,000	28.3
1984	(93,290,000)	(29.1)
1989	(105,400,000)	(29.0)
1991	114,000,000	32.0
1998	135,135,195	35.0

* 1951 and 1961 include the population of what became in 1971 Bangladesh.

			Cities (in thousands)		
	1951	1967	1972	1981	1996
Bahawalpur	42	128	134	178	
Faisalabad	179		823	1,092	
Gujrunwala	121	263	360	597	
Hyderabad	242	620	628	795	
Karachi	1,126	2,721	3,499	5,103	(10,119)*
Kasur	63		103	155	
Lahore	849	1,674	2,165	2,922	
Multan	190	525	542	730	
Peshawar	152	274	268	555	
Rawalpindi	237	423	615	806	

* Metropolitan area.

PHILIPPINES

	Total Population	Population Percentage of Population Urban
1950	20,551,000	27.1
1955	23,858,000	
1960	27,904,000	30.3
1965	32,491,000	
1970	37,540,000	33.0
1975	42,565,000	35.6
1980	48,098,000	36.0
1985	54,709,000	39.6
1989	60,097,000	41.0 (1987)
1991	62,868,000	42.4 (1990)
1998	77,725,862	55.0

Sources: *World Population Prospects: Estimates and Projections as Assessed in 1982* (New York: United Nations, 1982).
John Paxton, ed., *The Statesman's Year-Book, 1989–90,* 126th ed. (New York: St. Martin's Press, 1989).
Brian Hunter, ed., *The Statesman's Year-Book, 1993–94,* 130th ed. (New York: St. Martin's Press, 1993).

Cities (in thousands)

	1948	1960	1973	1980	1990	1995
Quezon City	108	398	896	1,166	1,667	1,670
Caloocan		146	326	468	761	
Cebu	168	251	385	490	610	610
Davao	111	226	464	592	850	
Manila	984	1,139	1,436	1,630	1,599	1,655

Sources: *U.N. Demographic Yearbook 1960, 1964, 1974.*
John Paxton, ed., *The Statesman's Year-Book, 1989–90,* 126th ed. (New York: St. Martin's Press, 1989).
Brian Hunter, ed., *The Statesman's Year-Book, 1993–94,* 130th ed. (New York: St. Martin's Press, 1993).

POLAND

	Total Population	Population Percentage of Population Urban
1950	24,614,000	39.8
1960	29,776,000	47.5
1970	36,642,000	52.3
1978	35,061,000	(58.4) (1980)
1984	37,026,000	60.0
1990	38,038,000	61.5
1998	38,606,922	64.0

Cities (in thousands)

	1950	1966	1978	1982	1985	1989	1994
Warsaw	804	1,261	1,555	(1,621)	1,649	1,655	1,643
Bydgoszcz	163	258	338	(354)	361	380	
Gdansk	195	324	442	(461)	467	465	
Katowice	175	287	349	(365)	363	367	
Krakow	344	525	694	(726)	716	748	745

POLAND (CONT.)

	1950	1966	1978	Cities (in thousands) 1982	1985	1989	1994
Lodz	620	745	823	(844)	849	852	833
Lublin	117	206	290	(312)	324	350	
Poznan	321	421	537	(559)	553	589	583
Szczecin		141	385	(390)	391	412	418
Wroclaw	309	477	598	(625)	636	642	642

PORTUGAL

	Total Population	Population Percentage of Population Urban
1950	8,405,000	19.3
1955	8,610,000	
1960	8,826,000	22.5
1965	9,235,000	
1970	8,628,000	26.2
1975	9,425,000	27.8
1981	9,833,000	29.7
1987	10,270,000	
1991	9,860,000	
1998	9,927,556	36.0

Sources: *World Population Prospects: Estimates and Projections as Assessed in 1982* (New York: United Nations, 1982).
John Paxton, ed., *The Statesman's Year-Book, 1989–90,* 126th ed. (New York: St. Martin's Press, 1989).
Brian Hunter, ed., *The Statesman's Year-Book, 1993–94,* 130th ed. (New York: St. Martin's Press, 1993).

	1950	1960	Cities (in thousands) 1972	1981	1987	1991
Lisbon	790	817	762	807	831	678
Porto	285	305	305	327	350	350

Source: *U.N. Demographic Yearbook 1960, 1964, 1974.*

ROMANIA

	Total Population	Population Percentage of Population Urban
1956	17,489,000	31.3
1966	19,103,000	38.2
1977	21,560,000	47.5
1983	(22,553,000)	(48.5) (1982)
1987	22,940,000	51.3

ROMANIA (CONT.)

	Total Population	Population Percentage of Population Urban
1990	23,207,000	54.3
1998	22,395,848	56.0

	Cities (in thousands)						
	1956	1966	1977	1982	1987	1989	1992
Bucharest	1,237	1,519	1,807	(1,979)	1,980	2,316	
Braila	103	145	196	(225)	235	248	
Brasov		265	256	(334)	347	364	324
Cluj-Napoca			263	(301)	310	329	328
Constanta	100	202	257	(307)	323	355	350
Craiova	97	175	221	(253)	275	300	
Galati	96	152	238	(279)	293	326	326
Iasi	113	196	265	(295)	314	347	342
Ploiesti	115	192	200	(228)	234	259	
Timisoara	142	194	269	(302)	319	351	334

SAUDI ARABIA

	Total Population	Population Percentage of Population Urban
1965	(6,750,000)	
1974	7,013,000	48.7 (1970)
1983	(10,421,000)	
1990	(12,250,000)	77.3 (1990)
1992	15,440,000	
1998	20,785,955	84.0

	Cities (in thousands)				
	1956	1965	1974	1986	1993
Riyadh	(150)	225	667	2,000	3,000
Damman				1,281	
Hofuf				1,011	
Jeddah	(160)	194	561	1,400	2,500
Mecca	(200)	185	367	618	
Medina			128	500	550
Ta'if				205	

REPUBLIC OF SOUTH AFRICA

	Total Population	Population Percentage of Population Urban
1946	11,416,000	38.5
1951	12,671,000	42.6
1960	16,003,000	46.7
1970	21,488,000	47.9
1980	24,886,000	53.6
1984	26,749,000	56.0 (1985)
1986	27,607,000	56.0 (1985)
1991	33,140,000	60.0
1998	42,834,520	50.0

	Cities (in thousands)					
	1951	1960	1970	1980	1985	1995
Cape Town	578	807	1,108		1,911	2,350*
Pretoria	285	422	563	547	823	1,080
Bloemfontein	109	145	182	256	233	
Durban	493	681	851	518	982	1,137
East London	92	116	125	164	193	
Germiston	153	214	222	155	166	
Johannesburg	884	1,153	1,441	1,534	1,609	1,916
Pietermaritzburg	36	128	161	187	192	
Port Elizabeth	189	291	476	562	652	
Springs	119	142	143	154	170	

* Cape Peninsula.

SPAIN

	Total Population	Population Percentage of Population Urban
1950	27,977,000	37.0
1960	30,431,000	42.9
1970	34,041,000	54.7
1981	37,746,000	
1986	38,891,000	
1991	38,872,000	
1998	39,133,996	77.0

	Cities (in thousands)					
	1955	1965	1974	1986	1991	1994
Madrid	(1,775)	2,559	3,520	3,124	2,910	3,041
Barcelona	(1,381)	1,697	1,810	1,694	1,625	1,631
Bilbao	(247)	334	458	378	369	
Las Palmas	(171)	215	328	372	342	
Málaga	(295)	312	403	595	512	

SPAIN (CONT.)

	1955	1965	Cities (in thousands) 1974	1986	1991	1994
Palma de Mallorca	(148)	170	267	321	297	
Seville	(410)	474	489	668	659	714
Valencia	(538)	502	713	739	753	764
Valladolid	(128)	165	275	341	328	
Zaragoza	(277)	358	547	596	586	

SWEDEN

	Total Population	Population Percentage of Population Urban
1950	7,042,000	47.5
1960	7,495,000	72.8
1970	8,076,000	81.4
1980	8,320,000	83.1
1985	8,360,000	
1989	8,500,000	
1992	8,644,000	83.4
1998	8,886,738	83.0

	1955	1966	Cities (in thousands) 1974	1984	1989	1992	1994**
Stockholm*	(1,044)	1,262	1,353	1,562	1,617	1,655	704
Boras			106	100	101	102	
Göteborg*	(433)	628	688	712	730	743	445
Jönköping			108	107	110	112	
Linköping			108	116	119	124	
Malmo	(215)	380	454	229	232	235	243
Norrköping			119	118	119	121	
Örebro			118	118	120	122	
Uppsala			138	153	162	171	181
Västerås		107	118	118	118	120	

* Metropolitan area.
** Not metropolitan area.

SYRIA

	Total Population	Population Percentage of Population Urban
1950	(3,215,000)	
1960	4,565,000	36.9
1970	6,305,000	43.5

SYRIA (CONT.)

	Total Population	Population Percentage of Population Urban
1981	9,046,000	47.1
1983	(9,606,000)	
1989	(11,350,000)	(50.0)
1991	(12,560,000)	(51.8)
1998	16,673,282	53.0

			Cities (in thousands)		
	1955	1966	1970	1981	1994
Damascus	(409)	618	923	1,112	1,550
Aleppo	(408)	579	639	985	1,591
Hama	(108)	199	137	177	229
Homs	(133)	143	215	347	644
Lattakia			126	197	307

TURKEY

	Total Population	Population Percentage of Population Urban
1955	24,065,000	28.8
1965	31,391,000	34.4
1975	40,348,000	41.8
1980	44,737,000	44.0
1990	56,473,000	48.4
1993	59,870,000	
1998	64,566,511	71.0

			Cities (in thousands)			
	1955	1965	1973	1985	1990	1995
Ankara	451	971	1,553	2,251	2,542	2,720
Adana	167	347	347	776	972	1,010
Bursa	129	308	427	614	775	950
Diyarbakir		308	251	305	371	
Gaziantep	125	234	353	466	574	684
Içel				314	414	
Istanbul	1,269	2,053	3,135	5,494	6,293	7,774
Izmir	297	573	819	1,490	2,319	1,921
Konya		242	324	439	543	
Kayseri		223	297	378	461	

UNITED KINGDOM

	Total Population	Population Percentage of Population Urban (England and Wales)
1951	48,854,000	80.8
1961	51,283,000	80.0
1971	53,979,000	78.2
1981	54,285,000	76.9
1991	53,920,000	
1998	58,970,119	89.0

	Cities (in thousands)				
	1951	1966	1973	1983	1992
London	8,348	7,914	7,281	6,754	6,680
Belfast	444	540	549	325 (1982)	
Birmingham	2,237	2,437	2,359	2,658	1,009
Bristol	443	429	422	388 (1981)	397
Edinburgh	469	469	450	441	440
Glasgow	1,758	980*	1,728	751	681
Leeds	1,693	1,728	1,736	2,059	722
Liverpool	1,382	1,373	1,226	1,501	479
Manchester	2,423	2,453	2,389	2,598	
Sheffield	513	486	512	534	435

* Excludes Greater Glasgow.

UNITED STATES OF AMERICA

	Total Population	Population Percentage of Population Urban
1950	151,868,000	64.0
1960	179,979,000	69.9
1970	203,984,000	73.6
1980	227,236,000	73.7
1990	248,710,000	74.0
1998	270,311,758	76.0

	Cities (in thousands; city district only)					
	1950	1960	1970	1980	1990	1996
Chicago	3,621	3,550	3,369	3,005	2,784	2,722
Dallas	434	680	844	904	1,007	1,052
Detroit	1,850	1,670	1,514	1,203	1,028	1,000
Houston	596	938	1,234	1,595	1,631	1,744
Los Angeles	1,970	2,479	2,812	2,967	3,485	3,554
New York	7,892	7,782	7,896	7,072	7,323	7,381
Philadelphia	2,072	2,003	1,949	1,688	1,586	1,478
Phoenix	107	439	584	790	983	1,159
San Antonio	408	588	654	786	936	1,068
San Diego	334	573	697	876	1,111	1,171

USSR (UNTIL 1991)*

	Total Population	Population Percentage of Population Urban
1959	208,827,000	47.9
1970	241,720,000	56.3
1979	262,436,000	62.3
1983	(272,500,000)	64.1
1989	286,717,000	65.9
1998	146,861,022	76.0

	Cities (in thousands)					
	1959	1967	1975	1983	1989	1996
Moscow	5,032	5,507	7,632	(8,396)	8,967	8,436
Baku	968	1,196	1,383	(1,638)	1,757	
Gorky	942	1,120	1,283	(1,382)	1,438	
Kharkov	934	1,125	1,357	(1,519)	1,611	
Kiev	1,104	1,413	1,947	(2,355)	2,587	
St. Petersburg	3,300	3,706	4,311	(4,779)	5,020	4,883
Minsk	509	772	1,147	(1,405)	1,589	
Novosibirsk	887 (1960)	1,064	1,265	(1,370)	1,436	1,418
Sverdlovsk	777	961	1,147	(1,269)	1,367	
Tashkent	911	1,239	1,595	(1,944)	2,073	

* After the breakup of the Soviet Union, Russia alone had a population of 148,041,000 (1990). Moscow's 1990 population was ca. 9 million.

VENEZUELA

	Total Population	Population Percentage of Population Urban
1950	5,035,000	53.8
1961	7,524,000	67.4
1971	10,721,000	75.7
1981	14,517,000	(76.1) (1980)
1983	(16,394,000)	—
1988	18,770,000	86.0 (1985)
1991	(20,230,000)	(90.0) (1990)
1998	22,803,409	86.0

	Cities (in thousands)				
	1950	1966	1971	1981	1990
Caracas*	694	1,764	1,663	2,944	2,784
Barcelona				156	
Barquisimeto	105	245	331	523	724
Cabimas		124		139	
Ciudad Guyana				314	
Maracay	65	166	367	388	
San Cristóbal		128	152	199	
Valencia	89	196	367	624	616

* Metropolitan area. City itself 1 million (1981).

VIETNAM

	Total Population	Percentage of Population Urban
1960	15,917,000	
1970	(21,154,000)	18.3
1979	52,742,000	
1984	(58,310,000)	
1989	(64,412,000	20.1
1992	(69,300,000)	21.9 (1990)
1998	76,236,259	19.0

Note: The 1960 and 1970 figures are for South Vietnam. In 1974, North and South were reunited.

	Cities (in thousands)				
	1955	1960	1973	1989	1992
Hanoi		644	1,400	1,089	2,961
Can Tho			(182)	208	
Da Nang	(100)		(492)	371	371
Haiphong		369		456	456
Ho Chi Minh City (Saigon)			(1,825)	3,169	4,000
Hué	(93)		(209)	211	211
Nha Trang			(216)	214	214

YUGOSLAVIA (UNTIL 1990)

	Total Population	Population Percentage of Population Urban
1953	16,991,000	18.5
1961	18,549,000	28.4
1971	20,523,000	38.6
1981	22,425,000	
1990	(24,107,000)	
1998	11,206,039	57.0

	Cities (in thousands)				
	1953	1961	1971	1981	1994
Belgrade	470	585	775	1,470	1,168
Ljubljana	139	134	213	305	
Nis			128	231	175
Novi Sad		102	163	258	180
Rijeka		101	132	193	
Sarajevo	136	143	271	449	
Skopje	122	166	313	505	
Split			153	181	
Zagreb	351	431	566	1,174	

CHAPTER 10

DICTIONARY OF POLITICAL TERMS, EVENTS AND ACTIONS, 1943–2000

Abadan Crisis 1951–54. The Iranian government, hoping to alleviate poverty with oil revenues, expelled the West from Abadan refineries, nationalizing the Anglo-Iranian Oil Company. However, falling production and exports undermined the position of Premier Mussadeq, who was ousted, and the oil company was placed under the control of an international consortium in August 1954.

ABC Countries 1950s term referring to the grouping of Argentina, Brazil and Chile.

Abu Musa Islands, sovereignty over which is disputed between the United Arab Emirates and Iran, which were seized by the latter in 1992, leading to fears that Iran was testing its position as the Gulf region's dominant power following Iraq's defeat in the GULF WAR.

ACP States States that, from the 1950s, were Atom Controlling Powers, able to promote nuclear fission and generate atomic energy for peaceful or military use: United States, 1945; USSR, 1949; Great Britain, 1952; France, 1960; China, 1964.

Afghanistan War Soviet troops occupied Afghanistan in December 1979, supporting the left-wing Armed Forces Revolutionary Council facing Muslim nationalist Mujaheddin resistance. Protracted guerrilla war continued while a third of the 15 million population fled to refugee camps in Pakistan and Iran. Unable to subdue the country, and with mounting losses, Russia announced in 1988 its intention to withdraw. The withdrawal was completed in February 1989. In 1992, Najibullah was ousted as Islamic rebels advanced on the capital and rebel groups began fighting one another for control. Eventually, in 1996, a group of Islamic students calling itself the Taliban emerged out of the chaos to

---

Note: Organizations are alphabetized by their acronyms.

seize control of Kabul and impose harsh fundamentalist laws. By fall 1998, Taliban controlled about 90% of the country, although only three governments—Pakistan, Saudi Arabia and the U.A.R.—recognize Taliban as Afghanistan's legitimate government. United Nations-sponsored peace talks broke down in 1998, and the UN continues to recognize the government of former president Burhanuddin Rabbani, who now heads the opposition alliance.

Afrikaner Resistance Movement (AWB)   A far-right neo-Nazi white extremist group in South Africa. Led by Eugene Terre Blanche, it vehemently opposes black rule and advocates a separate white homeland. It is believed to have considerable support within the government security services. In late 1993 it was reported to have agreed to cooperate with the INKATHA FREEDOM MOVEMENT to oppose the popular ANC (African National Congress). Inkatha, however, agreed at the last moment to participate in the April 1994 elections. The AWB has indicated that it will engage in violence to further its ends, and it is believed to be responsible for the car-bombings that took place just before the elections were held. As of May 1994, its support appeared to be shrinking rapidly.

Afro-Asian Conference   See BANDUNG CONFERENCE.

Agitprop   (Agitation-Propaganda)   Theatrical device employed by the political left in Europe and the United States in the 1950s and 1960s to convey a political message or political education. Seeking to interest and entertain, it developed into what is now termed "street theater."

Agrogorod   (Russ., "agro-town")   Agricultural institution in which farm workers would live in apartment blocks like city dwellers, and would have private plots grouped together in a common area. First proposed by Nikita Khrushchev in 1949, it was dropped after criticism in *Pravda* and at the Nineteenth Communist Party Congress. It was revived when Khrushchev became chairman of the Council of Ministers, and was put into effect between 1959 and 1965 under a different name.

Agudas Israel   Right-wing Israeli political party.

AID   (Agency for International Development)   Agency created by the United States government in 1961 for coordination and administration of United States economic aid.

Algiers Conference   1973. A meeting of Third World nations to consider more effective means of cooperative action.

Aliya   (Heb., "going up")   Among Jews, a call to read in the synagogue a passage from the Torah. The term is also applied to the "going up" or "return" of diaspora Jews to Israel.

Alliance For Progress   A program established in 1961 by the Kennedy administration to further economic development in Latin America, and thereby prevent the spread of communism.

Amethyst **Incident**   20 April to 31 July 1949. The British frigate *Amethyst* was shelled on the Yangtze River, a hitherto international waterway claimed exclusively by Chinese Communists. Seventeen crew members were killed. A failed rescue attempt led to further casualties. *Amethyst* remained moored on the river until successfully breaking out on 30/31 July.

Amnesty International   International organization founded by Peter Benenson, a British lawyer, in 1961. It campaigns for the release of political prisoners who have neither committed nor advocated acts of violence, seeks to help their families, and works to improve international standards of treatment of prisoners and detainees. Based in London, it is funded entirely by private subscription and was awarded the Nobel Peace Prize in 1972.

ANC   (African National Congress)   Party formed in Bloemfontein in 1912 to protect the interests of the black majority in South Africa. In 1926 it decided to work for a democratic and racially integrated South Africa. It was banned by the South African government in 1961. The ban was lifted in 1990 and Nelson Mandela *(q.v.)* released. The party is now the major political force in South Africa and is the majority party in the first post-apartheid government.

ANZUS Pact   Tripartite security treaty concluded on 1 September 1951 in San Francisco among Australia, New Zealand and the United States, providing for mutual collaboration should any of the three be subject to an armed attack in the Pacific area. The pact marked a new independence from British control in the foreign affairs of Australia and New Zealand. New Zealand was later to withdraw from the ANZUS Pact.

Apartheid   (Afrikaans, "apartness")   South African government policy based on the belief in white supremacy and racial purity, and involving total discrimination between blacks and whites. Some degree of racial segregation had existed in South Africa since the 17th century and was continued by the United Party of Smuts and Herzog after 1934. When the National Party came to power in 1948, oppressive measures against the majority nonwhite population steadily increased. These measures included the 1949 Prohibition of Mixed Marriages Act, the 1950 Suppression of Communism Act, the 1950 Group Areas Act, and the much-criticized 1963 "Ninety-Day Law" under which the police had powers of arbitrary confinement without recourse to the courts. The result was the suppression of all internal opposition to white supremacy. Recent years have seen the abandonment of much of this legislation. The last pillars of apartheid were dismantled in the early 1990s.

Arab League See p. 2.

Arms Race Continuous competition between the USSR and the West, particularly the United States, to establish technical and numerical superiority in arms production.

Arusha Declaration 1967. A call by Tanzanian president Julius Nyerere to develop the national economy through state ownership but locally administered village planning, and for the Tanzanian people to emulate his own simple lifestyle.

ASEAN See p. 4.

Aswan Dam Construction of this dam on the Nile River, central to Nasser's industrial and agricultural development program for Egypt, appeared thwarted when the United States and Great Britain withdrew a promise of aid on 20 July 1956, The latter action led to Nasser's nationalization of the Suez Canal on 26 July, the Suez Crisis, and Nasser's appeal to the USSR for funds, which were not received until 1970.

Atlantic Charter This declaration of principles for a postwar world and shared democratic ideals emerged from a meeting off Newfoundland between Roosevelt and Churchill on 9–12 August 1941. Among the principles agreed to by the Allies, including the USSR and 14 other states at war with the Axis powers, were open seas, equal access to trade and raw materials, lives without fear and want, renunciation of force as a means of settling disputes, and the creation of a means for securing world security, democratic government, the disarming of aggressors, and the easing of the international arms burden.

Austrian State Treaty 15 May 1955. The United States, USSR, Great Britain and France ended their joint occupation of Austria and withdrew all troops by 25 October 1955. Austria was restored to its frontiers of 1937, and union with Germany was forbidden. The treaty raised hopes of Soviet agreement to withdraw troops from Eastern Europe.

Awami League A political party proposing independence for East Pakistan, which won 167 seats out of 300 in the Pakistan general election held in December 1970. The Pakistani authorities refused to open the new National Assembly and civil war broke out. The leader of the Awami League, Sheikh Mujibur Rahman, became prime minister of the new nation of Bangladesh, but in January 1975 abolished all political parties and replaced them by a single party.

Ayatollah   Title given to the most renowned teachers and scholars of Islamic law in Shiite Iran. Demands for the return of exiled Ayatollah Khomeini led to the Islamic revolution in Iran in 1979. Since then, real power has lain with senior Shiite Muslim clergy of the Revolutionary Council.

Ayodhya   Site in northern India of a Muslim mosque that Hindus believe conceals the birthplace of the god Rama. A violent attempt by Hindu nationalists to tear down the mosque (inflamed by the revivalist Bharatiya Janata Party) brought about the fall of the Indian government in November 1990. Hindu militants seized the site in December 1992, provoking communal violence throughout India after the destruction of the mosque. It was estimated that more than 1,000 people died in the subsequent rioting.

Azad Kashmir   (Urdu, "Free Kashmir")   Pakistan's slogan for the campaign to detach the state of Kashmir from India.

Azania   Name used by some black nationalists to refer to South Africa.

Baader-Meinhof Group   (Red Army Faction)   Post–1968 West German urban guerrillas, emerging from the radical student movement, led by Andreas Baader and Ulrike Meinhof, responsible for six killings, 50 attempted killings, bombings of U.S. military installations, and bank raids. Its leaders, captured in June 1972, later died in prison, officially by suicide.

Baaskap   Afrikaans term for the belief in white supremacy, on which the former South African government policy of separate development, APARTHEID, was based.

Ba'athist   (Arabic, "revival" or "renaissance")   Arabic party founded in 1910 by Christian Syrian Michel Aflaq. The party officially adheres to a philosophy of pan-Arabism and principles of freedom, unity and socialism. It became the Ba'ath Socialist Party in 1952 after merging with the Syrian Socialist Party. However, Ba'athists are not confined to Syria, and pan-Arab philosophy is influential in Iraq, Jordan, Lebanon and the Persian Gulf states. Ba'athists were most influential during the period of the United Arab Republic (Egypt and Syria) of the 1950s, but became disillusioned by the authoritarianism of Egypt's president Nasser. A military coup in 1961 was followed by Syria's withdrawal from the union the same year. The Ba'athist cause suffered from the failure of this experiment and from antidemocratic tendencies of Ba'athist governments in Iraq and Syria since 1963.

Baghdad Pact   February 1955.   Providing for mutual defense and economic cooperation between Great Britain, Iran, Iraq, Pakistan and

Turkey, the pact, though it contained no formal guarantee of military assistance, was alleged by the USSR to have aggressive intentions. It was renamed the Central Treaty Organization (CENTO) when Iraq withdrew in 1959, following a left-wing coup. The organization is no longer in existence.

Balance of Terror   Mutual fear of starting a nuclear war, based on the assumption that no country will use nuclear weapons because of fear of retaliation by the other side. The concept is now questioned by proponents of a "limited" nuclear war, who believe that use of nuclear weapons can be closely controlled and restricted to certain areas without provoking massive retaliation.

Baltic States   Term used for Estonia, Latvia and Lithuania, part of the Soviet Union from 1940 to 1991. Having gained their independence following World War I, the Baltics were seized by the Soviet Union in 1940 as part of the 1939 Nazi-Soviet Pact. Growing agitation for independence in the late 1980s came to a head with the abortive 19 August 1991 coup in Moscow. Declarations of independence resulted in diplomatic recognition from Scandinavia, the European Community and, most important, the United States (on 2 September). All three countries have now become UN members.

Bamboo Curtain   Term given to the physical and ideological barrier to movement across the borders of the People's Republic of China. It seems to have been lifted since the end of the U.S. embargo on exports to China in 1971, admission of China to the UN, President Nixon's visit to China and establishment of official relations with the European Community (EC) in 1975. China had been partly isolated again in diplomatic terms after the TIANANMEN SQUARE massacre, although British prime minister John Major visited Beijing in September 1991 to discuss Hong Kong, which was returned to Chinese rule in July 1997.

Bandung Conference   17–24 April 1955.   An agreement reached at a conference held in Indonesia by 29 Afro-Asian states on economic and cultural cooperation, opposition to Dutch and French colonialism, and the development of a specifically Third World nonaligned and neutral political stance during the Cold War.

Banning Order   Sanction used in South Africa under APARTHEID to prohibit a person from doing certain jobs, being quoted (even posthumously) or giving interviews to the media.

Bantustan   White South African term, meaning "Bantu national homeland," denoting an area of land set aside for use and occupation by black Africans and granted a nominal independence that was not recognized outside South Africa. Examples were the Transkei and Bophuthatswana. The bantustans ceased to exist when majority rule came about in 1994.

Basic Treaty   21 December 1972.   A treaty of friendship and mutual recognition between the Federal Republic of Germany and the German Democratic Republic; the culmination of West German chancellor Willy Brandt's *Ostpolitik*, followed by entry of both to the UN in 1973.

Bassijis   Members of the Bassij (Farsi, "those who are mobilized"), formed in Iran in 1980 as a volunteer militia to fight in the 1980–88 war with Iraq. In 1993 they were remobilized and expanded as a militia force to fight "the enemy within" of growing Western influences.

Bay of Pigs   17–20 April 1961.   A CIA-backed invasion of Cuba by 1,500 anti-Castro exiles, who were confident they would spark an internal uprising. Planned under President Eisenhower, initially vetoed by President Kennedy, all participants were killed or captured. The invasion resulted in an increase in Castro's domestic popularity, Cuba's turning to the USSR for support and Kennedy's intensifying efforts to control CIA overseas activity in the future (see p. 447).

Begin Doctrine   Doctrine pronounced by Israeli prime minister Menachem Begin *(q.v.)* that the enemies of Israel must never be allowed to possess weapons of mass destruction. It prompted the Israeli air strike against Iraq's nuclear reactor in June 1981.

Benelux   Acronym for Belgium, Netherlands and Luxembourg, and the customs union between them established in 1948. A treaty establishing an economic union was concluded at The Hague in 1958 and came into force on 1 November 1960. This provided for free movement of goods, traffic, services and population between the three member states; a common trade policy and coordination of investment; and agricultural and social policies.

Bennite   Supporter of British Labour Party politician Tony Benn (1925–   ), member of Parliament for Chesterfield, former minister and member of the Labour Party National Executive Committee. The term has been misused to refer to all sections of the left indiscriminately, including the Trotskyist Militant Tendency, of which Benn is not a member. By 1991, Bennite influence in the Labour Party had considerably declined.

Berlin Blockade   June 1948 to May 1949.   With Berlin under four-power administration, the USSR, alleging the West had broken postwar agreements on German status, and hoping to force the United States, Great Britain and France out, imposed obstacles to road and river traffic entering the western sector of Berlin. The West responded with a round-the-clock airlift of fuel, food, mail and personnel to relieve the beleaguered city.

Berlin Wall The East Berlin riots of 1953 and the continuing disparity in living standards encouraged a stream of refugees from East to West Berlin. The communist authorities responded on 13 August 1961 by blocking 68 of 80 border crossing points and constructing a wire-and-concrete barrier that became a permanent feature of the city. All this changed with the revolutions in Eastern Europe in 1989. Dismantling of the wall began, and in October 1990 Berlin became the capital of a reunited Germany.

Bevanite Member of the British Labour Party supporting the position of Aneurin Bevan (1897–1960) on defense policy in the early 1950s. Bevan was defeated by the reformist Hugh Gaitskell in 1955. After opposing the shadow cabinet on defense issues in the early 1950s, Gaitskell was appointed shadow foreign secretary in 1957, and argued in favor of Britain retaining the H-bomb in opposition to the Bevanites at the party conference.

Bhopal Disaster 3 December 1984. Leakage of toxic gas from the Union Carbide pesticide plant near Bhopal, capital of the central Indian state of Madhya Pradesh, due to the buildup of pressure in an underground storage tank, led to 3,000 deaths and 200,000 severely injured persons.

Biafra War July 1967 to January 1970. The secession from Nigeria of Ibos under Colonel Ojukwu and the creation of the Biafra Republic in eastern Nigeria led President Gowon to order an attack on 7 July 1967, opening a civil war in which the United Kingdom and USSR supplied the federal government and France armed Biafra. The war ended in January 1970, with the territory placed under military administration (see p. 311–12).

Bicameral Composed of two legislative chambers. Generally consisting of upper and lower chambers. Both chambers can usually initiate legislation but the more important and controversial bills are generally introduced in the lower chamber.

Big Five Permanent members of the UN Security Council: United States, Russia (formerly USSR), Great Britain, China and France.

Big Three Leaders of the major Allied powers in World War II: Prime Minister Winston Churchill, Marshal Joseph Stalin, and President Franklin D. Roosevelt.

Birchers   Members of the right-wing John Birch Society in the United States in the late 1950s and early 1960s obsessed with the threat of communism to Christianity and American democracy.

Bisho Massacre   7 September 1992.   Troops opened fire on 70,000 African National Congress (ANC) demonstrators in the South African Ciskei "homeland," killing at least 28 and injuring 190. The massacre temporarily delayed the resumption of talks on the South African peace process, as both the ANC and the South African government charged each other with responsibility.

Bizonia   Economic union of British and American zones of Germany, 25 June 1947, following disagreement between the four occupying powers. The economic council of Bizonia in Frankfurt-am-Main had a quasi-governmental role, but remained under the ultimate authority of the occupying powers. France joined Bizonia in July 1948.

Black Africa   Sub-Saharan Africa; those African states under majority or black rule.

Black Berets   Soviet Interior Ministry troops. Used as "special forces" to suppress nationalism in Lithuania and Latvia in early 1991. The 62,000 OMON, or Black Berets, formed the central corps of troops of the Interior Ministry. Recruited from the Slav population, they were among the fittest, most politically reliable and best-trained troops in the Soviet Union. The failed coup of August 1991 left them discredited.

Black Consciousness   Movement in South Africa to reestablish confidence and pride in black people. The movement was banned by the South African government, and Steve Biko, its leader, died under suspicious circumstances in 1977 while in police detention.

Black Monday   Term applied to the collapse of the New York Stock Exchange on 19 October 1987, when the Dow Jones Industrial Average fell by 22.6 percent, bringing major falls in other markets around the world. It was the worst fall since 1929.

Black Muslims   Radical U.S. BLACK POWER movement led by Malcolm X that attained the height of its popularity in the 1960s.

Black Power   Movement that emerged in the United States in the 1960s to express the dissatisfaction of black people with their position in American society. It rejected integration and asserted the intellectual and cultural equality of blacks and whites. The movement was most aggressive in the late 1960s.

Black Saturday   Attack on Cairo's European quarter on 22 January 1952 by members of the Muslim brotherhood, socialists and students, using the slogans "Allah akbar" and "We want arms to fight for the (Suez) Canal." Four hundred buildings, including symbols of the British presence, were damaged and 17 Britons killed.

Black September   Palestinian terrorist organization founded in 1970. In February 1970 King Hussein of Jordan sought to curtail activities of the Palestine Liberation Organization, which responded with violence, leading to civil war (17–25 September). Government forces eventually imposed their authority. Black September, which was founded following these events, was responsible for the kidnapping attempt at the Munich Olympic Games in 1972 and other atrocities.

Bloody Sunday   30 January 1972.   Thirteen civilians were killed by British paratroops in Londonderry, Northern Ireland, while demonstrating in favor of a united Ireland.

Blunt Affair   Sir Anthony Blunt, a British intelligence officer from 1940 to 1945 and later the queen's personal advisor on art, confessed in 1964 to being a Soviet agent since the 1930s and to being the "fourth man" in the BURGESS-MACLEAN SCANDAL. Revelation in a book published in 1979 that he was granted immunity from prosecution forced Britain's prime minister Thatcher to confirm Blunt's role on 15 November. The queen annulled his knighthood the following day.

Boat People   Those who fled Vietnam after the victory of the Communist North Vietnamese over the south in 1975. They included many Chinese, and included those who were either political refugees or people simply unwilling to live in a communist state. Forced to take to sea in open boats, they tried to land in Malaysia, Hong Kong and elsewhere; thousands drowned or fell prey to pirates. The problem became acute again in the 1980s as economic hardship in Vietnam provoked further waves of refugees into Hong Kong. Against an international outcry, Great Britain began repatriation to Vietnam in December 1989.

Bofors Scandal   Political scandal in India surrounding arms purchases worth $1.3 billion from the Swedish Bofors Company. On 18 July 1989, a report cited corruption within the Indian government. Although Prime Minister Rajiv Gandhi was not involved, the scandal contributed to his election defeat in November 1989.

Boipatong Massacre   Township in South Africa, 40 miles from Johannesburg, scene of a massacre on 17 June 1992 of 42 men, women and children. The massacre was allegedly carried out by 200 INKATHA supporters with the connivance of the South African security forces.

Bokassa Affair   Amid embarrassing charges made in 1979 that French president Giscard d'Estaing had received gifts of diamonds and a hunting lodge from the self-proclaimed Emperor Bokassa, a corrupt, ostentatious and allegedly cannibalistic dictator of the Central African Republic, a former French colony, French troops were dispatched to hasten the emperor's ouster on 21 September 1979.

BOSS Bureau of State Security, the South African secret police force, accused of many illegal actions both within South Africa and abroad.

Braceros (Span.) Farm workers from Mexico legally admitted to the United States between 1942 and 1964 for temporary work. A scheme designed to stop illegal immigrants (sometimes called WETBACKS) by regulating immigration and conditions of employment was abandoned in 1964.

Brandt Report February 1980. "North-South: A Program for Survival," generated by the Brandt Commission, headed by the former West German chancellor, advocated a restructuring of the world economy, financial institutions, and development plans to stimulate growth, trade and confidence in order to avert divisions between North and South threatening eventual crisis.

Brazzaville Declaration January 1944. An agreement between Free French leader General Charles de Gaulle and representatives of French colonies on a postwar "French Union," in which colonies would participate in French parliamentary elections, with internal economic reform, local assemblies, but no independence—an agreement opposed by Algerian nationalists.

Bretton Woods July 1944. A United Nations monetary and financial conference on postwar trade and economic development, attended by 28 countries in New Hampshire, agreed on the formation of the International Monetary Fund, for individual countries to draw on to balance payments, and a World Bank, to make loans for national economic development. Both institutions were created to avoid a recurrence of the inter-war depression.

Brezhnev Doctrine An assertion by Soviet Communist Party first secretary Brezhnev of the legitimacy of intervention by one socialist state in the affairs of another when the central role of the Communist Party itself appeared threatened. The doctrine was demonstrated in the Warsaw Pact invasion of Czechoslovakia on 20–21 August 1968, which ended the liberalizing "Prague Spring."

Brinkmanship The policy of forcing a rival power to reach agreement by deliberately creating risk of nuclear war. John Foster Dulles, U.S. secretary of state (1953–59), told *Life* magazine in 1956 that "if you are scared to go to the brink you are lost."

Broederbond (Afrikaans, "brotherhood") Secret South African society formed shortly after the Boer War. The group sought to maintain dominance of Afrikaners over English South Africans in political, economic and cultural life.

Brussels, Treaty of 17 March 1948. A 50-year mutual guarantee among Belgium, Great Britain, France, Luxembourg and the Netherlands to provide military and other assistance in the event of attack; with the adherence of West Germany and Italy in May 1955, it became the Western European Union, intended to further West European unity.

Bundestag The former West German federal parliament, established by the "basic law" or constitution of 23 May 1949. Elected by universal suffrage for a fixed four-year term of office, its members pass federal laws and submit them to the upper chamber (Bundesrat). With the reunification of Germany in October 1990 it is the parliament for all Germany.

Burgess-Maclean Scandal Guy Burgess, second secretary at the British embassy in Washington, and Donald Maclean, head of the U.S. Department at the British Foreign Office, disappeared on 25 May 1951, resurfacing later in the Soviet Union, confirming they had been long-term communist agents, and leading to speculation on the identity of the "third man" who had warned them that their unmasking had been imminent. The "third man" was later revealed to be Kim Philby and the "fourth man" Sir Anthony Blunt. A "fifth man," John Cairncross, was exposed in 1991.

Busing The strategy adopted by some local school districts in the United States under court orders to integrate their schools. It involves transporting schoolchildren by bus from predominantly white or predominantly black neighborhoods to create racially mixed schools. The policy has attracted hostility from members of both groups.

Butskellism From the surnames of R. A. Buder, the British Conservative chancellor of the Exchequer, 1951–55, and Hugh Gaitskell, leader of the Labour Party, a term denoting agreement between parties and continuity between Labour and Conservative administrations in economic policy, specifically on the need for economic planning and for limited state ownership and interventions in industry.

Cairo Conference 22–26 November 1943. A declaration on 1 December by Roosevelt, Churchill and Jiang Kaishek demanded Japan's unconditional surrender to end the war in Asia. Japan was to be forced back to its 1894 boundaries; Taiwan was to be restored to China; and the Japanese presence in Korea and Manchuria was to be ended.

Camp David Talks   5–17 September 1978.   Peace talks among Egyptian president Sadat, Israeli premier Begin and U.S. president Carter resulting in a treaty signed in Washington on 25 March 1979, opening Egyptian-Israeli economic and diplomatic relations and agreeing to the return of occupied Sinai to Egypt. Hopes of developing an autonomous Palestinian state on the West Bank foundered in the face of Israeli internal opposition and PLO antagonism to the treaty.

CAP   Common Agricultural Policy of the EU (see p. 15), dictating farming and other primary production policies of member states. It allocates subsidies to various sectors of European agriculture.

Carnation Revolution   25 April 1974.   The Portuguese dictator Marcel Caetano was ousted by the army, with the carnation as a popular revolutionary symbol. General Spinola became provisional president in May 1974.

Casablanca Conference   14–24 January 1943.   A meeting between Roosevelt and Churchill at which the Anglo-American Allies reiterated their insistence on unconditional surrender by the Axis powers, decided to invade Italy through Sicily and to intensify bombing of Germany before mounting an attack on occupied France, and agreed that more British forces should go to the Far Fast following victory in Europe.

Casablanca Group   Representatives of the Algerian provisional government, Egypt, Ghana, Guinea, Libya, Mali and Morocco, who met in Casablanca in January 1961 to adopt the Casablanca Charter. The Charter, which had a radical socialist theme, aimed at creating an African Common Market and a joint military command structure.

Caudillismo   (Span., *caudillo*, "leader")   In Latin American politics, a system in which the *caudillo* as leader or head of state exercises almost absolute authority. It is related to the "personalismo" whereby a leader is glorified at the expense of party interest, ideology and constitution.

CENTO   See under BAGHDAD PACT.

Central African Federation   3 September 1953.   A British attempt to protect the interests of the white minority population and to encourage economic development by uniting the African territories of Nyasaland and Northern and Southern Rhodesia. Unpopular with the predominatly African population, it collapsed in 1963.

Cetnik   Serbian guerrillas (also rendered *Chetniks*) who at first opposed German occupation. Serbian rather than Yugoslavian nationalists, they opposed communism, and some commanders collaborated with the Germans and Italians during World War II.

CGT   (Confederation Generale du Travail)   The French national trade-union organization.

Charlottetown Accord   An attempt by Canadian premier Brian Mulroney to satisfy the aspirations of French-speaking Quebec by devolving greater power to the provinces, and thereby to encourage Quebec to remain in the confederation. The proposals were rejected in a national referendum.

Charter 77   A declaration signed by Czech human-rights activists, despite fears of intimidation, arrest and dismissal, arguing their claim for the individual liberties ostensibly recognized by the Soviet Union in the 1975 Helsinki Agreement.

Chechnya   Formerly the Chechen-Ingush Autonomous Soviet Socialist Republic, Chechnya declared independence from Russia after the breakup of the USSR in 1991. Three years later, Russia tried to regain control, and the long and bloody war resulted in over 70,000 casualties. When the war ended in 1996, Chechnya considered itself independent and held democratic elections in 1997. However, the international community still considers the area Russian. In 1999, Russia blamed Chechen rebels for bombings in Moscow and sent in ground troops as well as launching air strikes to destroy Chechen communications and infrastructure. Meanwhile, 125,000 Chechens have fled the region.

Chernobyl   April 1986.   A major accident in a Soviet light-water nuclear reactor in the Ukraine sent a radioactive cloud spreading through Scandinavia and Central Europe, contaminating agricultural produce. Though immediate casualties were said to be low (31 dead), by 1993 independent observers calculated that 5,000 had died of radiation and 350,000 were suffering radiation-related illnesses.

Chindits   (Burm., *Chinthe'*, a mythical winged beast of great ferocity)   A force raised by British general Orde Charles Wingate to operate behind Japanese lines in Burma in 1943 and 1944.

Christmas Revolution   Term applied to the popular uprising in Romania in December 1989 against the Ceausescu dictatorship. (See p. 244).

CIA   U.S. Central Intelligence Agency, established in 1947 to coordinate and analyze foreign intelligence reports to the president, to whom alone it is responsible. Under the directorship of Allen Dulles in the 1950s, the CIA moved into more active involvement in foreign affairs, initiating a series of "covert operations" designed to eliminate anti-American interests in such countries as Guatemala and Iran. The 1961 BAY OF PIGS debacle forced a reassessment of the CIA's function, and subsequent scandals and alleged domestic civil rights abuses have led to further calls for accountability and reform; however, despite criticism, the agency has maintained its controversial dual role of intelligence source and coercive arm for American interests.

Cienfuegos crisis   Intelligence gathered by American U-2 aircraft in September 1970 suggested that the Soviet Union was building a nuclear submarine base at Cienfuegos, Cuba, breaking the agreement that had ended the 1962 CUBAN MISSILE CRISIS. On 27 September the USSR assured the United States that no base would be bullt, and the United States reiterated its 1962 pledge not to overthrow the Cuban government.

CIS   See pp. 9–10.

Clintonomics   The initial economic policies of the newly elected U.S. president Bill Clinton (who took office in 1993) that emphasized the need for economic growth and the creation of jobs.

Closed Shop   A factory or other industrial establishment in which all the employees are members of a trade union. Various legislative attempts have been made to regulate the operation of closed shops in Great Britain. The closed shop was made illegal by the Thatcher government in the 1980s. In the United States they are prohibited by the Taft-Hartley Act, 1947.

CND   The Campaign for Nuclear Disarmament, launched on 17 February 1958 by Bertrand Russell and Canon L. John Collins to demand abandonment of nuclear weapons and a large reduction in British defense expenditures. The movement attracted support in 1960–61, after which it was much less successful, until 1979, following a NATO decision to site new nuclear missiles (cruise and Pershing) in Europe. After that its support increased considerably, but waned again with the ending of the Cold War.

CODESA   Convention for a Democratic South Africa. Discussions (1991–93) involving most of the significant black and white political forces in South Africa in an attempt to create an internationally recognized democratic constitution. See also NEGOTIATIONS FORUM.

Cod War   Popular term for diplomatic dispute, starting in 1958, between Great Britain and Iceland over the latter's unilateral decision to extend its 12-mile fishing limit to 50 miles.

Cohabitation   Term used to describe the political situation in France following the 1986 parliamentary election. With two years remaining before the end of President François Mitterrand's first term of office, the right won a majority of seats in parliament. The subsequent conservative government and socialist president tolerated and worked alongside each other. Mitterrand faced cohabitation again from 1993–95 during his second term in office.

Cold War   Protracted state of tension between the superpowers falling short of actual warfare. The term was first used in the U.S. Congress to describe deteriorating relations between the United States and the USSR. It describes the period of tension between 1946 and the early 1970s and the accompanying crises (Greek Civil War, Berlin, Cuba). The divisions were formalized by the creation of NATO (1949–50) and the WARSAW PACT (1955). With the advent of Gorbachev in the USSR, and the fall of communist regimes in Eastern Europe after 1989, it was effectively over. It was formally ended by the signing of the CONFERENCE ON SECURITY AND COOPERATION IN EUROPE (CSCE) on 19 November 1990.

Colombo Plan   January 1950. An attempt by British Commonwealth foreign ministers to encourage Southeast Asian development, with assistance in training, public administration, health, economic and scientific research programs, and the provision of essential equipment and personnel. It was joined later by the United States, which provided the bulk of the funds.

Colonels, Greek   Military junta that seized power in Greece on 21 April 1967. The coup was led by two colonels, George Papadopoulos and Stylianos Pattakos, who suspended the democratic constitution. The regime collapsed in July 1974, following its intervention in Cyprus.

Comecon   See p. 12.

Cominform   Information agency formed in 1947 and dissolved in 1956. Its members were the communist parties of Bulgaria, Czechoslovakia, France, Hungary, Italy, Poland, Romania, the Soviet Union and Yugoslavia (expelled in 1948), though membership was not obligatory for communist parties. It sought to promote party unity through dissemination of information.

Common Market   See under EU, p. 15.

Community Politics   Concentration on the local interests of voters rather than national issues, developed by the Liberal Party in Great Britain in the 1970s and imitated by major British parties.

Conakry Declaration   Charter signed by Ghana and Guinea on 1 May 1959 agreeing to create a union between the two countries as a preliminary to forming a wider African Union of States. Although joined by Mali on 1 July 1961, the attempt had no genuine political results.

Conducator   (Romanian, "leader")   The title used by the Romanian dictator, Nicolai Ceausescu *(q.v.)*.

Conference on Security and Cooperation in Europe   (CSCE) Major agreement of 19 November 1990, signed in Paris, that marked the formal end of the Cold War. Part of this agreement was the signing of the Conventional Forces in Europe (CFE) Treaty by 22 NATO and WARSAW PACT countries formalizing the biggest cuts in weapons and manpower since the end of World War II. In July 1992 the 52 CSCE members agreed to make CSCE an effective body in the prevention of war and the promotion of political stability.

Congress Party   Indian political party that grew out of the Hindu-dominated nationalist Congress movement of the independence struggle. It has dominated most of Indian political life since independence.

Constructive Engagement   The U.S. policy of attempting to produce change in South Africa by fostering good relations with Pretoria.

Containment   Policy adopted by the United States in 1947 in response to Russian expansion after World War II, with the aim of containing communist influence within its existing territorial limits.

Contras   Known collectively as the Nicaraguan Democratic Front, former Nicaraguan National Guardsmen who, following the 1979 overthrow of the rightist Somoza regime, fled to Honduras, from where they continued to oppose the Sandinista government. The contras received American military aid until June 1984; the Reagan administration's subsequent attempts to aid them covertly resulted in the "Iran-Contra" scandal. More recently, they have engaged in negotiations stemming from the 1987 Central American peace initiative. A cease-fire was eventually agreed to, and with the electoral defeat of the Sandinistas in February 1990 by Violetta Chamorro, the activities of the contras have effectively ceased.

CORE   Congress of Racial Equality, founded in the United States in 1942 to obtain civil rights for blacks.

COSAG   Concerned South Africans Grouping. A loose alliance led by Inkatha, representing conservative Zulus, the far-right Conservative Party, and Afrikaner separatist groupings, which disagreed with the decision of the NEGOTIATIONS FORUM on 2 July 1993 that South Africa would hold free multiracial elections on 27 April 1994.

Cruise Missile   An accurate and virtually undetectable nuclear missile with possible first-strike capability, the U.S. deployment of which in Western Europe from 1983 on encouraged a growth in antinuclear agitation, particularly in Great Britain, West Germany and the Netherlands.

CSCE See CONFERENCE ON SECURITY AND COOPERATION IN EUROPE.

Cuban Missile Crisis 16–22 October 1962. When U.S. intelligence revealed deployment of Soviet nuclear missiles in Cuba, President Kennedy demanded their withdrawal, mounting a naval blockade to prevent Russian ships from landing a further 42 missiles. Premier Khrushchev initially refused, but then agreed on condition that the U.S. remove its missiles from Turkey. Then, as war appeared imminent, the Soviet Union withdrew its missiles in return for Kennedy's promise not to invade Cuba.

Cult of Personality A political phenomenon whereby a leader, usually the head of state, is elevated above his colleagues to a position where he is seen as responsible for all the nation or party's achievements but for none of its failures. Such elevation is achieved by a massive propaganda exercise including posters and statues of the leader, the naming of towns after him, and so on. Joseph Stalin (1879–1953) set the pattern as Soviet leader but others have followed, for example Mao Zedong in China.

Cultural Revolution Term for the reassertion of Maoist doctrines in China between 1966 and 1976, following incitement to students by Marshal Lin Biao to adopt a critical attitude toward liberal and "Khrushchevian" elements in the Chinese Communist Party. A personality cult of Mao Zedong was also inaugurated.

Dáil Éireann (Ir., "assembly of Ireland") House of Representatives, lower chamber of the Irish Parliament (OIREACHTAS), with 144 members elected for five years by adult suffrage on a system of proportional representation. Often abbreviated to Dáil.

Dalai Lama (Tibetan, high ["ocean wide"] priest) Spiritual and temporal leader of Tibet, held always to be a reincarnation of the first Dalai Lama. In 1951 Chinese troops occupied Tibet and, following a rebellion in 1959, the Dalai Lama and some 9,000 followers fled to India. A delegation of lamas returned to Tibet in the 1980s, but the Dalai Lama remains in exile.

Death Squad An expression first used in the 1960s to describe unofficial units of the Brazilian police who tortured and killed criminals, turning in the late 1960s to action against political opponents. Similar squads have been active in Argentina, Haiti, Guatemala, El Salvador and Honduras. Terror activity of this type was an element of the "counter-insurgency" techniques taught by the U.S. military and the Central Intelligence Agency (CIA). Pentagon involvement in organization and finance has been alleged.

Delors Plan   Plan drawn up by the Delors Committee, set up in 1948 and headed by the president of the Commission of the European Economic Community, Jacques Delors. The Plan consisted of measures to create greater monetary and political unity in the EEC. The first phase projected creation of the European Monetary System (EMS), in which all countries would participate, and would also permit coordination of economic policies throughout the community. Phase two proposed setting up a European system of central banks that would gradually assume greater control over national monetary policy. Much of the plan was opposed by former British prime minister Margaret Thatcher (p. 516). Recent convulsions in the ERM (Exchange Rate Mechanism) have left much of the plan in disarray.

Demilitarized Zone   Zone along the 38th parallel dividing North and South Korea, established in 1953 following invasion of South Korea by the communist north in 1950. The term was also used between 1954 and 1975 with reference to the 17th parallel between North and South Vietnam.

Descamisados   (Span., "the shirtless ones")   The urban poor in Argentina, who supported Juan Domingo Perón (1895–1974), dictator in 1946 following civil disturbances by the *descamisados* the previous year aimed at securing his release from prison.

Destalinization   Process initiated at the 1956 Twentieth Party Congress in the USSR, following the death of Stalin in 1953, by Nikita Khrushchev (1894–1971), first secretary of CPSU, who criticized Stalin's personality cult and purges of the 1930s. Stalin's body was removed from Lenin's mausoleum, statues were removed and place names changed. Even in Albania, the last outpost of Stalinism, the process was complete by 1991.

Detente   (Fr., "relaxation")   Diplomatic term for diminution of strained relations between countries. Usually applied to improved relations between WARSAW PACT countries, led by the USSR, and the West, led by the United States, beginning in 1969 and inaugurated by Strategic Arms Limitation Talks (SALT).

Deutschmark   Originally the currency unit of West Germany and since 1991 of the united Germany. The growing strength of the Deutschmark since its creation in 1948 symbolized the success of the German postwar "economic miracle," and the currency became the monetary anchor of the European Exchange Rate in 1972. See also EXCHANGE RATE MECHANISM (ERM).

Dewline (acronym) Distant Early Warning Viewing Line, established in 1957 by North American Air Defense Command (NORAD). Section of radar systems built to detect approach of enemy missiles or aircraft. It stretches from the Aleutian Islands of Alaska across Canada to Iceland. The Soviet equivalent is the Tallinn Line.

Dirty War Term used to describe the repression by the Argentine military dictatorship between 1976 and 1983 of anyone deemed to be a guerrilla or subversive. An official enquiry in 1984 established that 9,000 people "disappeared" and thousands more were kidnapped and tortured by the military. A pardon in December 1990 that covered such leaders of the junta as Jorge Videla and Roberto Viola caused much controversy.

Disappeared Ones (Spanish, *desparecidos*) People in Latin American countries who have disappeared without trace as a result of government action. See DIRTY WAR.

Dissidents Those who refuse to conform to prevailing political and social mores. It is used to refer to individuals and groups in the former USSR who criticized abuse of human and civil rights.

Domino Theory Theory of early 1960s U.S. foreign policy that if South Vietnam became communist as a result of a North Vietnamese and Viet Cong victory, other Southeast Asian countries would follow. The premise was that all popular insurgencies or communist military efforts were directed by Moscow or Beijing as part of a worldwide plan.

Doves Americans advocating negotiation or reduction of U.S. involvement in Vietnam. The term is now applied to politicians taking moderate stances on foreign policy issues.

"Dries" Right-wing members of British Conservative Party supporting monetarist policies and opposing increases in public expenditure to alleviate social problems. They also support PRIVATIZATION, curtailment of trade union influence and a vigorous defense policy. (See also "WETS.")

Dual-Key System whereby both U.S. and host governments have to assent to the launching of American nuclear missiles based abroad.

Dual-Track NATO policy adopted in 1979 to deploy 572 medium-range missiles under U.S. control in Western Europe, while at the same time seeking bilateral negotiations between the United States and the USSR.

Dumbarton Oaks Conference August 1944. A Washington meeting of representatives from the United States, USSR, United Kingdom and China to outline international postwar security. Proposals published

7 October 1944 recommended creation of a United Nations organization to preserve world peace, including a Security Council on which the United States, USSR, United Kingdom, France and China would play a central role with veto powers.

Dumping   Sale of goods in a foreign market below the price in the home market or below production cost.

Dunkirk, Treaty of   4 March 1947.   An Anglo-French agreement to provide mutual assistance against any future German aggressive threats, together with consultation over economic relations, symbolizing postwar French reemergence as a major European power.

East Timor   The eastern part of the island of Timor in the Indonesian archipelago, East Timor was a Portuguese colony until 1975, when Indonesia annexed the area. While 90% of Indonesians are Muslim, East Timorese are primarily Roman Catholic. The people of East Timor began an independence movement almost immediately, and Indonesian military forces brutally repressed it for 25 years. More than 200,000 Timorese are reported to have died from famine, disease, and fighting since the annexation. The independence struggle received international attention in 1996, when two East Timorese activists received the Nobel Peace Prize for their efforts to bring about a peaceful resolution. In 1999, following General Suharto's departure from office, East Timorese voted overwhelmingly for independence from Indonesia in a UN–organized referendum. In the days following the election, pro-Indonesian militias kidnapped and murdered local residents and UN workers, and up to one-third of the population was forced out of the region. "Operation Warden," an Australian-led UN peacekeeping force, was sent in and the Indonesian army has promised to withdraw in phases, ending 25 years of Indonesian occupation of East Timor.

EC   See p. 14.

ECOSOC   Economic and Social Council of the UN. See p. 32.

ECU   (European Currency Unit)   A basket of European Union (EU) currencies, composed of amounts of members' currencies in proportion to their economic strength. The official ECU is used in the European Monetary System while a private ECU is used in banking and investment activity.

EDC   (European Defense Community)   Proposal in 1952 for an international army and budget, intended to be more coherent than NATO. The idea was abandoned when the French parliament refused to ratify a draft treaty.

EEC   See p. 14.

EFTA See p. 17.

Eisenhower Doctrine 5 January 1957. A proposal of President Eisenhower that the United States would provide military and economic aid to Middle East states threatened internally or externally by communism. Congress voted $200 million. Despite acceptance of U.S. troops by Jordan (1957) and Lebanon (1958), the policy lapsed in 1959 through general unpopularity in the region.

ELAS (Ethnikós Laíkós Apeletherotikón Stratós, Hellenic People's Army of Liberation) Founded by the communist resistance in wartime Greece, ELAS wished to achieve a communist government in postwar Greece along the lines of Tito's partisans. Great Britain and the United States had supported opposing promonarchist groups since 1943, and Britain sent troops to Greece in 1944 to prevent civil war, which eventually broke out following the return of the king in 1946. The Democratic Army, successor to ELAS, was defeated in 1949 by the royalists, backed by the United States and Great Britain.

END (European Nuclear Disarmament) A British-based movement formed in 1980, originally seeking removal of all nuclear weapons from Europe. It has since become a pressure group for a reunited Europe free of Soviet or American domination.

Enola Gay The aircraft, named after the pilot's mother, from which the first atomic bomb used in war was dropped on Hiroshima, 6 August 1945.

Enosis (Gk., "to unite") Greek Cypriot movement for the political union of Cyprus and Greece, dating from the 19th century, revived in 1954 by Archbishop Makarios III, and opposed by the Turkish minority on the island, and by the Turkish government. Turkey invaded and partitioned the island in 1975.

Entebbe, Raid on 3 July 1976. Half-hour battle in which Israeli commandos rescued 106 predominantly Jewish airline passengers at Entebbe Airport, Uganda, who were hijacked by Popular Front for Liberation of Palestine guerrillas demanding the release of 53 Arab terrorists. Twenty Ugandan soldiers, seven hijackers, three passengers and one Israeli soldier were killed.

EOKA (Ethnikí Orgánosis Kypriakoú Agónos, National Organization of Cypriot Struggle) Anti-British Greek Cypriot guerrilla movement. EOKA members of the National Guard overthrew Archbishop Makarios III and provoked Turkish invasion and partition of Cyprus.

Epuration (French, "purification" or "purge") The purge of suspected Nazi collaborators in France after 1945.

ETA   Acronym of Euzkadi Ta Askatasumar, meaning "Basque Home-land and Liberty." A radical group that split from the Basque Nationalist Party in 1959. It employs terrorist tactics. Police action in 1992 crippled ETA's central organization. Between 1968 and 1992 ETA was respon-sible for 701 deaths.

Ethnic Cleansing   Euphemism that emerged during the breakup of the former Yugoslavia in 1992 to describe the campaigns to remove minority ethnic groups by causing them to flee through terror and near-genocidal violence. Most often used to describe Serb actions against the Muslim community in Bosnia and the Albanians in Kosovo.

European Economic Area (EEA)   The world's largest free trade zone, which came into being on 1 January 1994, including 370 million people and covering 1.4 million square miles. The EEA created a single market between the 12 EC (European Union [EU] from 1 January 1994) states and five members of the European Free Trade Area (EFTA)— Austria, Finland, Iceland, Norway and Sweden. Liechtenstein later be-came a member. Austria, Finland and Sweden subsequently (1995) joined the EU.

Evian Agreements   March 1962.   Overwhelmingly ratified by refer-enda in France (April) and Algeria (July), the agreements ended the Al-gerian war of independence fought against France since 1954 with an immediate cease-fire and a guarantee of French withdrawal by the end of the year.

Exchange Rate Mechanism (ERM)   A system for maintaining values of European currencies at fixed rates to one another. There was origi-nally agreement that currencies could fluctuate within a narrow (2%) or wide (6%) band on either side of a predetermined central rate, but the whole ERM was thrown into question by currency turmoil in 1993.

Falange   Spanish Fascist party, founded in 1933 and merged with other groups by Franco in 1937 to form Falange Española Tradicion-alista. The only political party allowed in Spain in the Franco era, its influence declined in later years.

Falklands War   May–June 1982.   The British-ruled Falkland (Mal-vinas) Islands (population 2,000), claimed by Argentina, were occupied by Argentine forces on 2 April 1982. Great Britain responded with a 6,000-strong naval and military task force, which landed on 21 May and captured Port Stanley on 14 June. The Argentine garrison surren-dered; the discredited mainland military government fell shortly after.

Fedayeen   (Arab., "those who risk their lives for a cause")   Pales-tinian guerrillas who carried out raids in Israel under the leadership of the Grand MUFTI. Eventually subsumed into the PLO.

Fianna Fáil (Ir., "soldiers of destiny" or "Warriors of Ireland") Party formed by Eamon de Valera (1882–1975) in 1926 from moderate members of SINN FÉIN, reflecting a reversal of the previous opposition to dominion status for Ireland. One of two major Irish political parties.

Fine Gael (Ir., "Irish Tribe") Moderate national party and one of two major Irish political parties.

Finlandization Agreement under a 1948 treaty of friendship between the Soviet Union and Finland by which, effectively in return for its independence, Finland pledged to defend the Soviet Union if any power attempted invasion through Finland.

First Strike Tactic of nuclear warfare in which the aim is to destroy an enemy's missiles while they are still on the ground, thereby forestalling retaliation.

FNLA National Front for the Liberation of Angola, an independence movement that fought alongside UMTA against the ultimately victorious MPLA in the civil war begun in 1975. Funded from China, and initially from the United States and Zaire.

Folketing Danish parliament.

Force de Frappe (Fr.) Term for France's nuclear strike force.

Free Officers Army officers in Egypt who overthrew King Farouk in 1952.

Frelimo (Frente de Libertiçao de Mocambique) Marxist liberation movement that waged a guerrilla war against the Portuguese in Mozambique from 1964 to 1974, the dominant political force in the country after independence. By 1991, it appeared that its monopoly of political power might be ending.

Gahal Political block formed in Israel in 1965 through fusion of HERUT and the Liberal Party.

Gaitskellite British Labour Party member supporting the moderate policies of Hugh Gaitskell (1906–63) in the late 1950s and early 1960s. Gaitskell was elected leader in 1955 but was forced to abandon his idea of altering the party constitution, and he was defeated on defense issues by unilateralists in 1960.

Gama'a Al Islamiya (Islamic Group) Egyptian militant Islamic organization founded in the mid-1970s, allegedly responsible for the assassination of President Sadat *(q.v)* in 1981.

Gang of Four (1) Those radical Chinese leaders—Wang Hongvven, Zhang Chungqiao, Yao Wenyuan and Jiang Qing, Mao's widow—who were publicly denounced following the triumph of moderates in 1976.

A show-trial was held following a propaganda campaign and the arrest of the four on a charge of trying to take control of the army. Jiang Qing was given a suspended death sentence in 1981.

(2) In Great Britain, name popularly given to four prominent Labour Party politicians, Roy Jenkins, Shirley Williams, William Rodgers and David Owen, who left the party and formed the Social Democratic Party in 1981.

GATT   (General Agreement on Tariffs and Trade)   An international body aimed at reducing tariffs and other restrictions and fostering free trade. Eighty percent of world trade is now covered by GATT. Founded 1948, by 1993 over 108 countries were contracting parties and 29 others were applying GATT rules. It inaugurated the Kennedy Round (1964–67), the Tokyo Round (1973–79) and the Uruguay Round (1986–93). Negotiations were eventually concluded in 1993 and over 120 nations signed the GATT accord in April 1994. GATT was succeeded by the World Trade Organization in January 1995.

Gaullist   Follower of General Charles de Gaulle (1890–1970), although there is no precise definition of Gaullism. A short-lived mass movement under the Fourth French Republic centered on the Rassemblement du Peuple Français (RPF), an authoritarian anticommunist party with fascist tendencies, which enjoyed its greatest success in the late 1940s and early 1950s. The Union de la Nouvelle République (UNR) was formed from various Gaullist groups after establishment of the Fifth French Republic in 1958. Gaullism survived the general's retirement in 1969, and it provided a basis of support for his presidential successor, Georges Pompidou.

Gaza Strip   A strip of land (146 sq. miles) extending northeast from Egypt and bordered by Israel and the Mediterranean Sea. Temporarily occupied by Israel in the 1956 Suez Crisis, and occupied again during the 1967 SIX-DAY WAR, it remained in Israeli possession and became part of the controversy surrounding Israel's holding and settling of occupied territories. It has seen much violence during the INTIFADA. It is home to 700,000 stateless Palestinians. It is seen by Arabs as part of a future Palestinian state. Granted limited self-government in 1994 under the terms of the Israel-PLO accords.

Geneva Agreements   20 July 1954.   Negotiated during a two-month conference by the foreign ministers of the United States, USSR, Great Britain, France and the People's Republic of China, they ended the French colonial war in Laos, Cambodia and Vietnam, dividing Vietnam into two states along the 17th parallel.

Gibraltar Dispute   The British territory in southern Spain commanding entrance to the Mediterranean, which was captured by Britain in 1704 and formerly served as a strategically important naval base, was claimed by Spain in 1939. The UN recognized the claim in 1963; however, Great Britain asserted that the wish of the population, expressed overwhelmingly in a referendum, was to remain British. The Spanish government closed the frontier in 1969, but, following discussions from 1977 to 1980, ended the blockade.

Glasnost   The liberalizing "openness" of the Soviet intellectual atmosphere encouraged by Mikhail Gorbachev, following his appointment as Communist Party secretary in March 1985. *Glasnost* appeared to set few limits on the discussion of contemporary Soviet society and politics and of Soviet history, particularly the Stalin period. The failed coup of August 1991 has speeded its progress.

Golan Heights   Strategically important high ground in southern Syria overlooking Israeli territory, captured by Israel in the 1967 Six-Day War and occupied since. It has been occupied by some 9,600 Jewish settlers. Syria seeks its return.

Golkar   Official Indonesian political party in the Sukarno era.

Grand Coalition   (Grosse Koalition)   Term used in Central European politics to denote coalition of two major parties as opposed to a small coalition (Kleine Koalition) of one major party and a minor party. Such a coalition, between the conservative CDU/CSU and the social democratic SPD, governed West Germany from 1966, following the failure of the small coalition of CDU/CSU with the center-right FDP, until 1969, when SPD and FDP formed a small coalition and the BUNDESTAG elected Willy Brandt as chancellor. A grand coalition of the conservative OVP and the social democratic SPO governed Austria from 1945 to 1966.

Grand Design   Expression used to describe the early aspirations of U.S. president Kennedy *(q.v)* in international affairs. The Design envisaged a developing North Atlantic partnership, with an expanding European Economic Community becoming an equal partner with the United States. There was to be a multilateral nuclear force in NATO (see p. 21), and the KENNEDY ROUND would overcome trade barriers through tariff reductions. In practice, Europe remained divided and French president de Gaulle (q.v.) was suspicious of the plans.

Great Leap Forward   Chinese slogan for a series of radical changes in social and economic policy between 1958 and 1961. Private consumption was cut, material incentives withdrawn and massive agricultural communes were set up and serviced by light industrial and construction projects. The program failed following bad harvests and withdrawal of Soviet technical aid.

Great Society Phrase used by President Lyndon B. Johnson (1908–73) to describe the America his administration (1963–68) hoped to create by its ambitious program of social legislation.

Green Revolution Post–1945 improvement in agricultural yields in developing countries, as a result of application of pesticides, chemical-based fertilizers and high-yield crop seeds.

Greens Originally and principally the West German ecology party, which first emerged as a political force in Bremen in 1979, when environmentalists and antinuclear groups won 5.9% of seats in the Land (federal state) parliament. Greens have since been elected to other Land parliaments and to the BUNDESTAG, and similar parties have had success in other West European countries. The British Ecology Party changed its name to the Greens in 1985. They achieved more votes than the Liberal Democrats in the 1989 European elections, but declined rapidly thereafter.

Grenada Invasion See p. 337.

Group of Seven (G7) The world's leading industrialized nations (Britain, Canada, France, Germany, Italy, Japan, the United States), whose heads of state meet regularly to discuss world economic problems and attempt to coordinate action for their solution.

Guided Democracy Term given to the style of government of Sukarno in Indonesia.

Gulf War (1) Antagonism and border clashes between Islamic fundamentalist Iran and Ba'athist Iraq erupted into war on 22 September 1980, with initial Iraqi advances. A lull in 1981 was followed by Iranian counterattacks in May 1982. War continued to 1988, with massive casualties and allegations of use of chemical weapons and poison gas (see also p. 302–3). Cease-fire proposals were accepted by both sides in August 1988.

Gulf War (2) The UN–sponsored war to liberate Kuwait from Iraqi occupation that began in January 1991. See p. 304.

Haganah (Heb.) Armed force secretly formed by Jews in Palestine in 1936 for defense of their communes against Arab attacks. It later became the nucleus of the Israeli army.

Halabja Place in Iraq where Kurdish civilians were massacred by Iraqi forces using chemical weapons in March 1988.

Halloween Massacre 3 November 1975. Major reorganization of international policy posts in U.S. government carried out by President Gerald Ford *(q.v)*.

Hallstein Doctrine 1955. A West German assertion of its refusal to recognize East Germany, together with a declaration that it would resent any other state's doing so.

Hamas (Islamic Resistance Movement) Founded in December 1987 as a more active and fundamentalist rival to the PLO (Palestine Liberation Organization) in organizing the INTIFADA uprising against Israeli forces in the OCCUPIED TERRITORIES. It has bitterly opposed the PLO accord with Israel and has organized terrorist acts as retaliation for the HEBRON MASSACRE. Along with the Islamic JIHAD group, Hamas is known for using suicide bombers in public places. Although the PLO and Israel have since imposed strict security and harsh punitive measures, PLO chairman Yasir Arafat has tried to include Hamas in the political process, appointing Hamas members to leadership positions in the Palestinian Authority.

Hapoel Haniizrachi (Heb., "The Mizrach Worker") In Israel, a religious, moderately orthodox, center-left party. Joined with MIZRACHI in 1956 to form the National Religious Party.

Hartal (Hind., "shop" and "bolt") Ceylonese (i.e., Sri Lankan) general strike organized by Marxists in 1953 in protest at rapid price rises, particularly of rice. Repressive measures were introduced, and there were clashes between government forces and strikers. Prime Minister Senanayake, of the United National Party, was forced to resign, and the opposition Sri Lanka Freedom Party won the 1956 election.

Hawks American politicians who wished to continue, intensify or escalate the Vietnam War (1965–72). The term is now applied generally to politicians taking an aggressive stance on foreign policy issues.

Hebron Massacre Massacre of 50 Arabs by an extremist Jewish settler in March 1994. The massacre failed to derail the peace process, but led to retaliation by Hamas.

Helsinki Accords Result of the CONFERENCE ON SECURITY AND CO-OPERATION IN EUROPE (30 July–1 August 1975) attended by representatives of 35 countries. Agreement was reached on the prevention of accidental war, economic and technological cooperation, the desirability of increasing contact between citizens of East and West, and recognition of individual human rights.

Herut (Heb., "The Freedom Party") Extreme right-wing political group in Israel, founded by Menachem Begin and a successor to the Revisionist Party. Now part of GAHAL.

Hezbollah (Arab., "Party of God") An Iranian-supported terrorist group based in southern Lebanon. Active since the 1980s, its rocket attacks on Israeli settlements in northern Galilee helped provoke the massive Israeli bombardment of southern Lebanon in July 1993 (Operation Accountability), which in turn created a major refugee crisis as the Lebanese fled north toward Beirut. By the end of April 1999, Israel had made 41 air raids on Hezbollah guerrillas in Lebanon.

Histadrat (Heb., "Federation of Labor") Organizational body of the Israeli trade-union movement.

Historic Compromise Term used to describe the support given by the Italian Communist Party (PCI) to the governing Christian Democrats from 1976. The support marked the end of more than a generation of Communist exclusion from the governing coalitions of modern Italy and reflected the need to form a strong base with which to deal with growing problems of inflation and terrorism. From 1978 on the Communists were virtually unofficial members of the government, largely through the mediation of Aldo Moro, the Christian Democrat prime minister. His death in spring 1978 at the hands of terrorists, and that of the Communist leader Enrico Berlinguer in 1984, undermined a long-term arrangement.

Hot Line Direct communications link between Washington and Moscow intended to serve in times of international crisis. Similar links exist between London and Moscow and between Paris and Moscow.

Huks (Hukbalahap) Communist guerrillas in the Philippines. See p. 318.

Human Shield Term applied to the seizure of hostages by Saddam Hussein (p. 304) after the Iraqi invasion of Kuwait in order to deter military action by the Allies. Most were freed by Christmas 1990.

Hundred Flowers Government-sponsored movement in Communist China, 1956–57, aiming to attract constructive criticism of MAOISM. The flood of criticism that arose led to a government backlash.

Hung Parliament Parliament in which no one party has an overall majority, and which might result in the formation of a coalition or the formation of a minority government by the largest party, which would govern until defeated on a major piece of legislation.

Hungarian Uprising 23 October–4 November 1956. Student and worker demonstrations in Budapest on 23 October, in which Stalin's statue was destroyed, led to the appointment of Imre Nagy as prime minister, with the promise of reform and democratization. Russia appeared acquiescent and withdrew troops, but returned on 4 November after Nagy's announcement that Hungary would pull out of the Warsaw Pact to pursue a neutralist policy. Russian tanks shelled working-class areas; 100,000 refugees fled to the West; and Nagy and many of his supporters were executed (see p. 289).

ILO (International Labor Organization) Specialized agency of the UN created in 1919 to improve labor conditions, promote higher living standards and foster social justice.

Imjin River, Battle of 22–25 April 1951. Crucial and successful defensive battle fought by UN forces during the Korean War to hold back a Chinese–North Korean spring offensive.

Immorality Act South African apartheid legislation outlawing sexual relations between blacks and whites, making them an offense punishable by seven years' imprisonment. It was paralleled by the Prohibition of Mixed Marriages Act, which banned interracial marriage.

Indianismo Latin American intellectual movement for revival of Indian culture, arguing that in countries with an Indian majority, they form a separate element and should return to a dominant social, political and economic position.

Inkatha Freedom Movement A conservative, predominantly Zulu, sectarian rival to the more democratic and broadly based AFRICAN NATIONAL CONGRESS (ANC). Led by Chief Mangosuthu Buthelezi, it allowed itself to be used by the white South African government to divide the anti-apartheid movement. In late 1993 it was reported to have agreed to cooperate with the neo-Nazi AFRIKANER RESISTANCE MOVEMENT to oppose all-race elections favored by the ANC. At the last moment, however, it dropped its opposition and agreed to participate in the elections of April 1994.

Inkathagate A political scandal following from the revelation that the South African government had secretly funded the INKATHA FREEDOM MOVEMENT as a means to divide and weaken black opposition. Documents also revealed that the police were helping run an Inkatha-fronted trade union.

Internal Security Act September 1950. Also known as the McCarran Act, requiring all Communist Party and "front" organizations in the United States to register with the attorney general. It has been largely invalidated by the courts on constitutional grounds.

Intifada   Name given to the Arab uprising that began on 9 December 1987 in the Israeli-occupied GAZA STRIP and WEST BANK. By January 1991 it had claimed over 1,000 lives.

Iran-Contra Affair   Term used for scandal during the Reagan administration involving diversion of funds to contras in Nicaragua. See CONTRAS.

Iranian Hostage Crisis   Iranian students, with support of their government, seized the U.S. embassy and 63 staff members on 4 November 1979, demanding in exchange the return of the ousted shah for trial. An American rescue attempt failed disastrously on 25 April 1980. The hostages remained until 20 January 1981, the United States paying the Iranian government a substantial sum for their release.

Iraqgate   Revelations emerging in 1992 that the British and American governments had allowed the purchase and export of lethal weapons to Iraq since 1988 in contravention of their own laws and policies. The policies had originally been instituted in the 1980–88 Iran–Iraq war.

Iron Curtain   Term used to denote border between Soviet-dominated Eastern Europe and the West and, more specifically, constraints placed on movement and ideology by communist regimes in Eastern Europe. With the fall of Eastern European and Soviet communism it is now obsolete.

Iron Lady   Facetious term used first by Soviet leaders to describe former British Conservative prime minister Margaret Thatcher; later taken up by British journalists.

Janata   Alliance of opposition groups formed in India in 1977 to contest the elections against Mrs. Gandhi's Indian CONGRESS PARTY. It won the election, and Morarji Desai became prime minister until July 1979, when he was no longer able to control the coalition. After unsuccessful attempts by other Janata members to form a government, the Congress Party was returned to power in fresh elections in 1980. The Janata Dal rose to prominence again in 1989.

Jebalya   The Palestinian refugee camp in the GAZA STRIP, with a population of 60,000 in 1988. It was the site of riots on 9 December 1987 that marked the opening of the INTIFADA.

Jihad   Holy war of Muslims against nonbelievers in Islam.

Jordan Civil War   17–25 September 1970.   An attempted reassertion of authority over West Bank Palestinian refugees using Jordan as a base for PLO attacks on Israel provoked clashes between government and guerrilla forces, with heavy fighting around the capital, Amman, and in the north. The Palestinian bases were not overrun until July 1971.

KANU   (Kenya African National Union)   A political party led from June 1947 by Jomo Kenyatta (1897–1978), who became first prime minister of independent Kenya in 1963 and president in 1964. The party's strength lay in the Kikuyu, Kenya's most numerous tribe. Under Kenyatta, parties representative of other tribes were outlawed.

Karelia   Territory ceded by Finland to the Soviet Union in March 1940, following Finland's defeat in the Winter War. Russian president Boris Yeltsin *(q.v.)* refused to discuss the possibility of its return, despite Finnish offers of a cash payment and a multimillion-dollar aid program.

Kashmir Question   The ownership of Kashmir, a border area predominantly Muslim but two-thirds of which is controlled by India, is disputed between India and Pakistan. Wars in 1947, 1965 and 1971 have not resolved the problem.

Katanga Revolt   1960–63.   On the granting of independence by Belgium, Union Minière, a company with exclusive mining rights in the copper- and uranium-rich province of Katanga, encouraged it to secede from Congo on 11 July 1960 under Moise Tshombe. Using a white mercenary army to resist United Nations attempts to restore order, Katanga ended its rebellion in January 1963 (see p. 307).

Kennedy Round   Long, complex negotiations to encourage world trade through reduction of tariffs on industrial and agricultural imports, particularly in the United States and Europe, prompted by President Kennedy's message to Congress on 25 January 1963. A final compromise agreement was reached in Geneva on 15 May 1967. See GATT.

Khalsa   (Arab., "pure," "sincere," "free")   In India, the Sikh commonwealth of the Punjab; also, a land revenue collected directly by government officials.

Khmer Rouge   Cambodian communist movement that by 1974 had taken control of the Cambodian countryside, before capturing the capital city of Phnom Penh in 1975. Revolution ensued, and in 1976 a government led by Pol Pot was installed. The population of the entire country was forced onto the land to increase agrarian productivity, and there were reports of mass political killings. The government was replaced by the Vietnamese-backed Cambodian Liberation Front for National Renewal following the war of 1978–79. In the late 1980s, the Khmer Rouge was again a powerful guerrilla force in Cambodia. But after opposing the UN–sponsored peace settlement of 1991 and the multiparty elections in 1993 and continuing guerrilla warfare against the noncommunist coalition government formed after those elections, the Khmer Rouge suffered a series of military defeats. In 1995 many of their cadres accepted an offer of amnesty from the Cambodian government, and in 1996 several thousand guerrillas defected and signed a peace agreement with the government. See pp. 329–30.

Kilbrandon Report November 1973. Successes of Scottish and Welsh nationalists in British parliamentary elections prompted the Kilbrandon inquiry and a report recommending elected assemblies in Wales and Scotland. A Scottish referendum on the issue on 1 March 1979 proved indecisive; the Welsh, the same day, overwhelmingly rejected the proposed devolution of power.

King David Hotel 22 July 1946. Zionist guerrillas of the terrorist Irgun Zvai Leumi organization blew up the hotel housing the British administrative headquarters in Jerusalem, killing 91.

Knesset Israeli legislature, consisting of a single chamber of 120 members elected for four years by universal suffrage through a system of proportional representation.

Kolkhoz (abbrev. Russ., *kollektivnoye kbozyaistvo*, "collective farm") The term originated in the collectivization of agriculture in the USSR during the 1928–33 Five Year Plan when all individual farms and small holdings were combined into the kolkhoz system.

Komeito The "Clean Government Party" in Japan. See p. 235.

Komsomol (abbr. Russ., Kommunisticheskij Soyuz Nolodyezhi, Communist Union of Youth) Youth organization of the Communist Party of the Soviet Union.

Koreagate The name given to describe a South Korean scheme to influence U.S. legislators and top executive officials during the 1970s through cash bribes and campaign contributions totaling between $500,000 and $1 million annually. Park Tong Sun, a wealthy South Korean businessman, had entertained many Washington figures, some of whom were later indicted.

Korean War See pp. 321–22.

Kosovo Province in the former Yugoslavia that, although over 90% inhabited by ethnic Albanians, is seen by the Serbs as the cradle of their culture. Kosovo was an autonomous region within the Yugoslav federation until direct rule was imposed in 1989, which led to the formation of a Democratic League of Kosovo to agitate peacefully for complete independence. Tensions heated up again in 1996–97, when the Kosovo Liberation Army (KLA) began killing Serbian policemen in Kosovo. In

February 1998, President Milosevic sent Serbian troops to take back KLA–controlled areas, but many civilians were killed during the battle, outraging Kosovars and escalating the conflict. After several months of unsuccessful peace negotiations, in spring 1999, NATO launched a 78-day air campaign—the first time the organization stepped into the middle of a conflict between a sovereign nation and its own citizens. Serbia finally agreed to sign a UN-approved peace agreement with NATO over Kosovo in June 1999.

Kraków Declaration Declaration made by Czechoslovakia, Hungary and Poland on 5–6 October 1991 pledging attempt to integrate their forces into NATO (see p. 21) and to join the European Community (see p. 14).

Krugerrands South African gold coins introduced in 1967 as the first bullion coins to be produced for sale. A European Community ban on their import was imposed in 1986 but was later lifted.

Kuomintang (KMT) Chinese Nationalist Party founded in 1891 by Sun Yat-sen. After World War II the KMT departed from its original principles of democratic republicanism and became a corrupt and reactionary military oligarchy. The KMT regime collapsed and was replaced by the Communist Party in 1949, leaving its leader, Jiang Kaishek, and his followers to rule Taiwan, backed by the United States.

Kurdish Workers Party (PKK) Marxist-oriented guerrilla group fighting for an independent state in southeast Turkey. Its terrorist campaign accelerated in 1993, by which time 6,000 soldiers, rebels and civilians had died since 1984. The PKK leader is Abdullah "Apo" Ocalan, the son of Anatolian peasants, who exercises tight control of the organization.

Kurdistan Name of the independent homeland sought by the 25 million Kurds currently living in Turkey, Iraq, Syria, the former Soviet Union and Iran. See pp. 296–97.

Land (pl., *Länder*) German name for the constituent states of the Federal Republic of Germany (FRG). The term is also used in Austria.

Laogai The Chinese equivalent of the Soviet Gulag. China, as the largest abuser of human rights in the world, has an estimated 2,000 prison camps with perhaps 10 million prisoners forced to work prison farm, salt mines etc.

Lebanon, Civil War Ongoing clash erupting in 1975, with complex, constantly shifting alliances. The clash was initially between Phalangist Christians and left-wing Muslims backed by Palestinian guerrillas, and has involved successive Syrian and Israeli intervention, together with UN peacekeeping efforts (see pp. 301–2).

Liberation Election   Term used by black South Africans for the first multiracial election of 27–28 April 1994 that paved the way for majority rule in South Africa. The election resulted in a sweeping victory for the African National Congress (ANC).

Liberation Theology   The radical position adopted by many Catholic priests against oppressive regimes, especially in South America.

Libya Raid   14 April 1986.   U.S. F-111 bombers struck against "terrorist related" targets in Libya, following alleged Libyan links to a bomb attack on a West Berlin discotheque, 4 April 1986, resulting in the death of an American serviceman. The international opinion on the U.S. raid was divided. The raid was highly popular in the United States.

Likud   Alliance of various right-wing Israeli parties, which, under the leadership of Menachem Begin, won the general election of 1977, displacing the Israeli Labor Party for the first time in the country's history.

Liqoqo   Ruling council of state of Swaziland.

Little Rock   September 1957.   President Eisenhower sent federal troops into Little Rock, Arkansas, to enforce desegregation of schools under terms of a 1954 Supreme Court decision that had declared racial separation unconstitutional.

Lockerbie   See p. 373, "Air Piracy."

Lome Conventions   28 February 1975.   A trade agreement between the European Economic Community and (originally) 46 developing countries, by which the latter were granted tariff-free entry for their products into EEC territory together with increased aid and investment. LOME II, 31 October 1979, promised a further $7 billion in aid in 1980–85. The Lome agreements were further extended in the 1980s. LOME III was negotiated in 1984 between the EEC and 65 developing countries.

Loyalist   Term currently used to refer to the Protestants in Northern Ireland who support the maintenance of the union with Great Britain in opposition to those Catholics who wish to unite with the Republic of Ireland.

Maastricht   Summit held in December 1991 marking a new stage in moves toward European economic and political integration. It was ratified by all EC member states before 1 November 1993, when it came into force. The treaty established a European Union (EU), with Union citizenship for every person holding the nationality of a member state, introduced a central banking system, a common currency and a common foreign and security policy.

Majlis (Iranian National Consultative Assembly) Chief legislative body in Iran under the shahs. The last shah dissolved the assembly in 1961 after it had refused to pass his land reforms.

Malayan Emergency 1948–60. A successful British military/political operation against communists in Malaya, involving specialized jungle warfare units, the creation of tightly controlled village settlements to deny supplies to guerrillas, and economic, social and political reforms, culminating in independence in 1957 and the breaking of communist political power.

Malvinas Spanish name for the Falkland Islands, a British territory claimed by Argentina and the scene of armed conflict between that country and Great Britain in 1982 in which the latter was victorious.

Manhattan Project Code name for the World War II development of the atom bomb under Robert Oppenheimer by U.S., Canadian and British scientists at Oak Ridge, Tennessee.

Manila Treaty 8 September 1954. Australia, France, New Zealand, Pakistan, Philippines, Thailand, the United Kingdom and the United States formed the South East Asia Treaty Organization (SEATO) guaranteeing collective action against internal or external aggression together with economic cooperation.

Maoism System of communism adopted in China under Mao Zedong (1893–1976). Maoism envisages a more flexible system than Marxism-Leninism in which self-reliance is more important than state authority. The concept of revolutionary momentum, as expressed in the CULTURAL REVOLUTION, is more important than the state machine.

Mapai Miphiegeth Poalei Israel, or Israeli Workers' Party, founded in Palestine in 1930 and usually called the Labor Party. A moderate left-wing party.

Mapam United Workers' Party, an Israeli socialist party far to the left of MAPAI, drawing much of its support from the kibbutzim.

Marshall Plan 5 June 1947. U.S. secretary of state Marshall's offer of financial aid to reconstruct the postwar European economy was accepted by 16 nations. The communist states rejected it. The United States provided $17 billion in assistance between 1948 and 1952 through the European Recovery Program.

Mau Mau   Secret anti-European terrorist movement founded among the Kikuyu tribe of Kenya between 1948 and 1952. The movement had been largely stamped out by 1954.

May Events   1968. French students, demonstrating against education cuts in Paris on 2–3 May 1968, clashed with police, whose brutality triggered riots and increasingly radical demands, with 10 million workers coming out in a general strike in support of the students and their own opposition to President de Gaulle. As the strike and riots went on into June, threatening a potentially revolutionary situation, the government promised educational reform and wage increases to the workers, ending the events but presaging the end of de Gaulle's authority.

Meech Lake Accord   Series of constitutional amendments drawn up in 1987 by Canadian premier Brian Mulroney and the premiers of the 10 provinces in an attempt to make the 1982 constitution acceptable to the people of Quebec. The concessions made to Quebec separatist sentiment included recognition of French as the dominant language in Quebec, powers for Quebec to control immigration into the province and recognition that amendments to the constitution require the agreement of all 10 provinces. The Accord caused acute political disagreement in 1990 in such provinces as New Brunswick, Manitoba and Newfoundland. On 22 June 1990 the Accord failed when Manitoba and Newfoundland failed to approve it.

Mercosur   The South American Southern Core Common Market, founded in March 1991 by the Treaty of Asunción between Argentina, Brazil, Paraguay and Uruguay. Between 1990 and 1997, the trade value of the members leapt from $4 billion to $18 billion, and that success attracted Chile and Bolivia to sign free-trade agreements with Mercosur. However, in 1998, intra-Mercosur trade fell and for the first time output in its main economies has been falling simultaneously. Due to recessions in its two largest members, Brazil and Argentina, Mercosur is in danger of floundering.

Migrant Labor   Body of transient or nonnational laborers, sometimes contracted for on a seasonal basis. The term is applied to the black labor force in South Africa, which is housed in barracks or hostels by employers and separated from their families.

Minuteman   (1) Member of an extreme right-wing society founded in the United States in the 1960s to organize resistance to a feared communist invasion. It had several hundred members, mainly in California and Illinois, and was declared subversive by the attorney general in 1965.

(2) U.S. nuclear missile.

Mizrachi Right-wing political party in Israel; partner of HAPOEL HAM-IZRACHI in the National Religious Party.

MNR (Mozambique National Resistance) South African–backed guerrilla movement that fought to overthrow the Mozambican government. See NKOMATI ACCORD.

Mogadishu Raid 18 October 1977. Twenty-eight West German anti-terrorist police released 86 hostages held by BAADER-MEINHOF guerrillas at Mogadishu airport, Somalia, in a Lufthansa plane hijacked five days earlier. Three hijackers were killed and one hostage and one commando injured in a one-minute battle.

Morgenthau Plan 1944. A proposal at the QUEBEC CONFERENCES by U.S. treasury secretary Morgenthau that a defeated Germany be stripped of all industry, reverting to an agricultural nation. The plan was rejected on the grounds of the enormous amount of aid Germany would need to survive, but proved a useful propaganda weapon for the Nazis to urge Germany into fighting harder.

Moro Affair 16 March 1978. Aldo Moro, a former Italian premier and a major voice for conciliation between the Christian Democrat and Communist parties, was abducted in Rome by members of the Red Brigade, a left-wing urban terrorist league that had already carried out several actions against leading industrial and political leaders (see chapter 7). The drama that unfolded over the succeeding weeks had elements of both tragedy and farce: conflicting reports over Moro's whereabouts and condition, the apparent helplessness of the Italian police, tension between political factions, and a series of letters allegedly written by Moro himself, in which he pleaded with the government to exchange him for Red Brigade prisoners. The government refused the exchange, and on 9 May Moro's bullet-ridden corpse was found in Rome, in a car parked midway between the Communist and the Christian Democrat headquarters.

MPLA (People's Movement for the Liberation of Angola) A socialist movement that fought with UNITA and ENLA between 1961 and 1975 to secure Angolan independence from Portuguese rule. After independence (10 November 1975) it fought a civil war with UNITA and the ENLA for control. Its "People's Republic" was eventually recognized as the legitimate government of Angola.

Mufti Jurist trained in Islamic law who gives authoritative decisions on legal problems.

Muldergate 1978. After a South African National Party general election triumph, rumors of corruption surfaced, and an inquiry instituted by Premier P. W. Botha reported that Information Minister Dr. Connie Mulder, who was forced to resign, had misused secret propaganda funds. Some of the money had been used in support of conservative candidates in U.S. congressional elections.

Munich Massacre   5 September 1972. Black September Palestinian guerrillas attacked Israeli athlete quarters at the Munich Olympics, killing two and taking nine hostage. In the ensuing rescue attempt at Munich airport, two Germans, five Palestinians and the remaining athletes were killed.

Mutual Security Pact   2 December 1954.   The agreement between the United States and Nationalist China that the Seventh Fleet would guarantee protection from potential Communist Chinese threats remained effective until President Carter's recognition of Communist China in 1978.

My Lai Massacre   16 March 1968.   U.S. troops attacked a village suspected of harboring Viet Cong guerrillas and killed the inhabitants, leading to charges against Lt. William Calley of murdering 109 civilians. Calley, after a four-month trial, was found guilty and sentenced to life imprisonment on 29 March 1971; the sentence was later reduced.

NAFTA   North American Free Trade Agreement.   Free trade area set up by the United States, Canada and Mexico on 13 August 1992, enlarging an agreement that already existed between the United States and Canada. NAFTA was ratified by the three countries' national legislatures in 1993 and went into effect on 1 January 1994. It is intended to eliminate all duties, tariffs and other trade barriers between the three countries in 15 years.

Nassau Agreement   18 December 1962.   An agreement between President Kennedy and Prime Minister Macmillan on nuclear cooperation, by which the United States would supply Great Britain with Polaris missiles for submarines. The move antagonized French president de Gaulle, who interpreted it as a reassertion of Great Britain's American loyalties taking precedence over its bonds with Europe and who vetoed U.K. entry to the Common Market a month later.

National Salvation Front   The political movement led by Ion Iliescu in Romania that became the provisional government after the fall in December 1989 of the dictatorship of Nicolae Ceausescu.

NATO   See p. 21.

Negotiations Forum   Grouping of 26 parties, representing all races, that continued the work of CODESA in formulating constitutional arrangements for a post-apartheid South Africa. On 2 July 1993 the Forum agreed (with six parties dissenting) to hold multiracial elections on 27 April 1994 for a government of national unity to draft and adopt a new constitution. See also COSAG.

Neo-Nazism   Upsurge of organized racist violence in the newly united Germany. By 1999 there were 51,000 known neo-Nazi activists, and reported attacks on racial minorities increased from 270 in 1990 to 740 in 1999.

New World Order   Term favored by President Bush to describe the post–Cold War international order in which the United States would accept the Soviet Union as a normal part of the world order.

Nine, The   Members of the EEC between 1973, when Denmark, Great Britain and Ireland joined Belgium, the Federal Republic of Germany, France, Italy, Luxembourg and the Netherlands, and 1982, when Greece became the tenth member. Following the admission of Portugal and Spain in 1985 there were 12 members. Accession by Austria, Sweden and Finland in 1995 brings the current membership to 15.

Nkomati Accord   March 1984.   South Africa promised not to support the Mozambique rebel National Resistance Movement in return for Mozambique's agreeing not to back the outlawed African National Congress's activities in South Africa. The agreement did not end guerrilla warfare in Mozambique.

Nonproliferation Treaty   1968.   Agreement to discourage the spread of nuclear weapons, ratified in 1975 by 92 countries, but not by some possessing a nuclear potential, notably Pakistan, and also South Africa (until 1992).

Nuremberg Trials   1945–47.   Joint American, British, French and Soviet International Military Tribunal, which tried 177 Germans and Austrians for crimes against peace and humanity and for war crimes. Twenty-five were hanged, 35 acquitted and the rest imprisoned. The main trial, taking place between November 1945 and September 1946, was of 21 leading Nazis, of whom 10 were executed on 16 October 1946.

OAS   (1) Organisation de l'Armée Secrète, French terrorist organization, 1961–62, which posed a serious threat to the Fifth Republic. Most members were ex-Algerian colonists aggrieved at President Charles de Gaulle's desire to end the Algerian War (1954–62), which led to Algerian independence.
   (2) See p. 24.

OAU   See p. 23.

Occupied Territories The areas occupied by Israel during the June 1967 SIX-DAY WAR. The Golan Heights were taken from Syria, the West Bank from Jordan, and the Gaza Strip and the Sinai Peninsula from Egypt. Sinai was returned to Egypt in April 1982. Under the 1993 peace deal, the Gaza Strip and Jericho in the West Bank were to have limited self-government.

Oder-Neisse Line Boundary along the rivers Oder and Neisse between Poland and Germany giving to Poland a fifth of Germany's 1938 territory and a sixth of its population, provisionally agreed to by the United States, United Kingdom and USSR at Yalta and Potsdam; not officially recognized by West Germany until 18 November 1970, when the action was taken as part of Brandt's Ostpolitik (*q.v.*) reconciliation.

Ogaden Revolt Western Somali Liberation Front guerrillas, supporting the Somali government claim for Ethiopian Ogaden Province, captured the area in summer 1977, but were pushed out by Cuba/USSR–backed Ethiopian government forces January–March 1978. Fighting continues. See pp. 314–15.

Oireachtas (Ir., "national parliament") Parliament of the Irish Republic consisting of the president, DÁIL ÉIREANN and SEANED ÉIREANN.

Ombudsman (Swedish, "representative") Officer charged with investigating complaints against the central administration, introduced into Sweden in 1809, and adopted by Finland (1919), Denmark (1954), Norway (1962) and Great Britain (1965). In Britain the ombudsman has the official title "parliamentary commissioner for administration," and acts only at the request of an MP.

OPEC See p. 29.

"Open Skies" Treaty The Treaty on "Open Skies," which allows for observation flights to be made over the territory of other treaty signatories, was signed in Helsinki on 24 March 1992. All members of NATO signed, as did the five former Warsaw Pact East European states. Belarus, Georgia, Russia and Ukraine are the only republics of the former Soviet Union to have signed the treaty so far.

Operation Desert Shield The name for the U.S. military deployment to protect Saudi Arabia after the Iraqi invasion and annexation of Kuwait in 1990. See p. 304.

Operation Desert Storm Code name for the Allied military operation to liberate Kuwait. See p. 304.

Operation Restore Hope The name for the United States military deployment in Somalia. See p. 315.

Orangemen Members of the Orange Order, an Irish society formed in Ulster in 1795 to uphold Protestantism. Its name is taken from William III, Prince of Orange, who defeated James II at the battle of the Boyne in 1690. The society is bitterly anti-Catholic, maintains the Unionist Party and has branches outside Northern Ireland, particularly in Liverpool and Glasgow.

Osirak Iraqi nuclear site bombed by Israel in 1981.

Ostpolitik (Ger., "eastern policy") Policy of the German Federal Republic developed by Kurt Kiesinger as an attempt to normalize relations with communist countries other than the USSR, including recognition of the German Democratic Republic.

Palestine A territory of 10,429 square miles, formerly part of the Ottoman Empire, that became a British mandate from the League of Nations after World War I. In 1948, 8,048 square miles of the territory became Israel, and many Palestinians fled to neighboring Arab states. Without a resolution of its status no final settlement can be reached in the Middle East. See also PLO and INTIFADA.

Palmach Elite striking force of the HAGANAH, founded by Yitzhak Sadeli and imbued with his Marxist principles.

Pamyat A right-wing nationalist Russian organization that emerged in the late 1980s. There are anti-Semitic and fascist elements within it.

Panama Canal Zone Treaty 7 September 1977. Agreement between U.S. president Carter and Panamanian general Torrijos that the United States would evacuate the zone five miles on each side of the Panama Canal leased by the United States since 1903 and comprising 1% of Panamanian territory, on 1 January 2000.

Panama, Invasion of See p. 337.

Pan-Arabism The movement for Arab unity. Most notably the attempts by President Nasser *(q.v)* to unite the Arab world under Egyptian hegemony.

Panmunjom Negotiations 1951–53. Armistice talks to end the Korean War began at Kaesong on 8 July 1951 and moved to Panmunjom, where they continued inconclusively until an easing of tension following the death of Stalin. An agreement was reached confirming the division of Korea on 27 July 1953.

Partisans Armed bands offering resistance behind enemy lines. Particularly applied to Tito's communist guerrillas in wartime Yugoslavia.

Pass Laws 1952. Natives' (Abolition of Passes and Coordination of Documents) Act that consolidated and extended previous South African pass legislation of 1760, 1895 and 1923, with a provision that blacks over 16 should carry a "reference book" at all times, available for inspection by police on demand, with fines and imprisonment for failing to do so.

Pathet Lao The communist forces in the Laos civil war, which by 1973 controlled most of the country. Taking complete power at the conclusion of the Vietnam War, the Pathet Lao leader, Prince Souphanouvong, abolished the monarchy and became president of a Lao People's Democratic Republic in December 1975.

Patriotic Front See ZANU, ZAPU.

Perestroika From the Russian "restructuring," an attempt led by Mikhail Gorbachev (Communist Party general secretary 1985–88, president 1988–91) to regenerate the stagnant Soviet economy by encouraging market forces, decentralizing industrial management, and democratizing the party and government machinery. By 1991, against a background of political crisis and economic chaos, the future of *perestroika* was increasingly uncertain. However, the failure of the abortive coup of August 1991 made a return to the old Soviet system impossible.

Peronismo Political, economic and social program pursued by Argentinian dictator Juan Domingo Perón between 1946 and 1955 (also called *justicialismo*). In some ways analogous to fascism, it involved a five-year economic plan, extensive government control of economy and society, and an end to British influence on the economy.

Peshmerga From the Arabic word "those who confront death," a Kurdish guerrilla group in Iraq.

Philby Case Harold "Kim" Philby, a British Foreign Office official who resigned after admitting communist associations in July 1951, became a journalist, disappeared in Beirut in March 1963 and reappeared behind the Iron Curtain, confirming his role as the "third man" in the BURGESS-MACLEAN scandal.

Philippine Election 1986. Less than three weeks after an election held amid allegations of widespread fraud, Philippine president Ferdinand E. Marcos fled the country on 25 February 1986. Corazon Aquino, the widow of Benigno Aquino—the assassinated leader of the opposition to Marcos—had run against Marcos in the presidential election. Each candidate claimed victory and each held inauguration ceremonies on 25 February just hours before Marcos went into exile. Marcos's 20-year reign as president was brought to an end after two leading military allies resigned from their posts—Lieutenant General Fidel Ramos and Juan

Ponce Enrile, defense minister. On 24 February President Reagan had called on Marcos to resign and offered him a haven in the United States. The Marcos regime had been thoroughly corrupt, and the Philippine economy had stagnated under the rule of Marcos.

Plaid Cymru (Welsh, Party of Wales) Political movement founded in 1925. It hopes to separate Wales from the United Kingdom and thereby preserve Welsh language, culture and economy. The party has returned MPs in five elections. The Welsh people voted overwhelmingly against devolution in a referendum of 1979. Voters approved a regional assembly with limited powers, which was created in 1999.

PLO (Palestine Liberation Organization) Formed in Jordan in 1964 to unite Palestinian Arab groups in their struggle against Israel. Led by Yassir Arafat and dominated by the Syrian Al-Fatah group, the organization is recognized by the UN as the body representing Palestinians. Its support for Iraq during the Gulf War lost it much support, but in 1993 it agreed to a preliminary settlement with Israel including limited self-government in the Gaza Strip and Jericho. It is bitterly opposed by HA-MAS.

Poalei Agudas Yisrael The Agudas Workers of Israel. Left-wing, ultra-religious Israeli political party.

Postindustrial Society A term for Western societies, notably those of the United States and Great Britain, whose national economies appeared to have shifted by the 1980s from heavy industrial and manufactutring bases to service industries underpinned by computerization.

Potsdam Conference 17 July–1 August 1945. Final wartime meeting of Allied leaders Stalin, Truman (who had replaced Roosevelt on his death) and Attlee (who had defeated Churchill in a general election), reaffirming the agreements at Yalta that Germany should have no central government and should remain under Allied administration in four zones of occupation, with the German economy decentralized and the production of potential war materials restricted.

Poujadist Follower of Pierre Poujade, founder of a right-wing political movement violently active in France between 1954 and 1958 (Union de Défence des Commerçants et Artisans). The movement's membership was petit-bourgeois and its ideology antisocialist, anti-intellectual and anti-European. It won 52 seats in the National Assembly in 1956, but declined after de Gaulle's return to politics and the founding of the Fifth Republic.

Powellite Wing of the British Conservative Party that supported Enoch Powell (b. 1912) in the late 1960s, associated with monetarism and anti-EEC and anti-immigration positions. Powell was expelled from the Conservative Party and was an Ulster Unionist MP from October 1974 until 1987.

Prague Spring 1968. The period during which Alexander Dubček, appointed first secretary of the Czechoslovak Communist Party on 5 January 1968, attempted to create socialism "with a human face" by increasing individual and political liberty. Though he promised to remain within the Warsaw Pact, the Soviet Union exerted pressure to curtail reform, finally intervening with troops on 20–21 August 1968 on the grounds that counterrevolution was being planned.

Privatization Selling of nationalized industries and other parts of the public sector to private businesses and individuals. A hallmark of the Thatcher government in Great Britain and after 1986 of successive French governments. Its principles are now being applied to Eastern Europe.

Profumo Affair 1963. The most famous scandal in postwar British political history. Having initially denied in parliament his involvement with a prostitute who was having relations with the Soviet naval attaché, Tory war minister John Profumo admitted he had lied, resigning on 4 June. Though an inquiry concluded that national security had not been endangered, the affair appeared to discredit an already weak Conservative government.

Provos/Provisional IRA Wing of the IRA concerned with expelling British troops and government from Northern Ireland after 1968–69, when civil rights demonstrations by Catholics there provoked violent reprisals by Protestants, encouraging the IRA to renew its violent struggle for a united Ireland.

Pugwash Conferences of leading international scientists from the developed and developing countries to discuss the social responsibilities of science, held regularly since July 1957. The first was held in Pugwash, Nova Scotia, at the prompting of Bertrand Russell and Albert Einstein, and convened by the American industrialist and philanthropist Cyrus Eaton.

Quango (Quasi-Autonomous Nongovernmental Organization) A body in Great Britain that has the power to spend public money but is not under direct governmental control.

Quebec Conferences 1943–44. Strategic planning meetings between Roosevelt and Churchill. The first (19–24 August 1943) addressed the Normandy landings and operations in Italy and Southeast Asia; the second (13–16 September 1944) considered the advance into and post-war treatment of Germany and the defeat of Japan.

"Quebec Libre" (Free Quebec) Slogan of the Parti Quebecois, the voice of separatism in the predominantly French-speaking Canadian province of Quebec. French president de Gaulle encouraged separatist hopes in a speech in favor of "Quebec libre" in Montreal in July 1967. The Parti Quebecois won substantial electoral support in provincial elections throughout the 1970s.

Quemoy Incident August–September 1958. Quemoy, a Nationalist-held island six miles off the Chinese mainland, used as a base for Nationalist raiding parties 1953–58, was bombarded and threatened with invasion by Chinese Communists. A U.S. fleet moved in with supplies and a guarantee of military assistance.

Queremistas (Portuguese, *queremos Getulio*, "we want Getulio") Supporters of Getulio Vargas in the 1945 Brazilian presidential election. Vargas was dictator from 1937 to 1945 and from 1951 to 1954, when he committed suicide.

Quiet Revolution The period of the 1960–66 Liberal government in Quebec led by Premier Jean Lesage. Increased government involvement in the economy, improved welfare services, and school and hospital building encouraged a sense of communal self-awareness leading to separatist demands, the Liberals seeking "special status" within Canada and the more militant Parti Quebecois complete independence.

Rapacki Plan 14 February 1958. Polish foreign minister Rapacki proposed a ban on the manufacture and deployment of nuclear weapons in Czechoslovakia, Poland, East and West Germany, to be guaranteed by joint NATO–Warsaw Pact inspection. A renewal of the suggestion at the UN on 2 October 1958 met with U.S. and U.K. rejection, as the USSR would retain its conventional weapons superiority.

Reaganomics Term used somewhat derisively to refer to the economic policies of the Reagan administration (1981–89), which left the United States with a huge budget deficit.

Recruit Cosmos Political scandal in Japan in 1988 in which the information and property company Recruit Cosmos had offered cheap shares as bribes to politicians and civil servants. It caused the downfall of the finance and justice ministers. The prime minister, Takeshita, also eventually resigned, on 25 April 1989.

Red Army Faction Radical wing of BAADER-MEINHOF terrorist group.

Red Brigades (*Brigate rosse*)   Left-wing urban terrorist organizations active in Italy since the economic crisis of the early 1970s. An estimated 50 separate left-wing terrorist groups were operating in Italy in early 1982.

Red Guards   Young members of the People's Liberation Army of China who came to prominence during the CULTURAL REVOLUTION and were authorized to travel around the country helping to further revolution.

Red Monday   Term used to describe the sharp falls on world stock exchanges on 19 August 1991 when the anti-Gorbachev coup led by Yanayev took place in Moscow. The Dow Jones index fell 69.99 points; the FTSE 100 fell 80.5 points. The failure of the 61-hour coup saw shares rebound.

Red Sheepskin   The 1955 agreement between the CIA and the Greek government for the establishment of a resistance network against the possibility of an occupation by the Warsaw Pact. In 1990, the Greek government ordered an investigation into the circumstances of this agreement.

Republican Guard   Elite force of about 150,000 troops in Iraq under Saddam Hussein. Used to maintain his dictatorship, they were the subject of intense bombing by Allied air power in the GULF WAR.

Reykjavik Summit   11–12 October 1986.   Confused and inconclusive meeting between U.S. president Reagan and Soviet first secretary Gorbachev at which apparent initial agreement on strategic nuclear arms levels, numbers, mutual withdrawal of missiles from Europe and the eventual banning of all ballistic missiles foundered because of Soviet concerns about the U.S. Strategic Defense Initiative (Star Wars).

Rhodesia Rebellion   See UDI.

Rome, Treaty of   25 March 1957.   Signed by Belgium, France, Italy, Luxembourg, the Netherlands and West Germany, the treaty created the European Economic Community, a "Common Market" with the free movement of labor and capital, abolition of internal tariffs and unified external tariffs.

Rosenberg Case   1953.   Julius and Ethel Rosenberg were charged with passing American atomic secrets to the USSR during World War II, when the United States and the Soviet Union were allies. Following a trial, which raised doubts about the credibility of a prosecution witness, the Rosenbergs were electrocuted on 19 June 1953. The only American peacetime executions for espionage, they provoked worldwide protests.

RUKH   The name of the nationalist movement in the Ukraine that sought independence from Russia. Ukraine declared independence from the Soviet Union on 24 August 1991, confirmed by a referendum on 1 December.

Sabra and Shatila Massacre   On 16 September 1982, during the Israeli invasion of Lebanon and following the PLO evacuation of Beirut, Lebanese Christian militiamen attacked the Sabra and Shatila Palestinian refugee camps in west Beirut and killed hundreds of inhabitants. Israel came under international criticism for the attacks because the Christian militia were supported and armed by Israel. Israel itself conducted an investigation into the atrocities, which led to the resignation of several Israeli military officers who had been stationed in the area.

Sadat Assassination   Egyptian president Anwar al-Sadat was assassinated 6 October 1981 when a group of commandos in a grand military parade suddenly jumped off a truck and attacked him with grenades and machine-gun fire while he stood in a reviewing stand. Vice President Hosni Mubarak immediately became the ruler of Egypt. Mubarak had been at the side of Sadat at the time of the assassination but had escaped fatal injury. Sadat's assassins were Muslim fundamentalists opposed to Sadat's signing of the Camp David peace treaty with Israel.

Sadat Initiative   19–21 November 1977.   With heavy arms expenditure an increasing economic burden, Egyptian president Sadat undertook the first Arab diplomatic initiative to recognize Israel. His offer to visit the Israeli parliament in Jerusalem to put forward the Arab case was accepted by Premier Begin, though denounced by Syria, Libya and Algeria and the Palestine Liberation Organization. See CAMP DAVID TALKS.

Sagaing Massacre   Massacre in Burma (Myanmar) in 1988 of 300 pro-democracy demonstrators by the military regime.

Sajudis   The name of the nationalist movement in the Baltic Republic of Lithuania. Led by Vytautas Landsbergis, it declared independence from the USSR in 1989. Landsbergis became first president of Lithuania.

SALT Talks   November 1969–May 1972.   Strategic Arms Limitation Talks between the United States and the USSR, to reduce development and deployment of nuclear weapons. SALT I reached agreement on limitation of defensive missile systems. SALT II, negotiated from November 1974 to July 1979, reached agreement on missile types and numbers, but President Carter declined to submit it for ratification by the U.S. Senate following the Soviet invasion of Afghanistan.

Samizdat   (Russ., *sam*, "self"; *izdat'*, "publish")   Literature critical of the state written in secrecy by Soviet DISSIDENTS and distributed by hand.

Sandinistas   The Sandinista National Liberation Front, a radical Nicaraguan movement founded in 1961, which, after a long guerrilla campaign waged with support of trade unions, the middle classes and the Roman Catholic Church, overthrew the Somoza family dictatorship in July 1979. The Sandinistas were defeated in the elections of February 1990.

San Francisco Conference   25 April–26 June 1945.   Delegates of 50 countries, allies in the war against the Axis powers, discussed the formation of the United Nations. They drafted the UN Charter and the Statute of the International Court of Justice, and their decisions were ratified at the first meeting of the UN General Assembly in London on 24 October 1945.

Saniquellie Declaration   Principles on creating a Community of Independent African States agreed to on 19 July 1959 in the Liberian village of Saniquellie by President Nkrumah of Ghana, President Toure of Guinea and President Tubman of Liberia.

SAS   (Special Air Services)   Elite commando division in the British army, unorthodox in tactics and structure, and deliberately surrounded by secrecy.

Savak   Iranian secret police under the shah, dispersed after the Islamic revolution of 1979. Many former members were murdered by the people in revenge for crimes of torture and murder.

Schumann Plan   9 May 1950.   The first step toward creation of the European Economic Community, with the suggestion by French foreign minister Schumann that French and German coal and steel production be coordinated under a higher authority. The European Coal and Steel Community was created when Italy, Belgium, the Netherlands and Luxembourg widened the agreement in 1952.

Sea-bed Treaty   1971.   A guarantee by 25 states not to use the sea-bed beyond their 12-mile territorial waters for the dumping of nuclear waste.

Seanad Éireann   Irish Senate, consisting of 49 members elected by the universities and panels of candidates representing Irish society, and 11 nominated by the TAOISEACH. Elections must take place within 90 days of the dissolution of the DÁIL ÉIREANN.

Securitate   The Romanian secret police under the Ceausescu *(q.v.)* dictatorship. Its brutal suppression of disturbances in Timisoara in December 1989 sparked the Romanian revolution. Its loyalty and fanaticism caused hundreds of deaths in the civil war. Disbanded by the provisional government. See p. 119.

Sendero Luminoso   A Marxist-Maoist guerrilla movement founded in 1970. The title, which means "Shining Path," derived from the Peruvian Marxist Jose Carlos Mariategni's declaration that "Marxism-Leninism will open the shining path to revolution." By 1991, it was estimated that 21,500 people had died and over 10,000 were missing during the insurgency. The arrest of the movement's leader, Abimael Guzman, has led to a major decrease in violence.

Setif   Massacre of 6,000 Arabs in Algeria in 1945 by French police and European settlers in revenge for the Arab killing of 103 Europeans. The massacre helped provoke the struggle for Algerian independence from France that began in 1954.

Seventeenth Parallel   Dividing line at 170 north latitude between North and South Vietnam set by the terms of the Geneva Agreements in July 1954. Under the terms of the treaty the division was to have lasted only until national elections in 1956.

SHAPE   (Supreme Headquarters, Allied Powers in Europe)   NATO headquarters in Brussels.

Sharpeville Massacre   21 March 1960.   During black demonstrations against the South African apartheid pass laws near Johannesburg, the police opened fire, killing 67. The massacre provoked international condemnation and the withdrawal of some foreign capital, and brought South Africa close to civil war.

Shatt-al-Arab   The strategic waterway between Iraq and Iran, the dispute over which caused the Iran-Iraq war (see p. 302).

Shin Bet   Israeli security service.

Shuttle Diplomacy   Mediation between conflicting parties, involving constant travel by a representative from one antagonist to the other in order to achieve a settlement. Alternatively, the representative may be a third party, as was the case with Secretary of State Henry Kissinger on behalf of the United States in attempting to mediate in the Arab-Israeli conflict.

Sidra, Gulf of, Crisis   On 19 August 1981, a pair of U.S. Navy F-14 jet fighters downed two attacking Soviet-built Libyan SU-22s over the Gulf of Sidra, about 60 miles from the Libyan coast. Libya claimed part of the Gulf of Sidra as its territory, but the United States considered the area to be international waters. The confrontation occurred in the final hours of a two-day U.S. Navy military exercise in the southern Mediterranean and in the northern part of the Gulf of Sidra.

Sinn Féin (Ir., "ourselves alone") Irish nationalist movement founded by Arthur Griffiths in 1902, originally with the aim of securing independence from Great Britain. Griffiths was superseded by the more militant leaders James Connolly, Padraic Pearse and St Oliver Plunkett, who organized the 1916 "Easter Rising" in Dublin. Now influential as the political wing of the IRA.

Six, The   Name given to the original EC member states (Belgium, France, German Federal Republic, Italy, Luxembourg and the Netherlands) before accession of Great Britain, Ireland and Denmark in 1973.

Six Counties   The counties of Northern Ireland: Antrim, Armagh, Down, Fermanagh, Londonderry and Tyrone. With Cavan, Donegal and Monaghan, they originally formed the province of Ulster, but in 1923 these three were made part of the Dominion of Ireland, while the others remain part of the United Kingdom.

Six-Day War   5–10 June 1967. With Egypt having blockaded the TIRAN STRAITS and expelled the UN–peacekeeping force, and with Egyptian, Syrian and Jordanian armies mobilizing on Israeli frontiers, Israel struck the first blow, destroying Arab air forces on 6 June. Its tanks reached the Suez Canal on 7 June and its armies occupied Jordan's West Bank and the Syrian Golan Heights (see p. 299).

Slansky Trial   17–30 November 1950. The largest Stalinist show-trial outside the USSR, with Slansky, Czech vice premier and Communist Party secretary, and 13 others, 11 of whom were Jews, falsely charged with treason, Zionism, Titoism, Trotskyism and bourgeois nationalism. Eleven were found guilty, and Slansky was hanged on 2 December.

Social Chapter   Section of the 1991 Maastricht Treaty giving power to the European Commission to impose the terms of the SOCIAL CHARTER on common standards in employment policy without the possibility of a national veto. Great Britian has "opted out" of this clause, to the dismay of trade unionists.

Social Charter   The European Community (EC) Charter of Social Rights of Workers, setting a pattern for European labor law. Opposed by right-wing conservatives, especially in Great Britain. It guarantees such things as freedom of movement and equal treatment for workers throughout the community, the right to strike, a guaranteed "decent standard of living," freedom to join trade unions, the right to collective bargaining, and so on.

Solidarity   Name given to Poland's National Confederation of Independent Trade Unions, formed on 8 September 1980 under the leadership of Lech Walesa *(q.v.)* and representing 10 million industrial workers. Rural Solidarity was formed later in 1980. The union grew out of workers' reactions to rising food prices and was the focus of industrial unrest in Poland in 1980–81. On 13 December 1980, military rule was imposed in Poland; Solidarity was banned and went underground. With the collapse of communism in Eastern Europe, Solidarity has been vindicated. Despite splits in the movement, its leading figure, Lech Walesa, was elected president of Poland in 1990.

Solid South   U.S. political term used from Reconstruction to the 1960s; during this time Southern states tended to support Democrats in all local and national elections.

Sovkhoz   (Russ., *sovietskoye khozyaistvo,* "soviet farm") State–owned farm run by state employees in the USSR. There were 4,000 of them in the 1950s.

Soweto   South West Township, a black area near Johannesburg, scene of 16 June 1976 student demonstrations against government attempts to impose the Afrikaans language in education. The protest developed into three days of riots, with 236 nonwhites killed by police and two whites killed by rioters; on 6 July the government withdrew its proposal but the area remained a central flashpoint in antigovernment agitation.

Soyuz   Bloc of Soviet hard-liners who comprised conservatives from the military, directors of the nation's huge industrial complexes and all those in the communist hierarchy who were opposed to Gorbachev's broad democratic and market reforms. The failure of the August 1991 coup largely discredited their influence.

Special Relationship   The relationship between the United States and Great Britain, ostensibly based on a long-term shared culture and kinship rather than simple diplomatic interest. More often appealed to by British rather than American leaders.

Star Wars   Popular name given to the Reagan administration's Strategic Defense Initiative (SDI), after the popular science-fiction film of 1977.

START I   Strategic Arms Reduction Talks, a renewal of the SALT talks, begun in Geneva on 1 July 1982 between the United States and the USSR to discuss limitation of nuclear weaponry in Europe. The historic agreement was signed in July 1991 by Presidents Bush and Gorbachev. The Soviet Union agreed to cut its strategic nuclear arsenal by 35% (to 7,000 warheads), the United States by 25%.

START II   Wide-ranging agreement on reducing nuclear weapons signed by President Bush and President Yeltsin on New Year's Day, 1993. Building on START I, the accord obliges both sides to cut their arsenals from 10,000 warheads to 3,500 by the year 2003.

Stasi   The security police under the former communist regime in East Germany. It was disbanded in the revolution of 1989.

Stern Gang   Lohamei Herut Yisrael (Fighters for the Freedom of Israel), a Jewish guerrilla group founded by Avraham Stern. Operated in Palestine in the mid-1940s, it was responsible for the assassination of Count Bernadotte, UN mediator in Palestine, in 1945.

Stockholm Conference   1972.   Out of a growing recognition of their significance, representatives of 100 countries met to discuss the international implications of environmental issues.

Stormont   The former Northern Ireland parliament.

Storting   The Norwegian parliament, consisting of 150 representatives elected every four years by proportional representation. A quarter form the Lagring (upper house), and three quarters the Odelsting (lower house).

Student Revolt   A U.S. and European phenomenon of the late 1960s and early 1970s, which initially arose from demonstrations against U.S. involvement in Vietnam, but which then appeared to question the entire basis of the educational, political, social and economic system. The French MAY EVENTS of 1968 were the high point. Student activism waned with the end of the Vietnam War and the onset of the international depression in the late 1970s.

Suez Affair   Following Egyptian nationalization of the strategically important Suez Canal on 26 July 1956, Great Britain, France and Israel agreed secretly for Israel to attack Egypt through Sinai, while Britain and France occupied the Canal Zone on the pretext of separating the combatants. Israel attacked on 29 October, Britain and France on 31 October, provoking intense domestic and international criticism. The U.S. refusal to support Britain and France forced a cease-fire on 6 November and deployment of the UN Emergency Force. The affair confirmed British decline internationally and pushed Nasser closer to the Soviet Union (see p. 295).

Suppression of Communism Act   1950.   South African legislation banning the Communist Party, defining all persons advocating political, industrial, social or economic change as "Communists." The justice minister was empowered to impose banning orders on individuals, limiting their rights to publish, speak or meet others, and effectively providing for house arrest.

SWAPO (South West African People's Organization) Founded in 1960 by Sam Nujoma and Herman Toivo Ja Toivo. In 1920 Namibia was mandated by the League of Nations to South Africa, which later attempted to integrate it into its other territories. Afrer 1966 SWAPO mounted guerrilla actions against South African military units, following a UN resolution revoking South Africa's mandate. In 1971 the UN recognized SWAPO as the "sole authentic representative of the people of Namibia." SWAPO was excluded from the independence negotiation process in the 1970s, and a National Assembly and Council of Ministers were instituted by South Africa. Conflict between South Africa and SWAPO continued until 1989, when independence for Namibia was agreed upon for March 1990.

Taif Accord Agreement on new constitutional arrangements made in October 1989 at Taif, Saudi Arabia, by 70 surviving members of the last Lebanese parliament, elected in 1972. Maronite Christian dominance in government was to be reduced by having a president subject to a cabinet made up equally of Christian and Muslim members, with National Assembly membership also equally divided.

Taliban A faction of Islamic fundamentalist students who seized power in Kabul, the capital of Afghanistan, in September 1996, imposing harsh fundamentalist laws, including stoning for adultery and severing hands for theft. Women were required to cover themselves in public from head to toe. The Taliban's scorched-earth tactics and human rights abuses isolated it from the international community. Although the Taliban controlled about 90% of the country by 1998, only three governments—Pakistan, Saudi Arabia, and the U.A.E.—recognize the Taliban as Afghanistan's legitimate government.

Tanaiste (Ir., "second in line") Deputy prime minister of Ireland, appointed by the TAOISEACH.

Tangentopoli The "City of Bribes" corruption scandal that erupted in Italy in 1992, discrediting the entire political system and threatening to bring down the republic that had been founded in 1946. Large numbers of politicians from across the political spectrum were accused of accepting bribes from businessmen in return for contracts and favors.

Tanker War Attacks made on oil tankers in the Persian Gulf in the 1980–88 Iran–Iraq War. Iraq attacked ships trading with Iran in 1984; Iran replied with attacks on tankers using the ports of Iraq's Arab supporters.

Tan-Zam Railway   Chinese-aided project of the mid-1960s to provide landlocked Zambia with a rail route to the sea through Tanzania, avoiding dependence on the white regime in Rhodesia during the period of the UDI.

Taoiseach   (Ir.)   Prime minister of Ireland and head of government, appointed by the president on nomination of the DÁIL ÉIREANN.

Tashkent Agreement   January 1966.   Temporarily successful mediation by Soviet premier Alexei Kosygin between Lal Shastri of India and Mohammed Ayub Khan of Pakistan over the Kashmir dispute, following armed conflict between the two countries in 1965.

Tehran Conference   28 November–1 December 1943.   First meeting among Roosevelt, Churchill and Stalin, with agreement emerging on plans for the final attack on Germany, the invasion of occupied France, and initial discussions on the creation of a postwar United Nations.

Test-Ban Treaty   5 August 1963.   A U.S., Soviet and British agreement concluded after five years of negotiations to end nuclear tests in the atmosphere, in space or under water. Underground testing was allowed to continue. France and China refused to accept the treaty, but over 90 other countries signed in the following two years.

Tet Offensive   29 January–25 February 1968.   A mass attack by Viet Cong and North Vietnam armies under General Vo Nguyen Giap on U.S. and South Vietnamese forces, resulting in small territorial gains but large casualties on both sides. It encouraged a reassessment in Washington of the U.S. commitment, and an eventual reduction in military involvement.

Thatcherites   Supporters of former British Conservative prime minister Margaret Thatcher and her radical right-wing policies. They include the "DRIES."

Thirty-eighth Parallel   Latitude 38° north, which divides communist North Korea from South Korea, demarcation line established at the Yalta Conference of 1945 as a preliminary to the unification of Korea. Any hopes of unity were dashed by the Korean War (1950–53), when the North effectively invaded the South.

"Thousand Days"   Days in office of U.S. president John F. Kennedy (1917–63), who was inaugurated on 20 January 1961 and assassinated on 22 November 1963.

Three-Day Week   The result of the economic crisis in Great Britain in 1973 following increase in the cost of oil and miners', power workers' and railroad workers' overtime bans, resulting in declaration of a state of emergency by Edward Heath's Conservative government on 13 November 1973. Strict controls were introduced on domestic and industrial consumption of electricity, and from 1 January 1974 on, electricity could be supplied to industry only on three specified days a week. An election, which the Conservatives lost, was called to test support for the government policy.

Tiananmen Square   The main public square in Beijing. The location of mass prodemocracy demonstrations in the spring of 1989, and their violent repression by the Chinese government on 4 June.

***Tiger* Talks**   2–4 December 1966.   A meeting on the cruiser *Tiger* off Gibraltar between British premier Harold Wilson and Rhodesian rebel premier Ian Smith to reach settlement of the Rhodesian UDI. The talks failed, as did further ones on HMS *Fearless* in October 1968, through Smith's refusal to accept unimpeded progress toward black majority rule.

Tiran, Straits of   Seaway providing Israel's sole access to the Red Sea and Indian Ocean through the port of Eilat, blockaded by Egypt in 1956 and 1967.

Tonkin Gulf Resolution   7 August 1964.   The U.S. Congress, following an alleged North Vietnamese attack on the USS *Maddox* in the Gulf of Tonkin, authorized President Johnson to retaliate with bombing raids on oil refineries and air bases and to deploy U.S. forces to aid Southeast Asia Treaty Organization members under threat. The resolution was used by Johnson to deepen American involvement in the Vietnam War.

Totalitarian Capitalism   The attempt by the Communist Party in China to introduce a free-market capitalist economy without relinquishing its own power. Hence political liberty and free speech were not allowed. A symbol of this policy was the 1989 TIANANMEN SQUARE massacre. Following the opening of China's "second revolution" in 1978, the gross national product grew 8.7% annually while by 1993 the state sector accounted for only a third of economic output.

Treason Trial   December 1956.   One hundred and fifty-six opponents of apartheid were arrested and charged with membership in an "international Communist" conspiracy—the AFRICAN NATIONAL CONGRESS—to violently overthrow the South African state. The trial lasted to March 1961, at which time the remaining defendants were acquitted, but the ANC had become a banned organization.

Treuhand   The agency organizing the privatization of state enterprises in Germany.

Tripartism   Joint governments of Christian Democrats, Socialists and Communists formed in France and Italy immediately after World War II, reflecting their shared experience in the resistance against Germany. As the COLD WAR intensified, Communist ministers were dismissed from the French government in May 1947 and a Christian Democrat government was formed in Italy in April 1947.

Tripartite Agreement   May 1950.   An attempt by the United States, Great Britain and France to reduce the danger of war arising from continuing mutual Arab-Israeli hostility by guaranteeing the integrity of existing borders and limiting arms sales to potential antagonists.

Trizonia   Term used to denote combined British, French and United States occupation zones in Germany after July 1948, when France joined its occupation zone to BIZONIA.

Truman Doctrine   12 March 1947.   A shift to a more overt anticommunist policy with the guarantee by U.S. president Truman to provide financial aid to countries facing internal or external communist threats. Truman argued that not to do so would "endanger the welfare of our own nation."

TUC   Trades Union Congress, federation of some 72 British trade unions founded in 1868, whose basic function is to coordinate union action by means of annual conferences of union representatives where matters of common concern are discussed.

Tupamaros   Marxist urban guerrillas in Uruguay, about 1,000 in number, including many professional men. They were effective in creating unrest before 1972, when police and right-wing paramilitary groups carried out actions against them; since then they have been relatively inactive.

Twentieth Party Congress   February 1956.   A secret speech by Soviet Communist Party first secretary Khrushchev at the Congress denounced Stalin's "personality cult," the 1930s purges and other authoritarian excesses; acknowledged legitimacy of alternative roads to socialism than the Soviet model; and argued for "peaceful coexistence" with the West. The speech had repercussions for communist regimes in Eastern Europe and communist parties in Western Europe.

UDI   (Unilateral Declaration of Independence)   Declared by the Rhodesian Front government of Ian Smith on 11 November 1965, it was rejected by Great Britain and condemned by the UN, which saw it as a rebellion consequent upon Rhodesia's refusal to introduce black majority rule.

UN   See p. 31.

UNITA (National Union for the Total Independence of Angola) A group fighting alongside the MPLA and FNLA between 1961 and 1975 to achieve Angolan independence. Following independence in 1975 MPLA and UNITA set up rival governments, and a civil war broke out in which U.S.– and South African–backed UNITA and FNLA were defeated. UNITA forces still control some areas of southern Angola.

UNOMOZ United Nations Operation in Mozambique. UN troops were deployed in Mozambique to maintain the cease-fire and supervise demobilization following the end of the 16-year civil war between government Frelimo and rebel Renamo forces.

Uruguay Round See GATF.

U2 Incident 1 May 1960. U.S. pilot Gary Powers was captured when his U2 spy plane was shot down over Soviet territory, provoking a Russian walkout at the Paris Summit Conference when President Eisenhower refused Khrushchev's demand for an apology for the overflight. U2 flights were terminated and Powers was released in exchange for a Soviet spy in February 1962.

Vanunu Affair Allegations in the London *Sunday Times* by Mordechai Vanunu in October 1986 that Israel had developed nuclear weapons and was stockpiling them. Vanunu, who had worked at the Dimona plant in the Negev, was seized by agents of Mossad, the Israeli security agency, in Rome and imprisoned in Israel for treason.

Vatican II 1962–63. Summoned by Pope John XXIII, proceedings began on 11 October 1962 in the presence of over 8,000 Catholic bishops and observers from Anglican and Orthodox churches. The 16 decrees that emerged encouraged greater tolerance toward non-Catholic Christian churches and provided for the use of the vernacular rather than Latin in Catholic liturgy.

Velvet Divorce The division on 1 January 1993 of Czechoslovakia into the separate states of the Czech Republic (10 million population) and Slovakia (5 million population). So called because of the apparent amicable nature of the separation, but also an ironic reference to the 1989 VELVET REVOLUTION that overthrew communist rule.

Velvet Revolution Popular, nonviolent uprisings in Prague and other Czech cities in 1989, which overthrew the communist regime.

Viet Cong Name meaning "Vietnamese Communists" given by the South Vietnamese government to the armed forces of the Front for the Liberation of South Vietnam (founded in 1960). The Viet Cong took an active part in the Vietnam War (1965–73).

Viet Minh   Abbreviated form of Viet-Nam Doc-Lap Dong-Minh, the Vietnam Independence League, founded in May 1941 to resist Japanese occupation of Vietnam. It included noncommunist nationalists but was dominated by leading communist members Ho Chi Minh, Pham Van Dong and Vo Nguyen Giap. It declared a Democratic Republic of Vietnam following Japanese surrender in 1945, and following breakdown of negotiations with France it fought for Vietnamese independence (after 1951 as Viet Front).

Vietnam War   See p. 323–24.

Volkstaat   Afrikaans term for an independent white homeland that extremist right-wing white South Africans wish to see established.

Wafd   (Arab., "delegation")   Main nationalist party of inter-war Egypt. It was discredited by wartime cooperation with the British, and considered corrupt by Nasser and Sadat. Following its 1950 election victory, FREE OFFICERS encouraged civil unrest, and Wafd was dismissed by King Farouk before he himself was deposed, in 1952. Wafd and all other parties were dissolved in 1953.

Warsaw Pact   See p. 36.

Watergate   The name given to a series of scandals in the administration of President Richard M. Nixon, leading to Nixon's resignation on 9 August 1974. The Watergate hotel was the location of the Democratic Party national headquarters in Washington, D.C., which was burglarized on 17 June 1972. Five men arrested in the break-in and two of their accomplices were tried and convicted. James McCord, one of the convicted burglars, charged that there had been a cover-up of responsibility for the burglary. In the wake of the McCord accusation, and the investigative reporting of Carl Bernstein and Bob Woodward of the *Washington Post*, a special Senate committee chaired by Senator Sam Ervin (Dem., N.C.) held nationally televised hearings into the Watergate affair in the spring and summer of 1973. Former White House counsel John Dean charged that the Watergate break-in was approved by Attorney General John Mitchell and that White House aides H. R. "Bob" Haldeman and John Ehrlichman were involved in the cover-up. In May 1973, then–attorney general Elliot Richardson appointed Archibald Cox as a special prosecutor to investigate the entire "Watergate affair." Cox began to uncover evidence of improper conduct in the Nixon reelection committee, and illegal wiretapping by the administration. In July 1973, it became known that presidential conversations in the White House had been taped since 1971. In October 1973, when Cox tried to obtain these tapes from the president, Nixon fired him. This touched off calls for Nixon's impeachment from the press and from some in government. The

House Judiciary Committee began an impeachment inquiry, which ended in the adoption of three articles of impeachment against Nixon in July 1974. On 5 August 1974, Nixon released the transcripts of three of the recorded conversations that Special Prosecutor Leon Jaworski (whom Nixon had appointed to replace Cox) had sought from him. Nixon admitted that he had known about the Watergate cover-up shortly after the burglary and that he had tried to stop the Federal Bureau of Investigation's inquiry into the break-in. On 9 August 1974 Nixon resigned and Vice President Gerald R. Ford was sworn in as president. The next month, Ford pardoned Nixon for any crimes he might have committed as president; however, Mitchell, Haldeman, Ehrlichman and Dean were among those who were convicted for their part in the Watergate scandals.

Watts Riots   Week of riots in the predominantly black and Hispanic Watts district of southwest Los Angeles that began on 11 August 1965. Thirty-four people died and over 1,000 were injured in protests against economic deprivation, social injustice and military conscription for the Vietnam War. The events allegedly created a white backlash against progress blacks were attempting to make through the civil rights movement.

West Bank   Area on the west bank of the River Jordan occupied by Israel in the Six-Day War (5–10 June 1967) between Israel and Arab states. Palestinians regard it as a homeland, but Israelis retained possession of the area and have been colonizing it. It has been the scene of much violence during the INTIFADA. Under the 1993 Israeli–PLO agreement, Jericho (on the West Bank) gained limited self-government, effective from 1994.

Western European Union   See BRUSSELS, TREATY OF.

Westland Affair   Internal British government arguments in the winter of 1985–86 over the fate of the failing Westland Helicopter Co. broke into the open in January, with officially inspired leaks of sensitive Cabinet letters. This prompted the resignation of the defense and industry ministers, compromised traditional civil service neutrality, and undermined the reputation of Prime Minister Thatcher, who was accused of deeper involvement than she admitted.

"Wetbacks"   Derisory term applied to illegal immigrants entering the United States from Mexico, originally by swimming across the Rio Grande, providing cheap labor for California landowners, who encouraged them.

"Wets"   Derisory term applied to members of the British Conservative Party who did not support radical right-wing policies of former prime minister Margaret Thatcher.

WHAM   (Winning hearts and minds)   Propaganda exercises carried out by U.S. forces in the Vietnam War (1965–73) in an attempt to convince the Vietnamese people of the value of Western democracy and friendship with the United States. Coercion also played a part in the campaign.

White Revolution   Attempt begun in 1963 by the shah of Iran to modernize and Westernize his country, including extending the vote to women. The tensions this triggered played some part in his eventual overthrow in the 1979 revolution.

Whitewater   The controversy concerning the involvement of President Clinton (and Hillary Rodham Clinton) in a property development company in the northern Arkansas Ozark region after 1978, when Clinton was attorney general of Arkansas and soon to be governor. Among numerous allegations is the charge that money was diverted from a Little Rock savings bank into Whitewater and thence into Mr. Clinton's campaign funds. Linked to the mysteries of Whitewater was the death of Vince Foster, the deputy White House counsel, in July 1993.

"Winds of Change"   Phrase used by prime minister Harold Macmillan (1894–1986) in a speech to the South African parliament in 1960 to describe the growth of black national consciousness in Africa.

Wirtschaftswunder   (Ger., "economic miracle")   Rapid recovery of the West German economy after 1945.

Yalta Conference   4–11 February 1945.   Agreement among Roosevelt, Churchill and Stalin that set out the features of postwar Europe: East/West spheres of influence; a divided, disarmed and occupied Germany and Berlin following unconditional surrender; a "Declaration on Liberated Europe" guaranteeing democratic institutions in liberated states; and reaffirmation of the Atlantic and UN Charters. The United States was later criticized for effectively placing Eastern Europe under Soviet control.

Yom Kippur (October) War   6 October 1973.   While Israelis were observing the religious fast of Yom Kippur, Egyptian forces crossed the Suez Canal and Syrian troops penetrated the Golan Heights. Israeli troops counterattacked on 8 October, moving to within 65 miles of Cairo and 35 miles of Damascus. War was nominally ended by a UN cease-fire on 24 October. See p. 300.

Yongbyong   Site in North Korea of suspected nuclear facility. North Korea's refusal to open this site to international inspection has escalated tension on the Korean peninsula.

ZANU   (Zimbabwe African National Union)   Founded in 1963 by former ZAPU members to force the Rhodesian government to grant black majority rule, it was immediately banned. Failure of the Geneva talks on Rhodesia's future in 1976 led to increased guerrilla activity up to 1979, when the ban was lifted. In the 1980 elections, ZANU won 57 seats and 63% of the vote, and its leader, Robert Mugabe (p. 536), became leader of a coalition government that included ZAPU members. ZANU and ZAPU merged in 1987.

ZAPU (Zimbabwe African People's Union) Founded in 1961 by Joshua Nkomo (b. 1917) with the aim of achieving majority rule in Rhodesia, it was banned and undertook guerrilla activities with ZANU in a Patriotic Front alliance. In the 1980 elections, against hopes and expectations of Western governments, it won only 20 seats. It has been alleged by ZANU since 1982 that ZAPU seeks to overthrow the government, and by ZAPU that ZANU has committed atrocities in order to intimidate ZAPU. Nkomo fled the country in 1983. ZAPU and ZANU merged in 1987, making Zimbabwe a one-party state.

CHAPTER 11

BIOGRAPHICAL DICTIONARY

ACHESON, Dean G. (1893–1971)   U.S. secretary of state, 1949–53. Following a successful legal career, he served in the Roosevelt administration in various high-level posts, beginning in 1933, and he was appointed secretary of state by President Harry TRUMAN in 1947; he held that post for the duration of Truman's administration, advocating the "containment" of Soviet communism and helping to establish the North Atlantic Treaty Organization and other multinational pacts to further that goal. Despite his opposition to the expansion of communism, he was attacked by conservative Republicans, who blamed him and Truman for the fall of China to the Communists and criticized the Truman administration's handling of the Korean War. Acheson was also influential in the conduct of foreign affairs during the administration of President John F. KENNEDY (1961–63).

ADENAUER, Konrad (1876–1967)   West German chancellor (prime minister), 1949–63. Chief burgomaster of Cologne from 1917 to 1933 and a prominent member of the Catholic Center Party during the Weimar Republic, he was dismissed from office by the Nazis in 1933. He was founder and later chairman of the Christian Democratic Party (1945–66); elected as first federal chancellor in 1949, he served as foreign minister from 1951 to 1955, providing a defeated country with stable constitutional government and a place in NATO and the EEC.

AGNEW, Spiro T. (1918–96)   American vice president (1969–73). He was a surprise choice as Nixon's running mate, picked primarily to secure support from Southern states. He was forced to resign in 1973 when faced with prosecution for accepting bribes while governor of Maryland.

ALBRIGHT, Madeleine K. (1937–   )   First female U.S. secretary of state, appointed in January 1997. Born Marie Jana Korbel to a Czech diplomat, her family fled to England when the Nazis occupied Czechoslovakia in 1939. In 1997, she learned that her family was Jewish and that three of her grandparents died in German concentration camps. In the 1970s, Albright began her career as chief legislative assistant for Democratic senator Edmund Muskie and worked for President Jimmy Carter's national security advisor. She was a professor of international affairs at Georgetown University from 1982 to 1993, when she was named ambassador to the United Nations. The Senate unanimously confirmed her nomination as secretary of state in 1997.

ALLENDE GOSSENS, Salvador (1908–73)   President of Chile, 1970–73. A Marxist democrat who served as a Chilean Socialist Party deputy from 1937 to 1945 and senator from 1945 to 1970. After three unsuccessful attempts, he won the 1970 presidential election. His efforts to bring social reform by democratic means encountered increasing opposition and unrest, supported by the CIA. In 1973 he was overthrown in a military coup led by General PINOCHET, and he died during fighting at the presidential palace.

AMIN, Idi (1925–   )   President of Uganda from 1971 until 1979, when he was forced into exile. He moved up in the Ugandan armed forces, rising from the rank of private in 1946 to commander in chief in 1966. He came to political power in a coup in 1971, ousting Milton OBOTE from power. In 1972 he ordered the expulsion of most of Uganda's Asians. He earned a reputation as a vicious and murderous dictator. He is currently in exile in Saudi Arabia.

ANDROPOV, Yuri (1914–84)   General secretary of the Soviet Communist Party from 1982 to 1984. He had previously served as ambassador to Hungary (1954–57), where he played a major role in suppressing the 1956 uprising; secretary to the Central Committee of the Communist Party (1957–67); and chairman of the KGB (1967–82), in which position he became identified with the 1968 invasion of Czechoslovakia, the 1979 invasion of Afghanistan and the military crackdown in Poland. Although ill health dimmed his brief tenure as general secretary, he did initiate a drive for economic reform. His proposal for arms reduction was greeted with skepticism in the West.

ANNAN, Kofi Atta (1938–   )   Secretary-general of the United Nations (UN) since 1997. Annan began his UN career as a budget officer for the World Health Organization in Geneva in 1962, and he then served in several administrative posts. In 1993, he became undersecretary-general for peacekeeping organizations and coordinated the transition of operations from UN forces to NATO forces.

AQUINO, Corazon (Cory) (1933–   )   President of the Philippines 1986–92. Aquino lived in exile with her husband, Benigno, who led the opposition to President Ferdinand MARCOS from 1980 to 1983. After

Benigno Aquino's assassination on his return to Manila in 1983, she became increasingly active politically, and she was chosen as a compromise candidate to contest the presidential election against Marcos in 1986. Although Marcos claimed victory, international pressure in the face of widespread corruption led to his resignation and Aquino's accession to the presidency. Her administration faced five early attempted coups, but success in the 1987 plebiscite confirmed her as president until 1992. Further coup attempts occurred in 1989 and 1990, but U.S. support ensured her survival.

ARAFAT, Yasir (1929–)   Chairman of the Palestine Liberation Organization since 1968. Active in the League of Palestinian Students in the 1940s and 1950s, he formed the Al Fatah movement in 1956. Although the PLO has been associated with many terrorist incidents, Arafat has been regarded as a moderate Palestinian leader and, as such, has been recognized by much of the international community as someone with whom negotiations should take place. His support of Iraq (and its dictator, Saddam HUSSEIN) in 1990 did his cause little good. In 1993, however, he was instrumental in negotiating a peace accord with Israel, despite opposition from militants in Hamas and his own organization. In 1994, Arafat and Yitzhak RABIN and Shimon PERES of Israel were jointly awarded the Nobel Prize for Peace. Arafat moved toward Palestinian self-rule, but he was stalled when Benjamin NETANYAHU became prime minister of Israel. Arafat has pledge to continue the peace process with Netanyahu's successor, Ehud BARAK. Arafat was elected president of the Palestinian National Council in 1996 with nearly 90% of the popular vote.

AL-ASSAD, Hafez (1928–2000)   President of Syria from 1971 to 2000; minister of defense and commander of the air force, 1966–70; prime minister, 1970–71. Regarded as a hard-liner among Arab politicians, he has given active support to terrorist activity. Evidence of Syrian involvement in the attempted bombing of an El Al plane flying out of Heathrow Airport led Great Britain to break off diplomatic relations in 1986. Assad supported the Allies against Iraq in 1990, regaining lost diplomatic ground with the West. In February 1997 he was reported to be seriously ill. His death in June 2000 left the status of Syrian-Israeli relations unimproved in efforts to settle long-standing hostility. He was succeeded by his son Bashar.

ATTLEE, Clement (1883–1967)   British prime minister, 1945–51; member of parliament (Labour), 1922–55, representing Limehouse and then West Walthamstow. Elected leader of the Labour Party in 1935 when the party was in the doldrums, he held this position until 1955. Junior minister from 1930 to 1931, he served as lord privy seal (deputy prime minister) in the wartime coalition government (1940–45) and also as dominions secretary (1942–45). Prime minister of the first majority Labour government (1945–51), he was leader of the Opposition from 1951 to 1955. He was created Earl Attlee on his retirement.

AYUB KHAN, Mohammed (1907–74) President of Pakistan, 1958–69. A soldier commissioned in the British Indian Army in 1928, he rose to commander in chief (eventually field marshal) of the Pakistani army in 1951. Minister of defense from 1954 to 1955, he became head of state in 1958 when martial law was declared, and he won presidential elections in 1960 and 1965. Internal repression and lack of success in disputes with India led to riots in 1968 and to his resignation in 1969.

AZIKIWE, Benjamin Nnamdi (1904–96) President of Nigeria, 1963–66. An Ibo active in nationalist politics as editor of various newspapers and executive member of the Nigerian Youth Movement, 1934–41, he was elected a member of the Eastern Region House of Assembly, 1954–59, and premier, Eastern Region, 1954–59. He served as governor-general of Nigeria, 1960–63, and as first president of the republic, 1963–66. He ran unsuccessfully for president in 1979 and 1983.

BAKER, James Addison III (1930–) U.S. secretary of the treasury, 1985–88, under Reagan. Co-chairman of the campaign to elect George Bush president. Secretary of state from 1989 to August 1992, he faced a major test with the Gulf War of 1991. In 1997 he served as a UN special envoy to broker a peace settlement for Western Sahara.

BALEWA, Abubakar Tafawa (1912–66) Prime minister of Nigeria, 1960–66; federal minister of works, 1952–54; minister of trade, 1954; chief minister, 1957–59; federal prime minister, 1959; knighted, 1960; first federal prime minister of independent Nigeria, 1960–66; he was killed in a military coup in 1966.

BALLADUR, Edouard (1929–) French prime minister from 1993 to 1995. A lawyer and diplomat, he became a member of the Gaullist Rally for the Republic (RPR) and was appointed secretary-general to the presidency by President POMPIDOU in 1969. He left politics to work in industry and then acted as a councillor of state from 1984–88, serving as minister of state for economy, finance and privatization from 1986–88. Elected to the National Assembly in 1988, he became a prominent advocate of European financial union.

BANDA, Hastings Kamuzu (1906–97) President of Malawi from 1963 to 1994. After practicing medicine in the United Kingdom and Ghana, he returned to Nyasaland as president-general of the African National Congress in 1958. Imprisoned, 1959–60; leader, Malawi Congress Party, 1961; minister of natural resources and local government,

1961–63; prime minister of Nyasaland, 1963–64, and of independent Malawi, 1964–66. His dictatorial rule lost him the 1993 referendum. Due to widespread protests and the withdrawal of Western financial aid, Banda legalized other political parties in 1993 and was voted out of office in Malawi's first multiparty presidential elections the following year.

BAO DAI (1913–97)   Last emperor of Vietnam. Enthroned in 1932 (though he succeeded as emperor in 1926), he abdicated in 1945 under communist pressure and retired to Hong Kong, living a playboy existence. He returned as head of state in 1949 at the request of France. When a separate South Vietnam came into existence in 1954, he was nominal head of state, with NGO DINH Diem as prime minister. In 1955 he was deposed by Diem in a referendum held when he was out of the country.

BARAK, Ehud (1942–   )   Prime minister of Israel since May 1999. A centrist politician with a 35-year military career as Israel's most decorated soldier, he joined the Labor Party in 1995 as a protégé of then–prime minister Yitzhak RABIN. He served as interior minister under Rabin and foreign minister under Shimon PERES. He promised to end Israel's 17-year military presence in Lebanon, suggested territorial compromise with Syria and resumed peace talks with Yasir ARAFAT of the PLO. Barak resigned as prime minister in December 2000.

BATISTA y ZALDÍVAR, Fulgencio (1901–73)   President of Cuba, 1939–44; dictator, 1952–58. He joined the army, rising to the rank of sergeant before participating in a military coup against President Gerardo Machado. He promoted himself to colonel and established a Fascist-inspired corporate state. Elected president after permitting formation of rival political parties in 1939, he went into voluntary exile in 1944 after losing to Ramón Grau San Martín in the presidential elections. He returned to power in 1952 after a coup d'état, but after 1956, faced by Fidel CASTRO RUZ's left-wing partisan movement, he lost support in the army and was forced to flee in January 1959.

BEGIN, Menachem (1913–92)   Israeli prime minister, 1977–83. Having emigrated from Siberia to Palestine in 1941, he led Irgun Zvai Leumi, a paramilitary terrorist group. A member of the Knesset (parliament) from 1948, he was junior minister, 1967–70; leader of the right-wing Likud (Unity) Party from 1970; and prime minister, on winning the 1977 elections. His premiership was marked by his tough line against the PLO and on Israeli control of the West Bank of the Jordan, but also by relaxation of tension with Egypt, following talks with President SADAT in 1977. He was joint recipient of the Nobel Peace Prize (with Sadat) in 1978. He retired due to ill health in 1983.

BEN BELLA, Mohammed Achmed (1916–)   Prime minister of Algeria, 1962–66. Leader of the extremist Algerian National Movement in 1947, he was imprisoned by the French in 1950. He escaped in 1952 and founded the Front de Libération Nationale in 1954. He led the armed revolt against French rule, and he was captured and imprisoned by the French from 1956 to 1962. First prime minister of newly independent Algeria from 1962 to 1965, he was deposed by BOUMÉDIENNE's military coup and kept under house arrest until 1979. After ten years in exile, he returned to Algeria in 1990. The cancellation of the 1991 legislative election led to his exile for the second time, and his party was banned in 1997.

BEN GURION, David (1886–1973)   Israeli prime minister and minister of defense, 1948–53 and 1955–63. Born in Russia, he immigrated to Palestine in 1906. During the 1920s and 1930s he emerged as leader of the Labor Zionists and became leader of the Labor Party. In 1948 he proclaimed the creation of the state of Israel, becoming its first prime minister.

BERIA, Lavrenti (1899–1953)   Head of the Soviet Security Service, 1935–53. He organized a Bolshevik group during the Russian Revolution and directed the secret police in Georgia from 1921 to 1931. He was first secretary of the Georgian Communist Party, and he was appointed commissar for international affairs by Stalin in 1938 and head of the NKVD (Soviet Security Service) until after Stalin's death. He was dismissed and executed by other leading Communists, who believed he had been planning to succeed Stalin.

BERLUSCONI, Silvio (1936–)   Prime minister of Italy, 1994–95. A business tycoon, he owns the Fininvest group (with massive TV and newspaper interests, real estate etc.) and the AC Milan football club. Founder of Forza Italia, he is pro-free market, anti-immigrant and pro-decentralization. He headed the right-wing alliance that won the March 1994 election. He resigned amid allegations of corruption in business dealings and received a 16-month jail sentence in December 1995. In April 1996 Berlusconi ran unsuccessfully in the general election. He stood trial for tax evasion in February 1998 but was cleared of the charges.

BERNADOTTE, Count Folke (1895–1948)   President of the Swedish Red Cross and United Nations mediator. A Swedish soldier involved with the Red Cross in World War I, he arranged in World War II exchanges of sick and disabled prisoners at Göteborg in 1943 and 1944. He was used by Heinrich Himmler in 1945 as intermediary to seek surrender of German forces to the British and Americans, but the proposal was rejected in London and Washington. He was invited by

UN secretary-general Trygve LIE to serve as UN mediator in Palestine, where he was assassinated by Jewish terrorists in 1948.

BHUTTO, Benazir (1952–   )   The American-educated daughter of Zulfiqar Ali BHUTTO became the first woman leader of a Muslim nation, serving two terms as prime minister of Pakistan, in 1988–90 and in 1993–96. After the death of General ZIA UL-HAQ and the dissolution of his military dictatorship, Benazir Bhutto in December 1988 became prime minister after leading her Pakistan People's Party in the first democratic elections since her father's execution. In August 1990 she was removed from office by the president for "corruption and nepotism" (allegedly at the instigation of the military). After the October 1993 elections she again became prime minister. Under renewed charges of corruption, economic mismanagement, and a decline of law and order, her government was dismissed in November 1996 by President Farooq Leghari. In April 1999, Bhutto was sentenced to five years in prison for having taken kickbacks while in office.

BHUTTO, Zulfiqar Mi (1928–79)   President of Pakistan, 1971–73; prime minister, 1973–77. A barrister, he served under President AYUB KHAN from 1958 to 1966. Foreign minister from 1963 to 1966, he resigned over the Indo-Pakistan truce. Founder of the People's Party, which won a majority of seats in the assembly in 1970, he was elected president in 1971, when Pakistan was defeated in the war with India over Bangladesh. He led Pakistan out of the Commonwealth in 1972 (when Great Britain, Australia and New Zealand recognized the independence of Bangladesh). Under a new constitution introduced in 1973 he became prime minister. Accusations of ballot rigging led to riots in 1977, his overthrow by a military coup d'etat led by General ZIA UL-HAQ and his execution in 1979.

BIKO, Steve (1947–77)   South African nationalist leader, 1969–77; one of the founders of the Black Consciousness movement and president of the South African Students Organization established in 1969. He organized the Black Community Program banned by the South African government following the Durban strikes in 1973. He was arrested and died in police custody, his death causing major international concern.

BIN LADEN, Osama bin Mohammed (c. 1957–   )   Wealthy Islamic extremist allegedly responsible for orchestrating terrorist actions against U.S. military personnel in Saudi Arabia in 1995 and 1996, and bombings that destroyed American embassies in Kenya and Tanzania in 1998. Born in Saudi Arabia, bin Laden inherited a large fortune and, in 1979, he traveled to Afghanistan to help mujahideen fighters in their holy war against the Soviets. After being expelled by Saudi Arabia in 1991, he fled to the Sudan and allegedly operated terrorist training camps. The Sudan forced bin Laden to leave in 1996 and he returned to Afghanistan. In 1998, the United States fired missiles at one of bin Laden's alleged training camps in Afghanistan, and at an alleged nerve-gas manufacturing plant in the Sudan. The United States has asked for bin Laden's deportation, but Afghanistan's Taliban militia has said he will be prosecuted in Afghanistan only if the United States can supply evidence of bin Laden's terrorist participation.

BLAIR, Tony (1953–)   Prime minister of Great Britain from 1997. Born Anthony Charles Lynton Blair, he was first elected to Britain's House of Commons in 1983, where he served on various shadow cabinets of the Labour Party for the next decade. In July of 1994, he assumed leadership of the Labour Party. In 1997, Blair led his party to a landslide victory, ending 18 years of Conservative Party rule. He has produced constitutional reform leading to the formation of separate parliaments in Wales and Scotland.

BOTHA, Pieter (1916–)   State president of South Africa from 1984 to 1989. He held various federal government offices from 1958 to 1978. He led the National Party from 1978 until 1989. Prime minister from 1978 to 1984, he became state president when a constitutional change was introduced in 1984. Although a conservative, he introduced cautious reforms in the apartheid system. He remained caught between increasing international opposition toward South Africa and the diehard reactionaries in his party. His policy of modifying apartheid failed to satisfy black aspirations and international opinion but increasingly alienated his own right wing. He relinquished party leadership following a stroke in January 1989, retaining the presidency until his angry resignation in August 1989. He resigned from the National Party in May 1990 in protest at talks with the ANC.

BOUMÉDIENNE, Houari (1925–78)   President of Algeria, 1965–78. A soldier, he joined the Front de Libération Nationale in the war against France in 1955. Appointed minister of defense in 1962 by President M. A. BEN BELLA, he led a coup that overthrew Ben Bella in 1965. President of Algeria from 1965 until his death in 1978, he was responsible for the Four-Year Plan (1969–73), which developed industry, reformed agriculture and nationalized French oil interests.

BOURGUIBA, Habib (1903–)   President of Tunisia, 1957–87. A member of the Destour Party from 1921, he split away to form the Neo-Destour Party in 1934. Imprisoned by the French from 1934 to 1936 and from 1938 to 1943, he lived outside Tunisia from 1946 to 1949. On his return to Tunisia he was again imprisoned from 1952 to 1954. Prime minister in 1956 when Tunisia became independent, he was elected president in 1957.

BOUTROS-GHALI, Boutros (1922–)   Egyptian politician and international diplomat. secretary-general of the United Nations from 1992 to 1997. As a diplomat for Egypt (1977–91) he worked toward peace in the Middle East. After taking office at the UN he faced many challenges regarding the role of the UN in conflict areas such as Somalia, Rwanda and Haiti. In June 1996 the United States declared its intention to veto his reelection for a second term. He was replaced by Kofi ANNAN in December 1996.

BRANDT, Willy (1913–92)   West German chancellor (prime minister), 1969–74. An anti-Nazi social worker who fled to Norway in 1933, he acted as a link between the Norwegian and German resistance movements. He returned to Berlin in 1945 and entered the Bundestag in 1949. Mayor of West Berlin from 1957 to 1966, he became chairman of German Social Democrats (SPD) in 1964 and foreign minister in Kiesinger's Grand Coalition Government from 1966 to 1969. He was chancellor from 1969 to 1974 in a SPD/Liberal coalition. As foreign minister and chancellor he worked for reconciliation with the Eastern bloc. This *Ostpolitik* (q.v.) was marked by treaties with Poland and the Soviet Union in 1972, but his conciliatory gestures made him enemies, who exploited the security lapse that caused his downfall. He was awarded the Nobel Peace Prize in 1971.

BREZHNEV, Leonid (1906–82)   First secretary of the Soviet Communist Party, 1964–82; chairman of the presidium of the Supreme Soviet of the USSR (president of the USSR), 1972–82. Elected to the Supreme Soviet in 1950, he was appointed to the Party Central Committee and joined the Politburo in 1957. As Khrushchev's deputy from 1960 to 1964 he gained control of the party machine. From 1964 he gradually assumed increasing power at the expense of Prime Minister KOSYGIN. He was largely responsible for the decision to intervene in Czechoslovakia in 1968. On his death, in 1982, he was succeeded by Yuri ANDROPOV.

BULGANIN, Nikolai (1895–1975)   Prime minister of the USSR, 1955–58. Joining the Communist Party during the Revolution, he became chairman of the Moscow soviet (i.e., mayor) from 1931 to 1937. He succeeded STALIN as minister of defense in 1946. On Stalin's death he initially appeared to share power with KHRUSHCHEV but the latter rapidly assumed ascendancy and ousted Bulganin in 1958, becoming prime minister himself.

BUNCHE, Ralph (1904–71)   United Nations undersecretary, 1955–71. American academic and later State Department official, Bunche was active in the establishment of the UN, joining its secretariat in 1947 as director of the Trusteeship Division. He undertook special troubleshooting assignments for successive secretaries-general, notably in Palestine (for which he received the Nobel Peace Prize in 1950). He directed the UN peacekeeping operations in Suez (1956), Congo (1960) and Cyprus (1964).

BUSH, George Herbert Walker (1924–) Forty-first president of the United States. Republican politician. He was vice president, 1981–89, and then became the first vice president to be elected president since Martin van Buren in 1836. He inherited Reagan's legacy of massive budget deficit. Bush ordered the December 1989 invasion of Panama to overthrow the NORIEGA regime and seize the dictator. He was the driving force behind the Gulf War against Iraq's occupation of Kuwait. His popularity rose after this, but growing concern over the U.S. economy and other domestic issues helped the Democrats under CLINTON win the November 1992 presidential election.

BUSH, George W. (1946–) Son of former president George Bush. Governor of Texas since 1994. Won the Republican Party vote in the presidential primaries of March 2000 and won a majority of electoral votes to become 43rd president of the United States.

BUTHELEZI, Mangosuthu Gatsha (1928–) South African politician. Born into the Zulu royal family. Head of Buthelezi tribe since 1953. Rejected plan of South African government to make Zululand a "bantustan." Prime minister of Kwazulu, 1972. Leader of Inkatha Movement since 1977. Rivalry of Inkatha and Nelson Mandela's ANC has led to widespread deaths and disorder in the black townships. Buthelezi opposed the calling of the April 1994 multiracial elections and ordered his supporters to boycott the poll. Shortly before the elections, after much violence, he reversed this decision, and his Inkatha Freedom Party received about 10% of the total vote in the subsequent elections. He was subsequently appointed minister of home affairs. In December 1995 there were allegations that he had collaborated with the government during the apartheid period.

CAETANO, Marcelo (1906–80) Prime minister of Portugal, 1968–74. A minister under SALAZAR in the 1940s and 1950s, he retired from politics in 1959 to become rector of the University of Lisbon. He was recalled as prime minister on Salazar's retirement in 1968. Despite some liberal reforms, internal and external pressures led to revolution in 1974 and to Caetano's exile.

CAMPBELL, Kim (1948–) Canadian politician. First woman prime minister of Canada when she succeeded Brian MULRONEY in June 1993. Previously an academic, she was elected to parliament as a Conservative in 1988, and was appointed successively minister of Indian affairs, minister of justice and minister of defense. She failed to hold her seat in the electoral rout by the Liberals in October 1993, and resigned as party leader that December.

CARTER, Jimmy (1924–   )   President of the United States, 1977–81. A state senator (Democrat) in Georgia from 1962 to 1966, Carter was elected governor of Georgia in 1971. He gained the Democratic presidential nomination in 1976, beating President Gerald FORD in the ensuing election, and he took office in 1977. His inexperience in Washington politics marred Carter's relations with Congress, while contractions of world oil supplies posed an economic energy crisis he was unable to solve. His main achievements were the treaty between Israel and Egypt following talks at Camp David, the Panama Canal treaty, and Salt II (although not ratified). The seizure of American hostages at the American embassy in Iran, and the failure of a rescue mission, destroyed his standing with the American public and contributed to his defeat by Ronald REAGAN in 1980.

CASTRO RUZ, Fidel (1926–   )   Cuban revolutionary and premier of Cuba since 1959. As a young lawyer, Castro was an outspoken critic of the regime of President Fulgencio BATISTA. After two unsuccessful bids, he succeeded in toppling Batista on 1 January 1959. Initial American support eroded as Castro broadened his ties with the Soviet Union. In December 1961, shortly after the disastrous American-backed Bay of Pigs invasion, Castro declared himself to be a Marxist-Leninist. The Cuban Missile Crisis of 1962 added to international tensions, as President John F. Kennedy demanded that the Russians withdraw their offensive missiles from Cuban soil. The Russians complied but the world stood on the brink of war throughout the crisis. Castro's domestic policies—especially his nationalization of the economy—have been brought into question by such crises as the failed sugar harvest of 1970, while Cuban military involvement in Africa and elsewhere has drawn strong condemnation. The collapse of the Soviet Union in 1991 meant the end of generous subsidies to Cuba, and Castro subsequently allowed some economic liberation and free market activities, while retaining tight control over politics. In 1994, responding to the largest antigovernment demonstrations in 35 years, Castro lifted some restrictions on those wanting to leave the country and thousands fled to the United States.

CEAUSESCU, Nicolae (1918–89)   President of Romania, 1967 to 1989. He entered the underground Communist Party in 1936. After the Soviet invasion in 1944 his career was advanced. He joined the party secretariat in 1954, becoming effective deputy leader (under Dej) from 1957 to 1965. He was general secretary in 1965 and head of state after 1967. He frequently criticized Soviet policy (e.g., Soviet occupation of

Czechoslovakia in 1968), but made no attempt to take Romania out of the Warsaw Pact, thus minimizing the risk of Soviet intervention in Romania's internal affairs. He showed little sympathy for the liberalizing Soviet policies of Gorbachev. His corrupt regime and bankrupt economy provoked riots in 1989. Their savage repression led to the December 1989 "winter (or Christmas) revolution." He was executed by firing squad after a secret trial on 25 December 1989.

CERNIK, Oldrich (1921–94) Prime minister of Czechoslovakia, 1968–70. He held various posts in the Communist Party and government from 1948 to 1968. He then became associated with DUBČEK, who as first secretary introduced reform programs. Following the Soviet invasion Cernik continued in office until 1970, when, along with many other progressives associated with Dubcek, he resigned and was suspended from the Communist Party.

CHAMORRO, Violetta (1929–) President of Nicaragua from 1990 to 1997. Widow (since 1978) of the assassinated newspaper publisher Pedro Joaquin Chamorro, a tireless opponent of the Somoza dictatorship. Chamorro joined the five-member junta under ORTEGA after the Sandinista revolution, but she resigned disillusioned in April 1980. During her term in office, she tried to reverse the politics of the Sandinistas, advocating a return to ownership of private property, a free market economy, no press censorship and a de-emphasis on the military.

CHERNENKO, Konstanin (1911–85) General secretary of the Soviet Communist Party from 1984 to 1985. He was a protege of BREZHNEV, under whose regime he became a member of the Central Committee and Politburo, and his rise to general secretary after having been passed over for Andropov in 1982 was seen as the last stand of the old guard in Soviet politics.

CHERNOMYRDIN, Viktor (1938–) Russian prime minister from 1992 to 1998. He joined the Communist Party in 1961 and was a Central Committee functionary from 1978 to 1983. He was a deputy minister from 1983 to 1985, when he was appointed gas minister. He is a member of the centrist Civic Union, which advocates gradual change, with the state playing a major role. He supported YELTSIN against the September 1993 constitutional coup, but was caught up in the "Russian roulette" of revolving prime ministers during Yeltsin's last two years in office. In March 1998, during Russia's worst post-Soviet currency crisis, Yeltsin replaced Chernomyrdin with liberal energy minister Sergei Kiriyenko. That August, when it became clear that the economy was still suffering, he fired Kiriyenko and attempted to rehire Chernomyrdin, but parliament rejected his nomination and Chernomyrdin withdrew his name. Yeltsin went on to appoint and then fire two other prime ministers, Foreign Minister Yevgeny Primakov and Interior Minister Sergei Stepashin, before turning over the reigns to Vladimir PUTIN at the end of 1999.

CHIANG Ch'ing   See JIANG QING.

CHIANG KAI-SHEK   See JIANG KAISHEK.

CHILUBA, Frederick (1933–   )   President of Zambia since 1991. He became chairman of the Zambia Congress of Trade Unions in 1974 and was a leading opponent of the one-party state of President KAUNDA, becoming leader of the Movement for Parliamentary Democracy (MPD) formed in July 1991. He was elected to the presidency in November 1991 and called for sweeping economic reforms, including privatization and the establishment of a stock market. In 1996, parliament passed a bill that presidents may serve only two terms, and Chiluba was overwhelmingly elected to another five years.

CHIRAC, Jacques (1932–   )   President of France since 1995, and twice prime minister, from 1974 to 1976 and 1986 to 1988. Elected to the National Assembly in 1967, he held various government offices under presidents DE GAULLE and POMPIDOU from 1967 to 1974. He became prime minister under President GISCARD D'ESTAING from 1974 to 1976. Increasing tension between Chirac, as leader of the Gaullist Party, and Giscard led to his emergence as a political rival to Giscard. Elected mayor of Paris in 1977, he ran unsuccessfully in the 1981 presidential election against Giscard and MITTERRAND. Following a Gaullist victory in the 1986 parliamentary elections, he was appointed prime minister by socialist president Mitterrand. (See also Cohabitation, chapter 10.) He then served as mayor of Paris until he made his third run for the presidency in May 1995 and defeated the Socialist candidate, Lionel Jospin. Chirac provoked strikes and protests in 1995 and 1996, both for his austerity measures aimed at qualifying France for the EU's single currency program, and for the nuclear tests France conducted in the South Pacific. In 1996, his conservative coalition lost its majority in parliament and the Socialists formed a coalition government with Jospin as prime minister.

CHISSANO, Joaquim (1939–   )   President of Mozambique since 1986. Active in the Frente de Libertição de Mocambique (Frelimo) in the struggle against Portuguese rule, on independence in 1975 he was appointed minister of foreign affairs. He succeeded President MACHEL following Machel's death in an air crash in 1986. After Chissano failed to institute socialism, a new constitution was drafted in 1989, calling for three branches of government and granting civil liberties. In 1994, Chissano announced and won a multiparty general election, and his successful economic plan has won foreign confidence and aid. Mozambique became the first non-former-British colony to become a member of the British Commonwealth in 1995.

CHOU En-lai See ZHOU ENLAI.

CHRÉTIEN, Joseph Jacques Jean (1934–) Canadian politician and lawyer. Prime minister since October 1993. Liberal politician with extensive ministerial experience. Secretary of state for external affairs and deputy prime minister, June–September 1984. First elected to Commons, 1963. He won the leadership of the Liberal Party in 1990 and defeated Kim CAMPBELL in the 1993 election. Although a Quebecois, Chrétien is a strong supporter of national unity. His Liberal Party won the 1997 and 2000 elections.

CHRISTOPHER, Warren (1926–) U.S. secretary of state, 1993–1997. A lawyer and diplomat, he served as deputy secretary of state under President CARTER. He was an adviser to Bill CLINTON during his 1992 presidential campaign and acted as co-director of President Clinton's transition team. In 1993 he secured the signing of the Israeli–PLO peace agreement, and in 1995 brokered a peace agreement for Bosnia-Herzegovina. Christopher served as an advisor to Al Gore during the 2000 presidential election.

CHURCHILL, Winston Leonard Spencer (1874–1965) British statesman and great wartime leader. First elected to Parliament, 1900. Held office in World War I. First Lord of the Admiralty, 1939–40, then minister of defense and prime minister, 1940–45. He was leader of the opposition 1945–51, prime minister, 1951–55, and minister of defense, 1951–52. His natural dynamism inspired the country during World War II, but he was less in tune with the electorate's desire for postwar social reform, and he led his party to defeat in 1945. By 1951 he had come to terms with the demands of postwar Britain and led his party back to power.

CLARK, Joe (1939–) Prime minister of Canada, 1979–80; secretary of state for external affairs, 1984–93. Clark, from the province of Alberta in western Canada, was first elected to Parliament in 1972. He was elected leader of the then-opposition Progressive Conservative Party in 1976. His party unseated the government of Liberal prime minister Pierre Elliott Trudeau in 1979, only to lose control of the government to Trudeau and the Liberals the following year.

CLINTON, Bill (William Jefferson) (1946–) Forty-second president of the United States, having defeated George BUSH in the November 1992 presidential elections. Inaugurated January 1993 and elected to a second term in 1996. Governor of Arkansas 1979–80 and 1983–

92. Clinton's major foreign-policy ventures as president included helping to reinstate Haitian president Jean-Bertrand Aristide in 1994 after he had been ousted by the military in 1991; committing U.S. forces to a peacekeeping initiative in Bosnia and Herzegovina; and bombing the Yugoslav military in 1999 by NATO forces in order to end the Serbian occupation of Kosovo, Yugoslavia. Clinton failed to gain passage for his plan to overhaul the healthcare system in 1994, when Democrats lost control of both the Senate and the House of Representatives to the Republican Party for the first time in 40 years. He defeated Republican Bob Dole and Reform candidate Ross Perot in the 1996 elections. In 1998, after Clinton's much publicized affair with a young White House intern, the House brought two articles of impeachment against him for perjury and obstruction of justice. The Senate acquitted him of charges the following year.

COLLOR DE MELLO, Fernando (1950–)   President of Brazil, 1990–92. Elected mayor of Maceió in 1979, federal deputy for Alagoas in 1982, state governor in 1986. Left the Brazilian Democratic Movement (PMDB) to form the National Renovation Party as a vehicle for his presidential ambitions. He campaigned in 1990 pledging to end inflation, poverty and corruption. Despite his initial radical rhetoric, poverty, crime and inflation all increased during his period in office. He resigned in Decemher 1992 following a congressional investigation into allegations of corruption, and he was subsequently barred from holding public office for eight years. In 1998 he was acquitted on several counts of illegal activity.

CRESSON, Edith (1934–)   French socialist politician. Appointed France's first woman prime minister by François MITTERRAND in May 1991. She survived in office only briefly, resigning in April 1992 to be replaced by Pierre Beregevoy. Cresson was appointed to the European Commision in 1994.

D'AUBUISSON, Roberto (1943–92)   El Salvador politician, founder of the right-wing Arena Party. He joined the National Guard, moving to the armed forces general command in 1975. Dismissed following alleged involvement with right-wing paramilitary organizations, d'Aubuisson went into exile in Guatemala. He was acquitted on charges of attempting a coup in El Salvador in 1980. He formed Arena (Alianza Republicana Nacionalista) in 1981 and was president of the National Assembly from 1982 to 1983. He won 46% of the vote in the 1984 presidential election, his party gaining control of the National Assembly in 1988. He was unable to gain American financial support for the 1988 presidential campaign because of persistent allegations of his involvement in political murders.

DAYAN, Moshe (1915–81) Israeli minister of defense, 1967–74; foreign minister, 1978–79. An Israeli army officer until 1958, he entered politics and held various ministerial offices under BEN GURION. As the minister of defense he took much of the credit for the Israeli victory in the Six-Day War against Egypt, Jordan and Syria in 1967, but he was heavily criticized after Israeli reverses in the Yom Kippur War in 1973. He was dropped from the cabinet the following year, brought back as foreign minister by BEGIN in 1978, but he resigned in 1979 following policy disagreements.

DE GAULLE, Charles (1890–1970) President of France in 1945 and from 1958 to 1969. General de Gaulle refused to surrender to the Germans in 1940, leading the Free French forces from London. He returned to Paris in 1944, landing in Normandy a week after D-Day. His administration was recognized by the Allies in 1944, but he resigned in 1945 when his constitutional proposals were rejected. Returned to power on the collapse of the Fourth Republic in 1958 following a right-wing army revolt in Algiers, he became president under the new Fifth Republic constitution, strengthening his position in 1962 when the presidency became directly elected, thus confirming the ascendancy of his office over that of the prime minister. He conducted a rigorously independent foreign policy, granting independence to Algeria (1962), resisting British entry into the EEC (1963 and 1967) and withdrawing military support for NATO (1966–67). Student demonstrations in 1968 challenged his authority and, when his proposals for constitutional change were rejected in 1969, he resigned, being replaced by his increasingly assertive prime minister, Georges POMPIDOU.

DE KLERK, Frederik Willem (1936–) South African politician. President of South Africa, 1989–94. Succeeded P. W. BOTHA. Inaugurated far-reaching political changes in South Africa, releasing Nelson MANDELA from prison, dismantling apartheid legislation and opening a dialogue with the newly legalized ANC leading to the April 1994 elections. Shared Nobel Peace Prize (with Nelson Mandela) in 1993. In May 1995 he withdrew the National Party from the governing coalition. In August 1997 de Klerk resigned as leader of the National Party.

DELORS, Jacques (1925–) French president of the European Commission from 1985 to 1994. Joined the Banque de France in 1945. Held a number of senior civil service and advisory posts from 1962 on. In 1976 he became the Socialist Party's international economic affairs spokesman and in 1981 he was appointed economics and finance minister of France, playing a prominent part in formulating the austerity program introduced by the Socialist government in 1983. His appointment as president of the European Commission saw the post take on a much higher profile, particularly in the encouragement of European political and financial unity.

DENG Xiaoping (1904–97)   Long-serving Chinese official. As secretary-general of the Chinese Communist Party in the 1950s and 1960s, Deng played a major role in the ideological disputes with the USSR. Purged in the Cultural Revolution, he was reinstated in 1973 as deputy prime minister and was effective head of government during the months preceding the death of ZHOU Enlai. Though widely regarded as Zhou's likely successor, he again fell from power in 1976 when HUA Guofeng became prime minister. Reinstated in 1977, he led the attack on the "Gang of Four," and he promoted better relations with the United States. Although Deng nominally retired in 1980, he remained China's paramount leader during the 1980s. In November 1989, he resigned his last post (as chairman of the powerful Central Military Commission) but he still remained the "helmsman" of the nation until his death.

DESAI, Morarji (1896–1995)   Indian prime minister, 1977–79. Active in the civil disobedience movement led by M. K. GANDHI in the 1930s, he emerged as one of the leaders of the Congress Party after independence and held many senior government offices. Increasing conflict with Mrs. GANDHI led to his imprisonment from 1975 to 1977. Leading the Janata Party (an electoral alliance of noncommunist parties against Mrs. Gandhi) to victory in 1977, he inflicted the first defeat on the Congress Party since independence. Factionalism within the coalition led to his defeat in an election in January 1980.

Diem, NGO DINH.   See NGO DINH DIEM.

DOUGLAS-HOME, Sir Alec (1903–95)   British prime minister, 1963–64; foreign secretary, 1960–63 and 1970–74. He entered the House of Commons as a Conservative in 1931. Parliamentary private secretary to Prime Minister Neville Chamberlain from 1937 to 1939, he succeeded his father as 14th Earl of Home in 1951 and resigned from his seat in the Commons. He served as minister of state from 1951 to 1955; minister for commonwealth relations, 1955–60; leader of the House of Lords, 1957–60; and foreign secretary, 1960–63. Following MACMILLAN's resignation in 1963 he disclaimed his peerage to become prime minister as Sir Alec Douglas-Home (winning a by-election to return to the House of Commons). Following his defeat by Harold WILSON in the 1964 election, he became leader of the Opposition until 1965, when he stepped aside, being replaced by Edward HEATH. In 1970 he was appointed foreign secretary by Heath. Following a Conservative defeat in 1974, he was created a life peer as Lord Home of the Hirsel.

DUBČEK, Alexander (1921–92)   First secretary, Slovak Communist Party, 1968–69. Dubček joined the Communist Party in 1939 and fought with the Slovak resistance from 1944. Principal secretary of the Slovak Communist Party in 1958 and first secretary in 1968, Dubček favored change in the totalitarian character of the Communist Party and sought to reassure Soviet leaders that his reform program would not endanger Czechoslovak socialism. Nevertheless, the Russians invaded on 20/21 August 1968, and Dubček was arrested. Later released, he remained first secretary until 1969. He was expelled from the party in 1970. With the collapse of communism in 1989, Dubček was vindicated. He returned to public life as chairman (speaker) of the Czech parliament from December 1989 to his death in 1992.

DULLES, John Foster (1888–1959)   U.S. secretary of state, 1953–59. A lawyer long active in international affairs, he was appointed by Eisenhower as secretary of state in 1953. He built up NATO and created SEATO out of his belief in opposing the Soviets with the threat of massive retaliation. His inability to collaborate with Britain's Prime Minister EDEN led to tension in Anglo-American relations over Suez. He strongly opposed the Anglo-French invasion of Egypt in 1956.

EDEN, Anthony (1897–1977)   British prime minister, 1955–57. He entered the House of Commons in 1923 and served as foreign secrctary, 1935–38, 1940–45 and 1951–55, and deputy prime minister, 1951–55. Heir-apparent to Churchill for many years, he succeeded him as prime minister in 1955. Eden's main interests were always in foreign affairs. His premiership was marked by increasing tensions in the Middle East. Eden's hostility toward Nasser's Egypt led him to support Anglo-French military intervention in Suez. This divided the country, lost Eden the support of most Commonwealth leaders and aroused the ire of U.S. secretary of state DULLES. The Suez fiasco contributed to a collapse of his health and to his resignation in January 1957. He was created Earl of Avon in 1961.

EISENHOWER, Dwight D. (1890–1969)   President of the United States, 1953–61; supreme allied commander for the invasion of Europe in 1944; supreme commander, NATO, 1951. Although ostensibly not involved in politics, he was drafted by the Republican Party as a presidential candidate in 1952 and was elected with more popular votes than any previous candidate. With domestic policy entrusted to Sherman Adams and foreign policy to John Foster DULLES, Eisenhower's period in office was marked by a strengthening of the NATO alliance, drawing upon his earlier military experience. He chose to appear aloof from party politics, leaving this to his vice president, Richard M. NIXON.

ERHARD, Ludwig (1897–1977) West German chancellor, 1963–66. Head of an economics research institute before World War II and professor of economics at Munich University from 1945 to 1949. He was a Christian Democrat member of the Bundestag from 1949 to 1966. He became federal minister of economic affairs from 1949 to 1963, presiding over West Germany's "economic miracle," a transition from wartime devastation to prosperity. Deputy chancellor under ADENAUER from 1957 to 1963, he became chancellor on Adenauer's retirement in 1963. He lacked Adenauer's skill in international affairs and, fearing an economic recession, he proposed a series of tax increases in 1966, which led to his defeat. He resigned in 1966.

FAROUK, King (1920–65) King of Egypt, 1936–52. He attained his majority in 1938 and ousted the Wafd (see Chapter 10) government of Nahas Pasha, who had ruled following Farouk's father's death in 1936. He tried to launch schemes of land reform and economic advancement, but corruption was rife, and his earlier popularity rapidly dwindled. Strains in relations with Great Britain during and after World War II and failure of the army in Palestine in 1948 focused criticism against him, and he was forced to abdicate as a result of a military coup in 1952.

FORD, Gerald R. (1913–) President of the United States, 1974–77. A lawyer and Republican congressman from Michigan (1948–73), he was chosen by Richard NIXON as successor to Vice President Spiro AGNEW, who had been forced to resign. Ford was vice president during the mounting criticism of Nixon over Watergate *(q.v.)*. Following Nixon's resignation in 1974, Ford was sworn into office, becoming the only man in America's history to have held office as both president and vice president without being elected. He successfully gained the Republican nomination in 1976 but was defeated by Democrat Jimmy CARTER.

FRANCO, Francisco (1892–1975) Spanish head of state and dictator, 1936–75. Appointed chief of the general staff in 1934, he led the Fascist rebellion against the Republican government that began the Spanish Civil War. Head of the insurgent government in 1936, he structured his corporate state on the Italian model, with a single political party, the Falange. His refusal to modernize institutions or to relax his dictatorship led to mounting opposition from students, the Catholic hierarchy and the Basques. In 1969 he nominated Prince Juan Carlos to succeed him; this succession occurred in 1975, three weeks before Franco's death.

FUJIMORI, Alberto (1939–) President of Peru from 1990 to 2000. Born of Japanese immigrant parents, he was a university rector with no political experience before becoming the independent Cambio

90 group's 1990 presidential election candidate. Instituted an austerity program to deal with Peru's inflation and debt crisis. In April 1992 he closed parliament and began ruling with military backing. His New Majority-Change '90 coalition emerged as the leading party in November 1992 elections to a Democratic Constituent Congress to replace parliament and draft a new constitution. Under strong international pressure, he announced elections to a new congress, but they were boycotted by the principal opposition parties. Fujimori resigned in November 2000.

GANDHI, Indira (1917–84) Indian prime minister, 1966–77 and 1980–84. Daughter of NEHRU, she joined the Congress Party in 1939. Minister for broadcasting and information from 1964 to 1966, on SHASTRI's death (in 1966), she was elected leader of Congress and became prime minister. Her premiership was marked by significant social and economic progress, but also by tension with Pakistan (and war in 1971), and increasing internal discontent over her assumption of almost dictatorial powers on the declaration of an emergency in 1975. In 1977 Congress was defeated for the first time by the Janata coalition, united only in their opposition to Mrs. Gandhi. Within a few months she was on the road back to power, winning the election of 1980 with a promise of firm government, and demonstrating her popular appeal with ordinary people. She was assassinated in 1984 by Sikh extremists. Her son RAJIV GANDHI succeeded her.

GANDHI, Mohandas Karamchand, called "Mahatma" (great soul) (1869–1948) Indian national leader. He conducted passive resistance campaigns in protest at the Transvaal government's discrimination against the Indian minority settlers in South Africa from 1907 to 1914. He returned to India and emerged as leader of the Congress Party. He dominated the movement for Indian independence, advocating the boycotting of British goods and nonviolent civil disobedience (for which he was imprisoned four times). Gandhi collaborated with the last viceroys (Wavell and Mountbatten) in producing plans for the independence and partition of India. He was regarded as a saint by many of his Hindu followers, and his teaching of nonviolence has had great influence. He was assassinated in 1948.

GANDHI, Rajiv (1944–91) Indian prime minister from 1984 to 1989. An airline pilot who entered politics only on the death of his brother, Sanjay, in 1981, he held various ministerial offices under his mother, INDIRA GANDHI, from 1981 to 1984. He succeeded Mrs. Gandhi as prime minister on her assassination. Defeated in the December 1989 elections by a united opposition against him. He was assassinated in 1991 by Tamil militants during an election rally near Madras.

Giap, VO NGUYEN See VO NGUYEN GIAP.

GIBBS, Sir Humphrey (1902–90)   Governor of Rhodesia, 1960–69. A Rhodesian farmer, he remained loyal to the British Crown on the declaration of unilateral independence by Prime Minister Ian SMITH in 1965. He resigned in 1969 when Rhodesia became a republic.

GIEREK, Edward (1913–   )   Polish Communist Party leader, 1970–80. Following food riots in 1970, he replaced GOMULKA as party leader. He attempted to raise living standards through production of more consumer goods but encountered increasing opposition from dissident students and from the Catholic Church, encouraged by the election of Poland's Cardinal WOJTYLA of Cracow as pope in 1978. The emergence in 1980 of an independent trade union, Solidarity and further strikes raised doubts about his leadership, and he retired following a heart attack.

GISCARD D'ESTAING, Valéry (1926–   )   President of France, 1974–81. A member of the National Assembly from 1956 to 1974, he was leader of the Independent Republican Party, which supported the Gaullists after 1959 but retained its independence. Minister of finance under three successive prime ministers from 1962 to 1974, on the death of POMPIDOU in 1974 he was elected president, beating Gaullist and left-wing opponents. Though he was supported by Gaullists in the National Assembly, growing friction within the "majority," and alleged scandals, notably over gifts from Emperor Bokassa of the Central African Empire, weakened his campaign for reelection in 1981 and led to his defeat by MITTERRAND.

GOMULKA, Wladyslaw (1905–82)   First Secretary of the Polish Communist Party, 1956–70. In 1943 he became secretary-general of the Polish Workers' Party, which played a major role in the resistance movement. Minister responsible for territories annexed from Germany, from 1945 to 1947, he was dismissed in 1948. Readmitted to the party in 1956, he was elected first secretary after anti-Soviet riots in Poznan. Gomulka retained defense links with the Soviet Union but stopped agricultural collectivization and made limited political reforms. These were abandoned in 1962–63 for fear of internal unrest. Following food riots in 1970, he was replaced as first secretary by GIEREK.

GORBACHEV, Mikhail (1931–   )   Last president of the Soviet Union. A member of the Party Central Committee since 1971, the Secretariat (with responsibility for agriculture) from 1978, and the Politburo from 1980, Gorbachev emerged as a leading member under Yuri ANDROPOV (1982–84) and Konstantin CHERNENKO (1984–85). On Chernenko's death in 1985 he was chosen as general secretary, despite being the youngest member of the Politburo. Following over a decade of rule by old men, he brought a new dynamism to both domestic and foreign policy. His more open style won him international support and contributed to improved relations with President REAGAN, whom he met in Geneva in 1985, in Iceland in 1986 and in Moscow in 1988. His reforming policies, especially *perestroika (q.v)* and *glasnost (q.v)*, were threatened by nationalism in such areas as Azerbaijan and the Baltics. His policy of noninterference was vital in the 1989 revolution in Eastern Europe that overthrew the old communist regimes. Became executive president, 1990. Awarded Nobel Peace Prize, also in 1990. Granted extensive new powers, September 1990. These powers were further extended, 27 December 1990. His policies faced intense opposition from the Soyuz *(q.v)* conservatives (opposed to his reforms), radicals (such as Boris YELTSIN) and numerous nationalist groupings. The position of Gorbachev was drastically altered by the abortive 61-hour coup of 19 August 1991 led by Gennadi Yanayev. Gorbachev's position was effectively usurped by Yeltsin, president of Russia. With the Soviet Union visibly collapsing, Gorbachev resigned as general secretary of the party; the Communist Party itself was banned throughout the Soviet Union; and Gorbachev desperately tried to establish a new confederation to replace a Soviet Union that had, to all intents and purposes, collapsed. Gorbachev vowed to stay as president, but it was highly unclear what he was president of. He resigned on 25 December 1991.

GORE, Al (Albert, Jr.) (1948–) Vice president of the United States since January 1993. Running mate of Bill CLINTON. Former senator from Tennessee, as was his father. Won the Democratic Party vote in the presidential primaries of March 2000 and the popular vote in the November election but failed to obtain the necessary electoral votes to become president.

GOWDA, H. D. Deve (1933–) Prime minister of India from 1996 to 1997. Born as a member of the Vokkaliggas, a lower caste group whose name means "people of the plow," Gowda held a number of regional posts (member of Karnataka Legislative Assembly, 1962–82; chief minister of Karnataka, 1995–96) before becoming a member of parliament from 1991 to 1996. In June 1996, he became prime minister by default when two of his colleagues declined the post. He headed the United Front Alliance, a 13-party minority government comprised mostly of lower-caste Indians. In March 1997, Gowda resigned when Congress withdrew support for him due to high unemployment and the rise of Hindu radicals. However, the United Front Alliance continued in office, picking leftist candidate Inder Kumar Gujral to succeed Gowda as prime minister from 1997 to 1998.

GOWON, Yakuba (1934–) Head of the federal military government in Nigeria, 1966–75. An army officer involved in the successful coup to overthrow Tafawa BALEWA in 1966, he succeeded the coup's initial leader, Major-General Ironsi, who was killed a few months later. Between 1967 and 1970 his rule was dominated by civil war with the predominantly Ibo Eastern Region, which had proclaimed itself as independent Biafra. Economic difficulties led to a further military coup in 1975, led by Brigadier Murtula Mohammed, while Gowon was out of the country. Gowon retired to exile in the United Kingdom, returning to Nigeria in 1983.

GRIVAS, George (1898–1974) Commander of the Greek Cypriot National Guard. A right-wing Greek army officer, Grivas initiated the guerrilla campaign in Cyprus in 1953, creating a terrorist movement, EOKA, and he was later given command, against Archbishop MAKARIOS III's wishes, of the Greek Cypriot National Guard. Recalled to Athens in 1971, where he regarded Makarios's acceptance of Commonwealth membership as treason, Grivas later secretly returned to Cyprus (1971–74) and reorganized his followers against Makarios. His divisive legacy contributed to the disastrous coup and subsequent partition of Cyprus in July and August 1975.

GROMYKO, Andrei Andreyevich (1909–89) Soviet statesman. Gromyko served as Soviet ambassador to the United States from 1943 to 1946, and chief permanent Soviet delegate to the United Nations from 1946 to 1948. He was also ambassador to Great Britain from 1952 to 1953, and he served as Soviet foreign minister from 1957 until 1985. President from 1985 to 1988.

GROTEWOHL, Otto (1894–1964) First prime minister of the German Democratic Republic, 1949–64. A politician during the Weimar Republic, he laid low during the Nazi period. He refounded the German Social Democratic Party in 1945, joining the Communists under Soviet pressure and becoming prime minister in 1949.

GUEVARA, Ernesto ("Che") (1928–67) Latin American revolutionary. He became radicalized after witnessing American intervention in Guatemala in 1954. Guevara accompanied CASTRO to Cuba and played a prominent part in the guerrilla campaign (1956–59) leading to BATISTA's downfall. Minister for industries in Cuba, 1961–65, he resigned and went to the jungles of Bolivia to test his revolutionary theory. He was killed while leading a band of guerrillas against American-trained Bolivian troops in 1967. His rejection of both capitalism and orthodox communism made him a symbolic martyr for radical students throughout the world.

HABIBIE, Bacharuddin Jusuf "B. J." (1936–) President of Indonesia from 1998 to 1999. Trained as an aeronautical engineer, Habibie worked under President SUHARTO for 20 years, first as minister of state for research and later as vice president. Ten weeks after becoming vice president, Suharto resigned after 32 years and Habibie was handed the presidency. Habibie attempted to distinguish himself from his predecessor and win favor with the emerging opposition factions by promising free elections in 1999, but he withdrew his own candidacy days before the vote after losing the confidence of his party because of his alleged involvement in a banking scandal.

HAIG, Alexander (1924–) U.S. general and secretary of state, 1981–82. He commanded a brigade in Vietnam from 1966 to 1967. Military advisor to President Nixon from 1969 to 1973, he was commander in chief of American forces in Europe from 1974 to 1979 and supreme commander, NATO. Haig retired from the army to enter political life in 1979. He was appointed secretary of state by President Reagan in 1981. Haig's policy was often at variance with that of the president and other members of his administration; in 1982 Haig resigned after further differences with the president.

HAILE SELASSIE (1892–1975) Emperor of Ethiopia, 1930–74. Crowned emperor in 1930, he sought to modernize and centralize the government until forced into exile in 1936, when the Italians won the Abyssinian War. Allowed to return to Addis Ababa in 1941 after Allied successes, he resumed the task of converting Ethiopia into a modern state. He acted as elder statesman to the emergent African nations, but he increasingly lost touch with the social problems of Ethiopia. After his authority rapidly declined (1973–74) he was deposed in 1974 by left-wing army officers, and he died in 1975.

HAMMARSKJÖLD, Dag (1905–61) Secretary-general of the United Nations, 1953–61. Swedish politician, he was deputy foreign minister from 1951 to 1953. Elected secretary-general of the UN in 1953, he was reelected in 1957. The dignity and impartiality with which he conducted UN affairs, especially during the Suez crisis, enhanced the standing of the organization. In 1960 his conduct of the Congo crisis provoked hostility from the USSR. While seeking peace between the Congo and the secessionist province of Katanga, Hammarskjöld was killed in a plane crash. He was awarded the 1961 Nobel Peace Prize posthumously.

HAVEL, Vaclav (1936–) First president of the Czech Republic after its creation in January 1993 and president of the former Czechoslovakia after his unanimous election, 29 December 1989. Former dissident and political prisoner. Born in Prague; playwright; cofounder of Charter 77. Jailed for four months. Victim of smear campaign. Jailed again, 1979, for 4½ years for subversion. Cofounder of Civic Forum, November 1989. Accepted popular draft as presidential candidate, December

1989. As the Czechoslovak union faced dissolution in 1992, Havel, who opposed the division, resigned from office. The following year he was elected president of the new Czech Republic, but his political role was limited because Prime Minister Václav Klaus (1993–97) commanded more power. In 1998 Havel was reelected by a narrow margin.

HEATH, Edward (1916–)   British prime minister, 1970–74. MP for Bexley, 1950–74, and for Sidcup since 1974; Conservative chief whip, 1955–59. As lord privy seal (1961–63) he negotiated unsuccessfully for British entry into the Common Market. Leader of the Opposition from 1965–70, he was prime minister from 1970 to 1974. Heath successfully reopened negotiations for British membership in the European Community, and in 1973 Great Britain entered the EEC. His Industrial Relations Act got him into difficulty with the trade unions, and in 1974, after refusing to amend his incomes policy, miners' militant tactics forced Heath to put industry on a three-day week. Heath called a general election on this issue in February 1974 but failed to gain a majority and resigned. He was defeated in an election for the Conservative Party leadership by Margaret THATCHER in 1975.

HESELTINE, Michael (1933–)   British Conservative politician whose leadership challenge against Margaret THATCHER (though unsuccessful) precipitated her downfall in November 1990. Secretary of state for the enviromnent, 1979–83 and since 1990. Resigned as defense secretary over Westland Affair, 1986. Campaigned for reform of the poll tax (replacing it with a council tax). Became secretary of state for trade and industry under John MAJOR and was responsible for repealing the highly unpopular poll tax. He was appointed deputy prime minister following the July 1995 elections.

HO Chi Minh (1892–1969)   Vietnamese communist revolutionary and president of North Vietnam, 1954–69. Leader of the Vietnam revolutionary nationalist party, which struggled for independence from France before and after World War II, he proclaimed the Democratic Republic of Vietnam in 1945, following the defeat of Japan. However, the French returned to South Vietnam, and Ho was forced to fight an anti-colonial war of independence from 1946 to 1954. After the Geneva agreement recognized Ho's state in the north, he encouraged the Viet Cong resistance movement in the south. He increased industrial output in the north despite heavy American bombing after 1965. He was idolized by his people, and when Saigon fell to the communists in 1975, it was renamed Ho Chi Minh City.

HONECKER, Erich (1912–94)   Head of state, German Democratic Republic (East Germany) from 1976 to 1989. Having held various of-

fices in the East German Communist Party from 1958, he succeeded
ULBRICHT as first secretary in 1971, and in 1976 he became chairman
of the Council of State (head of state) and undisputed leader of East
Germany. Ousted from power when communism collapsed in 1989, he
faced numerous accusations of abuse of power, but he was partly protected by his failing health. He sought refuge in the Soviet Union and
eventually in Chile.

HOSOKAWA Morihiro (1938–) Japanese politician. Prime minister, 1993–April 1994. He left the LDP in 1992 to form the Japan New
Party with a commitment to eliminate corruption and reform the electoral process. Earlier he was a successful elected governor of Kumamoto.
He resigned in April 1994 after allegations of financial impropriety.

HOWARD, John Winston (1939–) Prime minister of Australia
since 1996 and leader of the Liberal Party since 1995. Member of parliament, 1974–75. Minster for business and consumer affairs, 1975–77.
Federal treasurer, 1977–83. Howard assumed leadership of the Liberal
Party in 1985, but in 1987, his coalition with the National Party failed
to unseat the Labor Party and he lost leadership of the Liberals in 1989.
In 1995 he regained leadership and led the Liberal-National coalition to
victory over Labor in 1996. During his first term in office, Howard was
confronted with national debates on immigration quotas and race relations, as well as the creation of the One Nation political party. He was
reelected in 1998 and voters supported his proposal to establish a republic and replace the English monarch with a president as head of state.

HOXHA, Enver (1908–85) First secretary, Albanian Communist
Party, 1941–85. After studying in France, where he joined the French
Communist Party, he returned to Albania and built up the Albanian
communist movement, becoming first secretary. He led the National Liberation Army from 1943 to 1944, occupying all the main Albanian
towns when the Germans pulled out of the Balkans in 1944. He headed
the Provisional Government of the Albanian Republic and established a
dictatorship on strictly Stalinist principles.

HUA Guofeng (1922–) Chairman of the Chinese Communist
Party, 1976–81, and Chinese prime minister, 1976–80. Elected to the
Central Committee of the party in 1969, he became a member of the
Politburo in 1973. Deputy premier in 1975, Hua became prime minister
in 1976 (following Zhou Enlai). When Mao died in 1976, Hua, who
had been critical of the Cultural Revolution, won the struggle for control
of the party and was recognized as chairman. He took immediate action
against the "Gang of Four," thus effectively countering the influence of
the radicals led by Mao's widow, JIANG Qing. He traveled widely abroad

but was not as influential in China as his hosts overseas believed. He was succeeded as prime minister in 1980, and surrendered chairmanship of the party in 1981.

HUSÁK, Gustav (1913–91)   President of Czechoslovakia from 1975 to 1989. He became first secretary of the Communist Party when DUB-ČEK was ousted from office in 1969, following the Soviet invasion. He retained this position when he became president in 1975, thus strengthening his ascendancy in the leadership. He fell from power after the "Velvet Revolution" of 1989. He was expelled from the Communist Party in February 1990.

HUSSEIN, King (1935–99)   King of Jordan since 1952. A generally pro-Western Arab leader with close personal ties with the United Kingdom and United States. Under political pressure over the Palestinian problem, Jordan contained many refugees and served as a base for guerrilla attacks on Israel. His attempts to control the guerrillas led to civil war in 1976 but the army remained loyal. Hussein supported a negotiated settlement of the Middle Eastern problem. He acted as intermediary after the Iraqi invasion of Kuwait in 1990. In the wake of the Israel–PLO accords of 1993, Hussein signed a bilateral peace treaty with Israel on 26 October 1994. At Hussein's death on 7 February 1999, he was succeeded by his eldest son, Abdullah, who became King Abdullah II.

HUSSEIN, Saddam (1937–   )   Iraqi dictator. Born in Takrit, 150 miles north of Baghdad. Joined the Ba'athist *(q.v)* cause. Involved in October 1959 assassination attempt against Brigadier Kassem. He fled to Egypt before returning to Syria and entering (by marriage) the Syrian Ba'athist leadership. He became president of Iraq in July 1979 and has run Iraq through a clique of Takriti family relations and by the ruthless use of terror. He has suppressed the Kurds (by use of gas and chemical weapons), launched an enormously bloody war against Iran (see p. 302) and provoked a world crisis by the invasion and annexation of Kuwait in August 1990 (see p. 304). Although defeated in the Gulf War, he remains in power and has continually refused to cooperate with UN arms inspectors as part of the cease-fire agreement. In 1998, the United States and Great Britain launched a four-day air strike against Iraq and both countries announced that they would support efforts of the Iraqi opposition to unseat Hussein.

IZETBEGOVIĆ, Alija (1922–   )   President of Bosnia and Herzegovina from 1990 to 1999. He spent a total of 14 years as a political prisoner for agitating for Muslim rights in the former Yugoslavia. Led the main Muslim party, the Party of Democratic Action (SDA), to victory in Bosnia and Herzegovina's first multiparty elections in 1990, supported by a majority of Muslim and Croat voters. In 1996, he was elected chairman of Bosnia's three-person national presidency, each representing one of the three ethnic groups. Bosnian Serbs, led by former president and war criminal Radovan Karadzic, ignored the December 1995 Dayton Peace Accord and Bosnian leaders have so far made little progress toward rebuilding the economy, resettling the estimated one million refugees still displaced, or establishing a working government. In 1999, Bosnian officials were caught up in a corruption scandal involving millions of dollars pilfered from international aid projects. That year, Ante Jelavic, a Bosnian Croat, was elected president, but Izetbegovic remained co-prime minister with Zivko Radisic, a Bosnian Serb.

JARUZELSKI, Wojciech (1923–) Prime minister of Poland from 1981 to 1989. An army general and minister of defense from 1968 to 1983, he was promoted to restore order following unrest in 1980–81, which gave rise to fears of Soviet intervention. Initially he made further concessions to the independent trade union, Solidarity, but having also become party leader, Jaruzelski proclaimed martial law in December 1981 and arrested Solidarity leaders. Some relaxation occurred the following year, but tension between the government and Solidarity led to sporadic outbursts of unrest. Elected president in 1989 but was succeeded by Lech WALESA in 1990.

JIANG Kaishek (1887–1975) Chinese Nationalist dictator, 1928–49. On establishinent of the Chinese Republic in 1911, Jiang assisted Sun Yat-sen in building up the army. On Sun's death in 1925, he established himself as leader of his party, the Kuomintang, and declared himself president in 1928. His dictatorship was frequently challenged by the Communists, by other factions within the army and by the Japanese, who occupied Manchuria in 1931 and launched a full-scale war in 1937. He was recognized as China's leader during World War II by Allied leaders, but civil war resumed in earnest after 1945. Beijing fell to the Communists, led by MAO Zedong, in 1949. Jiang withdrew to Taiwan, hoping to return to the mainland with U.S. military backing. This never occurred, but Taiwan prospered through its links with the United States and Japan.

JIANG Qing (1914–91) Wife of MAO Zedong. She was a leading pro-Maoist activist during the Cultural Revolution and wielded enormous power over all aspects of culture and propaganda. She was arrested as a member of the radical "Gang of Four" in 1976 (on Mao's death). Expelled from the Communist Party in 1977, she was sentenced to death, later commuted to life imprisonment, in 1981.

JIANG Zemin (1926–) Chinese Communist leader. As the party leader in Shanghai he was appointed party secretary by DENG Xiaoping following the ousting of Zhao Ziyang after the Tiananmen Square (*q.v.*)

massacre. State president since 1993. With Deng's death in 1997, Jiang became the paramount leader, introducing a privatization plan to reduce state control of some of China's industries and participating in the first U.S.-China summit in almost a decade.

JINNAH, Mohammed Ali (1876–1948)   First governor-general of Pakistan in 1948. A moderate leader of the Muslim League in India in the 1930s, he played a key role in discussions on Indian independence. His view that the Hindus and Muslims constituted two separate nations led to partition in 1947 and the creation of Pakistan. As the first governor-general, he wielded great power in the new state, but he died after only a year in office.

JOHN XXIII (1881–1963)   Pope (1958–63). Born Angelo Giuseppe Roncalli into an Italian peasant family and ordained in 1904, he rose through the echelons of Vatican diplomacy, becoming its first permanent observer at UNESCO, patriarch of Venice, and finally pope. As pope, he worked for world peace and favored the interchange of ideas with other religions. In 1962 he convened Vatican II (*q.v.*), an ecumenical council that called for greater religious tolerance and Christian unity and that brought about dramatic reforms within the Catholic Church.

JOHN PAUL II (1920–   )   Pope since 1978. A Polish parish priest ordained in 1946, Karol Wojtyla was created auxiliary bishop in 1958, archbishop in 1964 and cardinal in 1967. When John Paul I died only a few weeks after becoming pope, Cardinal Wojtyla became the first non-Italian pope since 1522, and he was invested as John Paul II in 1978. His pontificate has been marked by a conservative approach to theological questions, moral problems and church discipline, and by extensive and unprecedented traveling. He has survived two attempts on his life, in 1981 and 1982.

JOHNSON, Lyndon Baines (1908–73)   President of the United States, 1963–68. Elected senator from Texas in 1948, he became majority leader. Selected by John KENNEDY as his running mate in the 1960 presidential election, Johnson was sworn in as president on Kennedy's assassination in 1963. Gaining a large majority in the 1964 election, he followed a progressive policy at home in pursuit of his "Great Society." These achievements were offset, however, by the mounting unrest and protests resulting from the large-scale military commitments to the Vietnam War. Ill health and a sharp decline in his popularity induced Johnson to announce his retirement rather than contest the 1968 presidential election.

JUAN CARLOS I, King (1938–   )   King of Spain since 1975. Grandson of King Alfonso XIII, he was named by General FRANCO as the future king in 1969. Crowned in 1975 shortly before Franco's death, he encouraged restoration of democracy in Spain and established himself as a constitutional monarch, with effective power in the hands of an elected government.

KABILA, Laurent Desiré (1938–) President of the Democratic Republic of the Congo (formerly Zaïre) since 1997. A rebel leader who spent 30 years trying to overthrow MOBUTU, Kabila joined a Tutsi uprising in May 1997 that officially ousted the exiled dictator. Kabila assumed power as both chief of state and head of government, returning the name of the country to Democratic Republic of the Congo, its name before it became Zaïre in 1971. A member of the Mulubakat, a subgroup of the Luba tribe, Kabila joined the Katanga assembly and supported Zaïre's first prime minister, Marxist-Maoist Patrice LUMUMBA, in 1960. When President Joseph-Desiré Mobutu had Lumumba killed in a coup, Kabila and others fled into eastern Zaïre and, supported by the Soviet Union and China, launched rebellions against the Mobutu government. Kabila was briefly aligned with Argentine revolutionary Che GUEVARA, and in 1967 he helped establish the People's Revolutionary Party with forces that included exiled Rwandan Tutsi and Cuban troops. In 1975, Kabila's rebels kidnapped three American students and a Dutch researcher for an undisclosed ransom. Kabila disappeared in 1988 but reemerged as a rebel leader in October 1996, active over the government's removal of ethnic Tutsi from their land. In May 1997 Kabila's rebels toppled Mobutu's government, and Kabila took office as head of state. Anti-Kabila rebels have continued to fight on into 1999.

KÁDÁR, Janos (1912–89) First secretary of the Hungarian Communist Party, 1956–65, and prime minister, 1956–58 and 1961–65. Minister of interior from 1948 to 1950, he was arrested and imprisoned from 1951 to 1954. As first secretary in 1956, Kádár initially favored reform, but he later supported Soviet intervention, which crushed the Hungarian Uprising. He remained prime minister until 1958 and first secretary thereafter. Greater freedom of expression was allowed from 1959 on, and, when Kádár held the premiership for a second term from 1961 to 1965, he took positive measures of reconciliation and cautious liberalization.

KAIFU, Toshiki (1931–) Japanese prime minister, 1989–91. Virtually unknown to the outside world until he was elected to succeed the disgraced Sosuke Uno. Without a real power base within the ruling Liberal Democrats, he was widely perceived as an interim leader.

KASAVUBU, Joseph (1910–69) President of the Democratic Republic of the Congo (formerly Zaïre), 1960–65. Mayor of Leopoldville (Kinshasa) in 1957, when the Belgian Congo became independent, he became the first president, with LUMUMBA as prime minister. He remained in office during the civil war over the Katanga secession until 1965, when he was replaced by MOBUTU following a military coup.

KAUNDA, Kenneth (1924–)   President of Zambia from 1964 to 1991, he led the United Nationalist Independence Party in opposition to the Federation of Rhodesia and Nyasaland in 1960, which resulted in the end of the federation. Appointed prime minister of Rhodesia in 1964 and, having supervised the constitutional arrangements that won his country independence, he became president of Zambia 10 months later. Kaunda sought to hold in check militants opposed to the Ian SMITH regime in Rhodesia, but his strong hostility to racism led to periods of tension with Great Britain over this and other issues. He assumed autocratic powers in 1972 to prevent total breakup but, after a new constitution in 1973, his presidency was confirmed. He resigned after being defeated in the 1991 elections. In July 1995 he was elected president of the United Independence Party (UNIP). In May 1996 Kaunda was barred from future elections by the amended Zambian constitution. In 1998 he was placed under house arrest for allegedly concealing knowledge of an unsuccessful coup in October 1997. In June 1998 he was released.

KEATING, Paul (1944–)   Prime minister of Australia from 1991 to 1996. A union official in the 1960s, Keating was elected to the House of Representatives in 1969 and served as minister for Northern Australia in 1975. He was appointed federal treasurer on Labor's reelection to office in 1983 and became deputy prime minister. Keating won a party leadership election in December 1991.

KENNEDY, John F. (1917–63)   President of the United States, 1961–63. Kennedy served in the House of Representatives from 1946 to 1952. He was elected to the Senate in 1952. He won the Democratic Party presidential nomination in 1960, and in 1961 became the youngest and the first Roman Catholic president in U.S. history. He met with opposition to his civil rights and social reform program, but he achieved spectacular successes abroad—the Cuban Missile Crisis in 1962; the limited Test-Ban Treaty in 1963; his program of aid for Latin America; and establishment of the Peace Corps. His visit to the Berlin Wall in 1963 showed his breadth of vision, making him a symbol of hope and inspiration. After his assassination in Dallas in 1963, the grief and disillusionment extended far beyond the United States.

KENNEDY, Robert (1925–68)   U.S. politician. Kennedy acted as campaign manager for his brother in the 1960 presidential election. He served as attorney general from 1961 to 1964, and he was a strong champion of civil rights. Elected senator from New York in 1965, he began a campaign to secure the Democratic nomination for the presidency in 1968. He gained wide support from blacks and the underprivileged, but he was assassinated in Los Angeles after winning the California primary in 1968.

KENYATTA, Jomo (1897–1978)   President of Kenya, 1964–78. General secretary of the Kikuyu Central Association in 1928, he studied and worked, mainly in the United Kingdom, from 1931 to 1946. He returned to Kenya as a nationalist leader in 1946. President of the Kenya African Union in 1947, he was imprisoned during the Mau Mau emergency of 1952–61. On his release he became the first prime minister of a self-governing Kenya in 1963 and president of the Republic of Kenya on its inauguration in 1964. He remained in office until his death in 1978.

KHOMEINI, Ayatollah (1900–89)   Iranian religious leader. As ayatollah of Iran's Shiite Muslims, he vigorously condemned the shah's secularizing reforms, and especially the social emancipation of women. Arrested and exiled, from Paris in the late 1970s he called on the Iranian army to turn against the shah and establish an Islamic republic. Returned to Tehran after the shah left in 1979, he became de facto leader of Iran for 12 months. After the election of a president, Khomeini continued to enjoy a unique status.

KHRUSHCHEV, Nikita (1894–1971)   First secretary of the Soviet Communist Party, 1953–64. Concerned with Ukrainian affairs from 1938 to 1947, he became prime minister of the Ukrainian Soviet Republic from its liberation until 1947. Appointed by STALIN to reorganize Soviet agricultural production from 1949 to 1950, he succeeded Stalin as first secretary. Strong enough to attack Stalin and to survive both the independent tendencies of the Poles under GOMULKA and the Hungarian Uprising in 1956, he took over the premiership from BULGANIN in 1958 and continued to hold supreme posts in both party and state until 1964. Although willing to seek a relaxation in world tension, he alternated peaceful gestures with threats, e.g., the Cuban Missile Crisis of 1962. Deteriorating relations with China encouraged his party colleagues to oust him from office in 1964.

KIESINGER, Kurt (1904–88)   West German chancellor (prime minister), 1966–69. Christian Democrat member of the Bundestag, 1949–58, 1969–80; minister-president, Baden-Württemburg, 1958–66.

KIM Il Sung (1912–94)   Prime minister, Democratic People's Republic of Korea (North Korea), 1948–72; president since 1972. He led the Korean People's Revolutionary Army to victory against the Japanese from 1932 to 1945. When the Democratic People's Republic was proclaimed in 1948 he became premier. Following the Korean War (1950–

53), division of Korea continued and Kim maintained judicious neutrality between China and the USSR. He was the communist world's longest-lasting dictator, intent on establishing a dynasty, and his son, Kim Jong Il (1942–), was groomed as his successor.

KING, Martin Luther, Jr. (1929–68) American civil rights leader who, as a Baptist minister in Montgomery, Alabama, first gained prominence in a 1955–56 campaign against that city's segregated bus system. After this he helped to fonnd the Southern Christian Leadership Conference as the base for his civil rights actions. His policy of nonviolent resistance led to several arrests—one of them in the spring of 1963 shortly before a massive peaceful demonstration in Washington, D.C. He received the 1964 Nobel Peace Prize. He was assassinated in April 1968 while on a civil rights mission to Memphis, Tennessee. In the generation since his death, he has remained the major inspiration in the struggle for racial equality in the United States.

KISSINGER, Henry (1923–) U.S. secretary of state, 1973–77. Professor of government at Harvard from 1958 to 1971, he was advisor to President NIXON in the 1968 presidential campaign. As White House national security advisor from 1969 to 1973, he played a more prominent role than the secretary of state, traveling on peace missions to the Middle East, Vietnam, and southern Africa, and negotiating with the Soviet Union in SALT. He shared the Nobel Peace Prize for 1973 with Le Duc Tho (who refused the prize) for concluding the agreement that removed U.S. forces from the Vietnam War. He was appointed secretary of state in 1973, holding office for the remainder of Nixon's presidency and throughout President FORD's administration. Kissinger practiced a "Realpolitik" of great-power diplomacy.

KOHL, Helmut (1930–) Chancellor (prime minister) of the Federal Republic of Germany from 1982 to 1998; Christian Democrat minister-president, Rhineland Palatinate, 1969–76; leader of the opposition in the Bundestag, 1976–82. Presided over the reunification of Germany in 1990 and became first chancellor of a reunited Germany from 1990–94. In 1998, after 16 years of rule by Christian Democrat Kohl, Germans chose centrist Social Democrat Gerhard Schroeder as chancellor. In January 2000, Kohl resigned as honorary chairman of the Christian Democrats after criticism for his refusal to identify donors of more than $1 million in secret payments while he was chancellor and party leader in the 1990s.

KOSYGIN, Alexei (1904–80) Chairman of the Council of Ministers of the USSR (prime minister), 1964–80. A member of the Central Committee of the Communist Party in 1939, he was minister for economic planning, 1956–57; chairman of the state economic planning commission and first deputy prime minister, 1960. He succeeded Khrushchev in 1964 as prime minister. He collaborated closely with BREZHNEV, but the latter became increasingly dominant. Kosygin partially attained his objective of decentralizing control of industry and agriculture, but his hopes of producing more consumer goods remained largely unfulfilled. Ill health forced his resignation in 1980 and he died eight weeks later.

KRAVCHUK, Leonid Makarovich (1937–)   President of the independent Ukraine since 1991. As a member of the Soviet Communist Party in the Ukraine, he was given responsibility for ideology in October 1989. He became party second secretary in June 1990 but left the post in July to become chairman of the Ukrainian Supreme Soviet. Kravchuk resigned from the Politburo in August 1991 and took an increasingly nationalist stance as president.

KWASNIEWSKI, Aleksander (1954–)   President of Poland since December 1995. Kwasniewski joined the Communist Party in 1977 and edited the party youth newspapers. He was appointed to the Council of Ministers in 1985 and in 1987 was named minister of youth affairs and physical culture. He took part in the round-table discussions that ended communist rule in the late 1980s, heading the committee that dealt with trade unions. After the fall of communism, Kwasniewski founded the Democratic Left Alliance, which won a plurality of seats in the parliamentary elections of 1993. He then formed a ruling coalition with the Polish Peasant Party, which was similarly composed of former Communists. In the presidential elections, Kwasniewski capitalized on WALESA's waning popularity to upset his reelection bid and become the second president of post-communist Poland. He has pledged to continue Walesa's reform efforts toward a market economy and membership in NATO and the European Union.

LAGOS, Ricardo (1939–)   Socialist president of Chile since January 2000. An economist and lawyer who received a Ph.D. in the United States, Lagos returned to Chile to become a protégé of socialist president Salvador Allende GOSSENS. After the 1973 coup, Lagos went into exile in the United States until 1975 and worked for the United Nations from 1976 to 1984. He was a vocal opponent of Chilean dictator General Augusto PINOCHET. In the 1990s, Lagos served under President Aylwin and President Frei as education minister and public works minister. Lagos won the January 2000 elections by a narrow margin to become the first socialist executive in 27 years.

LEE Kuan Yew (1923–)   Prime minister of Singapore from 1959 until 1990. Founder and secretary-general of the People's Action Party in 1954, he was elected prime minister when Singapore gained internal self-government in 1959. Between 1963 and 1965, when Singapore was part of the Federation of Malaysia, he served as a member of the federal parliament. He remains an influential Commonwealth leader. When he resigned in 1990 after 31 years, he was the world's longest-serving premier. He was succeeded by the first deputy prime minister, Goh Chok Tong.

LIAQUAT, Ali Khan (1896–1951)   First prime minister of Pakistan, 1947–51. He was a leading member of the Muslim League in the 1920s and 1930s, working closely with JINNAH. After partition in 1947, he became prime minister and, following Jinnah's death, the most powerful figure in the new state. Criticized over his attempts to reduce tension with India and his refusal to declare Pakistan an Islamic state, he was assassinated by a fanatic in 1951.

LIE, Trygve (1896–1968)   Secretary-general of the United Nations, 1946–53. Norwegian Social Democratic politician serving in every government from 1935 to 1946, he was elected first secretary-general of the UN in 1946. He was an early but unsuccessful advocate of the admission of Communist China to the UN. He took the initiative in organizing UN forces to assist South Korea in checking aggression by North Korea in 1950. He resigned in 1953 and later reentered Norwegian politics.

LIN Biao (1908–71)   Chinese Communist soldier and MAO's designated successor. Lin fought with the Communists, commanding an army in the Long March, 1934–35. He gained victories over Jiang's Kuomintang troops in 1948, and he carried the war victoriously into central China in 1949. Created a marshal in 1955 and minister of defense in 1959, he assisted Mao in organizing the Cultural Revolution of the mid-1960s. Marshal Lin was declared Mao's designated successor by the Ninth Party Congress in 1966, but he was later killed in a plane crash in 1971 while escaping from China after an unsuccessful attempt to seize power in Beijing.

LIN Piao   See LIN BIAO.

LIU Shao-chi   See LIU SHAOQI.

LIU Shaoqi (1898–1974)   Chairman of the People's Republic of China (head of state), 1959–69. Elected to the Central Committee of the Communist Party in 1927, he was appointed a political commissar during the Long March. A principal vice chairman of the party on establishment of the Chinese People's Republic in 1949, Liu succeeded MAO as chairman of the People's Republic. He lost his position as heir apparent to Mao during the Cultural Revolution in 1966. Criticized for defending the importance of industrial workers as a spearhead of the revolution instead of the primacy of the peasantry, he was deprived of all his party offices in 1968, disappearing from public life the following year.

LON NOL (1913–85)   President of Khmer Republic (formerly Cambodia, then Kampuchea), 1972–75. A general who held various ministerial posts under Prince SIHANOUK, including prime minister (1966–67), he headed the government after Sihanouk was deposed in 1970, establishing close ties with the United States and South Vietnam (permitting their forces to operate in Cambodia). He assumed total power in the new republic in 1972, fleeing in 1975 as communist Khmer Rouge rebels marched on the capital.

LUMUMBA, Patrice (1925–61)   First prime minister of the Democratic Republic of the Congo (formerly Zaïre) in 1960. In the same year his party emerged as the largest in the national assembly, and the Belgians chose him to be the first prime minister, with Joseph KASAVUBU as president. During his four-month incumbency he faced various crises, notably the secession of Katanga province. He was dismissed for seeking Soviet help, arrested by the army and handed over to Katanga rebels, by whom he was murdered in 1961.

MacARTHUR, Douglas (1880–1964)   U.S. general; chief of staff of the U.S. Army, 1930–35. As supreme allied commander, South-West Pacific, in World War II, he accepted the Japanese surrender in 1945. Commander of occupation forces in Japan, 1945–51, he played a major part in reestablishing the defeated nation. As commander of UN forces during the Korean War in 1950, he made public his advocacy of carrying the war into China. This defiance of official policy led to his dismissal by President Harry TRUMAN in 1951. He received a hero's welcome on his return to Washington, but he failed to secure nomination for the presidential election campaign of 1952.

MACHEL, Samora (1933–86)   President of the Republic of Mozambique, 1975–86. A nationalist leader who joined Frelimo *(q.v)* in 1963, he was active in the guerrilla war against the Portuguese from 1964 to 1974. He became leader of Frelimo after the death of Eduardo Mondlane in 1969 and first president of the Republic of Mozambique in 1975. He was killed in a plane crash in South Africa in 1986.

MACMILLAN, Harold (1894–1986)   British prime minister, 1957–63; Conservative MP, 1924–29, 1931–64; minister of housing, 1951–54; minister of defense, 1954–55; foreign secretary, 1955; chancellor of the exchequer, 1955–57. Appointed to succeed EDEN as the prime minister following the Suez crisis, he restored Conservative fortunes to lead them to victory in the 1959 election. His period of office was marked by economic prosperity, although little was done to deal with some of the underlying problems of the British economy; and by a reassessment of Britain's role in the world (notably in Europe and in Africa). Great Britain's declining status was, however, masked by his own prestige, including the close relationship he established with President John KEN-

NEDY. He resigned due to ill health in 1963 and declined honors normally bestowed on retiring prime ministers until 1984, when he became Earl of Stockton.

MAJOR, John (1943–)   British Conservative prime minister from 1990 to 1997. He succeeded Margaret Thatcher. A Conservative member of Parliament for Huntingdon, 1979– ; chief secretary to the treasury, 1987–89; briefly foreign secretary, July–October 1989; chancellor of the exchequer, 1989–90. He was the youngest British prime minister since 1894. Unusual for a Conservative prime minister, he has no university education. He was rapidly faced with the Gulf War *(q.v)* crisis. At home, he faced problems over the economy, the poll tax and Conservative electoral unpopularity. He won the April 1992 election, only to become the most unpopular prime minister in recent British history as a result of the recession and a seemingly endless series of goverment blunders.

MAKARIOS III, Archbishop (1913–77)   President of the Cypriot Republic, 1960–77. Elected archbishop of the self-governing Orthodox Church in Cyprus in 1950, he accepted the role of national as well as spiritual leader. Arrested by the British military authorities, who thought he was the leader of the EOKA terrorists, and deported to the Seychelles in 1956, he returned in 1957 to become first president of the Cypriot Republic in 1960. After an attack on the presidential palace by Greek officers in 1974, he was forced into a five-month exile. He returned to a divided island, and he was unable to reassert Greek primacy over the Turkish Cypriots before his death in 1977.

MALAN, Daniel (1879–1959)   South African prime minister, 1948–54. Boer patriotism, hardened by Calvinist convictions, led Malan to champion Afrikaner nationalism, first as a Dutch Reformed Church preacher and from 1918 on as a Nationalist MP. As prime minister he was responsible for introducing the policy of apartheid, separating South Africans into white, black and colored races.

MANDELA, Nelson (1918–)   South African president from 1994 to 1999. Mandela practiced law until 1952, when hostility to apartheid led him to accept membership in the executive of the African National Congress (ANC). He traveled widely in South Africa, championing his ideal of a free, multiracial society in the 1950s. After the ANC was banned in 1961 he evaded arrest until 1962, when he was jailed for five years. In 1963 he was charged under the Suppression of Communism Act, and after an eight-month trial sentenced to life imprisonment. More than 25 years later he remained an important figure for black South Africans. His wife, Winnie, continued to take an active if controversial part in politics, traveling widely at home and abroad, championing Mandela's causes, despite restrictions on her freedom imposed by the South African government. The release of Mandela from detention in February 1990 paved the way for the CODESA talks between the ANC and President DE KLERK. Mandela was elected president of the ANC in 1991. He has been the architect of the new South Africa. His ANC won 252 seats in the April 1994 election and he became president. In 1993, he shared with De Klerk the Nobel Peace Prize. In May 1994 Mandela was inaugerated as president of South Africa. In December 1996 Mandela handed over leadership of the ANC to his deputy Thabo MBEKI. Mandela was succeeded as president by Thabo Mbeki in June 1999.

MAO Tse-tung   See MAO ZEDONG.

MAO Zedong (1893–1976)   Chairman of the People's Republic of China, 1949–76. A founding member of the Chinese Communist Party in 1921, he believed in a revolutionary elite within the peasantry, not the urban proletariat. Attacked by JIANG Kaishek, he led his followers in the Long March from 1934 to 1935 to northwest China, where they later defeated both the Japanese and Jiang, proclaiming a People's Republic in 1949. As the dominant figure in China for over 20 years, Mao favored radical policies, including the Great Leap Forward of 1958–59 (the commune movement) and the Cultural Revolution of 1966–76, with his *Thoughts* becoming the dogma of the Chinese masses. For the last five years of his life he was a figurehead, with ZHOU Enlai managing the unexpected reconciliation with President NIXON and the West.

MARCOS, Ferdinand E. (1917–89)   President of the Philippines, 1965–86. Lieutenant, later captain in the Philippine army and U.S. forces in the Far East during World War II, he was special assistant to President Manuel Roxas, 1946–47; member of the House of Representatives, 1949–59; of the Senate, 1959–66; and finally president of the Philippines. An authoritarian ruler who took tough action against political opposition, he was supported by the United States as an ally against communism. He governed by martial law after 1972. Growing international concern led to presidential elections in 1986 and, although he claimed victory, Marcos was forced into exile in the United States and died there. His wife, Imelda, became a byword for absurd extravagance. His body was returned to the Philippines in September 1993.

MARSHALL, George Catlett (1880–1959)   U.S. Army officer and cabinet member. U.S. Army chief of staff from 1939 to 1945, he was special ambassador to China from November 1945 to January 1947. As secretary of state (1947–49), he developed the European Recovery Program (also referred to as the Marshall Plan [*q.v.*]) to foster postwar economic recovery in Europe. He resigned as secretary of state in January 1949, but he came out of retirement to become secretary of defense in September 1950. He left that position in September 1951. Marshall, a graduate of the Virginia Military Institute, received the 1953 Nobel Peace Prize for his work on the Marshall Plan.

MASARYK, Jan (1886–1948)   Czechoslovak diplomat and foreign minister. He attended the Paris Peace Conference of 1919–20. He was Czech minister (i.e., ambassador) to London from 1925 to 1928. He resigned after the Munich Pact in 1938, spent the war years in London, as foreign minister and deputy prime minister of the Czech government in exile from 1941 to 1945, and on the liberation of Czechoslovakia he continued as foreign minister. Although he was out of sympathy with increasingly pro-Soviet policy, he remained in office after the communist coup in 1948 but died a few days later. The exact circumstances of his death remain a mystery.

MBEKI, Thabo (1942–   )   South Africa's president since June 1999, when he succeeded the popular nationalist leader, Nelson MANDELA. A leader of the African National Congress (ANC), Mbeki had already assumed many of Mandela's governing responsibilities when he won South Africa's first democratic elections in 1994. Mbeki's father, Govan, was arrested with Mandela in 1964 for their political work. When the ANC was banned in 1962, Mbeki went into exile. He received military training in Moscow and served as an ANC representative in several African countries before taking a place at the ANC headquarters in exile in Lusaka, Zambia.

MEIR, Golda (1898–1978)   Israeli prime minister, 1969–74. Active in Zionist socialist politics after immigrating to Palestine from the United States in 1921, on independence she became the first Israeli ambassador to the Soviet Union; minister of labor, 1949–56; and foreign minister, 1956–66. She was elected prime minister in 1969. Although she distrusted General Moshe DAYAN, she retained him as minister of defense until after the Yom Kippur War of 1973. She won the 1969 and 1973 elections but had to govern through coalitions. She resigned unexpectedly in 1974.

MENDERES, Adnan (1899–1961)   Prime minister of Turkey from 1950 to 1960. A lawyer until entering politics in 1932, he founded the Democratic Party in 1945 and was elected prime minister in 1950. He negotiated Turkey's entry into NATO and agreed to the independence of Cyprus from Great Britain in 1959. Following riots provoked by Turkey's failing economy, Menderes took dictatorial powers. He was deposed by the army and hanged for violating the constitution in September 1961.

MILOSEVIC, Slobodan (1941–   )   President of Serbia, 1990 to 1997. President of the new Federal Republic of Yugoslavia, consisting of Serbia and Montenegro since 1997. A Communist Party functionary from 1969 to 1982, then leader of the Belgrade Communist Party, he became chairman of the Serbian Communist Party in 1986. He became president of Serbia in 1989. In July 1990 he was elected president of the Socialist Party of Serbia (formerly the Communist Party) and was elected president of Serbia by a landslide in the first free elections in December 1990, his party taking an extreme nationalist "Greater Serbia" stance. Milosevic backed Serbian rebels throughout the three-year civil war, but the resulting economic crises led him to sign a peace agreement in 1995, ending the civil war in Bosnia. In December 1997, Milan Milutinovic was elected president of Serbia, but Milosovic refused to recognize the opposition's victory. Constitutionally barred from another term as president of Serbia, Milosevic became president of the Federal Republic of Yugoslavia in July 1997. In May 1998, Montenegro elected Milosevic opponent Milo Djukanovic as president. In October 2000, newly elected president Vojislav Kostunica took effective control of the Yugoslov government, following Milosevic's downfall.

MITTERRAND, François (1916–96)   President of France since 1981. Mitterrand entered politics in 1946 as Socialist deputy for the Nievre department. He was a left-wing candidate against President DE GAULLE in 1965. After disagreement among the French socialist parties in the late 1960s, he recovered his political authority and was accepted as leader of the left throughout the 1970s. Again unsuccessfully contesting the presidential election in 1974, finally, in 1981, he received 51.7% of the vote, defeating Valery GISCARD D'ESTAING. From 1981 until 1986 he was backed by a Socialist majority in the National Assembly but, following the parliamentary elections of 1986, he had to share power with a Gaullist majority led by Jacques CHIRAC as prime minister. He was reelected president in 1988, but his popularity waned as the Socialists were humiliated in the 1993 elections.

MOBUTU, Joseph   See MOBUTU, SESE SEKO.

MOBUTU, Sese Seko (1930–97)   President of Zaïre (now the Democratic Republic of the Congo), 1965–97. Chief of staff of the Congolese army in 1960, Mobutu took over the presidency in 1965, after the threat of a renewal of civil war. Mobutu imposed discipline harshly, but he gradually achieved an orderly government in Zaïre, an achievement that had seemed impossible in the 1960s. His regime was a byword for dictatorship, but, beginning in 1990, demands for a return to multiparty politics and the termination of U.S. aid put Mobutu in jeopardy of losing his office. He was overthrown in a coup led by Laurent KABILA in 1997 and died in exile shortly thereafter.

MOI, Daniel T. arap (1924–   )   President of Kenya since 1978. A teacher, he became a member of the Legislative Council in 1957 and chairman of the Kenya African Democratic Union from 1960 to 1961. He progressed through various ministerial posts in the 1960s: education, 1961–62; local government, 1962–64; and home affairs, 1964–68. He became vice president from 1967 to 1968 and president in 1978, on the death of Jomo KENYATTA. In 1991, he restored a multiparty system and in January 1993 he was declared winner in the first multiparty elections in 26 years.

MOUNTBATTEN, Earl (1900–79)   British admiral; during World War II, chief of combined operations, 1942; supreme allied commander Southeast Asia, 1943. Appointed last viceroy of India in 1947, he sped up the transition to independence and became first governor-general of India from 1947 to 1948. He resumed his naval career as first sea lord, 1955–59, and chief of defense staff, 1959–65. A cousin of the Duke of Edinburgh and a close advisor to the royal family, he was assassinated by Irish terrorists in 1979.

MUBARAK, Hosni (1928–   )   President of Egypt since 1981. Egyptian air force officer and politician, he was air force chief of staff from 1969 to 1972, commander in chief from 1972 to 1975 and vice president of Egypt from 1975 to 1981. He was vice chairman of the National Democratic Party (NDP) from 1976 to 1981 and secretary-general of the NDP and the Political Bureau, 1981–82. On the assassination of SADAT in 1981 he became president. Mubarak survived an assasination attempt in June 1995, and the ruling NDP won a clear victory in the December elections of that year.

MUGABE, Robert (1924–   )   Executive president of Zimbabwe since 1987. Deputy secretary-general of ZAPU (Zimbabwe African People's Union) in 1961, he was detained by Rhodesian authorities in 1962. He escaped to Tanzania and set up ZANU (Zimbabwe African National Union) in 1963. Detained by the Smith regime from 1964 to 1974, in 1976 he became joint head (with Joshua NKOMO) of the Patriotic Front, leading the Zimbabwe African National Liberation Army in guerrilla war from 1976 to 1979. After the cease-fire, Mugabe attended the Lancaster House Conference in 1979. He returned to Zimbabwe in 1980 to lead the ZANU election campaign, defeating both Nkomo and Abel MUZOREWA to become first prime minister of Zimbabwe from 1980 to 1987. He moved Zimbabwe toward a one-party state, merging ZANU and ZAPU in 1987. He became executive president the same year. By 1991 Mugabe was forced to abandon his commitment to a one-party Marxist state. In 1996 Mugabe was reelected president when the other candidates dropped out of the election.

MULRONEY, (Martin) Brian (1939–) Prime minister of Canada, 1984–93. A successfial lawyer and industrialist, Mulroney was elected leader of the Progressive Conservative Party in 1983. He was the first Conservative to attain the party leadership post without having previously run for public office, as well as the first Conservative leader to come from the province of Quebec in nearly 100 years. His platform emphasized deregulation and the encouragement of foreign capital and trade, and as such focused on establishing liberal trade agreements with the United States. His policies having become extremely unpopular due to the economic recession, he stepped aside in 1993 in the fruitless hope of averting a Conservative defeat in that year's general election.

MUSSADEQ, Mohammed (1881–1967) Prime minister of Iran, 1951–53. He served as foreign minister from 1922 to 1924. After withdrawing from politics, he was reelected to parliament in 1942. His militant nationalism triumphed in 1951 when the oil industry was nationalized, and he was appointed prime minister. The withdrawal of Western experts left the Iranians unable to produce oil, on which his promises of social revolution depended, and he was dismissed in 1953 and arrested in a coup d'état sponsored by the U.S. Central Intelligence Agency.

MUZOREWA, Bishop Abel (1925–) Zimbabwean churchman and politician. Bishop of the United Methodist Church in Southern Rhodesia in 1968, he was founder and president of the African National Council in 1971. Muzorewa mobilized African opinion against the proposed Rhodesia settlement of 1971–72. A member of the Executive Council of the transitional government in Zimbabwe-Rhodesia from 1978 to 1980, he was considered by the British government to be more conciliatory than his rivals, but he was soundly defeated by MUGABE in the 1980 election.

NAGY, Imre (1896–1958) Hungarian Communist; prime minister, 1953–55 and 1956. Minister of agriculture in the provisional government of 1945–46, when he was responsible for major land reforms, he became prime minister in 1953. Having instituted a more liberal regime, he was forced out of office following Georgy Malenkov's resignation as Soviet prime minister and expelled from the Communist Party. He was reappointed following the Twentieth Party Congress in 1956, but Soviet intervention overthrew his government a month later. He escaped to Yugoslavia but was arrested and executed in 1958.

NAKASONE Yasuhiro (1917–) Prime minister of Japan, 1982–87. Minister of transport, 1967–68; minister of state and director-general, defense agency, 1970–71; chairman of executive council, Liberal-Democratic Party (LDP), 1971–72; minister of international trade and industry, 1972–74; secretary-general of LDP, 1974–76 and chairman, 1977–80; minister of state, 1980–82.

NASSER, Gamal Abdel (1918–70)   President of Egypt, 1954–70. When Mohammed NEGUIB forced the abdication of King FAROUK in 1952, Nasser became a dominant figure in the ruling junta, succeeding Neguib in 1954. His nationalization of the Suez Canal led to a short-lived attack by British and French forces. Nasser's defiance of the West gave him great prestige and led to the creation of the United Arab Republic between Egypt and Syria, which he led from 1958 to 1961 (Egypt retaining the title until 1971). Internal criticism led him to mount the disastrous Six-Day War against Israel in 1967. He remained in office until his death in 1970, maintaining links with the USSR but also improving relations with the United States.

NEGUIB, Mohammed (1901–79)   President of Egypt, 1953–54. As brigadier in the Free Officers movement, he was responsible for overthrowing King Farouk in 1952. The first president of the Egyptian Republic in 1953, Neguib lacked the political skill of NASSER. He was gradually isolated by the younger army officers, resigning in 1954, and placed under house arrest.

NEHRU, Jawaharlal (1889–1964)   Indian prime minister, 1947–64. He became active in the Indian Congress movement after the Amritsar shootings of 1919. President of the Congress movement in 1929, he was chief tactician of the campaign for independence. He became prime minister and foreign minister on independence in 1947. Under his leadership, India made technical, industrial and social advances, and assumed moral leadership of the developing Third World, playing an important mediating role in various international crises. He died in office in 1964.

NETANYAHU, Benjamin (1949–   )   Prime minister of Israel from 1996 to 1999. Educated in the United States, Netanyahu began his career in the Israeli military and was elected to parliament as a Likud member in 1988. In 1991, he served in Yitzhak RABIN's coalition cabinet and was the Israeli spokesman during the Persian Gulf War. In 1993, he was elected leader of the Likud Party. After Rabin's assassination in 1995, Netanyahu became more popular for his opposition to the Israel–PLO peace accords and in 1996 he beat out incumbent Shimon PERES to become the youngest prime minister in Israeli history. But by 1998 Netanyahu was attacked from both sides of the political spectrum—the left accused him of intentionally thwarting the peace process and the right accused him of betrayal for giving up Israeli territory. In December 1998, Israel's parliament voted to dissolve Netanyahu's government and, in the following spring, Ehud BARAK of the Labor Party won the election.

NETO, Agostinho (1922–79) President of the Republic of Angola, 1975–79. Angolan doctor and nationalist leader. Imprisoned four times from 1952 to 1960, he was in the Cape Verde Islands from 1960 to 1962. President of the People's Movement for the Liberation of Angola (MPLA), he led the guerrilla war against the Portuguese from 1962 to 1974. He was the first president of the Republic of Angola in 1975, when Angola became independent in the midst of the civil war, defeating South African-backed rivals in 1976 with the assistance of Cubans.

NGO DINH Diem (1901–63) First prime minister and president of South Vietnam, 1954–63. A nationalist leader and civil servant from 1931, he was asked to be minister of the interior under HO Chi Minh. He declined the offer, living abroad until 1954. He became prime minister under BAO DAI in the new government of South Vietnam. In 1955 South Vietnam was declared a republic and he became head of state, replacing Bao Dai. His rule became increasingly harsh and repressive and, following international outrage at his treatment of Buddhists, he was overthrown in a military coup and murdered in 1963.

NGUYEN VAN Thieu (1923–) President of South Vietnam, 1967–75. Vietnamese army officer who rose to become South Vietnam's armed forces chief of staff, 1963–64; deputy premier and minister of defense, 1964–65; chairman of the National Leadership Committee and head of state, 1965–67. He was president of the Republic of (South) Vietnam from 1967 until the fall of Saigon in 1975.

NIXON, Richard M. (1913–94) President of the United States, 1969–74. Elected to the House of Representatives in 1946 and to the Senate in 1950, Nixon was vice president (under Eisenhower) from 1953 to 1961. Republican candidate in the 1960 presidential election, he lost narrowly to John KENNEDY. He gained the Republican nomination again in 1968 and became president in 1969. Assisted by his aide and later secretary of state, Henry KISSINGER, Nixon gradually reduced U.S. involvement in Vietnam, eased tensions with the USSR and improved diplomatic contacts with Communist China. His second term was dominated by controversy, first over his vice president, Spiro AGNEW, who resigned in 1973, and then over the Watergate conspiracies (*q.v.*, chapter 10), which eventually led to his own resignation in 1974, following the initiation of the impeachment process.

NKOMO, Joshua (1917–99) Zimbabwean nationalist and leader of the Zimbabwe African People's Union (ZAPU); president of the African National Congress (ANC), 1957–59; in exile, 1959–60; president, National Democratic Party, 1960; Nkomo helped form and became president of ZAPU. He was imprisoned from 1964 to 1974, during which time British emissaries visited him in their abortive quest for a Rhodesian settlement. Joint leader, with Robert MUGABE, of the Patriotic Front in the guerrilla war of 1976–79, after the Lancaster House Conference Nkomo returned home in triumph. ZAPU did not match ZANU's success in the first elections, however, and Mugabe appointed Nkomo his minister for home affairs, 1980–81. Tribal skirmishes continued and the uneasy Nkomo-Mugabe partnership finally broke down in February 1982. The rift with Mugabe ended in 1987, ZANU and ZAPU were merged and Nkomo returned to the cabinet as senior minister without portfolio. In April 1990 he became one of two national vice presidents.

NKRUMAH, Kwame (1909–72)   President of Ghana, 1960–66. Founder in 1949 of the Convention People's Party, which sought self-government for the Gold Coast colony, he was imprisoned from 1950 to 1951. Elected to parliament in 1951, he was prime minister of Gold Coast from 1954 to 1957 and of Ghana from 1957 to 1960 (after Ghana achieved dominion status). President from 1960 to 1966, when Ghana became a republic within the Commonwealth, he was a respected pan-African leader, although he was not accorded the position among African statesmen he sought. At home, his rule became increasingly dictatorial; government extravagance and a slump in cocoa prices led to inflation and economic chaos in 1965–66, and he was deposed by a military coup in 1966.

NORIEGA, General Manuel Antonio (1938–   )   Panamanian dictator with a military background. Became chief of G.2, the Panama intelligence agency, in 1969. After President Torrijos was killed in a plane crash in 1981, he took over control of the armed forces, becoming de facto ruler of Panama in 1983. Subverted 1984 presidential election. Indicted by a U.S. grand jury for drug trafficking and racketeering, 1988. Survived a coup attempt, October 1989. Fled U.S. invasion force seeking to capture him, December 1989, taking refuge in the Vatican embassy. He surrendered to U.S. forces on 3 January 1990 and was flown to Florida for trial. He was convicted in Miami in April 1992 and sentenced to a 40-year jail term.

NOVOTNY, Antonin (1904–75)   First secretary, 1953–68, and president, 1957–68, of the Czechoslovak Republic. He became a Communist in 1921 and was promoted to first secretary in 1953 (until replaced by DUBČEK in 1968). A dedicated Stalinist, he was never able to adjust to the new Khrushchev regime. His concentration on heavy industry led to a severe economic recession from 1961 to 1963, and student demonstrations in 1962 forced him to make political concessions. In 1968, in a last bid to check liberalization, he sought but was refused the backing of the Czech army, after which he withdrew from political life.

NUJOMA, Sam Daniel (1929–) Namibian nationalist leader. Led SWAPO guerrillas against South African forces. First president of independent Namibia, March 1990. In 1996, Nujoma traveled to South Africa to ask for investment funds, and an agreement was reached on how to cancel Namibia's pre-independence debt.

NYERERE, Julius (1922–99) President of Tanzania, 1964–85. He organized the moderate socialist Tanganyika African National Union (YANU) in 1950. TANU won elections in 1958 and 1960, and Nyerere became prime minister in 1961. Elected president when Tanganyika became a republic in 1962, he became president of the United Republic of Tanzania when Tanganyika and Zanzibar were united in 1964. Nyerere remained a respected Commonwealth statesman until his retirement in 1985.

OBOTE, Milton (1924–) President of Uganda, 1966–71 and 1980–85. A founding member of the Kenya African Union and member of the Uganda National Congress, 1952–60, he was elected to the Legislative Council in 1957. He helped form the Uganda People's Congress in 1960. Leader of the opposition in the Ugandan parliament, 1961–62, on independence he became prime minister, 1962–71. President of Uganda in 1966, he was deposed by a military coup in 1971 led by Idi AMIN. Following an invasion by Ugandan dissidents with the assistance of the Tanzanian army in 1979, Obote was elected president in 1980. Overthrown in July 1985 by General Tito Okello, he was subsequently exiled to Zambia.

OJUKWU, Chukwenmeka (1933–) President of Biafra, 1967–70. An army officer who served in the UN peacekeeping force in Congo in 1962, he became military governor of Eastern Nigeria in 1966, and proclaimed it to be the independent Republic of Biafra in 1967. President of Biafra and its leader in the war with federal Nigeria from 1967 to 1970, on the collapse of Biafra in 1970 he fled to Ivory Coast.

ORTEGA SAAVEDRA, Daniel (1945–) President of Nicaragua, 1981–90. Active in various underground resistance movements against the regime of Anastasio SOMOZA from 1959, he was imprisoned and tortured for revolutionary activities. A member of the National Directorate of FSLN (Sandinista Liberation Front), 1966–67, and imprisoned, 1967–74, he resumed his position with FSLN and became involved in further revolutionary activities. He fought a two-year military offensive, which overthrew the Somoza regime in 1979. A member of the Junta of National Reconstruction government since 1979, he was president from

1981 to his defeat by Violetta CHAMORRO in the elections of February 1990. After Chamorro's term expired in 1996, Ortega reemerged as the FSLN candidate for president, but he was defeated in the October elections by conservative candidate Arnoldo Aleman.

OWEN, Lord (David) (1938–)   A doctor, elected to parliament in 1966, he held a number of junior ministerial posts as a British Labour politician before serving as foreign minister from 1977 to 1979. A leading member of the breakaway group from Labour that formed the Social Democratic Party in 1981, he became SDP leader in 1983. He rejected the SDP's amalgamation with the Liberal Party following the failure of their electoral alliance in the 1987 general election, leading a rump SDP until its disbanding in 1990. He attempted unsuccessfully to negotiate a peaceful resolution of the Bosnian War in 1993 and 1994.

ÖZAL, Turgut (1927–93)   Turkish politician. After working as an economic advisor to the military government, he formed the Motherland Party (Anap) and became prime minister in 1983, a post he held until becoming president in 1989. His austerity program helped restore the economy, and by lifting state controls encouraged moves toward a free market system. He survived an assassination attempt in 1988. He died in office.

PERES, Shimon (1923–)   Polish-born Israeli politician who became prime minister from 1995 to 1996. Peres was active in the pre-independence resistance and, from 1952, in the defense ministry of his mentor David BEN GURION. Elected to the Knesset in 1959, he was active in the Labor Party, in which he held a succession of ministerial posts, culminating in defense minister in 1973. After leading Labor to a slim plurality in the 1984 elections, he was asked to organize a unity government in which he and Likud leader Yitzhak SHAMIR would alternate as prime minister. His first term ended in October 1986. Foreign minister since 1992, he was a key figure in the Israeli–PLO Peace Agreement of 1993. In 1994, Yasir ARAFAT, Yitzhak RABIN and Peres were jointly awarded the Nobel Prize for Peace. Following Rabin's assassination in 1995, Peres took over as prime minister, but he was narrowly defeated in his bid for reelection by Benjamin NETANYAHU of the Likud Party the following year. Peres declined to seek reelection as the leader of the Labor Party in 1997.

PEREZ DE CUÉLLAR, Javier (1920–)   UN secretary-general, 1982–1991. A Peruvian diplomat holding various posts from 1944 to 1978, he represented Peru at the UN from 1971 to 1975 and was president of the Security Council in 1974. He served as undersecretary-general for special political affairs from 1979 to 1981. In August 1988 he succeeded in negotiating a cease-fire between Iran and Iraq, at war since 1980.

PINOCHET, Augusto (1915–) A Chilean general, commander in chief of the armed forces from 1973 to 1980. He led the right-wing coup to depose President ALLENDE in 1973. President of the Government Council of Chile, 1973–74, he was president of Chile from 1974 until 1990. In October 1988 a referendum calling for new elections was adopted by popular vote. Pinochet subsequently gave up the presidency. Pinochet was arrested in October 1998 on Spanish warrants charging him with crimes against humanity during his leadership in Chile between 1973 and 1990. In January 2000, after 15 months under house arrest in London, the ailing 84-year-old Pinochet was deemed unfit to stand trial in Spain and will likely return to Chile, where he may still face trial.

PIUS XII (1876–1958) Pope, 1939–1958. Eugenio Maria Giuseppe Giovanni Pacelli. Ordained in 1899, most of his career was in the papal diplomatic service, where he became secretary of state and negotiated a Concordat with the German Nazi government in 1933. Politically neutral between the Allies and the Axis powers during World War II, he allowed asylum to refugees in Vatican City. A vehement anticommunist, he threatened excommunication to the party's supporters.

POL POT (1925–1998) Communist prime minister of Democratic Kampuchea (formerly Cambodia), 1976–79. He joined anti-French resistance under Ho Chi Minh in the 1940s. Following the communist Khmer Rouge victory in the civil war, he became prime minister in 1976, after the resignation of Prince Sihanouk. Pol Pot's ruthless regime was overthrown in 1979 after the Vietnamese invasion of Kampuchea. Charged with genocide and sentenced to death in absentia in 1979, he led guerrilla forces from 1979 to 1985. He was captured in 1997, but escaped in 1998, reportely to Thailand to avoid facing an international court for crimes against humanity. Cambodian authorities reported his capture in April 1998. Several days later reports of Pol Pot's death were confirmed.

POMPIDOU, Georges (1911–74) President of France, 1969–74. He was adviser to General DE GAULLE during World War II, and later on de Gaulle's return to power in 1959. Pompidou played a major role in the Algerian crisis and became prime minister in 1962. Initially subordinate to de Gaulle, he gradually established his own authority, particularly in responding to the demonstrations of students and trade unionists in 1968. Resentment over his growing prestige led to his dismissal by de Gaulle. When de Gaulle resigned in 1969, Pompidou was elected as his successor. He died in office in 1974.

PRODI, Romano (1939–)   Prime minister of Italy from 1996 to 1998. An industrial executive who became industry minister twice (from 1978 to 1979 and from 1993 to 1994), Prodi's Olive Tree coalition, a center-left alliance, won the 1996 elections to control the Italian Senate and gain a decisive plurality in the Chamber of Deputies. By 1998, Prodi appeared to be too much a candidate of the center, and Massimo D'Alema, a powerful member of the Democrats of the Left, won the October elections.

PUTIN, Vladimir (1952–)   Russian president since January 2000. A former KGB spy, Putin entered politics when the Soviet Union collapsed in 1990. Over the next decade, he held several titles, including vice mayor of St. Petersburg in 1994, deputy chief Kremlin administrator in 1997, head of Federal Security Service in 1998 and secretary of the presidential Security Council in 1999. In August 1999, Boris YELTSIN appointed Putin to be the fifth prime minister in 17 months. When Yeltsin resigned at the end of 1999, Putin took over and won the presidency by a narrow majority in the March 2000 elections. Putin has so far favored a strong military stance against rebels in Chechnya and has put nuclear arms reduction at the center of his foreign policy.

AL-QADDAFI, Muammar (1942–)   Libyan leader since 1969. As a young army officer he led a coup against the Libyan monarchy in 1969. Chairman of the Revolutionary Command Council from 1969 to 1977, he has been head of state since 1977, establishing a socialist republic. Using Libya's oil wealth to pursue a vigorously anti-Israeli foreign policy and to promote himself as a pan-Arab leader, he is recognized by the West as a patron of terrorists, responsible for bombings and hijackings of Israelis and others. This led to air strikes by the United States on Tripoli in 1986. Qaddafi's idiosyncratic style makes him one of the most unpredictable people in contemporary international politics.

QUAYLE, James Danforth (Dan) (1947–)   Vice president of the United States, 1989–93. He had been George BUSH's surprise choice for a running mate. Republican senator from Indiana, 1981–88.

RABIN, Yitzhak (1922–95)   Prime minister of Israel, 1974–77, and from 1992 to 1995. An army officer who rose to be chief of staff of the Israeli Defense Forces, 1964–68, he was a member of the Knesset since 1974. Leader of the Labor Party from 1974 to 1979, he was prime minister from 1974 to 1977, minister of communications from 1974 to 1975 and minister of defense after 1984. Under his premiership, Israel secured the historic peace agreement with the PLO in 1993 and with Jordan the following year. In 1994, Yasir ARAFAT, Shimon PERES and Rabin were jointly awarded the Nobel Prize for Peace. During a peace rally on 4 November 1995 Rabin was shot and killed by a Jewish extremist.

RAHMAN, Sheikh Mujibur (1920–75)   Prime minister of Bangladesh, 1972–75. Leader of the Awami League, he campaigned for the independence of East Bengal from Pakistan. Arrested several times and charged with treason in 1971, he was released following Indian military intervention against Pakistan. He returned to a hero's welcome on the establishment of the independent republic of Bangladesh at the end of 1971. As prime minister, the problems of creating a socialist state and parliamentary democracy in a desperately poor country proved too much, and he assumed dictatorial powers in 1975. Later that year the army staged a coup, and he was murdered.

RAHMAN, Tunku Abdul (1903–90)   Prime minister of Malaya, 1957–63, and of Malaysia, 1963–70. Leader of United Malaya's National Organization and chief minister from 1952 to 1957, he became first prime minister of independent Malaya in 1954 as a result of his ability to secure collaboration between Malay, Chinese and Indian groups. He played a major part in the creation of the federation between Malaya, Singapore, Sarawak and Sabah (Malaysia), becoming its first prime minister in 1963. Ethnic tensions caused riots in 1969, which necessitated suspension of the constitution. Further rioting led to his resignation in 1970. He remained the "founding father" of modern Malaysia.

RAKOSI, Matyas (1892–1971)   Hungarian Communist leader; prime minister, 1949–53 and 1955–56. Active in Communist resistance in the interwar years, he was sentenced to life imprisonment in 1935. He was released in 1940 to go to Moscow, where he led a committee of Hungarian Communists. From 1945 he led the party and government, presiding over the establishment of a Stalinist regime. Replaced by the more liberal Imre NAGY in 1953, by 1955 he had restored his control of the party. His repressive methods contributed to the unrest in 1956. In an attempt to appease the Hungarians, the USSR persuaded him to resign.

RAMAPHOSA, Cyril (c. 1953–)   South African black leader. Elected secretary-general, African National Congress, July 1991. A lawyer, he built up the National Union of Mineworkers as its secretary-general. A skilled negotiator, he has a reputation for toughness combined with pragmatism. Became chair of the Constitutional Assembly after the 1994 elections. He announced his resignation from active politics in July 1996.

RAO, Pamulaparti Venkata Narasimha (1921–)   Prime minister of India from 1991 to 1996, the first Indian prime minister to come from the south of the country. A scholar in the Nehru mold, he has held almost every senior office in government and the Congress Party, 1980–84. A highly successful foreign secretary under both Indira and Rajiv Gandhi, he was elevated to the premiership in the wake of Rajiv's assassination. Rao stepped down as prime minister in May 1996 after the Congress (I) Party was soundly defeated in parliamentary elections following a series of corruption scandals. Rao resigned as party chief that September, and the following year he was charged with corruption and bribery in an alleged vote-buying scheme dating from 1993. Rao was the first former Indian prime minister ever to face trial on criminal charges.

REAGAN, Ronald (1911–)   President of the United States from 1981 to 1989. A film star, he entered politics as a Republican, serving as governor of California from 1967 to 1974. In the 1980 presidential election he defeated Jimmy Carter, becoming president at the age of 70. His skill in communicating with ordinary Americans made him one of the most popular presidents in recent times. His second term in office, following a sweeping victory in 1984, was marked by a thaw in his previously strained relations with the USSR, helped by summits with GORBACHEV in Geneva and Reykjavík. At the same time, however, there was controversy concerning arms sales to Iran and support for the contra rebels in Nicaragua, as well as an ever-increasing budget deficit. He was succeeded by his vice president, George BUSH. In 2000, Reagan's family announced that he was in the final stages of Alzheimer's disease.

RHEE, Syngman (1875–1965)   President of South Korea from 1948 to 1960. He was in exile in the United States from 1912 to 1945, acting as spokesman for Korean independence. He returned to Korea in 1945 with U.S. support and was elected as first president following the division of Korea. He was a strong leader in the Korean War, but his increasingly dictatorial rule provoked unrest and riots, which led to his resignation in 1960. He retired in exile to Hawaii, where he died in 1965.

RUSK, David Dean (1909–94)   United States secretary of state, 1961 to 1969. After teaching political science in the 1930s and serving in World War II, Rusk followed his mentor George MARSHALL into the State Department, where he was named assistant secretary of state for Far Eastern affairs in 1950 and, under Dean ACHESON, played an important role in the formulation of policy during the Korean War. In 1952 Rusk left the State Department to become head of the Rockefeller Foundation. President John F. KENNEDY appointed him secretary of state in

1961; he retained that post under President Johnson. Rusk advocated worldwide economic cooperation and military opposition to communist expansion, becoming a prominent apologist for the escalation of the Vietnam War. In 1970, he became a professor of international law at the University of Georgia.

AL-SADAT, Anwar (1919–81) President of Egypt, 1970–81. A member of the Free Officers movement in 1948 and of the Revolutionary Command Council after an army coup in 1952, he was minister of state from 1955 to 1956, speaker in the United Arab Republic Assembly from 1961 to 1969, vice president from 1964 to 1966 and from 1969 to 1970, and president of Egypt in 1970 on the death of NASSER. His visit to Israel in 1977 to meet BEGIN in search of a Middle East settlement was a bold move that led to the Camp David peace treaty in 1978. He was assassinated in 1981.

SAKHAROV, Andrei (1921–89) Nuclear physicist (perhaps the main contributor to the Soviet H-bomb), utopian thinker, leading Soviet dissident. A prominent advocate of educational reform and intellectual freedom in the Soviet Union since the late 1950s, he gained international attention with a 1968 manifesto outlining peaceful steps toward a world community. Cofounder of the Committee for Human Rights in 1970, he received the Nobel Peace Prize in 1975, by which time he was a target of government condemnation. From 1980 to 1986 in internal exile in Gorky with his wife, activist Yelena Bonner, in 1986 he returned to Moscow, where, under the partial thaw of *glasnost*, he was permitted to resume limited scientific and human rights activities under the surveillance of authorities. He was eventually honored by the state shortly before his death.

SALAZAR, Antonio de Oliveira (1889–1970) Portuguese prime minister, 1932–68. Appointed minister of finance in 1928, he showed such skill at a time of political and economic crisis that he was made prime minister in 1932 and given virtually dictatorial powers. He ruled firmly through a quasi-Fascist, single-party system, retaining tight personal control on all areas of the government. He carried through a series of domestic reforms, but his hostility to political change at home and in the African colonies left a difficult legacy for his successor, Caetano, on his retirement in 1968.

SCHMIDT, Helmut (1918–) Chancellor (prime minister) of West Germany, 1974–82. An economist, he was a member of the Social Democratic Party (SPD) since 1946, a member of the Bundestag from 1953 to 1962 and, since 1965, chairman, SPD, 1967–69; minister of defense, 1969–72; and finance, 1972–74. He succeeded Brandt as chancellor in 1974, leading a coalition with the Free Democrats.

SCHWARZKOPF, H. Norman (1934–   )   U.S. general. Deputy commander, U.S. invasion of Grenada, 1983. Allied commander, Operation Desert Storm *(q.v)*, 1991. He retired from the army in August 1991.

SHAMIR, Yitzhak (1915–   )   Israeli politician. Born in Poland in 1935 he immigrated to Palestine, where he was active in the Irgun Zvai Leumi and, in the 1940s, operations chief of the terrorist Stern Gang. He served as senior staff member of Israeli intelligence (Mossad) from 1955 to 1965. Elected to the Knesset on the Likud slate in 1973, he became speaker in 1977, minister of foreign affairs in Menachem BEGIN's cabinet in 1980, and prime minister following Begin's 1983 resignation. In 1984 he entered into a coalition with the Labor Party, in which he agreed to share the post of prime minister with Labor leader Shimon PERES on a rotating basis. Foreign minister from 1984 to 1986, he resumed the premiership according to coalition agreement. He was defeated in the 1992 elections.

SHARIF, Nawaz (1948–   )   Pakistani prime minister from 1990 to 1993 and since 1997. A lawyer by profession, he was chief minister of the Punjab from 1985 to August 1990. Sharif's Islamic Democratic Alliance swept to victory in the 1990 general election, inflicting a crushing defeat on Benazir Bhutto, whose government was sacked for alleged corruption. Sharif himself was dismissed on corruption charges in 1993, and BHUTTO resumed power in the October elections, only to be ousted again in 1996. In 1997, Sharif's party, the Pakistan Muslim League (PML), returned him to power in a landslide parliamentary election. In 1998, following nuclear tests conducted by Israel, Pakistan exploded several bombs of its own, an act that concerned the international community all the more when, in October 1999, General Pervaiz Musharraf overthrew Sharif in a surprise military coup, suspending the constitution and dissolving parliament.

SHASTRI, Lal (1904–66)   Indian prime minister, 1964–66. He joined the Congress Party in 1920. Minister responsible for railroads and transportation in Nehru's cabinet, 1952–58, he was later minister of commerce and minister for home affairs. In 1963 he left office to work for the Congress Party, but he was brought back as Nehru's health was failing. Shastri succeeded Nehru as prime minister in 1964. Fighting between India and Pakistan in 1965 led to the Soviet-sponsored Tashkent talks between AYUB KHAN and Shastri. At the end of the meeting Shastri died suddenly of a heart attack.

SHEKHAR, Chandra (1927–   )   Prime minister of India, November 1990 to June 1991. A Socialist Party member in his youth, then active in Congress (I) after 1965. Split with Indira GANDHI, 1975. President of the Janata Party; however, on the merger that formed Janata Dal, he was passed over as leader. He led the rebellion (5 November 1990) against Vishwanath Pratap Singh that caused the fall of the government.

SHEVARDNADZE, Eduard (1928–) Russian foreign minister from 1985 until his shock resignation in December 1990 over increasing right-wing pressure. As Gorbachev's key lieutenant he presided over the ending of the Cold War and the freeing of the Eastern bloc from Soviet control. Born in Georgia, he established an earlier reputation for rooting out corruption and nepotism in Georgia. His resignation increased very considerably the pressures on Gorbachev. He returned briefly as foreign minister, November–December 1991. He became president of independent Georgia after October 1992 and acting prime minister, August 1993, in which office he has had to deal with a three-way civil war. Resigned in September 1993. In August 1995 he survived an assassination attempt in which a car bomb exploded near his motorcade as he traveled to a signing ceremony for a new Georgian constitution. He was elected president of Georgia in November 1995.

SHULTZ, George (1920–) U.S. secretary of state from 1982 to 1988. An economist, he was, under Richard NIXON, secretary of labor, 1969–70; director, Office of Management and Budget, 1970–72; and secretary of the treasury, 1972–74. He was appointed secretary of state by President REAGAN in 1982.

SIHANOUK, Prince Norodom (1922–) Cambodian leader, liolding various offices since 1940. King of Cambodia in 1941, he abdicated the throne in 1955 in order to become prime minister, an office he held until he was elected president in 1960. Deposed in 1970 by LON NOL with American support, he lived in exile in Beijing, where he campaigned in association with his former opponents, the communist Khmer Rouge. Restored as president in 1975 when Lon Nol was overthrown, he resigned the following year, having been arrested by POL POT. After 1982 he was head of state of the government of Democratic Kampuchea in exile, in territory held by Khmer Rouge soldiers along the Thai border. After the 1993 elections he returned yet again as king and head of state.

SINGH, Vishwanath Pratap (1931–) Prime minister of India from 1989 to November 1990. Former Congress (I) politician. Various posts, including defense minister, under Indira Gandhi. He broke with Congress in 1987; president of the Janata Dal coalition that ousted Rajiv Gandhi from power in the 1989 election. His minority government was rocked by growing Hindu nationalism. The violence over the Ayodhya mosque (q.v., chapter 10) led to the fall of his government.

SMITH, Ian (1919–   )   Rhodesian prime minister, 1964–78. A member of the Southern Rhodesia legislature from 1948 to 1953, he was a member of the federal parliament from 1953 to 1962, founder of the Rhodesian Front Party in 1962, and prime minister from 1964 to 1978. He declared independence for Southern Rhodesia unilaterally in 1965. After unsuccessful talks with British prime minister Harold WILSON in 1966 and in October 1968, Smith declared Rhodesia a republic in 1970. Forced by guerrilla war and external pressures to negotiate an internal settlement, he sought agreement with the moderates led by Bishop MUZOREWA, forming a joint white and black government in 1978. Smith became minister without portfolio in the Zimbabwe-Rhodesia government under Muzorewa in 1979 and came to London for talks that finally settled the Rhodesia crisis. He returned as one of the white members of the first parliament of independent Zimbabwe following the election won by Robert MUGABE.

SOMOZA, Anastasio (1925–80)   President of Nicaragua, 1967–72 and 1974–79. The last to rule of a family that controlled Nicaragua for 45 years. His imposition of martial law in 1972, suppression of opponents and violations of human rights led the United States to abandon support for Somoza, despite the risk of takeover by left-wing Sandinista guerrillas. Somoza fled the country in 1979 as Sandinista troops marched on the capital, Managua. He was assassinated in 1980.

SPAAK, Paul-Henri (1899–1972)   Belgian prime minister, 1938–40, 1947–49. Belgium's first Socialist prime minister in 1938, he was foreign minister of the government in exile after the Nazi invasion of Belgium in 1940. He played a great part in establishing Benelux, the Council of Europe, and the United Nations. First president of the UN General Assembly in 1946, he was also president of the Assembly of the Council of Europe, 1949–51; Belgian foreign minister, 1954–57; and secretary-general of NATO, 1957–61. He served again as Belgian foreign minister from 1961 to 1966, afterward retiring from politics.

STALIN, Joseph (1879–1953)   Soviet Communist Party secretary, 1922–53, and prime minister, 1941–53. Active in the October Revolution with Lenin, whom he replaced in 1923–24 as the dominant leader in the USSR, keeping out Trotsky. He was unchallenged in this position after 1927. During the 1930s he purged many veteran revolutionaries. Stalin directed the Soviet war effort in the 1940s, attending Allied conferences in Tehran, Yalta and Potsdam. After 1945, he retained as tight a grip on new socialist states in Eastern Europe as on the Soviet political machine. He died in office in 1953. He was denounced by his successor, KHRUSHCHEV, in 1956 for his "cult of personality" and his persecution of opponents in the 1930s.

STEVENSON, Adlai (1900–65)   United States ambassador to the United Nations, 1961–65. American politician, he was governor of Illinois from 1949 to 1952 and Democratic Party nominee for president in 1952 and 1956 (both times defeated decisively by Dwight D. Eisenhower). In 1961, President KENNEDY appointed Stevenson as the United States ambassador to the United Nations, a post Stevenson held until his death in 1965.

STRIJDOM, Johannes (1893–1958)   South African prime minister, 1954–58. Nationalist MP in 1929, he emerged as the extreme Afrikaner leader in 1934, succeeding MALAN as prime minister from 1954 until his death. A fanatical believer in apartheid, he was responsible for destroying the liberal traditions of South Africa's older and multiracial universities and for legislation depriving Cape coloreds of the vote.

SUHARTO, General (1921–   )   President of Indonesia from 1968 to 1998. Army chief of staff from 1965 to 1968, he assumed emergency powers in 1966, taking over from President SUKARNO in 1967 and being elected president himself in 1968. A right-wing dictator, he broke diplomatic links with China but restored stability, both domestically and in Indonesia's relations with its neighbors. Although elected unopposed to a sixth five-year term in 1993, Suharto stepped down in 1998 after 32 years in power due to economic troubles. Power then went to Vice President B. J. HABIBIE.

SUKARNO, Ahmed (1901–70)   President of Indonesia, 1950–68. Founding member of the national movement for Indonesian independence in 1927, he was in exile or prison from 1929 to 1944. President of the de facto Indonesian state in 1945, he was recognized as such by the Netherlands government in 1950. His authoritarian tendencies aroused increasing resentment from 1956 onward. Confrontation with Malaysia coincided with a period of economic stagnation from 1963 to 1965, and he lost executive power to General SUHARTO in 1967, although he retained the title of president until 1968.

SVOBODA, Ludwig (1895–1979)   President of Czechoslovakia, 1968–75. Commander of the Czechoslovak army corps attached to the Red Army from 1943 to 1944, he was minister of defense from 1945 to 1950. He joined the Communist Party in 1948 but disappeared from public affairs, as he was distrusted by Stalin, from 1952 to 1963. Rescued by Khrushchev, after his 70th birthday he was elected president to succeed NOVOTNY. He collaborated closely with DUBČEK, and he appears to have restrained the oppressive regime established after Soviet intervention in 1968, personally leading a delegation to Moscow. Although remaining president until 1975, he was little more than a distinguished figurehead for most of his term of office.

TAMBO, Oliver (1917–93)   President of the African National Congress (ANC), 1967–91. A lawyer in partnership with Nelson MANDELA, Tambo was ANC deputy president from 1958 to 1967, living in exile after March 1960. Appointed ANC president in 1967, he held the movement together, returning to South Africa in June 1991. He relinquished the post in July 1991 and took the largely honorary post of chairman, which he held until his death.

TENG Hsiao-p'ing   See DENG XIAOPING.

THANT, U (1909–74)   Secretary-general of the United Nations, 1962–71. A Burmese diplomat, he served in the UN from 1957. He assumed responsibilities as acting secretary-general in 1961, when he successfully sponsored a plan to reconcile Katanga and the Congo and helped to ease tension over the Cuban Missile Crisis. After his election in 1962 his initiatives included establishing UN peacekeeping forces in Cyprus, 1964; cease-fire arrangements after the Six-Day War of 1967; and acceptance of the Communist Chinese as members of the UN and the Security Council. He resigned in 1971.

THATCHER, Margaret (1925–)   British prime minister from 1979 to 1990. Conservative MP after 1959 and secretary of state for education and science from 1970 to 1974, she was elected leader of the Conservative Party in 1975, becoming the first woman prime minister in Great Britain in 1979. Her determination to stick to her rigid economic policies despite rising unemployment led to unpopularity, but she gained widespread respect for her leadership and strength of purpose in the Falklands War in 1982. This and divisions among her opponents led to a landslide victory in 1983. Although she showed greater flexibility after 1983, she dominated her government with an abrasive style, which cost her some electoral support, particularly after public disagreements within the cabinet early in 1986; still, despite this, she led the Conservative Party to another victory in the 1987 elections. However, by 1990 increasing dissatisfaction within her own party (over Europe, the poll tax and other issues) led to a leadership challenge by Michael HESELTINE. Faced with the evaporation of her support by Conservative backbenchers, she announced her resignation on 22 November 1990. She was succeeded by John MAJOR.

TITO, Josip (1892–1980)   President of Yugoslavia, 1953–80. He worked for the illegal Yugoslavian Communist Party in the 1920s and was jailed from 1928 to 1934. General secretary of the Yugoslav party from 1937, in 1941 he organized partisan forces against Hitler and Mussolini, liberating his country in 1943–45 and carrying through a communist revolution. In 1945 he became the first Communist prime minister and, in 1953, he became president, a post he held until his death in 1980. He successfully pursued an independent line for his country, experimenting with workers' self-government and refusing to accept uncritically every shift in Soviet policy. He denounced Soviet intervention in Hungary in 1956 and in Czechoslovakia in 1968.

TRUDEAU, Pierre Elliott (1919–2000)   Canadian prime minister, 1968–79 and 1980–84. He entered the federal parliament as a Liberal in 1965. Minister of justice and attorney-general in the government of Lester Pearson in 1967, he succeeded him as prime minister in 1968. Trudeau firmly opposed separatist tendencies in Quebec. Following defeat in the 1979 election, he was persuaded to remain in politics, regaining office in 1980.

TRUMAN, Harry S (1884–1972)   President of the United States, 1945–53. A senator from 1935 to 1944, he was Roosevelt's running mate in 1944, vice president, and president (on Roosevelt's death) in 1945. He had to assume immediate responsibility for the conduct of the war, and in 1945 he took the decision to drop the first atomic bomb on Japan. Unexpectedly, he won the 1948 election. Carrying the United States into NATO, its first peacetime military alliance, his strength of character led him to dismiss General MACARTHUR for exceeding his authority during the Korean War. At home he seized steel mills in order to prevent a strike. He retired in 1953.

TSHOMBE, Moise (1919–69)   Prime minister and president of the Democratic Republic of the Congo, 1964–65. Advocate of an independent but loosely federated Congo, he was president of the secessionist Katanga province from 1960 to 1963. Exiled from the Congo from 1963 to 1964, after UN intervention overthrew his regime, he returned as prime minister in 1964. His use of mercenaries and his apparent involvement in Patrice LUMUMBA's murder made him distrusted by African nationalists, and after blatantly corrupt elections and MOBUTU's coup in 1965, he went into exile. He was kidnapped in 1967 and taken to Algiers, where he died in prison in 1969.

ULBRICHT, Walter (1893–1973)   Head of state, German Democratic Republic, 1960–73. An active communist from 1919, he was a Reichstag member from 1928 to 1933. He immigrated to the USSR until 1945. The first organizer of the new communist movement in Berlin and effective head of the Socialist Unity Party from 1946 to 1971, he was chairman of the Council of State from 1960 to 1973. As a staunch Stalinist he was less accommodating to shifts in Soviet policy under Stalin's successors than any other East European leader.

VAJPAYEE, Atal Bihari (1926–)   Prime minister of India since 1998. First elected to parliament in 1957 as a member of the Jan Sangh, a forerunner of the Bharatiya Janata Party (BJP), Vajpayee was jailed along with thousands of opposition members during Indira GANDHI's rule. He helped found the BJP in 1980 and was sworn in as prime minister in May 1996, but he failed to attract needed support from other parties and lasted only 13 days. In 1998, the BJP formed an alliance with regional parties, many of which opposed Hindu nationalism, and the party won a record number of seats to put Vajpayee back in office. In May of that year, India exploded five nuclear bombs and relations with Pakistan quickly deteriorated as Pakistan retaliated with nuclear tests of its own. Vajpayee has not been deterred by economic sanctions from the United States and Japan and refuses to begin peace talks with Pakistan.

VANCE, Cyrus (1917–   )   A lawyer, he became U.S. secretary of the army in 1962, and deputy secretary of defense in 1964, in which post he strongly defended the Vietnam War. He was a member of the Vietnam peace talks negotiating team in Paris, 1968–69, and secretary of state from 1977 to 1980 under President CARTER. Vance supported diplomatic recognition of the united Vietnam. He resigned in 1980 following a failed attempt to rescue American hostages in Iran. He attempted unsuccessfully with Lord OWEN to negotiate a peaceful solution to the Bosnian problem in 1993.

VERWOERD, Hendrik (1901–66)   South African prime minister, 1958–66. A professor of sociology at Stellenbosch University from 1927 until he resigned in 1937 in protest at the admission to South Africa of Jewish refugees from Nazi persecution. He edited a nationalist newspaper until 1948. Elected senator in 1948, he was minister of native affairs in 1950, with responsibility for enforcing apartheid. Elected Nationalist Party leader and prime minister in 1958, he was a strong advocate of a South African republic and withdrawal from the Commonwealth, both of which he achieved in 1961. He was assassinated in 1966.

VO NGUYEN Giap (1912–86)   Vietnamese general and defense minister, 1954–82. Giap joined the Communist Party in 1933 and participated in risings against the French. He also helped HO Chi Minh organize guerrilla resistance to the Japanese from 1942 to 1945 and led the Viet Minh against the French from 1946 to 1954. His greatest victory was at Dien Bien Phu, in 1954, which precipitated the collapse of French rule in Indochina. He remained North Vietnamese commander in chief and defense minister throughout the Vietnam War, and he became a deputy premier on the establishment of the Socialist Republic of Vietnam in 1976 until his retirement in 1982.

VORSTER, Johannes (1915–83)   South African prime minister, 1966–78. Interned for pro-Nazi sympathies during World War II, he emerged as a Nationalist Party MP in 1953 and minister of justice from 1961 to 1966. Prime minister in 1966 on the assassination of VER-WOERD, his intensification of repressive measures and his strict maintenance of apartheid led to widespread condemnation of South Africa abroad, but the white South African voters endorsed his policies, and he won a landslide electoral victory in 1977. Ill health led to his resignation as prime minister in 1978, but he became president of the republic until forced to resign by the Muldergate Scandal (*q.v.*, chapter 10) in 1979.

WAHID, Abdurrahman (1940–   )   President of Indonesia since October 1999. Muslim cleric Wahid, commonly known as Gus Dur, became Indonesia's first freely elected president after B. J. HABIBIE withdrew his own candidacy days before the vote. In the nation's first democratic transfer of power, the electoral assembly chose Wahid over Megawati Sukarnoputiri, daughter of former president SUKARNO. Wahid, Megawati's political mentor and a leader famous for finessing coalitions, appointed her vice president the following day. Serious health problems, however, may interfere with Wahid's effectiveness as president. One of his first orders of business has been to appease Aceh separatists: Wahid has proposed a referendum on permitting Islamic law in the northern Sumatran region, but not independence.

WALDHEIM, Kurt (1918–   )   President of Austria, 1986–92. Secretary-general of the United Nations, 1971–82. Austrian diplomat, 1945–64; foreign minister, 1968–70; unsuccessful candidate in Austrian presidential election, 1971. He succeeded U THANT as secretary-general of the United Nations in 1971. Regional conflicts and mutual suspicion between the power blocs hampered Waldheim's efforts, especially in the Middle East, while he lacked any practical means of overcoming the procrastinating tactics of the South Africans over Namibia. He retired from the UN in 1982. In 1986 he was elected president of Austria amid controversy surrounding his alleged Nazi activities during World War II. In 1991 he announced that he would not run for reelection.

WALESA, Lech (1943–   )   President of Poland from 1990 to 1995. Leader of the Polish Solidarity movement after 1980. A shipyard worker in Gdansk, he was chairman of the strike committee in Gdansk in 1980. A founding member of the independent trade union Solidarity, which emerged in 1980 to negotiate major concessions from the Polish government, he was interned in 1981–82, following imposition of martial law by Gen. Wojciech JARUZELSKI. Although many of the concessions were lost, Walesa remained an internationally acclaimed symbol of freedom in a communist society, a reputation confirmed by the 1983 Nobel

Peace Prize. With the collapse of communism in Eastern Europe, and despite divisions within the ranks of Solidarity, Walesa was elected president of Poland, taking office on 22 December 1990. In 1995 he sought reelection but was narrowly defeated by the former Communist Aleksander Kwasniewski, head of the Democratic Left Alliance.

WILSON, Harold (1916–95) British prime minister, 1964–70 and 1974–76. Labour MP, 1945–83; president, Board of Trade, 1947–51 (resigning in 1951 over imposition of health care fees); Labour Party leader in 1963 (on death of Gaitskell). He led Labour to a narrow victory in 1964, winning a large majority in 1966. As prime minister from 1964 to 1970 he achieved many reforms, but his government was dogged by economic difficulties and he was criticized for his failure to solve the Rhodesian crises. After three and a half years in opposition, he returned to office as head of a minority government following the "crisis" election of February 1974. A second election in 1974 gave him an overall majority, which was sufficient to tackle rapidly rising inflation with a "social contract" with the trade unions. Unexpectedly, he retired in 1976, remaining an MP until 1983, when he accepted a life peerage.

YAHYA Khan (1917–80) President of Pakistan, 1969–71. Commanding general of the Pakistan army in 1966, he was appointed martial law administrator in 1969 by AYUB KHAN. He assumed the presidency in 1969. His refusal to accept the East Pakistani verdict, in the first open elections in 1970–71, in favor of the Awami League led to civil war over Bangladesh, a disastrous brief conflict with India, and to his precipitate resignation in 1971. He was detained under house arrest from 1972 until 1974.

YANAYEV, Gennadi (1937–) Nominal head of the abortive coup of 19 August 1991 that aimed to overthrow Gorbachev in the Soviet Union. Head of the Soviet Youth Organization (Komsomol) after 1980. A dour, uninspiring party *apparatchik*, he was a surprise choice as Gorbachev's vice president. Arrested in 1991 for the coup attempt, he was given amnesty in 1994.

YELTSIN, Boris Nikolayevich (1931–) Soviet and Russian politician; president of Russia from 1991 to 1999. Former Communist Party leader in Sverdlovsk, 1975. Promoted by Mikhail Gorbachev to be party leader in Moscow, 1985. At that time, seen as Gorbachev's chief radical ally. In 1987, after increasingly bitter disagreements with Gorbachev, he was forced to resign. In 1989, he was elected for the Moscow constituency with 90% of the vote. In May 1990, he was elected president of the Russian Federation, the largest republic within the Soviet Union. He resigned from the Communist Party in July 1990. A popular politician with his calls for more radical reform of the economy and greater independence for the Russian Federation, he became in 1991 the first directly elected president of the Russian Federation. The failure of the 19 August 1991 coup, due in large measure to Yeltsin's mobilization of popular opposition to it, transformed his power. In effect, from August 1991 he was the most powerful figure in the erstwhile Soviet Union. In December 1991 he helped found the Commonwealth of Independent States and the Soviet Union ceased to exist. In September 1993, Yeltsin was caught up in a constitutional coup, but remained in office. During his last two years as president, Yeltsin conducted a "Russian roulette" of revolving prime ministers. In March 1998, during Russia's worst post-Soviet currency crisis, Yeltsin replaced Viktor CHERNOMYRDIN with liberal energy minister Sergei Kiriyenko. That August, when it became clear that the economy was still suffering, he fired Kiriyenko and attempted to rehire Chernomyrdin, but parliament rejected his nomination and Chernomyrdin withdrew his name. Yeltsin went on to appoint and then fire two other prime ministers, Foreign Minister Yevgeny Primakov and Interior Minister Sergei Stepashin, before turning over the reins to Vladimir PUTIN at the end of 1999.

ZHIRINOVSKY, Vladimir Volfovich (1946–) Russian right-wing politician. Born in Alma-Ata. He became chairman in 1990 of the Liberal Democratic Parry, an extreme right-wing nationalist and anti-Semitic movement, which emerged as the largest party after the 1993 election. His image of a hysterical demagogue belies his appeal to the Russian masses. However, he saw support drop dramatically in the 1996 presidential election.

ZHIVKOV, Todor (c. 1911–98) Bulgarian Communist. As president of Bulgaria from 1954 to 1989, he was Eastern Europe's longest-serving political leader. He resigned his office as the revolutions in Eastern Europe spread to the streets of Sofia, the capital. He has been accused of founding Bulgaria's most notorious internment camps. In 1990 he was charged with embezzlement, and in 1992 he was sentenced to seven years under house arrest. He was released in January 1997.

ZHOU Enlai (1898–1976) Chinese prime minister, 1949–76. Zhou organized a Communist revolt in Shanghai in 1927 and became MAO Zedong's principal adviser on urban revolutionary affairs from 1931. He negotiated JIANG KAISHEK's release after the Sian kidnapping of 1936 and represented the Communists in talks with the U.S. mission (1945–47) to mediate in China's civil war. Prime minister of the People's Republic from 1949 until his death, he was also foreign minister until 1958. Zhou represented China at the Geneva Conference in 1954, and he remained the principal international spokesman for China, leading the detente with America during the Nixon-Kissinger period, 1969–74.

ZIA UL-HAQ, Mohammad (1924–88)   President of Pakistan from 1978 to 1988. An army general, he led a coup that ousted BHUTTO in 1977, following disturbances over allegations of electoral corruption. Under martial law he took tough action, including creation of an Islamic state. His position as president was confirmed in a referendum in 1984, and he was elected to office for a five-year term in 1985. He was killed in a plane crash in August 1988.

INDEX

Page numbers followed by *t* indicate tables.

596 World Political Almanac